COUR
CLUBS CHAM

RUGBY CLUB DIRECTORY 1988–89

Edited by BILL MITCHELL

A
Daily Mail
PUBLICATION

Published by Harmsworth Publications Ltd,
for Mail Newspaper plc
London EC4Y 0JA

ISBN No: 0 85144 473 3

Distributed by: Biblios,
Glenside Industrial Estate,
Partridge Green, Horsham, Sussex RH13 8LD

Typeset by MC Typeset Ltd, Gillingham, Kent, and printed by Richard Clay Ltd, Bungay, Suffolk.

EDITORIAL

THIS IS the first venture of its kind, although my friend and colleague Tony Williams has been highly successful in his efforts to produce two very readable soccer publications, both now well established.

This being a first venture, there have been problems, which will be less pronounced the second time around – by then we hope that clubs and photographers will realise that there is a big place for all of them, and that virtually everything they submit will be used. This book can only develop with the co-operation of Club Secretaries, who can supply us with extra information on the clubs, and freelance and professional photographers who can make the book livelier and even more attractive. We don't wish to be merely a statistical exercise – we want to have a lot to show you in terms of excitement and entertainment: we can't do it without your help.

Anyway, you can see from everything that follows that we have tried to give coverage to all clubs in the Courage Leagues, which have been such a boon to English rugby. If you like what you see, send us more material about your club in future, and enjoy it even more.

Meanwhile, we give a most heartfelt word of thanks to all those who have helped us with information, which has been invaluable. We are proud to present to you the first ever Courage League Clubs Directory.

BILL MITCHELL
Editor

Managing Editor: *Tony Williams*
Editor: *Bill Mitchell*

Executive Editorial Committee: *Tony Williams, Bill Mitchell, Ken Hole, Norman Flack, Sally Cartwright*

Contributors: *Terry O'Connor, Peter Jackson, Robert Kitson, Nick Cain, Michael Reynolds, Huw Richards, Steve Williams, Gordon Bunney, Colin Elsey, Chris Roberts, Peter Lea*

Editorial Assistants: *Pat Symons, Rhys Davies, Paula Mitchell*

BILL MITCHELL

BILL MITCHELL was born in 1932 and spent the first dozen years of his life in India, where his father worked. He was educated at Shrewsbury School, where they play the round ball version of football, but has been a regular fan of both codes for many years with greater emphasis on rugby more recently as soccer has more and more pressed its own "self-destruct" button. After Shrewsbury he did two years' National Service in the Army (Intelligence Corps) before a long spell working abroad in the pharmaceutical industry based at various times in West Africa, East Africa, Iran and the Canary Islands, from which he returned in 1981 and he has since worked as a freelance journalist – the last three years for Rugby World & Post.

ACKNOWLEDGEMENTS

IT IS My pleasure to acknowledge all the help we have been given in producing this Directory – starting with the encouragement we have received from Courage Ltd. and the Public Relations Director, Michael Reynolds. His assistance, along with that of courage's very efficient agents, Michael Humphreys, has been invaluable.

Our next message of thanks goes to Nigel Starmer-Smith, Editor of Rugby World & Post, who has been so helpful in providing us with the facilities to continue the job. Among those who helped to send out letters and forms were his very efficient team at Gallowtrees Common.

More helpers in the office were Pat Symons, Phys Davies and Paula Mitchell, all of whom we also thank.

The typesetters have been tremendous – thank you, Ken and May Culver at MC Typeset Ltd. Then there has been Allan Davies with his expertise as a top lay-out man. Thank you also, Steve Williams, for helping with photographs.

The first time is always the most difficult, but with plenty of help we cracked it!

CONTENTS

FOREWORD

THESE ARE exciting days for rugby football. Evolution, if not revolution, is in the air.

On the international scene, the success of the first World Cup guaranteed that it will become a permanent fixture in the rugby calendar; on the domestic front, the introduction of leagues to the English game is bringing a new edge of competitiveness, a new philosophy that can only produce higher standards at club and, eventually, international level.

Certainly, the dimensions reached by the Southern Hemisphere countries during and after the world competition underlined the gulf that now separates their rugby from ours. It will take time for that gap to be bridged, but the increased competition brought about by the Courage Clubs Championship will play a vital part in the rugby reformation.

I welcome the launch of the *Daily Mail's Rugby Club Directory*. It is a comprehensive guide to the clubs, featuring everything from the address of the Fixtures Secretary to detailed playing records. It even tells you how to reach the various grounds.

Among the fascinating articles is one by Terry O'Connor, the Daily Mail's No. 1 rugby writer, on why he believes the game is about to change dramatically.

Comprehensive statistics . . . informative reading . . . action pictures . . . this directory has something for everyone.

Enjoy it – and have a good season!

PETER LEA
Sports Editor, Daily Mail

COURAGE AND RUGBY

COURAGE'S major involvement with the game of Rugby Union Football started in 1965 with our sponsorship of the John Smith's Merit Tables.

These ran for two years and involved the top 24 clubs in the country. The Merit Tables formed the basis of the league structure now known as the Courage Clubs Championship.

Courage were pleased to be able to keep the continuity of rugby sponsorship when the Championship sponsorship started last season and the experience gained by everyone during the running of the Merit Tables proved invaluable when it came to the championship.

In the first season there were 106 leagues with 1128 clubs taking part, making it the largest league structure in the world, and one that needed an extraordinary amount of coordination and work to run effectively. As everyone now knows Leicester won the National Division 1 title in 1987/88 and so are the current Courage Clubs Champions, but it was the enthusiasm that the Championship received from ALL the clubs, and the positive attitude shown during the first season that led to its being such a success.

For Courage the natural association between the product and the sport is just one of the reasons for us to take on the sponsorship. As part of one of the largest brewing groups in the world, Courage are involved in sports and sponsorships which reflect our standing and in which we can take an active and helpful interest.

Courage have put a great deal of backing into the Championship providing detailed information books. Extra prizes (in the form of product!) for the clubs, team sheets, fixture posters, and structure charts are just some of the items in our bid to aid communications within the league.

UNION FOOTBALL

The overall coverage and support given to the leagues last season by local, regional and national press played a large part in ensuring the success of the first year, and we thank them for that support. The interest that they generated in the Championship was essential, and the constant flow of information that they provided showed how important the Championship is to the game of rugby as a whole.

The Championship has come so far in such a short time, it is difficult to realise that this is only the second year, and we at Courage are proud to have been involved in what is widely accepted as one of the most important developments in the history of the game. Hopefully the Championship will become the bedrock from which England can regain its position in the forefront of the rugby world.

It is an indication of the success of the Courage Championship that the Daily Mail are producing this book, and we thank them for taking such an interest.

The 1988/89 Courage Clubs Championship promises to be even bigger and better, with 1170 clubs taking part this year, and we are looking forward to an exciting season of rugby. We would like to thank our friends at the RFU and to say how much we have appreciated heir commitment and advice in building the Championship to its current position. We would also like to thank all those throughout the game who have worked so hard and to all those who will be involved in the future. We look forward to continuing our association with the RFU, all the clubs in the Courage Championship and with all who love and support the great game.

by Michael Reynolds

Leicester were the first winners of the Courage Rugby Club Championship. Les Cusworth (left) and Captain Paul Dodge, display the trophy.

REVIEW OF 1987–88 AND FUTURE PROSPECTS

SO FAR SO GOOD! That must be the verdict on the first season of leagues in England. An unqualified success? Well, almost. There were a few bugs in the system and most of these should be put right in the new season.

The main problem was only really seen in the top two divisions and the RFU could have been seriously embarrassed if Coventry had won their last game and thus left Waterloo relegated because they were – through no fault of their own – unable to play their final game.

But in the coming campaign we will have fixed Saturdays and there should be no repetition of such problems – or could we? There is such a thing as a severe winter and we can only keep our fingers crossed and hope that it will not create too many postponements. If it does it will be incumbent on the RFU to allow an extension of the season so that no ultimate injustices occur.

One thing we would not like to see in rugby is something akin to the long-running and undefying saga, which has brought League Football (with the round ball) into disrepute. With titles, promotion and relegation at stake in so many leagues we must avoid at all costs a situation where a virtual 'transfer market' comes into being. By all means we want to see the game become more 'professional', but we do not want a professional game. Everyone connected with it must work with enthusiasm and alertness to see that it stays that way. Not for us undignified television machinations, I hope.

During the past winter I was asked at a dinner why I thought rugby should stay amateur. It was a bit of a poser at short notice but by the end of the evening I was able to answer the question to our mutual satisfaction by pointing out that the speeches – although poor – had been made by decent, respectable people. How would he like a sport in which 'X' or 'Y' or 'Z' were the guests of 'honour' (and I mentioned a trio of self-publicity-seeking Football League chairmen)? The point was taken. In making this observation I exempt from criticism the majority of non-league officials, who are just as honourable as their rugby counterparts, but some of those League chairmen? Need I comment?

So, we want our game to stay amateur, which means that everyone connected with it has a duty and responsibility to maintain the game's image as a sport played by decent people on an amateur basis for decent people.

So, what of the season just ended? We could hardly have hoped for better as league and club officials strove successfully to make it work. At the end of the day we had three superb National champions in Leicester, Rosslyn Park and Wakefield with – appropriately enough – Rugby and an original old boys team – Askeans – gaining promotion from the Area Leagues.

Leicester have always been synonymous with enterprising rugby and in taking the title they showed a lot of courage in winning some very close matches against potential other champions.

Rosslyn Park showed why it is that London rugby after years of being something of a joke has now reached a status where its clubs can be under-estimated at the peril of detractors. Harlequins (with their John Player Special Cup triumph) have underlined this point.

The sad thing about Wakefield's success in the Third Division is that they cannot immediately benefit from their success and must go through it all again this coming season. It will not be easy for them, but they have some fine players to set up another strong campaign with Mike Harrison, Ray Adamson and Bryan Barley still there to take advantage of an excellent pack.

Further down the scale teams are just beginning to work out the ways and means of advancing their claims and one can now foresee senior status being gained by a number of unfashionable clubs and this is the exciting prospect that the leagues present.

From the area leagues we can confidently expect progress for such clubs as Durham City, Winnington Park or a resurgent Roundhay from the North along with Sidcup, Lydney and (it would not be before time) Camborne – mounting a challenge on behalf of Cornwall. Can the likes of Birkenhead Park, Broughton Park, Morley or Cheltenham recover to a position consistent with former glories?

In the divisions themselves there are some intriguing possibilities. Up North Aspatria and Tynedale have some fine cup performances behind them. Can they sustain these standards over a full season and emerge on the national scene? Again, what about Kendal, West Park, Otley or Halifax? How far can such high scoring clubs as De la Salle, Bolton, Mersey Police, Roundhegians and Bridlington progress from their present humble surroundings? Or Sheffield Oaks, Mowden Park and Whitby?

From the Midlands the name of Stoke emerges into the limelight – not the Stoke City of

Stanley Matthews but a very competent rugby side. Hereford one league down scored a massive 245 points in ten matches and Newark on the same level managed only two less. Teams to watch? West Midlands Police in North Midlands 4 achieved the huge total of 329 points from nine matches and they will be hard to halt at higher levels. Other heavy Midlands scorers were Shrewsbury, Selly Oak, All Spartans, Coventrians, Northampton Men's Own and Bedford Quins. Congratulations one and all.

The South-West has its own heroes with Redruth now joining fellow Cornishmen Camborne in Area League South, but watch out for Berry Hill from the Forest of Dean. They managed 290 points from ten matches in South West 2 and must be 'long shots' for a second promotion season. London Welsh – beaten by them in the John Player Cup – will endorse their credentials, but others to watch are Matson and Gordon League from Western Counties, the high-scoring Avon Old Boys from Gloucester–Somerset and Crediton from the Devon–Cornwall league. Other very high scorers were Spartans, Gloucester Old Boys (who still missed promotion from Gloucestershire 3), Swanage and Chippenham. Things certainly buzzed in the South-West where the response to our questions was the best of all. Well done, you secretaries.

London did not suffer by comparison with any of these clubs. Ealing comfortably won London 1 and now hope to advance through Area League South, but watch Ruislip this season. They did well in the John Player Cup. The high scoring Basingstoke, Barking and Purley will be challenging for better status this season along with Effingham of Surrey 2A, who only lost one match all season at any level. In the Eastern Counties divisions Campion (in 4) and Bancroft (in 5) both cleared 400 points in ten and eleven games respectively. Uckfield in Sussex 2 managed 252 in only seven! Others to score heavily were the Kent 1 champions Charlton Park, Haringey, Old Edwardians and Harrodians (will they now reduce prices as a celebratory gesture?)

Comparisons with golf are not invalid. In that game not only are the highest standards of behaviour demanded and enforced at all levels, but players by their handicapping system find their own targets to achieve and enjoy the game in the process.

That is the real message of the rugby system of leagues. Each club is set its own targets and there is no need for it to become a grim war of attrition to achieve them. The amateur ethos must prevail at all levels and it is good to see even those teams that have a rough time sticking to their guns. That is the right spirit which makes the game the fun that it is.

If the leagues can allow competition and enjoyment in equal measures they will not only be proved to be a success, but they will also show why the game has such a fine following with an almost complete absence of hooliganism. As long as the average club player or spectator can enjoy his Saturday afternoons without the problems of league soccer we have something decent to anticipate for the future.

Midlands giants Nottingham and Moseley launch the Courage Leagues on 5th September 1987. Chris Gray (Nottingham) is tackled by Moseley's Al Recardo (behind) and Mark Linnett. Photo: Colorsport.

WHICH WAY TELEVISION?

THE ONE good thing about the protracted negotiations over the rights to televise rugby was that they were carried out with dignity and decorum as befits the Rugby Union game, in marked contrast to soccer,whose officials succeeded in bringing the game into disrepute and ridicule by their antics, which against all reasonable moral standards gained that game more money than its reputation deserves. It is far more than will be paid to rugby.

At the end of the negotiations the BBC retained its right to stage the big games and it continues with its monopoly leaving ITV to seek other fields to exploit and in the light of subsequent statements by the latter's "big-wigs" it seems that the right decision was taken. Any organisation, whose top spokesman believes that events like The Derby should be staged at times to suit the demands of television, will find it hard to convince any people who have the interests of their sport at heart that they share that concern. TV has already dictated kick-off times at the soccer World Cup to the benefit of no-one except, perhaps, a few shareholders; we in rugby need that kind of interfernce as much as we need some other crippling illness.

But the BBC must avoid the temptation to rest on its laurels, because apart from their presentation of international matches they have very little to show which brings them any commendations. "Rugby Special" has for too many years merely been filling a vacant spot and the choice of matches that they have screened has at times be abysmal. The commentators have obviously been striving under severe handicaps with too few cameras available to give proper coverage of games.

The fact tht "Rugby Special" is now to be shown at a fixed time (5.00 p.m. on a Sunday) should make it possible for far more people to watch, but they must make sure that the quality of their matches and presentation is drastically improved. They must also be flexible in their approach, so that plans can be changed to make room for the really important matches to be shown at the appropriate times, rather than ones which happen to be conveniently close to TV crews which have been filming other events in the locality.

The BBC has done our game no favours, outside the internationals, by some of its presentation of lesser games and they will be under trial and close scrutiny over the next few years; and even now there is room for some further changes in attitudes. For a start it is not clear where Jonathan Martin, who controls sporting events for BBC TV, gained the idea that it is traditional not to start televising rugby before the first Saturday in October. The season starts in September and that is when television coverage should also commence.

The coverage of the World Cup in 1987 could also have been better and a little bit of humble investigation would have told the BBC that many more matches could have been screened live with huge viewing numbers than were actually shown. Fans will watch at inhospitable hours (as the Olympics always confirm) if an event is interesting enough.

The BBC cannot afford to be complacent. They are on probation and would do well to remember this fact. To pass with credit alone they must always be inovative all the time. An 'A' Grade will require a lot more than that.

COURAGE LEAGUE IMPRESSIONS

by Robert Kitson
(formerly of Hayters & The Daily Telegraph)

IMAGINE it is a Sunday afternoon in the autumn of 1998. You fancy watching some rugby on television. "Rugby Special", the paper reveals, will be featuring Courage Division One matches between . . . hold on a moment, what's this? Leicester v Stourbridge with highlights of Harlequins v Plymouth Albion and Sudbury v Bristol? Are they sure?

Well, you never know. After all, it's only five years since England beat the All Blacks at Twickenham! And look at what Bath have achieved in the last decade. Below the current upper strata of English clubs, rest assured, lurk a number of people with the ambition to match such fanciful dreams. For the senior clubs, the Courage Leagues have been a well-documented success from the start. Down at grassroots in those hundreds of clubs across the country, where TV cameras have never strayed, people are beginning to run out of superlatives.

Take Sidcup, a club with proud traditions but scarcely a rugby hotbed. After eight months hard work in Area League South, they suddenly found themselves on the threshold of promotion to National Division 3 or, in effect, playing for a direct ticket into the elite top 36 clubs in the country. Their opponents in the crucial final match, Lydney, making their first visit to suburban Kent, arrived to discover a committed crowd packing the touchlines and the national press well-represented, despite a clash with the County Championship and the Grand National to dissuade floating spectators and journos alike.

In the end, Sidcup blew it by missing a painful number of kicks at goal but that was scarcely the point. New friends were made, new pressures experienced yet, in time-honoured fashion, the result still faded into insignificance when the beer began to flow.

A quick unofficial poll in the packed clubhouse afterwards merely confirmed what everyone had been saying all season – leagues were the best thing to happen to English rugby since long shorts went out of fashion.

Similar case histories abound. At Sudbury on a lovely sunny afernoon in October, Lydney were once again the visitors. With little idea what to expect from their journey into East Anglia, the West Countrymen turned up with a side lacking one or two senior players who, allegedly, had not fancied traversing the country to pick up an easy win.

To cut a long story short, Lydney had their winger and touch judge sent off and lost 23–14. In their hosts' splendid modern clubhouse, built to replace the old one which had burnt down, one might have expected a bit of tension.

Instead, mostly kind words were exchanged and the subject turned to leagues. What a good idea, everyone said . . . should have come in years ago etc. Lydney, I bet, will be better prepared in future.

So what happened to those who said leagues would be a bad idea and the ruination of sociable, smaller clubs? Dissenters these days are virtually a protected species. At the excellent annual Combined London Old Boys dinner in the Rose Room, the new RFU President John Burgess was given a rough ride on what he might have regarded as safe home territory as he outlined his ideas for England's rugby future. Some less enlightened old boys were predictably none too keen on the streamlined structure outlined by Mr. Burgess and made their feelings clear.

Since then, apart from the odd disgruntled fixture secretary exasperated at the demolition of his long-established list and the extra work suddenly required, most of the hecklers have long since retreated quietly back into the woodwork. Those who declared they didn't give a XXXX for league rugby, even if it was sponsored by a brewery, are still in the bar delighted to discover that, socially at least, nothing much has changed.

On the field, the first year of leagues undoubtedly settled several arguments. False boasts were torpedoed, local rivalries settled at least for a year, and everyone found a yardstick by which to measure themselves.

Even the predicted fall off in entertainment never happened. Countless clubs reported staging some of their most exciting games for years and there was certainly no shortage of points scored. How many times for example have the likes of Billingham hit the headlines as they did last season for pasting luckless Hartlepool Athletic 146–0? Or Bancrofts, the top scorers throughout all the leagues with 447 points in winning Eastern Countires 5?

Clubs like Old Beccehamians and Eton Manner, intoxicated by fleeting glory at the Middlesex Sevens, at last had something more substantial to chew on and have enjoyed every minute despite missing out on promotion first time around.

It is probably true to say that several clubs took even themselves by surprise. In private, many are realistic enough to know that promotion, say, to Area League South with all the extra travelling that entails is more than they want or can afford. When, with a couple of games to go, at least two clubs found themselves staring a 600 mile round trip to Cornwall in the face the following season if they won promotion, the treasurers concerned admitted to severely divided loyalties. Whether by coincidence or design, both clubs suffered a mysterious loss of form in the run-in.

Sponsors do help to bridge the gap and several smaller clubs have got off the mark in this department with a speed that has put some of their better-known cousins to shame. There have been one or two unlikely liaisons – Ruislip for example were sponsored by a holiday firm specialising in skiing holidays which posed a few availability problems – but for the most part clubs are getting better at picking their way through financial difficulties. With a concrete league position to brandish at the property developer who wants to turn their ground into a theme park, clubs under pressure to vacate their premises also have more clout than hitherto.

The only losers, apart from the coaches who complain their players are becoming harder to motivate for non-league fixtures, seem to be student and hospital sides. Unlike Scotland where several universities co-exist happily in the national leagues, their English counterparts have made uncomfortable bedfellows. West London Institute, who failed to show up at Norwich on the day the host club had organised a pre-match Presidents lunch for former players, St. Thomas' Hospital, Brunel University, St. Mary's College and Hatfield Poly were all withdrawn for various reasons. Significantly, plenty of other clubs have been queuing up to take their places.

Discipline, of course, is what the old sweats loudly suggested would vanish out of the window the minute the first league scrum went down. The tally of sendings off in most counties tell an opposite story, however, and, if anything, the majority of dismissals have tended to come in non-league matches where the cost to the team of an individual being caught is less severe.

Several referees confirm the trend including Roger Quittenton, England's most experienced international official. His only worry is that crowd behaviour, particularly when promotion or relegation issues are at stake, could worsen, admitting that there are "one to two" grounds around the country where a young refereee could find the crowd pressure oppressive.

Such warnings apart, the future looks bright for the smaller club out to better itself. So what chance an international rising through the ranks with, say, Old Merchant Taylors or Aspatria, now that all clubs theoretically have the chance to "do a Wimbledon" and soar from obscurity to the top in a handful of seasons?

Sadly, unlike soccer, it is less likely to happen. Giantkillings in rugby happen much less frequently as the John Player Special Cup demonstrated over the years and there is plenty of pressure these days from bigger clubs with bigger resources of talented young players who want to progress in the game. Winning umpteen cans of beer for being part of a table-topping team scoring lots of points in the lower leagues may be tempting but probably isn't the ideal launch pad to an international cap.

So back to the murky crystal ball. Home and away fixtures between all clubs in the same season remains a possibility although it would be wrong to drive out all the traditional fixtures which still have a place in an amateur game. But which clubs are capable of upsetting the applecart and breaking into the senior clubs monopoly? The likes of Berry Hill, Maidenhead, Worthing and Southend might each be worth an outside bet – all they need is a bit of luck and a clubhouse big enough to hold all the free beer they should collect on the way up.

GOOD THING OR BAD?

Nick Cain (*Rugby World & Post*)
presents the case

THE general concensus at the end of the first season of league rugby in England was that it had been an almost unmitigated success – but, if we note the lessons of history, it is often the voices which dissent from the concensus that should be listened to most keenly.

Mid-way through the inaugural season of the Courage Clubs Championship, Andy Ripley, that larger-than-life modern Corinthian, embraced the misgivings of a small minority of English rugbymen towards the mammoth structure that had suddenly given the game a competitive framework with this appraisal:

'League rugby is like the Curate's Egg – the players basically like it, especially the team that's currently doing well. However, it's going to generate a down-side – notably a degree of professionalism will develop, which I'm not too sure the RFU in its current form is either aware of or can actually handle'.

Six months later the myths of merit table relegation have become hard-nosed reality in the brave new world of leagues and palace revolts have been set in motion by the prospect of failure . . .

In days of yore (i.e. up to a year ago) the prefix "first class" was one of those peculiarly English anachronisms whereby a club's status was determined almost entirely by past rather than present deeds – not least because there was no structure to provide an alternative yardstick. A first class club would probably react to a bad season by first consoling itself that it still retained its traditional fixture list, including a few crowd-pulling Anglo-Welsh and local derby trials-of-strength, and then pump itself up for "better things this time" with plenty of "let's pull-our-fingers-out" rhetoric. The election of a new captain would probably complete preparations for the new season.

But today that's not good enough – ask last season's Northampton committee. Being saved from relegation from National Division 2 to Division 3 only by the absurd inaugural season cut-out between the two divisions – the only non promotion-relegation clause in the whole league structure – proved too much for a group of Young Turks led by recently retired hooker Jon Raphael.

At this season's AGM he headed a group of seven former Northampton players who stood against the existing committee and ousted them from office with the overwhelming support of the club's rank-and-file (228–76).

The new players "consortium" made their first task the appointment of the RFU's former Midlands DTA, Barrie Corless, as new full-time manager at Franklin's Gardens. His job description involves responsibility for the promotion and efficient administration of the club with the objective of restoring the Saints to the top six clubs in National Division 1. It is Northampton's intention to fund Corless's salary through increased membership and sponsorship.

Re-organization like that ushered in by the "Northampton Seven" could represent just the tip of an iceberg. It seems inevitable that most clubs sooner or later will be tempted to pitch headlong into the same marketplace either in the hope of securing success or, at the very least, ensuring survival in the competitive world of league rugby.

And it is here that the "down-side" Ripley warned of becomes apparent: increased membership and sponsorship demand a successful "product". The spiral begins . . . the pressure is on clubs to attract and keep better players . . . the demands placed on those players in terms of the time and effort required to achieve professional sporting standards make full-time employment unrealistic . . . cash incentives become part of the packages on offer . . .

But is this push towards professionalism inevitable? And, given the increased demands the new competitive structure places on players, is it desirable?

The answers on both counts are a resounding "no!". Play-for-pay professionalism is not a foregone conclusion of a competitive league structure – nor is it desirable.

Highly competitive club leagues have been the cornerstone of all of New Zealand's major provincial unions for the past 100 years and in that time they have done no more to promote play-for-pay professionalism than boot money scandals in the UK.

What they have done is to provide a channel for competitive instinct and promoted the available talent to help New Zealand maintain its pre-eminence in the world game.

Whatever the rumours linking the phenomenal success of the current All Blacks with professionalism the truth is that in play-for-pay terms there is certainly no more abuse in New Zealand clubs and provinces than there is among the (non-league!) Welsh clubs that provided the opposition they annihilated in Christchurch and Auckland.

Where the New Zealanders have differed traditionally from the British pattern has been in the more professional approach to training and to achieving the higher standards of play and organization demanded by league structures.

This dedication has brought New Zealand's top rugby players its own rewards. They are national figures and enjoy celebrity status. Employers welcome them as good promotional assets. A star player like John Kirwan can endorse a product on TV without jeopardising his amateur status because he's so well known his rugby connection doesn't need a mention.

Kirwan, like all his fellow All Blacks, has a full-time job – albeit one that allows him to accommodate a rigorous four-hour-a-day training routine.

And, just as they are leading the way on the field, perhaps the New Zealanders are closer to getting the balance right off the field as well. Certainly the way their top players are adjusting to the increased pressures within the game have helped to highlight where the Regulations Relating to Amateurism are hopelessly outmoded and are likely to become increasingly unworkable.

It is incumbent on the RFU, now responsible for the largest league structure in rugby history, to make sure they are not left pushing the stable door shut while the "pro" horse is

Farewell old friend! Andy Ripley (Rosslyn Park, England, Middlesex, Barbarians and great character) has bowed out of the game at the age of 40. Photo: Colorsport.

Minis and a lady referee. Anyone can take part. Photo: Colorsport.

bolting for the finishing line. The stakes are high: it is essential not only for English rugby but the future of the world game.

Dismantling "petty amateurism" is one of the surest ways of blocking the play-for-pay avenue which has been, and will always be, the major threat to the union code. This would help to establish a bulwark against the threat of disgruntled players exploiting a divisive transfer market fed by cash incentives from over-ambitious clubs prepared to sacrifice amateur principles in favour of short-term success.

Recognizing the need for top players to gain some financial reward from an increasingly demanding game *does not* add up to abandoning the whole amateur ethos – it *does* mean adapting to the fact that the sporting climate has changed in the face of increasingly materialistic social conditions.

The Regulations Relating to Amateurism need to be re-drafted to allow for players to benefit by way of trust funds from off-field activities such as advertising and book-writing. Re-draw the amateur-professional axis along that line and then be prepared to prosecute play-for-pay transgressions mercilessly.

Otherwise, the dangers are clear. A professional split away from the amateur grass-roots will do our code no favours. The cheque-book will rule and a great sport could go the way of the win-at-all-costs bonus and the anti-game professional foul. You have only to look at the price soccer has paid to realise that a more complex contact sport like rugby union needs such "innovations" like a hole-in-the-head.

If English league rugby is to realise its potential as a force for constructive change in the game world-wide the RFU has to become "aware of and handle" the challenges that Andy Ripley alluded to. It's a matter of some urgency . . .

A REVIEW OF THE NATIONAL LEAGUES

NATIONAL LEAGUE DIVISION 1

APART from a few problems with rearrangement of fixtures the first season of the Courage League National Division 1 was a tremendous success and it produced some excellent rugby and worthy first champions in Leicester, who showed the real quality which is essential for success by winning those matches which really mattered – against Bath, Harlequins and Wasps – before Christmas, by which time they had virtually put themselves out of reach with seven consecutive victories.

The secret of their success was a fine back division which was adequately served by a pack, which – Dean Richards apart – contained no 'big names'. But those backs did their stuff from scrum-half Steve Kenney backwards through the evergreen Les Cusworth, Paul Dodge (when fit), Barry Evans, Rory Underwood and – inevitably – Dusty Hare, who just goes on and on breaking kicking records. It was a popular triumph for 'The Tigers'.

Wasps in the end finished only a point adrift although playing a game more, but the North London side sadly missed out on two trophies, having lost a John Player semi-final to Harlequins, who finished third after a poor start and fine late run. Both these talented sides can be expected to challenge for honours in the coming season along with Bath, whose loss of form can only be temporary.

Gloucester, Orrell (the only team to beat Leicester), Moseley, Nottingham (early leaders) and Bristol all had their moments as did Waterloo, who fell away badly after the New Year and only survived because Orrell won their final match at Coventry.

Coventry, whose players did so well in Warwickshire colours in the County Championship, could not cope with the opposition in the league and won only three games, so they play in Division 2 next season, although they cannot be down for too long.

Many expected big things from Sale, but the Brooklands club had a disastrous season losing all 11 matches and they too start the new season in the lower division.

Those who expected the new competitive edge to be too much for the discipline of the teams taking part were happily confounded. Hard indeed was the play, but indiscipline and rough play was not in any way prevalent.

Now that we will have fixed Saturdays we can look forward to a more even pattern of events and this should make for considerable excitement in the new season.

Leicester beat Waterloo and take the Division 1 title. Bates, well supported by Thornley, Dean Richards and Wells, goes over. Photo: Colorsport.

Wakefield 24 Fylde 21 – John Player Cup. Wakefield prop Clive Yemm crashes over for a try. Photo: Gordon Bunney.

NATIONAL LEAGUE DIVISION 2

THE success which attended the top Courage division also rubbed off on Division 2, where despite the original haphazard fixture arrangements the programme was virtually completed with only the game between Gosforth and Northampton left unplayed. The final result would have made no difference to promotion or relegation had it been played, but on this occasion the two bottom teams did not suffer the ignominy of demotion as had been stipulated at the beginning of the season.

From an early stage promotion was a 'three-horse-race' between Rosslyn Park, Liverpool St Helens and Saracens and all had their moments with the Roehampton team probably the best side in the competition and deserving their top place. With certain promising newcomers joining the club for the new season – notably Richmond's talented fly-half Simon Smith – they should hold their own in higher company even though it will be without Andy Ripley, who evidently considers that 40 really is too old an age for a first class rugby player – not that he looks that old.

Liverpool St. Helens also had an excellent season which made Saracens the unlucky ones, although the Southgate club has enough talent to continue their strong challenge for a top division place.

Headingley, Bedford and Richmond all showed improved form with Bedford providing in John Orwin the man who inspired England's improved forward play and also led the touring party in Australia.

The three exile clubs were disappointing but there is hope for 'Scottish' in the arrival at the Athletic Ground of Gavin Hastings, Paul Burnell (a most promising prop) and Derek White from Gala. 'Irish' also have some fine new recruits and ended the season in most promising form, but the same cannot be said for London Welsh, who had a dreadful time and at the moment do not seem to have the talent to survive at this level; they need some new players – now. Their existing talent, although willing enough, is just not good enough – Mark Douglas, Richard Wintle and Stuart Russell apart.

Gosforth can do better, but they will need to improve to avoid 'the drop', which surely will befall Blackheath uless they show a dramatic improvement. Northampton should not be where they are but their recent 'palace revolution', which leaves Barry Corless in charge, may 'work the oracle' for them.

Division 2 can expect some exciting times in the new season with fixed Saturdays again making it easy to follow progress.

NATIONAL LEAGUE DIVISION 3

FOR sheer excitement the battle at the top of Division 3 was possibly the most exciting of all the competitions, which was astonishing when nothing but pride was at stake. Promotion was not on the agenda, which meant that it was in many ways a pointless exercise.

This did not deter the teams from having a 'battle royal' for the title and at various times Plymouth Albion (who also had a fine John Player Cup run), Sheffield, Vale of Lune and – then – West Hartlepool all looked possible winners before at the last gasp Wakefield 'came up on the rails' to snatch the title on points difference from 'West'.

Wakefield had their own selection of stars, none of whom had been enticed there by any blandishments other than a wish to play for the club. By the end of the season Mike Harrison had added to his tally of England caps and Bryan Barley went to Australia along with full back Ray Adamson with the former returning to the full international side. Graham Marshall did some brave deeds for Scotland 'B', whilst there were many county honours for the club.

West Hartlepool have for years been one of the leading lights of the North East and they too played excellently to keep up the excitement.

Further down the table Metropolitan Police did less well than they had done in 1986–87, but they will come again; their facilities are superb. Fylde – with Wade Dooley and Steve Bainbridge – are another team to watch and Maidstone came through their first season in real senior company bravely.

Exeter at one time seemed likely candidates for the dreaded drop, but made a remarkable late recovery with three vital wins that not only meant a retention of status, but future possibilities? Nuneaton were always struggling but not as much as Morley, who only won one match, and the wretched Birmingham who won none at all. Both the latter two are making brave noises and mean to fight their way back.

It was Division 3 for thrills and it could happen again in 1988–89.

NATIONAL DIVISIONS

COURAGE CLUBS CHAMPIONSHIP

DIVISION 1

	P	W	D	L	F	A	Pts
Leicester	10	9	0	1	225	133	37
Wasps	11	8	1	2	218	136	36
Harlequins	11	6	1	4	261	128	30
Bath	11	6	1	4	197	156	30
Gloucester	10	6	1	3	206	121	29
Orrell	11	5	1	5	192	153	27
Moseley	11	5	0	6	167	170	26
Nottingham	11	4	1	6	146	170	24
Bristol	10	4	1	5	171	145	23
Waterloo	10	4	0	6	123	208	22
Coventry	11	3	1	7	133	246	21
Sale	11	0	0	11	95	374	11

Coventry and Sale are relegated to Division 2 and replaced by Rosslyn Park and Liverpool-St. Helens.

DIVISION 2

	P	W	D	L	F	A	Pts
Rosslyn Park	11	8	2	1	155	83	37
Liverpool-St Helens	11	8	1	2	154	97	36
Saracens	11	7	2	2	228	86	34
Headingley	11	6	2	3	202	104	31
Bedford	11	6	2	3	152	139	31
Richmond	11	6	0	5	140	156	29
London Scottish	11	4	1	6	141	158	24
London Irish	11	4	1	6	120	177	24
London Welsh	11	3	2	6	153	185	22
Gosforth	10	2	1	7	99	129	17
Blackheath	11	2	0	9	102	187	17
Northampton	10	1	0	9	81	226	13

Gosforth have had three points and one win deducted for fielding ineligible player against Bedford.

DIVISION 3

	P	W	D	L	F	A	Pts
Wakefield	11	10	0	1	308	90	41
West Hartlepool	11	10	0	1	249	105	41
Plymouth	11	8	0	3	276	125	35
Sheffield	11	7	1	3	134	161	33
Vale of Lune	11	7	0	4	183	149	32
Fylde	11	6	0	5	269	170	29
Met Police	11	5	0	6	130	128	26
Maidstone	11	4	0	7	134	162	23
Exeter	11	3	2	6	128	197	22
Nuneaton	11	2	1	8	94	157	18
Morley	11	1	1	9	109	235	15
Birmingham	11	0	1	10	46	381	12

AREA LEAGUE NORTH

	P	W	D	L	F	A	Pts
Rugby	10	9	0	1	184	100	18
Durham	10	8	0	2	165	100	16
Roundhay	10	6	2	2	131	67	14
Preston G'hoppers	10	5	1	4	178	149	11
Northern	10	5	1	4	121	137	11
Broughton Park	10	5	0	5	152	106	10
Stourbridge	10	5	9	5	132	134	10
Lichfield	10	4	0	6	150	165	8
Birkenhead Park	10	4	0	6	117	179	8
Derby	10	2	0	8	136	169	4
Solihull	10	0	0	10	59	219	0

AREA LEAGUE SOUTH

	P	W	D	L	F	A	Pts
Askeans	s10	8	1	1	141	83	17
Sidcup	10	7	2	1	130	72	16
Lydney	10	7	0	3	173	99	14
Camborne	10	5	2	3	113	119	12
Havant	10	5	0	5	116	102	10
Stroud	10	5	0	5	112	114	10
Southend	10	5	0	5	63	108	10
Sudbury	10	3	2	5	125	106	8
Salisbury	10	3	1	6	84	94	7
Cheltenham	10	3	0	7	95	152	6
Streatham/ Croydon	10	0	0	10	70	173	0

Rugby and Askeans are promoted to Division 3. Morley and Birmingham are relegated.

NATIONAL LEAGUE – DIVISION 1

Where's the ball? The glances of Leicester's Mann (left), Bath's Cronin and Leicester's Redfern ('A') suggests that no-one is sure. Have you spotted it? Photo: Colorsport.

LEICESTER

Aylestone Road, Leicester LE2 7LF. Tel: 0533 541607
Founded: 1880
President: K.P. Andrews
Chairman: B.T. Small
Coach: G.G. Willars
Secretary: J.A. Allen, 60 Dorchester Road, Leicester. Tel: 858407 (H) or 471234 (W)
Fixtures Secretary: J.H. Berry, Bunnystone Cottage, Bunnison Lane, Colston Bassett. Tel: 0949 81258 (H) or 0949 81428 (W)
Club captain (1987–88): P. Dodge
Club captain (1988–89): P. Dodge
No. of teams: Senior 3. Youth & Minis 1
Directions to Ground: Exit 21 of M1 – A46 towards Leicester. 1 mile turn right at traffic lights (Post House Hotel on corner), after 1 mile T-junction, turn left. 2 miles towards city. On entry into one-way system ground on right
Ground capacity: 15,200. Stand, 9,200
Colours: Scarlet/white/green. (*Change colours:* Red with green and white hoop)
Nickname: Tigers
Floodlights: Yes
Admission: £1.80 adults
Membership: £22 full, £11 OAP & Junior
Programme: 40p (Editor: D.M.W. Berry)
Local newspaper: Leicester Mercury
League: Div. 1
Final position (1987–88): 1st
Playing record (1987–88): P 38, W 32, L 6, F 1077, A 422
Competitions won: John Player Cup 1979, 1980, 1981. Courage League Div. 1 1987/88

Most capped players: (for England unless otherwise stated): L. Cusworth 12, P.W. Dodge 32, W.H. Hare 25, R.V. Stirling 19, P.J. Wheeler 41, Woodward 21.
(for Ireland): G.R. Beamish 12.

Players' appearances, 1987–88: W.H. Hare 31, T. Buttimore 21, M. Foulkes Arnold 24, L. Cusworth 25, J. Wells 25, S. Redfern 37, P. Dodge 18, R. Tebbutt 20, W. Richardson 29, N. Youngs 8, T. Smith 31, C. Tressler 8, D. Richards 17, R. Underwood 15, B. Evans 30, S. Kenney 26, I. Bates 35, H. Roberts 27, M. Charles 7, I. Smith 5, S. Povoas 16, C. Dexter 16, J. Harris 16, P. Burnell 6, R. Lane 1, P. Thornely 19, A. Marriott 12, S. Burnhill 20, K. McDonald 1, L. Richardson 2, D. Grewcock 7, P.J. Mann 18, P. Coltman 1, R. Nockles 4, D. Hopper 3, T. Thacker 3, C. Gerald 2, A. Gissing, T. Underwood, G. Collins 1.

Leading scorers, 1987–88: *Points*: W.H. Hare 374 (1 t, 71 pens, 74 cons, 3 d.g.); J. Harris 109 (5 t, 8 pens, 22 cons, 7 d.g.); B. Evans 80 (20 t). *Tries*: B. Evans 20, R. Underwood 12, C. Dexter 12, D. Richards 10.

International & representative honours 1987–88: L. Cusworth, R. Underwood, D. Richards, B. Evans, T. Buttimore, J. Wells.

Leicester show why they are champions as Paul Dodge (letter 'P') – a replacement against Waterloo – passes inside to John Wells. Photo: Colorsport.

A rare break-out by Waterloo against Leicester as Heslop (with ball and supported by veteran Connor) seems to have escaped the attentions of John Wells (Leicester). Photo: Colorsport.

Results: League Division 1

[1]*John Player Cup*

[2]*Courage Championship*

Sept 5	Bedford	A	W	29–9
Sept 8	Nuneaton	H	W	52–0
Sept 12	[2]Bath	H	W	24–13
Sept 19	London Welsh	H	L	6–9
Sept 26	[2]Harlequins	A	W	12–9
Oct 3	[2]Coventry	H	W	32–16
Oct 10	Richmond	A	W	20–6
Oct 17	Northampton	A	W	47–0
Oct 21	Oxford University	A	W	17–6
Oct 24	Swansea	H	L	9–17
Oct 31	Llanelli	A	L	15–20
Nov 7	Cardiff	H	W	27–19
Nov 10	Cambridge University	H	W	64–6
Nov 14	[2]Nottingham	A	W	22–13
Nov 21	[2]Wasps	H	W	12–9
Nov 28	[2]Moseley	A	W	21–3
Dec 5	Gloucester	H	W	19–12
Dec 12	Blackheath	A	W	16–15
Dec 19	[2]Bristol	H	W	15–10
Dec 28	Barbarians	H	W	48–30
Jan 2	Headingley	H	W	37–6
Jan 9	Gloucester	A	L	16–30
Jan 16	Bedford	H	W	42–9
Jan 23	[1]Rosslyn Park	A	W	15–0
Jan 30	London Welsh	A	W	41–6
Feb 6	London Scottish	H	W	34–15
Feb 13	[1]Bath	H	L	6–13
Feb 20	[2]Orrell	A	L	6–30
Feb 27	Northampton	H	W	35–9
Mar 5	Saracens	A	W	28–8
Mar 8	R.A.F.	H	W	51–0
Mar 12	Coventry	A	Cancelled	
Mar 15	Loughborough Students	H	Cancelled	
Mar 18	Lansdowne	H	W	38–13
Mar 26	[2]Sale	H	W	42–15
Apr 2	Ballymena	A	W	19–16
Apr 4	[1]Waterloo	H	W	39–15
Apr 9	Bristol	A	W	15–12
Apr 16	Gosforth	H	W	65–0
Apr 23	Mosley	H	W	41–3
Apr 30	J.P.S. Final			

New Zealand mudlark. The famous photo of Sale prop Fran Cotton during the 1977 Lions tour. Photo: Colorsport.

Mark Bailey (Wasps) beats the Bath cover as Simon Halliday seems to gasp with dismay. Photo: Colorsport.

WASPS

Repton Avenue, Sudbury, Middlesex. Tel: 01-902 4220
Founded: 1867
President: Mike Cutter
Chairman: Peter Yarranton
Coach: Rob Smith
Secretary: Ivor Montlake, Roebuck Cottage, Wych Cross, Forest Row, East Sussex. Tel: 034 282 2980.
Fixtures Secretary: Neville Compton, 29 Dukes Wood Avenue, Gerrards Cross, Bucks. Tel: 0753 885507.
Club captain (1987–88): David Pegler
Club captain (1988–89): Rob Lozowski
No. of teams: Senior 10, Youth 2.
Directions to Ground: 10 mins walk from Sudbury Town Station (Piccadilly Line)
Ground capacity: 4000. Stand, 900.
Clubhouse: Modern 2 storey, new trophy room, medical room, gym, sponsors room, bars, shop, pressroom, etc.
Colours: Black and gold wasp. (*Change colours:* Same but hoops).
Floodlights: Yes
Admission: £2.
Membership: £30
Programme: 50p. (Editor: N. Compton)
Local newspaper: Harrow Observer
League: 1st
Final position (1987–88): 2nd
Playing record (1987–88): P 37, W 27, D 2, L 8. F 744, A 429.
Competitions won: JP Cup runners up 1986 & 1987. Middlesex 7s winners 1948, 1952, 1985.
Most capped players: (*for England unless otherwise stated*): M. Colclough 25, R.M. Uttley 23, G.H. Davies 21, N. Horton 20, R. Andrew 20, D.J. O'Brien 20 for Ireland, G.J. Fay 20 for Australia, R.V. Stirling 18, P. Rendall 17, K.G. Simms 15.

Leading scorers, 1987 88. *Points*: C.R. Andrew 136 (7 t, 4 d.g., 22 pens, 15 cons.), N. Stringer 135 (1 t, 29 pens, 22 cons), D. Richardson 90 (14 pens, 22 cons). *Tries*: S. Smith 13, J. Ellison 10, M. Bailey 9, C.R. Andrew 7, R. Pellow 7.

International & representative honours 1987–88: R. Andrew 6, P. Rendall 7, J. Probyn 7, K. Simms 2, N. Melville 4 (England); S. O'Leary 2, M. Rose, K. Simms (England B); P. Rendall (President of Japan's XV). R. Andrew, K. Sims, P. Rendall, J. Proby, N. Melville, S. O'Leary, M. Rose, M. Bailey, C. Pinnegar (England Final Trial). A. Simmons (Barbarians).

Unsung heroes – so far! Wasps hooker Simmons passes to scrum-half Bates against Bath – 14.11.87. Photo: Colorsport.

It's a forwards' game? Ask Wasps' and Bath's Hill, Pinnegar, Dawe, Redman and Bonner. Photo: Colorsport.

Results: League Division 1

[1] *Div 1.*
[2] *John Player Cup*

Sept 5	Maesteg	s H	W	39–7
Sept 6	Metropolitan Police	A	W	24–6
Sept 12	Richmond	A	W	4–0
Sept 16	Bedford	H	W	22–12
Sept 19	Liverpool St Helens	H	W	43–10
Sept 26	Headingley	A	W	26–12
Oct 3	Blackheath	H	W	45–3
Oct 10	[1] Bristol	A	D	12–12
Oct 17	Vale of Lune	H	W	15–13
Oct 18	Côte Basque	A	L	16–22
Oct 24	Askeans	H	W	57–7
Nov 7	Saracens	H	W	37–6
Nov 14	[1]Bath	H	W	19–15
Nov 21	[1]Leicester	A	L	9–12
Nov 28	[1]Nottingham	H	W	17–9
Dec 5	Rosslyn Park	H	L	6–12
Dec 12	Rugby	H	L	6–28
Dec 19	Northampton	H	W	15–12
Jan 2	[1]Harlequins	H	W	17–16
Jan 9	Llanelli	A	L	0–15
Jan 16	[1]Gloucester	A	L	13–22
Jan 23	[2]Aspatria	A	W	13–9
Jan 30	Nottingham	A	W	13–9
Feb 5	[1]Moseley	A	L	12–19
Feb 1	[2]Gloucester	A	W	24–13
Feb 20	Fylde	H	A	60–11
Feb 27	[2]Plymouth Albion	A	W	26–4
Mar 5	[1]Coventry	H	W	20–4
Mar 12	[1]Sale	A	W	14–6
Mar 19	Loughborough Students	H	W	44–10
Mar 26	[2]Harlequins	H	L	16–20
Apr 1	Birkenhead Park	A	W	29–15
Apr 2	[1]Waterloo	A	W	22–13
Apr 4	New Brighton	A	D	10–10
Apr 9	London Welsh	A	W	26–20
Apr 16	Coventry	H	W	49–6
Apr 23	Orrell	H	W	23–15

Season's review: Runners-Up in Division One, Losing Semi-Finalists to the eventual Winers of the John Player Cup, only 8 defeats in 37 matches, 6 players capped for England plus 2 for England 'B'.

In Division One, we did suffer in having anything between 5 and 13 players removed by representative calls in about half the Matches and this resulsted in a loss v Moseley, which had a critical effect on our eventual position. But we did lose to Leicester away by 9–12, the difference being that they took their one chance and we failed to take ours – so no complaints.

Our Cup run ended in the last minute of extra time after a nail biter with Harlequins 16–20 and they went on to win in style at Twickenham.

Perhaps our best performance of all was a defeat 16–22 by the Cote Basque in France, a side containing no less than 7 current French Internationals including Blanco, Lescarboura and Condom.

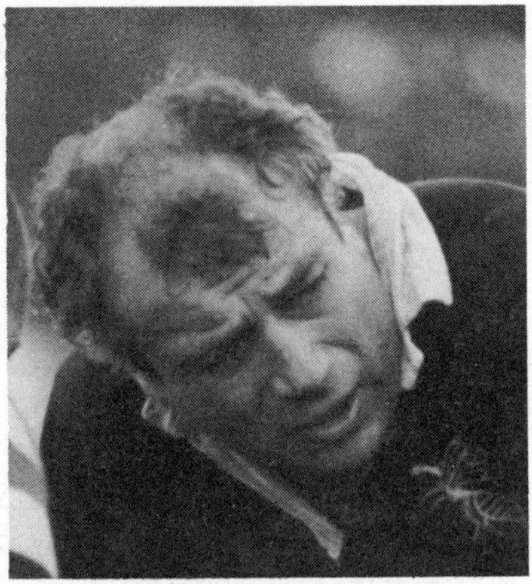

Paul Rendall, Wasps loosehead prop. Photo: Chris Roberts.

Mark Bailey (Wasps) outpaces a Bath defender – 1987–88. Photo: Chris Roberts.

The rise and the decline. Harlequins' Everton Davis passes against hitherto unbeatable Waterloo at the Stoop Memorial Ground and out of the John Player Cup go the Blundellsands team (37–4). For good measure Quins take four league points from the match. Photo: Colorsport.

HARLEQUINS

Stoop Memorial Ground, Craneford Way, Twickenham.
Founded: 1866
President: K.H.C. Chapman
Chairman: R.F. Looker
Coach: R. Best
Secretary: C.M. Herridge, 11 Langley Avenue, Surbiton, Surrey. Tel: 01s-390 0201 (H). 0932 569166. (W)
Fixtures Secretary: R.F. Read, Brookside, Lodge Lane, Salfords, Redhill, Surrey. 0293 783711 (H). 01-661 5107 (W).
Club captain (1987–88): J. Olver
Club captain (1988–89): J. Olver
No. of teams: Senior 4. Youth & Minis 2.
Directions to Ground: A316 from London on dual carriageway and turn first left into Egerton Road and right into Craneford Way.
Ground capacity: 4000. Stands, 600.
Clubhouse: 4 changing rooms, weights room, 3 bars, refreshments.
Colours: L blue, magenta, chocolate, Fr. grey black and light green.
Nickname: Quinns
Floodlights: Yes. Will be installed in August/September.
Admission: £3 incl. car park
Membership: £40 non playing. £25 playing.
Programme: 50p. (Editor: C.M. Herridge)
Local newspaper: Richmond & Twickenham Times
League: 1st Division
Final position (1987–88): 3rd.
Playing record (1987–88): P 33, W 22, L 9, D 2. F 869, A 438.
Competitions won: John Player Cup, Surrey Sevens, Middlesex Sevens.
Most capped players: (For England unless otherwise stated): W.W. Wakefield 31, J.D. Currie 25, C.B. Stevens 25, R.W.D. Marques 23, W.J.A. Davies 22 + 3 for British Isles, R.J. Dixon 22 + 3 for British Isles, J.G.G. Birkett 21, R.B. Hiller 19; W. Cuthburton 20 for Scotland; R.C.C. Thomas 26 for Wales + 2 for British Isles.
Players' appearances, 1987–88: R. Moon 27, A. Thompson 27, N. Edwards 26, A. Mullins 25, P. Ackford 22, T. Bell 22, E. Davis 22, J. Olver 20, J. Salmon 22, R. Langhorn 20, S. Thresher 20.
Leading scorers, 1987–88: *Points*: S. Thresher 146 (8, 16 pens, 33 cons); J. Salmon 98 (10 t, 8 pens, 17 cons); M. Rose 86 (3 t, 8 pens, 25 cons); J. Eagle 72 (18 t); R. Moon 52 (13 t). *Tries*: J. Eagle 18, R. Moon 13, E. Davis 12, N. Edwards 10

Player of the Year 1987–88: Neil Edwards.

Forwards nowadays are athletic and mobile as shown here by Quins' Neil Edwards against Bristol, whose Simon Hogg tries to tackle him in the John Player Cup Final. Photo: Colorsport.

Harlequins crush Waterloo in their "double-header". Everton Davis (Quins) watched by Adrian Thompson seems to have beaten off another tackle. Photo: Colorsport.

Richard Moon (Harlequin) passes to a colleague in the John Player Cup Final at Twickenham watched pensively by Bristol's David Thomas. Photo: Colorsport.

Results: League Division 1

[1] *League matches*
[2] *John Player Cup*

Sept 5	Glasgow & District	H	W	29–22
Sept 12	Northampton	A	L	4–15
Sept 19	Llanelli	H	W	26–15
Sept 26	[1]Leicester	H	L	9–12
Oct 3	Swansea	H	W	19–17
Oct 17	Rosslyn Park	H	W	7–21
Oct 24	Cardiff	H	L	12–21
Oct 31	London Welsh	A	W	26–4
Nov 7	London Irish	A	W	32–19
Nov 14	Gosforth	A	D	33–4
Nov 21	[1]Gloucester	A	D	9–9
Nov 24	Oxford University	A	W	29–14
Nov 28	Cambridge University	A	W	28–9
Dec 5	Blackheath	A	W	36–16
Dec 12	Bedford	A	W	54–0
Dec 19	Rugby	A	D	9–9
Dec 28	Richmond	A	W	46–20
Jan 2	[1]Wasps	A	L	16–17
Jan 17	Saracens	A	W	34–6
Jan 23	[2]Maidenhead	A	W	40–0
Feb 7	[1]Orrell	A	L	6–12
Feb 13	[2]Berry Hill	A	W	17–4
Feb 20	Headingley	A	W	68–6
Feb 27	[1,2]Waterloo	A	W	37–4
Mar 5	[1]Moseley	A	W	32–11
Mar 19	[1]Coventry	A	W	15–12
Mar 26	[2]Wasps	A	W	20–16
Apr 1	[1]Nottingham	A	W	34–8
Apr 1	Swansea	A	L	16–38
Apr 4	Llanelli	A	L	44–23
Apr 9	[1]Bath	A	L	9–21
Apr 23	Sale	A	W	66–0
Apr 30	[1,2]Bristol	A	W	28–22

International & representative honours 1987–88: J. Salmon, M. Rose, W. Carling, M. Skinner (England); J. Olver (England B); R. Cramb (Scotland); R. Cramb, D. Butcher (Scotland B); N. Edwards, S. Hunter, J. Oliver, M. Rose, J. Salmon, M. Skinner (London Division); W. Carling; Barbarians: W. Carling, R. Cramb, J. Olver (Northern Division); T. Bell, P. Curtis, R. Dudman, S. Sheasby, C. Smith, A. Thompson (Middlesex); P. Ackford, P. Brady, D. Butcher, S. Cooke, E. Davis, N. Edwards, M. Green, S. Hunter, A. Woodhouse (Surrey); M. Sly (Sussex); M. Skinner, S. Thresher (Kent); W. Carling (Durham).

Season's review: Winners of the John Player Cup; Winners of the Middlesex Sevens for the third successive year; scored more points than any other club in the National League 1st Division.

Harlequins' Tim Bell. Photo: Colorsport.

That man Everton Davis (Quins) evades a tackle by England scrum-half Richard Harding (Bristol) in the John Player Cup Final. Photo: Colorsport.

Bath at Wasps and on the attack. David Trick waits for a pass as Wasps flanker Ellison (bending) and Probyn size up the situation. Photo: Colorsport.

BATH

Recreation Ground, Bath. Tel: 0225 25192
Founded: 1865
President: N.P. Halse
Chairman: G.W. Hancock
Coach: J. Rowell
Secretary: C.D. Howard, Horseshoe Cottage, Faulkland, Bath BA3 5XA. Tel: 0373 87 501 (H) or 0225 62827 (W)
Fixtures Secretary: J.W.P. Roberts, Grove Hosue, Ashley, Box, Wilts. Tel: 0225 742251 (H)
Club captain (1987–88): R.J. Hill
Club captain (1988–89): S. Barnes
No. of teams: Senior 3. Youth & Minis 6
Directions to Ground: Off Pulteney Street in city centre
Ground capacity: 7,500. Stand, 1,000
Clubhouse: Recreation Ground, Bath
Colours: Blue/black/white. (*Change colours:* White)
Floodlights: Yes
Admission: £2
Programme: 30p (Editor: C.D. Howard)
Local newspaper: Bath and West Evening Chronicle
League: Nat. Div. 1
Playing record (1987–88): P 44, W 29, D 4, L 11, F 1098, A 549
Competitions won: John Smith's Merit Table 1986/87, John Player Special Cup 1983/84, 1984/85, 1985/86, 1986/87

Most capped players: J.P. Hall 19, S. Barnes 8, R.J. Hill 8, G.J. Chilcott 7, S.J. Halliday 6, A.H. Swift 6, N.C. Redman 5, C.R. Martin 4 (for England).

Players' appearances, 1987–88: J. Guscott 37, M.R. Lee 36, R. Cue 28, J.S.C. Morrison 28.

Leading scorers, 1987–88: *points*: S. Barnes 184 (6 t, 26 cons, 30 Pens, 6 d.g.); P. Cue 154 (6 t, 35 cons, 19 pens, 1 d.g.); J. Guscott 111 (21 t, 9 cons, 2 pens, 1 d.g.). *Tries*: J. Guscott 21.

Player of the Year: A. Robinson.

International & representative honours 1987–88: England: S. Barnes, G.J. Chilcott, D.W. Egerton, S.J. Halliday, A. Robinson. Scotland: D.F. Cronin.

Season's review: Did not win the John Player Cup nor the Courage League! Bath's most memorable win at Leicester in Cup. Individually more International caps have been gained and a complete Bath team can now be fielded composed of players (still playing) who have gained caps whilst playing for Bath.

Which way is the right way Gareth Chilcott (Bath's prop) is looking? There is a clue.
Photo: Chris Roberts

Fly-half Stuart Barnes (Bath and England), who regained his international place on the summer tour – against Fiji. Photo: Colorsport.

GLOUCESTER

Kingsholm, Worcester Street, Gloucester, Tel. 0452 20901
Founded: 1873
President: Canon H.M. Hughes, BA
Chairman: P.J. Ford
Coach: K. Richardson
Secretary: T.R. Tandy, 48 Cotteswold Road, Gloucester GL4 9RQ. Tel: 0452 23049
Fixtures Secretary: P.J. Ford, Rivermead, Sandhurst Lane, Gloucester. Tel: 0452 424101 (H). 0452 23580 (W).
Club captain (1988–89): Marcus Hannaford
No. of teams: Senior 2. Colts 1.
Directions to Ground: Use inner ring road, Kingsholm is signposted.
Ground capacity: 12,000. Stands, 1100.
Clubhouse: Tel: 0452 20901/28385. 2 dressing rooms, dining room and bars.
Colours: Cherry and white. *Change colours:* Yellow.
Floodlights: Yes.
Admission: £2
Membership: £20 (ground). £25/£40 (stands).
Programme: 30p. (Editor: P. Arnold)
Local newspaper: Citizen
League: Division 1 National
Final position (1987–88): 3rd.
Playing record (1987–88): P 47, W 32, L 12, D 3. F 973, A 591.
Competitions won: National Knock-out Cup: 1971/2, 1977/8, 1981/2 (shared), John Smith Merit Table 1985/86.
Most capped players: (For England unless otherwise stated): A.T. Voyce 27 (+2 for British Lions), D. Rutherford 14 (+1 British Lions), G.W.D. Hastings 13.
Players' appearances, 1987–88: J. Breeze 36, M. Preedy 36, M. Hannaford 35, M. Hamlin 35, K. Dunn 31, I. Smith 30, N. Scrivens 29, R. Pascall 29, J. Brain 27, D. Morgan 27, D. Cummins 26, J. Ethridge 26.
Leading scorers, 1987–88: T. Smith 136 (2 tries, 22 pens, 31 cons), N. Marment 108 (4 tries, 18 pens, 19 cons)
Most tries: J. Breeze 25, D. Morgan 15, M. Hannaford 15.

International & representative honours 1987–88: Mike Hamlin – S.W. Division R. Mogg – Barbarians

Season's review: By normal standards this was a good season for Gloucester, but Gloucester are not a normal club, and a successful season for them is one where they win something, so the final "bottom line" reports no successes but in terms of overall results a satisfactory season. They will look to an improvement on fourth place in the Courage National League Division 1 and would also hope to do better in the new Pilkington Cup than the fourth round achieved last season when Wasps won at Kingsholm (24–13). The talent is there, spearheaded by a fine pack with an excellent front row.

Winning try. Gloucester's Ian Smith goes over against Bristol despite the attentions of Harding and Doubleday. Photo: Colorsport.

ORRELL

Edgehall Road, Orrell, Wigan, WN5 8TL. Tel: Up Holland 623193
Founded: 1927
President: G. Southworth
Chairman: R.J. Pimbleat
Coach: W. Lyon
Secretary: J. Arrowsmith, 1 Fisher Drive, Orrell, Wigan. Tel: 0942 216879
Fixtures Secretary: J.B. Cooper. Tel: Bursc?? 893239
Club captain (1987–88): Simon Langford
Club captain (1988–89): Simon Langford
No. of teams: Senior 4. Youth & Minis 7
Directions to Ground: M6 junction 26, left at TL, left at next TL (Stag Inn), left at next TL (Church St), 200 yds left into Edgehall Road
Ground capacity: 5,000. Stand, 300
Clubhouse: Member's lounge, President's lounge, Sponsor's loung, clubroom
Colours: Black & amber. (*Change colours:* Amber or Red/white)
Floodlights: Yes
Admission: £2 (Div. 1 games)
Membership: £27 (£30 joint husband/wife)
Programme: 30p (Editor: F. Holcroft. Tel: Wigan 225077)
Local newspaper: Wigan Observer – John Benn
League: Div. 1
Final position (1987–88): 6th
Competitions won: Lancashire Cup 87/88 and previously 7 times. Glengarth 7's

Most capped players: Frank Anderson 1, John Carleton 26, Fran Clough 3, Dave Cusani 1, Peter Williams 4 all for England.

Players' appearances, 1987–88: Sammy Southern completed 550 appearances for Orrell plus 51 for Lancashire.

Leading scorers, 1987–88: Gerry Ainscough 304 (20 t, 46 cons, 42 pens, 2 d.g.)

Player of the Year 1987–88: D. O'Brien.

International & representative honours 1987–88: D.V. Southern (capt), S. Langford, D. O'Brien, G. Ainscough, D. Fell, D. Cleary, P. Williams, D. Cusani, N. Hitchen, R. Kimmins, Lancashire County Championship.

Strange but true!

ON 27th March 1971 Scotland met England at Murrayfield – exactly 100 years after the first ever international match at Edinburgh's Raeburn Place to the day. The presentations ended early and the kick-off was advanced. Scotland's Jock Turner kicked the ball deep and it was fielded by England full back Bob Hiller, who unintentionally started a passing movement which ended with captain Spencer dropping the ball which was hacked on by Scotland's John Frame, who scored a try, which was converted by Arthur Brown. The try was timed as having been scored in 13 seconds and Scotland led before the advertised time of kick-off – eventually winning (26–6).

WALES, who now beat England at Twickenham more often than not, did not avoid defeat there until their eighth appearance in 1931 and won for the first time there in 1933. Since then Wales have won nine times, England eight times and there have been seven draws in matches between the two countries at Twickenham, but England last won in Cardiff in 1963 and Wales lead the series overall with 46 wins to 36 for England with 12 games drawn.

Kimmins (Orrell) wins a line-out against Richmond.

MOSELEY

The Reddings, Redding Road, Mosley, Birmingham B13 8IW. Tel: 021 449 2149.
Founded: 1873
President: N.R.E. Morris
Chairman: J.C. White
Coach: V.D. Protherough
Secretary: B.J. Main, 59 Spiceland Road, Birmingham B31 1NL. Tel: 021 476 6890
Fixtures Secretary: D.A. Evans, 22 Brooks Road, Wylde Green, Sutton Coldfield, West Midlands B71 1HP. Tel: 021 354 5076
Club captain (1987–88): I.R. Metcalfe
Club captain (1988–89): S. Robson
No. of teams: Senior 5. Youth & Minis 11.
Directions to Ground: South Birmingham – A38 – Take Priory Road, traffic lights, county cricket ground on left, island, right into Russell Road, 100 yards left intoMoorcroft road into Reddings Road.
Ground capacity: 9,999. Stand, 1800.
Clubhouse: Tow members bars, public bar, players bar.
Colours: Red and black. (*Change colours:* white (red and black hoop)
Nickname: "Mose"
Floodlights: Yes
Admission: £2.50
Membership: £42 non-playing, £24 playing
Programme: 28 page programme, colour cover, 45p. (Editor: Peter Woodrooke).
Local newspaper: Birmingham Post
League: Division 1
Final position (1987–88): 7th
Playing record (1987–88): P 43, W 24, D 1, L 18. F 718, A 678.
Competitions won: United XV won Midlands Division League
Most capped players: Nigel Horton 20, P.G.D. Robbins 19, Peter Cranmer 16, Nick Jeavons 14, John Finlan 13, J.F. Byrne 13, Jan Webster 11, Martin Cooper 11, C.W. McFadyean 11, K.J. Fielding 10, for England.
Players' appearances, 1987–88: John Goodwin 39, Peter Shillingford 34, Carl Arntzen 19, Kevin Hickey 19, Adrian James 37, Simon Robson 20, Chris Allen 22, Adrian Parsons 25, Richard Denhardt 32, Graham Smith 33, Chris Barbor 20, Jon Desborough 26, Sam Masters 29, Bob Barr 29, Mark Linnett 28, Richard Tuckwood 27.

Leading scorers, 1987–88: *Points*: John Goodwin 135 (15 t, 15 cons, 15 pens); Murray Jones 132 (3 t, 18 cons, 28 pens); Peter Shillingford 72 (18 t); Carl Arntzen 46 (2 t, 20 cons, 6 pens). *Tries*: Peter Shillingford 18; John Goodwin 15; Kevin Hickey 10.

Player of the Year 1987–88: Graham Smith.

International & representative honours 1987–88: J. Domachi, Richard Tuckwood, P. Shillingford, A. Parsons, (N. Midlands); C. Allen (Gloucestershire); Simon Robson (Midland Division, Staffordshire); Mark Linnett (England B, Combined Services Tour NZ, Warwickshire, British Police); Kevin Hickey (Warwickshire); Tim Exeter (Scottish A and B, Anglo-Scots).

Season's review: Knocked Bath out of the John Player Cup quarter finals (4–3). Highest score v. Bedford 37–0. Had the award for 3 tries by Peter Shillingford v. Wasps. Double over Coventry and Newport. Captain Ian Metcalfe injured v. Swansea in 3rd match of the season leading to his retirement from the game.

The opening afternoon. Nottingham and Moseley launch the Courage National League – 5th September 1987. Moseley's Tim Exeter feeds Carl Arntzen followed by Nottingham's Gary Rees. Left: Moseley scrum-half Steve Cookson in action against Nottingham. Photos: Colorsport.

Results: League Division 1
[1] *John Player Cup*
[2] *Friendly*

Sept 2	[2]Newbridge	A	W	31–4
Sept 5	Nottingham	A	L	12–21
Sept 12	[2]Swansea	H	L	10–18
Sept 19	Bath	A	L	0–14
Sept 26	[2]Northampton	H	W	32–1
Sept 30	[2]Nuneaton	A	W	36–3
Oct 3	Sale	A	W	19–15
Oct 10	Orrell	H	W	28–10
Oct 11	[2]Petone (NZ Tourists)	H	L	8–22
Oct 17	[2]Aberavon	A	D	9–9
Oct 14	Coventry	H	W	26–3
Oct 31	[2]Cardiff	A	W	114–1
Nov 7	[2]Newport	H	W	16–1
Nov 14	[2]Ldn Welsh	H	W	18–3
Nov 18	[2]Fylde	H	W	32–9
Nov 21	[2]Rosslyn Park	A	L	6–31
Nov 28	Leicester	H	L	3–21
Dec 5	[2]Headingly	H	W	22–1
Dec 12	Bristol	A	L	10–21
Dec 14	[2]Bedford	H	H	37–0

Dec 26	[2]Coventry	H	W	19–10
Jan 1	Gloucester	A	L	12–18
Jan 2	[2]Glam Wors	H	L	18–20
Jan 9	[2]Neath	A	L	8–30
Jan 15	[2]Saracens	H	L	13–19
Jan 23 30	[1]Wakefield	A	W	14–4
Feb 5	Wasps	H	W	19–12
Feb 13	[2]Gosforth	H	W	33–9
Feb 20	[2]Roundhay	A	W	11–10
Feb 27	[1]Bath	H	W	4–3
Mar 5	Harlequins	H	L	11–32
Mar 9	[2]Abertillery	H	W	13–12
Mar 12	[2]Ldn Irish	A	L	19–34
Mar 17	[2]St Marys Coll Dublin	H	L	12–21
Mar 26	[1]Briston (S.F.)	H	L	6–34
Mar 30	[2]Rugby	A	W	21–19
Apr 2	[2]Gloucester	H	L	10–19
Apr 4	[2]Nottingham	H	L	12–25
Apr 9	[2]Newport	A	W	19–16
Apr 16	[2]Bridgend	H	W	19–12
Apr 23	[2]Leicester	A	L	3–41
Apr 26	Waterloo	H	W	27–3
Apr 30	Llanelli	A	L	26–22

NOTTINGHAM

Ireland Avenue, Dovecote Lane, Beeston, Nottingham NG 1JD. Tel: 0602 254238.
Founded: 1877
President: David W. Roberts
Chairman: Jim B. Bourke FRCS
Coach: Jim Robinson
Secretary: John Drapkin, "Crailing", Wellin Lane, Ed Walton, Nottingham NG12 4AH. Tel: 0602 231662.
Fixtures Secretary: J.H. Addison, Wycliffe Mills, High Church street, New Basford, Nottingham NG7 7JP. Tel: 0602 785466.
Club captain (1987–88): Simon Hodgkinson
Club captain (1988–89): Brian Moore
No. of teams: Senior 3. Youth & Minis 11.
Directions to Ground: M1 (Junction 25) A52 Dir. north, 1 roundabout exit 3 B6003, at T junction turn left onto A6055, pass dual carriageway, Barton's bus depot, Turn right at next crossroad into Dovecote Lane. imm. turn right into Ireland Avenue.
Ground capacity: 5000. Stand, 550.
Clubhouse: 2 clubhouses, 3 bars, open to all spectators.
Colours: Green and white. (*Change colours:* yellow and white).
Floodlights: Yes
Admission: £2
Membership: £23
Programme: 40p. (Editor: Hon. Sec.)
Local newspaper: Nottingham Evening Post
League: Nat. Div. 1
Final position (1987–88): 8th
Playing record (1987–88): P 42, W 24, D 1, L 17. F 814, A 505.
Most capped players: V.H. Cartwright 12, G. Rees 17, B.C. Moore 12, C.R. Andrew 5, H.A. Hodges 3, J. Pallant 3, C. Oti 2, for England.
Players' appearances, 1987–88: D. Kaye 39, G. Mosses 38, M. Freer, R. Byrom 35, P. Cook, C. Jones 39, G. Hartley 38, S. Hodgkinson 25, G. Koral 22, B. Moore and C. Gray 21, G. Rees, D. Hindmarch 20, D. Bell, G. Wyatt 19.

Leading scorers, 1987–88: *Points*: S. Hodgkinson 237 (2, 3 d.g. 29 cons, 54 pens); C. Jones 68 (17 t); M. Sims 54 (6 t, 4 cons, 4 pens); P. Swannick 51 (3 t, 9 cons, 7 pens). *Tries*: C. Jones 17; G. Hartley 11.

Player of the Year 1987–88: Richard Byrom.

International & representative honours 1987–88: Rees, Moore, Oti (England); Cook, Hartley, Hodgkinson (England B); Gray (Scotland B); Hartley, Hodgkinson, Jones, Moore, Rees, Northard. (Middlesex Division); Cook (North); Gray (Anglo-Scots).

Results: League Division 1

5 Sept	Moseley	H	W	21.12
12 Sept	Sale	A	W	17.0
26 Sept	Orrell	H	D	12–12
30 Sept	Coventry	A	W	20–15
10 Oct	Bath	H	W	25–15
17 Oct	Waterloo	A	L	9–10
31 Oct	Bristol	H	L	3–16
14 Nov	Leicester	H	L	13–22
28 Nov	Wasps	A	L	9–17
2 Apr	Harlequins	A	L	8–34

John Player Cup

23 Jan	[1]Waterloo		L	6–19

The ball or a piece of soap? Plenty of Nottingham and Moseley bodies – Chris Gray (left), Greg Koral (6) and Kevin Hickey (aloft) – but do any of them get possession? Photo: Colorsport.

BRISTOL – 1987–88 (Their Centenary Season)

Cup Final action. Who wins this ruck? Probably Bristol this time. Photo: Colorsport.

BRISTOL

Memorial Ground, Filton Avenue, Horfield, Bristol BS7 0AQ. Tel: (0272) 514448
Founded: 1888
President: T.A.B. Mahoney, TD
Chairman: E.J. Blackman
Coach: R. Hesford
Secretary: T. Wynne Jones, 31 Bromley Heath Road, Downend, Bristol BS16 6HY. Tel: 56961
Fixtures Secretary: B.W. Redwood, 205 Stoke Lane, Westbury on Trym, Bristol BS9 3RX. Tel: 684342
Club captain (1987–88): N.J. Pomphrey
Club captain (1988–89): A. Dun
No. of teams: Senior 2. Youth & Minis 1
Directions to Ground: Exit 2, M32, follow signs for Horfield
Ground capacity: 8,000. Stand, 1,500
Clubhouse: Bristol Football Social Club, Memorial Ground. Tel: 514134
Colours: Blue/white. (*Change colours:* Slate/yellow/brown)
Floodlights: Yes
Admission: Ground £2.50. Stand £5
Membership: Ground £25. Stand £50
Programme: 30p
Local newspaper: Western Daily Press/ Evening Post
League: Nat. Div. 1
Final position (1987–88): 9th
Playing record (1987–88): P 48, W 37, D 2, L 9, F 1101, A 554
Competitions won: John Player Cup 1982/83

Most capped players: (for England unless otherwise stated): J.V. Pullin 42 + 2 British Isles, J.S. Tucker 27, M. Rafter 17, L.J. Corbett 16, W.R. Johnston 16, G.G. Gregory 13, R.M. Harding 12, J.M. Webb 11, D.M. Rollitt 11, R. Hesford 10.

Players' appearances, 1987–88: R. Knibbs 39, J. Doubleday 36, H. Duggan 34, D. Palmer, W. Hone 32.

Leading scorers, 1987–88: *points*: J. Webb 275 (8 t, 66 cons, 37 pens); S. Mogg 141 (8 t, 14 cons, 20 pens, 7 d.g.). *Tries*: J. Carr 19; D. Woodman 16; Crane and H. Duggan 11.

Player of the Year: Wayne Hone

International & representative honours 1987–88: England: J.M. Webb, R.M. Harding (captain v Fiji).
S.W. Division: J.M. Webb, R.M. Harding, A. Dun, R. Knibbs.
County Championship: Gloucester J. Watson, Devon P. Lander, Somerset N. Hutton.
Scotland U19: A. Sharp.

Season's review: After a disappointing start when defeats were suffered against Cardiff, Swansea, Gloucester and Bath the Centenary Season took off after an exciting draw against the Barbarions.

From November up to the pulsating John Player Special Final against Harlequins the 1st XV were defeated only by Glamorgan Wanderers, Leicester (2), Coventry and Harlequins. From late December to early April 21 consecutive matches were won.

In March the 1st XV played, and defeated, opponents from Wales, Scotland, France, Japan and England. The international flavour of the season was continued in May with an undefeated tour of Spain.

Bristol's reputation in Seven-a-Side rugby was enhanced by winning the Bournemouth and Oxford Tournaments, and narrowly losing the Harlequins in the Final of the Middlesex 7's.

Centenary Captain Nigel Phomphrey has retired. In Season 1988/99 the Club Captain will be Andy Dun with David Thomas as Vice-Captain.

Bristol entertain Gloucester and go down narrowly despite the efforts of Richard Harding, seen here evading Polledri and passing out to his backs. Photo: Colorsport.

Men of letters! Bristol v. Gloucester – along with Leicester – prefer literacy to being numerate. Photo: Colorsport.

Results: League Division 1
[1] Courage Championship
[2] Friendly

Sept 1	[2]Cheltenham	A	W	50–3
Sept 5	[2]Cardiff	H	L	15–20
Sept 12	[2]Newport	H	W	15–5
Sept 19	[2]Swansea	A	L	12–26
Sept 22	[2]Weston-S-Mare	A	W	61–0
Sept 26	[1]Gloucester	H	L	16–21
Sept 30	[2]Met. Police	H	W	33–12
Oct 3	[2]London Irish	A	W	35–18
Oct 10	[1]Wasps	H	D	12–12
Oct 17	[1]Bath	A	L	9–15
Oct 21	[2]Barbarians	H	D	20–20
Oct 24	[1]Sale	H	W	37–3
Oct 31	[1]Nottingham	A	W	16–3
Nov 4	[2]Glam. Wanderers	A	L	6–26
Nov 7	[2]Bridgend	H	W	25–14
Nov 21	[2]London Welsh	A	W	14–3
Nov 26	SW Police	H	W	38–0
Dec 5	[2]Newport	A	W	14–11
Dec 12	[1]Moseley	H	W	21–10
Dec 19	[1]Leicester	A	L	10–15
Dec 26	[2]Weston-S-Mare	H	W	36–3
Dec 28	[2]Llanelli	H	W	19–15
Dec 30	[2]Clifton	H	W	9–8
Jan 2	[2]Bedford	A	W	25–3
Jan 9	[2]Coventry	H	W	14–11
Jan 16	[2]Aberavon	A	W	30–14
Jan 23	Bedford	A	W	21–4
Feb 5	[2]Gloucester	A	W	13–10
Feb 13	Richmond	H	W	34–0
Feb 20	[2]Richmond	A	W	24–13
Feb 27	Sale	A	W	19–15
Mar 1	[2]Cardiff	A	W	12–10
Mar 4	[2]Kelso	A	W	26–3
Mar 6	[2]Selkirk	A	W	19–12
Mar 12	[2]London Scottish	A	W	24–6
Mar 18	[2]Begles	H	W	13–6
Mar 22	[2]Clifton	A	W	30–3
Mar 26	Moseley	A	W	34–6
Mar 30	[2]Toshiba	H	W	62–31
Apr 2	[2]Bath	H	W	16–15
Apr 4	[2]Glam. Wanderers	H	W	42–16
Apr 9	[2]Leicester	H	L	12–15
Apr 12	[2]Exeter	A	W	22–3
Apr 17	[2]Combn. Services	H	W	18–16
Apr 20	[2]Stroud	A	W	17–12
Apr 23	[1]Coventry	A	L	3–25
Apr 30	[1]Harlequins (J.P. Final)		L	22–28

Harlequins during their tour of Waterloo in the John Player Cup and Courage League "double-header" in March. (Photo: Colorsport).

WATERLOO

St. Anthony's Road, Blundellsands, Liverpool L23 8TW. Tel: 051-924-4552
Founded: 1882
President: B.H. Calvert
Vice President: D.G. Bowman
Coach: R.G. Hopkin
Secretary: K. Alderson, 66 St. Michaels Road, Blundellsands, Liverpool L23 7UW. Tel: 051-924-1168
Fixtures Secretary: G.V. Poynton, 19 Lakeside Gardens, Rainford, St. Helens, Merseyside WA1 18HH. Tel: 074488 4128
Club captain (1987–88): J.P. Syddall
Club captain (1988–89): S. Gallagher
No. of teams: Senior 5. Youth & Minis 10
Directions to Ground: End of M57 – follow signs for Crosby, then signs Waterloo FC to ground
Ground capacity: 10,000. Stand, 950
Clubhouse: Two large bars, function room, gym, hospitality lounge, changing rooms, bathing area
Colours: Myrtle/scarlet/white hoops. (*Change colours:* Red/white collar)
Floodlights: No
Admission: £1.20
Membership: £34
Programme: 30p (Editor: A. Cove)
Local newspaper: Crosby Herald/Liverpool Echo/Daily Post
League: Div. 1
Final position (1987–88): 10th

Playing record (1987–88): W 27, D1, L 9

Most capped players: (for England unless otherwise stated): Joe Periton 14, Jack Heaton, H. "Bert" Toft, Alan Ashcroft, Gordon Rimmer, Reg Bazley.
(for Wales): Watcyn Thomas 14.

Players' appearances, 1987–88: C. Dew 33, P. Colley 32, I. Aitchison 31, D. Carfoot 31, J. Tickle 31, N. Allott 30, S. Gallagher 29, M. Cotter 26, S. Peters 26, N. Wilkinson 26, N. Heslop 25, L. Connor 24, P. Jenkins 24, J. Syddall 24, P. Hackett 20, D. Reed 19, I. Taylor 17, R. Angell 16, G. Hawkins 14, M. Molyneaux 12, J. Whitehead 10.

Leading scorers, 1987–88: *Points*: I. Aitchison 315 (7 t, 43 cons, 50 pens, 17 d.g.); P. Cooley 96 (24 t); R. Angell 73 (4 t, 15 cons, 8 pens, 1 d.g.). *Tries*: P. Cooley 24, N. Heslop 13, M. Cotter 12.

Player of the Year: S. Gallagher.

International & representative honours 1987–88: S. Peters, P. Hackett (North); N. Heslop, P. Jenkins, S. Gallagher, I. Aitchison (Lancashire); J. Ashcroft, A. Bowman, S. Bracegirdle (Lancashire U21); P. McCrave, N. Thompson (Cheshire).

Season's review: Waterloo made an excellent start to the season and by the New Year would have been everyone's favourite at least to finish in the top three in the new Courage First Division and probably even to win it. The club won the *Rugby World & Post* Senior award for the month of December 1987 and their flanker Sean Gallagher was subsequently chosen as Whitbread's Player of the Month for January 1988. Then things went terribly wrong. Although the team somewhat unconvincingly reached the last eight of the John Player Cup the campaign came to an ignominious end with a very heavy defeat at the Stoop Memorial Ground (37–4) and the poor form continued right up to the end of the season when there was a distinct possibility of relegation which would have happened if Coventry had not lost their final match at home to Orrell. Had that happened Waterloo might well have been tempted to take the issue to court as the archaic rules of the Lancashire RFU had prevented them from playing their final match. In the end the club survived and they are now hoping that the early season form of last year will be followed right through the season – and then something might be achieved.

Leicester thrash Waterloo and take the title. (Photo: Colorsport).

Results: League Division 1

[1] *John Player Cup*
[2] *Friendly*
[3] *Lancs Cup*

Sept 2	[2]Rotherham	H	W	48–12
Sept 5	[2]Richmond	H	W	32–25
Sept 12	[2]Nuneaton	H	W	52–7
Sept 19	[2]Blackheath	A	W	28–6
Sept 26	[2]Sheffield	H	W	32–6
Oct 3	[2]Wanderers	H	W	23–6
Oct 10	[2]Vale of Lune	A	W	38–15
Oct 17	Nottingham	H	W	10–9
Oct 24	[2]Saracens	A	W	10–9
Oct 31	Gloucester	H	W	16–6
Nov 7	[2]L.S.H.	A	W	18–3
Nov 14	[2]Bedford	H	W	27–4
Nov 21	[2]London Irish	A	W	39–18
Nov 28	[2]Rosslyn Park	A	W	9–6
Dec 5	[2]Manchester	H	W	60–4
Dec 12	Bath	A	W	17–10
Dec 19	[2]Roundhay	H	L	12–15
Dec 27	[2]Birkenhead Park	A	W	28–0
Jan 2	Sale	H	W	29–13
Jan 9	[2]Wakefield	A	D	22–22
Jan 16	[2]Headingley	H	W	30–15
Jan 23	[1]Nottingham	H	W	19–6
Jan 30	[2]West Park	H	W	48–0
Feb 7	Coventry	A	L	10–15
Feb 13	[1]Gordon League	A	W	11–9
Feb 20	[2]Met. Police	H	W	27–7
Feb 27	[1]Harlequins	A	L	4–37
Mar 12	[2]Ruthin	H	W	48–0
Mar 26	[3]Northampton	A	W	23–17
Apr 2	Wasps	H	L	13–22
Apr 4	Leicester	A	L	15–39
Apr 7	[3]Fylde	H	W	34–12
Apr 13	[3]Lancs Cup	H	W	13–6
Apr 16	Orrell	A	L	6–30
Apr 20	[3]Orrell	A	L	7–9
Apr 23	[2]Pontypool	H	L	9–22
Apr 26	Moseley	A	L	3–27

Coventry – 1987–88: (Back-row) (l to r): J. Butler (Hon. fixtures secretary), L. Johnson, T. Gulliver, P. Rowland, J. Hyde, G. Robbins, P. Suckling, H. Walker (Hon. match secretary), J. Burgum (Touch judge); (Middle-row): P. Rossborough (Playing administrator), J. Broderick (Coach), A. Savage, C. Prescott (President), M. Fairn (Capt.) P. Jackson (Hon. secretary), D. Jones, R. Rowan, S. Wilkes, J. Mauchlen (Committee); (Front-row): J. Williamson, G. Colleran, S. Hall, J. Minshull, J. Graham, A. Farrington
Photo: Coventry Evening Telegraph.

COVENTRY

Coundon Road, Coventry. Tel: 0203 591274.)
Founded: 1873
President: Harry Walker
Chairman: Eric Blackburn
Coach: Peter Rossborough
Secretary: Peter Jackson, 147 Chester Road, Castle Bromwich, Birmingham. Tel: 021 747 2498.
Fixtures Secretary: John Butler, 62 Spring Lane, Whittington, Nr. Lichfield, Staffs. Tel: 0543 432654.
Club captain (1987–88): Martin Fairn
Club captain (1988–89): Martin Fairn
No. of teams: Senior 1. Colts 1.
Directions to Ground: Take Birmingham Road off Inner Ring Road, right at first traffic lights, bear left, ground on lefe over level crossing from A45. Take L fork onto Holyhead road, left 2nd set of major traffic lights right at next set too Barkers Butts Lane, ground on right 200 yards.
Ground capacity: 10000. Stand, 1100.
Clubhouse: Open Saturday, Monday and Thursday evenings. Sunday lunchtime.
Colours: Blue and white. (*Change colours:* Dark Blue.
Nickname: "Cov".
Floodlights: Yes
Admission: Stand £3.30. Ground £2.20.
Membership: Vice President £30.
Programme: 40p. (Editor: John Butler, as above).
Local newspaper: Coventry Evening Telegraph
League: Div. 2
Final position (1987–88): 11th (Div 1)
Playing record (1987–88): P 41, W 18, D 1, L 22. F 632, A 743.
Competitions won: Cup Winners 1972/73 and 1973/74.
Players' appearances, 1987–88: Martin Fairn 38, Andy Parton 36, Steve Wilkes 36, Tony Gulliver 35, Peter Rowland 33, Stuart Hall 33, Andy Farrington 30, Julian Hyde 28, Lee Johnson 25.

Leading scorers, 1987–88: *Points*: Steve Thomas 118, Martin Fairn 96, Ian Potter 67, Andy Parton 44, Stuart Hall 44.

Player of the Year 1987–88: Paul Suckling.

International & representative honours 1987–88: Lee Johnson (England B), 12 players in Warwickshire County Final Side.

Season's review: Relegated to Courage National Division 2. First time in over 50 years we had more defeats in the season than victories.

Results: League Division 1
[1] *Division 1*
[2] *Friendly*

Sept 1	[2]Lichfield	H	L	6–9
Sept 5	[2]Newport	H	W	19–9
Sept 12	[1]Gloucester	A	L	3–39
Sept 19	[2]Cardiff	H	W	21–14
Sept 16	[1]Sale	H	W	24–19
Sept 26	[1]Nottingham	H	L	15–20
Oct 3	[1]Leicester	A	L	16–32
Oct 10	[2]Wanderers	A	W	19–18
Oct 17	[2]Bridgend	H	L	13–49
Oct 24	[1]Moseley	A	L	3–26
Oct 31	[2]Blackheath	A	W	15–9
Nov 7	[2]London Welsh	H	W	30–3
Nov 14	[2]Northampton	A	L	6–44
Nov 18	[2]Nuneaton	A	W	24–0
Nov 21	[1]Bath	H	D	9–9
Nov 28	[2]Bedford	H	W	61–13
Dec 2	[2]London Irish	H	W	11–3
Dec 5	[2]Richmond	A	W	22–9
Dec 12	[2]Liverpool St Helens	A	L	12–16
Dec 19	[2]Gloucester	H	W	17–6
Dec 26	[2]Moseley	H	L	10–19
Dec 30	[2]Wales Police	H	W	10–7
Jan 2	[2]Neath	H	L	10–18
Jan 9	[2]Bristol	A	L	11–14
Jan 17	[2]Newbridge	A	L	4–8
Jan 30	[1]Tynedale	H	W	7–6
Feb 7	Waterloo	H	W	15–10
Feb 13	[1]Sale	H	L	0–13
Feb 19	[2]Northampton	H	W	29–12
Feb 27	[2]Fylde	A	L	26–33
Mar 5	[2]Wasps	A	L	4–20
Mar 19	Harlequins	H	L	12–15
Mar 23	[2]Bedford	A		Post.
Mar 26	[2]Maesteg	A	L	12–36
Mar 30	[2]Nuneaton	H	W	26–3
Apr 2	[2]Gosforth	H	W	37–15
Apr 4	[2]Headingley	A	L	13–14
Apr 9	[2]Llanelli	A	L	9–65
Apr 13	Wasps	A	L	6–49
Apr 16	[2]Pontypool	H	L	9–10
Apr 23	Bristol	H	W	25–3
Apr 30	Orrell	H	L	11–24

England prospect? Sale forward John Howe. Photo: Colorsport.

SALE

Heywood Road, Sale. Tel: 061-973-6348
Founded: 1861
President: A.D. Thomson
Chairman: D.S. Craven
Coach: Richard Trickey
Secretary: Desmond Smith, 2 Riddings Road, Hale, Altrincham WA15 9DS. Tel: 061-941-1717
Fixtures Secretary: Andy Lawson, 1 Oakenrod Villas, Bury Road, Rochdale. Tel: 0706 525440
Club captain (1987–88): Mike Kenrick
Club captain (1988–89): Andy Simpson
No. of teams: Senior 4. Youth & Minis 1
Directions to Ground: Off Marshland Road, near to "Little B" pub
Ground capacity: 4,000. Stand, 400
Clubhouse: 3 executive suites available for sponsors
Colours: Blue & white hoops. (*Change colours:* Plain dark blue)
Floodlights: Yes
Admission: £2
Membership: £30 non-playing
Programme: 30p. (Editor: Dr. R.E. Cook. Tel: 061-973-5114)
Local newspaper: Sale and Altrincham Guardian
League: Nat. 1
Final position (1987–88): Bottom (relegated)
Playing record (1987–88): P 40, W 20, D 1, L 19, F 808, A 730

Most capped players: A.M. Bond 6, F.E. Cotton 31, E. Evans 30, S.J. Smith 28, P.A. Davies 1, V.S.J. Harding 6, J. Mycock 5, W.M. Patterson 2, J. Roberts 18, J.E. Williams 9 for England.
E.C. Davey 23, W. Wooller 18 for Wales.
K.C. Fyfe 10, K.H.D. McMillan 4, G.D. Shaw 6, P.K. Stagg 28 for Scotland.
F.E. Cotton 7, G.M. Isherwood 3, W.M. Patterson 1, P.K. Stagg 3 for British Lions.

Leading scorers, 1987–88: *Points*: G. Jenion 223 (5 t, 40 cons, 41 pens); P. Jee 121 (3 t, 29 cons, 17 pens); C. Rafferty 61 (10 r, 7 d.g.). *Tries*: M. Fitton 15.

Player of the Year 1987–88: Graham Jenion.

International & representative honours 1987–88: John Bentley (England, Australain tour).

Season's review: Defeated by Bristol in quarter-finals of the John Player Cup. Wins over London Irish and Coventry. Failed to win any games in Division 1 and relegated. Sale Colts won Cheshire Championship.

Martin Whitcombe (Sale and Yorkshire) helps to spearhead a strong promotion bid. Photo: Colorsport.

Results: League Division 1

[1] John Player Cup
[2] Friendly

Sept 2	[2]Kendal	A	L	0–25
Sept 5	[2]Morley	A	W	39–3
Sept 9	[2]Orrell	H	L	7–10
Sept 12	Nottingham	H	L	0–17
Sept 16	[2]Broughton P	H	W	21–6
Sept 19	[2]W Hartlepool	A	W	26–6
Sept 26	Coventry	A	L	19–24
Oct 3	Moseley	H	L	15–19
Oct 10	[2]Neath	A	L	11–29
Oct 17	[2]Richmond	H	W	17–8
Oct 24	Bristol	A	L	3–37
Oct 31	[2]Saracens	H	W	21–15
Nov 5	Orrell	A	L	0–19
Nove 14	[2]Ldn Scottish	H	W	26–9
Nove 21	[2]Birkenhead Park	H	W	37–4
Nov 28	[2]Halifax	H	W	65–10
Dec 5	[2]Pontypridd	A	L	12–24
Dec 12	[2]New Brighton	H	W	68–6
Dec 19	[2]Headingly	A	D	4–4
Dec 26	[2]Wilmslow	H	W	20–0
Dec 28	[2]Broughton P	A	W	20–6
Jan 2	Waterloo	A	L	13–29
Jan 9	[2]Bedford	H	W	54–6
Jan 16	[2]Winnington P	A	W	41–0
Jan 23	[1]Ldn Irish	A	W	16–3
Jan 30	[2]Broughton P	H	W	31–19
Feb 6	[2]L'pool St Helens	H	W	43–6
Feb 13	[1]Coventry	A	W	13–0
Feb 20	[2]Hawick	H	W	22–12
Feb 27	[1]Bristol	H	L	15–19
Mar 5	[2]Gosforth	A	L	14/29
Mar 12	Wasps	H	L	6–14
Mar 19	[2]Northampton	H	W	23–3
Mar 26	Leicester	A	L	15–42
Apr 1	[2]Vale of Lune	H	W	25–20
Apr 2	[2]Wakefield	A	L	12–22
Apr 9	[2]Pontypodd	A	L	10–52
Apr 16	Gloucester	A	L	7–16
Apr 23	Harlequins	A	L	0–66
Apr 30	Bath	H	L	17–46

Rosslyn Park – 1987–88. Division 2 Champions.

The other men of letters – Leicester – beat Rosslyn Park in the John Player Cup – mud and all. Photo: Colorsport.

ROSSLYN PARK

Priory Lane, Roehampton, London SW15. Tel: 01-876 1879
Founded: 1879
President: Geoffrey Dodds
Chairman: Alan Taylor
Coach: Hugh McHardy
Secretary: David E. Whittam, FRCS, 37 Queens Road, Kingston-upon-Thames KT2 7SL. Tel: 01-549 4209 (H) or 01-672 1255, ext. 52052 (W)
Fixtures Secretary: Colin Horgan, 96 Thames Street, Sunbury-on-Thames, TW16 6AG. Tel: 0932-78-5012
Club captain (1987–88): Tony Brooks
Club captain (1988–89): Tony Brooks
No. of teams: Senior 9. Youth & Minis 2
Directions to Ground: Ground situated at the Junction of the Upper Richmond Road (South Circular Road) and Roehampton Lane, London SW15
Ground capacity: 3,500. Stand, 630
Clubhouse: Large public bar, Members bar, Presidents bar, kit and souvenir shop, cafeteria, changing rooms, first-aid room, offices
Colours: Red and white hoops. (*Change colours:* Dark blue with red band)

Nickname: The Park
Floodlights: Yes
Admission: £2.50
Membership: Playing £32.20, non-playing £25.75
Programme: 12 pages, 50p (Editor: Martin Sturgis)
Local newspaper: Richmond & Twickenham Times/Surrey Comet
League: Nat. Div. 1/Promoted Div. 2
Final position (1987–88): Top of Div. 2
Playing record (1987–88): P 32, W 21, D 2, L 9, F 543, A 361
Competitions won: Courage Div. 2 Championship

Most capped players: J.P. Scott 34, M.J. Colclough 25, A.G. Ripley 24, C.E. Winn 8, P.J. Warfield 6, C.P. Kent 5, T.C. Wintle 5, A. Obolensky 4 (for Englang).

Players' appearances, 1987–88: J. Graves 29, J. Ager 28, A. Brooks 27, D. Barnett 25, S. Foulds 25, P. Essenhigh 25, R. Luddington 23, C. Freeman 21, A. Ripley 20.

The mud has won. Leicester change jerseys against Rosslyn Park in the John Player Cup Third Round at Roehampton. The Tigers also win – 15–0. Photo: Colorsport.

Leading scorers, 1987–88: *Points*: J. Graves 210, A. Brooks 52, P. Tayler 28, J. Ager 24, M. Jermyn 23, M. Summers 20, R. Luddington 20, A. Ripley 12, P. McMahon 12, A. Harris 12. *Tries*: A. Brooks 13, P. Taylor 7, J. Ager 6, M. Summers 5, R. Luddington 5, A. Ripley 3, P. McMahon 3, A. Harris 3.

International & representative honours 1987–88: Jason Hoad (Capt); Gavin Thompson (England Colts).

Season's review: Winners of the Courage Division 2 championship and promotion to Division 1. Ran the Second World Schools Sevens Tournament in March 1988 – won by Wales.

Results: League Division 2

[1] *Courage*
[2] *Friendly*
[3] *John Player Cup (3rd round)*

[2]North Walsham	W	21–3
[2]Metropolitan Police	W	14–3
[1]Gosforth	W	14–3
[1]London Welsh	W	16–15
[2]Orrell	L	7–15
[1]London Scottish	W	15–6
[2]Harlequins	W	21–7
[2]Surrey County Clubs	W	48–9
[1]Headingley	D	12–12
[1]London irish	W	20–3
[2]Abertillery	W	21–20
[2]Gloucester	L	6–16
[2]Cambridge University	W	23–3
[2]Moseley	W	31–6
[2]Waterloo	l	6–9
[2]Wasps	W	12–6
[1]Richmond	W	20–12
[1]Liverpool/St. Helens	W	13–3
[1]Blackheath	W	14–8
[2]Nottingham	W	11–3
[2]Cross-Keys	L	15–20
[3]Leicester	L	0–15
[2]Bath	L	15–19
[2]Maesteg	W	14–4
[1]Saracens	D	6–6
[1]Bedford	L	3–15
[2]West Hartlepool	W	43–6
[1]Northampton	W	22–0
[2]Old Wesley	W	17–16
[2]London Scottish	W	28–13
[2]Bridgend	L	16–44
[2]Cardiff	L	22–38

LIVERPOOL ST. HELENS

Moss Lane, Windle, St. Helens. Tel: 0744 25708
Founded: 1857
President: Richard A. McCullagh
Chairman: Terry B. Ryan
Coach: Mike Slemen
Secretary: B.G. Cragg, 9 Mulberry Avenue, St. Helens. Tel: 0744 59345
Fixtures Secretary: Ira Daglish, 8 Cooper Avenue, Liverpool L18 LPG
Club captain (1987–88): Brian Wellans
Club captain (1988–89): Brian Wellans
No. of teams: Senior 6. Youth & Minis 3
Directions to Ground: M6 to A580 towards Liverpool, traffic lights A570 turn right to Southport, immediate first left into Moss Lane
Ground capacity: 2,000. Stand, 200
Clubhouse: Lounge, main bar, Sponsors suite
Colours: Red/black/white/blue hoops. (*Change colours:* White or red)
Nickname: L.S.H.
Floodlights: Yes
Admission: £2
Membership: £30
Programme: 30 pages, 30p (Editor: G. Duckworth)
Local newspaper: Liverpool Daily Post, Echo, St. Helens Reporter/Star
League: Nat. 1
Final position (1987–88): 2nd (Nat. 2)
Playing record (1987–88): P 44, W 29, D 2, L 13, F 785, A 596

Most capped players: (for England unless otherwise stated): M.A.C. Slemen 31, A.F. Blakiston 17, R.W. Poulton 17, R. Higgins 13, M. Regan 12, C.E. Allen 9.
Ireland: C.E. Allen 21, R.A. Lloyd 19, H.J. Knox 10.
Scotland: F.H. Turner 15.

Players' appearances, 1987–88: Ian Gibbons 36, Peter Buckton 35, Paul Robbins 34, Nick Simms 32, John Hescott 31, John Ingram 31, Keiron Rabbitt 31, Tim Shaw 29, John Shinwell 27, Jeff Rienall 27, Tony Askew 26, Brian Welland 26, Andy McGowan 26, Chris O'Toole 21, Wayne Pugh 21, Gareth Jones 18, Andy Edwards 16, Colin King 13, Mark Bate 12, Nick Birt 11, Gary Chubb 11, Stuart Harmes 10.

Leading scorers, 1987–88: *Points*: Nick Simms 124 (3 t, 14 cons, 25 pens, 3 d.g.); Brian Wellans 87 (7 t, 7 cons, 14 pens, 1 d.g.); Tony Askew 83 (2 t, 12 cons, 16 pens, 1 d.g.); Stuart Harmes 60 (4 t, 10 cons, 8 pens). *Tries*: Ian Gibbins 13, John Shinwell 8.

Player of the Year: Peter Buckton.

International & representative honours 1987–88: P. Buckton (Yorkshire); C. King, B. Wellans, C. O'Toole (Lancashire); K. Rabbitt, N. Simms, P. Robbins (Lanarkshire); G. Rignall, G. French (Lancashire U21).

Season's review: The highlight of the season must be gaining promotion into Division 1, finishing 2nd to Rosslyn Park. Followed by the commencement of major improvements to the ground and clubhouse. A first class set of floodlights has been erected, terracing has been extended to cover both sides of the ground. A sponsors suite has been developed to give a panoramic view of the 1st team pitch while new changing facilities for players and referees have been constructed.

During the close season a start will be made on the construction of a new stand which will incorporate further sponsor facilities.

The playing squad has been strengthened notably by J. O'Driscoll (London Irish), D. Morris (Winnington Park), P. Hamer (Vale of Lune), P. Bruchez (Widnes) and the return of H. Howard from Australia. The squad to be coached by Mike Slemen.

SARACENS

Bramley Road Sports Ground, Chaseside, Southgate, London N14. Tel: 01-449 3770
Founded: 1876
President: R.B.W. Smith
Chairman: J.P. How
Coach: A. Russ
Secretary: B.D.W. Richards, 36 Stone Hall Road, Winchmore Hill, London N21 1LP
Fixtures Secretary: D.H.J. Grammer, 75 Roundwood Lane, Harpenden, Herts AL5 3EX
Club captain (1987–88): L. Adamson
Club captain (1988–89): F. Steadman
No. of teams: Senior 7
Directions to Ground: From Junction on M25 head to Southgate, ground on the left, or take Piccadilly line to Southgate and walk along Chaseside to ground, bus 298
Ground capacity: 2,500 approx. Stand, 300
Clubhouse: Lounge bar area and cafeteria – open to all visitors
Colours: Black with red star and crescent. (*Change colours:* Black/white/red hoops)
Nickname: Sarries
Floodlights: Yes, but training facilities only
Admission: £2.50 (inc. prog) to ground £3
Membership: Players £26, non-players £16
Programme: Incl. in admission (Editor: Chris Johnson)
Local newspaper: Enfield Gazette
League: Div. 2
Final position (1987–88): 3rd
Playing record (1987–88): P 38, W 19, D 2, L 17, F 626, A 522

Most capped players: Vic Harding 6.

Leading scorers, 1987–88: *Points*: Ben Rudling 134 (1 t, 14 cons, 34 pens). *Tries*: Dave McLagan 15.

Player of the Year 1987–88: Sean Robinson.

International & representative honours 1987–88: John Buckton (North, England B, toured Australia with England); Laurence Smith (London); Dean Ryan (Combined Services & British Police tour of New Zealand).

Season's review: Saracens useful set of forwards coupled with the outstanding ability of their centres John Buckton and Laurence Smith saw them narrowly miss promotion. In their opening matches they beat Headingley and London Irish but lost to London Welsh. Their promotion prospects were severely dented when they lost 13–10 to Liverpool and drew 7–7 with Gosforth during the Divisional Championship when they were missing Smith, Buckton and hooker John McFarland.

Even so, they could still have snatched promotion when they dominated their match with Rosslyn Park but could only draw 6–6. They recorded five wins in their final six matches.

While their attacking brand of rugby was good to watch it should have produced a more fruitful season and this could be put down largely to the inadequacies of their goalkicking.

One major strength in the Saracens side was long-serving scrum-half Floyd Steadman who is captain for the coming season.

Saracens – 1987–88. Captain – L. Adamson (with ball); Coach: A. Russ.

Headingly – 1987–88. Winners of Yorkshire Cup. Photo: Gordon Bunney.

Headingley 41 Fylde 7. John Howarth and England's Peter Winterbottom start another attack. Photo: Gordon Bunney.

HEADINGLEY

Clarence Field, Bridge Road, Kirkstall, Leeds. Tel: 0532 755029.
Founded: 1878
President: J.D.H. Kitchen
Chairman: C.M.R. Shipley
Coach: P.G. Nash
Secretary: J.M. Beaumont, 44 Larkfield Avenue, Rawdon, Leeds LS19 6EN. Tel: 0532 596574.
Fixtures Secretary: V.G. Barley, 32 West Park Crescent, Leeds 8. Tel: 0532 665292.
Club captain (1987–88): J. Howarth
Club captain (1988–89): P. Huntsman
No. of teams: Senior 5. Youth & Minis 1.
Directions to Ground: A65 to Ilkley out of the centre of Leeds. Two miles out of centre turn left at traffic lights, immediatly on left.
Ground capacity: 5,000. Stand, 650.
Clubhouse: Main bar and tea facilities downstairs. Sponsors bar upstiars. Squash club with three courts attached to club house.
Colours: Green, black and white.
Floodlights: Yes
Admission: £2
Membership: £20 ordinary membership
Programme: 20p. (Editor: V.G. Barley)
Local newspaper: Yorkshire Post

League: National 2
Final position (1987–88): 4th
Playing record (1987–88): P 39, W 23, D 2, L 13.
Competitions won: 1987–88 winners of Yorkshire Cup and Tetley Sevens.

Most capped players: (for England unless specified otherwise). I. R. McGeechan (Scotland) 32, P.I. Winterbottom 29, P.H. Thompson 17, J.S. Spencer 14, J.A. King 12, F. Williams (Wales) 11

Players' appearances, 1987–88: S. Shortland, P. Johnson 34; P. Huntsman 33; j. Howarth 32; N. Hargreaves 31; A. Fraser 30; N. Summers, A. Machell 29; P. Sellar, S. Irving 27, M. Appleson 26.

Leading scorers, 1987–88: *Points*: M. Appleson 194 (11 t, 21 cons, 36 pens); J. Howarth 136 (2 t, 1 d.g., 25 cons, 25 pens). *Tries*: S. Irving 15; M. Appleson, N. Summers, P. Johnson 11.

Representative honours 1987–88: P.J. Winterbottom (England, Division, County); P. Huntsman (Division, County); A. Fraser (County); P. Sellar (County).

Headingley 41 Fylde 7. Martin Pepper and Dave Parsonage of the home team swoop on loose ball. Photo: Gordon Bunney.

Headingley 41 Fylde 7. Steve Brugger, Steve Worral and Neil Hargreaves (Headingley) set up another attack. Photo: Gordon Bunney.

Bedford's greatest day. John Player Cup victory over Rosslyn Park in 1975. Recognise Bedford's immortal flanker Budge Rogers? Photos: Colorsport.

BEDFORD

Goldington Road, Bedford. Tel: (0234) 47511
Founded: 1886
President: A.P. Goodman
Chairman: K.W. Phillips
Coach: R. Chadwick
Secretary: R.E. Evans, 16 Bushmead Avenue, Bedford. Tel(54884 (H) or 64321 (W)
Fixtures Secretary: J.R. Saunders, College Farm, Oakley, Beds. Tel. Oakley 2328
Club captain (1987–88): J. Orwin
Club captain (1988–89): J. Orwin
No. of teams: Senior 5. Youth & Minis 11
Directions to Ground: From town centre follow road signs to Cambridge (A428), the ground is about half a mile out of town on Goldington Road on left hand side
Ground capacity: 5,000 approx. Stand, 900
Clubhouse: Two clubhouses – one is open lunchtimes and evenings every day except Sunday and Tuesday
Colours: Oxford/Cambridge blue hoops/ navy shorts. (*Change colours:* White)
Nickname: Blues
Floodlights: Yes
Admission: Under revision
Membership: Vice Presidents £32
Programme: 30p (Editor: R. Forsyth)
Local newspaper: Bedfordshire Times/ Bedfordshire-on-Sunday
League: Nat. Div. 2
Final position (1987–88): 5th
Playing record (1987–88): P 42, W 22, D 2, L 18, F 723, A 800
Competitions won: R.F.U. Knockout Competition 1974/75

Most capped players: D.P. Rogers 34 (for England).

Players' appearances, 1987–88: S. Batty 28, S. Binnington 21, J. Chandler 32, J. Davidson 19, P. Ellam 36, A. Finnie 30, B. Gabriel 33, C. Glanville 36, S. Harris 23, M. Howe 31, D. Jancey 20, P. McCarthy 24.

Leading scorers, 1987–88: *Points*: A. Finnie 226 (1 t, 36 cons, 45 pens, 5 d.g.); S. Batty 62 (11 t, 6 cons, 2 pens); S. Cunningham 57 (2 t, 5 cons, 9 pens, 4 d.g.); B. Gabriel 44 (7 t, 5 cons, 2 pens). *Tries*: S. Batty 11, J. Chandler 9, B. Gabriel 7, D. Jancey 7.

John Orwin – helped to revive both Bedford and England last season. Photo: Colorsport.

Young Player of the Year 1987–88: Cameron Glanvill.

International & representative honours 1987–88: J. Orwin (England, Captain on tour of Australia); J. Orwin, M. Howe (Barbarians); Andy Walford, John Davidson, Andy Tucker, Mark Howe, Andy Finnie, Steve Binnington, Steve Cunningham (East Midlands).

Season's review: Captain John Orwin played for England against France, Wales, Scotland and Ireland (twice). At the end of the season he was elected captain of England on the summer tour of Australia and Fiji. Bedford finished with the best playing record for years. Amongst these statistics the club savoured the wins over Gloucester and Nottingham and the fact that both sides promoted from the second division, Rosslyn Park and Liverpool St. Helens, fell at Goldington Road. This has however to be contrasted with the disappointment of not being promoted due mainly to the poor away form that saw defeats at Saracens and Richmond with a draw at London Irish.

Budge Rogers (Bedford) evades a Rosslyn Park tackle in their successful 1975 John Player Cup Final

RICHMOND

Athletic Ground, Richmond, Surrey TW9 2SS. Tel: 01-940 0397.
Founded: 1861
President: R.D.F. Robins
Coach: Stefan Czerpak
Secretary: K.G. Cresswell, 7 Connaught Avenue, East Sheen, London SW14 7RH. Tel: 01-878 4401 (H & W).
Fixtures Secretary: Dr T.E. Roberts, 7 Homestead Road, Basingstoke, Hants. Tel: 0256 464999 (H).
Club captain (1987–88): John Cullen
Club captain (1988–89): John Cullen
No. of teams: Senior 4. Youth & Minis 12.
Directions to Ground: Approx. 3 minutes walk from Richmond BR & LT Station in Old Deer Park. 100 yards from Richmond Roundabout on A316 Twickenham Road.
Ground capacity: 10,000. Stands, Main 1,000. North, 750
Clubhouse: Main bar, members bar, cafeteria, 14 changing rooms, showers, weights room, secretariat, 7 pitches (including 3 floodlit training pitches)
Colours: Old gold, black hoops. (*Change colours:* white).
Floodlights: Yes
Admission: £2 to ground (50p for mainstand)
Membership: £25
Programme: Free on admission. (Editor: E.W. Brown)
Local newspaper: Richmond and Twickenham Times
League: National 2
Final position (1987–88): 6th
Playing record (1987–88): P 24, W 13, D 2, L 20. F449, A619.
Competitions won: None.

Most capped players: England: C.W. Ralston 21 + 1 British Isles, M.P. Weston 29 + 6 British Isles (9 + 6 with Richmond), N.M. Hall 17, P. Cranmer 16, E.T. Gurden 16, C. Gurden 14, F.M. Stout 14, W.E. Bromet 12, Alan Rotherham 12, A.L. Bucknall 9, J.P.A.G. Janion 9. Scotland: P.W. Kininmonth 21 + 3 British Isles. South Africa: T.P. Bedford 25. Wales: A.S. Gould 27.

Players' appearances, 1987–88: David Sole 32, Simon Pennock 30, John Cullen 29, Simon Smith, 28, Andy Hampel 25, John Heaton 25, Martin Slagter 22, Robert Rydon 19, Mike Harrisex 17, Dave Kenningham 17, Steve Winduse 17, Nicky Preston 16, Peter Combe 14, Tim Marvin 12, Chris Mills 12, Doug Cooper 11, Alan Maxwell 11, Rod Crerar 10, Ricky Forde 10, Dave Gavins 10, Jim Thorn 19.

Most Promising Player of the Year 1987–88: (Nim Hall Trophy): Paul Seccombe

Season's review: By finishing half-way Richmond did rather better than expected and if they can keep up the effort they should continue to progress in the near future. They would be the first to admit to themselves that they do not at the moment have a team which is good enough for the top division, but they are working at it.

In recent seasons there was the distinct danger that the club was in a state of poor morale and many thought they could slide into oblivion of the kind that the lower divisions provide, but there is a new spirit at the Athletic Ground and they can only improve under some inspiring captaincy from John Cullen. Others in whom they have placed many hopes are two forwards, who must first complete courses at Oxbridge – Victor Obogu (Oxford) and Charles Vyvyan, the Cambridge no. 8. There are others of promise also. A replacement for fly-half Simon Smith is needed.

In the John Player Cup Richmond had their best result of the season when they defeated Liverpool-St. Helens in a tense thriller played in appalling conditions, but this form was not repeated in the next round where Bristol proved to be too strong. But it was an indication of possibilities.

Richmond – 1987–88

London Scottish usually do well in sevens. Here at Twickenham in 1987 they put pressure on Rosslyn Park. Photo: Colorsport.

LONDON SCOTTISH

New Foot Road, Richmond, Surrey
Founded: 1878
President: R.I. Marshall
Coach: R. Wilson
Secretary: W.R. Luke, 105 Palewell Park, London SW14 8JJ. Tel: 01-876 9228
Fixtures Secretary: N.R.H. Stanners, 70 Farningham Road, Caterham, Surrey CR3 6LJ
Club captain (1987–88): T. Paterson-Brown
Club captain (1988–89): C. Richardson
No. of teams: Senior 11. Youth & Minis 4.
Directions to Ground: London transport (tube) District Line. BR (Southern) from Waterloo Road to Kew Foot Road.
Ground capacity: 2,000. Stand, 500
Clubhouse: Extensive facilities.
Colours: Blue jersey, white shorts, red socks. (*Change colours:* White).
Nickname: "Scottish"
Floodlights: No
Admission: £2
Membership: £30 playing, £24 non-playing
Programme: With admission
Local newspaper: Richmond & Twickenham Times
League: National 2
Final position (1987–88): 7th

Playing record (1987–88): P 30, W 10, D 2, L 18. F 389, A 468.

Competitions won: Sevens Comps won Sevenoaks, Worthing, Sterling County, London Floodlight (Rosslyn Park)

Most capped players: (all for Scotland) A.F. McHarg 44, I.H.P. Laughland 31, J.P. Fisher 25, M.A. Biggar 24, M.J. Campbell-Lamerton 23 (plus 8 for British Isles), W.C.C. Steele 23 (plus 2 for British Isles), S. Wilson 22 (plus 5 for British Isles), R.G. McMillan 21, A.J.W. Hinshelwood 21 (plus 4 for British Isles).

Players' appearances, 1987–88: N. Weir 27, D. Caskie 24, S. Glen 24, I. Kirk 22, D. Tosh 21, D. Buchanan 21, T. Borthwick 19, T. Paterson-Brown 19, I. Morrison 18, A. Rhodes 20.

Leading scorers, 1987–88: N. Chesworth (1 d.g., 14 pens., 10 cons.) 65 points, A. Mitchell (1 try, 1 d.g., 9 pens., 5 cons.) 44 points, L. Renwick (7 tries) 28 points, D. Buchanan (7 tries) 28 points, A. Tutor (7 pens, 3 cons.) 27 points, T. Paterson-Brown (5 tries) 20 points.

International & representative honours 1987–88: (for Scotland unless specified otherwise)
G. Hastings (England), J. Campbell-Lamerton (Romania *World Cup*, Zimbabwe *World Cup*, Barbarians v Newport), L. Renwick (Reserve in Ireland, France, Wales, England; Scotland 'B' v France 'B' and v Italy 'B'; Anglo-Scots District Side), J. Macklin (Scotland XV v France XV, Barbarians v Newport; Anglo-Scots District Side), T. Paterson-Brown (Scotland 'B' v

That ace sevens expert Hugh McHardy, now coach at Rosslyn Park, evades a challenge from Harlequins in the 1987 Middlesex Sevens and goes over for a try for Blackheath. Photo: Colorsport.

That ace sevens expert Hugh McHardy, now coach at Rosslyn Park, evades a challenge from Harlequins in the 1987 Middlesex Sevens and goes over for a try for Blackheath. Photo: Colorsport.

Club details (cont.)
France 'B' and v Italy 'B' Anglo-Scots), J. Beazley, D. Millard, I. Kirk, I. Morrison, I. Abercrombie, D. Tosh and C. Russell (Anglo-Scots).

Season's review: 1987–88 was a period of grim disappointment with hopes of promotion vanishing early inthe season and a second round disaster in the John Player Cup, when a visit to Tynedale saw an embarrassing defeat – and elimination. Earlier Sudbury had been narrowly beaten in the same event.

League results were also very modest with an early thrashing of Northampton the only bright spot.

Sevens results were far more encouraging with victories at Sevenoaks, Worthing, Stirling County and Rosslyn Park (in the London Floodlit competition). A semi-final place was also achieved in the Middlesex Sevens at Twickenham, when both sevens qualified for the final day.

There are high hopes fort he new campaign after the return of Gavin Hastings from Edinburgh and the likely arrival from Gala of the Scotland forward Derek White. They must make a difference and a settled team will also help; some 61 players appeared for th 1st XV last season.

Results: London Scottish 4
[1] *Courage League II*
[2] *John Player Cup*

1	Camborne	W	26–6
2	Orrell	L	12–14
3	[1]Headingley	L	6–22
4	[2]Sudbury	W	9–3
5	[1]Northampton	W	50–3
6	[1]Rosslyn Park	L	6–15
7	[1]Blackheath	W	18–9
8	[2]Tynedale	L	9–11
9	London Irish	W	6–3
10	Cambridge University	L	15–19
11	Sale	L	9–26
12	Richmond	L	6–9
13	Oxford University	W	19–7
14	Bath	L	13–23
15	Edinburgh Acad.	W	25–9
16	Birkenhead Park	W	16–9
17	Cannot read		
18	[1]Gosforth	W	13–8
19	Hawick	L	18–12
20	Leicester	L	15–34
21	Otley	L	15–30
22	[1]Bedford	L	9–21
23	Met. Police	W	28–3
24	Richmond	L	0–20
25	Bristol	L	6–24
26	Nottingham	L	6-24
27	Rosslyn Park	L	13–28
28	[2]London Welsh	D	30–30
29	[1]Liverpool/ St. Helens	L	3–10
30	[1]Saracens	L	0–34

LONDON IRISH

The Avenue, Sunbury-on-Thames, Middx. Tel: 0932 783034
Founded: 1898
President: Hugh Brady
Chairman: Air Comm. J.R. Forsyth
Coach: L. Flye
Secretary: Pat Barragry, 155 Hemmingford Road, Islington, N1. Tel: 01-607 394 (H) or 01-631 1355 (W)
Fixtures Secretary: Mike Tewksbury, 48 Bingley Road, Sunbury-on-Thames, Middx. Tel: 0932 780278
Club captain (1987–88): Mike Gibson
Club captain (1988–89): David Fitzgerald
No. of teams: Senior 10. Youth & Minis 7
Directions to Ground: Trains from Waterloo to Sunbury-on-Thames at 04 and 34 mins past the hour
Stand capacity: 400
Colours: Green and white
Nickname: The Irish
Floodlights: No
Admission: £2
Membership: £30 playing, £35 non-playing, £2.00 life
Programme: 50p (Editor: Brendon Quirke)
League: Nat. Div. 2

Final position (1987–88): 7th
Playing record (1987–88): P 32, W 11, D 1, L 20, F 395, A 420

Most capped players: K. Kennedy, J. O'Driscoll, M. Molloy, J. Richie, A. Mulligan, M. Gibson, H. McNeill, R. Roe, J. Daly, T. Reid.

Leading scorers, 1987–88: J. Staples.

International & representative honours 1987–88: Mike Gibson, Hugo McNeill (Ireland).

Season's review: A modest season but this could be attributed to a poor start and the team did come on strongly at the end. A late run of victories took them off the bottom of the table and they have recruited a sufficient number of good players to be able to say that their future prospects should at the very least be promising. Players like Neil Francis can only get better and as long as good Irish players who come to the South East of England continue to play at Sunbury they should at least be able to maintain their position amongst the game's elite clubs.

London Irish's Alistair McKibbin during his side's John Player Final bid against Leicester in 1980, when they lost (21–9). "Irish" have recruited well in the summer and could challenge for promotion. Photo: Colorsport.

London Welsh R.F.C. 1986–87: Back Row: E. Thomas (Match Sec.), N. Connell, M. Lewis, S. Page, G. Llewelyn, S. Russell, J. Ford, P. Michaelson, R. Russell (Referee), K. Brickell (Trainer). Middle Row: A. Rees, M. Hall, J. Davies, C. Price (Captain), W.G. Thomas, B. Bradley, B. Light. Front Row: P. Roblin, S. Pill, J. Wiltshire, C. Williams. Absent (15 games or more): J. Evans, T. Jones, M. Douglas, C. Leleu, H. Evans, J. Price, J. Hughes.

Mathew Watkins seems in danger of losing his shirt, but Mark Douglas surges through the Baa-Baas defence in characteristic style.

LONDON WELSH

Old Deer Park, Kew Road, Richmond, Surrey. Tel: 01-940 2520
Founded: 1885
President: Vic Watkins
Chairman: Colin Bosley
Coach: Haydn Morgan
Secretary: Roland Hobbs, 73 Downs Road, Epsom, Surrey KT18 5JT. Tel: 037 27 22252
Fixtures Secretary: John Manfield, 13 Prices Lane, Reigate, Surrey RH2 8BB. Tel: 97372 40390
Club captain (1987–88): Mark Douglas
Club captain (1988–89): Mark Douglas
No. of teams: Senior 7. Youth & Minis 11
Directions to Ground: Next to Kew Gardens in Kew Road leading from Richmond to Key Bridge
Ground capacity: 8,000. Stand, 1,300
Clubhouse: Large multi-use unit incorporating Richmond cricket and squash clubs
Colours: Scarlet. (*Change colours:* Green)
Nickname: The Welsh or Exiles
Floodlights: No
Admission: £1.50
Membership: £23
Programme: 30p (incorporates advertising with team and club news) (Editor: Paul Beken)
Local newspaper: Richmond and Twickenham Times
League: Nat. 2
Final position (1987–88): 9th
Playing record (1987–88): P 38, W 10, D 2, L 26, F 550, A 804

Most capped players: J.P. Williams 55, Gerald Davies 46, Mervyn Davies 38, B.V. Meredith 34, Wick Powell 27, John Taylor 26, Arthur Harding 20 (for Wales).

Players' appearances, 1987–88: M. Douglas 33, J. Davies 29, T. Waldron 28, N. Humphreys 27, R. Wintle 27, G. Llewelyn 24, S. Pill 21, P. Robin 19, N. Jenkins 18, B. Light 17, R. Thomas 17.

Guy Leleu breaks free from his Bath pursuers, with Jeremy offering timely support.

Leading scorers, 1987–88: *Points*: N. Humphreys 107 (9 t, 4 cons, 20 pens, 1 d.g.); P. Turner 96 (3 t, 15 cons, 18 pens); C. Price 59 (3 t, 10 cons, 9 pens). *Tries*: M. Douglas 14, N. Humphreys 9, R. Wintle 9.

International & representative honours 1987–88: S. Russell, R. Wintle (Wales); R. Wintle, M. Douglas (Welsh Trial).

Season's review: For anyone with the club's best interests at heart, last season was a lacerating experience. The rare moments of fleeting brilliance served only to bring later disappointments into sharper focus. By March the Welsh could ponder on an unprecedented 19 defeats from 20 games, the worst first-team playing record since 1938–39, and an abject home record – without parallel in the club's history – they even had the misfortune to lose at home in the John Player Cup to a Junior Club, Berry Hill.

Results: League Division 2

[1] *John Player Cup*
[2] *Friendly*

Sept 5	[2]Plymouth Albion	A	W	26–14
Sept 6	[2]Torquay Athletic	A	W	34–9
Sept 12	[2]Saracens	A	W	23–7
Sept 19	[2]Leicester	A	W	9–6
Sept 23	[2]Met. Police	H	W	44–0
Sept 26	Rosslyn Park	A	L	15–16
Sept 30	Bedford	A	D	6–6
Oct 3	Richmond	H	L	22–26
Oct 10	[2]Bridgend	A	W	16–15
Oct 17	[2]Llanelli	H	L	6–20
Oct 24	[2]Neath	H	L	9–33
Oct 31	[2]Harlequins	H	L	4–26
Nov 7	[2]Coventry	A	L	3–30
Nov 14	[2]Moseley	A	L	3–18
Nov 21	[2]Bristol	H	L	3–14
Nov 28	[2]Newport	H	L	18–25
Dec 5	[2]Aberavon	H	L	10–27
Dec 12	[2]Cardiff	A	L	21–27
Dec 19	[1]London Irish	H	L	6–13
Dec 26	[2]Llanelli	A	L	13–44
Jan 2	Northampton	A	W	16–14
Jan 9	[2]Bath	H	L	11–35
Jan 16	Liverpool St. Helens	H	L	10–27
Jan 23	[1]Berry Hill	H	L	10–13
Jan 30	[2]Leicester	H	L	6–41
Feb 6	[2]Cardiff	H	L	7–38
Feb 13	[2]Bridgend	H	L	9–16
Feb 21	[2]Pontypridd	A	L	9–35
Feb 27	[2]Swansea	A	L	13–40
Mar 5	[2]Maesteg	H	W	34–10
Mar 12	Blackheath	A	L	7–22
Mar 19	Headingley	H	L	10–18
Mar 26	[2]Swansea	H	W	37–13
Apr 2	[2]Aberavon	A	L	4–23
Apr 4	[2]Newport	A	L	18–21
Apr 9	[2]Wasps	H	L	20–26
Apr 13	London Scottish	H	D	24–24
Apr 23	Gosforth	A	W	14–12

The Welsh were at their resilient best in the home victory over Swansea. In one of the most amazing recoveries of modern times, the Welsh won 27–21 after being 18 points behind at one stage. In this line-out action, World Cup captain, Richard Moriarty is failed by Richard John and Glyn Llewelyn.

Mitre

GOSFORTH

North Road, Gosforth, Newcastle upon Tyne NE3 2DT. Tel: 091 2856915
Founded: 1877
President: John H. Gray
Chairman: R.W. Wood
Head of Coaching: A. McConnell
Secretary: Tom Farrell, 1 Parklands, Darras Hall, Ponteland, Newcastle upon Tyne NE20 9LL. Tel: 0661 24557 (H) or 091 2646464 (W)
Fixtures Secretary: J.M. Smith, 3 Oaklands Avenue, Gosforth, Newcastle upon Tyne NE3 4YJ. Tel: 091 285 3377 (H) or 091 265 5193 (W)
Club captain (1987–88): D. Davidson
Club captain (1988–89): G.G. Smallwood
No. of teams: Senior 6. Youth & Minis 9
Directions to Ground: 3 miles north of Newcastle upon Tyne along the Great North Road A6125
Ground capacity: 2,000. Stand, 400
Clubhouse: 3 bars, lounge, players and sponsors
Colours: Green and white. (*Change colours:* Blue)
Floodlights: No
Admission: £1.50
Membership: £30 – full membership
Programme: 20p (Editor: W.M.H. Dix)
Local newspaper: Newcastle Chronicle & Journal
League: Nat. 2
Final position (1987–88): 10th
Playing record (1987–88): P 41, W 25, D 1, L 15, F 719, A 588
Competitions won: John Player Cup Winners 1976 & 1977. Northumberland RFU Challenge Cup – 26 times winners

Most capped players: (for England unless otherwise stated): R.J. McLoughlin 40 (Ireland), A. Smith 33 (Scotland), R.M. Uttley 23, P.J. Dixon 22, S. Bainbridge 16, D.F. Madsen 14 (Scotland), M. Young 10.

Players' appearances, 1987–88: R. Petyt 40, K. Westgarth 37, D. Davidson 36, T. Roberts 36, N. Frankland 31, D. Johnson 31, R. Parker 30, G. Smallwood 30, A. Elliott 29, D. Nunn 29, D. Waler 26, J. Whisber 25, R. Wilkinson 21.

Leading scorers, 1987–88: *Points*: D. Johnson 283 (1 t, 36 cons, 59 pens, 10 d.g.); D. Walker 72 (18 t); R. Petyt 65 (6 t, 7 cons, 9 pens). *Tries*: D. Walker 18, A. Elliott 11.

Player of the Year 1987–88: Richard Petyt.

International & representative honours 1987–88: Northern Division U21 – R Petyt; County Championship Northumberland – G.G. Smallwood, J. Whisker, S. Smith, D. Clegg; Yorkshire – N. Frankland.

Season's review: A disappointing season with too many matches lost late in the game. However occasional glimpses of potential, with wins against good opposition. Team rebuilding continues with the aim of adding experience to a young 1st XV squad. A new coaching structure for the new season carries the promise of better things to come and at the end of 1988/89 season who knows? We might just find ourselves with a brand new clubhouse and playing facilities to match.

Results 1987/88:
League: W 3, D 1, L 6, F 124, A 145
John Player Cup: F 27, A 32
Northumberland Senior Cup: W 2, L 1, F 51, A 29
Friendlies: W 19, L 7, F 517, A 382

Gosforth – 1987–88

BLACKHEATH

Rectory Field, Charlton Road, London SE3
Founded: 1858
President: J.B. Williamson
Chairman: F. McCarthy
Secretary: P. Rossiter-Marvell, Flat 2, 157 Victoria Way, London SE7 7NX. Tel: 01-858 0646 (H) or 01-485 4100, ext. 258 (W)
Fixtures Secretary: P.J.S. Blacklock, Home Farm, Smeeth, Ashford, Kent. Tel: Sellinge 3104 (H)
Club captain (1987–88): D. Hursey
Club captain (1988–89): T.P. Fenby
No. of teams: Senior 6. Youth 2
Directions to Ground: From Central London take direction of South Circular Road, follow A207 towards Dartford. Ground is new park on right. Also go by BR to Blackheath
Clubhouse: Old clubhouse with excellent bar, dressing rooms, etc
Colours: Red and black (*Change colours:* Black)
Nickname: Club
Membership: £35 players, £25 non-players
Local newspaper: Mercury
League: Nat. 2
Final position (1987–88): 11th
Playing record (1987–88): P 28, W 10 L 18, F 390, A 450

Most capped players: N.S. Bruce 31 (for Scotland). C.N. Lowe 25, A.L. Horton 7, T.P. Wright 13 (for England)

International & representative honours 1987–88: Several players for Kent

Results: League Division 2
[1] *John Player Cup*
[2] *Kent Cup Final*

Bedford	A	L	0–6
London Scottish	A	L	9–18
Headingley	A	L	9–21
Richmond	H	L	3–4
Rosslyn Park	A	L	8–14
Liverpool St. Helens	A	L	0–15
Northampton	H	W	19–12
London Irish	H	L	12–16
Gosforth	A	L	8–26
London Welsh	H	W	22–7
Saracens	H	L	12–48
[1]1st Round v Letchworth	A	W	26–0
[1]2nd Round v Redruth (after extra time)	A	W	13–9
[1]3rd Round v Saracens	A	L	3–15
[2]Maidstone		D	9–9
[2]Maidstone (replay)		L	0–29

Season's review: Blackheath finished eleventh in the Second Division of the National League with two wins from 11 matches played, but they are a good club and can with the right will do better and find a place for themselves amongst the game's elite. Of course, the unthinkable could also happen and they could also descend and in the process lose many of thier prized fixtures; if there had been promotion and relegation between the second and third divisions this descent would already be underway. Apart from their poor league showing they also failed in the Kent County Cup by losing the final to Maidstone. They drew one match, but then with virtually an Extra 2nd XV they were well beaten in the replay. The 1st XV was playing a prestige fixture in New Zealand.

The remedy for clubs like Blackheath, which have seen better days, is in their own hands. We would like next year to be able to report a vast improvement.

Gary Pearce, Northampton's captain and England's most capped prop. in action against Scotland in 1985. Photo: Colorsport.

NORTHAMPTON

Franklins Gardens, Weedon Road, St. James, Northampton. Tel: 0604 51543
Founded: 1880
President: G.R. Allen
Coach: T. Burwell/P. Bryant
Secretary: R. Horwood, Church Lane Cottage, Little Billing, Northampton. Tel: 0604 410326 (H) or 0604 790777 (W)
Fixtures Secretary: R.B. Taylor, 82 Bridgewater Drive, Northampton. Tel: 0604 38626
Club captain (1987–88): G. Steele-Bodger
Club captain (1988–89): G. Pearce
No. of teams: Senior 4
Directions to Ground: From Junction 16 from M1 (A45) to Northampton, Weedon Road
Ground capacity: 6,000. Stand, 2,000
Clubhouse: Sturtridge Pavilion
Colours: Black/green/gold hoops. (*Change colours:* White)
Nickname: Saints
Floodlights: Yes
Admission: Ground £2 (OAPs/Under 18s £1), Stand £2.50 (OAPs/Under 18s £1.20)
Membership: Player £12.50, youth £6.50
Local newspaper: Chronicle & Echo
League: Div. 2
Playing record (1987–88): P 40, W 14, D 0, L 26, F 573, A 738

Most capped players: Garry Pearce 35.

Players' appearances, 1987–88: *Points*: P. Larkin (25 cons, 15 pens). *Tries*: F. Packman 18, P. Alston 17.

Player of the Year: Phil Pask.

International & representative honours 1987–88: Gary Pearce (England, England B (captain)); Michael Ord (England Under 19); Jan Dohnalek (England Under 16).

Season's review: The "Saints" have know better days. In fact this must have been one of the worst seasons in the club's history and the only stroke of good fortune that they encountered was the fact that there is to be no relegation and promotion between Divisions 2 and 3 until next season so they live to fight another day. Is it a sign of things to come? The result of their disasters was made apparent when the AGM took place and the whole committee was voted out of office. A "modern" set-up is now taking the place of the old system with Barry Corless in charge, but it remains to be seen whether this will bring a change in fortunes, because if it does not one of England's most famous clubs could find themselves in Division 3 when the 1989/90 season begins and this will have the inevitable consequence of the better players looking for the better placed clubs.

Results: League Division 2
[1] *John Player Cup*
[2] *Friendly*
[3] *Courage Club Championship*

Sept 5	[2]Vale of Lune	A	L	7–12
Sept 7	[2]Louisville, Kentucky	H	W	70–6
Sept 12	[2]Harlequins	H	W	15–4
Sept 15	[2]Nottingham	A	L	0–22
Sept 19	[3]Richmond	H	L	3–16
Sept 26	[2]Moseley	A	L	19–32
Sept 29	[2]Rugby	H	W	10–9
Oct 3	[3]London Scottish	A	L	3–50
Oct 10	[2]Cardiff	H	L	7–14
Oct 17	[2]Leicester	H	L	0–47
Oct 24	[2]Oxford University	A	W	22–19
Oct 27	[2]Nuneaton	A	L	3–6
Oct 31	[2]Cambridge University	A	L	3–12
Nov 7	[2]Aberavon	H	W	19–9
Nov 14	[2]Coventry	H	W	44–6
Nov 21	[3]Bedford	A	K	16–17
Nov 28	[2]Ebbw Vale	H	W	14–12
Dec 5	[2]Llanelli	H	L	15–24
Dec 12	[3]London Irish	H	W	15–13
Dec 19	[2]Wasps	A	L	12–15

Dec 26	[2]Saracens	H	W	48–12
Jan 2	[3]London Welsh	H	L	14–16
Jan 9	[2]Bective Rangers	H	W	15–6
Jan 17	[3]Blackheath	A	L	12–19
Jan 23	[1]Plymouth Albion	A	L	7–14
Jan 30	[2]Bristol	A	Cancelled	
Feb 7	[3]Saracens	A	L	6–22
Feb 13	[2]Cambridge University	H	W	35–4
Feb 19	[2]Coventry	A	L	12–29
Feb 27	[2]Leicester	A	L	9–35
Mar 4	[2]Gloucester	H	L	12–13
Mar 6	[3]Liverpool St. Helens	H	L	9–13
Mar 12	[3]Rosslyn Park	H	L	0–22
Mar 15	[2]Royal Air Force	H	Cancelled	
Mar 19	[2]Sale	A	L	3–23
Mar 22	[2]Met. Police	H	W	12–6
Mar 26	[2]Waterloo	H	L	17–23
Apr 1	[2]Aberavon	A	L	0–51
Apr 2	[2]Llanelli	A	L	13–27
Apr 9	[2]Morley	H	W	44–3
Apr 13	[2]Bedford	H	W	23–6
Apr 16	[3]Headingley	A	L	3–38
Apr 19	[2]Birmingham	A	W	36–7
Apr 23	[2]Bective Rangers	A	W	28–19
Apr 30	[2]Cheltenham	H	W	24–4

Reliable boot. Ray Adamson (Wakefield) helps Yorkshire in their successful 1986–87 season. Photo: Colorsport.

Mike Harrison – captain of Wakefield, Yorkshire and England – on another determined run. Photo: Gordon Bunney.

WAKEFIELD

College Grove, Wakefield. Tel: 0924 372038
Founded: 1901
President: B. Guest
Chairman: A. Calvert
Coach: M. Dearman
Secretary: R. Foster, 27 Carr Lane, Sandal, Wakefield WF2 6HJ. Tel: 0924 250116.
Fixtures Secretary: B. Halstead, 84 Whitcliffe Road, Cleckheaton BD19 3DR. Tel: 0274 872710.
Club captain (1987–88): M. Rawnsley
Club captain (1988–89): M. Rawnsley
No. of teams: Senior 4. Colts 1.
Directions to Ground: Into the centre of Wakefield and ask for Pinderfields/Stanley Royd Hospitals. Ground is 250 yds from these buildings.
Stand capacity: 500
Ground capacity: 3,500/4,000
Clubhouse: Lounge with bar and sports room with bar. The Rugby Club is part of a 6-sports complex, i.e. The Wakefield Sports Club.
Colours: Black and gold. (*Change colours:* All black, all gold, all red)
Floodlights: Yes
Admission: £2 per adult, £1 Senior Citizen, 59p transfer to stand.
Membership: £30
Programme: 20p. Editor: Phil Hodson.
Local newspaper: Wakefield Express
League: National 3
Final position (1987–88): 1st
Playing record (1987–88): P 43, W 36, D 1, L 6, F 1179, A 422.
Competitions won: Harlequins/Lord Taverners Sevens, 1987; National Table Three Championship (but no promotion).

Most capped players: Mike Harrison 15, Bryan Barley 7 for England.

Leading scorers, 1987–88: Ray Adamson 257 points (6 t, 55 cons, 41 pents) – club record.

Player of the Year 1987–88: Steve Townend

Representative honours 1987–88: Mike Harrison, Bryan Barley (England, North, Yorkshire); Ray Adamson (England B, North, Yorkshire); Graham Marshall (Scotland B, Anglo-Scots, Yorkshire).

Season's review: Fourteen players gained representative honours with Yorkshire, Yorkshire B and Yorkshire U21 fifteens, with Mike Harrison, Bryan Barley and Ray Adamson England Tourists and Graham Marshall selected as a Scottish Tourist to Zimbabwe. But he, and Harrison, had to pull out through injuies. Wakefield coach, Mich Dearman, has been invited onto the RFU Coaching Panel. Wakefield won the Harlequins/Lord Taverners Sevens in September £987 and the National Table Three Championship.

WEST HARTLEPOOL

Brierton Lane, Hartlepool. Tel: 0429 272640/233149.
Founded: 1881
President: N. Brown
Chairman: R. Bateman
Coach: J. Clark
Secretary: F. Gibbon, Regent House, York Road, Hartlepool. Tel: 0429 234455.
Fixtures Secretary: L. Smith, 2 Elm Grove, Hartlepool. Tel: 0429 231000.
Club captain (1987–88): P. Stacey
Club captain (1988–89): P. Stacey
No. of teams: Senior 5. Youth & Minis 6.
Directions to Ground: Exit A689 from A19 into Hartlepool. Cross first roundabout, proceed ½ mile and turn left into Brierton Lane as duel carriageway begins to swing right opposite "Travellers Rest". Ground 400 yds on left.
Ground capacity: 5,500. Stand, 600
Clubhouse: 2 bars, 4 squash courts.
Colours: Green, red and white. (*Change colours:* Blue and white).
Floodlights: Yes
Admission: £1.50
Membership: £15
Programme: Free on admission. (Editor: S. Smith Tel: 0429 233149)
Local newspaper: Hartlepool Mail
League: National 3
Final position (1987–88): 2nd
Playing record (1987–88): P 42, W 31, D 0, L 11. F880, A580.
Competitions won: Northern Merit Table 1983/4. Durham Cup 1932–6.

Most capped players: C.D. Aarvold 16 (+ 5 Lions). J.T. Taylor 11 (Captain). (All with England)

Players' appearances, 1987–88: D. Evans 40, M. Baggs 35, P. Stacey 35, D. Mitchell 35.
Leading scorers, 1987–88: J. Stabler (t 4, cons 38, pen 43, dg 2, 242 pts), O. Evans (t 23, 92 pts), P. Robinson (t 20, 80 pts)
Player of the Year 1987–88: P. Stacey
Representative honours 1987–88: Durham – S. Hackney (also Barbarians), J. Dixon, A. Mitchell, J. Stabler (also Combined Series to New Zealand).
Season's review: Finished Runners-up in division 3 on points difference though no promotion. Fine first year for new coach John Clark.

PLYMOUTH ALBION

Beacon Park, Plymouth
Founded: 1876
President: D.J.L. Gabbitass, FCI Arb.
Chairman: V.J. Pinches
Coach: N. Sparrow
Secretary: W.J. Foster, 4 Stopford Place, Stoke, Plymouth PL1 4QT. Tel: 0752 559703.
Fixtures Secretary: R. Evans, 4 Brynmoor Walk, Higher Compton, Plymouth. Tel: 0752 771825.
Club captain (1987–88): R. Westlake
Club captain (1988–89): K. Norris
No. of teams: Senior 3. Youth & Minis 9.
Stand capacity: 480
Ground capacity: 4,000
Clubhouse: 3 bars
Colours: Cherry/white/red. (*Change colours:* Red)
Floodlights: Yes
Programme: Editor: M. Glanville
Local newspaper: Western Evening Herald, Western Morning News
League: National 3
Final position (1987–88): 3rd
Playing record (1987–88): P 43, W 30, L 12, D 1, F 1055, A 578
Competitions won: Devon Cup Winners 1974, 1977, 1983, 1984, 1985, 1986, 1987, 1988.

Most capped players: E. Stanbury 16, W.A. Mills 11, R.H. Sparks 9, S.G. Williams 7, R.A. Jago 5, J. Peters 5. (For England.)

Leading scorers, 1987–88: *Points:* M. Livesey 217 (37 pens, 53 cons). *Tries:* S. Walklin 22, I. Russell 21, K. Norris 20.

Player of the Year 1987–88: Ian Russell.

Representative honours 1987–88: K. Turton, N. Leonard, I. Harrison, I. Russell, S. Walklin, B. Priday, B. Fairgrieve, R. Bailey, K. Norris (Devon).

Season's review: Devon Cup winners for the 8th time. In the John Player Cup beat Northampton and Blackheath but lost to Wasps.

Sheffield 13 Fylde 12. Steve Grieve (Sheffield) dives through the visitors' defence at Abbeydale. Photo: Gordon Bunney.

SHEFFIELD

Abbeydale Park, Dore, Sheffield S17 3LJ. Tel: 0742 367011.
Founded: 1902
President: P.J. Tear
Secretary: J. Goulding, Buck Trap, Andwell Lane, Sheffield S10 4QF. Tel: 0742 308838 (H) 0742 763555 x 4632 (W).
Fixtures Secretary: R. Dean, 92 Riverdale Road, Sheffield S10 3FD. Tel: 0742 301021 (H) 0709 371234 (W).
Club captain (1987–88): B. Reichwald
Club captain (1988–89): B. Reichwald
No. of teams: Senior 5. Youth & Minis 2.
Stand capacity: 100
Ground capacity: 1,000
Clubhouse: Sports club with separate restaurant/dance room. Lounge for wives and children.
Colours: Blue/white hoops, navy blue shorts, red socks. (*Change colours:* Red shirts)
Floodlights: Yes (training only)
Admission: £2
Membership: Players 19 over £15, non-players £30.
Programme: On admission. Editor: Andy Reichwald.

Local newspaper: Yorkshire Post
League: National 3
Final position (1987–88): 4th
Playing record (1987–88): P 35, W 21, D 1, L 13, F 533, A 403.
Competitions won: South Yorkshire 2nd XV Cup, 1988.

Players' appearances, 1987–88: D. Watson, D. Fairclough, W. Reichwald, A. Harrison, S. Grieve, R. Parr, M. Pierce, A. Mezulis, R. Goodliffe, A. Reichwald, S. Hodgson.

Leading scorers, 1987–88: *Points:* R. Goodliffe 135, D. Fairclough 128, C. Saul 111. *Tries:* D. Fairclough 31, R. Taylor 15, K. Morley 13, J. Murphy 13.

Player of the Year 1987–88: Rob Parr

Season's review: This season's results have guaranteed our place in Division 3 and an automatic entry into the Pilkington Cup Competition – in spite of 1987/88 being a transitional season which saw the first team change half its personnel.

Vale of Lune – 1987–88. Photo: Lancaster & Morecombe Newspapers Ltd.

VALE OF LUNE

Powder House Lane, Lancaster. Tel: 0524 64029, 0524 63151 (coin box).
Founded: 1900
President: R. Benjamin
Secretary: J.E. Cowper, 53 Tormsholme Road, Lancaster LA1 2UA. Tel: 0524 65800.
Fixtures Secretary: F.W. Swarbrick, "Oxendale", Wyresdale Road, Lancaster.
Club captain (1987–88): A. Higgin
Club captain (1988–89): T.B.A.
No. of teams: Senior 5. Youth & Minis 8.
Directions to Ground: Leave M6 and Junc 34. Follow signs for Morecambe. 1 mile after crossing river, turn right down Penrhyn Road (which becomes Powder House Lane). This turning is 250 yds beyond "The Lancastrian Hotel".
Stand capacity: 300
Ground capacity: 10,000
Clubhouse: Club bar, lounge bar, open all year – every evening and Sunday lunchtime.
Colours: Cherry and white hoops.
Nickname: The Vale
Floodlights: No
Admission: Varies
Membership: V.P. £12, Patron £7, Playing £15.
Programme: 10 pages (10p). Editor: P. Lovatt-Horn
Local newspaper: Lancaster Guardian, The Visitor
League: National 3
Final position (1987–88): 5th
Playing record (1987–88): P 39, W 18, L 21, F 624, A 646.

Leading scorers, 1987–88: *Points:* Andy Higgin 279 (4 t, 43 cons, 52 pens, 7 d.g.). *Tries:* Ian Ralston.

Representative honours 1987–88: Sam Hodgson, Les Dent, Richard Taylor, Malcolm Brown (Cumbria); Andy Higgin (Lancashire); Steve Gill (Cheshire); Sam Hodgson (Barbarian).

Season's review: Following a promising start in Division 3 with only one defeat from 6 games before Christmas, a combination of injuries and heavy grounds resulted in Vale only winning 2 of their 5 remaining Courage games. Highlight of the season was Sam Hodgson's selection as a Barbarian, first against East Midlands and then for the Easter Tour. He became the Vale's first Barbarian. Mark Hancock was elected captain of Cambridge University for the coming season. Although the weather did its best to spoil the occasion the Vale hosted the semi-final of the Toshiba County Championship when Lancashire defleated Gloucestershire.

FYLDE

The Woodlands Memorial Ground, Blackpool Road, Ansdell, Lytham St. Annes, Lancashire.
Founded: 1919
President: R. Blackledge
Chairman: R. Woolley
Coach: I. Geary
Secretary: P. Makin, 5 Ribblesdale Place, Preston. Tel: 0772 59625.
Fixtures Secretary: Col. K. Scragg, 30 Howick Cross Lane, Penwortham, Preston. Tel: Preston 747572.
Club captain (1987–88): M. Dixon
Club captain (1988–89): M. Hesketh
No. of teams: Senior 6. Youth & Minis 9.
Directions to Ground: Leave M55 (Ext.4) on to A583 (Preston Kirkham) to traffic lights and turn sharp right into Whitehill Road to next lights and turn left onto Queensway. Ground about 3 miles on left (after Blossoms Pub and Church on right).
Stand capacity: 500
Ground capacity: 7,000
Clubhouse: Clubroom, Tea Bar, Loung and Players Bars, Toilets and Sponsors and Committee Rooms.
Colours: Claret, gold and white. (*Change colours:* Maroon)
Floodlights: No
Admission: £1.80, £1 OAP, 20p Juniors, Members free.
Membership: Adults £35 (under 21 £7)
Programme: 20p. Editor: L.B. Jones, BEM
Local newspaper: Evening Gazette (Blackpool)
League: National 3
Final position (1987–88): ?
Playing record (1987–88): P 40, W 20, D 2, L 18, F 889, A 802.
Competitions won: Losing finalists Manchester Sevens 1987/88.
Most capped players (for England unless otherwise stated): Bill Beaumont 34, 7 British Lions; Malcolm Phillips 25, Wade Dooley 23, Steve Bainbridge 19, 2 British Lions.

Fylde – 1987–88: (Back-row) (l to r): S. Townsend (Touch judge), A. Little, P. Faulkner, A. Macfarlane, W. Dooley, S. Bainbridge, M. Dixon, M. Hesketh, S. Frost, D. Newman, J. Nicholson; (Front-row): Ian Greenhalgh, M. Fielden, M. Preston, S. Gough, B. Hanavan, S. Burnage, M. Weir. Photo: "Evening Gazette", Blackpool.

Players' appearances, 1987–88: Micky Weir 39, Steve Burnage 36, Mark Hesketh 34, Ian Greenhalgh 34.

Leading scorers, 1987–88: *Points:* Steve Burnage 387 (12 t, 78 cons, 58 pens, 3 d.g.). *Tries:* Mark Preston 32, Bendan Hanavan 22.

Representative honours 1987–88: W Dooley (Lancashire, North), S. Bainbridge (Lancashire, North), S. Holmes (Cumbria, England Students (captain), D. Ward (Cumbria, England Students), R. Moffatt (Cumbria), M. Dixon (Cumbria), B. Hanavan (Lancashire, British Police), M. Fielding (North U21, Lancashire), J. Pond (Lancashire), S. Kember (Lancashire).

Season's review: A good first half of the season, fell away in the second half due to several key players being injured and unavailable. A highlight of the season was the United Stated Tour to Boston – Fylde won 4 games and lost 1.

METROPOLITAN POLICE

Metropolitan Police fly-half and captain Ian Burrell scores an early new season try at Wasps as Buster White fails to stop him. Can Met. Police add to London's strength in National Division 2? Photo: Chris Roberts.

Police Sports Club, Ember Lane, East Molesey, Surrey.
Founded: 1923
President: C.B.J. Sutton, QPM
Chairman: K.J. Will
Coach: A.V. Boddy
Secretary: D. Barham, MPAA Office, Room G11, Wellington House, 67–73 Buckingham Gate, London SW1E 6BE. Tel: 01-230 7108.
Fixtures Secretary: P. Hudson, 44 Avondale Road, Mortlake, London SW14 8PT. Tel: 01-878 0645.
Club captain (1987–88): S. O'Reilly
Club captain (1988–89): D. Kyffin
No. of teams: Senior 3.
Directions to Ground: A3 to "Scilly Isles" Roundabout then A.309 (Hampton Court Way) to first roundabout, turn left into Ember Court Road and ground faces in 300 yards; or British Rail to Thames Ditton or Esher, then 10 minutes walk.
Stand capacity: 750
Ground capacity: 3500
Clubhouse: At present a general sports ground (not specifically rugby).
Colours: Dark blue shirts, blue shorts, dark blue stockings. (*Change colours:* Navy blue and white hoops, blue shorts, light blue stockings)
Floodlights: Yes
Admission: £2, children (U16) & OAPs £1.
Membership: £10
Programme: with admission. Editor: A. Reynolds.
Local newspaper: Kingston Informer/Surrey Comet
League: National 3
Final position (1987–88): 7th
Playing record (1987–88): P 38, W 17, L 21.
Competitions won: Middlesex Cup 1972/3 and 1980/81, National Merit Table 'C' Winners 1985/86, John Player Cup quarter-finalists 1972/73 and 1980/81.

Most capped players: D.S. Wilson (8 for England); A.M. Rees (13 for Wales).

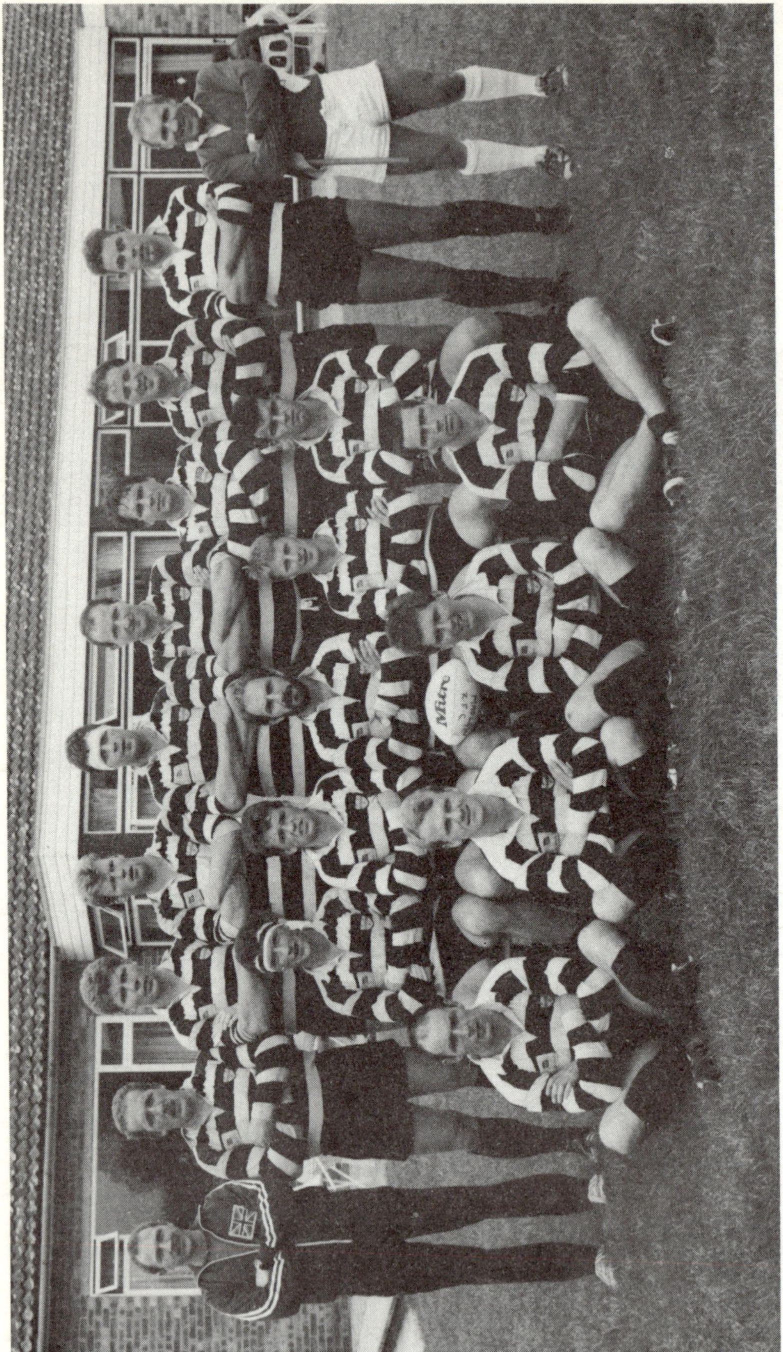

Maidstone – 1987–88.

Players' appearances, 1987–88: D. Barham 33, S. O'Reilly 32, N. Sinclair 28, S. Jones 27, J. Kerr 26, A. Mercer 26.

Leading scorers, 1987–88: *Points:* A. Mercer 78 (5 t, 5 cons, 14 pens, 2 d.g.); M. Wood 75 (5 t, 11 cons, 11 pens); N. Sinclair 50 (4 t, 8 cons.)

Player of the Year 1987–88: Paul Switzer.

Representative honours 1987–88: S. O'Reilly, D. Barham, S. Dear, An. Mercer, C. Malone (Middlesex); C. Malone (Scottish U21); J. Wells (Yorkshire U21).

Season's review: A frustrating season for the Metropolitan Police in which territorial advantage was not converted into points. Consequently results were generally poor and ample opportunity squandered.

MAIDSTONE

William Day Memorial Ground, Willow Way, Maidstone, Kent. **Founded:** 1880
President: J.V. Harrisson
Chairman: Harry Green
Coach: Andy Cushing
Secretary: Geoffrey Burr, Hush Heath Oast, Hush Heath Hill, Cranbrook, Kent. Tel: 0580 211661 (H) 0622 690691 (W).
Fixtures Secretary: Tony Morris, 7 Camden Street, Maidstone, Kent. Tel: 0622 673120 (H).
Club captain (1987–88): Andrew Cushing
Club captain (1988–89): Andrew Cushing
No. of teams: Senior 6. Youth & Minis 8.
Directions to Ground: From the centre of the town, go out on the Ashford Road. ½ mile from centre turn right at traffic lights, opposite Ford dealers Haynes Bros, into Square Hill Road. Second left into Mote Avenue, and then turn right into Willow Way before the Mote Park entrance. Ground on left.
Stand capacity: 100
Colours: Red, white & black hooped jerseys, black shorts, red stockings. (*Change colours:* Bottle green jerseys).
Floodlights: Training floodlights
Admission: £2 per league match, (Members £1). Non-league £1 (Members 50p).
Membership: £25 playing, £15 non-playing.
Programme: Included in admission. (Editor: Ray Vale)
Local newspaper: Kent Messenger
League: National 3.
Final position (1987–88): 7th
Playing record (1987–88): All matches: P 37, W 20, D 2, L 15, F 508, A 337. Courage Div 3: P 11, W 4 L 7. F 134, A 162. Kent Cup P 5, W 4, D 1. F 116, A 36.

Competitions won: Kent County Cup Winners, beating Blackheath 29–0 in the replay at Maidstone after a 12–12 draw at Dartfordians RFC.

Leading scorers, 1987–88: *Points*: Rob Kift 97 (14 cons, 23 pens); Phil Davies 81 (4 d.g., 6 cons, 19 pens). *Tries*: James Hall 11, Andy Cushing 10.

Representative honours 1987–88: Peter Catt, Clive Cashell (Kent).

Player of the Year: Ross Whatley.

Season's review: Fears that Maidstone's nomination to the Courage National Division 3 league may be too much for them were without foundation. Losing to the previous season's winners of Table 'C' the Vale of Lune by 14–16 in injury time, though disappointing, was the boost they needed.

They beat Nuneaton, Exeter, Moreley and Birmingham and besides Vale of Lune had narrow defeats against Met Police 6–9, Fylde 10–12, West Hartlepool 10–12, Sheffield 3–10 and only suffering heavier defeats at the hands of Wakefield and Plymouth Albion.

Maidstone's strength was undoubtedly in the forwards who were ably coached and led by Andy Cushing, the former London Scottish and Cambridge University player.

Maidstone also won the Kent Cup against Blackheath by 29–0 after a replay. Full Kent County caps were won by Peter Catt (lock) and Clive Cashell (flank).

Exeter – 1987–88: (Back-row) (l to r): L. Budd (Trainer), G. Meldon, B. Loughman, C. Grandfield, J. Tutchings, M. Bleasdale, G. Stratton, M. Collins; (Middle-row): P Holman (Coach), T. Vinnicombe (Match secretary), D. Ratley, S. Tutchings, M. Kee, D. Hartland, H. Langley, G. Sluman, A. Maunder, R. Withers, A. Green, C. Mills (Coach), J. Snell (Coach), B. Staddon (Director of coaching), J. Baxter (Chairman of selectors); (Front-row): R. Huxtable (Fixtures secretary), G. Bess, A. Cole (Chairman), M. Bodnar (Capt.), J. Challenger (President), P. Drewett (Vice-capt.), N. Gunter (Secretary), M. Cathery, S. Williams (Treasurer).

EXETER

The County Ground, St. Thomas, Exeter. Tel: 0392 78759.
Founded: 1782
President: L.J.B. Challenger
Chairman: A.R. Cole
Coach: R.C. Staddon
Secretary: N.R. Gunter, 2 Church Lane, Whitestone, Exeter. Tel: 0392 81419.
Fixtures Secretary: R. Huxtable, 21 Somerset Avenue, St. Thomas, Exeter. Tel: 0392 77385.
Club captain (1987–88): N. Bodnar
Club captain (1988–89): D. Hartland
No. of teams: Senior 4. Youth & Minis 4.
Directions to Ground: Main entrance at rear of St. Thomas Church, Cowick Street, Exeter.
Stand capacity: 800
Ground capacity: 10,000
Clubhouse: The Rugby Memorial Club. Open during Rugby season.
Colours: All black. (*Change colours:* White)
Floodlights: Yes
Admission: £1.50
Membership: £18
Programme: 30p. Editor: T.J. Turner
Local newspapers: Express and Echo, Western Morning News

League: National 3
Final position (1987–88): 9th
Playing record (1987–88): P 39, W 17, D 5, L 17, F 539, A 585.

Most capped players: M.A. Underwood 5, R.J.P. Madge 4, D.C. Manley 4, P.L. Nicholas 3, A.A. Brown 1, for England. J.R. Buchanan 16, for Scotland.

Leading scorers, 1987–88: *Points:* A. Green 140 (7 t, 8 cons, 22 p.g., 6 d.g.), S. Tutchings 91 (3 t, 8 cons, 22 p.g.), A. Maunder 60 (15 t). *Tries:* A. Maunder 15.

Player of the Year 1987–88: A. Maunder

Representative honours 1987–88: Nick Bodnar, Andy Green (Devon), Phil Bye (Devon U21s), Dave Furzer (Devon Colts).

Season's review: A XV – P 32, W 16, D 0, L 16, F 481. A 514. B XV – P 30, W 20, D 1, L 9, F 567, A 359. Colts XV – P 32, W 16, D 1, L 15, F 468, A 420. Under 16s – P 19, W 6, D 2, L 11, F 192, A 309. All sides improved during season and gained best results after Xmas.

NUNEATON

The Harry Cleaver Ground, Attleborough Road, Nuneaton. Tel: 0203 383206/383925.
Founded: 1879
President: N. Peckett
Chairman: Dr C.J. McKeown
Coach: N. Barker
Secretary: D.D. Swarbrigg, 70 Chetwynd Drive, Nuneaton. Tel: 0203 327426 (H) 0203 852643 (W).
Fixtures Secretary: J. Davies, 3 Saints Way, Nuneaton CV10 0UU. Tel: 0203 370011 (H) 0203 344800 (W).
Club captain (1987–88): R. Massey
Club captain (1988–89): R. Burton
No. of teams: Senior 3. Youth & Minis 11.
Directions to Ground: Nuneaton Town Centre. Attleborough Road.
Stand capacity: 490
Ground capacity: 5,000
Clubhouse: Bar, 2 lounges, kitchen, dining area
Colours: Black, red, white hoops. (*Change colours:* Blue or black)
Nickname: Nuns
Floodlights: Yes
Admission: £1.50
Membership: Vice Presidents £20
Programme: 30. Editor: N.R.F.C.
Local newspaper: Evening Tribune
League: National 3
Final position (1987–88): 10th
Playing record (1987–88): P 38, W 9, D 2, L 27.
Competitions won: Warwickshire Colts Cup.

Most capped players: W.A. Holmes (16 for England).

Leading scorers, 1987–88: *Points:* B. Massey, 84. *Tries:* B. Boffey, 6.

Player of the Year 1987–88: M. Bloxham

Representative honours 1987–88: Bob Massey, Andy Ellis (Warwickshire)

Season's review: As a consequence of injuries and non-availability 60 players were used in the 1st XV. A close examination of results reveals that if we had won the games we *should* have won and perhaps some of the games we *could* have won, Nuneaton would have been in the top three of the division.

MORLEY

Scatcherd Lane, Morley, Leeds. Tel: 0532 533487.
Founded: 1878
President: R. Binks
Chairman: J. Mellor
Coach: J. Shepherd
Secretary: Bob Lloyd, 5 Shepley Bridge, Mirfield, West Yorkshire WF14 9HR. Tel: 0924 494612 (H) 0204 21971 (W).
Fixtures Secretary: T. Richmond, 101 Carlinghow Hill, Batley, West Yorkshire WF17 0AG. Tel: 0924 472705 (H) 0274 480741 (W).
Club captain (1987–88): A. Rivett
Club captain (1988–89): T.B.A.
No. of teams: Senior 5. Youth & Minis 10.
Stand capacity: 1,000
Ground capacity: 6,000
Clubhouse: 3 bars, function suite, Presidents lounge, physio room and all usual facilties.
Colours: Maroon. (*Change colours:* Cambridge blue)
Floodlights: Yes
Admission: £1.50
Membership: £20
Programme: 30p. Editor: Belinda Mellor
Local newspapers: Morley Advertiser, Morley Observer, Yorkshire Post, Evening Post
League: National 3
Final position (1987–88): 11th (relegated)
Playing record (1987–88): P 41, W 10, D 2, L 29, F 440, A 857.

Most capped players: G.H. Marsden 3, J.P. Shooter 4, for England.

Players' appearances, 1987–88: Tony Clark 41, Jon Clark 38.

Leading scorers, 1987–88: *Points:* Jamie Grayson 120 (23 pens, 24 cons, 1 d.g.), Jon Clark 75 (4 t, 15 pens, 7 cons). *Tries:* Tony Clark 16, Dennis Tocker and Tony Donoghue 7.

Representative honours 1987–88: P. White (English Universities), R. Szabo (British Police), G. Stokes (England Schools 16 group).

Season's review: Won only one Division 3 game and relegated to Area League North. A yong side, average age 21. Highlight of the season was beating Headingley 16–14. John Shepherd coached Yorkshire and Yorkshire U21. Marie Griffiths (physio) made history by being the first woman physio to tread the hallowed turf at Twickenham for the Yorkshire U21.

BIRMINGHAM

Portway, Forshaw Heath Lane, Earlswood, W. Midlands B94 5LH. Tel: 0564 822955.
Founded: 1911
President: J. Goodman
Chairman: J. Brockeshaw
Coach: B. Wallace
Secretary: I. Howell-Jones, 59 Hazelhurst Road, Kingsheath, Birmingham B14 6AB. Tel: 021 444 2032 (H) 032 427 2141 (W).
Fixtures Secretary: A. Morden, 134 Old Station Road, Hampton in Arden, Solihull, B92 0HF. Tel: Hand in Arden 2462 (H) 021 643 2736 (W).
Club captain (1987–88): W. Hart
Club captain (1988–89): T.B.A.
No. of teams: Senior 3.
Directions to Ground: Junction 3, M42, signposted.
Stand capacity: 150
Ground capacity: Thousands
Clubhouse: 3 bars, 3 pairs changing rooms, main clubhouse and bar, sponsors lounge, press room.
Colours: Red shirts, red and black, white shorts, white stockings. *(Change colours:* Black and gold hoops)
Floodlights: No
Admission: £1.50
Membership: Full playing £25, ordinary £20
Programme: 20p. Editor: Trevor Woolley.
Local newspaper: Birmingham Post
League: National 3
Final position (1987–88): Bottom (relegated)
Playing record (1987–88): P 31, W 4, D 2, L 25, F 599, A 924.

Andy Macfarlane (Fylde) starred for the North and was on the verge of England selection as a no. 8. Photo: Colorsport.

The Rugby Football Club. Champions of Area League North 1987–88.

AREA LEAGUE NORTH

IF YOU were a supporter of Rugby the Area League North season was a story of triumph and the name of the town from which the game originated will in future feature in the National Divisions, which – among other things – is useful propaganda for the game. Rugby have been improving quietly over recent seasons under the benevolent influence of Mal Malik and Steve Brain and lost only one match.

They were hotly pursued by another improved club – Durham City – and we can expect more good performances by the North-East side, which did have the consolation of winning their county cup and a place in this coming season's Pilkington Cup.

Roundhay, after a shocking season in 1986–87, made a fine recovery in the Area League and can be expected to challenge for honours, whilst Preston Grasshoppers, Northern, Broughton Park and Stourbridge all showed signs of being able to compete with the best if given the opportunity.

Lichfield, after several promising seasons, struggled at this level as did Birkenhead Park, whose fame deserves better reward. Unfortunately, fame no longer is a passport to the 'big time'.

Adrift at the bottom were Derby and Solihull, who failed to win any of their ten matches, so both must try their luck at a lower level until they can find the necessary talent for a renewed challenge.

Any league, which can produce an average score of around 28 points per game, must provide entertaining rugby and this was certainly the case here.

TABLES 1987–88

AREA LEAGUE NORTH

	P	W	D	L	F	A	Pts
Rugby	10	9	0	1	184	100	18
Durham	10	8	0	2	165	100	16
Roundhay	10	6	2	2	131	67	14
Preston G'hoppers	10	5	1	4	178	149	11
Northern	10	5	1	4	121	137	11
Broughton Park	10	5	0	5	152	106	10
Stourbridge	10	5	9	5	132	134	10
Lichfield	10	4	0	6	150	165	8
Birkenhead Park	10	4	0	6	117	179	8
Solihull	10	0	0	10	59	219	0

Rugby and Askeans are promoted to Division 3.
Morley and Birmingham are relegated.

AREA LEAGUE NORTH

THE RUGBY FOOTBALL CLUB

Webb Ellis Road, Rugby. Tel: 0788 54907.
Founded: 1873
President: Peter Galliford, OBE
Chairman: David Rees
Coach: Andy Johnson, Sports Injury Specialist, Ivor Field
Secretary: John W. Llewellyn, 11 Rokeby Street, Rugby. Tel: 0788 72287.
Fixtures Secretary: Malcolm W.T. Palmer, Virginia Cottage, High Street, Grandborough, Rugby CV23 8DQ. Tel: 0788 812326 (H), 05642 4454 (W)
Club captain (1987–88): Steve E. Brain, England, Warks.
Club captain (1988–89): Steve Brain
No. of teams: Senior 3. Youth & Minis 6.
Directions to Ground: From town centre take A4071 Bilton Road. Webb Ellis Road is 2nd turning right. Ground on right.
Ground capacity: 3000. Stand, 200 (but facilities exist for temporary stands on special occasions to increase capacity).
Clubhouse: Changing rooms, bath and shower facilities. Gymnasium, squash courts, bar, function room, conference room, meals, snacks.
Colours: White, red yoke, red lion motif. (*Change colours:* Navy blue, lion motif (red).
Nickname: Lions
Floodlights: Yes
Admission: £1.75 (incl programme 30p).
Membership: £25, season, £30 vice-president, £40 family VP, £60 (corporate VP), £260, life.
Programme: 30p. (Editor: David Rees, Roy Batchelor)
Local newspaper: Rugby Advertiser and Coventry Evening Telegraph
League: Area League North
Final position (1987–88): 1st. Now promoted National Division 3 88/89
Playing record (1987–88): P 42, W 30, D 1, L 11. F 1047, A 516.
Competitions won: Area League North title, 26 March 1988. Warwickshire Cup, 17 April, 1988. Have been invited as the guest side to finals day of the Middlesex. 7's May 1989.

DURHAM CITY

Green Lane, Durham City. Tel: 091 3861172
Founded: 1872
President: H. Sedgewick
Coach: E. Wood
Secretary: C. Warbrick, 19 Neville Dale Terrace, Durham City. Tel: 091 3847531.
Fixtures Secretary: J. Thompson, West View, Market Place, Crook, Co. Durham. Tel: 0388 528 071.
Club captain (1987–88): J. Bland
Club captain (1988–89): H. Nicholson
No. of teams: Senior 5. Youth & Minis 9.
Directions to Ground: Centre of Durham, turn into Old Elvet at Royal County Hotel, left at Magistrate's Court. Ground 150 yards on right.
Ground capacity: 3000. Stand, 500.
Colours: Navy blue and gold. (*Change colours:* White or navy blue).
Floodlights: Yes
Admission: £1
Membership: £20
Programme: £1. (Editor: G. Moore)
Local newspaper: Durham Advertiser, Newcastle Journal, Northern Echo
League: Area Leage North
Final position (1987–88): 2nd
Playing record (1987–88): P 39, W 25, D 2, L 12. F 778, A 464.
Competitions won: Durham County Senior Cup 1885, 88, 1910, 21, 29, 32–34, 36, 53, 57, 58, 62–67, 88.

ROUNDHAY

Chandos Park, Lidgett Lane, Leeds LS8 1QX. Tel: 0532 661815.
Founded: 1924
President: R.A. Bidgood, JP
Coach: Robin Kay
Secretary: Norman Gray, 6 Ayresome Terrace, Leeds LS8 1BJ. Tel: 0532 662742 (H), 0532 463240 (W)
Fixtures Secretary: David Fawcett, 433 Meanwood Road, Leeds LS. Tel: 0532 453606.
Club captain (1987–88): R. Burman
Club captain (1988–89): R. Burman
No. of teams: Senior 4.
Directions to Ground: North of Leeds, Lidgett Lane, Off Harrogate Road at Moortown Corner.
Ground capacity: 2000. Stand 400.
Clubhouse: Members bar, general bar, committee room, dining room.
Colours: Scarlet, emerald, white. (*Change colours:* Red, white shorts).
Nickname: Roundhay
Floodlights: Yes
Admission: £1
Membership: £10
Programme: 30p. (Editor: Ray Peycke)
Local newspaper: Yorkshire Post and Yorkshire Evening Post
League: Area L. North
Final position (1987–88): 3rd
Playing record (1987–88): P 39, W 22, D 2, L 16. F 621, A404.
Competitions won:

PRESTON GRASSHOPPERS

Lightfoot Green, Fulwood, Preston PR4 0AP. Tel: 0772 863546, 0772 863027, 0772 861605 (Press box)
Founded: 1869
President: T.B. (Barry) Leeming
Chairman: Robert Eastham
Coach: Malcolm Alden, Michael Hill
Secretary: Les Anson, Oak Tree, 110 Whittingham Lane, Broughton, Preston PR3 5DD. Tel: 0772 862250.
Fixtures Secretary: John Rowell, 121 Bare Lane, Bare, Morecambe LA4 4RD. Tel: 0524 424514.
Club captain (1987–88): Roy Dransfield
Club captain (1988–89): Roy Dransfield
No. of teams: Senior 6. Youth & Minis 11.
Directions to Ground: M6, Junction 32. Turn left towards Preston. Left again in 50 yards. follow Ingol signs. Ground less than 1 mile from motorway.
Ground capacity: 3000 (approx). Stand, 250.
Clubhouse: Large main bar, lounge, committee room, 6 dressing rooms, musical room, admin office, 4 squash courts.
Colours: Navy, white hoops. (*Change colours:* Emerald green).
Nickname: Hoppers
Floodlights: No
Admission: £1.50 (inc programme)
Membership: Social (non voting) £5. Ordinary £12. Playing £25. Juniors £5. Student £12. Rugby/squash £45.
Programme: Inc. in admission. (Editor: Les Anson)
Local newspaper: Lancashire Evening Post
League: Area North
Final position (1987–88): 4th
Playing record (1987–88): P 39, W 22, D 3, L 14. F 687, A 491.
Competitions won: Lancashire Cup finalists 1983/4, 1985/6. Lancashire Colts Cup Winners 1983/4, 1987/8. Finalists 1984/5, 1986/7.

NORTHERN

McCracken Park, Great North Road, Newcastle-u-Tyne. Tel: 091 2363369.
Founded: 1876
President: I.H. Percy
Chairman: R.S. Appleby
Coach: TBA
Secretary: E. Wilkins, 27 Kingsley Avenue, Melton Park, Newcastle-u-Tyne. Tel: 091 2365557.
Fixtures Secretary: E. Armstrong, The Fawdon, Red House, Newcastle NE3 2AH. Tel: 091 2857449.
Club captain (1987–88): J. Baldwin
Club captain (1988–89): J. Baldwin
No. of teams: Senior 6. Youth & Minis 6.
Directions to Ground: On Great North Road (old A1). North of Gosforth.
Ground capacity: 1000. Stand: 200)
Clubhouse: 2 bars, function rooms, changing facilities, squash.
Colours: White shirts, blue shorts, red socks. (*Change colours:* white, red and blue hoops on shirts).
Floodlights: No
Admission: £1.50 (inc. programme)
Membership: £35 playing, £20 non-playing.
Programme: Incl in admission. (Editor: R.S. Appleby)
Local newspaper: Journal and Evening Chronicle
League: Area League North
Final position (1987–88): 5th
Playing record (1987–88): P 43, W 15, L 26, D 2. F 580, A 765.
Competitions won: County Sevens

BROUGHTON PARK

Chelsfield Grove, Chorlton, Manchester M21 2SU. Tel: 061 881 2481.
Founded: 1882
President: R.W. Greenall
Chairman: J.G. Parry
Coach: B. Jackson
Secretary: R.W. Greenall, 260 Barlow Moor Road M21 2HA. 061 861 0457.
Fixtures Secretary: K.R. Hanham, 1 Broad Meadow, Bromley Cross, Bolton, Lancs. Tel: 0204 56524.
No. of teams: Senior 4. Youth & Minis 8.

Directions to Ground: From south M6 leave Junction 19 – M56. Continue to A5103 slip road to Chorlton right. North M62–63 leave at Junction 7. A56 right at Edge Lane left at park to Church at junction. Ground on left.
Ground capacity: 3000. Stand, 600.
Colours: Black, white hoops. (*Change colours:* Red).
Nickname: Park
Floodlights: No
Admission: £1.50
Membership: £25
Programme: 30p. (Editor: A.H. McCallum)
Local newspaper: M/C Evening News
League: Area League North
Final position (1987–88): 6th
Playing record (1987–88): P 41, W 28, L 12, D 1.

STOURBRIDGE

Bridgnorth Road, Stourton, Stourbridge. Tel: 0384 393889.
Founded: 1876
President: N. Glover
Coach: D. Fourness
Secretary: R.M. Baker, 33 Lychgate Avenue, Pedmore, Stourbridge. Tel: 0562 883835.
Fixtures Secretary: A. McCreadie, 24 Leavale Road, Norton Stourbridge. Tel: Stourbridge 0386.
Club captain (1987–88): J. Shaw
Club captain (1988–89): K. Astley
No. of teams: Senior 6. Youth & Minis 9.
Directions to Ground: On A458 Brignorth Road out of Stourbridge approx 3 miles.
Colours: Navy blue, white hoops. (*Change colours:* Red, yellow hoops)
Floodlights: Yes
Programme: £1. (Editor: J. Standish)
Local newspaper: Stourbridge News, Express & Star, Birmingham Post and Mail
League: Area League North
Final position (1987–88): 7th
Playing record (1987–88): P 36, W 26, D 1, L 9. F 666, A 353
Competitions won: Rugby World Junior Club of Year 85/86. North Midlands Cup Winners 1981, 1983, 1984 1985, 1986.

LICHFIELD

Cooke Fields, Tamworth Road, Lichfield. Tel: Lichfield 263020
Founded: 1874
President: P.N. Martin
Chairman: D. Lewis
Coach: A. Gouldstone
Secretary: C.R. Smith, The Old Schoolhouse, Edingale, Tamworth, Staffs. Tel. 082 785 673
Fixtures Secretary. A.G. Young, 5 Covey Close, Lichfield, Staffs. Tel. 0543 262832
Club captain (1987–88): Mark Davis
Club captain (1988–89): Paul Massey
Directions to Ground: On A51, Tamworth Road out of Lichfield
Ground capacity: Approx 2000
Clubhouse: New facilities
Colours: Myrtle Green
Floodlights: No
Membership: £24.00 pa
Programme: Varies. (Editor: A. Wilson)
Local newspaper: Lichfield Mercury
League: Area League North
Final position (1987–88): 8th
Playing record (1987–88): P 34, W 22, D 0, L 12
Competitions won: Manchester 7s, Stafforshire 7s

BIRKENHEAD PARK

The Upper Park, Park Road North, Birkenhead, Merseyside.
Founded: 1871
President: G.B. Porter Esq MA, MP.
Chairman: A.R. Abraham
Coach: D. Buttery
Secretary: Not yet decided.
Fixtures Secretary: Graeme Marrs, 501 Tower Building, Liverpool L3 1BL. Tel: 051-236-3191 (Bus.), 051-652-1536 (Home).
Club captain (1987–88): A. Chapman
Club captain (1988–89): Not yet elected.
No. of teams: Senior 5, Youth & Minis 2
Directions to Ground: (Train) Mersey rail to Birkenhead Park, then 5 mins walk. (Road) M53 Exit 1, follow signs to B'Head, turn rt up Mallaby Street into Park Road North. M62 9 M58, through B'Head Tunnel (4 lane).
Ground capacity: 8,000
Colours: Red, white & blue stripes, white shorts, red stockings. (*Change colours:* Black shirts, red collar, white shorts, red stockings)
Nickname: "Park"
Floodlights: Yes
Admission: £1.50, 50p for children.
Membership: £30 p.a. for full membership.
Programme: 16 page, 20p. (Editor: Michael Davies)
Local newspaper: Birkenhead News, Liverpool Daily Post, Liverpool Echo.
League: North 1
Final position (1987–88): 9th
Playing record (1987–88): P 40, W 15, D 1, L 24.
Competitions won: Runners-up Cheshire Cup last three years.

Most capped player: J.R. Paterson (Scotland) 21.

SOLIHULL

Sharmans Cross Road, Solihull. Tel: 705 7995.
Founded: 1933
President: A. Abercrombie
Chairman: R. Wharrod
Secretary: E.J. Sheridan, 9 Mayhurst Close, Hollywood, Birmingham B47 5QH. Tel: 021 230 2315.
Fixtures Secretary: H. McCormick, 3 Western Close, Dorridge, Solihull. Tel: 05695 4068.
Club captain (1987–88): S. Jervis
Club captain (1988–89): J. Houlton
No. of teams: Senior 5. Youth & Minis 9.
Directions to Ground: Sharmans Cross Road, off Streetbrook Road, Solihull.
Colours: Gold and black. (*Change colours:* Gold, black collars
Floodlights: No
Membership: £40
Programme: 50p
Local newspaper: Solihull News, Solihull Times.
League: Area League North
Final position (1987–88): Bottom

AREA LEAGUE SOUTH

THIS was the story of what might have been – and what should have been. Sidcup – in a very closely fought division – had their noses in front for much of the season until Askeans took the lead, but the final match for the Kent side should have been a formality as they were at home to Lydney, whose own challenge had faded.

However, sport is full of stories of anti-climax (remember that sad Doug Sanders missed put at St. Andrews in 1970!) and Sidcup contrived to miss kick after kick, whilst the brave men from Gloucestershire managed three to take home the points and deprive the home side of promotion. Another team from Kent – Askeans – will play in Division 3 next season instead.

Askeans are an ambitious club and should hold their own in better company, but in the new season which teams should we consider as the best prospects? Sidcup again, of course. Lydney also, since they did win the highly competitive county cup as a bonus.

Cornwall have few reasons for satisfaction at a club level at the moment, but either Camborne or promoted Redruth could put that right. Havant, Stroud and Southend are all capable of challenging the top teams in the league and, if tradition means anything, so should Cheltenham, who have produced some excellent youth teams recently.

Salisbury could be strengthened by the arrival of the Army champion side in their area, but Sudbury may struggle. Poor Streatham–Croydon were out of their depth and lost all their games, but they have the facilities and will to come back.

The average score per game in this league was less than that of their Northern counterparts, but the overall standard may have been more even and this would account for the difference.

TABLES 1987–88

AREA LEAGUE SOUTH

	P	W	D	L	F	A	Pts
Askeans	s10	8	1	1	141	83	17
Sidcup	10	7	2	1	130	72	16
Lydney	10	7	0	3	173	99	14
Camborne	10	5	2	3	113	119	12
Havant	10	5	0	5	116	102	10
Stroud	10	5	0	5	112	114	10
Southend	10	5	0	5	63	108	10
Sudbury	10	3	2	5	125	106	8
Salisbury	10	3	1	6	84	94	7
Cheltenham	10	3	0	7	95	152	6
Derby	10	2	0	8	136	197	4
Streatham/ Croydon	10	0	0	10	70	173	0

AREA LEAGUE SOUTH

ASKEANS

60H Broad Walk, Kidbrooke, SE3. Tel: 01-856 1025.
Founded: 1929
President: B.L. Sarson
Chairman: Col K.P. Walker, OBE, TD
Coach: S.A. McKinney
Secretary: A.L.M. Eastick, 97 Heathlee Road, Blackheath, SE3 9HS. Tel: 01-852 8596.
Fixtures Secretary: M. Sidgwick, 53 Borkwood Way, Orpington, Kent. Tel: 0689 57436.
Club captain (1987–88): A.M. Bond
Club captain (1988–89): A.M. Bond
No. of teams: Senior 5. Youth & Minis 4.
Directions to Ground: Just off a2 betwen Blackheath and Eltham
Ground capacity: 1500. Stand, 300.
Colours: Blue, black, white. (*Change colours:* Red).
Nickname:
Admission: £2 – Courage League and John Player. £1 others.
Membership: £10
Programme: Admittance with programme. (Editor: M.J. Blake)
Local newspaper: Kentish Times
League: Area League South
Final position (1987–88): 1st
Playing record (1987–88): P 31, W 25, D 1, L 5. F 739, A 323.
Competitions won: Area League South, Tamdem Computers, Seven Counties Merit Table.

SIDCUP

Sydney Road, Sidcup, Kent. Tel: 01-300 2336.
Founded: 1883
President: A.H. Marsh
Coach: B. Pinder
Secretary: D.A. Ash, 282A High Street, Orpington, Kent. Tel: 01-464 0953 (H), 0689 25674 (W).
Fixtures Secretary: R.D.P. Henderson, 35 Spurrel Lane, Bexley, Kent. Tel: 0322 54920 (H).
Club captain (1987–88): P. Bensley
Club captain (1988–89): P. Dwyer
No. of teams: Senior 6. Youth & Minis 13.
Directions to Ground: From a20, take A222. Turn left at Police Station, turn left into Sydney Road.
Stand capacity: 200
Clubhouse: 2 bars, toilets and changing rooms.
Colours: White, maroon monogram. (*Change colours:* Maroon shirts).
Floodlights: No
Admission: By programme

Membership: £35, playing, £10 non playing, £5 ladies and SCs, £3 joining fee.
Programme: Variable. (Editor: Steven Haggarty, 7 Hatherley Road, Sidcup.
Local newspaper: Sidcup Times
League: Area League South
Final position (1987–88): 2nd
Playing record (1987–88): P 30, w 22, d 2, L 6. F 450, A 267.
Competitions won: 2nd in Tandem Computers Merit Table (Seven Counties).

LYDNEY

Regentsholm, Regent Street, Lydney, Glos GL15 5RN. Tel: 0594 42479.
Founded: 1887
President: Mrs John H. Watts
Chairman: A.S.P. Wolfe
Coach: P. Kiely
Secretary: A.J. Jones, 5 Kimberley Close, Lydney, Glos GL15 5AE. Tel: 0594 42709 (H), 0594 42777 (W).
Fixtures Secretary: D. Nelmes, Pine View, Forest Road, Bream, Glos. Tel: 0594 562038.
Club captain (1987–88): Adrian Knox
Club captain (1988–89): Rhodri J. Lewis
No. of teams: Senior 3. Youth & Minis 6.
Directions to Ground: Centre of town, 100 yards off main A48 trunk road.
Ground capacity: 2500 plus. Stand, 260 covered.
Clubhouse: Fully carpeted main lounge bar, players dining room/bar, sponsors bar.
Colours: Black and white hoops. (*Change colours:* red).
Nickname: The Severnsiders
Floodlights: Yes
Admission: £1
Membership: £15 season ticket.
Programme: 20p. (Editor: D. Nelmes)
Local newspaper: Lydney Observer, The Citizen
League: Area League South
Final position (1987–88): 3rd
Playing record (1987–88): P 46, W 28, L 17, D 1.
Competitions won: Flowers County Cup won by 1st Fifteen. Forest of Dean Competition won by 2nd Fifteen.

CAMBORNE

The Recreation Ground. Tel: 0209 713227
Founded: 1878
President: J.M. Trott
Chairman: L. Ptifrsuc
Coach: R.G. Tonkin
Secretary: S.C. West, "Shalimar", Shorts Hill, Treslothan, Camborne. Tel: 0209 716665 (H). 0209 713170 (W).
Fixtures Secretary: E.T. Pascoe, 51 St. Meriadoc Road, Camborne. Tel: 0209 718158.
Club captain (1987–88): P. Trudgeon
Club captain (1988–89): C. Alcock
No. of teams: Senior 3. Youth & Minis 5.
Directions to Ground: Leave A30 Camborne/Redruth by-pass at junction 'Camborne West'. enter town from west follow signs marked 'Recreation Ground'.
Ground capacity: 2000. Stand, 600.
Clubhouse: ½ mile approx from ground at 5 South Terrace, Camborne. Tel: 0209 712684.
Colours: Cherry and white. (*Change colours:* Blue).
Floodlights: No
Admission: 80p and 40p OAPs. (Different prices for some games).
Membership:
Programme: Produced per match 20p. (Editor: S.C. West)
Local newspaper: Camborne/Redruth Packet and West Briton.
League: Area League South
Final position (1987–88): 4th
Playing record (1987–88): P 38, W 23, L 12, D 3. F 782, A 468.
Competitions won: Cornwall Merit Table Champions 77/78, 78/79, 79/80, 80/81, 81/82, 84/85 and 85/86. County Cup Winners 77/78, 84/85 and 86/87.

HAVANT RFC

Hooks Lane, Fraser Road, Bedhampton, Havant, Hants PO9 3DT. Tel: (0705) 477843
Founded: 1951
President: Bob Iverson
Chairman: Dave Platt
Coach: Brian Powell
Secretary: Jim Doyle, 62 Corbett Road, Waterlooville, Portsmouth, Hants PO7 5TA. Tel: (0705) 259787
Fixtures Secretary: Mick Chalk, 16 Highclere Avenue, Leigh Park, Havant. Tel: (0705) 472239.
Club captain (1987–88): Andy Perry
Club captain (1988–89): Andy Perry
No. of teams: Senior 7. Youth & Minis 6.
Directions to Ground: Off A3M on M27 for Havant, near Bedhampton Station.
Colours: Shirts – Navy and white hoops, Shorts & socks – Navy. *Change colours:* Shirts – Red.
Floodlights: No.
Membership: £25.
Programme: Teams and adverts. 50p. Editor: Dave Platt, 9 Brookside Road, Bedhampton, Havant.
Local newspaper: The News (Portsmouth)
League: Area South
Final position (1987–88): 5th
Playing record (1987–88):
Competitions won: Hampshire Cup 20/3/88 (and previous 4 years).

STROUD

Fromehall Park, Stroud, Glos Tel: 04536 3019)
Founded: 1873
President: C.G. Woodruff
Chairman: W.J. Silverthorne
Secretary: M.F. Hall, 1 Elm Terrace, Foxmoor Lane, Ebley, Stroud, Glos. Tel: Stonehowe (045382) 4321.
Fixtures Secretary: R.J. Hillier, Marijon, Paganhill Lane, Stroud, Glos. Tel: Stroud 4381.
Club captain (1987–88): A. Dix
Club captain (1988–89): A. Dix
Directions to Ground: A46, 1 mile south of Stroud at Golden Cross.
Ground capacity: 4000. Stand, 100.
Clubhouse: Clubroom, 3 bars, changing rooms, 2 squash courts.
Colours: Blue and white hoops. (*Change colours:* All blue).
Floodlights: No
Admission: £1
Membership: Between £5 (social) to £20 (patron)
Programme: 20p. (Editor: N.F. Hall)
Local newspaper: Stroud News & Journal
League: Area League South
Final position (1987–88): 6th
Playing record (1987–88): P 41, W 23, D 1, L 12. F 690, A 488.
Competitions won: Stroud Junior Combination Cup (3rd team)

SOUTHEND

Warners Park, Sutton Road, Southend-on-Sea, Essex SS2 5RR. Tel: 0702 546682.
Founded: 1870
President: F. Dyton
Chairman: T. Webb
Coach: P. Lane
Secretary: J.D. Barty, 12 Broad Close, Hockley, Essex SS5 5DE. Tel: 0702 294793 (H), 0702 364394 (W).
Fixtures Secretary: T. Webb, 28 St James Gardens, Westcliffe on Sea, Essex SS0 0BU.
Club captain (1987–88): I. Grimsell
Club captain (1988–89): N. Branch
No. of teams: Senior 6. Youth & Minis 2.
Directions to Ground: A127 to Southend at roundabout after Bell Pub. Go straight on past Access Head Office to next traffic lights. Turn left, go to next roundabout, turn left, follow road to club house.
Ground capacity: 5000 v Gloucester John Player Cup
Clubhouse: Brick built approx 8 years old.
Colours: Brown shirts, white shorts. (*Change colours:* Brown and white hoop shirts).
Floodlights: Yes
Membership: £20 playing + match fee. £20 non players. £7.50 colts.
Programme: £1. (Editor: G. Lamb)
Local newspaper: Southend Evening Echo
League: Area League South
Final position (1987–88): 7th
Playing record (1987–88): P 32, W 18, D 2, L 12.
Competitions won: London Welsh 7s

SUDBURY

Mootfield, Rugby Road, Gt Cornard, Sudbury, Suffolk. Tel: 0787 77547.
Founded: 1925
President: R.G. Newton
Chairman: T.F. McNeil
Coach: R.P. Day
Secretary: C.R. Donnelly, 1 Prince Charles Close, Acton Lane, Sudbury, Suffolk CO10 6YT.
Fixtures Secretary: G. Underwood, Mill Cottages, 11 Bures Road, Sudbury, Suffolk.
Club captain (1987–88): R. Sumner
Club captain (1988–89): R. Sumner
No. of teams: Senior 5. Youth & Minis 5.
Directions to Ground: A12 to Colchester A134 to Sudbury. At roundabout take 1st left (Northern Road). After ½ mile turnright, follow signposts.
Ground capacity: 1000+
Clubhouse: Bar, kitchen, toilets, 8 changing rooms, 2 baths, showers, squash court, weights gymn.
Colours: Navy blue, broad white hoop. (*Change colours:* Claret with navy blue hoop).
Floodlights: Yes
Admission: 50p/£1
Membership: £30 playing member (includes squash court and weights room)
Programme: Admission. (Editor: R.P. Day)
Local newspaper: Suffolk Free Press, East Anglian Daily Times
League: Area League South
Final position (1987–88): 8th
Playing record (1987–88): P 32, W 19, D 3, L 10. F 618, A 264.
Competitions won: 24/1/88 Suffolk cup. 23/4/88 Eastern Counties Cup. Signpost Paints Floodlit Cup.

SALISBURY

Castle Road, Salisbury, Wilts. Tel: 0722 25317.
Founded: 1923
President: Peter Jamieson
Chairman: C. Evans
Coach: Vacant
Secretary: Richard Larcombe, Spindleberry, Stratford-sub-Castle, Salisbury, Wilts SP2 3LG. Tel: 0722 336712 (H). 0985 215345 (W).
Fixtures Secretary: R. Rowland, 1 Lode Hill, Downton, Salisbury, Wilts. Tel: 0725 22064.
Club captain (1987–88): David Morley
Club captain (1988–89): David Morley
No. of teams: Senior 4. Youth & Minis 10.
Directions to Ground: From town centre A345 north towards Amesbury, over one roundabout, ground on left before Old Sarum monument.
Ground capacity: Unlimited
Clubhouse: One main, two lounge bars, six changing rooms (+ referees)
Colours: Green & white. (*Change colours:* All white).
Floodlights: Yes.
Admission: By programme
Membership: £15
Programme: 50p. (Editor: R. Rowland)
Local newspaper: Salisbury Journal
League: Area League South
Final position (1987–88): 9th
Playing record (1987–88): P 36, W 16, D 4, L 16. F 514, A 390.

CHELTENHAM

Prince of Wales Stadium, Tommy Taylors Lane, Cheltenham. Tel: 0242 525393.
Founded: 1889
President: E. Nicholas
Chairman: Barrie Lewis
Coach: Richard Akenhead
Secretary: Tom Parker, 39 Long Mynd Avenue, Cheltenham GL51 5QT. Tel: 0242 521076.
Fixtures Secretary: Mike Edwards, 2 Greenbank Cottages, Piccadilly, Guiting Power, Cheltenham, Glos. Tel: 04515 396.
Club captain (1987–88): Mike Steele
Club captain (1988–89): Cyril Kelly
No. of teams: Senior 2. Youth & Minis 11.
Directions to Ground: Leave motorway (M5 at exit 20 and follow signs to Recreation Centre.
Ground capacity: 3000. Stand, 500 covered.
Clubhouse: Large 1st floor clubhouse and bar. Built 6 years ago. 2 floodlit pitches.
Colours: Red, black. (*Change colours:* White).
Floodlights: Yes
Admission: £1.50
Membership: £20 VP
Programme: 20p. (Editor: Club Secretary)
Local newspaper: Gloucestershire Echo, Cheltenham (Evening)
League: Area League South
Final position 10th
Playing record (1987–88): P 42, W 16, L 26. F 468, A 818.

STREATHAM – CROYDON

159 Breestock Road, Thornton Heath CR4 7JP. Tel: 01 684 1502.
Founded: 1871
President: A.E.P. Bain
Coach: S. Kelleher
Secretary: R.A. MacLennan, 31 Northwood avenue, Purley CR2 2ER. Tel: 01 660 2070. 01 658 2333.
Fixtures Secretary: R.J. Towers, 24 Earnest Grove, Beckenham, Kent.
No. of teams: Senior 6. Youth & Minis 1.
Directions to Ground: BR Thornton Heath Station. 10 mins walk. London Transport Thornton Heath Garage 2 minutes walk.
Ground capacity: 2000+. Stand, 200.
Clubhouse: Bar, tea room.

Area League South

Membership: £30
Colours: cardinal, white. (*Change colours:* Blue).
Floodlights: No

Local newspaper: Croydon Advertiser, South London Press
League: Area League South
Final position (1987–88): 11th (relegated to London 1)
Playing record (1987–88): P 33, W 11, L 22. F 466, A 509.

Fylde's England lock Wade Dooley in action at Slough in a Charity Match in memory of the home team's chairman Brian Sterry. Photo: Chris Roberts.

Yorkshire and Sale centre John Bentley – one of the country's heroes in their championship-winning 1987 team. Photo: Colorsport.

NORTH DIVISION

THE North Division contributes two dozen leagues to the Courage structure starting with two main leagues – North 1 and 2 – followed by two higher leagues covering the North West and North East – both with 1 and 2 suffixes – and these are themselves followed by regional leagues for the North West and county leagues over the East of the Pennines – six from Yorkshire and another four from Durham and Northumberland.

The leagues have been well assessed but it does mean that any ambitious club in the lower reaches of, say, Yorkshire 6 is going to spend some dozen years reaching a fixture list that would include the likes of Harlequins, Waterloo and Bristol.

But who cares? Each team will in most cases be satisfied like the average golfer in reaching their targeted potential, which is probably well short of playing at Twickenham. The leagues tell clubs where they are in the national – or divisional – 'pecking order' and most will be happy to have dreams at night and get on with enjoying themselves in broad daylight.

However, there are clubs which can in time make it to the top – or near there – and those to watch are clubs like Winnington Park and Aspatria. Conversely, others with proud histories will be under pressure to hold what they have and it is sad to see clubs like Middlesbrough and Manchester fall into this category. But it is all for the good of the game as a whole.

NORTH LEAGUES

THE first club to take advantage of the promotion and relegation system to improve their status is Winnington Park, who won a keenly contested North 1 from the strong challenge of Kendal and West Park.

At the other end of the table it is sad to see Widnes and Middlesbrough descend, but they are replaced by worthy clubs in Aspatria and Halifax with Bradford and Bingley most unluckily pipped for promotion on points difference by the other two.

Manchester and Wilmslow were out on their own at the foot of North 2 and start the new season in the North West top division. They will surely fight their way back.

TABLES 1987–88

NORTH 1

	P	W	D	L	F	A	Pts
Winnington Pk	10	8	0	2	211	74	16
Kendal	10	7	0	3	135	104	14
West Park	10	7	0	3	135	107	14
Otley	10	5	1	4	194	122	11
Harrogate	10	5	0	5	147	113	10
Tynedale	10	5	0	5	96	116	10
Wigton	10	4	2	4	80	135	10
Hartlepool R	10	4	1	5	104	162	9
Hull & ER	10	3	1	6	96	128	7
Widnes	10	3	0	7	80	143	6
Middlesbrough	10	1	1	8	81	155	3

NORTH 2

	P	W	D	L	F	A	Pts
Aspatria	10	8	0	2	263	60	16
Halifax	10	8	0	2	225	83	16
Bradford & Bingley	10	8	0	2	144	80	16
Sandal	10	6	0	4	142	92	12
Alnwick	10	6	0	4	121	75	12
Lymm	10	6	0	4	111	119	12
New Brighton	10	4	0	6	108	157	8
Huddersfield	9	4	0	5	79	171	8
Davenport	9	3	0	6	78	142	6
Manchester	10	1	0	9	55	140	2
Wilmslow	10	0	0	10	42	249	0

NORTH 1

WINNINGTON PARK

Burrows Hill, Hartford, Northwich, Cheshire. Tel: 0606 74242.
Founded: 1907
President: S. Bowden
Chairman: D.A. Gray
Coach: D.K. Hill and A. Burchel
Secretary: T.R. Palin, Woodville, Dalefords Lane, Whitegate, Northwich, Cheshire. Tel: 0606 882052 (H). 0928 87226 (W).
Fixtures Secretary: C.F. Gleave, Westerley, West Road, Weaverham, Cheshire. Tel: 0606 853999 (H) or Lynam 2016 (W).
Club captain (1987–88): Keith Curbishley
Club captain (1988–89): Roy Allcock
No. of teams: Senior 6. Youth & Minis 8.
Directions to Ground: One mile from Hartford turn on A556, turn left at traffic lights by Hatford Church, then right into Beech Road. B5152. First left is Burrows Hill, ground on right.
Ground capacity: 5000
Clubhouse: Two storey modern clubhouse built 1974.
Colours: White with royal and sky blue circlet. (*Change colours:* Blue or red and white hoops).
Nickname: Park
Floodlights: Yes
Admission: £1
Membership: £20

Programme: £1. (Editor: D.A. Gray)
Local newspaper: Northwich Guardian and Chronicle
League: Area North 1
Final position (1987–88): 1st
Playing record (1987–88): P 30, W 30, L 7. F 893, A 315.
Competitions won: Courage North 1 Winners, Cheshire Cup Winners

KENDAL

Mintbridge, Kendal, Cumbria. Tel: 0539 24239
Founded: 1905
Secretary: P.E.S. Briggs, 22 Long Meadow Lane, Natland, Kendal, Cumbria. Tel: 05395 61103 (H). 0539 20136 (W)
Fixtures Secretary: R.A. Short, Cockin Farm, Whinfell, Kendal, Cumbria. Tel: 053 984 251 (W)
League: North 1
Final position (1987–88): 2nd

WEST PARK

Eccleston Hill, Prescot Road, St. Helens, Merseyside WA10 3AG. Tel: 26138.
Founded: 1947
President: H.G. Huyton
Chairman: M.J. Worsley
Coach: A. Ward/A. Collins
Secretary: W. Bold, as club – evenings
Fixtures Secretary: J.E. Briers, 5 Daresbury Road, Eccleston, St. Helens, M/Side. Tel: 34665.
Club captain (1987–88): G. Hughes
Club captain (1988–89): G. Hughes
No. of teams: Senior 6, Youth & Minis 7
Directions to Ground: A58 from St. Helens to Liverpool. Next to Carmel College. Opp. Hattons Garage.
Ground capacity: 1200. Stand, 300
Clubhouse: Large concert room. Small lounge for members.
Colours: Green & gold. (*Change colours:* Red)
Floodlights: No
Admission: 50p to £1.
Membership: £12 + VAT (Senior) Juniors vary from £2.50 to £4.
Programme: inc. in ground entrance (Editors: as fixture Sec. + A.J. Tipping)
Local newspaper: St. Helens Reporter, St. Helens Star, St. Helens Leader.
League: North Div. 1
Final position (1987–88): third
Playing record (1987–88): P 38, W 23, D 1, L 14, F 700, A 504.
Competitions won: none (semi-final Lancs Cup).

OTLEY

Cross Green, Otley. Tel: Otley 461180
Founded: 1865
President: G. Matthewman
Chairman: M. Anderton
Secretary: G. Hinchcliffe, 22 Cyprus Drive, Thackley, Bradford. Tel: 0274 615543 (H). 0274 724282 (W)
Fixtures Secretary: C. Wright, 10 Weston Drive, Otley. Tel: Otley 465589
Club captain (1987–88): W. Holdsworth
Club captain (1988–89): W. Holdsworth
No. of teams: Senior 6. Youth & Minis 11.
Directions to Ground: Take Pool Road out of Otley, ground about 800 yards on left.
Ground capacity: 5500. Stand, 850.
Colours: Black and white. (*Change colours:* Red).
Floodlights: No
Admission: £1.50
Membership: £29
Programme: 20p. (Editor: K. Thompson)
Local newspaper: Airedale & Wharfdale Observer
League: North 1
Final position (1987–88): 4th
Playing record (1987–88): P 39, W 23, D 2, L 14.

HARROGATE

The County Ground, Claro Road, Harrogate, North Yorkshire. Tel: Harrogate (0423) 66966.
Founded: 1871
President: John A. Englefield
Chairman: Michael Newport
Coach: Peter J. Clegg
Secretary: Allen M. Tattersfield, 23 St Helens Road, Harrogate. Tel: 0423 885710 (H). 0532 469655 (W)
Fixtures Secretary: John M. Ashman, 38 Hollins Lane, Hampsthwaite, Harrogate. Tel: 0423 770354 (H). 0423 505023 (W).
Club captain (1987–88): Garry J.M. Irving
Club captain (1988–89): Garry J.M. Irving
No. of teams: Senior 5. Youth & Minis 10.
Directions to Ground: Claro Road goes directly from the A59 Skipton/Harrogate/York Rd and is between the County and Grasby Hotels, both of which face onto the A59. The ground is directly behind the Granby Hotel and Granby Park flats.
Ground capacity: 4000. Stand, 500.
Clubhouse: Full catering facilities. Main bar and cocktail bar. Two hospitality rooms.
Colours: Red, amber and black. (*Change colours:* White)
Floodlights: No
Admission: £1.50
Membership: £27
Programme: 20p. (Editor: Michael A. Hymas)
Local newspaper: Harrogate Advertiser and Harrogate Herald.
League: North 1
Final position (1987–88): 5th
Playing record (1987–88): P 40, W 18, D 1, L 21.
Competitions won: Yorkshire County Cup Winners 1905, 1907, 1949, 1965 and 1981.

TYNEDALE

Tynedale Park, Corbridge, Northld. NE45 5AY. Tel: 0434 71 2996/7.
Founded: 1876
President: John Clark
Chairman: Edward Robson
Coach: George Haldane
Secretary: James Chapman, Temperley Grange, Corbridge, Northld. NE45 5RX. Tel: 0434 71 2943 (H), 091 261 1841 (W).
Fixtures Secretary: J.A. Suddes, Glendalough, 2 West Hextol Close, Hexham, NE46 2BS. Tel: 0434 603989 (H), 0660 20200 (W).
Club captain (1987–88): A.T. Gledson
Club captain (1988–89): A.T. Gledson
No. of teams: Senior 4.
Directions to Ground: Immediately adjoining BR Corbridge.
Ground capacity: 5000. Stand, 2000.
Clubhouse: Brick built. 2 social rooms.
Colours: Blue and white horiz. stripes, white shorts. (*Change colours:* White).
Floodlights: Yes, training only.
Admission: £1.50
Membership: £25 full, £10 social, £6 juniors, £3 colts, £2 ladies
Programme: 50p
Local newspaper: Hexham Courant, Newcastle Journal, Newcastle Evening Chronicle
League: North 1
Final position (1987–88): 6th
Playing record (1987–88): P 35, W 23, D 1, L 11. F 552, A 370.
Competitions won: Northumberland Senior Cup, Northumberland County Cups (1, 2 & 3)

The North's fly-half Rob Andrew gets his backs going against the Midlands at Northampton. Photo: Colorsport.

Aspatria's scrum-half George Doggart – now with Sale – was a prime reason for his club's cup run and league success. Photo: Colorsport.

Tops at their specialities. North and England scrum-half Nigel Melville spins out another long pass watched by international referee Roger Quittenton. Photo: Colorsport.

WIGTON

Lowmoor Road, Wigton. Tel: 0965 42206.
Founded: 1882
President: David Everett
Chairman: Alan Robson
Coach: John Wood
Secretary: Michael Penrice, 6 Wheatsheaf Lane, Wigton. Tel: 0965 42206.
Fixtures Secretary: Alan Robson, 2 Station Hill, Wigton. Tel: 0965 42310.
Club captain (1987–88): Neil Carruthers
Club captain (1988–89): Neil Carruthers
No. of teams: Senior 3, Youth & Minis 6
Directions to Ground: Leave M6 Penrith and drive up the B530 to Wigton (signposted). Cross staggered X roads over A596 and bear right to Rugby Club.
Ground capacity: 2,000. Stand, 120
Clubhouse: Built 1969
Colours: Green tops, white shorts. (*Change colours:* White)
Floodlights: Yes only on training pitch.
Admission: £1
Membership: £20 full membership. 16–19 £5, U.16 £2, Social £2.
Programme: Programme given with admission charge. (Editor: Michael Penrice)
Local newspaper: Cumberland News/Evening News & Star.
League: North 1
Final position (1987–88): 7th
Playing record (1987–88): P 29, W 13, D 5, L 11, F 390, A 310.
Competitions won: Cumberland Cup 1965, '70, '71, '72, '73, '79, '86. Cumberland Colts Cup 1986–87 and 1987–88 plus 40 Sevens tournaments since 1960 including Northumberland County, Isle of Man.

HARTLEPOOL ROVERS

The Friarage, Westview Road, Hartlepool, Cleveland. Tel: 0429 267741
Founded: 1879
President: J.H. Peart
Chairman: A.J. Hill
Coach: Brian Edwards, Billy Archbold
Secretary: K. Lister, 24 Egerton Road, Hartlepool, Cleveland. Tel: 0429 267246.
Fixtures Secretary: C. Winspear, Welldeck Road, Hartlepool, Cleveland.
Club captain (1987–88): Allan Calvert
Club captain (1988–89): Kevin Robinson
No. of teams: Senior 4. Youth & Minis 6.
Directions to Ground: Enter Hartlepool from either A689 or A19. Head for the Headland Rovers on Westview Road.
Ground capacity: 5000. Stand, 500.
Clubhouse: Bar/lounge.
Colours: White shirts, red socks, black shorts. (*Change colours:* Red, black and white hooped shirts.
Nickname: The Rovers
Floodlights: Yes
Admission: £1
Membership: £15
Programme: £1
Local newspaper: Hartlepool Mail
League: North Div 1
Final position (1987–88): 8th
Playing record (1987–88): P 36, W 15, L 19, D 2.

HULL & EAST RIDING

Sports Club, The Club, The Circle, Anlaby Road, Hull. Tel: 0482 507098/918
Founded: 1901
Secretary: C.K. Rockingham, 30 St. Margarets Avenue, Cottingham, North Humberside HU16 5NF. Tel: 0482 844146 (H)
Fixtures Secretary: S. Elliot, 73 Kingtree Avenue, Cottingham, North Humberside HU16 4DR. Tel: 0482 847485
League: North 1
Final position (1987–88): 9th
Playing record (1987–88): P 39, W 18, D 5, L 16, F 537, A 518

WIDNES

Heath Road, Ditton, Widnes, Cheshire. Tel: 051-424-2575.
Founded: 1924
President: J.A. Lambert
Chairman: J. McCann
Coach: M. Ryan
Secretary: A. Roberts, 21 Belmont Road, Widnes. Tel: 051-424-0654.
Fixtures Secretary: Dave Skinner, 25 Farmdale, Widnes. Tel: 051-424-6860.
Club captain (1987–88): C. Greaves
Club captain (1988–89): G. Forshaw
No. of teams: Senior 4, Youth & Minis 1
Directions to Ground: Exit Junct. 7 M62, follow signs for Liverpool, turn left 1st set lights.
Ground capacity: 2,000
Clubhouse: Large clubroom, luxurious lounge bar.
Colours: Red & black hoops. (*Change colours:* White)
Nickname: "The Wids"
Floodlights: No
Admission: £1, £1.50, League & cup £1.50.
Membership: Playing £15, Social £6.
Programme: Extensive 20p (Editor: R. Wasson Press Officer)
Local newspaper: Widnes Weekly News, Widnes World, Liverpool Daily Post.
League: North 1
Final position (1987–88): 10th (relegated from North One)
Playing record (1987–88): P 42, W 24, D1 , L17, F 582, A 486.
Competitions won: Girobank Lancashire Trophy March 1988, Lancashire Cup April 1976, Lancashire Colts Cup 1978, Rugby World & Post Junior Team of the Month November 1987.

MIDDLESBROUGH

Acklam Park, Green Lane, Middlesbrough. Tel: 0642 818567.
Founded: 1872
President: N.P. Clarkson
Chairman: S. Foster
Coach: B. Coyne
Secretary: D. Brydon, 20 Westwood Avenue, Linthorpe, Middlesbrough. Tel: 0642 819954.
Fixtures Secretary: M. Wright, 30 Margill Close, Marton, Middlesbrough. Tel. 0642 310711.
Club captain (1987–88): A.D. Duff
Club captain (1988–89): A.D. Duff
No. of teams: Senior 5. Youth & Minis 9.
Directions to Ground: A19 (to Acklam turnoff). Follow signs to Middlesbrough (left fork, across main road, 500m on right).
Stand capacity: 400
Ground capacity: 2500 normally
Clubhouse: 2 bars, 1 lounge.
Colours: Maroon shirts, white shorts. (*Change colours:* White shirts)
Nickname: Boro
Floodlights: No
Admission: £1
Membership: £12.50
Programme: 20p (Editor: D. Brydon)
Local newspaper: Evening Gazette
League: North 1
Final position (1987–88): Bottom
Playing record (1987–88): P 39, W 14, D 3, L 22, F 434, A 561.

ASPATRIA

Bower Park, Station Road, Aspatria, Cumbria. Tel: 0965 20420.
Founded: 1875
President: R.J. Hanvey
Chairman: D.G. Miller
Coach: D. Robley
Secretary: J.M. Hanley, 7 King Street, Aspatria, Cumb. CA5 3AD. Tel: 0965-20420 (H), 0461-37757 (B).
Fixtures Secretary: P. Gray, 4 Queen Street, Aspatria, Cumbria. Tel: 0965-21760.
Club captain (1987–88): T. Borthwick
Club captain (1988–89): P. Jackson
No. of teams: Senior 3, Youth & Minis 2
Directions to Ground: Situated 20 miles south of Carlisle, accessible from M6 at Penrith.
Ground capacity: Unlimited. Stand, 300
Clubhouse: 250 limit, consists of lounge, entertainment, and committee rooms.
Colours: Black/red hoops. (*Change colours:* Red shirts)
Nickname: The Black/reds
Floodlights: Yes
Admission: £1
Membership: £3 Social, £10 Players
Programme: Weekly–24 pages, 25p (Editor: M. Hanley)
Local newspaper: Cumberland News
League: North 2
Final position (1987–88): Top position
Playing record (1987–88): P 37, W 31, L 6, F 860, A 244.
Competitions won: North League 2, Cumbrian Senior Cup, Rugby World & Post Junior Team on the month January 1988.

HALIFAX

Standeven Memorial Ground, Ovenden Park, Keighley Road, Halifax. Tel: 0422 65926
Founded: 1873
Secretary: G.E. Milnes, 2 Glen View, Clover Hill, Halifax. Tel: 0422 46364
Fixtures Secretary: R.A. Childs, Riley Lane, Halifax. Tel: 0422 244608
League: North 2
Final position (1987–88): 2nd
Playing record (1987–88): P 43, W 22, D 0, L 21, F 642, A 642

BRADFORD AND BINGLEY

Wagon Lane & Aire View, Cottingley, Bingley, W. Yorks. Tel: 0274 563480.
Founded: BFD 1866, Bing'y 1876
President: S. Crossley-Smith
Chairman: J.D.V. Cook
Coach: M. Elford
Secretary: W.P. Dennis, 2 Hesp Hills, Beckfoot Lane, Bingley BD16 1AR.
Fixtures Secretary: W.K. Wilkinson, Green Acres, Station Lane, Birkenshaw, Bradford, W. Yorks. Tel: 0274 681231.
Club captain (1987–88): J.W. Fletcher
Club captain (1988–89): J.W. Fletcher
No. of teams: Senior 6, Youth & Minis 6
Directions to Ground: A650 Bfd to Bingley, turn right immediately.
Ground capacity: 3000. Stand, 150
Clubhouse: 4 Ale bars (2)
Colours: Red, amber & black hoops. (*Change colours:* Red or blue)
Nickname: The Bees
Floodlights: No
Admission: £1
Membership: £15
Programme: (Editor: E. Cummins & Co.
Local newspaper: Telegraph & Argus – BFD
League: N 2
Final position (1987–88): Joint 1st (promoted)
Playing record (1987–88): P 39, W 25, L 12, D 2, F 550, A 550.

SANDAL

Milnthorpe Green, Standbridge Lane, Sandal, Wakefield. Tel: 0924 250661.
Founded: 1927
President: J. Adams
Chairman: R.M. Holmes
Coach: M. Shuttleworth
Secretary: S.J. Powers, 39 Durkar Low Lane, Wakefield. Tel: 0924 252148.
Fixtures Secretary: P. Tunningley, 6 High Ash Close, Notton, Nr Barnsley. Tel: 0226 722123.
Club captain (1987–88): N. Powell
Club captain (1988–89): N. Powell
No. of teams: Senior 5. Youth & Minis 11.
Directions to Ground: M1 junction 39, A636 towards Wakefield. Asdale Road to Standbridge Lane.
Ground capacity: 3000. Stand 200.
Colours: Maroon, amber, white. (*Change colours:* Amber, maroon and white).
Floodlights: Yes
Admission: £1.50
Membership: £9.50
Programme: 20p
Local newspaper: Wakefield Express
League: North 2
Final position (1987–88): 4th
Playing record (1987–88): P 37, W 30, L 6, D 1. F 821, A 328.

ALNWICK

Greensfield, Alnwick, Northumberland. Tel: 0665-60.
Founded: 1962
President: N. Burn
Chairman: R. Robinson
Coach: P. Scurfield
Secretary: S. Brierley, East Cawledge Farm, Alnwick, Northumberland NE66 2HB. Tel: 0665-602426.
Fixtures Secretary: A. Bell, Greensfield Farm, Alnwick. Tel: 0665-608891.
Club captain (1987–88): C. Blythe
Club captain (1988–89): J. Black
No. of teams: Senior 5, Youth & Minis 4
Directions to Ground: A1 15 North of Morpeth take 1st left into Alnwick, left again ground on left.
Ground capacity: 3000+. Stand, 200
Colours: Blue shirts, white shorts, blue & gold socks. (*Change colours:* Gold shirts)
Floodlights: Yes
Admission: £1.00 League games.
Membership: £15.00 player
Local newspaper: Newcastle Journal & Northumberland Gazette.
League: North 2
Final position (1987–88): 4th
Playing record (1987–88): P 39, W 27, L 12, F 623, A 302.

LYMM

Founded: 1960
Secretary: K. Etherington, 73 Booths Lane, Lymm, Cheshire WA13 OPF. Tel: 0925 75 5008 (H) or 061 872 5959 (W)
League: North 2
Final position (1987–88): 6th
Playing record (1987–88): P 33, W 24, D 3, L 6, F 487, A 309

NEW BRIGHTON

Reeds Lane, Leasowe Road, Moreton, Wirral, Merseyside L46 3RH. Tel: 051-677-1873.
Founded: 1875
President: Bernard Murphy
Chairman: Denis Morgan
Coach: D. Ferguson/W. Vance
Secretary: Joe Pinnington, 91 Telegraph Road, Heswall, Merseyside L60 0AE. Tel: 051-342-7773 (H), 0244-390-440 (W).
Fixtures Secretary: David Pennington, 62 Broadway Avenue, Wallasey, Merseyside. Tel: 051-638-8379.
Club captain (1987–88): J. Houghton
Club captain (1988–89): J. Houghton
No. of teams: Senior 5, Youth & Minis 7
Directions to Ground: Junction 1 on the M53 To New Brighton. 1st left to Moreton/Hoylake. 1 mile at SHELL garage turn left. Ground 200 yards on left.
Ground capacity: 6000. Stand, 600
Clubhouse: 2 Bars, open every night. Plus 8 Squash courts.
Colours: Dark Blue/white shorts. (*Change colours:* White)
Nickname: "Brighton" or Seasiders
Floodlights: Yes
Admission: £1.00, 50p for OAP & children.
Membership: £40.00 full playing
Programme: 16 pages plus advertisements (Editor: Joe Pinnington)
Local newspaper: Liverpool Daily Post
League: North 2
Final position (1987–88): 7th
Playing record (1987–88): P 39, W 14, D 1, L 24, F 444, A 750.

HUDDERSFIELD

The Tandem, Waterloo, Huddersfield. Tel: 23864.
Founded: 1909
President: J.E. Wade
Chairman: J.M. Brown
Coach: E. Whitwam
Secretary: M. Noble, Wheatfield House, Brockholes, Huddersfield HD7 7AG. Tel: 0484 662006.
Fixtures Secretary: B. Starbuck, 2 The cottages, Upper Thong, Holmfirth. Tel: Hudd. 686059 (H). Hudd. 682266 (W).
Club captain (1987–88): G. Workman
Club captain (1988–89): J.D. Sharpe
No. of teams: Senior 5. Youth & Minis 5.
Directions to Ground: Follow Sheffield/Wakefield signs from centre of Huddersfield. Approx 2 miles from Huddersfield Roads dissect at Waterloo. Take Wakefield Road. Ground 200 yds on left.
Ground capacity: 2000. Stand, 400.
Clubhouse: Brick/wood structure. All facilities, bar, changing rooms, baths and showers.
Colours: White, claret and gold. (*Change colours:* Maroon).
Floodlights: No
Admission: £1.50
Membership: £20
Programme: 10p. (Editor: B.N. Webster)
Local newspaper: Huddersfield Examiner
League: North 2
Final position (1987–88): 7th
Playing record (1987–88): P 38, W 8, L 30.
Competitions won: April 1988 winners Heath RFC 7-A-Side Tournament

DAVENPORT

Bridge Lane Memorial Ground, Headlands Road, Bridge Lane, Bramhall, Stockport, Cheshire. Tel: 061 439 2150
Founded: 1923
Secretary: J. Curzon, 26 Axminster Walk, Bramhall, Stockport, Cheshire SK7 2QT. Tel: 061 439 5478 (H). 061 344 3278 (W)
Fixtures Secretary: M.W. Roe, 138 Moor Lane, Woodford, Cheshire SK7 1PJ. Tel: 061 440 8536
League: North 2
Final position (1987–88): 9th
Playing record (1987–88): P 32, W 11, D 1, L 20, F 312, A 463

MANCHESTER

Grove Park, Grove Lane, Cheadle Hulme, Cheadle, Cheshire. Tel: 061 485 1115.
Founded: 1860
President: Dr J.K. Mills
Chairman: R.H. Jenkins
Coach: TBA
Secretary: G.T. Dodds, Brigfield, 8 Dennison Road, Cheadle Hulme, Cheadle, Cheshire SK8 6LW. Tel: 061 485 2104.
Fixtures Secretary: D.W. Partington.
Club captain (1987–88): R. Smith
Club captain (1988–89): TBA
No. of teams: Senior 5. Youth & Minis 6.
Directions to Ground: Along A34 turn into Stanley Road at traffic lights at Belfrey Hotel, Cheadle Hulme. Ground ½ mile on right.
Ground capacity: 4–5000. Stand 300.
Clubhouse: Players bar, lounge bar, badminton and functions hall, 6 squash courts, kitchen.
Colours: Red and white hoops. (*Change colours:* red shirts).
Floodlights: Yes, for training
Admission: £1
Membership: £34 playing.
Programme: Notes teams and adverts. Included in admission. (Editor: Secretary)
Local newspaper: Stockport Messenger, Manchester Evening News
League: North 2
Final position (1987–88): 10th

WILMSLOW

Kings Road, Wilmslow. Tel: 0625 522274.
Founded: 1884
President: J.B. Fisher
Chairman: R.E.S. Green
Coach: C. Kynnersley
Secretary: G. Coles, 21 Woodlands Road, Handforth, Wilmslow. Tel: 0625 523860.
Fixtures Secretary: G. Mitchell, Green Bank Farm, Smallwood. Tel: Smallwood 329.
Club captain (1987–88): N.J. Burrows
Club captain (1988–89): N.J. Burrows

North 2

No. of teams: Senior 5, Youth & Minis 11
Directions to Ground: From Junction 6 on M56 take A538 towards Wilmslow. Kings Road is 4 miles on right immediately after Texaco Petrol Station.
Ground capacity: 3/4000. Stand, 500
Clubhouse: Large players bar & cocktail bar.
Colours: Sky blue, maroon & white hoop. (*Change colours:* Navy)
Floodlights: Yes
Admission: £1.00 (50p member)
Membership: Players £20.00, Patrons £10.00
Programme: Free
Local newspaper: Wilmslow World
League: North 2
Final position (1987–88): Bottom (relegated)
Playing record (1987–88): P 40, W 6, D 1, L 33, F 254, A 1004.

NORTH WEST LEAGUE

NO FEWER than 11 leagues under the prefix 'North West' are fighting for a better status starting with North West 1, which pays farewell to Carlisle and Wirral, champions and runners-up respectively. Wigan were their nearest challengers and must make a strong bid for promotion next season.

Down into North West 2 go Netherhall and Blackburn and they have been no mean clubs in recent seasons. Their replacements are Old Aldwinians – champions of East/North 1 – and Mersey Police, who won North West West 1.

The rest of the North West is then split into three regional sections – East, North and West – and the promotion process has seen rises for clubs from and within those groupings with outstanding teams being De la Salle in NW East 1 and Bolton in the same area's Second Division; both won all their matches.

Up in the North of the North West Windermere won all their games in Division 1, but Thornton Cleveleys needed points difference to win the Second Division from British Steel, although both go up.

Mersey Police in West 1 were another side with a perfect record as mentioned, but the outstanding performance after them came in Division 3 where Halton won all nine games and scored 229 points in the process. Where will they be in, say, 1990–91?

TABLES 1987–88

NORTH WEST 1

	P	W	D	L	F	A	Pts
Carlisle	10	9	0	1	195	58	18
Wirral	10	8	0	2	133	99	16
Wigan	10	6	2	2	140	103	14
Caldy	10	6	0	4	119	111	12
Chester	10	5	1	4	118	99	11
Mid-Cheshire	10	5	0	5	129	123	10
Rochdale	10	4	1	5	110	112	9
Egremont	10	3	1	6	138	128	7
Southport	10	3	0	7	72	168	6
Netherhall	10	2	1	7	64	146	5
Blackburn	10	1	0	9	69	140	2

NORTH E/NORTH 1

	P	W	D	L	F	A	Pts
Old Aldwinians	10	8	1	1	209	47	17
Vickers	10	8	0	2	214	47	16
Furness	10	7	1	2	134	97	15
Moresby	8	7	0	1	120	63	14
Fleetwood	10	5	2	3	133	77	12
Oldham	10	5	0	5	99	70	10
Eccles	9	3	1	5	69	93	7
Littleborough	9	3	1	5	81	129	7
Toc H	9	2	0	7	62	94	4
Calder Vale	10	1	0	9	82	174	2
Colne & Nelson	10	1	0	9	47	359	2

NORTH WEST 2

	P	W	D	L	F	A	Pts
Sedgley Park	10	8	1	1	183	74	17
Sandbach	10	8	0	2	195	64	16
Macclesfield	10	7	0	3	122	62	14
Leigh	10	6	0	4	110	135	12
Burnage	10	5	1	4	97	110	11
Workington	10	5	1	4	94	131	11
Cockermouth	10	4	1	5	167	124	9
Penrith	10	3	1	6	108	106	7
Newton le Willows	10	3	1	6	108	148	7
Heaton Moor	10	1	1	8	46	144	3
Warrington	10	1	1	8	35	167	3

NW EAST 1

	P	W	D	L	F	A	Pts
De la Salle	10	10	0	0	252	42	20
Metrovick	10	8	0	2	153	70	16
Ashton on Mersey	10	6	0	4	159	70	12
Tyldesley	10	5	1	4	116	67	11
O Salians	10	5	1	4	108	96	11
O Bedians	10	5	1	4	88	81	11
Kersal	10	5	0	5	124	75	10
Congleton	9	3	0	6	58	129	6
Ashton-under-Lyne	10	3	0	7	50	146	6
N Manchester	10	2	1	7	52	262	5
Bowden	9	0	0	9	76	198	0

NW EAST 2

	P	W	D	L	F	A	Pts
Bolton	9	9	0	0	216	53	18
Crewe & Nantwich	9	7	0	2	142	59	14
Gtr Man Fire Serv	9	6	2	1	92	58	14
Broughton	9	5	2	2	173	80	12
Bury	9	4	0	5	126	134	8
Manchester YMCA	9	3	0	6	83	143	6
Oldham Coll	8	2	1	5	67	109	5
Chorley	8	2	1	5	56	100	5
Dukinfield	9	2	0	7	94	135	4
Marple	9	0	0	9	40	238	0

NW NORTH 1

	P	W	D	L	F	A	Pts
Windermere	9	9	0	0	214	41	18
Keswick	9	8	0	1	129	46	16
Kirkby Lonsdale	9	6	0	3	185	92	12
Rossendale	9	6	0	3	153	97	12
Creighton	9	4	0	5	98	197	8
St Benedicts	9	3	1	5	87	107	7
Blackpool	9	3	0	6	65	129	6
Carnforth	9	2	2	5	73	138	6
Millom	9	1	1	7	41	135	3
Whitehaven	9	1	0	8	105	162	2

NW NORTH 2

	P	W	D	L	F	A	Pts
Thornton Cleveleys	7	6	0	1	145	41	12
British Steel	7	6	0	1	88	56	12
U Eden	7	5	0	2	115	62	10
Ambleside	7	4	0	3	98	79	8
Silloth	7	3	0	4	64	67	6
Smith Bros	6	2	0	4	81	100	4
Clitheroe	7	1	0	6	33	132	2
Lanc Moor Hosp	6	0	0	6	35	122	0

● *The tables are published from information supplied. Any queries should be directed to the appropriate league secretary*

NW WEST 1

	P	W	D	L	F	A	Pts
Mersey Police	10	10	0	0	239	69	20
Liverpool Coll	10	8	0	2	109	72	16
Ormskirk	10	5	0	5	116	82	10
Old Parkonians	10	5	0	5	102	94	10
Douglas (IOM)	10	5	0	5	127	146	10
Aspull	10	4	0	6	122	145	8
St Edwards OB	10	4	0	6	108	143	8
Birchfield	10	3	2	5	85	132	8
Eagle	10	4	0	6	65	136	8
Oldershaw	10	3	1	6	119	125	7
Old Anselmians	10	3	1	6	103	151	7

NW WEST 2

	P	W	D	L	F	A	Pts
Old Instonians	10	7	1	2	155	74	15
Ruskin Park	10	7	1	2	170	98	15
Vulcan	10	7	1	2	168	97	15
Sefton	10	6	1	3	142	78	13
Hightown	10	4	3	3	118	120	11
S Liverpool	10	4	2	4	101	113	10
Port Sunlight	10	3	3	4	146	113	9
Chester Coll	9	4	1	4	120	132	9
St Mary's OB	9	2	2	5	51	128	6
Moore	10	1	1	8	79	205	3
Wallasey	10	0	2	8	72	136	2

NW WEST 3

	P	W	D	L	F	A	Pts
Halton	9	9	0	0	229	38	18
Old Rockferrians	8	7	0	1	152	38	14
Helsby	9	5	2	2	134	83	12
Mossley Hill	9	6	0	3	99	97	12
Shell (Stanlow)	9	4	2	3	129	67	10
Hoylake	9	4	0	5	110	113	8
Prescot	9	1	4	4	59	84	6
Wigan Tech	9	1	1	7	55	146	3
Agecroft	9	1	1	7	47	199	3
Burtonwood	8	1	0	7	50	199	2

NORTH WEST 1

CARLISLE

Warwick Road, Carlisle. Tel: 0228 21300
Founded: 1873
Secretary: W.A. Swarbrick, 5 St. Aidans Road, Carlisle. Tel: 0228 29287 (H) or 23456 (W)
League: North West 1
Final position (1987–88): 1st
Playing record (1987–88): P 33, W 25, D 0, L 8, F 658, A 214
Competitions won: North West 1

WIRRAL

Thornton Common Road, Clatterbridge, Wirral. Tel: 051 334 1309
Founded: 1937
Secretary: R.T. Backhouse, 35 Raby River, Raby Mere, Wirral, Merseyside L63 0NQ. Tel: 051 334 6591 (H) or 0244 350682 (W)
League: North West 1
Final position (1987–88): 2nd
Playing record (1987–88): P 33, W 20, D 1, L 12, F 520, A 407

WIGAN

"Douglas Valley" Leyland Mill Lane, Wigan, Lancs. Tel: (0942) 42556.
Founded: 1913
President: Brian Leigh
Chairman: Cliff Brookwell
Coach: John Coombs
Secretary: John Gee, 27 Brookside Road, Standish, Wigan. Tel: (0257) 422397.
Fixtures Secretary: Frank Morgan, 37 Wigan Road, Standish, Wigan. Tel: (0257) 422977.
Club captain (1987–88): Carl Gray
Club captain (1988–89): Andrew Knowles
No. of teams: Senior 4, Youth & Minis 4

Directions to Ground: Leave the M6 at Exit 27 (Standish) drive into Standish, turn right at traffic lights in Standish, drive towards Wigan, turn left at Cherry Gardens Hotel.
Ground capacity: Stand 50+
Clubhouse: Clubroom, lounge + 2nd unfinished lounge.
Colours: Irregular black & white hoops. (*Change colours:* Red)
Floodlights: Training lights only.
Admission: £1 for Cup & League. 50p Friendly.
Membership: £20 Senior Player, £10 Patrons etc, £1 Junior/Colt.
Programme: Club News + Teams (inc. in admission) (Editor: Brian Leigh)
Local newspaper: Wigan Observer, Evening Post, "Reporter", "Leader".
League: NW1
Final position (1987–88): 3rd
Playing record (1987–88): P 39, W 22, D 2, L 15.

CALDY (formerly Old Caldeians R.F.C.)

Paton Field, Lower Caldy Crossroads, West Kirby, Wirral, Merseyside. Tel: 051-625 8043.
Founded: 1924
President: John Butler
Chairman: Alan Jeffcoat
Rugby Manager: Tony Atherton
Coach: Danny Hughes
Secretary: Frank Price, 6 Graham Road, West Kirby, Wirral. Tel: 051 632 5232.
Fixtures Secretary: Ollie Farrell, 15 Leachway, Irby, Wirral. Tel: 051 648 3085.
Club captain (1987–88): Roy Farebrother
Club captain (1988–89): Gary Devaney
No. of teams: Senior 7, Youth & Minis 8
Directions to Ground: On the A540 West Kirby to Chester Road just outside West Kirby.
Ground capacity: 3000 + suitable car parking
Clubhouse: 2 bars + changing facilities for 5 matches.
Colours: Sable, claret, gold + silver hoops. (*Change colours:* Claret, gold + silver)
Floodlights: Yes on 2nd XV pitch.
Admission: By donation for programme.
Membership: £20 playing membership
Programme: Donation (Editor: David Nunn)
Local newspaper: Liverpool Echo, Liverpool Daily Post, Wirral News, Wirral Globe.
League: North West 1
Final position (1987–88): Fourth
Playing record (1987–88): P 43, W 29, D 2, L 12, F 850, A 495.
Competitions won: 1987–88 Nightfreight Wirral Floodlit Cup, Cheshire Cup 1971, National Old Boys Seven-A-Side Winners 1969–70, Wirral Floodlit Cup Winners 1984–85, 1986–87, 1987–88. Had a record season in 1987–88 with 29 Wins. Caldy host the Merseyside Seven-A-Side Tournament and have done so for the past 45 years. 1988 winners Glasgow High (An invitation side). 2 Paraguayan Internationals playing for Caldy in 1987–88.

CHESTER

Hare Lane, Vicars Cross, Chester. Tel: 336017.
Founded: c1925
President: David Roberts
Chairman: Michael J. Lord
Coach: Mark Allen
Secretary: Stephen Maddox, 8 Fairfield Road, Hoole, Chester. Tel: Chester 45438 (H). 051 638 7070 (W).
Fixtures Secretary: Craig Cawthorn, 21 Oaklands Drive, Tattenhall. Tel: Tattenhall 70498.
Club captain (1987–88): David Williams
Club captain (1988–89): David Williams
No. of teams: Senior 6. Youth & Minis 11.
Directions to Ground: Approaching Chester on A56 ground is located on the right immediately before arriving at A41 ring road.
Ground capacity: c 3000. Stand, c 900.
Colours: Red. (*Change colours:* Blue).
Floodlights: No
Membership: £31.50
Local newspaper: Chester Chronicle, Chester Observer
League: North West 1
Final position (1987–88): 5th
Playing record (1987–88): P 34, W 12, D 2, L 20. F 411, A 495.

MID CHESHIRE COLLEGE

Moss Farm Leisure Complex, Moss Road, Northwich, Cheshire. Tel: 0606-79987.
Founded: 1965
President: Derek Campbell
Chairman: John Chappell
Coach: Roger Blake
Secretary: Ron McLaverty, 7 Pear Tree Drive, Wincham, Northwich, Cheshire CW9 6EZ. Tel: 056 589-3997.
Fixtures Secretary: Keith Naylor, 272 London Road, Leftwick, Northwich, Cheshire. Tel: 0606-43482.
Club captain (1987–88): Rick Dodd
Club captain (1988–89): Rick Dodd
No. of teams: Senior 5, Youth & Minis 4
Directions to Ground: Top of Castle Hill in Northwich – Turn right into Moss Road, ground on right.
Clubhouse: Changing rooms/bar/function room.
Colours: Black shirts/black shorts. (*Change colours:* Gold shirts/black shorts)
Floodlights: No
Membership: £20
Local newspaper: Northwich Guardian/Northwich Chronicle.
League: North West 1
Final position (1987–88): 5th
Playing record (1987–88): P 34, W 21, D 1, L 12, F 619, A 368.
Competitions won: Cheshire Plate – April 1988.

ROCHDALE

Moorgate Avenue, Bamford, Rochdale. Tel: 0706 46863.
Founded: 1921

North West 1

President: H. Deasey
Chairman: J. Cooper
Coach: C. Simkins
Secretary: I.R. Coates, 16 Woodcock Close, Bamford, Rochdale. Tel: 0706 58413.
Fixtures Secretary: I.R. Coates, 32 Links View, Rochdale. Tel: 0706 59980.
Club captain (1987–88): K. Thornton
Club captain (1988–89): J. Deasey
No. of teams: Senior 5, Youth & Minis 5
Directions to Ground: Junction 20, M62 at second roundabout follow Blackburn. At traffic lights turn left (to Bury). Moorgate Avenue third on right.
Ground capacity: Stand, 100
Clubhouse: 3 lounges
Colours: Maroon/white
Floodlights: Yes
Membership: £23
Programme: £1
Local newspaper: Rochdale Observer
League: North West 1
Final position (1987–88): 7th
Playing record (1987–88): P 38, W 18, D 2, L 18, F 439, A 401.

EGREMONT

Bleach Green, Egremont, Cumbria. Tel: 0946 820645
Founded: 1878
Secretary: W.H.F. Morgan, 58 Dent View, Egremont, Cumbria CA22 2ET. Tel: 0946 822119 (H) or 0940 28333 (W)
League: North West 1
Final position (1987–88): 8th
Playing record (1987–88): P 31, W 17, D 3, L 11, F 561, A 279

SOUTHPORT

Waterloo Road, Southport. Tel: 69906.
Founded: 1872
President: S. Wilson
Chairman: J. Winn
Coach: G. Jackson
Secretary: R. Fischer, 66 Southbank Road, Southport. Tel: 43654.
Fixtures Secretary: K. Shorrock, 28A Alexandra Road Southport. Tel: 37420.
Club captain (1987–88): I. MacPherson
Club captain (1988–89): P. Jones
No. of teams: Senior 4, Youth & Minis 4
Directions to Ground: Adjacent to A565 Southport to Liverpool (½ mile from Hillside Station) in southerly direction.
Ground capacity: 4,000. Stand, 250
Clubhouse: Bar (main) & cocktail, kitchen, 5 changing rooms, 3 bath & showers.
Colours: Red amber black. (*Change colours:* Blue and blue white hoops)
Floodlights: Yes training only.
Membership: £25 player, £10 patron.
Local newspaper: Southport Visitor
League: NW 1
Final position (1987–88): 2nd from last.

NETHERHALL

Netherhall Park, Netherhall Road, Maryport, Cumbria. Tel: 815833
Club and office: Crosby Street, Maryport, Cumbria. Tel: 81 3845.
Founded: 1960
President: Dr B.J. Havard
Chairman: J.J. Eve
Coach: J. Humes
Secretary: A. Scholey, Hillmore House, High Street, Maryport. Tel: 813935.
Fixtures Secretary: B. Edmondson, 76 Thirlmere Avenue, Workington. Tel: 3398.
Club captain (1987–88): G. Petre
Club captain (1988–89): L. Rumney
No. of teams: Senior 3. Youth & Minis 4.
Directions to Ground: On east side of A596(T).
Clubhouse: 6 changing rooms, showers, baths, function room, bar, kitchen.
Colours: Claret and gold. (*Change colours:* Red).
Floodlights: No
Admission: Collection
Membership: £6 full.
Programme: Free. (Editor: P. Porter)
Local newspaper: West Cumbria Evening News & Star
League: North West 1
Final position (1987–88): Bottom (relegated)
Competitions won: Cumbria Under 17 1986/87, Workington Under 17 Floodlit 7-A-Side 1986/87.

BLACKBURN

Ramsgreave Drive, Blackburn BB1 8NB. Tel: 0254 47669
Founded: 1877
Secretary: P.S. Gabriel, 5 Ottowa Close, Blackburn, Lancs BB2 7ER. Tel: 0254 678 678 (H) or 0254 64294 (W)
Fixtures Secretary: P. Dixon, 113 Brownhill Road, Blackburn. Tel: 0254 47669
League: North West 1
Final position (1987–88): 11th (bottom, relegated)

NORTH WEST 2

SEDGLEY PARK

Park Lane, Whitefield, Manchester. Tel: 061-766-5050.
Founded: 1932
President: A.G. Smith
Chairman: D.H. Smith
Coach: To be appointed
Secretary: M.J. Glover, 5 Glendevon Place, Whitefield. Tel: 061-796-9779.
Fixtures Secretary: D.W. Morton, 34 Delaunays Road, Manchester M8 6QS. Tel: 061-795-1644.
Club captain (1987–88): R. Hall
Club captain (1988–89): R. Hall
No. of teams: Senior 4, Youth & Minis 6
Directions to Ground: M62, Jnct 17, A56 Bury bear left at lights, left again at next lights (Park Lane).
Clubhouse: Large 2-storey clubhouse completed 1980.
Colours: Claret & gold. (*Change colours:* Yellow)
Nickname: Tigers
Floodlights: No
Admission: Free
Membership: £20 (Senior playing member)
Programme: Free (at 1st team matches) (Editor: D.W. Morton)
Local newspaper: Prestwich & Whitefield Guide, The Bury Times.
League: NW2
Final position (1987–88): Top of NW2 (promoted)
Playing record (1987–88): P 39, W 21, D 1, L 17, F 517, A 476.
Competitions won: Courage NW2 (1987/88); Girobank NW West 1 (1986/87).

Sandbach – 2nd in North NW2 – 1987–88 – and promoted. Photo: Sandbach Chronicle.

SANDBACH

Bradwall Road, Sandbach, Cheshire CW11 9AP. Tel: 0270 762475.
Founded: 1956
President: Mike Hopkins
Chairman: John Cooper
Coach: Phil Bell
Secretary: John Frayling, 6 Blackacres Close, Sandbach CV11 9DR. Tel: 0270 764007 (H), 0782 811041 (B).
Fixtures Secretary: Steve Clayton-Barker, 68 Abbey Road, Sandbach CW11 9MB. Tel: 0270 762679.
Club captain (1987–88): Alex Burton
Club captain (1988–89): Paul Brough
No. of teams: Senior 5, Youth & Minis 8
Directions to Ground: From M6, Junction 17 head towards Sandbach, turn right into Longleton Road, turn right at keep left signs into Offley Avenue then right again into Bradwall Road.
Ground capacity: 500. Stand, None
Clubhouse: 2 bars, 6 changing rooms, 2 baths, showers, sauna, multi gym, injury treatment area.
Colours: Emerald with 6″ red chest band.
Floodlights: No
Admission: 50p
Membership: £12.50 Social, £17.50 Playing, £6 Student, £4 Mini/junior.
Programme: 24 pages advertising, match notes (Editor: Chris Allen – 0260 273547 (B))
Local newspaper: Sandbach Chronicle
League: NW1
Final position (1987–88): 2nd in NW2 Promoted.
Playing record (1987–88): P 38, W 23, D 4, L 11, F 530, A 328.
Competitions won: Runners up NW2, Semifinalists Cheshire Cup.

MACCLESFIELD

Priory Park, Priory Lane. Tel: 0625 827899
Founded: 1927
Secretary: R. Farrimond, 8 Pool End Close, Tytherington, Macclesfield, Cheshire. Tel: Macclesfield 28308 (H) or Congleton 275333 (W)
League: NW West 2
Final position (1987–88): 3rd
Playing record (1987–88): P 35, W 24, D 0, L 11, F 554, A 278

LEIGH

Round Ash Farm, Hand Lane, Leigh, Lancs. Tel: 0942 673526
Founded: 1948
Secretary: G. Burrows, 6 Fern Close, Atherton, Manchester M29 9AA. Tel: 0942 870119 (H) or 061 247 3263 (W)
League: North West 2
Final position (1987–88): 4th
Playing record (1987–88): P 34, W 21, D 1, L 13, F 370, A 372

BURNAGE

Varley Park, Battersea Road, Heaton, Mersey, Stockport SK4 3EA. Tel: 061 432 2150
Founded: 1936
Secretary: I. Hodgson, Kimberley End, 22 Capesthorne Close, Holmes Chapel, Crewe, Cheshire CW4 7EN. Tel: 0477 33406 (H) or 061 881 0012 (W)
Fixtures Secretary: R. Howarth, 159 Arnesby Road, Sale, Cheshire. Tel: 061 969 8866
Club captain 1987–88: L. Georgiou
Club captain 1988–89: L. Georgiou
No of teams: Senior 5. Youth & Minis 6.
Directions to Ground: Junction 12 – M 63. turn left on A5145 to Station Road and then Heaton Mersey Industrial Estate.
Clubhouse: Two bars and 6 changing rooms.
Colours: Black. (*Change colours:* Amber.)
Nickname: Buffaloes
Floodlights: Training
Membership: £25.
Local newspaper: Manchester Evening News
League: North West 2
Final position (1987–88): 5th
Playing record (1987–88): P 36, W 22, D 2, L 12. F 476, A 319.
Competitions won: Toc H '7's, 1st May 1988.

WORKINGTON

Ellis Sports Ground, Mossbay Road, Workington CA14. Tel: 0900-2625.
Founded: 1877
President: G. Nicholson
Chairman: K. Dixon
Coach: G. McCrickerd
Secretary: M. Heaslip, 32 Elizabeth Street, Workington. Tel: 0900 66339.
Fixtures Secretary: J. Heaslip, 3 St. Michael's Road, Workington. Tel: 0900-2449.
Club captain (1987–88): M. Tweddle
Club captain (1988–89): S. Thompson
No. of teams: Senior 4, Youth & Minis 2
Directions to Ground: Off B5296 ½ mile south of Town Centre.
Ground capacity: 17,000. Stand, 2,000.
Clubhouse: Bar, lounge, functions & catering.
Colours: Black/white hoops. (*Change colours:* All black)
Nickname: Zebras
Floodlights: Yes
Admission: Varies
Membership: £12.65 Players; £5.75 V. Presideurs.
Programme: 8 pages 50p (Editor: J. Murray, 35 Clifton Court, Workington. Tel: 0900-62496)
Local newspaper: West Cumberland Times & Star
League: NW2
Final position (1987–88): Sixth
Playing record (1987–88): P 36, W 15, D 2, L 19, F 335, A 374.
Competitions won: Cumberland Cup 1900, 1907, 1908, 1909, 1920, 1921, 1922, 1924, 1925, 1926, 1931, 1950, 1953, 1954, 1955, 1962. Girobank League N.W. (North) Div. One: 1986.

COCKERMOUTH

Leithwaite, Cockermouth.
Founded: 1878
President: Mrs Audrey Lee
Chairman: David Coulthand
Coach: John Cusack
Secretary: Bill McDowell, 10 The Green, Cockermouth. Tel: 0900 824274.
Fixtures Secretary: Andrew Quarey, 15 Beech Lane. Tel: 0900 824282.
Club captain (1987–88): Mark McDowell
Club captain (1988–89): Mark McDowell
No. of teams: Senior 3, Youth & Minis 2
Directions to Ground: Workington Road, Cockermouth.
Ground capacity: 500. Stand, 100
Colours: Black and amber. (*Change colours:* Red)
Nickname: Wasps
Floodlights: No
Admission: 50p
Membership: £10
Local newspaper: West Cumbria Times and Star.
League: North West 2
Final position (1987–88): 6th
Playing record (1987–88): P 24, W 20, D 1, L 13.
Competitions won: Runners up Cumbria Cup, Moresby Seven A Side Winners, Girobank/Times and Star Team of Month, March.

PENRITH

Winters Park, Penrith, Cumbria. Tel: 0768-63151.
Founded: 1881
President: W. Mounsey
Coach: M. Arragon
Secretary: M. Hendrie, 25 Frenchfield Way, Penrith, Cumbria. Tel: 0768-65791.
Fixtures Secretary: W. Mounsey, The Luham, Eden Hall, Penrith, Cumbria. Tel: Lanewithby 202.
Club captain (1987–88): M. Sanderson
Club captain (1988–89): G. Robertson
No. of teams: Senior 3, Youth & Minis 5
Directions to Ground: M6 leave at Junction 40 – take A66 towards Scotch Corner – next roundabout travel towards Alston Club on left ½ mile from roundabout.
Ground capacity: 5,000. Stand, 350/400.
Clubhouse: Club/bar/dance hall/4 squash courts/tennis courts.
Colours: Myrtle green and white
Floodlights: No
Membership: £17.00 full rugby membership.
Programme: Free
Local newspaper: Cumberland and Westmorland Herald
League: NW2
Final position (1987–88): 8th
Playing record (1987–88): P 32, W 11, L 17, D 4, F 326, A 391.
Competitions won: 1st XV Semi-Finals Girobank, Cumbria Cup.

NEWTON-LE-WILLOWS

Crow Lane East, Newton-Le-Willows, Merseyside. Tel: (09252) 4591.
Founded: 1947
President: Mrs B. Southern
Chairman: W. Roberts
Coach: C. Bailey & J. Gilchrist
Secretary: R. Pearson, 12 Birley Street, Newton-Le-Willows. Tel: (09252) 4055.
Fixtures Secretary: M. Parker, 2 Warrington Road, Golborne Dale, Newton-Le-Willows. Tel: (09252) 6679.
Club captain (1987–88): J. Stuart
Club captain (1988–89): S. Chesworth
No. of teams: Senior 4, Youth & Minis 9
Directions to Ground: From M6/A580 intersection (Jnct. 23) follow A49 south along Ashton Road. At Oak Tree P.H. turn right into Crow Lane East, clubhouse 300 yds on right.
Ground capacity: 500. Stand, N/A.
Clubhouse: Two bars, dance hall, 5 changing rooms. (Also cricket, tennis, bowls, and ladies hockey)
Colours: Royal blue & gold stripes. (*Change colours:* Royal blue)
Nickname: Newts
Floodlights: No only for training
Admission: Collection
Membership: £10
Programme: 10p
Local newspaper: Newton & Golbourne News
League: North West 2
Final position (1987–88): 9th
Playing record (1987–88): P 34, W 9, D 2, L 23.
Competitions won: Lancashire County Plate Winners 1984–85 season.

HEATON MOOR

Green Lane, Heaton Moor, Stockport, Cheshire. Tel: 061 432 3407.
Founded: 1899
President: R.D. Howard
Chairman: G.B. Costello
Coach: J. Ashley
Secretary: Ian Sinclair MC, 13 Norman Road, Heaton Moor, Stockport, Cheshire SK4 4HJ.
Fixtures Secretary: J.W. James, 22 Hillcrest Road, Bramhall, Stockport, Cheshire SK7 3AE.
Club captain (1987–88): J.G. Ashley
Club captain (1988–89): D. Beckley
No. of teams: Senior 4. Youth & Minis 3.
Directions to Ground: Any motorway to join M63 for Airport and Stockport. Leave at J12. Hard left on A5145 1 mile right at sign to Heaton Moor, right into Green Lane at cross roads.
Clubhouse: First class, brick, separate bathhouse and dining area.
Colours: Red, black and amber hoops. (*Change colours:* red, gold or black.
Nickname: The Moor
Floodlights: Yes, for training.
Membership: £25 playing + match tax. £10 Patrons.
Programme: 50p (inc. admission) (Editor: D.H. Huxstep)
Local newspaper: Stockport Express, Stockport Messenger, Heaton Moor Guardian
League: North West 2
Final position 10th
Playing record (1987–88): P 37, W 8, D 1, L 28. F 264 A 571.

WARRINGTON

Bridge Lane, Appleton, Warrington. Tel: 0925 64591
Founded: 1923
Secretary: J.K. Fletcher, 472 Manchester Road, Paddington, Warrington, Cheshire. Tel: 0925 814182 (H) or 0925 31244 (W)
Fixtures Secretary: W.K. Wilkinson, 5 Osborne Road, Lower Walton, Warrington WA4 6JD. Tel: 0925 07964
League: North West 2
Final position (1987–88): 11th (bottom, relegated)

NW E/NORTH 1

OLD ALDWINIANS

Audenshaw Park, Droylsden Road, Audenshaw, Nr. Manchester. Tel: 061-301-1001.
Founded: 1936
President: M. Wilson
Chairman: W. Thorpe
Coach: Len Deacon/Phil Lord
Secretary: G. Hatton, Oak Drive Post Office, 655 Manchester Road, Denton, Manchester M34 2NA.
Fixtures Secretary: Barry Ross (Future) Tel: 061-301-3814 and Alan Whalley (Present) Tel: 061-370-0921.
Club captain (1987–88): Gordon Longley
Club captain (1988–89): Gordon Longley
No. of teams: Senior 6, Youth & Minis 8
Directions to Ground: Ground and Club off Manchester – Ashton-U-Lyne. Road entrance off A662, easily accessible from A635 M/C – Ashton-U-Lyne.
Ground capacity: 1st pitch fully enclosed approx 3500–4000 + 3 other pitches. Stand, 200.
Clubhouse: Large function room, 2 members lounges, 3 bars, 8 changing rooms + large bathing area + showers.
Colours: Shirts red/white hoops, navy shorts, red socks. (*Change colours:* Black/white hoops or navy blue)
Nickname: Shaw
Floodlights: Yes Floodlit training area.
Membership: Playing £25. Social £3.

NW E/North 1

Local newspaper: The Reporter Group and The Advertiser (Tameside)
League: North West E North 1
Final position (1987–88): Promoted as Champions.
Playing record (1987–88): P 45, W 35, D 1, L 8, F 745, A 272.
Competitions won: League North West/East North Division One Champions.

VICKERS

Hawcoat Park, Hawcoat Lane, Barrow-in-Furness. Tel: 0229 25296.
Founded: 1930
President: Dr R. Leach
Chairman: K. Mills
Coach: J. Richardson
Secretary: E. France, 20 Rydal Avenue, Barrow-in-Furness. Tel: 0229-24536.
Fixtures Secretary: C.J. High, 19 Cowlarns Road.
Club captain (1987–88): J. Steele
Club captain (1988–89): J. Steele
No. of teams: Senior 4, Youth & Minis 1
Directions to Ground: Leave M6 at Junction 36 take A590 to Barrow, turn right at first set traffic lights, ground ½ mile on the left.
Ground capacity: 500
Clubhouse: Multi Sports Club, 12 changing rooms.
Colours: Maroon & White. (*Change colours:* Blue or Maroon)
Floodlights: No
Membership: £6.20
Local newspaper: Evening Mail
League: East North 1
Final position (1987–88): 2nd (promoted)
Playing record (1987–88): P 34, W 28, L 6, F 669, A 231.
Competitions won: Rugby World & Post Junior Club of the Month – February 1988.

FURNESS

Strawberry Grounds, Abbey Road, Barrow-in-Furness, Cumbria. Tel: 0229 25226
Founded: 1902
Secretary: D. Jenkins, 83 Hartington Street, Barrow-in-Furness, Cumbria LA14 5SS. Tel: 0229 30924
League: NW E/North 1
Final position (1987–88): 3rd
Playing record (1987–88): P 32, W 13, D 1, L 18, F 399, A 361

MORESBY PARKS

Walkmill Park, Moresby Parks, Whitehaven, Cumbria. Tel: Whitehaven 5984.
Founded: 1915
President: M.G. Bawden
Chairman: C. Denwood
Coach: F. Fee
Secretary: M. Simpson, 54 Thornton Road, High Meadows, Whitehaven.
Fixtures Secretary: S. Bray, Care of Secretary.
Club captain (1987–88): J. Peet
Club captain (1988–89): J. Peet
No. of teams: Senior 3
Directions to Ground: Follow A595 to Distington, turn left at Castle Inn – 2 miles to Moresby.
Clubhouse: Pre-fabricated building – 2 main rooms & changing facilities.
Colours: Red shirts/white shorts. (*Change colours:* Red/white hooped shirts)
Nickname: The Red Devils
Floodlights: No
Membership: Playing member £10. Social £1.50.
Local newspaper: Times & Star, Whitehaven News.
League: NW E/N 1
Final position (1987–88): Second (promoted)
Playing record (1987–88): P 29, W 23, D 2, L 4.
Competitions won: Floodlit Cup – Nov 87.

FLEETWOOD

Molbourne Avenue, Fleetwood. Tel: 03917 4774
Founded: 1932
Secretary: T.M. Jones, The Cottage, Derby Road, Poulton le Fylde, Nr. Blackpool, Lancs. Tel: 0253 899352 (H) or 03917 3030 (W)
League: NW E/North 1
Final position (1987–88): 5th

OLDHAM

Manor Park, Bryth Road, Bardsley, Oldham. Tel: 061 624 6383
Founded: 1904
Secretary: T.J. Brown, 27 Esther Street, Green Acres, Oldham, Lancs OL4 3EP. Tel: 061 620 1878 (H) or 061 248 6161 (W)
Fixtures Secretary: S.J. Kenney, 32 Sholver Hill Close, Oldham, Lancs. Tel: 061 633 7900
League: NW E/North 1
Final position (1987–88): 6th

ECCLES

Guildford Road, Peel Green, Eccles, Manchester. Tel: 061 789 2613
Founded: 1897
Secretary: M. Dutton, 10 Ashley Drive, Swinton M27 3AX. Tel: 061 794 2904 (H) or 061 480 0634 (W)
League: NW E/North 1
Final position (1987–88): 7th
Playing record (1987–88): P 36, W 17, D 1, L 18, F 298, A 364

LITTLEBOROUGH

Rakewood, Hollingworth Lane, Littleborough, Lancs. Tel: 0706 70220
Founded: 1930
Secretary: A. Fletcher, 12 Heron Close, Pheasant Wood, Cleveleys, Lancs F75 2JJ. Tel: 0253 824054 (H) or 0204 389274 (W)
League: NW E/North 1
Final position (1987–88): 8th

DISBURY TOC H

Simon Field, Ford Lane, Didsbury, Manchester M20. Tel: 061-445 2146
Founded: 1924
President: P.J.M. Bradley
Coach: Alan Cupello
Secretary: Rudy Speed, 9 Moorfield Road, West Didsbury, Manchester M20 8UZ. Tel: 061 434 2956 (H) or 061 872 5919 (W)
Fixtures Secretary: Rudy Speed, as above
Club Captain (1987–88): Steve Popeola
Club Captain (1988–89): Steve Popeola
No. of teams: Senior 4. Youth & Minis None.
Directions to ground: Near Didsbury Village, Manchester
Clubhouse: New clubhouse on ground.
Colours: Black and amber. (*Change colours:* Maroon.)
Nickname: TOC
Floodlights: No
Membership: £15 playing member, senior. £5 U-21 and unemployed.
Programme editor: Geoff Green

NW E/North 1

Local newspaper: South Manchester Reporter/ Manchester Evening News
League: NW E/North 1
Final position (1987–88): 9th
Playing record (1987–88): P 35, W 16, D 1, L 18. F 415, A 486

CALDER VALE

Holden Road, Roadby, Burnley. Tel: 0282 24337
Founded: 1926
Secretary: A. Finnan, 27 Barnfield Avenue, Worsthorne, Burnley BB10 3JQ. Tel: 0282 21935 (H) or 36317 (W)
Fixtures Secretary: T.F. Boyle, 352 Coalclough Lane, Burnley. Tel: 0282 24218 (H) or 0282 36317 (W)
League: NW E/North 1
Final position (1987–88): 10th
Playing record (1987–88): P 33, W 8, D 3, L 22, F 306, A 564

COLNE & NELSON

Holt House, Colne, Lancs. Tel: (0282) 863339.
Founded: 1926/27
President: Dr J.D. Robertson
Chairman: F. Cook
Coach: G. Ratcliffe
Secretary: Kit Hornton, 12 Camden Street, Nelson, Lancs. Tel: (0282) 63612 (H), (0282) 22527 (W).
Fixtures Secretary: J. Tindall, 108 Skipton Road, Colne, Lancs.
Club captain (1987–88): G. Wilson
Club captain (1988–89): G. Tindall
No. of teams: Senior 3, Youth & Minis 1
Directions to Ground: From M65 turn left at roundabout off new section of motorway. Ground and club at end of Harrison Drive, Colne.
Clubhouse: Bar/kitchen/clubroom for approx 150, 2 changing rooms with communal shower area.
Colours: Black & white hoops. (*Change colours:* Maroon)
Floodlights: No
Membership: £16.50 p.a.
Local newspaper: Nelson Leader/Colne Times
League: NW East 1
Final position (1987–88): 11th in NW division EN.1 Relegated to E1)
Playing record (1987–88): P 36, W 7, D 0, L 29, F 186, A 537.

NW EAST 1

DE LA SALLE

Lancaster Road, Salford. Tel: 061 789 2261.
Founded: 1946
President: Rev Bro. Phillip
Chairman: J. Collins
Secretary: K. Hazeldine, 37 Granary Lane, Worsley, Manchester. Tel: 061 794 4409.
Fixtures Secretary: J.L. Hibbert, 2 Duchy Avenue, Worsley, Manchester. Tel: 061 799 0143.
Club captain (1987–88): Paul Andrews
Club captain (1988–89): Paul Andrews
No. of teams: Senior 4. Youth & Minis 4.
Directions to Ground: First exit off M602, turn left. Third set of traffic lights, turn left into Lancaster Road, 200 yards on left.
Colours: Scarlet and old gold hoops, black shorts. (*Change colours:* Blue)
Floodlights: No
Admission: Free
Membership: £17
Programme: 50p. (Editor: K. Hazeldine)
Local newspaper: Salford Advertiser
League: NW East 1
Final position (1987–88): 1st (Promoted)
Playing record (1987–88): P 41, W 30, D 2, L 9.
Competitions won: Lancs Trophy Finalist League East Div 1 (Champions), finalist TOC H "7".

METROVICK

Finney Bank Road, Sale, Cheshire. Tel: 061 973 7061
Founded: 1923
President: D. Edwards
Chairman: J. Ward
Coach: G. Hawkins
Secretary: Dr J. Fewster, 61 Grappenhall Road, Warrington WA4 2AR. Tel: 0925 66219 (H).
Fixtures Secretary: C. Barton, 4 Oulderhill Drive, Rochdale, Lancs. 0706 350312 (H). 0706 623627 (W).
Club captain (1987–88): T. Gedrych
Club captain (1988–89): S. Diamond
No. of teams: Senior 5. Youth & Minis 0.
Directions to Ground: M63, junction 6. A56 towards Sale. Right at first lights into Glebelands Road. Second right into Finney Bank Road.
Clubhouse: Changing for 8 teams, baths, showers.
Colours: Black, white hoops. (*Change colours:* Blue).
Nickname: MV
Floodlights: Yes, training.
Membership: £18
Local newspaper: Manchester Evening News
League: NW East 1
Final position (1987–88): 2nd (Promoted)
Playing record (1987–88): P 34, W 18, D 3, L 13. F 355, A 306.

ASHTON ON MERSEY

Barrock Lane, Off Carrington Lane, Ashton on Mersey, Sale, Cheshire. Tel: 061 973 6637
Founded: 1930
Secretary: F.M.S. Ashton, 188a Ashley Road, Hale, Altrincham, Cheshire WA15 0SF. Tel: 061 941 3796 (H) or 061 928 4647 (W)
Fixtures Secretary: J. Evans, 50 Cloverley, Brooklands, Sale, Cheshire. Tel: 061 962 7080 (H) or 061 962 3611 (W)
League: NW East 1
Final position (1987–88): 3rd

TYLDESLEY

Well Street, Tyldesley. Tel: 0942 882967
Founded: 1881
Secretary: M.P. Taylor, "Garthmere", Garthmere Road, Atherton, Lances. Tel: 0942 883237 (H) or 0942 870893 (W)
League: NW East 1
Final position (1987–88): 4th
Playing record (1987–88): P 39, W 24, D 2, L 13, F 507, A 323

OLD SALIANS

Rookwood, Clarendon Crescent, Sale, Cheshire. Tel: 061 973 7250.
Founded: 1944
President: H.W. Thomas
Chairman: A.T. Roberts
Coach: R. Alderson
Secretary: A.N. Frost, Limehurst, 35 Priory Road, Sale, Cheshire. Tel: 061 976 2607.
Fixtures Secretary: K.F. Sheldon, 4 Oban Drive, Sale, Cheshire. Tel: 061 962 2878.
Club captain (1987–88): M. McCarthy
Club captain (1988–89): G. Middlebrook
No. of teams: Senior 5, Youth 9 Minis 1
Directions to Ground: Exit M63 Jct 8 turn 1st right into Dane Road, Club half mile on left.
Ground capacity: 400+
Clubhouse: 3 bars, facilities for cricket, tennis, hockey + function room
Colours: Navy with white band. (*Change colours:* Green red & white hoops)
Nickname: "Sealions"
Floodlights: No Planning permission applied for.
Admission: Nil
Membership: £22 playing. £7 social.
Local newspaper: S.A.M. & Guardian
League: NW E1
Final position (1987–88): 5th

OLD BEDIANS

Millgate Lane, Didsbury. Tel: 061 445 8862
Founded: 1954
Secretary: J. Dunn, 1 Lynmouth Avenue, Withington, Manchester. Tel: 061 228 1100
League: NW East 1
Final position (1987–88): 6th

KERSAL

Stelfox Avenue, Timperley, Altrincham, Cheshire. Tel: 061 973 9157
Founded: 1879
Secretary: A. Forbes, 6 Crampton Drive, Hale Barns, Cheshire. Tel: 061 980 3661 (H) or 061 834 8161 (W)
Fixtures Secretary: A. Long, 59 Dennison Road, Hazel Grove, Stockport, Cheshire. Tel: 0625 873360
League: NW East 1
Final position (1987–88): 7th
Playing record (1987–88): P 41, W 21, D 1, L 19, F 506, A 426

CONGLETON

Park Street. Tel: (0260) 273338.
Founded: 1860
President: M. Wright
Chairman: D. Ingham
Coach: To be appointed
Secretary: M. Dale, 34 Howey Hill, Congleton. Tel: (0260) 277718.
Fixtures Secretary: K. Williams, 2 Sprink Lane, Buglawton, Congleton, Cheshire. Tel: (0260) 279202.
Club captain (1987–88): N. Cardall
Club captain (1988–89): N. Cardall
No. of teams: Senior 4
Directions to Ground: Follow signs to Leisure Centre
Ground capacity: Open park land.
Clubhouse: Ex Public House – The Woodman, Park Street, Congleton.
Colours: Red/white/black hoops. (*Change colours:* Red or blue/white hoops)
Floodlights: No
Membership: £20
Programme: Free monthly newsletter (Editor: D.J. Thorley)
Local newspaper: Congleton Chronicle
League: NW East 1
Final position (1987–88): 8th
Playing record (1987–88): P 33, W 19, L 14.

ASHTON-UNDER-LYNE

Gambrel Bank, Ashton-Under-Lyne
Founded: 1884
President: B. Fisher
Chairman: I. Cricket
Coach: M. Walsh
Secretary: M.W. Crebbin, "Grasmere", High Grove Road, Grasscroft, Oldham OL4 4HG.
Fixtures Secretary: P. Newton, 128 St Albans Avenue, Ashton-Under-Lyne.
Club captain (1987–88): W. Blomely
Club captain (1988–89): S. Hett
No. of teams: Senior 3. Youth & Minis 1.
Directions to Ground: From market up Henrietta Street to St. Albans Avenue.
Clubhouse: Two storey.
Colours: Red, amber, black hoops. (*Change colours:* Red).
Floodlights: Yes, for training
Membership: £18
Local newspaper: Ashton Reporter or Advertiser
League: NW East 1
Final position (1987–88): 9th
Playing record (1987–88): P 35, W 15, D 1, L 19. F 301, A 376.

NORTH MANCHESTER

Victoria Avenue East, New Moston, Manchester. Tel: 061-682-9234.
Founded: 1983-84
President: E. Riley
Chairman: M. Skinner
Coach: B. Wilson
Secretary: B.H. Stott, 8 Ballea Avenue, New Moston, Manchester M10 0WL. Tel: 061-682-0541.
Fixtures Secretary: P. Riley, 51 Boardman Fold Road, Alkrington, Middleton. Tel: 061-653-7257.
Club captain (1987–88): P. Stokes
Club captain (1988–89): P. Stokes
No. of teams: Senior 2, Youth & Minis 1
Colours: Sky blue/gold/scarlet hoops
Floodlights: No
Membership: £25
Local newspaper: Middleton Guardian & Manchester Evening News
League: NW East 1
Final position (1987–88): Ninth

BOWDEN

Clay Lane, Timperley, Cheshire
Founded: 1877
Secretary: C.D. Fall, 10 Malvern Drive, Altrincham, Cheshire WA14 4NQ. Tel: 061 928 8276 (H) or 061 236 7212 (W)
Fixtures Secretary: J. Daldrey, 77 Navigation Road, Altrincham. Tel: 061 928 8672 (H) or 061 236 7212 (W)
League: NW East 1
Final position (1987–88): 15th (bottom, relegated)

BOLTON

Mortfield Pavillion, Avenue Street, Bolton.
Founded: 1974
President: T. Holden
Chairman: D. Pepper
Coach: A.A. Catterall
Secretary: R.D. Pemberton, Grasmere House, 23 Wilkinson Street, Leigh. Tel: 0942 678257.
Fixtures Secretary: D. Patchett, Badger Cottage, 2 Richmal Terrace, Ramsbottam. Tel: 0706-82-6298.
Club captain (1987–88): L. Towler
Club captain (1988–89): L. Towler
No. of teams: Senior 4
Directions to Ground: ¼ mile out of Bolton on Chorley Old Road turn into Avenue Street.
Colours: Red–white hoops. (*Change colours:* Navy)
Floodlights: No
Membership: £15
Local newspaper: Bolton Evening News
League: N/W East 2
Final position (1987–88): Won (promoted)
Playing record (1987–88): P 31, W 15, D 3, L 13.

CREWE AND NANTWICH

Whitehouse Lane, Nantwich, Cheshire CW5 6HH. Tel: 0270-626155.
Founded: 1922
President: D. Potts
Chairman: S.M. Flood
Coach: A. Pinkney
Secretary: A.G. Jones, 9 Gingerbread Lane, Nantwich, Cheshire CW5 6NH. Tel: 0270-625737.
Fixtures Secretary: R. Holland, 88 Rope Lane, Wistaston, Crewe. Tel: 0270-666773.
Club captain (1987–88): R. Foden
Club captain (1988–89): R. Foden
No. of teams: Senior 4, Youth & Minis 5
Directions to Ground: Ground – Barony Park Nantwich (Clubhouse in Whitehouse Lane, Nantwich)
Clubhouse: Bar, social room + changing rooms.
Colours: White with black hoop. (*Change colours:* Red)
Floodlights: Yes
Membership: Non-players £6.00, Senior players £30.00.
Programme: N/A
Local newspaper: Nantwich Chronicle
League: (1987/88) North West East Div. 2
Final position (1987–88): 2nd (promoted)
Playing record (1987–88): P 33, W 18, D 0, L 15, F 460, A 368.
Competitions won: Won promotion to North West League East Div. 1.

GREATER MANCHESTER FIRE SERVICE

Old Strets F.C., Highfield Grove, Stretford, Manchester. Tel: 061 865 0146.
Founded: 1965
Chairman: C. Rooney
Secretary: G.R. Smith, 22 Fistral Crescent, Stalybridge, Cheshire.
Fixtures Secretary: C. Clinkard, 36 Torkington Road, Gatley, Manchester. Tel: 061 428 3597.
Club captain (1987–88): R. Saunders
Club captain (1988–89): R. Saunders
No. of teams: Senior 2
Directions to Ground: Come off M63 at Jnc. 7 head towards Manchester. Ground is 200 yds on right.
Clubhouse: Guests at Football Club.
Colours: Red shirts. (*Change colours:* Amber & black)
Nickname: Fire Balls
Floodlights: No
League: North West East 2
Final position (1987–88): 2nd
Playing record (1987–88): P 32, W 20, L 8, D 4.
Competitions won: National Fire Service XV a side competition Winners.

BROUGHTON

Yew Street, Broughton, Salford M7 9HL. Tel: 061 792 2920.
Founded: 1913
President: W. McGloughlin
Chairman: P. Tyson
Coach: P. Smith
Secretary: W.C. Lorains, 191 Longhurst Lane, Mellor, Stockport. Tel: 061 427 2250.
Fixtures Secretary: A. Murphy, Contact club for new address. Tel: 061 792 2920.
Club captain (1987–88): D. Smyth
Club captain (1988–89): D. Smyth
No. of teams: Senior 4. Youth & Minis 1.
Directions to Ground: M63 motorway network. M602 to Salford – signs Salford University, Yew Street off Lower Broughton Road.
Clubhouse: 4 changing rooms, 2 bars, committee room, stewards accommodation.
Colours: Navy blue, maroon, gold hoops. (*Change colours:* Yellow strip).
Nickname: Old Salfordians
Floodlights: No
Membership: £12
Local newspaper: Salford City Reporter
League: NW East 2
Final position (1987–88): 3rd

BURY

Radcliffe Road, Bury. Tel: 061 764 1528
Founded: 1875
Secretary: M.D. Jones, 7 Bramley Road, Bramford, Rochdale, Lancs. Tel: 0706 352041 (H) or 061 236 9378 (W)
Fixtures Secretary: K. Punshon, 24 Newcombe Road, Holcombe Brook, Bury. Tel: Tottington 4886
League: NW East 2
Final position (1987–88): 5th
Playing record (1987–88): P 34, W 13, D 0, L 21, F 365, A 577

MANCHESTER Y.M.C.A.

Princess road, Alexandra Park, Manchester. Tel: 061 226 6814
Founded: 1905
Secretary: B. Reece, 42 Edgeworth Road, Fallowfield, Manchester M14 6RS. Tel: 061 248 6289 (H) or 061 429 8060 (W)
League: NW East 2
Final position (1987–88): 6th

OLDHAM COLL

Chapel Road, Oldham. Tel: 061 665 2149
Founded: 1967
Secretary: K. McGuire, 24 Newbury Grove, Hopwood, Heywood, Lancs. Tel: 0706 622203 (H) or 061 236 8500 (W)
League: NW East 2
Final position (1987–88): 7th

NW East 2

CHORLEY

Brookfields, Chancery Road, Astley Village, Chorley, Lancs. Tel: (02572) 68806.
Founded: 1972
President: J. Lucas
Chairman: T. Callander
Coach: B. Ingham
Secretary: M. Walkden, 18B The Farthings, Astley Village, Chorley. Tel: 02572 72825.
Fixtures Secretary: D. Edwards. Tel: 0772 424403.
Club captain (1987–88): D. Muir
Club captain (1988–89): D. Muir
No. of teams: Senior 3. Youth & Minis 2.
Ground capacity: 1000
Clubhouse: Brick built, club room, lounge, 2 changing rooms, showers.
Colours: Black/white hoops. (*Change colours:* Blue/green hoops)
Floodlights: No
Membership: £25 full, £3.50 social.
Local newspapers: Chorley Citizen/Chorley Guardian
League: NW East 1
Final position (1987–88): 7th
Playing record (1987–88): P 32, W 8, D 1, L 23.
Competitions won: Multipart Veterans Trophy.

DUKINFIELD

Blockcaffs, Birch Lane, Dukinfield, Cheshire.
Founded: 1880
President: M.B. Cuttle
Chairman: A.E. Taylor
Coach: C. Samuels
Secretary: A.E. Hilton, Old St Georges Vicarage, Penine View, Heyrod, Stalybridge, Cheshire SK15 3BT. Tel: 061 338 3410.
Fixtures Secretary: As above.
Club captain (1987–88): M. McQuillan
Club captain (1988–89): M. McQuillan
No. of teams: Senior 3. Youth & Minis 2.
Directions to Ground: Recreation grounds next to Dukinfield Baths on the B6170 that runs between A635 at Ashton to A57 at Hyde.
Clubhouse: Own clubhouse with new large extension.
Colours: Royal blue and gold hoops. (*Change colours:* red and black hoops).
Nickname: Originally Dukinfield Tigers
Floodlights: Yes, training only
Membership: £20
Local newspaper: Dukinfield Reporter
League: NW East 2
Final position (1987–88): 7th
Playing record (1987–88): P 39, W 18, D 1, L 20. F 365, A 431

MARPLE

Braybyns Park, Marple Bridge, Cheshire
Founded: 1971
Secretary: K. Abbot, 136 Station Road, Hadfield via Hyde, Cheshire SK14 7AA. Tel: 061 832 5705 (H)
League: NW East 2
Final position (1987–88): 10th (bottom, relegated)

NW NORTH 1

WINDERMERE

Longlands, Bowness-On-Windermere, Cumbria LA23 3AS. Tel: W'mere 3066.
Founded: 1921 (official) Oridinally 1886 – not continuous from this date.
President: Ian R. Alexander
Chairman: Alan L. Jones
Coach: Graham Smith/Ian Rukin
Secretary: R. Nigel Rimmer, Langrigge Close, Langrigge Drive, Bowness-On-Windermere, Cumbria LA23 3AF.
Fixtures Secretary: Guy W. Aspinwall, 40 Oakthwaite Road, Windermere, Cumbria LA23 2BD.
1st XV captain (1987–88): David Fletcher
1st XV captain (1988–89): David Fletcher
No. of teams: Senior 2
Directions to Ground: Follow directions to Windermere (A591) follow signs to Bowness turn.
Ground capacity: Not sure. Stand, 50
Colours: Amber shirts/black shorts. (*Change colours:* Black shirts)
Floodlights: Yes for training.
Membership: £8 (Players) plus match fees. Patrons £3 minimum.
Local newspaper: Westmorland Gazette
League: NW North 1
Final position (1987–88): First
Playing record (1987–88): P 38, W 28, D 0, L 10, F 731, A 336.
Competitions won: NW Div North 1 Winners; Westmorland & Furness Cup 22/4/88 (S. Cumbria)

KESWICK

Davidson Park, Keswick. Tel: 0596 72823
Founded: 1879
Secretary: M.E. Brownman, 3 Briar Rigg, Keswick, Cumbria CA12 4NW. Tel: 0596 72461 (H) & (W)
League: NW North 1
Final position (1987–88): 2nd
Playing record (1987–88): P 31, W 20, D 1, L 10, F 397, A 286

KIRKBY LONSDALE

Underleypark, Kirkby Lonsdale, Carnforth, Lancs. Tel: 9468 71780.
Founded: 1877
President: M. Hastenwell
Chairman: M.J. Neal
Coach: M.E. Nelson
Secretary: W.M. Martindale, 89 Fairgarth Drive, Kirkby Lonsdale, Carnforth, Lancs LA6 2DT.
Fixtures Secretary: N.R. Winn, Ferry Cottage, Arkholme, Carnforth, Lancs. Tel: 0468 21489.
Club captain (1987–88): N.A.P. Meadows
Club captain (1988–89): I.S.H. Wade
No. of teams: Senior 3.
Directions to Ground: M6 Junction 36. A65 Skipton left at Kirkby Lonsdale sign ¾ mile left for. B 6254 out of town ½ mile. Turn right rhough road "Raygarth".
Ground capacity: 1500. Stand, 50.
Clubhouse: New 1987 – 4 teams changing.
Colours: Red, amber and black. (*Change colours:* Red and white hoops).
Floodlights: No
Admission: Free (collection)
Membership: £10
Local newspaper: Westmorland Gazette and Lancaster Guardian
League: NWN1
Final position (1987–88): 3rd
Playing record (1987–88): P 36, W 16, D 0, L 20. F 480, A 493.
Competitions won: Westmorland & Furness Cup Winners 1970/71, 72/73, 1985/86. Winners Nat Girobank League N. Area Div 2 1986/87.

ROSSENDALE

Sports Centre, Newchurch Road, Rawtenstall, Rossendale. Tel: 07062 216635
Founded: 1970
Secretary: P. Brotherton, 47 Poulton Avenue, Accrington, Lancs BB5 5EP. Tel: 0254 34310 (H) or 0282 72511 (W)
League: NW North 1
Final position (1987–88): 4th
Playing record (1987–88): P 45, W 32, D 0, L 13, F 765, A 394

CREIGHTON

Canns Field, Off Newtown Road, Carlisle. Tel: 0228 21169.
Founded: 1927
President: W. Grieve
Chairman: M. Simpson
Secretary: D.J. Thomlinson, 146 Moorhouse Road, Carlisle. Tel: 0228 35111 (H), 24379 (B).
Fixtures Secretary: J.W. Graham, 4 Carlton Gardens, Carlisle. Tel: 0228 26705.
Club captain (1987–88): C. Whalley
Club captain (1988–89): C. Whalley
No. of teams: Senior 3
Directions to Ground: Follow directions to Cumberland Infirmary, ground 300 yds further.
Clubhouse: Basic
Colours: Navy blue. (*Change colours:* Blue & white hoops)
Floodlights: No
Membership: £10
Local newspaper: Cumberland News
League: NW North 1
Final position (1987–88): 5th
Playing record (1987–88): P 32, W 23, L 9.
Competitions won: Creightons Sevens (No other clubs invited!)

ST. BENEDICTS

Newlands Avenue
Founded: 1974
Secretary: W. Dougan, 9 Crow Park, Loop Road South, Whitehaven, Cumbria CA28 7SF. Tel: 0946 66679 (H)
League: NW North 1
Final position (1987–88): 6th

BLACKPOOL

Fleetwood Road, Norbreck. Tel: 0253-3308.
Founded: 1959
President: E. Schools
Chairman: P. Isaacs
Coach: H. Williams
Secretary: Cliff Wainscott, 213 Kingscote Drive, Blackpool. Tel: 0253-35072.
Fixtures Secretary: I. Taylor, 3 Gosforth Road. Tel: 58183.
Club captain (1987–88): A.J.R. Hopton
Club captain (1988–89): A.J.R. Hopton
No. of teams: Senior 3, Youth & Minis 3
Directions to Ground: M55 – (Leave J4). A583 (to Blackpool) right at Oxford Square, B5124, joins A587 (signs to Fleetwood) ground on right ½ mile past Red Lion.
Clubhouse: Bar, lounge, showers, 4 changing rooms.
Colours: Red & blue hoops. (*Change colours:* Dark blue)
Floodlights: Yes (for training only)
Membership: £18
Programme: New this season – format not finalised. 50p (Editor: P. Isaacs)
Local newspaper: Evening Gazette
League: North West North 1
Final position (1987–88): 7th
Playing record (1987–88): P 38, W 13, D 1, L 24, F 307, A 559.

CARNFORTH

Carnforth High School, Kellet Road, Carnforth
Founded: 1980
Secretary: J.S. Marsdens, "Whinfell" Eden Mount Way, Carnforth, Lancs LA5 9XN. Tel: 0524 734832 (H)
League: NW North 1
Final position (1987–88): 8th
Playing record (1987–88): P 33, W 17, D 2, L 14, F 584, A 389

MILLOM

The Dunes, Haverigg, Millom, Cumbria. Tel: 0657 2832
Founded: 1873
Secretary: F. Eccles, 14 St. Lukes Road, Haverigg, Millom, Cumbria LA18 4HB. Tel: 0657 2606 (H)
League: NW North 1
Final position (1987–88): 9th
Playing record (1987–88): P 32, W 6, D 1, L 25, F 220, A 657

WHITEHAVEN

The Playground, Whitehaven. Tel: 5253
Founded: 1876–7
President: W.G. Anderson
Chairman: H. Connor
Coach: C. Murdock
Secretary: E. McConnell, 38 Loop Road South. Tel: 0946 2225.
Fixtures Secretary: H. Diamond, 20 Lakeland Avenue, Whitehaven. Tel: 0946 63579.
Club captain (1987–88): N. Harrison
Club captain (1988–89): TBA
No. of teams: Senior 1. Youth & Minis 3.
Ground capacity: 1500. Stand, 400.
Colours: Maroon, white hoops. White shorts. (*Change colours:* Maroon, white shorts
Floodlights: No
Membership: £10
Local newspaper: Whitehaven News
League: North West North 1
Final position (1987–88): Bottom
Playing record (1987–88): P 32, W 2, L 30. F 266, A 672.

THORNTON CLEVELEYS

Fleetwood Road North, Thornton Cleveleys, Lancashire. Tel: 0253-854104.
Founded: 1927
President: E. Nicol
Chairman: M. Brennand
Coach: C. Ashcroft
Secretary: M. Boardman, 41 Roylen Avenue, Carleton, Poulton-Le-Fylde. Tel: 0253-890099.
Fixtures Secretary: B. Hirst, 30 Harewood Close, Carleton, Poulton-Le-Fylde. Tel: 0253-892856.
No. of teams: Senior 4, Youth & Minis 3
Directions to Ground: Off M55, Junction 3, A585 towards Fleetwood approx. 7 miles right at roundabout on B5268 through traffic lights, Windmill on left, Club is ½ mile further on, on left.
Ground capacity: 300
Clubhouse: Wooden pavilion, changing, bar, social & kitchen areas.
Colours: Red, black and amber. (*Change colours:* Yellow or blue)
Floodlights: No
Membership: £5 + £3 p.w. playing subs.
Programme: A4 sheet, free (Editor: P. Moran)
Local newspaper: W. Lancashire Evening Gazette
League: N.W., North 1
Final position (1987–88): 1st in North 2 (promoted)
Playing record (1987–88): P 34, W 23, D 2, L 9, F 582, A 321.

BRITISH STEELS

Moss Bay, Workington, Cumbria. Tel: 0900-3570.
Founded: 1953
President: A. Williams
Chairman: T. Moore
Coach: M. Rafferty
Secretary: B. Rumney, 14 Walls Road, Salterbeck, Workington.
Fixtures Secretary: D. Milligan, 226 Mossbay, Workington. Tel: 0900-66870.
Club captain (1987–88): M. Jeffery
Club captain (1988–89): M. Jeffery
No. of teams: Senior 2
Directions to Ground: Off M6 at Penrith to Workington, distance 30 mls.
Ground capacity: 500
Clubhouse: Bar, lounge, singing room.
Colours: Red-blue-white hoops. (*Change colours:* Blue white hoops)
Nickname: Steels
Floodlights: No
Admission: £1, 50p child, OAP.
Membership: £5
Programme: 50p (Editor: B. Rumney (Hon. Sec.))
Local newspaper: Cumbria Evening News and Star
League: North North West 2
Final position (1987–88): 2nd
Playing record (1987–88): P 32, W 22, D 3, L 7.
Competitions won: Moresby 7's Winners, Cumbria Shield Semi-Finalists.

UPPER EDEN

Westgarth Road, Kirkby Stephen, Cumbria. Tel: 07683 71585.
Founded: 1975
President: D. Lawrence
Chairman: C. Sowerby
Coach: C. Sowerby
Secretary: S. Moffat, 1 The Arcade, Market Street, Kirkby Stephen, Cumbria CA17 4QN. Tel: 07683 71794.
Fixtures Secretary: G. Todd, Mellbecks House, Kirkby Stephen, Cumbria CA17 4AB. Tel: 07683 71562.
Club captain (1987–88): I. Collinson
Club captain (1988–89): I. Collinson
No. of teams: Senior 2
Directions to Ground: From Town Centre turn right off High Street through Broughm Lane & Cross to Westgarth Road. Ground at end of road.
Colours: Black/white hooped shirts. (*Change colours:* Black shirts)
Floodlights: No
Membership: £7
Local newspaper: Cumberland & Westmorland Herald
League: NW North 2
Final position (1987–88): 3rd
Playing record (1987–88): P 34, W 22, D 1, L 11.
Competitions won: Westmorland Furness Cup 1984.

AMBLESIDE

Galava Park, Borrans Road, Ambleside, Cumbria. Tel: 0966 32536
Founded: 1874
Secretary: J.P. Stead, Gale Crescent Hotel, Low Gale, Ambleside. Tel: Ambleside 32284 (H) or 0966 32066 (W)
League: NW North 2
Final position (1987–88): 4th

SILLOTH

Marshalling Yard, Eden Street, Silloth. Tel: 0968 32299
Founded: 1973
Secretary: R.G. Edwards, Mayfair, Beckefoot, Silloth, Cumbria. Tel: Silloth 31382 (H) or Carlisle 23422 (W)
League: NW North 2
Final position (1987–88): 5th

SMITH BROS

Seven Fields, Bransty
Founded: 1964
Secretary: W. Barwise, 101 Bransty Road, Bransty, Whitehaven, Cumbria CA28 6HF. Tel: 62567
League: NW North 2
Final position (1987–88): 6th

CLITHEROE

Littlemoor Park, Littlemoor Road. Tel: Clitheroe 22261
Founded: 1978
Secretary: J. Hyde, Moorhey Cottage, Knowle Green, Longridge, Preston PR3 2XE. Tel: Ribchester 402 (H) or Burnley 24201 (W)
League: NW North 2
Final position (1987–88): 7th

LANCASTER MOOR HOSPITAL

c/o Secretary
Founded: 1980
President: M. Bonnett
Chairman: F. Roome
Secretary: J.T. Mills, 9 Lily Grove, Scotforth, Lancaster, Lancs. LA1 4TR. Tel: 0524 39114 (H), 0524 65240 Ext 304 (B).
Fixtures Secretary: F.W. Swarbrick, 'Oxensale', Wyresdale Road, Lancaster. Tel: 0524 37601 (H), 0524 64055 (B).
Club captain (1987–88): I. Poole
Club captain (1988–89): N/K at this time
No. of teams: Senior 1
Directions to Ground: No ground at present. Have been renting Vale of Lane facilities.
Clubhouse: Have own clubhouse at Lancaster Moor Hospital.
Colours: Black & white hoops. (*Change colours:* All black)
Floodlights: No
Membership: £10 includes membership of Hospital Social Club.
Local newspaper: Lancaster Guardian
League: North NW2
Final position (1987–88): Bottom (relegated)
Playing record (1987–88): P 26, W 8, D 0, L 18, F 283, A 447.

NW WEST 1

MERSEYSIDE POLICE

Merseyside Police Sports, Club House, Riversdale Road, Aigburth, Liverpool 19. Tel: 051-427-2208.
Founded: 1960
President: Sir Kenneth Oxford CBE, QPM, Chief Constable
Chairman: Chief Constable Mr David Howe B.A., Assistant Chief Constable
Coach: Sgt. W. Harris
Secretary: Det. Sgt. D.H. Dafnis, St. Andrews, 72 Bertram Drive, Meols, Wirral, Merseyside L47 0LJ. Tel: 051-632-5927 (H), 051-777-3632 (W).
Fixtures Secretary: Det. Superintendent R.G. Corker, 47 Broadway, Bebbington, Wirral. Tel: 051-608-1876.
Club captain (1987–88): Alex Donkor
Club captain (1988–89): Alex Donkor
No. of teams: Senior 4
Directions to Ground: M62, Queens Drive South, Allerton Road, Mather Avenue, right along Booker Avenue, Holmefield Road, cross Aigburth Road into Riversdale Road.
Ground capacity: Open ground round pitch.
Clubhouse: Bar, 4 changing rooms. Capacity 200/300.
Colours: Blue. (*Change colours:* Blue and gold hoops)
Floodlights: No
Admission: Nil
Membership: £5.00
Programme: Nil (Editor: Fred Evans)
Local newspaper: Liverpool Daily Post and Echo
League: N.W. West 2
Final position (1987–88): Top West 1
Playing record (1987–88): W 34, D 2, L 3, F 933, A 282.
Competitions won: Police Athletic Association National Police Cup 21.4.88. Lancashire Rugby Union Girobank Plate Competition 17.4.88. Vine Street Metropolitan Police Invitation Sevens 27.9.87. Courage League Northern area West 1 (Top – all ten games won).

LIVERPOOL COLLEGIATE OLD BOYS

The Pavillion, Sandforth Court, Off Queens Drive, Liverpool L13 0DQ. Tel: 051 228 7132.
Founded: 1925
President: J. Lucas
Chairman: B. Graham
Secretary: I. Mason, 46 Balmoral Road, Fairfield, Liverpool L6 8NF. Tel: 051 263 6688.
Fixtures Secretary: G. Lloyd, 39 Glenbank Close, Liverpool L9 2BR. Tel: 051 525 1491.
Club captain (1987–88): P. Walsh
Club captain (1988–89): J. Lloyd
No. of teams: Senior 3
Directions to Ground: We are in the process of getting a new ground.
Colours: Navy/sky blue hoops. (*Change colours:* Maroon)
Floodlights: No
Membership: £20
Local newspaper: Liverpool Echo
League: NW West 1
Final position (1987–88): 2nd
Playing record (1987–88): P 40, W 32, L 7, D 1, F 691, A 268.
Competitions won: Hoylake 15 a side competition, Rockferry 15 a side competition.

ORMSKIRK

Green Lane, Ormskirk. Tel: 0695 27523
Founded: 1926
Secretary: R. Porter, 51 Rivington Drive, Burscough, Ormskirk, Lancs L40 7RN. Tel: 0704 892653 (H) or 0695 24234 (W)
League: NW West 1
Final position (1987–88): 3rd

OLD PARKONIANS

Holm Lane, Oxton, Birkenhead. Tel: 051 652 3105
Founded: 1928
Secretary: J.S. Jackson, 8 Morris Court, Bidston Road, Oxton, Merseyside L43 6XG. Tel: 051 652 9813 (H)
League: NW West 1
Final position (1987–88): 4th

DOUGLAS (I.O.M.)

Club House, Port-e-Chee, Meadows, Douglas. Tel: 0624 76493
Founded: 1949
Secretary: P.E. Garrett, 15 St. Georges Street, Douglas, I.O.M. Tel: 0524 29037 (H) or 0624 24535 (W)
League: NW West 1
Final position (1987–88): 5th

ASPULL

Woodshaw Park, Woods Road, Aspull, Wigan. Tel: 0942 831611
Founded: 1947

NW West 1

Secretary: K. Gretton, 7 Fieldbrook Walk, Westhoughton, Bolton, Lancs. Tel: Bolton 696551 (Bolton)
League: NW West 1
Final position (1987–88): 6th

ST EDWARDS OLD BOYS

St Edwards College, Sandfield Park, West Derby, Liverpool. Tel: 051-228-1414.
Founded: 1950
Chairman: F.N. Nelson
Coach: N. Melville
Secretary: D. Phoenix, 11 Linden Drive, Huyton, Merseyside L36 5TT. Tel: 051-489-1221.
Fixtures Secretary: R. Reilly, 130 Quarry Street, Woolton L25 6HQ.
Club captain (1987–88): P. Falconer
Club captain (1988–89): P. Falconer
No. of teams: Senior 4
Directions to Ground: From "Jolly Miller" on Queens Drive down Mill Lane turn right at playing field into Eaton Road. Further 300 yards right along Sandfield Park Road alongside Walkers playing fields, Club & School 200 yards up.
Colours: Blue, broad yellow horizontal stripe.
Floodlights: Yes training – not playing.
Membership: £18
Local newspaper: Liverpool Echo
League: NW West 1
Final position (1987–88): 7th
Playing record (1987–88): P 28, W 16, L 12, F 452, A 382.

BIRCHFIELD

Moor Lane, Witton, Birmingham. Tel: 356 2142
Founded: 1957
Secretary: J. Wingate, Flat 3, 7 Rotton Park Road, Edgbaston, Birmingham B16 9JH. Tel: 021 454 1388 (H) or 841 1411 (W)
League: NW West 1

EAGLE

Thornton Road, Gt. Sankey, Warrington. Tel: 0925-32926.
Founded: 1962
President: B. Morris
Chairman: D. Atten
Coach: V. Sandwell
Secretary: J. Lasko, 3 Colville Grove, Sale, Cheshire M33 4FW. Tel: 061-969-7808.
Fixtures Secretary: B. Lawton, 9 Mullion Grove, Padgate, Warrington. Tel: 0925-811639.
Club captain (1987–88): V. Sandwell
Club captain (1988–89): V. Sandwell
No. of teams: Senior 4
Directions to Ground: Follow A562 from Warrington towards Widnes turn left at Lane Ends traffic lights.
Colours: Black and white. (*Change colours:* Green)
Floodlights: No
Membership: £16
Local newspaper: Warrington Guardian
League: N.W. West 2
Final position (1987–88): 8th in N.W. West 1
Playing record (1987–88): P 37, W 21, L 16, D 0, F 453, A 457.

OLDERSHAW

Belvedere Road, Wallasey. Tel: 051 638 4379
Founded: 1924
Secretary: G.A. Webster, 96 Rullerton Road, Wallasey, Wirral. Tel: 051 638 2053 (H) or 051 236 6066 (W)
League: NW West 1
Final position (1987–88): 9th

OLD ANSELMIANS

Malone Field, Village Road, Eastham, Wirral. Tel: 051 327 1613
Founded: 1947
Secretary: M. Quail, 8 Elm Road, Prenton, Birkenhead, Merseyside L42 9NY. Tel: 051 608 5492 (H) or 051 647 9821 (W)
League: NW West 1
Final position (1987–88): 11th (bottom, relegated)

NW WEST 2

OLD INSTONIANS

The Pavilion, The Fender, Woodchurch Road, Penton
Founded: 1935
Secretary: C.G. Williams, Ivy Cottage, Little Storeton Lane, Wirral, Merseyside. Tel: 051 608 3396 (H) or 653 5858 (W)
League: NW West 2
Final position (1987–88): 1st (promoted)
Competitions won: NW West 2 1987–88

RUSKIN PARK

Ruskin Drive, St. Helens, Lancs. Tel: 0744 22893.
Founded: 1954
President: John Dootson
Chairman: Brian Forsyth
Coach: E. Halton
Secretary: J.P. Middlehurst, 10 Upholland Road, Billinge, Wigan, Lancs. Tel: 0744 892114.
Fixtures Secretary: G. Bath, 14 Orville Street, St. Helens. Tel: 0744 815719.
No. of teams: Senior 4
Directions to Ground: Pilkington Recreation Ground, Dentons Green, St. Helens, 1 mile from A580 and Junct. A570.
Ground capacity: Sports Ground (unlimited). Stand, 50 (All Standing).
Clubhouse: Pavillion/games/function room/changing facilities. Exceptionally high standard.
Colours: Blue black white hoops.
Nickname: Ruskin
Floodlights: No
Membership: Company employee £3, Outside £15.
Programme: (Editor: Rugby Management/used cup games only)
Local newspaper: St Helens Reporter/Star
League: NW West 2
Final position (1987–88): West Div. 2 Runners Up
Competitions won: Chester Vets Competition 24/April 88.

VULCAN

The Sportsground, Off Wargrave Road, Newton-Le-Willows, Merseyside. Tel: 09252 4180.
Founded: 1956
President: No such position
Chairman: Dave Ashton
Secretary: A.D. Stockton, 58 Westover Road, Padgate, Cheshire WA1 3JP.
Fixtures Secretary: J. Bajer, 5 Heylock Close, Newton-Le-Willows, Merseyside. Tel: 09252 6533.
Club captain (1987–88): R. Brown
Club captain (1988–89): M. Hayes
No. of teams: Senior 4
Directions to Ground: Junction 23 M6 (A580 interchange) to Newton-Le-Willows. 1 mile to small roundabout at Oak Tree Public House after ½ mile turn left into Victoria Road proceed under Railway Bridge and continue to the Wargrave Public House. Turn left into Sports Ground opposite pub.
Ground capacity: Unrestricted
Colours: Black and amber. (*Change colours:* Red)
Floodlights: No
Membership: £8.50 p.a.
Local newspaper: Newton & Golborne News (Warrington Guardian Series)
League: NW West 2
Final position (1987–88): 3rd

SEFTON

Thornmead Lane, Layfield Road, West Derby, Liverpool 12. Tel: 051 228 9092
Founded: 1907
Secretary: T.J. Beggs, 38 Plattsville Road, Mossley Hill, Liverpool LT8 0HZ. Tel: 051 722 6986 (H) or 051 546 2961 (W)
League: NW West 2
Final position (1987–88): 4th
Playing record (1987–88): P 37, W 16, D 1, L 22, F 469, A 555

HIGHTOWN

Sandy Lane, Hightown, Merseyside. Tel: 051 929 2769
Founded: 1921
Secretary: L. Crawford, 2 The Nurseries, Formby, Merseyside L37 4JG. Tel: 07048 79159 (H) or 0836 510880 (W)
League: NW West 2
Final position (1987–88): 5th

S. LIVERPOOL

Speke Hall Avenue, Speke, Liverpool. Tel: 051 486 2991
Founded: 1963
Secretary: J.B. McPoland, 15 Faringdon Close, Hunts Cross, Liverpool L25 9PX. Tel: 051 486 6445 (H) or 051 427 8331 (W)
League: NW West 2
Final position (1987–88): 6th

PORT SUNLIGHT

Leverhulme Playing Fields, Green Lane, Bromborough. Tel: 051334 3677
Founded: 1908
Secretary: T. Bennion, 12 Grasville Road, Higher Tranmere, Wirra LH2 5PU. Tel: 051 645 9548 (H)
League: NW West 2
Final position (1987–88): 7th

CHESTER COLLEGE

Cheyney Road, Chester CH1 4BJ. Tel: 0244 375444.
Founded: 1889
President: P.E. Grinter
Secretary: P.E. Grinter, The College, Cheyney Road, Chester. Tel: 0244 35091 (H) 0244 375444 (W).
Fixtures Secretary: A. Proctor, The College, Chester.
Club captain (1987–88): R. Thomas
Club captain (1988–89): S. Robertson
No. of teams: Senior 2.
Directions to Ground: Signposted from Chester Northgate Roundabout.
Colours: White/green/black. (*Change colours:* green)
Local newspapers: Chester Chronicle, Cheshire Observer.
League: North West 2
Final position (1987–88): 7th

ST MARY'S O.B.

17 Moore Lane, Crosby, Liverpool 23. Tel: 051 924 1774.
Chairman: James McInerney
Coach: Bernard Gavan
Secretary: Mark Cunningham, 48 Cambridge Avenue, Crosby L23 7XW. Tel: 051 924 5201.
Fixtures Secretary: John Baker, 21 Water Street, Liverpool 23. Tel: 051 924 5090.
Club captain (1987–88): Bernard Gavan
Club captain (1988–89): Bernard Gavan
No. of teams: Senior 3. Youth & Minis 1.
Directions to Ground: A 565 Liverpool to Southport Road. Signs Crosby and High Town.
Clubhouse: Open all week.
Colours: Maroon, blue, yellow hoops. (*Change colours:* White).
Floodlights: Yes
Membership: £12
Local newspaper: Crosby Herald
League: NW West 2
Final position (1987–88): 9th

MOORE

Moss Lane, Moore, Nr. Warrington. Tel: (092574) 473.
Founded: 1968
Chairman: M.W. Butler
Coach: P. Moran
Secretary: J. Horton, 4 Selworthy Drive, Thelwall, Warrington. Tel: 0925 65625.
Fixtures Secretary: R. Johnson, 53 Shepperton Close, Appleton, Warrington. Tel: 0925 604191.
Club captain (1987–88): S. Craven
Club captain (1988–89): S. Woollacott
No. of teams: Senior 3
Directions to Ground: M56, Junction 11, A56 towards Warrington, follow signs for Moore, turn off main road in village, into Moss Lane.
Clubhouse: Usual facilities.
Colours: Black & amber. (*Change colours:* Red)
Floodlights: No
Membership: £7
Local newspaper: Warrington Guardian
League: NW West 2
Final position (1987–88): 10th (relegated)
Playing record (1987–88): P 36, W 6, D 2, L 28.

WALLASEY

Cross Lane, Leasowe Road, Wallasey, Merseyside. Tel: 051 638 1486.
Founded: 1926
President: Hedley Rees
Coach: Mike Chatham
Secretary: John Burton, 14 Seaview Lane, Irby, Wirral, Merseyside. Tel: 051 648 4341 (H), 061 236 3707 (W).

NW West 2

Fixtures Secretary: Andy Rae, 8 Inchcape Road, Wallasey. Tel: 051 638 6903.
Club captain (1987–88): Eddy Raftery
Club captain (1988–89): Neil McEwan
No. of teams: Senior 5, Youth & Minis 2
Directions to Ground: From M53 Junction 1 (Bidston Flyover) take Spur Road to New Brighton/Wallasey take 2nd exit road & turn right at traffic lights into Cross Lane.
Colours: Red black white hoops.
Floodlights: Yes training only.
Membership: £25 pa
Local newspaper: Wallasey News
League: North West West 3
Final position (1987–88): (West 2 bottom)
Playing record (1987–88): Censored but expect to do better in 1988–89.

NW WEST 3

HALTON

League: NW West 3
Final position (1987–88): 1st
Competitions won: NW West 3

OLD ROCKFERRIANS

The Pavilion, Prenton Dell Road, Prenton, Birkenhead. Tel: 051 608 1501
Founded: 1928
Secretary: B.P. Meehan, 11 Kings Drive, Irby, Wirral, Merseyside. Tel: 051 648 5695 (H). 051 645 6917 (W)
League: NW West 3
Final position (1987–88): 2nd

HELSBY

Bicc Athletic and Social Club, Chester Road, Helsby. Tel: Helsby 2553.
Founded: 1962–3
President: R. Highcock
Chairman: J. Gregory
Coach: M. Buck
Secretary: E. Lamb, 41 Brackendale, Elton, Cheshire. Tel: Helsby 4039.
Fixtures Secretary: P. Ashton. Tel: Helsby 4416.
Club captain (1987–88): D. Orme
Club captain (1988–89): P. Ashton
No. of teams: Senior 3.
Clubhouse: Athletic and Social Club (Private Membership)
Colours: Black/Amber Hoops. (*Change colours:* All black strip).
Floodlights: No
Membership: £10 includes Social Club Membership.
Local newspaper: Chester Chronicle, Runcorn Weekly News
League: NW 3
Final position (1987–88): 3rd

MOSSLEY HILL

PO Box 9, Mossley Hill Road, Liverpool L18 8DX. Tel: 051 724 4377.
Founded: 1986
Chairman: John Parr
Secretary: Keith Spencer, 82 Stevenson Street, Wavertree, Liverpool L15 4HB.
Fixtures Secretary: Secretary
Club captain (1987–88): Simon Edge
Club captain (1988–89): Simon Edge
No. of teams: Senior 3
Directions to Ground: 2½ miles south from end of M62 Motorway – signposted for Mossley Hill Station closeby.
Clubhouse: Multi Sports Facility
Colours: Maroon/gold quarters. (*Change colours:* Red/black/blue stripes)
Floodlights: No
Membership: £24
Local newspaper: Liverpool Echo
League: NW West 3
Final position (1987–88): Joint 3rd
Playing record (1987–88): P 36, W 21, D 3, L 12, F 463, A 341.

SHELL (STANLOW)

Chester Road, Whitby, Ellesmere Port, Cheshire. Tel: 051 355 2704.
Founded: 1948
Chairman: E. Kilshaw
Coach: R. Edwards
Secretary: G. Pugh, 23 Vale Road, Ellermere Port, Cheshire. Tel: 051 355 5795.
Fixtures Secretary: N. Marrs. Tel: 0606 853010.
Club captain (1987–88): S. Lundstrum
Club captain (1988–89): S. Lundstrum
No. of teams: Senior 4
Clubhouse: Social Club
Colours: Amber. (*Change colours:* Blue)
Floodlights: No
Local newspaper: Ellesmere Port Pioneer
League: NW West 3
Final position (1987–88): 5th
Playing record (1987–88): P 36, W 20, L 13, D 3.

HOYLAKE

Melrose Avenue
Founded: 1922
Secretary: A. Warren, 8 Redhouse Bank, West Kirkby, Wirral, L48 5EH. Tel: 051 625 2178 (H). 051 236 2616 (W)
Fixtures Secretary: G. Guest, 8 School Lane, Meols, Wirral. Tel: 051 632 2794
League: NW West 3
Final position (1987–88): 6th

PRESCOT

Victoria Terrace, Rainhill, Nr. Prescot. Tel: 051 426 2805
Founded: 1949
Secretary: M.S. Hughes,, 12 Grebe Avenue, Eccleston Park, St. Helens, Merseyside. Tel: 0744 56452 (H). 061 998 7919 (W)
League: NW West 3
Final position (1987–88): 7th

WIGAN COLLEGE TECHNOLOGY

Christopher Park, Wigan Lower Road, Standish Lower Ground, Wigan. Tel: 0942 41140.
Founded: 1925
President: Terry Sweeny
Chairman: John Grimes
Coach: Jack Dewhurst
Secretary: Ian Parker, 5 Bengairn Close, Wigan WN1 3YW. Tel: 0942 493902.

NW West 3

Fixtures Secretary: Neil Smith, c/o Smith & Grimes Engineering, Brook Lane, Orrell. Tel: 0942 213084 Daytime.
Club captain (1987–88): Ian Smith
Club captain (1988–89): Neil Smith
No. of teams: Senior 2
Directions to Ground: Follow B5375 Woodhouse Lane, out of Wigan, cont. through junction with Scot Road, onto Wigan Lower Road. Christopher Park is ½ mile along on right, next to new houses.
Clubhouse: Bird In Hand Public House, Gidlow Lane, Wigan.
Colours: Black. (*Change colours:* Black red white irregular hoops)
Floodlights: No
Membership: £5
Local newspaper: Lancashire Evening Post
League: NW West 3
Final position (1987–88): 8th
Playing record (1987–88): P 32, W 18, L 12, D 2.

AGECROFT

Littleton Road, Playing Fields, Salford 7
Secretary: A. Price, 17 Kerrier Close, Eccles, Manchester. Tel: 788 9907
League: NW West 3
Final position (1987–88): 9th

BURTONWOOD

Firtree Lane, Burtonwood, Cheshire. Tel: 09252 4480
Founded: 1964
Secretary: D. Cheney, 4 Melrose Avenue, Burtonwood, Cheshire, WA5 4LZ. Tel: 09252 3717
League: NW West 3
Final position (1987–88): 10th (bottom)

NORTH EAST LEAGUES

THE two senior North East Leagues – 1 and 2 – provided some stiff competition with Wharfedale from Division 1 moving upwards along with Rotherham, whilst Novocastrains and Stockton move up from Division 2 replacing Ripon – no wins in 10 matches – and Blaydon, whose points difference was inferior to those of Keighley and Westoe.

The strugglers in Division 2 were Barnsley, who descend into the Yorkshire league, with the unfortunate Newcastle University, also through an inferior points difference, moving down into the Durham-Northumberland league. Roundhegians from Yorkshire 1 and Blyth from Durham–Northumberland 1 are their replacements, the former having won all their 10 games with a total points score from their team of 256.

Other unbeaten teams were Bridlington in Yorkshire 3, Halifax Vandals (100% in Yorkshire 5), Sheffield Oaks (a perfect record in Yorkshire 6 and an astonishing 293 points from nine matches), Whitby (winners of all their nine games in Durham–Northumberland 3) and Wensleydale (who scored 176 points in winning all their seven Durham–Northumberland 4 matches).

The traumas of Armthorpe are reported elsewhere, but they epitomised the spirit of the new leagues by playing all their fixtures in spite of their lack of success.

TABLES 1987–88

NORTH EAST 1

	P	W	D	L	F	A	Pts
Wharfdale	10	9	0	1	140	55	18
Rotherham	10	8	0	2	173	52	16
Gateshead Fell	10	7	0	3	122	79	14
O Crossleyans	10	6	1	3	143	105	13
Morpeth	10	6	0	4	90	84	12
Thornesians	10	6	0	4	115	117	12
O Broadleians	10	3	1	6	88	126	7
Westoe	10	3	0	7	98	139	6
Keighley	10	3	0	7	65	118	6
Blaydon	10	3	0	7	107	177	6
Ripon	10	0	0	10	74	163	0

NORTH EAST 2

	P	W	D	L	F	A	Pts
Novocastrians	10	9	1	0	137	72	19
Stockton	10	9	0	1	190	76	18
Pontefract	10	6	1	3	146	144	13
O Hymerians	10	6	0	4	104	95	12
Beverley	10	5	0	5	144	85	10
Selby	10	4	0	6	86	78	8
York	10	4	0	6	105	112	8
Ryton	10	3	0	7	91	134	6
Pocklington	10	3	0	7	94	157	6
Newcastle Univ	10	3	0	7	123	191	6
Barnsley	10	2	0	8	82	158	4

YORKSHIRE 1

	P	W	D	L	F	A	Pts
Roundhegians	10	10	0	0	256	72	20
Bramley	10	8	1	1	193	71	17
Hemsworth	10	7	1	2	169	80	15
W Pk Bramhope	10	5	1	4	135	99	11
Driffield	10	4	1	5	143	111	9
Goole	10	4	0	6	76	115	8
Castleford	10	4	0	6	123	193	8
Cleckheaton	10	4	0	6	81	162	8
Moortown	10	4	0	6	57	147	8
York Rl	10	2	0	8	95	169	4
Scarborough	10	1	0	9	49	158	2

YORKSHIRE 2

	P	W	D	L	F	A	Pts
N Ribblesdale	10	9	0	1	152	70	18
Huddersfield YMCA	10	7	0	3	196	81	14
Doncaster	10	7	0	3	171	74	14
Wheatley Hills	10	7	0	3	174	84	14
Wath	10	6	2	2	122	69	14
Malton & Norton	10	4	1	5	97	91	9
Ilkley	10	4	1	5	84	140	9
Sheffield Tigers	10	3	0	7	62	122	6
Ionians	10	3	0	7	114	205	6
O.Otliensians	10	2	1	7	80	130	5
Leodiensians	10	0	1	9	31	217	1

YORKSHIRE 3

	P	W	D	L	F	A	Pts
Bridlington	10	9	1	0	245	38	19
Marist	10	7	0	3	151	95	14
Basildon	10	6	0	4	143	109	12
Knottingley	10	5	1	4	72	50	11
Heath	10	5	0	5	82	166	10
Leeds CSSA	10	4	1	5	97	121	9
Airebronians	10	4	1	5	114	142	9
Yarnbury	10	3	1	6	107	100	7
Rodillians	10	3	1	6	65	103	7
Bradford Salem	10	3	0	7	63	135	6
Northallerton	10	3	0	7	74	154	6

YORKSHIRE 4

	P	W	D	L	F	A	Pts
Wibsey	10	9	0	1	234	50	18
O Modernians	10	8	0	2	199	92	16
Dinnington	10	6	1	3	164	77	13
Hessle	10	6	1	3	141	81	13
West Leeds	10	6	0	4	139	87	12
Hullensians	10	4	1	5	89	106	9
Wetherby	10	3	1	6	85	168	7
Leeds YMCA	10	3	0	7	76	146	6
Yorkshire CW	10	3	0	7	85	208	6
Burley	10	3	0	7	62	189	6
Skipton	10	2	0	8	92	162	4

YORKSHIRE 5

	P	W	D	L	F	A	Pts
Halifax Vandals	10	10	0	0	196	35	20
O Rishworthians	10	8	0	2	233	52	16
Phoenix Pk	10	8	0	2	156	52	16
Leeds Corinthians	10	6	0	4	121	96	12
Ossett	10	6	0	4	144	133	12
BP Chemicals	10	4	0	6	89	133	8
Yorkshire Main	10	3	0	7	93	98	6
Hornsea	10	3	0	7	80	152	6
Rowntrees	10	3	0	7	83	164	6
Willernsea	10	3	0	7	71	182	6
Knaresborough	10	1	0	9	38	207	2

YORKSHIRE 6

	P	W	D	L	F	A	Pts
Sheffield Oaks	9	9	0	0	293	7	18
Bridon	10	9	0	1	304	34	18
De la Salle	10	7	1	2	176	83	15
Sheff Steels	10	6	0	4	115	98	12
Stocksbridge	10	5	0	5	83	121	10
Granville Coll	10	5	0	5	99	169	10
Sheff Medicals	9	4	0	5	173	85	8
Adwick	10	3	1	6	143	171	7
Markham	10	3	9	7	73	128	6
Maltby OB	10	2	0	8	95	272	4
Armthorpe R	10	0	0	10	52	438	0

DURHAM/NORTHUMBERLAND 1

	P	W	D	L	F	A	Pts
Blyth	10	8	0	2	138	99	16
Rockcliff	10	6	1	3	70	74	13
Ponteland	10	6	0	4	95	13	12
Ashington	10	5	1	4	117	96	11
Darlington	10	5	1	4	91	74	11
Seghill	10	5	1	4	100	89	11
Acklam	10	4	2	4	105	62	10
Redcar	10	4	1	5	118	84	9
Horden	10	4	1	5	129	124	9
Winlaton	10	3	0	7	74	132	6
Percy Pk	10	0	2	8	60	150	2

DURHAM/NORTHUMBERLAND 2

	P	W	D	L	F	A	Pts
Mowden Pk	10	9	0	1	259	60	18
Hartlepool	10	9	0	1	196	81	18
Bishop Auckland	10	8	0	2	245	87	16
Sunderland	10	5	1	4	160	117	11
Consett	10	5	1	4	109	122	11
Seaham	10	4	2	4	158	109	10
Wallsend	10	3	2	5	128	146	8
Medicals	10	3	0	7	83	139	6
N Durham	10	3	0	7	80	162	6
Hartlepool BBOB	10	3	0	7	105	247	6
Houghton	10	0	0	10	46	299	0

DURHAM/NORTHUMBERLAND 3

	P	W	D	L	F	A	Pts
Whitby	9	9	0	0	256	56	18
Billingham	9	7	0	2	159	78	14
Guisborough	9	6	0	3	100	58	12
Seaton Carew	9	4	0	5	96	99	8
Wearside	9	4	0	5	85	112	8
Chester-le-Street	9	4	0	5	71	120	8
Darlington RA	9	3	1	5	94	75	7
N Shields	9	3	1	5	117	143	7
Hartlepool TDS OB	9	3	0	6	59	113	6
Washington	9	1	0	8	51	234	2

DURHAM/NORTHUMBERLAND 5

	P	W	D	L	F	A	Pts
Wensleydale	7	7	0	0	176	21	16
Prudhoe	8	7	0	1	113	84	14
S Tyneside Coll	7	5	0	2	183	65	10
Barnard Castle	7	4	0	3	113	88	10
Richmondshire	8	3	1	4	94	65	7
Jarrovians	8	3	0	5	87	105	6
C Serv Durham	8	2	0	6	54	244	4
Newton Aycliffe*	7	0	1	6	31	109	3

**2 points awarded*

NORTH EAST 1

WHARFEDALE

Wharfeside Avenue, Threshfield, Skipton, N. Yorks.
Founded: 1923
President: J.S. Spencer
Chairman: F.W. House
Coach: M. Wright
Secretary: P.W. Hartley, 46 Shortbank Road, Skipton, N. Yorks. Tel: 0756-4929.
Fixtures Secretary: M. Harrison, Oldhall Farm, Threshfield, Skipton, N. Yorks. Tel: 0756-752777.
Club captain (1987–88): L. Ingham
Club captain (1988–89): L. Ingham
No. of teams: Senior 4, Youth & Minis 7
Ground capacity: 1000 approx.
Colours: Green. (*Change colours:* Maroon)
Floodlights: Yes
Admission: £1.00
Membership: £10.00
Programme: Free with admission fee (Editor: P.W. Hartley)
Local newspaper: Craven Herald & Pioneer, Yorkshire Post.
League: North East 1
Final position (1987–88): Champions
Playing record (1987–88): P 36, W 28, D 1, L 7, F 628. A 267.
Competitions won: Champions North East Div. 1 1987/88.

ROTHERHAM

Clifton Lane, Rotherham. Tel: (0709) 370763.
Founded: 1923
President: J. Clark
Chairman: P. Hind
Coach: B. Forster
Secretary: J.W. Clay, 66 Warren Road, Wickersley, Rotherham. Tel: (0709) 549111.
Fixtures Secretary: A. Williams, 116 Grange Road, Rotherham. Tel: (0709) 364190.
Club captain (1987–88): S. Cousins
Club captain (1988–89): R. Selkirk
No. of teams: Senior 4, Youth & Minis 8
Directions to Ground: Leave M1

Ground capacity: 1000
Clubhouse: V. Good
Colours: Maroon & sky hoops
Floodlights: Yes
Admission: 50p (£1 League)
Membership: £15 playing
Programme: 25p (Editor: M. Salter)
Local newspaper: Rotherham
League: North East 1
Final position (1987–88): 2nd
Playing record (1987–88): P 34, W 27, D 0, L 7.

GATESHEAD FELL

Hedley Lawson Park, Eastwood Gardens, Gateshead NE9 5UB. Tel: 091-4875739.
Founded: 1907
President: W.R. Johnston
Chairman: I. Willis
Coach: A. Thompson
Secretary: J. McMillan, 95 Kells Lane, Gateshead NE9 5XX. Tel: 091-4870355.
Fixtures Secretary: Dr W.L. Hetherington, 97 Kells Lane, Gateshead NE9 5XX. Tel: 091-4879128.
Club captain (1987–88): R.W. Ward
Club captain (1988–89): R.W. Ward
No. of teams: Senior 4, Youth & Minis 2
Directions to Ground: From South aim A69 to A6127 to Gateshead turn right into Keus Lane/Dryden Road. (Eastwood Gdns runs parallel & East Dryden Road)
Ground capacity: 2000. Stand, 350
Clubhouse: Lounge & bar, bar & functions hall, committee room & cellar.
Colours: Dark blue & light blue (narrow rings). (*Change colours:* Red)
Nickname: "Fell"
Floodlights: Yes training only
Membership: £12.00
Programme: 10 pages, 3 articles, 1 page club officials, rest–adverts.
Local newspaper: The Journal, Evening Chronicle
League: North East 1
Final position (1987–88): 3rd
Playing record (1987–88): P 38, W 27, D 2, L 9, F 653, A 333.
Competitions won: J&B Journal Trophy – Division 1 April 1988.

OLD CROSSLEYANS

Standeven House, Broomfield Avenue, Saville Park, Halifax. Tel: 0422 63000
Founded: 1923
Secretary: J. Broadbent, Thistledom Old Lane, Ripponden, Halifax. Tel: 0422 822224 (H) or 0422 54186 (W)
Fixtures Secretary: K. Davies, 23 School Close, Ripponden, Halifax. Tel: 0422 823662
League: North East 1
Final position (1987–88): 4th
Playing record (1987–88): P 32, W 21, D 2, L 9, F 530, A 307

MORPETH

Grange House Field, Mitford Road, Morpeth NE61 1RJ.
Founded: 1947
President: D. Pringle
Chairman: H. Kennedy
Coach: W. Hewitt
Secretary: K. Fraser, Solway House, De Merley Road, Morpeth NE61 1HZ. Tel: 0670 511208.
Fixtures Secretary: W. Hewitt, The Birches, Lane Head Farm, Felton.
Club captain (1987–88): Andy Brown
Club captain (1988–89): Ian Pledger
No. of teams: Senior 6. Youth & Minis 10.
Directions to Ground: From Newcastle through Town Centre travelling north. Left onto Nutford road after telephone exchange. Club on right after school entrance.
Clubhouse: Clubroom, cocktail bar, 2 squash courts, kitchen.
Colours: Scarlet and white hoops. (*Change colours:* Blue).
Floodlights: No
Membership: £25
Programme: Free. (Editor: M. Barry)
Local newspaper: Newcastle Journal, Morpeth Herald and Gazette.
League: North East 1
Final position (1987–88): 5th
Playing record (1987–88): P 39, W 22, D 2, L 15. F 553, A 447.

THORNENSIANS

The Clubhouse, Coulman Street, Thorne. Tel: 0405 812746
Founded: 1939
Secretary: W. Mellors, 65 Kirton Lane, Thorne, Doncaster, Yorks. Tel: 0405 812836 (H)
League: North East 1
Final position (1987–88): 6th
Playing record (1987–88): P 34, W 18, D 1, L 15, F 429, A 422

OLD BRODLEIANS

Woodhead Park, Denholmegate Road, Hipperholme, Halifax, West Yorkshire HX6 37G. Tel: 0422-202708.
Founded: 1930
President: D.A. Robertshaw
Chairman: B.C. Young
Coach: To be appointed
Secretary: G. Pearson, 203 Wakefield Road, Lightcliffe, Halifax, West Yorkshire. Tel: 0422-206266.
Fixtures Secretary: P.R. Sugden, 112 Woodhouse Lane, Brighouse, West Yorkshire. Tel: 0484-721860.
Club captain (1987–88): A.J. Shippin
Club captain (1988–89): J. Murphy
No. of teams: Senior 6, Youth & Minis 11
Directions to Ground: Junction 26 M62, A58 to Halifax (4 miles turn right on Keighley Road at Hipperholme traffic lights. Club ½ mile on left.)
Ground capacity: 3000. Stand, 100

Clubhouse: Bar, catering facilities, large lounge, dancing area, 8 changing rooms & multi-gym.
Colours: Black shirts with red & white hoops. (*Change colours:* All red or all light blue)
Nickname: "Brods"
Floodlights: No
Admission: £1
Membership: £15
Programme: 50p (Editor: B.M. Deadman)
Local newspaper: Halifax Courier & Brighouse Echo.
League: North East 1
Final position (1987–88): 7th
Playing record (1987–88): P 39, W 18, D 3, L 18.
Competitions won: "Calderdale" annual sevens tournament 1968 & 1981.

WESTOE

Green Road, South Shields. Tel: 091 4561506
Founded: 1875
Secretary: J.R. Wells, 240 Mowbray Road, South Shields. Tel: 091 4552260 (H) or 091 456003 (W)
Fixtures Secretary: R.A. Mills, 146 King George Road, South Shields, Tyne & Wear. Tel: 091 4553090
League: North East 1
Final position (1987–88): 8th
Playing record (1987–88): P 35, W 12, D 1, L 22, F 413, A 653

KEIGHLEY

Skipton Road, Otley, Keighley. Tel: 0535 602174
Founded: 1919
Secretary: M.T. Greaves, 24 Devonshire Street, Keighley, W. Yorks BD21 2BD. Tel: 0535 53192 (H) or 0535 605646 (W)
Fixtures Secretary: J. Midgley, 21 Woodville Road, Keighley. Tel: 0535 602414 or 0535 605311 (W)
League: North East 1
Final position (1987–88): 9th
Playing record (1987–88): P 37, W 14, D 3, L 20, F 430, A 437

BLAYDON

Crowtrees, Hexham Road, Swalwell, Newcastle-upon-Tyne NE16 3BM. Tel: 091 414 2528
Founded: 1888
Secretary: T.N. Brown, 5 The Avenue, Axwell Park, Blaydon-on-Tyne, Tyne & Wear NE21 5ND. Tel: 091 4143698 (H) or 091 2683838 (W)
Fixtures Secretary: J.M. Huxley, The Mount, Sunniside, Newcastle-upon-Tyne. Tel: 091 488 7280
League: North East 1
Final position (1987–88): 10th
Playing record (1987–88): P 37, W 15, D 4, L 18, F 447, A 503

RIPON

Mallorie Park Drive, Ripon, N. Yorks. Tel: 4675.
President: F.M. Metcalfe
Chairman: H.W. Proud
Coach: J. Horsell
Secretary: K.L. Green, Byland House, Copt. Hewick, Ripon. Tel: 3443.
Fixtures Secretary: H.W. Proud, Lurebank Terrace, Ripon. Tel: 5474.
Club captain (1987–88): J. Platt
Club captain (1988–89): H. Renshaw
No. of teams: Senior 4, Youth & Minis 3
Colours: Blue & white hoops. (*Change colours:* Green & white hoops)
Floodlights: No
Membership: Playing £16, Non playing £10.
Programme: 20p (Editor: L.S. Couldwell)
Local newspaper: Ripon Gazette
League: NE1
Final position (1987–88): Bottom (relegated)
Playing record (1987–88): P 39, W 10, D 3, L 26, F 349, A 506.
Competitions won: Yorkshire Shield Winners 1976–77.

NORTH EAST 2

NOVOCASTRIANS

Sutherland Park, The Drive, High Heaton, Newcastle Upon Tyne, NE7 7SY. Tel: 091-2661247.
Founded: 1899
President: G.R.L. Parkinson
Chairman: C. Magnay
Secretary: C.S. Lawson, 10 Westfield Drive, Newcastle Upon Tyne NE3 4XU. Tel: 091 2852630 (H).
Fixtures Secretary: R.J. Fay, 10 Lyndhurst Crescent, Gateshead, Tyne & Wear NE9 6BA. Tel: 091 4873393 (H).
Club captain (1987–88): J.A. Pollock
Club captain (1988–89): G. Ward
No. of teams: Senior 7, Youth & Minis 4
Directions to Ground: The ground is in the vicinity of the DHSS headquarters near the junction of the A191 and A188 (Four Lane Ends), and is approached up the drive which is off the A188 approx ¼ mile south of Four Lane Ends.
Clubhouse: Clubroom and bar, cocktail bar, spectators verandah.
Colours: Red, white and black hoops. (*Change colours:* Plain blue)
Nickname: Novos
Floodlights: Yes training lights
Membership: Playing £32.00, Non playing £10.00, Student £6.00.
Programme: (Editor: c/o The President)
Local newspaper: The (Newcastle) Journal, The Evening Chronicle
League: 1987–88 N.E.2
Final position (1987–88): Winners (promoted)
Playing record (1987–88): P 40, W 29, D 3, L 8.
Competitions won: Winners – N.E. League Div. II. Winners – Northumberland Fifth Team Cup.

STOCKTON

Station Road, Norton. Tel: 0642 554031
Founded: 1873
President: J.Y. Glover
Chairman: D. Trotter
Coach: J. Moore
Secretary: D. Chisman, 16 Dunettar Avenue, Eaglescliffe. Tel: 0642 781339.
Fixtures Secretary: B. Waller, 37 Albert Road, Eaglescliffe. Tel: 0642 780197.
No. of teams: Senior 4. Youth & Minis 8.
Directions to Ground: Off Junction Road Norton Cleveland.
Stand capacity: 200
Colours: Red. (*Change colours:* Blue).
Floodlights: No
Admission: £1
Membership: £5
Programme: 25p

Local newspaper: Evening Gazette
League: North East 2
Final position (1987–88): 2nd

PONTEFRACT

Moor Lane, Carleton, Pontefract. Tel: 0977 702650
Founded: 1947
Secretary: M.T. Izon, West Hill House, North Road, Wentbridge, Pontefract WF8 3JJ. Tel: 0977 620277 (H) or 702029 (W)
League: North East 2
Final position (1987–88): 3rd
Playing record (1987–88): P 34, W 20, D 3, L 11, F 486, A 406

OLD HYMERIANS

Haworth Court, Beverley High Road, Hull. Tel: 0482-802119.
Founded: 1925
Chairman: R.H. Gore
Coach: P.J.E. Wildsmith
Secretary: M.A. Harness, The Cottage, 48 George Street, Cottingham HU16 5QP. Tel: 0482-842138.
Fixtures Secretary: M. McDonald, 10 Chilton Rise, Kirkella HU10 7NA. Tel: 0482-657091.
Club captain (1987–88): M. Dye
Club captain (1988–89): A.J. Woods
No. of teams: Senior 4
Directions to Ground: A63 follow the signs for Ring road to Beverley High Road/Sutton Road traffic lights turn left 2nd road on the right – Emmott Road follow this road to this ground.
Ground capacity: Stand, 150.
Colours: Chocolate/gold. (*Change colours:* Navy)
Floodlights: Yes training only.
Membership: £16
Programme: £1 (Editor: R.P. Ashton)
Local newspaper: Hull Daily Mail
League: NE2
Final position (1987–88): 4th
Playing record (1987–88): P 34, W 22, L 12.

BEVERLEY

Beaver Park, Norwood, Beverley. Tel: 0482-870306.
President: F.J. Ankrett
Chairman: P. Cartwright
Coach: To be appointed
Secretary: A.J. Winter, 8 Old Road, Leconfield, Beverley. Tel: 0964-550411.
Fixtures Secretary: R. Jenner, 3 Spark Mill Terrace, Beverley. Tel: 0482-868944.
Club captain (1987–88): G.S. Hodgson
Club captain (1988–89): I. Marlow
No. of teams: Senior 4, Youth & Minis 3
Directions to Ground: Follow signs through Beverley for Hornsea. Ground on the left just before the railway crossing and behind Lady Le Gros Public House.
Colours: Brown green and white.
Nickname: The Beavers
Floodlights: No
Membership: £15
Local newspaper: Hull Daily Mail and Beverley Guardian
League: N.E.2
Final position (1987–88): 5th
Playing record (1987–88): P 37, W 23, D 0, L 14, F 623, A 307.
Competitions won: Yorkshire Silver Trophy 1974/75. Yorkshire Shield 1985/86. Humberside Cup 1983/4 and 1986/87.

SELBY

Sandhill Lane, Selby, N. Yorks. Tel: 0757 703608
Founded: 1933
Secretary: M.W.M. Blackwell, Top End House, Cliffe, Selby, N. Yorks. Tel: 0757 638666 (H) & (W)
League: North East 2
Final position (1987–88): 6th
Playing record (1987–88): P 34, W 13, D 2, L 19, F 503, A 465

YORK

Clifton Park, Shipton Road, York. Tel: 0904 23602
Founded: 1928
Secretary: B. McClure, 6 Alwyne Drive, York YO3 RS. Tel: 0904 32744 (H) or 0904 653022 (W)
League: North East 2
Final position (1987–88): 7th
Playing record (1987–88): P 36, W 22, D 1, L 15, F 533, A 389

RYTON

Emma Sports Complex, Barmoor, Ryton, Tyne & Wear. Tel: 091 4133820.
Founded: 1880
President: R.T. Thoburn
Chairman: R.J. Holmes
Coach: I. Nesbitt
Secretary: I. Graham, 5 Coronation Street, Crookhill, Ryton, Tyne & Wear NE40 3EW. Tel: 091 4137646.
Fixtures Secretary: S. Richards, 64 Leander Avenue, Chester-Le-Street, Co. Durham. Tel: 091 3889535.
Club captain (1987–88): W.J. Mordue
Club captain (1988–89): K. Dobson
No. of teams: Senior 4, Youth & Minis 2
Directions to Ground: Take A695 from A1M just after Birtley Service Station continue on through Blaydon Clubhouse on Main Road through Ryton.
Clubhouse: Bar, lounge, presidents room, games room, 11 changing rooms + bath + shower room.
Colours: Royal blue. (*Change colours:* Red)
Floodlights: No
Membership: £13 Playing member, £7 Full member, £2.50 Social member.
Programme: 25p (Editor: President)
Local newspaper: Newcastle Journal + Evening Chronicle
League: NE 2
Final position (1987–88): 8th
Playing record (1987–88): P 35, W 17, D 1, L 17, F 318, A 423.
Competitions won: 1927 Durham Senior Cup, 1985/86 4th Tuam Shield.

POCKLINGTON

Percy Road, Pocklington. Tel: 07592 3358
Founded: 1928
Secretary: M.B. Herring, 34 Hill Rise Drive, Market Weighton, York YO4 3JZ. Tel: 07592 3358
League: North East 2
Final position (1987–88): 9th
Playing record (1987–88): P 38, W 18, D 0, L 20, F 497, A 509

NEWCASTLE UNIVERSITY

University of Newcastle, Physical Education & Sports Department, Kings Walk, Newcastle-upon-Tyne. Tel: 2320323.
League: North East 2
Final position (1987–88): 10th

BARNSLEY

Wombwell Lane, Stairfoot, Barnsley. Tel: 0226 284344
Founded: 1902
Secretary: J. Reed, 79 Roehampton Rise, Ardsley, Barnsley, S. Yorks. Tel: 0226 284688
League: North East 2
Final position (1987–88): 11th (bottom)
Playing record (1987–88): P 33, W 15, D 2, L 16, F 342, A 373

YORKSHIRE 1

ROUNDHEGIANS

Chelwood Drive, Leeds 8. Tel: 0532-667377.
Founded: 1928
President: W.O. Boddy
Chairman: G. Read
Coach: A. Green
Secretary: A. Rowell, 43 West Park Road, Leeds 8. Tel: 0532-665906.
Fixtures Secretary: M.J. Fletcher, 15 Tynwald Mount, Leeds 17. Tel: 0532-687346.
Club captain (1987–88): P. Armstrong
Club captain (1988–89): P. Armstrong
No. of teams: Senior 5, Youth & Minis 4
Directions to Ground: From junction of Moortown Ring Road and A6 (Harrogate Road) turn towards city centre – at first traffic lights turn left onto Street Lane – Chelwood Drive ¾ mile on left.
Ground capacity: ? 2000
Clubhouse: 2 bars, sports hall, changing rooms, showers, baths etc.
Colours: Green, black & white. (*Change colours:* Red)
Nickname: Hegians
Floodlights: Yes for training
Admission: £1 for league & cup games
Membership: £10 Social + £6 rugby (£16 total).
Programme: Free team sheet with brief comment. (Editor: G. Read)
Local newspaper: Yorkshire Post, Skyrack Express
League: Yorkshire 1
Final position (1987–88): 1st (promoted)
Playing record (1987–88): P 37, W 30, L 7, F 757, A 312.
Competitions won: Yorkshire Cup 1957–58. Yorkshire Shield 1937–38 + 1982–83. Courage Championship Yorks. Div. 1 1987–88.

BRAMLEY

The Warrels, Grosmont Terrace, Warrels Road, Bramley, Leeds 13. Tel: 0532 577787.
Founded: 1921
Secretary: D.A. Nesham, 40 Water Lane, Farnley, Leeds 12. Tel: 0532 576208 (H). 0532 463795 (W).
League: Yorkshire 1
Final position (1987–88): 2nd
Playing record (1987–88): P 40, W 33, D 1, L 6. F 757, A 262.

HEMSWORTH

Lowfield Road, Hemsworth. Tel: 0977 610078.
Founded: 1961
President: Brian May
Chairman: Les Kemp
Coach: Grant Smith
Secretary: Mike Illingworth, 87 West Lane, Sharlston, Wakefield. Tel: 0924 862947.
Fixtures Secretary: Peter Turgoose, 27 Grange Avenue, S. Elmsall. Tel: 0977 47309.
Club captain (1987–88): Les Kemp
Club captain (1988–89): Mick Murgtagh
No. of teams: Senior 3
Directions to Ground: Turn right off Station Road into Lowfield Road and to end of housing estate, over railway bridge onto car park.
Ground capacity: 1500
Clubhouse: Changing and bar facilities
Colours: Navy blue. (*Change colours:* Red or red & white hoops)
Floodlights: No (soon)
Admission: £2
Membership: £20 (£5 rebate before Oct.)
Local newspaper: Hemsworth & South Elmsal Express
League: Yorkshire 1
Final position (1987–88): Third
Playing record (1987–88): P 35, W 24, D 2, L 9, F 591, A 273.

WEST PARK BRAMHOPE

The Sycamores, Bramhope, Leeds 16. Tel: 0532 671437.
Founded: 1959
President: M.J. Fisk
Chairman: J.W. Hadwin
Coach: P.J. Knowles
Secretary: W.W. Barrack, Lynholme, 15 Eastgate Close, Bramhope, Leeds LS16 9AA. Tel: 0532 842540.
Fixtures Secretary: M. Openshaw, 5 Victoria Grove, Horseforth, Leeds. Tel: 0532 587338.
Club captain (1987–88): B. Norcliffe
Club captain (1988–89): B. Norcliffe
No. of teams: Senior 4. Youth & Minis 9.
Directions to Ground: Take A660 out of Leeds towards Otley. After passing the Parkway Hotel on the right look for a Shell Filling Station on the left. One mile later turn left immediately in front of the filing station.
Stand capacity: 200
Clubhouse: 2 well appointed bars. Excellent changing facilities.
Colours: Black with gold band. (*Change colours:* Gold)
Floodlights: No
Admission: £1 (League and Cup games only)
Membership: £18
Programme: 20p (Editor: R. Gibson)
Local newspaper: Wharfedale & Airedale Observer
League: Yorkshire 1
Final position (1987–88): 4th
Playing record (1987–88): P 33, W 20, D 1, L 12, F 424, A 180.
Competitions won: Pocklington Sevens 1988; Sheffied Tigers Sevens 1988.

DRIFFIELD

The Clubhouse, Kelley Thorpe, Driffield, E. Yorks. Tel(0377-46598. (Address for correspondence)
Founded: 1925
President: John 'J.U.' Burdass
Chairman: P.R.B. 'Pip' Megginson
Coach: Roger Iveson
Secretary: Ross Weekes, 8 Kings Mill Road, Driffield, E. Yorks YO25 7TT. Tel: 0377-43832 (H), 0377-43631 (W).
Fixtures Secretary: John Harrison, 9 Parsonage Close, Nafferton, Driffield, E. Yorks. Tel: 0377-43032 (H), 0377-43631 (W).
Club captain (1987–88): Ali(stair) Brumfield

Club captain (1988–89): Charlie Burdass
No. of teams: Senior 4, Youth & Minis 2
Directions to Ground: From south west (A163) clubhouse on first roundabout after El Alamein Army Camp. From north & east follow signs for A163 clubhouse on 3rd roundabout. From south (A164) follow signs for A163 clubhouse on right – unmistakeably. From west (A166) follow signs for A163 clubhouse on 2nd roundabout.
Ground capacity: Hundreds. Stand, Not just yet.
Clubhouse: Large, well furbished, numerous changing rooms, dance area, 2 bars, 1 V. large.
Colours: Black, white & blue hoops. (*Change colours:* Yellow or red)
Floodlights: Yes
Admission: Negotiable
Membership: £20 p.a. Senior players. £12 Non players.
Programme: Variable. (Editor: See Sec./Press Officer.
Local newspaper: Driffield Times – gives much generous coverage to DRUFC
League: Yorkshire 1
Final position (1987–88): 5th
Playing record (1987–88): P 41, W 28, D 2, L 11.
Competitions won: Erstwhile winners of the Yorkshire Shield Compet. (1971) The Humberside Cup.

GOOLE

Murham Avenue, Goole. Tel: 0405 768621
Founded: 1928
Secretary: I.R. Higgins, 30a Pasture Road, Goole, N. Humberside DN14 6EZ. Tel: 0405 76821 (W).
League: Yorkshire 1
Final position (1987–88): 5th
Playing record (1987–88): P 33, W 18, D 0, L 15. F 440, A 363.

CASTLEFORD

Whitwood Common Lane, Castleford, West Yorkshire. Tel: Castleford 554762.
Founded: 1870
President: H. Schumm
Coach: 1st XV Captain
Secretary: D. Timmins, 12 Parker Avenue, Altofts, Normanton, West Yorks. WF6 2NS. Tel: Wakefield 892155.
Fixtures Secretary: M. Beedle, 87 Cherry Tree Road, Walton, Wakefield. Tel: Wakefield 255701.
Club captain (1987–88): J. Davies
Club captain (1988–89): S. Davies
No. of teams: Senior 4, Youth 1
Directions to Ground: Leave M62 at Junction 31; Take A655 towards Castleford. Clubhouse within ½ mile on right hand side.
Ground capacity: 1000. Stand, None.
Colours: White, blue, red hoop. (*Change colours:* Red)
Floodlights: No
Admission: None
Membership: £12 Playing member
Programme: 50p (Editor: Secretary)
Local newspaper: Pontefract and Castelford Express.
League: Yorkshire 1
Final position (1987–88): Seventh
Playing record (1987–88): P 32, W 10, D 1, L 21, F 348, A 579.
Competitions won: 3 Sevens 'Plate' Tournaments – Bridlington; West Park Bramhope; and Wakefield Metropolitan District. All in April 1988.

COURAGE
CLUBS CHAMPIONSHIP

CLECKHEATON

Moorend, Cleckheaton. Tel: 0274 873410.
Founded: 1924
Chairman: R. Moore
Secretary: A. Potter, 337 Whitehall Road, Cleckheaton. Tel: 0274 870917 (H) 0274 877853 (W).
Fixtures Secretary: J. Wood, 705 Halifax Road, Cleckheaton. Tel: 0274 873532 (H).
Club captain (1987–88): A. Bentley
Club captain (1988–89): T. Evans
No. of teams: Senior 4. Youth & Minis 6.
Directions to Ground: M62 Junction 25, then A628. Can be seen from roundabout.
Stand capacity: 250 plus.
Colours: Red/white hoops. (*Change colours:* All red)
Floodlights: Training only
Admission: Collection only
Membership: £13 playing
Programme: 40p (Editor: A. Potter)
Local newspapers: Spenboro' Guardian, Bradford T&A, Yorkshire Evening Post.
League: Yorkshire 1
Final position (1987–88): 8th
Playing record (1987–88): P 35, W 12, D 2, L 21.

MOORTOWN

Moss Valley
Founded: 1932
Secretary: C. Williams, 12 West Parade, Leeds LS1 6AZ. Tel: 9532 789915 (H). 0532 577397 (W).
League: North Yorkshire 1
Final position (1987–88): 9th
Playing record (1987–88): P 32, W 12, D 1, L 19. F 261, A 390.

YORK R.I.

New Lane, Acomb, York. Tel: 0904-798930.
Founded: 1932
President: No separate RU President
Chairman: Chris Smith
Coach: Changing
Secretary: Jim Cooper, 8 Otterwood Bank, York YO2 3JS. Tel: 0904-797858.
Fixtures Secretary: Bill Cooper, 'Moorcroft', Lucycroft Drive, Baildon, West Yorks BD17 5BG.
Club captain (1987–88): Mark Schumacher
Club captain (1988–89): Neil Exley
No. of teams: Senior 4, Youth & Minis 2
Directions to Ground: New Lane, off Holgate Road, off Tadcaster Road (A64).
Ground capacity: Part of Communal Sports Complex. Stand, none.
Clubhouse: Bar, changing rooms, baths, showers etc.
Colours: Blue & white hoops. (*Change colours:* Red)
Floodlights: Yes
Admission: Free
Membership: £16
Programme: Only for cup competition organised by club. (Editor: N. Lowrey)
Local newspaper: Yorkshire Evening Press
League: Yorks 1
Final position (1987–88): 10th (relegated)

SCARBOROUGH

Scarboro RuFc, The Clubhouse, Scalby Road, Newby, Scarboro.
Founded: 1926
President: C.A. Hurd
Chairman: J. Evans
Coach: M.E. Holder
Secretary: B.M. Clayton, 49 Scalby Avenue, Newby, Scarboro. YO12 6HW.

Fixtures Secretary: A.R. Elliott, 29 Porritt Lane, Irton, Scarboro.
Club captain (1987–88): R.W. Chisholm
Club captain (1988–89): C.A. Burnard
No. of teams: Senior 4, Colts 1, Mini 4
Directions to Ground: Two miles North of Scarboro. on the Whitby Road – opposite Newby Service Station.
Ground capacity: 2,000. Stand, 200
Clubhouse: Bar, games room, snooker, capacity 200 (Fire reg.)
Colours: Maroon, white, blue hoops. (*Change colours:* Mid blue)
Floodlights: No training ground only.
Admission: None (collection)
Membership: £15 p.a.
Programme: Free (paid for by adverts) (Editor: D. Campbell)
Local newspaper: Scarboro Evening News and Mercury.
League: Yorkshire 1
Final position (1987–88): Bottom (relegated)
Playing record (1987–88): P 35, W 12, L 21, D 2.

YORKSHIRE 2

N. RIBBLESDALE

Grove Park, Settle, Yorkshire. Tel: 07292 2755.
Founded: 1923
Secretary: J.W. Smith, 7 Sandholme Close, Giggleswick, Settle, N. Yorks. Tel: 07292 2403 (H). 0942 714109 (W).
League: Yorkshire 2
Final position (1987–88): 1st
Playing record (1987–88): P 37, W 24, D 3, L 10. F 464 A 387.
Competitions won: Yorkshire 1st

HUDDERSFIELD YMCA

Laund Hill, Salendine Nook, Huddersfield. Tel: 0484 654052.
Founded: 1927
Secretary: D.B. Tomkins, 3 Celandine drive, Salendine Nook, Huddersfield, W. Yorks HD3 3UT. 0484 655523 (H).
League: Yorkshire 2
Final position (1987–88): 2nd

DONCASTER

Sandall Beat Lane, Off Armthorpe Road, Doncaster. Tel: 0302 831388
Founded: 1875
Secretary: D.A. Exley, MBE, 24 Newtree Drive, Wadworth, Doncaster. Tel: 0302 854362.
Fixtures Secretary: A. Bowes, 1 Dunscroft Grove, Old Rossington, Doncaster. Tel: 0302 831388.
League: Yorkshire 2
Final position (1987–88): 3rd
Playing record (1987–88): P 35, W 16, D 1, L 18. F 350, A 452.

WHEATLEY HILLS

Co-op Social Club. Tel: 0302 784484.
Founded: 1962
President: M.J. Tiplady
Chairman: A.R. Dunkerley
Secretary: T.S. Tuck, 91 Campton Avenue, Doncaster DN5 8EF. Tel: 0302 786998 (H).
Fixtures Secretary: P. Cooke, 23 Tutbury Gardens, Doncaster DN4 6RZ. Tel: 0302 536032 (H)
Club captain (1987–88): M. Spoor
Club captain (1988–89): M. Spoor
No. of teams: Senior 4. Youth & Minis 4.
Directions to Ground: N out of Doncaster A638 left at B & Q. Follow road after first right.
Colours: Maroon and gold quarters.
Floodlights: No
Membership: £14
Programme: 20p. (Editor: c/o the Committee)
Local newspaper: Yorkshire Post and Doncaster Star
League: Yorkshire 2
Final position (1987–88): 4th
Playing record (1987–88): P 35, W 22, L 13, D 0. F 481, A 447.

WATH

Moor Road, Wath upon Dearne, Rotherham, South Yorks. Tel: 0709 872399
Founded: 1930
Secretary: G. Scherdel, Newburn House, 61 Rig Drive, Swinton, Rotherham, S. Yorks. Tel: 0709 873398 (H). 0709 584368 (W).
League: Yorkshire 2
Final position (1987–88): 5th
Playing record (1987–88): P 32, W 16, D 6, L 10. F 388, A 331.

MALTON & NORTON

Peasey Hill Ground, Pasture Lane, Peasey Hill, Malton. Tel: 0653 694657.
Founded: 1953
President: John Seekings
Chairman: John Brown
Coach: Nick Cooke
Secretary: John Charman, Beechwood, Middlecave Road, Malton. Tel: 0653 694007.
Fixtures Secretary: Chris Wilson, Keldhead Hall, Middleton Road, Pickering. Tel: 0751 72754.
Club captain (1987–88): Stephen Riddolls
Club captain (1988–89): Stephen Fothergill
No. of teams: Senior 4
Directions to Ground: Into Malton on the A64 follow signs to Helmsley and take last right turn before leaving town. Club is approximately 400 yards on the left hand side.
Ground capacity: Not known. Stand, 100.
Clubhouse: Modern, 4 changing rooms, Ref's room, 2 baths and showers.
Colours: Black, red & white hoops. (*Change colours:* Blue)
Floodlights: No
Membership: £20.00
Local newspaper: Malton Gazette & Herald/Ryedale Mercury
League: Yorkshire II
Final position (1987–88): 6th
Playing record (1987–88): P 40, W 17, D 3, L 20, F 493, A 374.
Competitions won: 1984/85 North Yorkshire Cup. 1985/86 Yorkshire Silver Trophy.

ILKLEY

Stack's Field, Denton Road, Ilkley. Tel: (0943) 607037.
Founded: 1899
President: D.R. Sayers
Chairman: J.S. Pack

Yorkshire 2

Coach: Ian Pack
Secretary: J.A.L. Hope, Oak Royd, Oak Avenue, Burley In Wharfedale, Ilkley. Tel: (0943) 863377.
Fixtures Secretary: J.K. Bernard, 36 Dale View, Ilkley. Tel: (0943) 602945.
Club captain (1987–88): Rory Wilson
Club captain (1988–89): Blair Nixon
No. of teams: Senior 4, Youth & Minis 6
Directions to Ground: From traffic lights at parish church in town centre turn towards River Wharfe/Middleton. Ground easily visible about 200 yds on right.
Ground capacity: 2,000
Clubhouse: At ground/Websters/available for private hire.
Colours: White, red, black. (*Change colours:* Black)
Floodlights: Yes (training only)
Local newspaper: Ilkley Gazette/Wharfe Valley Times
League: Yorks 2
Final position (1987–88): 7th
Playing record (1987–88): P 33, W 16, D 2, L 15.
Competitions won: AIRE-WHARFE Cup 1988.

SHEFFIELD TIGER

Hathersage Road, Dore Moor S17 3AB. Tel: (0742) 360075.
Founded: 1933
President: Dr. S. Blower
Chairman: N/A
Coach: T.B.A.
Secretary: Stewart Devitt, 12 Bramwith Road, Nethergreen, Sheffield S11 7EZ. Tel: (0742) 304186.
Fixtures Secretary: Fred Senior, 5 Ashurst Road, Sheffield S6 5LP. Tel: (0742) 341306.
Club captain (1987–88): Mark Heaton
Club captain (1988–89): Mark Heaton
No. of teams: Senior 5, Youth & Minis 2
Clubhouse: Bar facilities
Colours: Maroon, black shorts. (*Change colours:* Maroon & white hoops)
Nickname: "Tigers"
Floodlights: No
Membership: £30.00 Playing, £20 Non-playing.
Local newspaper: Sheffield Star
League: Yorkshire 2
Final position (1987–88):
Playing record (1987–88): P 33, W 10, D 1, L 22.

IONIANS

Brantingham Lane, Elloughton, nr Hull, North Humberside.
Founded: 1926
President: P. Tremere
Chairman: D. Coates
Coach : D. Mil
Secretary: C. Wilkinson, 83 Hall road, Sproatley, nr Hull, Yorks, HU11 4PZ. Tel: 0482 811347 (H).
Fixtures secretary: R. Gosling, 11 Ransome Way, Elloughton, nr. Hull. Tel: (0482) 668655.
Club captain (1988–89): J. Cartmell
No. of teams: 12 in all
Directions to ground: Two hundred and fifty yards out of Elloughton village towards Brantingham.
Stand capacity: 250
Colours: Blue, green, white. (*Change colours:* black).
Floodlights: Yes.
Membership: £15
Local newspaper: Hull Daily Mail
League: Yorkshire 2
Final position (1987–88): 9th
Playing record (1987–88): P 37, W 9, D 0, L 28. F 388, A 759.
Competitions won: Humberside Cup, Bridlington Sevens, Pocklington Sevens, Ionians Sevens!

OLD OTLIENSIANS

Chaffer's Fields, Pool Road, Otley. Tel: 0943 461476.
Founded: 1927
Secretary: J. Kerby, Flat 2, Cecil Court, Valley Drive, Harrogate, N. Yorks. Tel: 0423 515123 (H). 0423 885959 (W).
League: Yorkshire 2
Final position (1987–88): 10th
Playing record (1987–88): P 31, W 13, D 2, L 16. F 389, A 411.

LEODIENSIANS

Crag Lane, Off Kings Lane, Alwoodley, Lees. Tel: 0532 673409.
Founded: 1906
Secretary: B. White, 397 Gledhow Lane, Leeds 7. Tel: 0532 625484 (H). 450733 (W).
Fixtures Secretary: J.M. Crook, 40 Cookridge Drive, Leeds 16. Tel: 0532 673651.
League: Yorkshire 2
Final position (1987–88): 11th (bottom, relegated)
Playing record (1987–88): P 32, W 10, D 4, L 18. F 236, A 436.

YORKSHIRE 3

BRIDLINGTON

Queensgate, Bridlington. Tel: 0262 676405.
Founded: 1926
President: G. Morrice
Chairman: D. Boddington
Coach: T.B.A.
Secretary: P. Preston, Los Gigantes, Eastgate, Rudston, Driffield. Tel: 0262 82435.
Fixtures Secretary: S. Wright, 15 Shaftesbury Avenue, Bridlington. Tel: 675230.
No. of teams: Senior 4. Youth & Minis 4.
Directions to Ground: Off Quay Road.
Stand capacity: 200
Ground capacity: 5000
Clubhouse: Open each evening Midweek & Saturday 7–11; Sat Lunchtime 12–2.30; Sun 12–2, 7–10.30.
Colours: Blue and gold (*Change colours:* Yellow)
Floodlights: Yes
Membership: £12 full + wife; £10 associate + wife; £8 full + ass; £2 jun.
Local newspaper: Bridlington Free Press
League: Yorkshire 3
Final position (1987–88): 1st
Playing record (1987–88): P 33, W 26, L 7 (Club record)
Competitions won: Yorkshire Silver Trophy 1988; Champions, Yorkshire Division 3; Bridlington 7's Winnter (Easter).

MARIST

Cranbrook Avenue, Hull. Tel: 0482 859216.
Founded: 1958
Secretary: N.R. Dixon, 82 New Village Road, Cottingham, E. Yorks HU16 4NE. Tel: 0482 841549 (H). 0430 40185 (W).
League: Yorkshire 3
Final position (1987–88): 2nd
Playing record (1987–88): P 33, W 19, D 2, L 12. F 480, A 341.

BASILDON

League: Yorkshire 3
Final position (1987–88): 3rd

KNOTTINGLEY

Howards Field, Marsh Lane, Knottingley. Tel: 0977 82438.
Founded: 1963
Secretary: M. Henderson, 4 Wellington Place, Knottingley, W. Yorks WF11 8LG. Tel: 0977 85754 (H). 0924 829511 (W).
League: Yorkshire 3
Final position (1987–88): 4th
Playing record (1987–88): P 34, W 20, D 2, L 12. F 458, A 322.

HEATH

North Dean, Stainland Road, West Vale, Halifax, W. Yorks. Tel: 0422 72920.
Founded: 1928
President: J.S. Robertshaw
Chairman: D.W. Bradley
Coach: J. Smith
Secretary: Craig Bedford, 58 Hollins Lane, Sowerby Bridge, Halifax, W. Yorks HX6 2RP. Tel: 0422 834473 (H), 0422 73462 (B).
Fixtures Secretary: Derek Shackleton, 16 Banks End Road, Elland, Halifax, W. Yorks. Tel: 0422 75339 (H), 0422 831751 (B).
Club captain (1987–88): P. Stewart
Club captain (1988–89): P. Stewart
No. of teams: Senior 3
Directions to Ground: Leave M62 junction 24, follow Halifax signs at roundabout, turn left at Calder & Hebble Pub (approx 2 mile down hill). ½ mile later turn left at garage.
Clubhouse: 2 storey building with changing groundfloor, bar 1st floor.
Colours: Emerald, claret, gold. (*Change colours:* Emerald)
Nickname: Heathens
Floodlights: No
Membership: £26
Local newspaper: Halifax Evening Courier
League: Yorks 3
Final position (1987–88): 5th
Playing record (1987–88): P 29, W 13, L 14, D 2, F 284, A 380.
Competitions won: Yorkshire Shield 78/79.

LEEDS CSSA

Civil Service Sports Club, Newton Road, Leeds LS7 4HX. Tel: (0532) 624178.
Founded: 1962
President: Jack Moverley
Chairman: Paul Bettison
Coach: H. Nemyria
Secretary: Steve Sykes, 96 Leasowe Road, Leeds LS10 2EZ. Tel: (0532) 779156.
Fixtures Secretary: Dr R.W. Marshall, 38 Barthorpe Crescent, Leeds LS17 5PE. Tel: (0532) 685755.
Club captain (1987–88): Hrysko Nemyria
Club captain (1988–89): Hyrsko Nemyria
No. of teams: Senior 3
Directions to Ground: From S(A61) 9 W(A58) to Chapeltown Road. Right onto Newton Road at RL HQ. From E(A64) & NE(A58) Right onto Harehills Lane, Left onto Newton Road at Hospital. From N Harrogate Road to Chapel Town Road. Left onto Newton Road.
Ground capacity: 200
Clubhouse: Bar, snooker room (3 tables), ballroom. Detached changing rooms.
Colours: Red/yellow hoops. (*Change colours:* Navy blue)
Floodlights: No
Admission: No charge
Membership: Rugby section £1.50, Main club (compulsory) £8.40 – £16.80 depending on grade of membership.
Programme: 1st XV – 10p (Editor: Steve Sykes (address above)
Local newspaper: Yorkshire Post/Yorkshire Evening Post.
League: Yorks 3
Final position (1987–88): 6th
Playing record (1987–88): P 35, W 19, L 14, D 2.
Competitions won: Yarnbury Sevens 24.4.88.

AIREBRONIANS

Upper Mill Cottages, Esholt Lane, Esholt, Shipley, W. Yorks. Tel: 0274 587792.
Founded: 1960
Secretary: J.M. Race, 12 Deighton Road, Wetherby, W. Yorks. Tel: 0397 64750 (H). Bradford 881082 (W).
League: Yorkshire 3
Final position (1987–88): 7th
Playing record (1987–88): P 29, W 12, D 3, L 14. F 349, A 416.

YARNBURY

Brownberrie Lane, Horsforth, LS18 5HB. Tel: Horsforth 581346.
Founded: 1872
Secretary: P.M. Clark, 48 Newlaithes Gardens, Horsforth, Leeds LS18 4JU. Tel: 021 784 5312 (H). 021 772 2361 (W).
League: Yorkshire 3
Final position (1987–88): 8th
Playing record (1987–88): P 33, W 12, D 2, L 19. F 332, A 432.

RODILLIANS

Manley Park, Lee Moor Road, Stanley, Wakefield. Tel: 0924 82361.
Founded: 1960
Secretary: R.J. Matthews, 27 Newlands Walk, Stanley, Wakefield WF3 4DT. Tel: 0924 828727 (H). 0924 823135 (W).
League: Yorkshire 3
Final position (1987–88): 9th

BRADFORD SALEM

Shay Lane, Heaton, Bradford BD9 6SL. Tel: 0274 496430.
Founded: 1924
Secretary: J.C. Dobson, 2 Highfield drive, Heaton, Bradford BD9 5PW. Tel: 0274 487517 (H). 0274 247521 (W).

Yorkshire 3

Fixtures Secretary: R.M. Birkett, 9 Shay Crescent, Heaton, Bradford BD9 5PW. Tel: 0274 43479 (H). 0274 75511 (W).
League: Yorkshire 3
Final position (1987–88): 10th
Playing record (1987–88): P 30, W 7, D 1, L 22. F 214, A 419.

NORTH ALLERTON

Brompton Lodge, North Allerton Road, Brompton, North Allerton, N. Yorks. Tel: 0609 3496.
Founded: Present club elected to RFU in 1961, Rugby has been played in North Allerton for over 100 years.
President: R.C. Lovelace
Chairman: J.S. Turner
Coach: J. Williamson
Secretary: S. Hague, 14 The Stone Bow, Thornton-Le-Beans, North Allerton, North Yorks. DL6 3SR. Tel: 0609 774325.
Fixtures Secretary: A. Bradley, 15 Borrowby Avenue, North Allerton, N. Yorks. Tel: 0609 2743.
Club captain (1987–88): G. Appleyard
Club captain (1988–89): D. Bowes
No. of teams: Senior 4, Youth & Minis 3
Directions to Ground: On arriving in North Allerton follow road signs to Teesside (A19)/Brompton, then further signs to Brompton.
Clubhouse: Address as above – changing rooms & clubhouse on same site as ground. Serves the best Tetley's in the area.
Colours: Green/amber. (*Change colours:* Amber)
Nickname: "North"
Floodlights: No. Only training lights.
Membership: Player £23. Vice President £11. Social £3. Juniot £3.
Programme: Donation (Editor: J.S. Turner)
Local newspaper: North Yorkshire News, Darlington & Stockton Times, Northern Echo, Middlesborough Evening Gazette, Yorkshire Post.
League: Yorkshire 3
Final position (1987–88): Last
Playing record (1987–88): P 34, W 8, L 25, D 1, F 290, A 580.
Competitions won: Yorkshire Trophy 1977, North Yorkshire Trophy 1979.

YORKSHIRE 4

WIBSEY

143 High Street, Wibsey, BFD. Tel: 0274 671643.
Founded: 1931/32
President: M. Spencer
Coach: S. Griffin
Secretary: D. Hartley, 143 High Street, Wibsey, Bradford. Tel: 0274 677255 (H), 0274 675231 (W).
Fixtures Secretary: A. Deacon, 18 Overton Drive, BFD 6. Tel: 0274 574905.
Club captain (1987–88): M. Macabe
Club captain (1988–89): Not yet selected.
No. of teams: Senior 3
Directions to Ground: From end of M606 to Odsal roundabout turn left on 3 exit carry about 2 mile over two roundabouts. Turn right 2 hundred yards past Horse and Groom Hotel.
Ground capacity: 200
Clubhouse: Tetleys beer, open all week, address as above.
Colours: Green & red hoops. (*Change colours:* Blue)
Floodlights: No
Admission: Collection
Membership: £10
Local newspaper: Telegraph & Argus
League: Yorks 4
Final position (1987–88): First (promoted)
Playing record (1987–88): P 36, W 25, D 0, L 11.
Competitions won: Finalists Yorks Silver Trophy.

OLD MODERNIANS

Cookridge Lane, Leeds LS16 7ND. Tel: 0532-671075.
Founded: 1963
President: G. Castle
Chairman: C. Smart
Coach: M. Barker
Secretary: D. Moran, 11 Stanhope Avenue, Horsforth, Leeds LS18 5AR. Tel: 589163.
Fixtures Secretary: D. Carter, 81 Green Lane, Cookridge, Leeds 16. Tel: 679718.
Club captain (1987–88): P. Day
Club captain (1988–89): P. Day
No. of teams: Senior 3
Directions to Ground: Take Otley Old Road out of Leeds. Ground is on right hand side on Cookridge Lane going towards Bramhope.
Ground capacity: 100
Clubhouse: Lounge, games room, guest room – capacity 200 persons.
Colours: Red & black hoops. (*Change colours:* Black shirts)
Nickname: The "Mods"
Floodlights: No
Membership: £10.00
Local newspaper: Wharfe Valley Times + Yorkshire Post.
League: Yorks 4
Final position (1987–88): Runners up
Playing record (1987–88): P 36, W 20, L 15, D 1, F 426, A 328.
Competitions won: Yorkshire Silver Trophy Winners 1986, Yorkshire Div. 4 Runners Up 1987–88.

DINNINGTON

Lodge Lane, Dinnington, Sheffield. Tel: 0909-562044.
Founded: 1968
President: G. Tierney
Chairman: E. Taylor
Coach: A. Donkin
Secretary: I.W. Goold, 7 New Road, Firbeck, Rotherham. Tel: 0709-362170.
Fixtures Secretary: Bill Gilbody. Tel: 0909-562997.
Club captain (1987–88): J. Whaling
No. of teams: Senior 4
Directions to Ground: M1 Exit 31 – A57 towards Worksop – Turn left at lights – "T" junction turn right past school.
Colours: Blue-white-gold hoops. (*Change colours:* Black)
Floodlights: No
Membership: £15
League: Yorks 4
Final position (1987–88): 3rd
Playing record (1987–88): P 35, W 18, D 2, L 15, F 614, A 424.

HESSLE

The Foreshore, Livingstone Road, Hessle, E. Yorks. Tel: 0482 643430.
Founded: 1926
President: A.O. Sellers
Chairman: J.R. Grayson

Coach: N. Chapman
Secretary: P.J. Love, 41 Oaklands Drive, Hessle, E. Yorks. Tel: 0482 646857.
Fixtures Secretary: P. Denton, 45 Maplewood Avenue, Hull. Tel: 0482 572124.
Club captain (1987–88): C. Spicer
Club captain (1988–89): C. Spicer
No. of teams: Senior 4. Youth & Minis 6.
Directions to Ground: Follow directions to Humber Bridge Country Park, when on Livingstone Road, Clubhouse on left.
Colours: Green, black, white irregular hoops. (*Change colours:* Black shirts).
Floodlights: No
Membership: £15 playing members
Local newspaper: Hull Daily Mail, Beverely Guardian
League: Yorkshire 4
Final position (1987–88): Joint 3rd

WEST LEEDS

Blue Hill Lane, Wortley, Leeds. Tel: 0532 639869.
Founded: 1926
Secretary: D. Brealey, 124 New Laithes Road, Horsforth, Leeds LS18 2AY. Tel: Leeds 581314 (H). Leeds 446731 (W).
League: Yorkshire 4
Final position (1987–88): 5th
Playing record (1987–88): P 34, W 18, D 1, L 15. F 428, A 440.

HULLENSIANS

Springhead Lane, Anlaby Common, Hull HU4 7RU. Tel: 0482 505656.
Founded: 1924
President: Paul Camm
Chairman: L. Wilcock
Coach: T.B.A.
Secretary: Andrew P. Newton, 32 Goodmanham Way, Cottingham, Hull HU16 5LJ. Tel: (0482) 841101.
Fixtures Secretary: Chris Martin, 20 St Peters Avenue, Anlaby, HU10 7AP. Tel: (0482) 650696.
Club captain (1987–88): K. Osborne
Club captain (1988–89): N. Hare
No. of teams: Senior 3, Youth 1
Directions to Ground: Follow sign posts for Anlaby, look for the "Haltemprice Sports Centre" Rugby club 1½ miles down Springfield Way on the left after the church.
Ground capacity: 2000
Clubhouse: Cap. 120 (2 changing rooms, 1 bath, 1 bar lounge)
Colours: Red and black. (*Change colours:* Yellow)
Floodlights: No
Admission: Nil
Membership: £7.50
Local newspaper: Hull Daily Mail
League: Yorks 4
Final position (1987–88): 6th
Playing record (1987–88): P 35, W 16, L 15, D 4.

WETHERBY

H.M.Y.C.C., York Road, Wetherby. Tel: 0937 65141.
Founded: 1966
Secretary: J.M. Hopkins, 1 Almsford Close, Harrogate, W. Yorks HG2 8EF.
League: Yorkshire 4
Final position (1987–88): 7th

LEEDS Y.M.C.A.

Lawnswood Playing Fields, Otley Road, Leeds. Tel: (0532) 678168.
Founded: 1926
President: E. Peck
Chairman: B. Marston
Coach: Ian Pateman
Secretary: L. Wilcock, 12 Winding Way, Leeds LS17 7RA. Tel: (0532) 675341.
Fixtures Secretary: J. Eyre, 142 Birchwood Hill, Leeds 17. Tel: (0532) 665689.
Club captain (1987–88): Sean Rath
Club captain (1988–89): John Greenwood
No. of teams: Senior 3
Directions to Ground: Situated near Leeds University Sports Ground on A660 Leeds – Otley Road.
Clubhouse: On ground
Colours: Light & dark blue hoops. (*Change colours:* Red)
Floodlights: No
Membership: £15
Local newspaper: Yorkshire Post
League: Yorks 4
Final position (1987–88): 7th
Playing record (1987–88): P 28, W 10, D 1, L 17, F 310, A 430.
Competitions won: McBride Trophy 1985, 1986 & 1987.

YORKSHIRE CW

Pontefract Road, Stanton, Leeds LS10. Tel: 701715 or 701107.
Founded: 1952
Secretary: M. Coleman, 113 Wood Lane, Rothwell, Nr Leeds. Tel: Leeds 820578 (H). 701104 (W).
League: Yorkshire 4
Final position (1987–88): 9th

BURLEY

Abbey Road, Kirstall, Leeds 5. Tel: 757400.
Founded: 1921
Secretary: E. Holdsworth, 15 Carlton Gate, Leeds LS7 1HW. Tel: 0532 442786.
League: Yorkshire 4
Final position (1987–88): 10th

SKIPTON

Sandy Lands, Carleton, New Road, Skipton. Tel: Skipton 3148.
Founded: 1874
Secretary: R. Lumley, 10 Parkwood Drive, Skipton, N. Yorks. Tel: 60766 (H). 0535 36116 (W).
League: Yorkshire 4
Final position (1987–88): 11th (bottom, relegated)

HALIFAX VANDALS

League: Yorkshire 5
Final position (1987–88): 1st
Competitions won: Yorkshire 5

OLD RISHWORTHIAN

The Club House, Copley, Halifax, West Yorkshire. Tel: 0422 53919.
President: J.F. Dawson
Secretary: D.W. Butler, Keepfens Shaw Lane, Holywell Green, Halifax, West Yorkshire. Tel: 0422 71672.
Fixtures Secretary: M. Procter, 138 Wakefield Road, Lightcliffe, Halifax, West Yorkshire. Tel: 0422 201730.
No. of teams: Senior 3
Colours: White/black/maroon hoops. (*Change colours:* Maroon)
Floodlights: No
Membership: £12 p.a.
Local newspaper: Halifax Courier
League: Yorkshire 5
Final position (1987–88): Runners up Yorkshire 5 (promoted)
Playing record (1987–88): P 32, W 19, L 13, F 470, A 260.

PHOENIX PARK

The Oval Ball, Stony Road, Farsley, Leeds. Tel: 0532 553439.
Founded: 1937
Secretary: M. Ryan, 280 Whitehall Road, Lyke, Bradford BD12 9dX. Tel: 0274 735099 (W).
League: Yorkshire 5
Final position (1987–88): 3rd

LEEDS CORINTHIANS

Middleton District Centre, Leeds 10. Tel: 0532 711574.
Founded: 1956
Secretary: F. Boon, 39 Neville Grove, Swillington, Leeds LS26 8QN. Tel: 0532 867833 (H). 0532 701107 (W).
League: Yorkshire 5
Final position (1987–88): 4th

OSSETT

c/o B. Crossland, 87 Broadowler Lane, Ossett WF5 0QG. Tel: 0924-275646 (H), 0924-375444 (W).
Founded: Re-Formed 1979
President: D.C. Jowett
Chairman: D.C. Jowett
Coach: To be advised
Secretary: B. Crossland, 87 Broadowler Lane, Ossett WF5 0QG. Tel: 0924-275646 (H), 0924-375444 (W).
Fixtures Secretary: C. Hampshire, 58 Barnes Avenue, Wakefield. Tel: 0924-361445.
Club captain (1987–88): S. Spurr
Club captain (1988–89): S. Spurr
No. of teams: Senior 2
Directions to Ground: From M1 towards Ossett on Queens Drive under motorway bridge turn right at Spring Mill 9 hole golf course.
Clubhouse: Ossett Cricket & Athletic Club, Pavillion, Queens Terrace, Ossett.

John Bentley (Sale) – soon to be capped by England – races away to score a try for Yorkshire in the Under-21 County Championship Final against Gloucestershire. Yorkshire won 22–11. Photo: Colorsport.

Colours: Black & white. (*Change colours:* Red)
Floodlights: No
Membership: Playing members £12.50
Local newspaper: Wakefield Express
League: Yorkshire 5
Final position (1987–88): 5th

B.P. CHEMICALS

Saltend, Hull. Tel: 0482 896113.
Founded: 1973
Chairman: K. Smith
Coach: P. Richards
Secretary: S. Ladd, 4 Chavler Street, Hull HU8 8NA. Tel: 0482 706502.
Fixtures Secretary: S. Peat, 10 Albina Garth, Hedon HU12 8LY. Tel: 0482 897428.
Club captain (1987–88): G. McKinley
Club captain (1988–89): G. McKinley
No. of teams: Senior 2
Directions to Ground: Follow signpost A1033 Hedon, just on outskirts of Hull.
Colours: Maroon & Gold. (*Change colours:* Blue & white hoops)
Floodlights: No
Local newspaper: Hull Daily Mail
League: Yorks 5
Final position (1987–88): 6th

YORKSHIRE MAIN

Yorkshire Main Miners Welfare Club, Edlington Lane, Edlington, Doncaster. Tel: 0709
Founded: 1983
Chairman: Gary Makuch
Secretary: Steve Derrick, 172 Cedar Road, Warmsworth, Doncaster. Tel: 0302 850981.
Fixtures Secretary: H.R. Whiteley, 53 Thompson Avenue, Edlington, Doncaster. Tel: 0709 863446.
Club captain (1987–88): Brian Wilson-Storey
Club captain (1988–89): Brian Wilson-Storey
No. of teams: Senior 2
Directions to Ground: Along A1 to A630 head towards Roth & Sheffield, turn left at 1st traffic lights to Edlington, 1 mile on left.
Ground capacity: 300
Colours: Green & black. (*Change colours:* Red & black)
Floodlights: No
Admission: Nil
Membership: £12.50
Local newspaper: Doncaster Star
League: Yorkshire 5
Final position (1987–88): 7th

HORNSEA

Hollis Recreation Ground, Atwick Road, Hornsea. Tel: Hornsea 534181.
Founded: 1924
President: T. Tomlinson
Chairman: R. Scruton
Secretary: G. Steven, 59 Hornsea Road, Leven. Tel: 0964 543868.
Fixtures Secretary: G. Edmond, Corner Stones, Football Green, Hornsea. Tel: Hornsea 535714.
Club captain (1987–88): I. Naylor
Club captain (1988–89): M. Seymour
No. of teams: Senior 3.
Directions to Ground: Off Atwick Road, Hornsea.
Ground capacity: 1000. Stand, 30.
Colours: Black, green on white hoop. (*Change colours:* Green).
Floodlights: No
Admission: Free
Membership: £20
Local newspaper: Hornsea Gazette
League: Yorkshire 5
Final position (1987–88): 8th
Playing record (1987–88): P 29, W 6, D 1, L 22.

ROWNTREE

Millecrux Sports Ground, Haxby Road, York. Tel: 0904 623933.
Founded: 1894. Refounded 1984
President: R.A. Kaner
Chairman: P.M. Cregan
Coach: A. Warriner
Secretary: P.K. Knowles, 6 St Oswalds Close, Wilberfoss, York YO4 5NF. Tel: 07595 8190.
Fixtures Secretary: T. Lax, 31 Rosslyn Street, Clifton, York YO3 6LG. Tel: 0904 638884.
Club captain (1987–88): N. McLeay
Club captain (1988–89): N. McLeay
No. of teams: Senior 2, Youth & Minis 1
Directions to Ground: Out of York on Haxby Road, past Rowntree Factory on right.
Colours: Red, white & black hoops. (*Change colours:* Red)
Floodlights: No
Membership: £16
Local newspaper: York Evening Press
League: Yorkshire 5
Final position (1987–88): 9th
Playing record (1987–88): P 10, L 7, W 3.

WITHERNSEA

Highfield Ground, Queen Street, Withernsea.
Founded: 1938
Secretary: A. Ellis, 11/17 Seaside Road, Withernsea, N. Humberside HU10 2DL.
League: Yorkshire 5
Final position (1987–88): 10th

KNARESBOROUGH

Knaresborough Squash Club, Manse Lane, Knaresborough, N. Yorks.
Founded: 1982
Secretary: P. Drew, 45 st Catherines road, Harrogate HG2 8LA. Tel: 889034 (H). 867355 (W).
League: Yorkshire 5
Final position (1987–88): 11th (bottom, relegated)

YORKSHIRE 6

SHEFFIELD OAKS

Myers Grove School, Wood Lane, Sheffield S6 1HG
Founded: 1978
Secretary: R.J. Walton, 1 Little Matlock Way, Stannington, Sheffield S6 6FX. Tel: 0742 349421 (H). 0742 557331 (W)
League: Yorkshire 6
Final position (1987–88): 1st (promoted)
Competitions won: Yorkshire 6

BRIDON

Bridon Sports Ground, Carr Hill, Balby, Doncaster DN4. Tel: 0302 344010
Founded: 1970
Secretary: P. Varley, 29 Bahram Road, Bessacarr, Doncaster DN4 7BG. Tel: 0302 530875
League: Yorkshire 6
Final position (1987–88): 2nd
Competitions won: Runners up Yorkshire 6

DE LA SALLE

Beauchief Hall, Beauchief Abbey Lane, Sheffield 8. Tel: 367756
Founded: 1956
Secretary: Mrs. M. Buckley, 93 Ingram Road, Sheffield S2 2SB. Tel: 0742 20246 (H)
League: Yorkshire 6
Final position (1987–88): 3rd

SHEFFIELD STEELS

HQ Prince of Wales Hotel, Ecklington, Derbys
Founded: 1928
Secretary: Darren Shaw, 10 Chesterfield Road, Ecklington, Sheffield S31 9BD. Tel: 0246 432456
League: Yorkshire 6
Final position (1987–88): 4th

STOCKSBRIDGE

634 Manchester Road, Stocksbridge, Sheffield. Tel: 0742 885078.
Founded: 1963
Chairman: H. Everson
Coach: A. Smith
Secretary: G. Brailsford, 15 Shelley Close, Penistone, Sheffield S30 6GT. Tel: 0226 766160.
Fixtures Secretary: C. Lambert, 21 Haywood Avenue, Deepcar, Sheffield S30 5QD. Tel: 0742 885525.
Club captain (1987–88): M. Taylor
Club captain (1988–89): M. Taylor
No. of teams: Senior 3.
Directions to Ground: A57 from Sheffield at Deepcar follow Car Road to Bolsterstone. Turn right 500 yards on left.
Clubhouse: Converted chapel, not on ground.
Colours: Royal blue, 2 white hoops. (*Change colours:* Red, light blue, white hoops).
Floodlights: No
Membership: £13
Local newspaper: Sheffield Star
League: Yorkshire 6
Final position (1987–88): 5th
Playing record (1987–88): P 23, W 8, L 15.

GRANVILLE COLLEGE

Ash House Lane, Dore, Sheffield. Tel: 0742 620332
Founded: 1966
Secretary: R.F.C., Granville College, Granville Road, Sheffield S2 2RL. Tel: 0742 738441
League: Yorkshire 6
Final position (1987–88): 6th

SHEFFIELD MEDICALS

Medical Society Office, The Medical School, Beech Hill Road, Sheffield S10. Tel: (0742) 766222 Ext. 2493.
Founded: 1953
President: W. Morris-Jones Mch FRCS
Coach: David Rogers
Secretary: Paul Kirk, 70 Bower Road, Sheffield S10 1ER. Tel: (0742) 683573.

Yorkshire 6

Fixtures Secretary: Tim Parkin, 40 Wayland Road, Sheffield. Tel: (0742) 670737.
Club captain (1987–88): Paul Kirk
Club captain (1988–89): David Potter
No. of teams: Senior 3
Directions to Ground: University playing fields, Norton, via Chesterfield Road.
Clubhouse: University sports pavillion.
Colours: Blue/white hoops. (*Change colours:* Black with gold hoop)
Floodlights: No
Admission: Nil
Membership: £5.00 – £15.00
Local newspaper: Sheffield Star + Yorkshire Post
League: Yorkshire 6
Final position (1987–88): Fifth
Playing record (1987–88): P 25, W 15, L 8, D 2.

ADWICK-LE-STREET

(See Clubhouse)
Founded: 1965
President: W.B. Johnson
Chairman: D. Bibby
Coach: D. Bibby
Secretary: R.J. Terry, 27 Sherwood Drive, Skellow, Doncaster. Tel: 0302 727580.
Fixtures Secretary: D. Patrickson, 41 Ridge Balk Lane, Woodlands, Doncaster. Tel: 0302 725687.
Club captain (1987–88): R. Maskrey
Club captain (1988–89): R. Maskrey
No. of teams: Senior 2
Directions to Ground: 4 miles North of Doncaster on the A638 Road, Tally Ho! Pub/changing rooms.
Clubhouse: c/o Tally Ho!, Great North Road, Woodlands, Doncaster. Tel: 0302 722372.
Colours: Navy/sky hoops. (*Change colours:* Navy/sky quarters)
Floodlights: No
Membership: £5
Local newspaper: Doncaster Evening Star/Doncaster Free Press
League: Yorks 6
Final position (1987–88): 7th
Playing record (1987–88): P 30, W 10, L 18, D 2, F 336, A 404.

MARKHAM

Welfare Cricket Ground, Church Street, Armthorpe
Founded: 1981
Secretary: J. Moncur, 74 Doncaster Road, Armthorpe, Doncaster, S. Yorks. Tel: 0302 834269
League: Yorkshire 6
Final position (1987–88): 9th

MALTBY OLD BOYS

Maltby Comp School, Braithwell Road, Maltby. Tel: 0709 812580
Founded: 1980
Secretary: G.A.C. Barnes, 153 Morthen Road, Wickersley, Rotherham SG6 0DX. Tel: 0709 543684 (H). 0246 417941/2 (W)
League: Yorkshire 6
Final position (1987–88): 10th

ARMTHORPE ROVERS

c/o Club Secretary
Founded: 1968
President: Stuart Robinson
Chairman: Terry Cook
Coach: Tony MacNally
Secretary: Barry Jones, 98 Laburnum Drive, Armthorpe, Doncaster, Yorks. Tel: Don. 832804.
Fixtures Secretary: 49 Laurel Road, Armthorpe, Doncaster.
Club captain (1987–88): S. Christian
Club captain (1988–89): T. Cook
No. of teams: Senior 1
Directions to Ground: Junction 4 off the M18 towards Doncaster, left at the first roundabout brings you into Armthorpe, change Armthorpe Comp. School.
Clubhouse: Tadcaster Arms, Armthorpe.
Colours: Red, white, black hoops. (*Change colours:* White)
Nickname: The Rovers
Floodlights: No
Membership: £10
Local newspaper: Doncaster Star
League: Yorks 6
Final position (1987–88): 11th
Playing record (1987–88): P 10, L 10, W 0. (league only)

DURHAM/NORTHUMBERLAND

BLYTH

Plessey Road, Blyth, Northumberland. Tel: 0670-352063.
Founded: 1961
President: A.F. Heinzman
Chairman: A.F. Heinzman
Secretary: S.W. Bainbridge, 5 Eddleston Avenue, Newcastle-upon-Tyne NE3 4SJ. Tel: 091-2855317.
Fixtures Secretary: D. Grey, 12 Winchester Avenue, Blyth, Northumberland. Tel: 0670-369591.
Club captain (1987–88): C. Correia
Club captain (1988–89): G. Sinton
No. of teams: Senior 4, Youth & Minis 6
Directions to Ground: Principal route – From A189 via 1061 into Blyth (Newcastle Road) to Plessey Road.
Clubhouse: Yes! We have one!
Colours: Emerald & black. (*Change colours:* Red)
Floodlights: No
Membership: £20
League: Durham & North 1
Final position (1987–88): First
Playing record (1987–88): P 37, W 20, D 1, L 16, F 585, A 462.
Competitions won: Winners Courage Durham & Northumberland League Div. I: Winners Blyth 7's.

ROCKLIFF

Lovaine Avenue, Whitley Bay, Tyne & Wear. Tel: 091 251 3704.
Founded: 1887
President: J.D. Reid
Chairman: I.G. Firth
Coach: W. Curley
Secretary: P.A. Heppell, 7 Rothley Way, W/bay. Tel: 091 252 9308.
Fixtures Secretary: D. Johnstone, 9 Western Way, W/bay. Tel: 091 253 3590.
Club captain (1987–88): A. Robertson
Club captain (1988–89): M. Wylie
No. of teams: Senior 4. Youth & Minis 3.
Directions to Ground: Off Hill Heads Road along Lovaine Avenue. (Behind Cricket Club).
Ground capacity: 1000
Clubhouse: Spacious clubhouse, spearate changing block.
Colours: Cardinal red and gold. (*Change colours:* various).
Floodlights: No
Membership: ranging from £25 to £3.
Local newspaper: Whitley Bay Guardian (weekly).
League: Northumberland/Durham 1

Final position (1987–88): 2nd
Playing record (1987–88): P 34, W 17, D 1, L 16. F 374, A 481.

PONTELAND

Castlewood Sports Centre, Ponteland. Tel: 0661 25441
Founded: 1967
Secretary: J. Kilgallon, 29 Wolveleigh Terrace, Gosforth NE3 1UP. Tel: 091 285848 (H). 091 2731121 (W)
League: DUR/NORTH 1
Final position (1987–88): 3rd
Playing record (1987–88): P 31, W 16, D 0, L 15, F 419, A 447

ASHINGTON J.W.

Recreation Ground, High Market, Ashington, Northumberland. Tel: 0670-814123.
Founded: 1922
President: A.F. Bewick
Chairman: R. Turnbull
Coach: J. Harbottle
Secretary: J.D. Evans, 'Cartref' 20 Blackdene, Ashington, Northumberland. Tel: 0670-811250.
Fixtures Secretary: J.S.E. Brown, 23 Coomside, Cramlington, Northumberland. Tel: 0670-716847.
Club captain (1987–88): M. Lillico
Club captain (1988–89): D. Turner
No. of teams: Senior 4, Youth 1
Directions to Ground: ½ mile north on the A1068 to Ellington.
Colours: Royal blue/amber hooped shirts, white shorts, royal blue socks. (*Change colours:* Yellow)
Nickname: Ash
Floodlights: under way
Membership: £12.50
Local newspaper: The Journal
League: Northumberland and Durham 1
Final position (1987–88): 4th
Competitions won: Winner Northumberland County Colts Cup Competition 1987–88.

DARLINGTON

"Lingfield", McHoulen Road, Darlington, Co. Durham. Tel: 0325 466974.
Founded: 1963
President: D.G. Gardner
Chairman: B. Robson
Coach: A.R.W. Sansom
Secretary: A.P.F. Foster, "Cadogan", 45 Hartford Road, Darlington DL3 8HF. Tel: 0325 466501 (H) 0325 381818 (W).
Fixtures Secretary: D.G. Gardner, Balder View, Cotherstone, Barnard Castle.
Club captain (1987–88): T.V. Miller
Club captain (1988–89): G. Elgey
No. of teams: Senior 4. Youth & Minis 6.
Directions to Ground: Turn off A66 bypass along Yarm Road. Club on outskirts of town.
Clubhouse: Bar capacity 120, lounge 100.
Colours: Black & white hoops. (*Change colours:* Blue)
Floodlights: Yes (training)
Admission: T.B.A.
Membership: £20 full members
Programme: Editor: A. Gunnell
Local newspaper: Northern Echo
League: Durham/Northumberland 1
Final position (1987–88): 4th

SEGHILL

Welfare Park, Seghill, Cramlington, Northumberland NE23 7ER. Tel: 091 2370414.
Founded: 1921
President: J. Archbold
Chairman: E. Grainger
Coach: K. Watson
Secretary: J.N. Atherton, 20 Oakfield Way, Abbots Lea, Seghill, Cramlington, Northumberland NE23 7HH. Tel: 091 2370113.
Fixtures Secretary: P. Harvey, 1 Springville, East Sleekburn, Bedlington, Northumberland NE22 7AZ. Tel: 0670 825792.
Club captain (1987–88): P. Harvey
Club captain (1988–89): R. Hedley
No. of teams: Senior 4, Youth & Minis 2
Directions to Ground: Through Tyne tunnel, North on A1 Spine Road, 2nd left after Coast Road roundabout signposted Seghill.
Ground capacity: 500
Clubhouse: Lounge
Colours: Scarlet & black hoops. (*Change colours:* All black shirt)
Floodlights: No
Admission: Collection
Membership: £2 + playing fee £2 per game.
Local newspaper: Newcastle Chronicle + Journal
League: Northumberland & Durham 1
Final position (1987–88): 6th
Playing record (1987–88): P 34, W 18, L 12, D 4.
Competitions won: Under 21 McEwans League Champions.

ACKLAM

Talbot Park, Saltersgill Avenue, Middlesborough, Cleveland
Founded: 1976
Secretary: I. McMullan, 16 Linden Grove, Linthorpe, Middlesborough, Cleveland TS5 5NE. Tel: 0642 826945 (H). 0642 245432 (W)
League: DUR/NORTH 1
Final position (1987–88): 7th
Playing record (1987–88): P 32, W 14, D 4, L 14, F 379, A 283

REDCAR

Mackinlay Park, Green Lane, Redcar, Cleveland TS10 3RW. Tel: 482733.
Founded: 1920
President: T.H. Jackson
Chairman: J.S. Fawcett
Coach: A. Evans
Secretary: L. Welburn, 174 Laburnum Road, Redcar. Tel: 471746.
Fixtures Secretary: R. Atkinson, 27 Richmond Road, Redcar. Tel: 471740.
Club captain (1987–88): A. Evans
Club captain (1988–89): M. Trodden
No. of teams: Senior 4, Youth & Minis 10
Directions to Ground: Redcar – East end of coast road to Marske A1085.
Ground capacity: 5 pitches, 23 acres. Stand, 250
Clubhouse: 3 bars, pool room, recreation room, squash courts etc.
Colours: White with broad red band. (*Change colours:* Chocolate blue white hoops)
Floodlights: No
Admission: Collection
Membership: £12
Local newspaper: Evening Gazette
League: Durham/Northumberland 1
Final position (1987–88): 8th
Playing record (1987–88): P 30, W 12, D 1, L 17.

HORDEN COLLIERY WELFARE

Welfare Park, P/Lee. Tel: (091) 5863501.
Founded: 1925
President: P.G. Dunn
Chairman: J. Fenwick
Coach: R. Muir
Secretary: L. Applegarth, 63 Eastdene Way, Peterlee, Co. Durham. Tel: (091) 5862477.
Fixtures Secretary: R. Brownless, 20 Manorway, P/ Lee. Tel: (091) 5864464.
Club captain (1987–88): D. Turner
Club captain (1988–89): D. Turner
No. of teams: Senior 4, Youth & Minis 2
Directions to Ground: Welfare Park – through P/Lee into centre of Horden.
Ground capacity: 300
Clubhouse: Northumberland St Horden.
Colours: Maroon & sky blue
Nickname: Yackers
Floodlights: No
Membership: £10
Local newspaper: Hartlepool Mail
League: Durham & North 1
Final position (1987–88): 9th
Playing record (1987–88): P 34, W 17, L 17, D 1, F 521, A 424.

WINLATON VULCANS

Axwell View, Winlaton, Tyne & Wear. Tel: 091 4142502.
Founded: 1896
President: R. Archer
Chairman: A. Archer
Secretary: M.A. Brown, 20 Clockburnsyde Close, Whickham, Tyne & Wear NE16 5UR. Tel: 091 4886081.
Fixtures Secretary: I. Bilclough, 8 Holly View, Winlaton Mill, Tyne & Wear. Tel: 091 4148560.
Club captain (1987–88): I. Bilclough
Club captain (1988–89): T. Rutherford
No. of teams: Senior 3, Youth & Minis 1
Directions to Ground: Off A1 follow signs Newcastle/ G'Head and then N/CLE West sign turn off at sign for Swalwell, then right at roundabout, straight over at next roundabout, continue for 1 mile then left up Wincaton Bank, club at top of bank.
Clubhouse: Own clubhouse, lounge + bar + changing rooms (3) + baths.
Colours: Black
Floodlights: Yes
Membership: £10
Local newspaper: Evening Chronicle
League: Northumberland & Durham 1
Final position (1987–88): 9th

PERCY PARK

Preston Avenue, North Shield. Tel: 0632 575710
Founded: 1872
Secretary: A.C. Baker, 30 The Garth, Winlaton, Tyne & Wear. Tel: 0912 577007 (H). 091 4144869 (W)
Fixtures Secretary: G.R. Moore, 32 Agricola Gardens, Wallsend NE28 9RX. Tel: 0632 2340657
League: DUR/NORTH 1
Final position (1987–88): 11th (bottom, relegated)
Playing record (1987–88): P 34, W 1, D 2, L 31, F 169, A 876

DURHAM/NORTHUMBERLAND 2

MOWDEN PARK

22 Yiewsley Drive, Darlington, Co. Durham DL3 9XS Tel: 0385 465932.
Founded: 1946
President: A.F.W. Hammond
Chairman: P.D. Warne
Coach: M. Lindley
Secretary: M. Cambell, 491 North Road, Darlington, Co. Durham DL1 3AB.
Fixtures Secretary: D.P. Howland, 33 Enterpen Close, Yarm, Cleveland. Tel: Eaglescliff 788023.
No. of teams: Senior 4. Youth & Minis 6.
Directions to Ground: B6279 from Darlington. Turn left into Barnes Road at top turn right. Yiewsley Drive 2nd on right.
Ground capacity: 5000. Stand, 300.
Colours: Blue and white hoops. (*Change colours:* Maroon).
Floodlights: No
Membership: £15 playing, £10 other male, £2 ladies. £3 country member (over 25 miles); £1 juniors, £4 over 65s.
Local newspaper: Northern Echo
League: Durham/Northumberland 2
Final position (1987–88): 1st
Competitions won: Rugby World & Post Junior Club of the Month for May, top in Durham/Northumberland 2.

HARTLEPOOL BOYS BRIGADE OLD BOYS

Old Friarage, Headland, Hartlepool.
President: J. Waller
Chairman: T.G. Rennie
Coach: E. Arnell
Secretary: G.K. Faint, 11 Nesbyt Road, Hartlepool, Cleveland TS24 9NB. Tel: 0429 265674.
Fixtures Secretary: I. Mulrooney, 65 Percy Street, H.Pool. Tel: 0429 278082.
Club captain (1987–88): P. Ainslie
Club captain (1988–89): K. Hetherington
No. of teams: Senior 2
Directions to Ground: From North or South – Approach H.Pool along A19 trunk road taking the A179 H.Pool turn off. Straight on over 4 roundabouts following signs "A1049" & "Headland". Old Friarage is next to tennis courts & bowling green.
Colours: White with broad black band. (*Change colours:* Blue)
Nickname: Brigade
Floodlights: No
Admission: No charge
Membership: £2 p.a.
Local newspaper: Hartlepool Mail
League: Durham/Northumberland 2

Durham/Northumberland 2

Final position (1987–88): 10th
Playing record (1987–88): P 32, W 16, D 1, L 15, F 450, A 538.
Competitions won: Durham County Junior Cup 1937/73/74/77/78/81/83/84. Junior Club Merit Table 1986.

BISHOP AUCKLAND

Peel Street, Bishop Auckland. Tel: 0388 602922
Founded: 1976
Secretary: J.W.H. Gill, 38 Kenilworth Avenue, Bishop Auckland, Co. Durham DL14 0NJ. Tel: 0388 602337 (H). 0325 462133 (W)
League: DUR/NORTH 2
Final position (1987–88): 3rd

SUNDERLAND

Ashbrooke West Lawn, Sunderland. Tel: 091 528 4536
Founded: 1873
Secretary: S.N. Harrison, 9 Gillside Grove, Roker, Sunderland SR6 9PQ. Tel: 091 522 6188
League: DUR/NORTH 2
Final position (1987–88): 4th
Playing record (1987–88): P 34, W 13, D 1, L 23, F 466, A 700

CONSETT

Belle View Park, Medonsley Road, Consett, Co. Durham. Tel: 504261
Founded: 1923
Secretary: N.J. Hodson, 9 Kempton Close, Derwent Braes, Shotley Bridge, Consett, Durham DH8 0UB. Tel: Con 500722 (H). Newcastle 828520 (W)
League: DUR/NORTH 2
Final position (1987–88): 5th

SEAHAM

Azelia Terrace, Seaham, Co. Durham. Tel: 078381 2331
Founded: 1980
Secretary: G. Turns, 17 Stavordale Street, West Seaham, Co. Durham SR7 7RA. Tel: 07838 19908
League: DUR/NORTH 2
Final position (1987–88): 6th

WALLSEND

Wallsend Sports Centre, Bigges Main, Wallsend
Founded: 1959
Secretary: L. Dunne, 2 Lilac Road, Walkerville, Newcastle NE6 4TL. Tel: 091 263 5398 (H). Blyth 352441 (W)
League: DUR/NORTH 2
Final position (1987–88): 7th

MEDICALS

Cartington Terrace, Heaton, Newcastle Upon Tyne. Tel: 265 6321.
Founded: 1898
President: Dr M. McQuillin
Chairman: Dr M. McQuillin
Secretary: C.J. Belfield, c/o Dental School, Framlington Place, Newcastle Upon Tyne.
Fixtures Secretary: P. Fisher. Tel: 4901515 (Work).
Club captain (1987–88): P. Brantingham
Club captain (1988–89): J. Foster
No. of teams: Senior 4
Directions to Ground: Take the coast road East and turn right at the Corner House.
Ground capacity: 500. Stand, 100
Clubhouse: Bar + kitchen.
Colours: Maroon shirts, white shorts. (*Change colours:* Blue shirts)
Nickname: Medics
Floodlights: No
Membership: £11
Programme: (Editor: J. Kelly)
Local newspaper: Journal + Sunday Sun
League: Northumberland & Durham 2
Final position (1987–88): 7th
Playing record (1987–88): P 26, W 13, L 13.

NORTH DURHAM

Prince Consort Road, Gateshead, Tyne & Wear. Tel: 091 4783071.
Founded: 1875
President: W.J. Barnes
Chairman: C. Stafford
Coach: J. Banks
Secretary: R. Thompson, 3 Ancroft Place, Newcastle Upon Tyne NE5 2HN. Tel: 091 2746041.
Fixtures Secretary: T.N. Tate, 21 Lynnholme Gardens, Gateshead. Tel: 091 4773567.
Club captain (1987–88): D. Tate
Club captain (1988–89): N. Wilde
No. of teams: Senior 3, Youth & Minis 2
Directions to Ground: A1(M) to North. Main road to Gateshead. Turn left at Springfield Hotel. Ground on left of dual carriageway to Newcastle Upon Tyne.
Ground capacity: 2000
Clubhouse: Two storey building, bar & lounge upstairs. Changing accm downstairs.
Colours: Red & white hoops. (*Change colours:* Green)
Floodlights: No
Membership: £12.50
Local newspaper: Gateshead Post, Newcastle Journal & Evening Chronicle.
League: Northumberland/Durham 2
Final position (1987–88): Ninth
Playing record (1987–88): P 30, W 4, D 1, L 25, F 160, A 480.

HARTLEPOOL

Mayfield Park, Easington Road, Hartlepool. Tel: 35399
Founded: 1893
Secretary: M. Westhorp, 4 Newquay Close, Cliffords Green, Hartlepool, Cleveland. Tel: 33605 (H). 862412 (W)
League: DUR/NORTH 2
Final position (1987–88): 2nd
Playing record (1987–88): P 35, W 19, D 0, L 16, F 508, A 483

HOUGHTON

Dairy Lane, Houghton. Tel: 091 5841 460
Founded: 1875
Secretary: T. Roberts, "Jelta", Gilpin Street, Houghton Le Spring, Tyne & Wear DH4 5DR. Tel: 091 584 2659 (H)
League: DUR/NORTH 2
Final position (1987–88): 11th (Bottom, relegated)

WHITBY

The Showfield, Whiteleys, Whitby, North Yorks. Tel: (0947) 603433.
Founded: 1951
President: J.A. Stalker
Chairman: P.C. Brown
Coach: C. Hayes
Secretary: T.M. Marshall, "Heatherdene", Fairhead, Grosmont, Nr. Whitby YO22 5PN. Tel: 0947 603433 (W), 0947 85427 (H).
Fixtures Secretary: L. Bentley, 11 Normanby Terrace, Whitby. Tel: 0947 603982.
Club captain (1987–88): Darryl Grason
Club captain (1988–89): Darryl Grason
No. of teams: Senior 3, Youth & Minis 2
Directions to Ground: Off A171 Stakesby Road, ½ mile town centre.
Clubhouse: New modern clubhouse open 7 days a week.
Colours: Maroon & black. (*Change colours:* Black & white hoops)
Floodlights: No
Admission: Free
Membership: £10 playing, £3.75 social.
Local newspaper: Whitby Gazette
League: Northumberland/Durham 3
Final position (1987–88): First (promoted)
Playing record (1987–88): P 33, W 28, D 1, L 4, F 942, A 283.
Competitions won: Northumberland Durham 3 Champions. Pernod Atack Try Award.

BILLINGHAM

Synthonia Sports Club, Belasis Avenue, Billingham, Stockton. Tel: 523788.
Founded: 1923
President: J.W.C. Taylor
Chairman: L. Jack
Coach: B. Woodhouse
Secretary: N. Taylor, 64 Melrose Avenue, Billingham, Cleveland. Tel: 0642 554786.
Fixtures Secretary: J. McCoy, 242 Cotswold Crescent, Billingham, Cleveland. Tel: 0642 533554.
Club captain (1987–88): C. Daley
Club captain (1988–89): M. Riby
No. of teams: Senior 3
Directions to Ground: Going North A19 take Billingham turn off straight up Central Avenue. Ground on left. Going South A19 etc.
Ground capacity: Unlimited. Stand, 50–60.
Clubhouse: Shared with other sections in Synthonia Sports Club.
Colours: Green & white hoops.
Nickname: Synners
Floodlights: No
Membership: £12
Local newspaper: Evening Gazette & Hartlepool Mail
League: Northumberland & Durham 3
Final position (1987–88): 2nd
Playing record (1987–88): P 33, W 19, L 14, F 617, A 385.

GUISBOROUGH

Belmangate, Guisborough, Cleveland. Tel: 0287-32966.
Founded: 1968
President: W. Henderson
Chairman: A.W. Neville
Coach: No appointment
Secretary: D.F. Childs, 32 Boston Drive, Marton, Cleveland. Tel: 0642-314081.
Fixtures Secretary: C.B. Hanson, 7 Primrose Close, Guisborough, Cleveland. Tel: 0287-33051.
Club captain (1987–88): A. Notman
Club captain (1988–89): H. Peacock
No. of teams: Senior 3, Youth & Minis 2
Directions to Ground: A19 to Teesside; A172 at Tontine; A173 to Guisborough at Stokesley.
Colours: Black & amber. (*Change colours:* Amber)
Nickname: Priorymen
Floodlights: No
Membership: £16
Local newspaper: Evening Gazette
League: Northumberland & Durham 3
Final position (1987–88): 3rd
Playing record (1987–88): P 34, W 12, D 2, L 20, F 274, A 436.

SEATON CAREW

Petrus Park, Elizabeth Way, Seaton Carew, Hartlepool, Cleveland. Tel: 0429 60945
Founded: 1921
Secretary: J. Holland, 14 Berwick Street, Seaton Carew, Hartlepool, Cleveland. Tel: 0429 60945
League: DUR/NORTH 3
Final position (1987–88): 4th

WEARSIDE

Thorney Close School, Telford Road. Tel: 091 528 0149
Founded: 1954
Secretary: J.G. Watson, 67 Torrens Road, Thorney Close, Sunderland SR3 4JD. Tel: 901 514 0659 (W)
League: DUR/NORTH 3
Final position (1987–88): 5th

CHESTER-LE-STREET

Riverside Sports Complex, Chester-le-Street, Co. Durham. Tel: 0385 884121
Founded: 1979
Secretary: A. Warren, 10 Carrowmore Road, Chester-le-Street, Co. Durham. Tel: 091 388 7855
League: DUR/NORTH 3
Final position (1987–88): 6th

DARLINGTON RA

Brinkburn Road, Darlington. Tel: 68125
Founded: 1925
Secretary: S.G. Allison, 2 Rochester Way, Darlington. Tel: 0325 288616 (H)
League: DUR/NORTH 3
Final position (1987–88): 7th

NORTH SHIELDS

Preston Playing Fields, Preston Village, North Shields, Tyne & Wear. Tel: 091 257 7352.
Founded: 1922
President: J.R. Smith
Chairman: P. Taylor
Coach: P. Martin
Secretary: D. Daniels, 1 Highcross Road, North Shields, Tyne & Wear.
Fixtures Secretary: A.G. Shield, 9 Cresswell Avenue, North Shields. Tel: 091 2590402.
Club captain (1987–88): T. Gallon
Club captain (1988–89): T. Gallon
No. of teams: Senior 4, Youth & Minis 1
Directions to Ground: At junction of main A1 and A1058 North of Tyne tunnel follow signs to Tynemouth. At second roundabout turn right and right again. Club beside Swimming Baths.
Clubhouse: Small clubhouse with bar/lounge, four changing rooms/showers/weights room.
Colours: Royal blue/white 2″ hoops, white shorts, hooped socks. (*Change colours:* Royal blue shirts)
Floodlights: No
Membership: Playing membership £20 p.a.
Local newspaper: Newcastle Evening Chronicle/Journal
League: Northumberland & Durham 3
Final position (1987–88): 7th
Playing record (1987–88): P 39, W 14, D 1, L 24.

WEST HARTLEPOOL TDS OLD BOYS

Wiltshire Way, Hartlepool, Cleveland. Tel: 233548.
Founded: 1953
President: J.S. Howard
Chairman: D. Sweeting
Secretary: D. Bramley, 63 Hutton Avenue, Hartlepool.
Fixtures Secretary: A. Cheshire, 22 Doyalty Road, Hartlepool. Tel: 234659.
Club captain (1987–88): D.S. Burns
Club captain (1988–89): J. Dove
No. of teams: Senior 4
Clubhouse: Club bar/lounge/3 changing rooms/showers
Colours: Royal blue
Nickname: "Tech"
Floodlights: No
Membership: £10
Local newspaper: Hartlepool Mail
League: Northumberland/Durham 3
Final position (1987–88): 9th

WASHINGTON

Washington School, Spout Lane, Washington, Co. Durham.
Founded: 1976
President: R. Boyes, MP
Chairman: T.I. Hall
Secretary: W. Cowan, 5 Valebrooks Avenue, Sunderland SR2 7HS.
Club captain (1987–88): J.A. Forsyth
Club captain (1988–89): J.A. Forsyth
No. of teams: Senior 2.
Directions to Ground: Northumbria Centre, Northern Area Playing Fields, Washington.
Colours: Amber & gold hoops. (*Change colours:* Amber)
Floodlights: No
Membership: £6.50
Local newspapers: Sunderland Echo, Newcastle Journal.
League: Northumberland & Durham 3
Final position (1987–88): 2nd bottom

DURHAM/NORTHUMBERLAND 4

WENSLEYDALE

Caukill Park, Wensley Road, Leyburn, N. Yorks. Tel: 0969 23067.
Founded: 1968
President: E.Hough
Chairman: E. Lowther
Secretary: D. Ward, 3 Kelberdace Terrace, Leyburn.
Fixtures Secretary: I. Burrow, Lane House Farm, Jervaulx, Ripon. Tel: 0617 60226.
Club captain (1987–88): P. Orton
Club captain (1988–89): H. Rose
No. of teams: Senior 3.
Directions to Ground: A684 through Leyburn and ¾ mile on the left.
Colours: Black and amber. (*Change colours:* Blue).
Nickname: Rams
Floodlights: No
Membership: £15 playing
Local newspaper: Darlington & Stockton Times
League: Northumberland/Durham 4
Final position (1987–88): 1st (promoted)
Playing record (1987–88): W 20, D 3, L 11. F 450, A 241.
Competitions won: Durham IV Champions 1987–88. Yorkshire Silver Trophy 1981–82. North Yorks Trophy 1985–86.

PRUDHOE HOSPITAL

Founded: 1982
Secretary: J.R. Nichol, 11 Park Avenue, Prudhoe, Northumberland NE24 5BA.
League: DUR/NORTH 4
Final position (1987–88). 2nd

SOUTH TYNESIDE COLLEGE

St. Georges Avenue, South Shields, Tyne & Wear, Tyneside. Tel: (091) 4560403.
Founded: 1946
President: College Principal Dr D.T. Turnbull
Secretary: R. Smith, 87 Colman Avenue, South Shields, Tyne & Wear NE34 9AG. Tel: (091) 4542359.
Fixtures Secretary: C. Moule, 2 Portland Close, Chester Le Street, Co. Durham. Tel: (90) 3887548.
Club captain (1987–88): K. Stodhart
Club captain (1988–89): G. McAlpine
No. of teams: Senior 2
Directions to Ground: From South side of Tyne tunnel travel due East to S. Shields to Westoe area (N3 miles).
Clubhouse: Martec Club, adjacent pitch.

Colours: Black with 3 narrow hoops – 2 red and 1 gold between.
Floodlights: No
Local newspaper: Gazette (South Tyneside)
League: Durham/Northumberland 4
Final position (1987–88): 4th
Playing record (1987–88): P 25, W 12, L 11, D 2.

BARNARD CASTLE

(Former YMCA Building) Birch Road, Barnard Castle, Co. Durham.
Founded: 1975
President: F. Leishman
Chairman: J. Stead
Secretary: T. Worley, 29 Stainton Village, Barnard Castle, Co. Durham.
Fixtures Secretary: M. Worley, 4 Stainton Village, Barnard Castle, Co. Durham. Tel: 0833-38923.
Club captain (1987–88): P. Kelsall
No. of teams: Senior 2, Youth & Minis 1
Colours: All Black. (*Change colours:* Gold)
Nickname: Castle
Floodlights: No
Membership: £10 playing, £2 associate.
Local newspaper: Teesdale Mercury
League: Northumberland/Durham 4
Final position (1987–88): Fourth
Playing record (1987–88): P 7, W 4, L 3.

RICHMONDSHIRE

The Terrace Hotel, Maison Dieu, Richmond, N. Yorkshire.
Secretary: J. Tomlinson, 12 Laburnham Close, Richmond. N. Yorkshire. Tel: 0748 833501 (W).
League: Durham/Northumberland 4
Final position (1987–88): 5th

JARROVIANS

Lukes Lane, Hebburn, Tyne & Wear. Tel: 0632 693716
Founded: 1961
Secretary: S. Gallagher, 25 Jervis Street, Hebburn, Tyne & Wear NE31 2XP.
League: DUR/NORTH 4
Final position (1987–88): 6th

DURHAM CIVIL SERVICE

Civil Service Sports Ground, Belmont, Durham.
Secretary: C. Cummins, 5 Ash Terrace, Bowburn, Co. Durham.
League: Durham/Northumberland 4
Final position (1987–88): 7th

NEWTON AYCLIFFE

Moor Lane. Tel: 312768
Founded: 1958
President: G. Robson
Chairman: R.P. Shepherd
Coach: D. Pass
Secretary: Rev D. Capron, The Vicarage, St Cuthberts Way. Tel: 0325 313613.
Fixtures Secretary: G. Burn, 53 Seymoor Grove, Eaglescliffe. Tel: 0642 785098.
Club captain (1987–88): D. Kelly
Club captain (1988–89): S. Donnelly
No. of teams: Senior 3.
Colours: Green, maroon, old gold. (*Change colours:* Purple).
Floodlights: No
Membership: £2
Local newspaper: Northern Echo
League: Durham/Northumberland 4
Final position (1987–88): 6th

Luckless England scrum-half Nigel Melville on a happy day as the North retain their Divisional title against the Midlands at Northampton – 23–15. Photo: Colorsport.

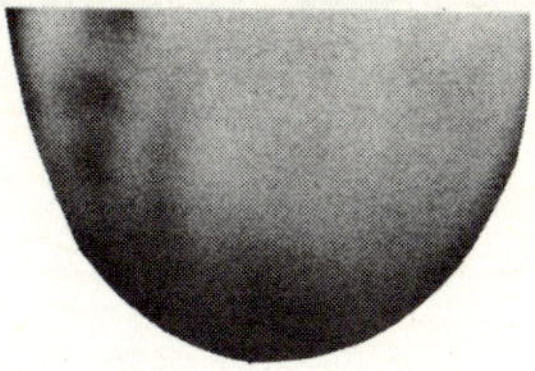

Midlands fly-half Les Cusworth against the North on 19th December 1987. It was an Indian Summer for Les – one of the game's geniuses. Photo: Colorsport.

MIDLANDS DIVISION

THE Midlands Division produced a different style from the North with their clubs spread over 24 leagues, starting with a top division followed by two strong regional sections – ie Midlands 1, Midlands 2 West and 2 East.

The leagues were then divided along traditional county lines as prevails in the County Championship – with Notts., Lincs. and Derbys, Staffordshire, North Midlands, Warwickshire, Leicestershire and East Midlands all providing their own leagues.

Traditionally, the Midlands have centred on a few very strong senior sides such as Leicester, Moseley, Coventry, Bedford, Nottingham and Northampton and all the other teams have been classed as 'juniors', but with promotion and relegation in existence several clubs are due shortly to 'shake up' the teams at the top.

The first of these challengers are Stoke, more famous for their soccer team and Stanley Matthews, but strong junior teams like Barker's Butts, Mansfield and Paviors can soon be expected to make their mark. The whole concept of senior and junior teams could undergo quite a change.

MIDLANDS LEAGUES

STOKE are the first team from the Midlands to make an upward move as they won eight of their ten matches, but had to overcome a strong challenge from both Barker's Butts and Mansfield. At the foot of the Division 1 table were Hinckley and the pointless Peterborough and they are replaced by Midlands 2 West winners Hereford, who lost only one match out of 10 played and were four points clear of all opposition, and Newark, who had the same record, but only beat off the challenge of Vipers by two points.

The basement teams in the two leagues were Leamington and Evesham (West) and Loughborough and the pointless Wigston (East).

TABLES 1987–88

MIDLANDS 1

	P	W	D	L	F	A	Pts
Stoke	10	8	0	2	128	83	16
Barker's Butts	10	7	0	3	166	87	14
Mansfield	10	7	0	3	106	98	14
Paviors	10	6	0	4	119	92	12
Walsall	10	5	1	4	183	100	11
Westleigh	10	5	1	4	135	114	11
Stockwood Pk	10	5	1	4	118	122	11
Wolverhampton	10	5	0	5	116	149	10
Stafford	10	3	0	7	110	166	6
Hinkley	10	2	1	7	111	157	5
Peterboro	10	0	0	10	71	195	0

MIDLANDS 2 WEST

	P	W	D	L	F	A	Pts
Hereford	10	9	0	1	245	54	18
Dixonians	10	7	0	3	117	80	14
S Coldfield	10	7	0	3	125	125	14
Dudley	10	6	0	4	96	76	12
Tamworth	10	6	0	4	97	86	12
Bromsgrove	10	4	1	5	97	91	9
Burton	9	4	0	5	81	85	8
Worcester	10	4	0	6	106	138	8
Newbold	10	3	1	6	56	125	7
Leamington	10	2	0	8	87	155	4
Evesham	9	1	0	8	36	128	2

MIDLANDS 2 EAST

	P	W	D	L	F	A	Pts
Newark	10	9	0	1	243	72	18
Vipers	10	8	0	2	172	77	16
Matlock	10	7	1	2	173	97	15
Syston	10	6	0	4	163	98	12
L Buzzard	10	5	2	3	112	114	12
Kettering	10	5	0	5	145	88	10
Lincoln	10	5	0	5	89	127	10
Stoneygate	10	3	1	6	115	115	7
Stamford	10	3	0	7	103	190	6
Loughboro	10	2	0	8	74	257	4
Wigston	10	0	0	10	49	208	0

STOKE-ON-TRENT

Hartwell Lane, Barlaston, Stoke-on-Trent. Tel: Barlaston 2807.
Founded: 1884
President: A. Walker
Chairman: M. Mosley
Coach: N. McPherson
Secretary: I.P. Godfrey, 78 Caverswall Road, Blythe Bridge, Stoke-on-Trent. Tel: 0782 393307 (L) 0283 216161 (W)
Fixtures Secretary: P. Daniels, 78 Eastbourne, Northwood, Stoke-on-Trent. Tel: 0782 279911 (H) 0782 395959 (B)
Club captain (1987–88): D. Tatton
Club captain (1988–89): S. Teasdale
No. of teams: Senior 4. Youth & Minis 1.
Directions to Ground: From the North – leave M6 at Junc 15, follow A34 south and then follow sign to Barlaston. Go through village and ground is 1 mile on the right. From the South – leave M6 at Junc 14, follow A34 north, directions then as above.
Ground capacity: 5,000
Clubhouse: Changing facilities for 6 teams, bar, seating capacity 120, separate private function room for 50.
Colours: Cambridge/navy blue shirts, black shorts, navy blue socks. (*Change colours:* Black)
Nickname: The Potters
Floodlights: Yes
Admission: £1
Membership: £25
Programme: Editor, S. Beck.
Local Newspaper: The Sentinel (Hanley, Stoke-on-Trent)
League: Midlands 1
Final position (1987–88): Winners (promoted)
Playing record (1987–88): P 32, W24, L8.
Competitions won: Mercian Merit Table 1980/81, 1984/85; Courage Midlands Div 1 1987/88.

BARKERS' BUTTS

Pickford Grange Lane, Allesley, Coventry CV5 9AR. Tel: Meriden 22192.
Founded: 1947
President: W.J. Gittings
Chairman: A.R. Gibbs
Coach: Panel under captain
Secretary: R.G. Coward, Pickford Grange Lane, Allesley, Coventry CV5 9AR. Tel: Meriden 22192.
Fixtures Secretary: T.H. Jones, Stonehaven, Tamworth Road, Coventry. Tel: Keresley 2015.
Club captain (1987–88): S.R. Hall
Club captain (1988–89): N. Brown
No. of teams: Senior 4, Youth & Minis 5.
Directions to Ground: From Coventry A45 towards Birmingham – turn off left towards Meriden – first left. From Birmingham A45 – follow Pickford Green sign off to right.
Ground capacity: 2,000
Clubhouse: Brick built – two bars – gymnasium
Colours: Royal blue & gold. (*Change colours:* Amber)
Floodlights: Full training lights only.
Membership: £10
Programme: 8 page: 20p (Editor Hon. Sec.)
Local newspaper: Coventry Evening Telegraph
League: Midlands 1
Final position (1987–88): 2nd
Playing record (1987–88): P 35, W 29, L 6, D 0
Competitions won: Coventry Minor Cup (U21's).

MANSFIELD

Eakring Road, Mansfield, Notts. Tel: 0623–649834
Founded: 1956
President: Ted Lane
Chairman: Byron Edwards
Coach: Dave Doig
Secretary: Dylan Howells, 273 Nottingham Road, Mansfield, Notts. Tel: 0623–35722
Fixtures Secretary: Kevin Swithenbank, 40 Summercourt Drive, Ravenshead, Notts. Tel: 0623–793726
Club captain (1987–88): Pete Emberson
Club captain (1988–89): Pete Emberson
No. of teams: Senior 5, Youth & Minis 4.
Directions to Ground: Take A617 S.E. from Mansfield Centre; turn left after 1–2 miles at first lights after joining dual carriageway; turn right at 2nd mini-roundabout after 1 mile onto Eakring Road; ground on right after ½ mile.
Ground capacity: No Stand
Clubhouse: Large lounge, large clubroom, 7 changing rooms, 2 sets of showers.
Colours: Blue & white hoops.
Floodlights: Training lights only.
Admission: Nil
Membership: £19
Programme: Match programme for most home games (Editor: Byron)
Local newspaper: CHAD
League: Midlands 1
Final position (1987–88): 3rd
Playing record (1987–88): P 32, W 24, D Nil, L 8, F 501, A 310.
Competitions won: Winners Notts Pennant League 1978–79, 1979–80, 1981–82, 1982–83, 1983–84, 1984–85, 1985–86. Winners Notts Cup 1977–78, 1984–85. Winners Notts Colts Cup 1982–83, 1984–85, 1985–86, 1987–88.

PAVIORS

Burntstump Hill, Arnold, Nottingham. Tel: 0602–630384.
Founded: 1922
President: R. Rossin
Chairman: M. Sudbury
Coach: R. O'Brien
Secretary: P. Evans, 86B Redhill Road, Arnold, Nottingham. Tel: 0602–269930.
Fixtures Secretary: C. Whitworth, 1 Southpark Avenue, Berry Hill, Mansfield. Tel: Mansfield 648871.
Club captain (1987–88): M. Lacey
Club captain (1988–89): M. Lacey
No. of teams: Senior 5.
Directions to Ground: Off A614, 4 miles north of Nottingham.
Ground capacity: 400
Clubhouse: New one being built Summer 1988.
Colours: Green jersey, red band.
Nickname: "PAVS"
Floodlights: Yes
Membership: £25
Programme: 30p (Editor: P. Sallis)
Local newspaper: Nottingham Evening Post
League: Midlands 1
Final position (1987–88): 4th
Playing record (1987–88): 1st XI P 33, W 19, L 13, D 1

WALSALL

Delves Road, Walsall. Tel: Walsall 26818.
Founded: 1926
President: W.F. Perkins
Chairman: John King
Secretary: D.E. Horton, 53 Stonnall Road, Aldridge. Tel: 55320.
Fixtures Secretary: T. Day, 20 Daffodil Place, Walsall. Tel: 611729.
Club captain (1987–88): Nick Archer
Club captain (1988–89): Rob Harding
No. of teams: Senior 5, Youth & Minis 7.
Directions to Ground: Jnc. 7, M6, turn left at Crest

Motel, 600 yrds on right hand side.
Ground capacity: Stand, 100
Clubhouse: all facilities.
Colours: Scarlet shirts/socks, black shorts.
Floodlights: No
Admission: by programme
Membership: £2.50
Programme: 25p
Local newspaper: Walsall Observer
League: Midlands 1
Final position (1987–88): 4th
Playing record (1987–88): P 33, W 19, D 3, L 11, F 523, A 349.

WESTLEIGH

Lutterworth Road, Blaby, Leics. Tel: 0533 771010.
Founded: 1904
President: B.W. Ball
Chairman: N. Otter
Coach: B. Howell
Secretary: R.D.R. Wain, 12 Talbot Lane, Leicester. Tel: ?533 518139.
Fixtures Secretary: C.J. Barker, 66 Carisbrooke Road, Leicester. Tel: 0533 708676.
Club captain (1987–88): D.K. Mills
Club captain (1988–89): L. Clifford
No. of teams: Senior 5. Youth & Minis 5.
Directions to Ground: A46 from Leicester to Lutterworth; leaving Blaby Village on RHS.
Colours: Black and white. (*Change colours:* Various/ County shirts)
Floodlights: Yes
Membership: Playing £25
Local newspaper: Leicester Mercury
League: Midlands 1
Final position (1987–88): 6th

STOCKWOOD PARK

London Road, Luton, Beds. Tel: Luton 28044.
Founded: 1946
President: L.G. Carr
Chairman: M.T. Bronson
Coach: S. Askew
Secretary: C.A. Chatwin, 30 Honeygate, Luton LU2 7EP, Luton Tel: (0582) 29954 (H), 01-492-8872 (B).
Fixtures Secretary: R. Poulter, St. Helier, Kings Walden Road, Offley, Hitchin, Herts. Tel: Offley 656 (H), Hitchin 54801 (B).
Club captain (1987–88): M.A. Lovell
Club captain (1988–89): M.A. Lovell
No. of teams: Senior 6, Youth & Minis 9.
Directions to Ground: M1 to Junction 10 exit, turn left at roundabout, follow sign for Luton, 1st set of lights turn left into Stockwood Park. Clubhouse on right.
Clubhouse: Red and yellow brick, two downstairs bars. Upstairs room with panoramic views over pitches.
Colours: Red shirts with yellow band, navy shorts, red socks. (*Change colours:* Yellow shirts)
Nickname: Park
Floodlights: Yes **Admission:** Nil
Membership: £18
Programme: Donation (Editor: John Humphries)
Local newspaper: Herald, Luton News
League: Midlands 1
Final position (1987–88): 7th
Playing record (1987–88): P 36, W 22, D 2, L12
Competitions won: East Midlands Cup, beating Leighton Buzzard 17–15, Hertford floodlight competition beating Harlow 6–4.

WOLVERHAMPTON

Castlecroft Road, Wolverhampton, WV3 8NA. Tel: 0902 763900.
Founded: 1875
Secretary: S.J. Fraser, 31 Catholic Lane, Sedgley, Dudley, West Midlands. Tel: 09073 5638 (H); 038-482 3391 (W).
Fixtures Secretary: J. Hurst Knight, 6 Westgate Villas, Bridgnorth, Shropshire. Tel: 07462 5563.
Colts Secretary: R.C. Davies, 35 Woodfield Heights, Tettenhall, Wolverhampton. Tel: 0902 752122.
Local newspaper: Express & Star
League: Midlands 1
Final position (1987–88): 8th

STAFFORD

Castlefields, Newport Road, Stafford. Tel: 0785 211433.
Founded: 1876
President: Lord Stafford
Chairman: Ken Bailey
Coach: Brian Malpass
Secretary: Dai Bryant, 26 Springvale Rise, Parkside, Stafford. Tel: 0785 49590.
Fixtures Secretary: Derek Warbrick, 7 Beech Close, Haughton, Stafford. Tel: 0785 780592.
Club captain (1987–88): Andy Lewis
Club captain (1988–89): Glyn Williams
No. of teams: Senior 5. Youth & Minis 5.
Directions to Ground: A518 Newport Road. ½ mile RHS from Town Centre.
Stand capacity: 300
Ground capacity: 3000
Clubhouse: Lounge and players bar.
Colours: Black/amber
Floodlights: No
Admission: £1
Membership: £25
Programme: Free
Local newspaper: Stafford Newsletter
League: Midland 1
Final position (1987–88): 9th (relegated)
Playing record (1987–88): P 32, W 8, D 0, L 24

HINCKLEY

Leicester Road, Hinckley. Tel: 0455-615010.
Founded: 1893
President: R.S. Palmer
Chairman: D.J. Barratt
Coach: A. Ottey
Secretary: G. March, Tinkers Cuss, Sharnford, Leics. Tel: 045527-2380.
Fixtures Secretary: G. Targett, 14 Grange Drive, Burbage, Hinckley.
Club captain (1987–88): P. Adams
Club captain (1988–89): P. Green
No. of teams: Senior 2
Directions to Ground: Left hand side of A47 towards Leicester.
Colours: Black & Amber.
Floodlights: Yes
Admission: Collection
Membership: £10
Local newspaper: Hinckley Times
League: Midlands 1
Final position (1987–88): 11th
Playing record (1987–88): P 34, W 16, D 2, L 16
Competitions won: 5 times winners of Leicestershire Cup – twice runners up.

PETERBOROUGH

Second Drove, Fengate, Peterborough. Tel: 0733 69413.
Founded: 1924
Secretary: I. McN Hamilton, 73 Garton End Road, Peterborough PE1 4EZ. Tel: 0733 45240 (H) 0733 310101 (W).
League: Mids 1
Final position (1987–88): 11th

HEREFORD

Wyeside, Hereford. Tel: (0432) 273410.
Founded: 1922
President: J.F. Escott
Chairman: J.C.E. Farr
Coach: W.J. Watkins
Secretary: J.A. Butler, 3 Longworth Road, Tupsley, Hereford. Tel: (0432) 266449 (H), (0432) 359881 (B).
Fixtures Secretary: M.D. Osborne, 3 The Courtlands, Wimforton, Hereford. Tel: 054-46-749.
Club captain (1987–88): W.J. Watkins
Club captain (1988–89): A.J. Hill
No. of teams: Senior 3, Youth 2.
Directions to Ground: On the riverside (Wye) ¼ mile above New Bridge.
Ground capacity: 3,000
Clubhouse: Old school pavilion
Colours: Red (*Change colours:* White)
Floodlights: Yes
Membership: £20
Local newspaper: Hereford Times
League: Midlands 2 West
Final position (1987–88): Winners
Playing record (1987–88): P 34, W 30, D 1, L 3, F 876, A 236.
Competitions won: North Midlands KO Cup 10.4.88, Worcester RFC Floodlit Trophy 13.4.88.

DIXONIANS

Wassell Grove Lane, Wassell Grove, Hagley, Worcs. Tel: 0562 882288.
Founded: 1913
President: A.J. Kendrick
Chairman: R. Burton
Coach: A. Miles
Secretary: K. Brittain, 'The Brambles', Hollywell Lane, Bayton Common, Clows Top, Worcs DY14 7NR. Tel: 029922 255.
Fixtures Secretary: D. Hall, 32 Jerrard Drive, Sutton Coldfield, West Mids. Tel: 021-378 2839.
Club captain (1987–88): G. Viney
Club captain (1988–89): J. Larkin
No. of teams: Senior 4. Youth & Minis 0.
Directions to Ground: Junction 3 on M5, A456 towards Kidderminster, at 4th island turn right, ½ mile on RHS.
Ground capacity: All standing (1000)
Clubhouse: Bar for 150, changing 6 teams, shower, bath.
Colours: Bottle green/red stripe. (*Change colours:* Maroon)
Floodlights: No.
Membership: £35
Local newspaper: Express and Star
League: Midlands 2 West
Final position (1987–88): 2nd
Playing record (1987–88): P 39, W 25, D 2, L 12, F 513, A 443.

SUTTON COLDFIELD

Walmley Road, Sutton Coldfield. Tel: 021 351 5243.
Founded: 1921
President: P. Maxwell-Jones
Chairman: R. Smoldon
Coach: A. Wilkes
Secretary: T. Gallagher, 11 The Rise, Great Barr, Birmingham B42 2BP. Tel: 021 358 5243.
Fixtures Secretary: R. Smoldon, 263 Boldmere Road, Sutton Coldfield. Tel: 021 373 2539.
Club captain (1987–88): P. Proctor
Club captain (1988–89): K. Lewis
No. of teams: Senior 6. Youth & Minis 12.
Ground capacity: 3,000
Clubhouse: 2 storey, 3 bars, 8 changing rooms.
Colours: Emerald green. (*Change colours:* Blue)
Nickname: Suts
Floodlights: Yes
Membership: £10 p.a.
Programme: Available free. Editor: A. Wilcock.
Local newspaper: Sutton Coldfield News
League: Midland 2 West
Final position (1987–88): 3rd
Playing record (1987–88): P 31, W 17, D 1, L 13, F 467, A 396.
Competitions won: Warwickshire 7's 1981/82; Warwickshire 2nd XV 1985.

DUDLEY

Heath Brook, Swindon Road, Wall Heath, W. Mids. Tel: Kingswinford 287006.
Founded: 1927
Secretary: D. Evans, 156 Common Road, Wombourne, W. Midlands WV5 0LX. Tel: 0902 894463 (H) 0902 22431 (W).
Fixtures Secretary: R. Connett, Barnet House, Wordsley Green, Wordsley, Stourbridge, W. Midlands DY8 5PD. Tel: 0384 295296 (H) 0384 278130 (W).
League: Mids 2 West
Final position (1987–88): 4th
Playing record (1987–88): p 37, W 24, D 1, L 12, F 543, A 249.

TAMWORTH

Wiggington Park, Tamworth, Staffs. Tel: 0827 68794.
Founded: 1925
Secretary: T.R. Wakelin, 10 Witherley Road, Atherstone, Warks CV9 1LZ. Tel: 0827 2472.
Fixtures Secretary: A. Farmer, 45 Bever Close, Glascote Heath, Tamworth. Tel: 0827 287764 (H) 021 558 0275 (W).
League: Mids 2 West
Final position (1987–88): 5th

BROMSGROVE

Finstall Park, Bromsgrove, Worcs. Tel: 0527 74690.
Founded: 1872
Secretary: K.R. Hurst, Wormash Farmhouse, fockbury Lane, Dodford, Bromsgrove B61 9AT. Tel: 0527 33987 (H) 021 552 1541 (W).
League: Mids 2 West
Final position (1987–88): 6th
Playing record (1987–88): P 32, W 20, D 2, L 10, F 533, A 291.

BURTON ON TRENT

Peel Croft, Lichfield Street, Burton on Trent, Staffs. DE14 3RH. Tel: Burton (0283) 64510.
Founded: 1870
President: D.H. Mayger
Coach: D.M. Williams
Secretary: A. Wilson, 5 Hornbrook Road, Burton on Trent, Staffs. DE13 0XE. Tel: 0283 61342.
Fixtures Secretary: P.E. Richard, 20 Olton Road, Mickleover, Derby DE3 5PL. Tel: 0332 516901.
Club captain (1987–88): Neil Thompson
Club captain (1988–89): Andy Peach
No. of teams: Senior 6, Youth & Minis 5 of each.
Directions to Ground: Just off the Lichfield end of the High Street (B5121) and distinguishable by its ten floodlight pylons from any angle.

Ground capacity: 1970 County Championship Final housed appx. 5,000 (Staffs beat Gloucestershire), but there were a few crushed toes: 10 of them mine. Stand, appx. 250
Clubhouse: Main clubroom with bar, kitchen, changing rooms and rather nice lounge.
Colours: White with black diagonal band over right shoulder, shorts white, stockings black with white tops. (*Change colours:* Red jerseys)
Nickname: Crofters
Floodlights: Yes (HQ of Staffs County Championship home games, senior and under 21).
Admission: Non-gate taking club. (County Championship games (see above) and Staffs County Cup Final determined by Staffs ??).
Membership: Ordinary members £8.50; patrons/patronesses £15; players (snr) £22; players (under 19 on 1st Sept, schoolboys, college students, OAPs £5; ladies £5; juniors (under 17 on 1st Sept.) £2.50.
Programme: Teams, ref (and society) advertisements, club notes, no charge (copy enclosed). (Editor: Mr D.M. Williams)
Local Daily Evening newspaper: Burton Daily Mail, 65–68 High Street, Burton on Trent, Staffs DE14 1LE. Tel: 0283-512345]Sports Editor: Mr Rex Page]
League: Midlands 2 West
Final position (1987–88): 7th (out of 11)
Playing record (1987–88): P 38, W 16, L 20, D 2, F 474, A 570.
Competitions won: Sadly – none 1987–88; Staffs County Cup Winners 1971 – slightly downhill since, I fear.

WORCESTER

Sixways, Pershore Lane, Hindlip, Worcester. Tel: 0905 51173.
Founded: 1871
President: R.G. Kimberley
Chairman: L.A. Lee
Coach: P. John
Secretary: W.J.L. Best, The Flat, Sixways, Pershore Lane, Hindlip, Worcester.
Fixtures Secretary: R. Paul, 139 Liverpool Road, Worcester. Tel: 0905 355565.
Club captain (1987–88): J.N. Wootten
Club captain (1988–89): J.N. Wootten
No. of teams: Senior 7, Youth & Minis 10.
Directions to Ground: Off M5 junction 6 onto B4538.
Ground capacity: Vast, Stand, small open stand
Clubhouse: Lounge, Club room – 2 bars – changing rooms etc.
Colours: Navy & gold
Floodlights: Yes
Membership: £20
Local newspaper: Worcester Evening News
League: Midlands 2 West
Final position (1987–88): 8th
Playing record (1987–88): P 31, W 15, D 1, L 15, F 379, A 418

NEWBOLD-ON-AVON

Parkfield Road, Rugby, Warwickshire. Tel: 0788 565811.
Founded: 1894
President: D.C. Pope
Chairman: P.E. Fereday
Coach: A.R. Spooner
Secretary: R. Yapp, 55 Long Furlong, Rugby, Warwickshire CV22 5QT. Tel: 0788 814879.
Fixtures Secretary: C. Cramphorn, 262 Lower Hillmorton Road, Rugby, Warwickshire CV21 4AB. Tel: 0788 73632.
Club captain (1987–88): Paul Fereday
Club captain (1988–89): John Wallace
No. of teams: Senior 3, Youth & Minis 1
Directions to Ground: Two miles from M6, junction 1
Colours: Red & black hoops
Floodlights: No
Local newspaper: Rugby Advertiser
League: Midland 2 West
Final position (1987–88): Ninth
Playing record (1987–88): P 35, W 17, D 2, L 16, F 474, A 429

LEAMINGTON

'Moorefields', Kenilworth Road, Leamington. Tel: 0926 25584.
Founded: 1926
President: M. Goymer
Chairman: R. Maycock
Coach: D. Scannell
Secretary: P.G. Payne, 14 Lillington Road, Leamington Spa, CV32 5YR.
Fixtures Secretary: P.G. Payne, as above.
Club captain (1987–88): A. Davies
Club captain (1988–89): P. Gray
No. of teams: Senior 6. Youth & Minis 8.
Ground capacity: 3000
Colours: Royal blue with single scarlet/gold hoop. (*Change colours:* Red)
Floodlights: Yes
Admission: Optional by programme
Membership: £20 (players). £3 (non-players).
Programme: 50p. Editor: TBA.
Local newspaper: Leamington Courier
League: Midlands 2 West
Final position (1987–88): 10th (relegated)
Playing record (1987–88): W 18, L 20.
Competitions won: Warwickshire 2nd XV Cup; Warwickshire Colts 7's Cup, Veterans Cup (over 35's), 3rd place in Try Pernod Attack Awards.

EVESHAM

Evesham Sports Club, Albert Road, Evesham. Tel: 0386 6469.
Secretary: J.P. Hartley, Nightingale House, Bishampton, Pershore, Worcs WR10 2NH. Tel: 038 682 325 (H) 03805 54848 (W).
League: Mids 2 West
Final position (1987–88): 11th (bottom)

Nottingham's Gary Rees – one of the top flankers in the Midlands and for England. Photo: Colorsport.

Dying but not dead. The County Championship keeps going and produces thrillers like this semi-final – Warwickshire 31 Surrey 19 at Coventry. Warwicks' Steve Thomas (No. 9) receives from prop Lee Johnson. Photo: Colorsport.

NEWARK

The Clubhouse, Kelham Road, Newark, Notts. Tel: 0636 702355.
Founded: 1919
President and Chairman: P. Butler
Coach: C. Fehrs
Secretary: R.J.H. Ewens, Timber Top, Main Street, Thoroton, Notts NG13 9DS.
Fixtures Secretary: L. Dukes, 47 King Street, Southwell, Notts. Tel: 0636 813542.
Club captain (1987–88 and 1988–89): A. King
No. of teams: Senior 5. Youth & Minis 11.
Directions to Ground: From Newark Castle take signs to Mansfield (left over railway crossing). Ground is ½ mile along on RHS.
Stand capacity: 250
Ground capacity: Approx. 3000
Colours: Royal blue shirts with single white hoop/blue shorts.
Floodlights: Yes
Admission: Nil
Membership: £20
Programme: 50p (Editor: K. Hunter)
Local newspaper: Newark Advertiser
League: Midlands 2E
Final position (1987–88): Winnners (promoted)
Competitions won: Midlands Div 2 (East), Notts Cup, Notts, Lincs and Derbys Cup.

VIPERS

Blaby By Pass, Whetstone, Leicester. Tel: 0533 864777.
Founded: 1920
Secretary: G. Rossb, 5 Broomleys, Countesthorpe, Leicester LE8 3RW. Tel: 0533 779431 (H).
League: Mids 2 East
Final position (1987–88): 2nd

MATLOCK

Cromford Meadows, Cromford, Matlock. Tel: Wirksworth 2821.
Founded: 1926
President: C. Loeber
Chairman: J.G. Lowry
Coach: Niel Mantell
Secretary: Kevin Archer, Stoneridge Barn, The Knoll, Tansley. Tel: Matlock 4319.
Fixtures Secretary: D.J. Pearson
Club captain (1987–88): Chris Roome
Club captain (1988–89). Chris Roome
No. of teams: Senior 4, Youth & Minis 1
Directions to Ground: Off A6, opposite Cromford Church on Crick Road.
Ground capacity: Lots
Clubhouse: Bar/bass, 6 changing rooms/showers, dining room.
Colours: Royal Blue. (*Change colours:* Scarlet)
Floodlights: No
Membership: £25 playing. £10 vice president/social.
Programme: Donation (Editor: Mr A. Wragg)
Local newspaper: Matlock Murcury/Derbyshire Times/ Derby Evening Telegraph
League: Midlands 2 East
Final position (1987–88): 3rd
Playing record (1987–88): P 35, W 25, L 8, D 2, F 677, A 354
Competitions won: Derbyshire Cup (7), Notts, Lincs & Derbys Cup (10), Derbyshire Sevens (13), Newark Sevens (1), Loughborough Sevens (2), TOC H (Manchester) Sevens (1), Buxton Sevens (2), Pernod "Try" Attack (2), Tigger Price Memorial Plaque (7), John Player Cup qualifyers (3).

SYSTON

Fosseway, Syston. Tel: 0533 625707. (New ground Dec 1988: Barkby Road, Queniborough.)
Founded: 1887
President: F.R. Fryer
Chairman: D. Loughran
Coach: E. Walker
Secretary: F.R. Fryer, 1 Festival Avenue, Thurmaston LE4 8JB.
Fixtures Secretary: C. Borderick, 25 Turn Street, Syston. Tel: 0533 007552.
Club captain (1987–88): P. Smith
Club captain (1988–89): D. Rennie
No. of teams: Senior 5. Youth & Minis 5.
Clubhouse: Moving to new ground, Dec. 88, at Barkby Road, Queniborough.
Colours: Navy & saxe blue hoops. (*Change colours:* red)
Floodlights: Yes
Membership: £16
Programme: Free (Editor: E. Wheeler)
Local newspaper: Leicester Mercury
League: Midlands East 2
Final position (1987–88): 4th
Competitions won: Oakham 7's, Newark 7's Plate.

LEIGHTON BUZZARD

Leighton Road, Stanbridge, Leighton Buzzard, Beds LU7 9HR. Tel: 0525 371322.
Founded: 1934/35
President: H. Burchell
Chairman: A. Hodey
Coach: D. Hyde
Secretary: J. McCormack, 15 Neptune Gardens, Leighton Buzzard, Beds LU7 8NW. Tel: 0525 378194.
Fixtures Secretary: A. Hodey, 36 Woodmans Close, Leighton Buzzard, Beds. Tel: 0525 379976.
Club captain (1987–88): J. Goodier
Club captain (1988–89): J. Fraser
No. of teams: Senior 6. Youth & Minis 11.
Directions to Ground: From North: M1 Junction 13 – Woburn – Leighton Buzzard – Stanbridge. From South: M1 Junction 9 – A5 through Dunstable – turn off to Tilsworth and Stanbridge. Ground between Stanbridge and Leighton Buzzard.
Clubhouse: 7 changing rooms, referee's room, members bar, main hall and bar, Steward's accommodation.
Colours: Navy/white regular hoops. (*Change colours:* Myrtle green)
Nickname: The Buzzards
Floodlights: No
Membership: £20
Programme: 25p (Editor: R. Harper)
Local newspaper: Beds and Bucks Observer, The Herald
League: Midlands 2 East
Final position (1987–88): 5th
Playing record (1987–88): P 40, W 26, D 2, L 12.
Competitions won: Bedfordshire Cup 1980/81, 1985/6, 1986/87, 1987/88. East Midlands Championship 1985/86, 1986/87.

KETTERING

Waverley Road, Kettering, Northants. Tel: 0536 85588.
Founded: 1875
President: J. Cutthel
Chairman: P.H. Dodson
Coach: P. Searle
Secretary: J.D.E. Stephens, 8 High Street, Cranford, Kettering, Northants. Tel: 0536 78737.

Fixtures Secretary: R. Bowpey, Messuage Farm, 10 Lower Benefield, Peterborough. Tel: Bus 0536 72281, Home 08325 382.
Club captain (1987–88): S.A. Bridgeman
Club captain (1988–89): S.A. Bridgeman
No. of teams: Senior 5, Youth & Minis 6
Directions to Ground: From A6 through town left or right turn onto Pipers Hill Road, 2nd right onto Waverley Road.
Colours: Blue/white hoops. (*Change colours:* Blue)
Floodlights: No
Admission: Nil
Membership: £35
Programme: 50p (Editor: M. Naylor/W. Linnel)
Local newspaper: Evening Telegraph
League: Midlands 2 East
Final position (1987–88): 6th
Playing record (1987–88): P 37, W 24, D 1, L 12, F 634, A 363
Competitions won: Beach Villas Cup, Corby 7's Casuals 7's Bert White Shield, Hospitals Cup.

LINCOLN

The Lindum Sports Ground, Wragby Road, Lincoln. Tel: 0522 26592.
Founded: 1921
President: A. Beatham
Chairman: M. Rossington
Coach: R. Whittaker
Secretary: B.R. Hunt, 3 St Giles Avenue, Lincoln. Tel: 0522 23743.
Fixtures Secretary: E.A.F. Coulthard, 25 Queensway, Lincoln. Tel: 0522 33666.
Club captain (1987–88): D. Hughes
Club captain (1988–89): M. Wilson
No. of teams: Senior 4. Youth & Minis 3.
Directions to Ground: Top of the hill near the Cathedral, Wragby Road ← St. Giles Avenue.
Colours: White, red collars. (*Change colours:* Red)
Nickname: Imps
Floodlights: No
Membership: £30
Programme: Editor: John Grove
Local newspaper: Lincoln Echo
League: Mid East 2
Final position (1987–88): 6th
Playing record (1987–88): P 31, W 11, D 1, L 19, F 467, A 452.

STONEYGATE

Covert Lane, Scraptoft Lane, Leicester. Tel: 0533 419188.
Founded: 1888
President: M.J. Astill
Chairman: R.D. Foxon
Coach: J. Hall
Secretary: S.G. Mounfield, 89 Curzon Avenue, Birstall, Leicester LE4 4AG. Tel: 0533 674410 (H).
Fixtures Secretary: R.D. Foxon, 7 Church Street, Rothley, Leicester.
Club captain (1987–88): D. Hope
Club captain (1988–89): D. Hope
No. of teams: Senior 5. Youth & Minis 5.
Directions to Ground: A47 to East of Leicester. Follow signs for Scraptoft then ask!
Ground capacity: 16 acres
Clubhouse: 2 storey
Colours: Cardinal & white hoops. (*Change colours:* Grey, black, pink)
Nickname: 'Gate
Floodlights: Training only
Membership: £45
Local newspaper: Leic Mercury
League: Midlands 2 East
Final position (1987–88): 8th
Competitions won: Leicestershire County Cup, Westleigh Sevens, Loughborough Sevens.

STAMFORD

Hambleton Road, Stamford, Lincs. Tel: 0780 52180.
Founded: 1902
Secretary: A.E. Lawrence, 97 Casterton Road, Stamford. Tel: 0780 52689 (H) 0780 64387 (W).
League: Mids 2 East
Final position (1987–88): 9th

LOUGHBOROUGH

Derby Road Playing Fields, Loughborough, Leics. Tel: 0509-216093.
Founded: 1891 (Re-founded 1929)
President: J.F.G. Charles
Chairman: J.F.G. Charles
Coach: W.D. Gray
Secretary: T. Cameron-Smith, 31 Knighthorpe Road, Loughborough. Tel: 0509-268326.
Fixtures Secretary: P.V.J. Harlow, 26 Hathern Road, Longwhaton. Tel: 0509-842411.
No. of teams: Senior 5, Youth & Minis 10.
Directions to Ground: Just off the main road from Loughborough to Kegworth (A6).
Clubhouse: Bar, lounge, changing rooms, bath, showers, toilets, kitchen, etc.
Colours: Blue & Gold (hoops). (*Change colours:* Yellow (plain).
Floodlights: No
Membership: £20.00
Local newspaper: Loughborough Echo
League: Midlands 2 East
Final position (1987–88): 10th from 11 (Relegated).
Playing record (1987–88): P 10, W 2, D 0, L 8.

WIGSTON

Leicester Road, Countesthorpe, Leics. Tel: 0533 771153.
Founded: 1946
Secretary: P. Williams, 33 Newton Lane, Wigston, Leicestershire. Tel: 0533 22619 (H) 0533 22619 (W).
League: Mids 2 East
Final position (1987–88): 11th (bottom)

STAFFORDSHIRE LEAGUES

STAFFORDSHIRE were one of the weaker leagues in the division with only two divisions consisting of seven and nine clubs respectively. Trentham in Division 1 won all their six matches, whilst Uttoxeter took the Division 2 title, also with a perfect record in eight games, but they did it in style by scoring an amazing 201 points.

The county needs a few more clubs to strengthen its structure, although it does provide several teams for the senior divisions.

TABLES 1987–88

STAFFORDSHIRE 1

	P	W	D	L	F	A	Pts
Trentham	6	6	–	–	94	24	12
Rugeley	6	5	–	1	129	44	10
Burntwood	6	4	–	2	96	57	8
Cannock	6	3	–	3	96	77	6
Linley	6	1	–	5	40	42	2
Wednesbury	6	1	–	5	38	137	2
Wulfrun	**6**	**1**	**–**	**5**	**20**	**132**	**2**

STAFFORDSHIRE 2

	P	W	D	L	F	A	Pts
Uttoxeter	8	8	–	–	201	27	16
G E C	8	7	–	1	192	38	14
Rubery Owen	8	5	–	3	163	64	10
Michelin	8	4	2	2	77	68	10
Eccleshall	8	4	1	3	82	96	9
W'ton Aston	8	2	1	5	68	93	5
Old Oaks	8	2	–	6	54	143	4
Cheadle	8	2	–	6	49	148	4
St Matthews	8	–	–	8	36	245	0

STAFFORDSHIRE 1

TRENTHAM

Oaktree Road, Trentham. Tel: 0782 642320.
Founded: 1948
Secretary: M.S.M. Riley, 23 Kersbrook Close, Trentham, Stoke-on-Trent ST4 8XL. Tel: 0782 615381 (W).
League: Staffs 1
Final position (1987–88): 1st

RUGELEY

Hagley Park, Rugeley. Tel: 08894 79985.
Founded: 1947
Secretary: D.W. Pemberton, 16 Crestwood Rise, Etchinghill, Rugeley, Staffs. Tel: 08894 77666 (H) 05438 78141 (W).
League: Staffs 1
Final position (1987–88): 2nd

BURNTWOOD

Chasetown Clubhouse, Burntwood. Tel: Burntwood 2222.
Founded: 1972
President: H. Cooper
Chairman: P. Blockley
Coach: M. Thomas
Secretary: M.B. Thomas, 16 Thorpe Street, Chase Terrace, Walsall WS7 8NE. Tel: 0543 75284.
Fixtures Secretary: M. Steele, 26 Foxhill Close, Heath Hayes, Nr. Cannock. Tel: Heath Hayes ????
Club captain (1987–88): P. Watkins
Club captain (1988–89): C. Martin
No. of teams: Senior 3. Youth & Minis 2.
Directions to Ground: Burntwood Recreation Centre, Lichfield–Cannock Road, turn left at SonKey's Corner onto High St, Chasetown to Recreation Centre.
Clubhouse: Shared with Chasetown F.C., Church Road, Burntwood, Walsall.
Colours: Scarlet & Emerald Green
Nickname: Nailers
Floodlights: No
Membership: £10
Local newspaper: Lichfield Mercury
League: Staffordshire 1
Final position (1987–88): 3rd
Competitions won: Rugeley 7s.

CANNOCK

Cannock Stadium, Pye Green Road, Cannock.
Founded: 1982
Secretary: C. Webb, 90 Hatherton Road, Cannock, Staffs. Tel: 05435 6105 (H) 021 358 6296 (W).
League: Staffs 1
Final position (1987–88): 4th

LINLEY

Red Lion, Goldenhill, Stock-on-Trent, Staffs.
Founded: 1962
Chairman: Alan Currie
Coach: Dave Jennings
Secretary: Alan Hodgkinson, 50 Greenbank Road, Tunstall, Stock-on-Trent ST6 7EY. Tel: 88201.
Fixtures Secretary: Tim McGough, 8 Fegg Hayes Road, Chell, Stoke-on-Trent. Tel: 827170.
Club captain (1987–88): Dave Jennings
Club captain (1988–89): Geoff Morrey
No. of teams: Senior 3.
Directions to Ground: Stoke-on-Trent north to town of Kidsgrove follow signs to Ski Hut Kidsgrove.
Clubhouse: Ski Hut Kidsgrove change/drink – Red Lion Goldenhill.
Colours: Green/gold V. (*Change colours:* Yellow/green hoops)
Floodlights: No
Membership: £15
Local newspaper: Evening Sentinel
League: Staffordshire 1
Final position (1987–88): 5th
Playing record (1987–88): P 32, W 4, D 2, L 26

WEDNESBURY

14 Bridge Street, Wednesbury. Tel: 021-502-2477.
Founded: 1921
President: Derek Rogers
Chairman: Robert Slater
Coach: Ian McDermott
Secretary: Peter Hughes, 28 Alder Road, Wednesbury. Tel: 021-556-5005.
Fixtures Secretary: Michael Hawkins, 3 Heathfield Drive, Bloxwich, Walsall. Tel: 0922-401329.
Club captain (1987–88): S. Vickers
Club captain (1988–89): G. Phillips

Staffordshire 1

No. of teams: Senior 2.
Directions to Ground: Take directions to Wednesbury from junction 9 on M6 – take 6th turning on left, follow road for approx one mile – ground lies to the right on Hydes Road.
Clubhouse: About ½ mile from ground at address above.
Colours: Black/white hoops. (*Change colours:* Red).
Floodlights: No
Local newspaper: Express & Star; Sandwell Evening Mail.
League: Staffs 1
Final position (1987–88): 6th (Relegated)
Playing record (1987–88): W 13, L 16, D 1

WULFRUN

Hilton Main Sports & Social Club, Cannock Road, Fetherstone.
Founded: 1963
President: R. Smith-Dawson
Chairman: D. Hargreaves
Coach: J. Withers
Secretary: C. Withers, 138 Old Park Road, Dudley. Tel: Dudley 835472.
Fixtures Secretary: A. Wilkinson, 162 Aldersley Road, Wolverhampton. Tel: 0902 758509.
Club captain (1987–88): J. Withers
Club captain (1988–89): J. Withers
No. of teams: Senior 4. Youth & Minis 3.
Directions to Ground: Adjacent to M54, Junction 1. Follow signs to Wolverhampton, entrance 200 yds on right.
Ground capacity: 200
Clubhouse: Bar, clubroom, snooker room.
Colours: Emerald green shirts with black trim.
Floodlights: No
Membership: £10
Local newspapers: Express & Star
League: Staffordshire 1
Final position (1987–88): 7th (bottom)

STAFFORDSHIRE 2

UTTOXETER

Oldfields Ground, Springfield Road, Uttoxeter.
Secretary: W.M.M. Howieson, 6 Lichfield Court, Lichfield Road, Walsall, W. Midlands.
League: Staffs 2
Final position (1987–88): 1st
Competitions won: Staffordshire 2

G.E.C. ST LEONARDS

G.E.C. Ltd, St Leonards Works, Stafford ST17 4LX. Tel: (0785) 58070.
Founded: 1977
President: M.A. Hughes
Chairman: T. Griffin
Coach: K. Mottershead
Secretary: K. Richards, 19 Clifton Drive, Kingston-Hill, Stafford ST16 3U2. Tel: (0785) 59873.
Fixtures Secretary: K. Richards, as above for club secretary.
Club captain (1987–88): P. Sargeant
Club captain (1988–89): M. Tucker
No. of teams: Senior 3.
Directions to Ground: Riverway playing fields, off the Lichield Road, Stafford.
Clubhouse: St. Leonards Sports & Social Club.
Colours: Black & gold. (*Change colours:* Red & black)
Floodlights: No
Membership: £5.00
League: Staffordshire 2
Final position (1987–88): second

RUBERY OWEN

Little Cross Street, Darlaston, West Midlands WS10 8ET. Tel: 021 526 3515.
Founded: 1957
Chairman: D. Brawn
Coach: J. Osborn
Secretary: I.F. Blake, 32 Crossway Lane, Birmingham B44 8DN. Tel: 021 356 6053.
Fixtures Secretary: M. Alberts, 28 Lime Road, Wednesbury, West Midlands WS10 7NG. Tel: 021 556 2080.
Club captain (1987–88): J. Osborn
Club captain (1988–89): J. Osborn
No. of teams: Senior 4.
Directions to Ground: M6 junction 10, towards Wolverhampton, 2nd left (Lane Arms) then ½ mile on left.
Clubhouse: Yes
Colours: Red. (*Change colours:* Blue and white hoops)
Floodlights: No
Membership: £11 per annum.
Local newspaper: Wolverhampton Express and Star
League: Staffs 2
Final position (1987–88): 3rd

MICHELIN

Mac Sports Centre, Rosetree Avenue, Trent Value, Stoke-on-Trent. Tel: 0782 642369.
Secretary: P. Ibbs, 78 Grosvenor Avenue, Oakhill, Stoke-on-Trent ST4 5BO. Tel: 0782 414574.
League: Staffs 2
Final position (1987–88): 4th

ECCLESHALL

Drake Hall, Nr Eccleshall.
Founded: 1979
Secretary: M. Turnbull, 25 West Close, Walton, Stone, Staffs. Tel: 0785 817295.
League: Staffs 2
Final position (1987–88): 5th

WHEATON ASTON

Wheaton Aston Sports & Social Club, Lapley Road, Wheaton Aston, Stafford. Tel: 0785 840440.
Secretary: K.A. Ingham, 30 Brookhouse Way, Gnosall, Stafford ST20 0HS. Tel: 0785 822904.
League: Staffs 2
Final position (1987–88): 6th

OLD OAKS

The Shire Oak School, Walsall Road, Walsall.
Founded: 1983
Secretary: R. Sollom, 7 Silver Court Gardens, Brownhills, Walsall WSA 6EJ. Tel: 0543 377733 (H) 021 359 687314 (W).
League: Staffs 2
Final position (1987–88): 7th

CHEADLE

The Level, Freehay, Cheadle.
Founded: 1983

Staffordshire 2

Secretary: Mrs G.C. Kaminski, 22 Conway Street, Shelton, Stoke-on-Trent, Staffs ST4 2BL. Tel: ?782 415489 (H).
League: Staffs 2
Final position (1987–88): 8th

ST MATTHEWS

League: Staffs 2
Final position (1987–88): 9th (bottom)

NORTH MIDLANDS LEAGUES

THE North Midlands had 43 teams playing in four leagues and it also produced three outstanding performances with Old Yardleians drawing only one of their 10 matches and winning the rest to take the top league title. Selly Oak took North Midlands 3 by winning all 10 matches and in winning nine North Midlands 4 games the West Midlands Police were clearly in a different class as they scored 329 points.

There was a tough battle in North Midlands 2 with Shrewsbury just beating off Malvern by a single point, but both will expect to do well in higher company.

TABLES 1987–88

NORTH MIDLANDS 1

	P	W	D	L	F	A	Pts
O Yardleians	10	9	1	0	143	67	19
Whitchurch	10	7	0	3	118	75	14
Kidd'rm'ter	10	6	0	4	135	93	12
Kings Norton	10	6	0	4	124	100	12
Newport	10	5	0	5	144	90	10
Camp Hill	9	5	0	4	111	74	10
Bridgnorth	10	4	1	5	115	99	9
O Halesonians	9	4	1	4	69	112	9
Luctonians	10	3	9	7	80	95	6
Erdington	10	2	1	7	83	144	5
Edwardians	10	1	0	9	34	207	2

NORTH MIDLANDS 2

	P	W	D	L	F	A	Pts
Shrewsbury	10	8	0	2	221	63	16
Malvern	10	7	1	2	143	70	15
Ludlow	10	6	1	3	152	77	13
Woodrush	10	6	0	4	110	85	12
Aston OE	10	5	1	4	138	119	11
Droitwich	10	5	1	4	110	85	11
Telford	10	4	1	5	74	90	9
Pershore	10	4	1	5	80	137	9
Bourneville	10	3	0	7	63	132	6
Old Saltleians	10	2	0	8	52	153	4
Old Centrals	10	2	0	8	55	187	2

NORTH MIDLANDS 3

	P	W	D	L	F	A	Pts
Selly Oak	10	10	0	0	254	50	20
Five Ways OE	10	9	0	1	172	77	18
B'ham C'Off	9	7	0	2	188	89	14
Old Griffinians	8	6	0	2	117	66	12
B'ham Welsh	9	5	0	4	100	150	10
Warley	9	4	0	5	137	85	8
Redditch	10	4	0	6	110	115	8
Kynoch	10	3	0	7	100	166	6
Ledbury	10	2	1	7	117	227	5
Yardley & Dist	10	1	1	8	78	197	3
Old Moseleian	10	0	0	10	61	212	0

NORTH MIDLANDS 4

	P	W	D	L	F	A	Pts
W Mids Police	9	9	0	0	329	49	18
Veseyians	9	8	0	1	280	53	16
Birchfield	9	6	0	3	165	110	12
Upton	9	6	0	3	98	87	12
Bromyard	9	4	1	4	106	90	9
Tenbury	9	3	1	5	81	190	7
Witton	9	2	0	7	71	158	4
Bewdley	9	2	0	6	28	209	4
B'ham Civ Ser	9	2	0	7	49	159	4
Ross-on-Wye	9	1	0	7	62	164	2

NORTH MIDLANDS 1

OLD YARDLEIANS

Tilehouse Lane, Shirley, Solihull, West Midlands. (021) 744-3380.
Founded: 1927
President: L. Cox
Chairman: M. Goode
Coach: S. Sidwell
Secretary: I. Wallace, 20 St Pauls Avenue, Balsall Heath, Birmingham B12 8LU. Tel: (021) 440-1090.
Fixtures Secretary: S. Painter, 26 Shrewley Crescent, Marston Green, Birmingham. Tel: (021) 779-4192.
Club captain (1987–88): S. Chinn
Club captain (1988–89): S. Chinn
No. of teams: Senior 4, Youth & Minis 3
Ground capacity: 120
Colours: Maroon old gold & green ¼'s, navy shorts. (*Change colours:* Yellow or green jerseys)
Nickname: The Y's
Floodlights: No
Membership: £20
Programme: 50p (Editor: C. Thompson)
Local newspaper: Solihull News/Times, Birmingham Evening Mail, Sunday Murcury
League: North Midlands 1

North Midlands 1

Final position (1987–88): 1st – Promoted to Midlands West Div 2.
Playing record (1987–88): P 44, W 33, D 4, L 7, F 762, A 388.

WHITCHURCH

Edgeley Park, Whitchurch, Salop. Tel: 0948 3316.
Founded: 1936
Secretary: R.S. Lewis, Fountain House, Sedgeford, Whitchurch, Shropshire SY13 1EX. Tel: 0948 2054 (H) 0727 72688 (W).
League: North Mids
Final position (1987–88): 2nd

KIDDERMINSTER CAROLIANS

Marlpool Lane, Kidderminster, Worcs. Tel: 0562 740043.
Founded: 1969
President: P. Knowles
Chairman: M. Bryce
Coach: A Higley
Secretary: K. Woodham, 20 Comberton Avenue, Kidderminster. Tel: 0562 515888.
Fixtures Secretary: P. Taylor, 1 Falcon Close, Kidderminster. Tel: 0562 600615.
Club captain (1987–88): P. Taylor
Club captain (1988–89): A. Stooksbury
No. of teams: Senior 1. Youth & Minis 7.
Directions to Ground: Follow signs to Kidderminster Town Centre, follow signs A442 to Bridgnorth, turn off A442 into Marlpool Lane at Bull and Bush Public House.
Colours: Black & gold hoops. (*Change colours:* Gold)
Floodlights: No
Membership: Playing £27 p.a.
Local newspaper: Kidderminster Shuttle
League: North Midlands 1
Final position (1987–88): 3rd
Playing record (1987–88): P 35, W 19, D 0, L 16, F 533, A 452.

KINGS NORTON

Ash Lane, Hopwood, Alvechurch, Nr Birmingham. Tel: 021 445 3340.
Founded: 1923
Secretary: R.E. Adams, 122 Osmaston Road, Harborne, Birmingham B17 0TN. Tel: 021 427 3563 (H) 021 745 3119 (W).
League: North Mids
Final position (1987–88): 4th
Playing record (1987–88): P 34, W 19, D 1, L 14, F 404, A 352.

NEWPORT (SALOP)

The Showground, Forton Road, Newport, Shropshire. Tel: (0952) 810021.
Founded: 1946
President: Gavin Goulson
Chairman: Christopher Cann
Coach: Michael Trumper
Secretary: David Wassell, 54 Ford Road, Newport, Shropshire. Tel: (0952) 820221 (H), (0952) 820202 (B).
Fixtures Secretary: Peter Hardy, 145 Hadlry Park Road, Leegomery, Telford. Tel: (0952) 47358 (H). (Confirmations) David Vasilionka, 12 Norbroom Drive, Newport. (Tel: (0952) 810755 (H).
Club captain (1987–88): Andrew Crow
Club captain (1988–89): Michael Trumper
No. of teams: Senior 4, Youth & Minis 2.
Directions to Ground: From the Town Centre take A719 Eccleshall Road, turn left (by Showground sign) just past the Ryland's Nursing Home. If approaching the club from the bypass take the A719 into Newport, turn right not far past Plough Farm Nursery.
Clubhouse: There is a good bar and ample changing.
Colours: Shirts maroon & white hoops, white shorts, plain maroon socks.
Floodlights: No
Membership: £20
Programme: We are just starting a programme this year (Editor: Richard Butter Tel: (0952) 47443 (H).
Local newspaper: Newport Advertiser
League: North Mids Division 1
Final position (1987–88): 5th
Playing record (1987–88): P 36, W 24, D 1, L 11, F 557, A 321.
Competitions won: The Colts won the Shropshire.

CAMP HILL

Haslucks Green Road, Solihull. Tel: 021 744 4175.
Founded: 1893
Secretary: A. Mucklow, 51 Shakespeare Drive, Solihull, W. Mids B90 2AN. Tel: 021 744 3872 (H) 0203 416510 (W).
Fixtures Secretary: D.J. Smith, 106 Wakefield Court, Hayfield Road, Birmingham B13 0LQ. Tel: 021 449 4278 (H) 021 454 1275 (W).
League: North Mids
Final position (1987–88): 6th
Playing record (1987–88): P 37, W 21, D 1, L 15, F 516, A 373.

BRIDGNORTH

"The Bull", Bridge Street, Bridgnorth. Tel: 2796.
Founded: 1962
President: E. Davies
Chairman: J. Peake
Coach: B. Greaves
Secretary: T.B.A.
Fixtures Secretary: A. Stoll, The School House, Vicarage Road, Penn, Wolverhampton. Tel: 0902 332025.
Club captain (1987–88): J. Price-Jones
Club captain (1988–89): J. Price-Jones
No. of teams: Senior 4. Youth & Minis 8.
Directions to Ground: Find Bridgnorth. Find River Severn. Club House is next to bridge over River Severn.
Colours: Black. (*Change colours:* Green)
Membership: £30
Local newspaper: Bridgnorth Journal
League: North Midlands 1
Final position (1987–88): 6th
Playing record (1987–88): W 20, L 18, D 2, F 530, A 454.

OLD HALESONIANS

Wassell Grove, Hagley, West Midlands. Tel: Hagley 883036.
Founded: 1930
President: M. Churchill
Chairman: P. Worsley
Coach: I. Glendenning
Secretary: T. Walters, Bury's Hill, Ounty John Lane, Stourbridge, West Mids. Tel: Hagley 882363.
Fixtures Secretary: D. Cooper, 34 Hyperion Road, Stourton, Stourbridge, W Mids. Tel: St 374635.
Club captain (1987–88): S. Cullwick
Club captain (1988–89): R. Foulds
No. of teams: Senior 5. Youth & Minis 8.
Directions to Ground: From Junction 3 M5 take A456 to Wassell Grove (4 miles).
Ground: 4 pitches, 2 hockey pitches, 1 cricket pitch.
Clubhouse: 8 changing rooms, showers, bath, large club room and members lounge.

North Midlands 1

Colours: Royal blue with gold hoop (*Change colours:* Red)
Floodlights: No
Membership: £17
Local newspaper: County Express
League: N.M.1
Final position (1987–88): 7th
Playing record (1987–88): P 32, W 13, D 3, L 16, F 340, A 482.

LUCTONIANS

Mortimer Park, Kingsland, Leominster. Tel: 0568-81-345.
Founded: 1948
President: P. Sparey
Chairman: P. Burgoyne
Coach: G. White
Secretary: J. Russell, Upper House, Tillington, Hereford. Tel: 0432 760203.
Fixtures Secretary: R. East, 402 Buckfield Road, Leominster. Tel: 0568 4426.
Club captain (1987–88): G. Monkley
Club captain (1988–89): S. Green-Price
No. of teams: Senior 4, Youth 1
Directions to Ground: Off A44 approx 4 miles west of Leominster.
Ground capacity: 5,000, Stand N/A.
Clubhouse: Brick
Colours: Black & white hoops. (*Change colours:* Green)
Nickname: Lucs
Floodlights: Yes
Admission: Free
Membership: £25.00
Local newspaper: Hereford Times
League: North Mids 1
Final position (1987–88): 9th
Playing record (1987–88): P 37, W 13, D 1, L 23, F 382, A 487.

ERDINGTON

Birches Green Playing Fields, Kingbury Road, Erdington, Birmingham. Tel: 021-373 7567.
Founded: 1924
President: B. Tinney
Chairman: E. Lewis
Secretary: D. Owen, 129 Bradbury Road, Solihull, West Midlands B92 8AL. Tel: 021-706 4699.
Fixtures Secretary: K. Robinson, 5 Ullenhall Road, Walmley, Sutton Coldfield B76 8QG. Tel: 021-351 2740.
Club captain (1987–88): R. Lee
Club captain (1988–89): T.B.A.
No. of teams: Senior 4. Youth & Minis 2.
Directions to Ground: Follow Kingsbury Road from Junction 6 of the M6. Cross Bromford Lane, approx ½ mile on left.
Colours: White shirts with one blue hoop/blue shorts.
Floodlights: No
Local newspaper: Birmingham Evening Mail
League: North Midlands 1
Final position (1987–88): 10th

EDWARDIANS

Streetsbrook Road, Solihull, W. Midlands. Tel: 021 744 6831.
Founded: 1882
Secretary: D.J. Brewer, Wixford Villa, Wixford, Alcester, Warwickshire B49 6DA. Tel: 0789 77 2754 (H) 0527 29002 (W).
Fixtures Secretary: J.G. Bayliss, 43 Westbourne Road, Olton, Solihull, W. Midlands. Tel: 021 706 2482 (H).
League: North Mids
Final position (1987–88): 11th (bottom, relegated)

NORTH MIDLANDS 2

SHREWSBURY

Sunborne Castle, Shrewsbury. Tel: 0743-53380.
Founded: 1908
President: John Jones
Chairman: Chris MacDonald
Coach: Elwyn Williams
Secretary: John Dodds, 58 Preston Street, Shrewsbury. Tel: 0743-236417.
Fixtures Secretary: Martin Heiron, Ashfield, All Stretton, Church Stretton, Shropshire. Tel: Church Stretton 722509.
Club captain (1987–88): Keith Faulkner
Club captain (1988–89): Keith Faulkner
No. of teams: Senior 4, Youth & Minis 7
Directions to Ground: 3 miles north west of Shrewsbury on B5062 Newport Road.
Ground capacity: 1500
Clubhouse: Own clubhouse with clubroom, lounge, bar, kitchen and changing facilities.
Colours: Navy blue. (*Colour change:* Red shirts)
Floodlights: Yes
Membership: Player £20, vice president £5.
Programme: 20p (Editor: Martin Jones, 47 Queen Street, Castlefields, Shrewsbury. Tel: 0743-64629.
Local newspaper: Shropshire Star, Shrewsbury Chronicle
League: North Midlands 2
Final position (1987–88): 1st in North Midlands League 2 (promoted).
Playing record (1987–88): P 37, W 21, D 2, L 14, F 647, A 438.
Competitions won: Won North Mids league Div 2. Won Shropshire Sevens competition in April 1988.

MALVERN

Spring Lane, Malvern. Tel: 06845 3728.
Founded: 1934
Secretary: Miss K. Fry, 347 Worcester Road, Malvern Link, Worcs WR14 1AN. Tel: 06845 63985 (H) 06845 2700 (W).
League: North Midlands 2
Final position (1987–88): 2nd

LUDLOW

Linney Fields, Ludlow, Shopshire. Tel: 0584 5762.
Founded: 1933
President: Doug Hanson
Chairman: Richard Griffiths
Coach: Philip Norton
Secretary: Laurie Wallace, 49 Newington Way, Craven Arms SY2 9PS. Tel: 05882 2450 (H), 0584 4465 (B).
Fixtures Secretary: Ian Smith, 71 Temesdo, Ludlow. Tel: 0584 2726 (B).
Club captain (1987–88): Simon Melvin
Club captain (1988–89): Simon Melvin
No. of teams: Senior 4, Youth & Minis 6.
Directions to Ground: Ask for Recreational area below Ludlow Castle.
Ground capacity: 1000
Clubhouse: Bar, 4 changing rooms, showers etc.
Colours: Red shirt/black shorts. (*Change colours:* All black)
Floodlights: No
Admission: Nil

North Midlands 2

Membership: £15.00
Programme: Free, team list plus update of league. (Editor: Roger Evans)
Local newspaper: Ludlow Advertizer
League: North Mids 2
Final position (1987–88): Third
Playing record (1987–88): P 40, W 24, D 3, L 13.
Competitions won: Runner up Shrewsbury 7s 1st May.

WOODRUSH

Icknield Street, Forhill, Birmingham.
Founded: 1966
President: H.J. Toogood
Chairman: J.C. Johnston
Coach: I. Smith
Secretary: R. Caley, 75 Midhurst Road, Kings Norton, Birmingham.
Fixtures Secretary: J. Miah, 45 Lodgehill Road, Selly Oak, Birmingham B29 9NU. Tel: 021 472/7435.
Club captain (1987–88): S. Baker
Club captain (1988–89): P. Cox
No. of teams: Senior 4, Colts 1
Colours: Emerald green/white hoops
Floodlights: No
Membership: £25
Programme: Free (Editor: S. Peace)
Local newspaper: Birmingham Evening Mail/Redditch Indicator
League: N. Mids 2
Final position (1987–88): 3rd
Playing record (1987–88): P 34, W 24, L 10, F 550, A 290.
Competitions won: Sutton 7's BRMB/TSB 7's

ASTON OLD EDWARDIANS

Sunnybank Avenue, Perry Common, Birmingham B44 0HP.
Founded: 1889
President: Neil Gamble
Chairman: Eric Collis
Coach: Mike Collis
Secretary: John Silverwood, 120 Brambling, Wilnecote, Tamworth B77 5PP. Tel: Tamworth 282164.
Fixtures Secretary: Tony Stafford, 5 Skelton Walk, Lake View, Northampton NN3 1PU. Tel: 0604 48529.
Club captain (1987–88): Gary Smith
Club captain (1988–89): Gavin Cairns
No. of teams: Senior 4, Youth 1.
Directions to Ground: Sunnybank Avenue is off College Road A453 travelling away from Birmingham city centre.
Colours: Red, white & green narrow hoops, white shorts, green socks. (*Change colours:* White shirts)
Floodlights: No
Membership: £20
Programme: (Editor: Brian Roberts)
Local newspaper: Sutton Coldfield News.
League: North Midlands 2
Final position (1987–88): 5th
Playing record (1987–88): P 36, W 17, D 2, L 17, F 604, A 478.

DROITWICH

Hanbury Road, Droitwich, Worcs. Tel: 0905 770384.
Founded: 1972
Secretary: A. Hodgkiss, 24 Princes Avenue, Droitwich, Worcs. Tel: 0905 775476 (H) 0905 54229 (W).
League: North Midlands 2
Final position (1987–88): 6th

PERSHORE

Mill Lane, Wyre Piddle. Tel: Pershore 554105.
Founded: 1963
President: C.R. Askew
Chairman: R. Warton
Coach: S. Guy
Secretary: A. Jenkinson, 12 Eltric Road, Worcester.
Fixtures Secretary: S. Guy, The Firs, Throckmorton Road Hill, Evesham.
Club captain (1987–88): C. Hemmings
Club captain (1988–89): C. Hemmings
No. of teams: Senior 4
Directions to Ground: Leave M6 junct 6 Evesham Road to Wyre Piddle turn at cross into lane.
Clubhouse: Freehold
Colours: Black, two scarlet hoops. (*Change colours:* Green)
Nickname: Persh
Floodlights: No
Membership: £25
Local newspaper: Evesham Journal, Worcester Evening News
League: NM 2
Final position (1987–88): 7th
Playing record (1987–88): P 36, W 17, D 3, L 16.
Competitions won: Templar Trophy 1987 and 1988 N. Mids Cup semi-final 1987.

BOURNVILLE

Pavillion, Heath Road, B30 1HH. Tel: 021-458-1711.
Founded: 1909
President: S.G. Foley
Chairman: W. Joyner
Coach: R. Cox
Secretary: S.P. Hinton, 76 Lye Avenue, B32 3UE. Tel: 021-422 3090.
Fixtures Secretary: C. Champken, 94 Wharf Road, B30 3LP. Tel: 021-459-3700.
Club captain (1987–88): G. Bailey
Club captain (1988–89): G. Bailey
No. of teams: Senior 4, Youth & Minis 1
Directions to Ground: To Birmingham – take Bristol Road Sth. Turn off at Bournville Lane, playing fields on right 500 yds.
Clubhouse: R.C.T. charity owned. Changing & bar facilities, Banks brewery.
Colours: Maroon/blue/gold. (*Change colours:* Yellow/ white)
Nickname: Bourn's
Floodlights: No
Membership: £20 per season.
Programme: Free (Editor: N. Suddaby)
Local newspaper: Evening Mail
League: North Mids 2
Final position (1987–88): 9th
Playing record (1987–88): P 33, W 15, D 1, L 17, F 301, A 355.
Competitions won: B.R.M.B. (Midlands) merit table div 2 winners 1985–86.

OLD SALTLEIANS

Watton Lane, Waterorton, Nr Birmingham. Tel: 021-748 3380.
Founded: 1933
President: J. Harradence
Coach: J. Kelly
Secretary: R. Heighway, Amberley, Vicarage Hill, Tamworth-in-Arden, Solihull B94 5EA. Tel: 05644 2262.
Fixtures Secretary: G. Phipps, 254 Orphanage Road, Wylde Green, Birmingham B24 0BE. Tel: 021-350 5204.
Club captain (1987–88): J. Kelly
Club captain (1988–89): P. Brugger
No. of teams: Senior 5. Youth & Minis 7

North Midlands 2

Directions to Ground: Adjacent M42 at Coleshill off A446 turn into Watton Lane.
Clubhouse: 4 changing rooms, baths, showers, lounge, cloakroom.
Colours: Red and yellow hoops. (*Change colours:* Green or blue jerseys).
Nickname: Old Salts
Floodlights: Training lights only
League: North Midlands 2
Final position (1987–88): 10th
Playing record (1987–88): P 32, W 8, D 1, L 23.

OLD CENTRALS

Bourne Vale, Little Hardwick Road, Aldridge, West Mids. Tel: 021 353 2856.
Founded: 1913
President: C. Fullard
Chairman: M. Toone
Coach: M. Chambers
Secretary: M. Harris, 32 Barker Road, Sutton Coldfield, West Mids B74 2NZ.
Fixtures Secretary: M. Halloran, 86 Eastern Road, Sutton Coldfield. Tel: 021 355 3770.
Club captain (1987–88): K. Carter
Club captain (1988–89): W. Ward
No. of teams: Senior 4. Youth & Minis 1.
Colours: Maroon/green/gold.
Nickname: C's
Floodlights: Yes
Membership: £15
League: North Midlands 2
Final position (1987–88): 11th

NORTH MIDLANDS 3

SELLY OAK

Moorgreen Recreation Ground, Holders Lane, Moseley, Birmingham. Tel: 021-449-7950.
Founded: 1964
President: A. Badsby
Chairman: L. Winkett
Secretary: M. Spinner, 3 Ashbrook Grove, Stirchley, Birmingham. Tel: 021-471-4769 (H), 021-233-2001 (W).
Fixtures Secretary: B. Pearce, 9 Langford Avenue, Great Barr, Birmingham.
Club captain (1987–88): S. Williams
Club captain (1988–89): A. McGill
No. of teams: Senior 4
Directions to Ground: From Edgbaston cricket ground towards Moseley, a roundabout turn right along Russell Road, at cross road turn right on Moor Green Lane, 1st right Holders Lane.
Colours: Blue & white hoops. (*Change colours:* Red shirts)
Floodlights: No
Membership: £10
Local newspaper: Evening Mail
League: North Mids 3
Final position (1987–88): 1st (promoted)
Competitions won: North Midlands Div 3 Champions 1987–88.

FIVE WAYS OLD EDWARDIANS

"Masshouse", Ash Lane, Hopwood, Birmingham B48 7BD. Tel: 021-445 4909
Founded: 1892
President: A.G. Boggust
Chairman: D. Roach
Coach: M. Collis
Secretary: R.G. Lisseter, 138 Chatsworth Road, Halesowen, W Mids B62 8TH.
Fixtures Secretary: P. Hipkiss, 37 The Crescent, Cradley Heath, W. Mids. Tel: 021-550 4280.
Club captain (1987–88): J. Woolley
Club captain (1988–89): J. Woolley
No. of teams: Senior 4. Youth & Minis 1.
Directions to Ground: Junction 2 M42, right at garage in Hopwood, end of Ash Lane.
Clubhouse: "Masshouse", 6 changing rooms, 2 baths, shower, large clubhouse upstairs, kitchen, committee room.
Colours: Navy blue and amber. (*Change colours:* White)
Floodlights: No
Admission: Nil
Membership: £23
Local newspaper: Birmingham Evening Mail
League: North Midlands 3
Final position (1987–88): 2nd (promoted)
Playing record (1987–88): P 34, W 22, L 11, D 1, F 514, A 345.

BIRMINGHAM CITY OFFICIALS

Sedeemere Road, Yardley, Birmingham 26. Tel: 021 783 2694.
Founded: 1927
Secretary: T. Dunne, 253 Church Road, Sheldon, Birmingham B26 3TH. Tel: 021 743 0109.
League: North Mids 3
Final position (1987–88): 3rd

OLD GRIFFINIANS

Moundsley Hall, Walkers Heath Road, Kings Norton. Tel: 021 458 2408.
Secretary: A. Johnson, 13 St Georges Court, Bournville, Birmingham. Tel: 021 472 1860.
League: North Mids 3
Final position (1987–88). 4th

BIRMINGHAM WELSH

Clock Lane, Bickenhill, Solihull. Tel: 06755 2995.
Founded: 1936
Secretary: A. Coates, 6 Brutus Drive, Coleshill, Birmingham B46 1UF. Tel: 0675 65659 (H) 0753 872164 (W).
League: North Mids 3
Final position (1987–88): 5th

WARLEY

Birchley Island, Wolverhampton Road, Oldbury, Warley. Tel: 021-552 1644.
Founded: 1972
President: L.T. Barnfield

North Midlands 3

Chairman: K.S. Jordan
Coach: M. Lewis
Secretary: P.C. Jordan, 7 Station Drive, West Hagley, Worcs DY9 0NX. Tel: 021-429 6417 (W) 2 882176 (H).
Fixtures Secretary: P. Davies. Tel: 021-420 3141.
Club captain (1987–88): G. Strong
Club captain (1988–89): I Moss.
No. of teams: Senior 4. Youth & Minis 1.
Directions to Ground: On Junction 2 M5 with Wolverhampton Road.
Clubhouse: Bar, toilets.
Colours: Red & White hoop. (*Change colours:* Blue).
Floodlights: No
Membership: £18
League: North Midlands 3
Final position (1987–88): 5th

REDDITCH

Bromsgrove Road, Redditch. Tel: 0527 62807.
Founded: 1966
Secretary: N. Pritchard, 254 Birchfield Road, Webheth, Redditch. Tel: 0527 44763 (H).
League: North Mids 3
Final position (1987–88): 7th

KYNOCH

Holford Drive, Perry Barr, Birmingham. Tel: 021-356 4369.
Founded: 1924
President: John Allen
Chairman: John Thompson
Coach: Dave Quinn
Secretary: John Ross, 127 Leopold Avenue, Handsworth Wood, Birmingham B20 1EX. Tel: 021-358 3277.
Fixtures Secretary: Pat Nugent, 17 Chestnut Drive, Erdington, Birmingham B24 0DN. Tel: 021-382 4902.
Club captain (1987–88): Bob Cox
Club captain (1988–89): Dave Thompson
No. of teams: Senior 4
Directions to Ground: Holford Drive, off Aldridge Road (A453), Perry Barr, Birmingham.
Ground capacity: 200
Clubhouse: Part of large works sports complex.
Colours: Black and white. (*Change colours:* Red)
Nickname: Kays
Floodlights: Yes
Membership: £7.00
Programme: None (Press officer: Martin Stevenson)
Local newspaper: Sutton Coldfield Observer
League: North Midlands 3
Final position (1987–88): 8th
Playing record (1987–88): P 31, W 11, D 1, L 19, F 345, A 503.

LEDBURY

Ross Road Playing Fields, Ledbury.
Founded: 1946
Secretary: F.I. Stoddart, Richmond Villa, Newstreet, Ledbury, Herefordshire. Tel: Ledbury 4451 (H) Ledbury 4601 (W).
League: North Mids 3
Final position (1987–88): 9th

YARDLEY & DIST.

Tile House Lane, Shirley, West Midlands. Tel: 021 745 9311).
Founded: 1971
Secretary: T.W. Draycott, 143 Manor Road, Stechford, Birmingham 33 8DH. Tel: 021 784 5312 (H) 021 772 2361 (W).
League: North Mids 3
Final position (1987–88): 10th

OLD MOSELEIANS

Luatrout Lane, Solihull. Tel: 021-705-7847.
Founded: 1927
President: Pat Shough
Chairman: John Barker
Coach: Tony Howell
Secretary: John Stefani, 26 Beauchamp Road, Warwick.
Fixtures Secretary: Mick Fielding, 33 Fiora Road, Hammils, Birmingham.
Club captain (1987–88): Nick Kennedy
Club captain (1988–89): Ugo Muin
No. of teams: Senior 3, Youth & Minis 1
Directions to Ground: A41 Solihull bypass signs for Catherine De Barnes along lane turn into Field Lane, Luatrout Lane crosses Field Lane at bottom. Ground at junction.
Colours: Black with red/white band. (*Change colours:* Yellow)
Nickname: Mo's
Floodlights: No
Membership: £18 per annum.
Local newspaper: Solihull News
League: North Mids 3
Final position (1987–88): Bottom N.M. 3 (relegated)

NORTH MIDLANDS 4

WEST MIDLANDS POLICE

Tally Ho! Pershore Road, Edgbaston, Birmingham. Tel: 021 472 3201.
Founded: 1974
President: Chief Constable – Mr G.J. Dear, QPM, LLB, DC.
Chairman: Assistant Chief Constable Mr Jones
Coach: Insp. I. Darnel
Secretary: Superintendent M.G. Joiner, Chelmsley Wood Police Station, Ceolmund Crescent, Chelmsley Wood, Birmingham B37 5UB. Tel: 021-770-5381.
Fixtures Secretary: Sgt Hussey. Tel: 021-440-1111.
Club captain (1987–88): DC C. Lee
Club captain (1988–89): DC C. Lee
No. of teams: Senior 3
Directions to Ground: Tally Ho!, Pershore Road, Edgbaston, Birmingham – Next to the Warwickshire County Cricket ground.
Clubhouse: Tally Ho!. Tel: 021-472-3201.
Colours: Red top. (*Change colours:* Blue)
Floodlights: No
Local newspaper: Birmingham Mail
League: N. Mids. 4
Final position (1987–88): Top Div 4 (promoted)
Competitions won: N. Mids Div. 4 league.

VESEYIANS

Little Hardwick Road, Sutton Coalfield. Tel: 021 353 5388.
Founded: 1928

North Midlands 4

Secretary: R.J. Mason, 8 Tudor Road, Sutton Coalfied. Tel: 021 354 1630 (H) 021 233 2001 (W).
League: North Mids 4
Final position (1987–88): 2nd

BIRCHFIELD

Moor Lane, Witton, Birmingham. Tel: 356 2142.
Founded: 1957
Secretary: J. Wingate, Flat 3, 7 Rotten Park Road, Edgbaston, Birmingham B16 9JH. Tel: 021454 (H) 841 1411 (W).
League: North Mids 4
Final position (1987–88): 3rd

UPTON-UPON-SEVERN

As Secretary
Founded: 1981
President: Ian Llewellyn
Chairman: Colin Williams
Secretary: Peter Barker, Tiltridge Farm, Upton-upon-Severn. Tel: 06846 2906.
Fixtures Secretary: Nigel Banwell, 16 Riverside Close, Upton-upon-Severn. Tel: 06846 2046.
Club captain (1987–88): Will Clive
Club captain (1988–89): Phil Humphreys
No. of teams: Senior 2/3
Directions to Ground: Opposite church with spire in Upton-upon-Severn.
Ground capacity: Unlimited
Clubhouse: Shared with Sports Club.
Colours: Black & white quarters. (*Change colours:* Green)
Floodlights: No
Membership: £17
Local newspaper: Malvern Gazette, Upton News (Free)
League: N. Mids. 4
Final position (1987–88): 4th

BROMYARD

c/o Bromyard Cricket Club. Tel: 0885 488152.
Founded: 1981
President: G. Williams
Chairman: G.D. Houghton
Coach: D. Redpath
Secretary: G. Charters, Dumbleton Cottage, 24 Church Street, Bromyard, Herefordshire HR7 4DP. Tel: 0885 483296 (H), 0885 488300 (W).
Fixtures Secretary: D.A. Wilson, Ferny Cottage, Little Cowarne, Bromyard. Tel: 0885 86232.
Club captain (1987–88): S. Irwin
Club captain (1988–89): R.I. Ridley
No. of teams: Senior 2
Directions to Ground: A465 out of Bromyard to Hereford. Ground is one mile on the right.
Ground capacity: It is a field.
Clubhouse: Cricket Club.
Colours: Green with gold band. (*Change colours:* Dark blue)
Floodlights: No
Membership: £14
Local newspaper: Hereford Times
League: N. Mids 4
Final position (1987–88): 5th
Playing record (1987–88): P 30, W 13, D 3, L 14, F 371, A 296.

TENBURY

c/o The Sports Club, Worcester Road, Tenbury Wells, Worcs. Tel: 0584 810456.
Founded: 1958
President: M. Hoar
Chairman: D. James
Coach: Pat James
Secretary: R. Bowkett, c/o Bowketts (Tenbury) Ltd, Bromyard Road, Tenbury Wells, Worcs. WR15 8DE.
Fixtures Secretary: S. Spurway, 2 Hillend Road, Twyning, Tewkesbury, Glos. GL20 6JL.
Club captain (1987–88): Phil James
Club captain (1988–89): Pat James
No. of teams: Senior 2
Directions to Ground: Along A456 from Kidderminster/Worcester, enter Burford (signposted) R.H.S. Large building – Hospital, immediately past, next building, Tenbury Sports Club.
Colours: Black & green hoops. (*Change colours:* Black & white hoops)
Floodlights: No
Membership: £10 – players
Local newspaper: Tenbury Wells Advertiser
League: North Midlands 4
Final position (1987–88): 6th
Playing record (1987–88): P 26, W 11, L 14, D 1.

WITTON

Ansells Sports & Social Club, Alridge Road, Perry Barr, Birmingham. Tel: 021 356 4296.
Founded: 1918
Secretary: P. Jones, 137 Dunedin Road, Great Barr, Birmingham B44 9DL. Tel: 021 378 4158 (H) 021 236 1678 (W).
League: North Mids 4
Final position (1987–88): 7th

BEWDLEY

The Playing Fields, Spennells Valley, Kidderminster, Worcs. Tel: 0562 822717.
Founded: 198?
Chairman: Glyn McAdam
Coach: Stuart James
Secretary: Andrew Napier, 33 St John's Avenue, Kidderminster, Worcs. Tel: 0562 822717.
Fixtures Secretary: Andy Foster, Lime-Kilns, Pensax, Worcs.
Club captain (1987–88): Tim Blythe
Club captain (1988–89): Steve Owen
No. of teams: Senior 2
Directions to Ground: From Worcester underneath railway viaduct (in Kidderminster) along Spennells Valley Road, Pitch/chaning rooms clearly visable on right hand side (with road off to the right).
Colours: Blue yellow 'V'. (*Change colours:* Yellow blue 'V')
Floodlights: No
Admission: None
Membership: Playing £15, Social £5
Local newspaper: Kidderminstrer Shuttle, Kidderminster Chronicle, Severn Source.
League: N. Mids. 4
Final position (1987–88): 8th
Playing record (1987–88): P 29, W 10, L 18, D 1.

BIRMINGHAM CIVIL SERVICE

Old Damson Lane, Solihull. Tel: 021-779-2136.
Founded: 1928
President: Jack Tempest
Chairman: John Archer
Coach: Les Barwood
Secretary: Mark Darby, 40 Kingsdown Road, Northfield, Birmingham B31 1AH. Tel: 021-475-4798.
Fixtures Secretary: Bill Pratt, 108 Redstone Close, Church Hill, Redditch B92 9AF. Tel: Redditch 68649.
Club captain (1987–88): Mark Howard

North Midlands 4

Club captain (1988–89): Mark Howard
No. of teams: Senior 4, Youth & Minis 1 under 17's.
Directions to Ground: Just off the Coventry Road, opposite Birmingham International Airport.
Clubhouse: Sports Club
Colours: Red & one white hoop jerseys/navy shorts. (*Change colours:* Black shirts)
Floodlights: No
Membership: £16.00
Local newspaper: Evening Mail (Birmingham)
League: North Mids. 4
Final position (1987–88): 8th
Playing record (1987–88): P 33, W 8, L 24, D1.

ROSS-ON-WYE

Station Street, Ross-on-Wye. Tel: 0989 63256.
Founded: 1873
Secretary: M. Pearce, 'Uplands', Bromsash, Ross-on-Wye, Herefordshire. Tel: 0989 981 338 (H) 0594 542 421 (W).
League: North Mids 4
Final position (1987–88): 10th (bottom)

Nottingham and Moseley struggle for possession in the inaugural Courage National League match on 5th September 1988. Photo: Colorsport.

NOTTINGHAMSHIRE, LINCOLNSHIRE AND DERBYSHIRE LEAGUES

THE three counties provide five leagues (there is a geographically divided fourth league) embracing 51 clubs and the best performance came from All Spartans in the third league as they won all 10 games and scored 227 points with a miserly 29 conceded. Ashbourne in the western section of the fourth league also ended with a perfect record from seven matches and 199 points scored.

Elsewhere, the competition was stiff with Moderns only winning the top league on points difference from Chesterfield and Amber Valley doing the same to East Retford in the second league – the actual winning margin being only four points! Both are promoted.

Barton won a strongly contested east section of the fourth league, even though they could only draw with Yarborough.

TABLES 1987–88

NOTTS, LINCS & DERBYS 1

	P	W	D	L	F	A	Pts
Moderns	10	9	0	1	203	40	18
Chesterfield	10	9	0	1	204	55	18
Scunthorpe	10	8	0	2	225	64	16
W Bridgford	10	6	0	4	133	72	12
Southwell	10	5	1	4	120	100	11
Worksop	10	5	0	5	76	134	10
Kesteven	10	4	0	6	48	129	8
Glossop	9	3	0	6	67	113	6
Mellish	9	2	1	6	53	116	5
Boston	10	2	0	8	58	165	4
Grimsby	**10**	**0**	**0**	**10**	**41**	**240**	**0**

NOTTS, LINCS, DERBYS 4 WEST

	P	W	D	L	F	A	Pts
Ashbourne	7	7	0	0	199	26	14
Hope Valley	8	6	1	1	153	31	13
Buxton	7	5	0	2	186	68	10
Melbourne	8	5	0	3	144	60	10
Leesbrook	7	4	0	3	122	71	8
East Leake	8	3	1	4	99	78	7
Tupton	8	2	0	6	36	187	4
Bolsover	7	1	0	6	47	126	2
Whitwell	**8**	**0**	**0**	**8**	**7**	**346**	**0**

NOTTS, LINCS, DERBYS 2

	P	W	D	L	F	A	Pts
Amber Valley	10	8	1	1	142	43	17
E Retford	10	8	1	1	144	49	17
Market Rasen	10	7	0	3	105	85	14
Sleaford	9	6	1	2	150	52	13
Spalding	10	6	1	3	137	85	13
Keyworth	10	5	0	3	117	119	10
Casuals	10	4	0	6	80	114	8
Ilkeston	9	3	1	5	90	127	7
Nott'hamians	10	2	0	8	32	165	4
Dronfield	10	1	1	8	72	134	3
Notts Police	10	1	0	9	71	167	2

NOTTS, LINCS, DERBYS 4 EAST

	P	W	D	L	F	A	Pts
Barton	8	7	1	0	180	29	15
Meden Vale	8	6	0	2	154	38	12
Ollerton	7	6	0	1	126	53	12
Yarborough	7	5	1	1	99	30	11
Cleethorpes	8	4	0	4	104	80	8
Rainworth	8	3	0	5	81	72	6
Harworth Coll	8	2	0	6	73	130	4
Bourne	8	1	0	7	26	243	2
Horncastle	8	0	0	8	32	200	0

NOTTS, LINCS, DERBYS 3

	P	W	D	L	F	A	Pts
All Spartans	10	10	0	0	227	29	18*
Long Eaton	10	8	0	2	202	61	16
Belper	10	8	0	2	169	55	16
Ashfield Swans	10	6	0	4	104	79	12
Boots	10	5	1	4	87	102	11
NKOB	9	4	1	4	88	93	9
Gainsboro	10	3	1	6	79	141	7
Skegness	10	3	1	6	59	142	7
Rolls Royce	10	3	0	7	76	77	6
Bakewell	9	1	1	7	26	204	3
Bingham	**10**	**0**	**1**	**9**	**21**	**155**	**1**

**Two points deducted*

MODERNS

Ferry Field, Main Road, Wilford, Nottingham. Tel: (0602) 811374.
Founded: 1956
President: S. Lewis
Chairman: B. Walls
Coach: N. Highfield
Secretary: J. Mapp, 57 Chaworth Road, West Bridgford, Nottingham. Tel: (0602) 814093.
Fixtures Secretary: A. Clarke, 33 Homefield Road, Arnold. Tel: (0602) 263865.
Club captain (1987–88): G. Rudkin/G. Price
Club captain (1988–89): B. Blakeway
No. of teams: Senior 4, Youth & Minis 1
Directions to Ground: Towards Nottingham (S) ring road, Clifton Bridge – Wilford. From Nottingham over Trent Bridge towards M1 – Wilford.
Colours: Cherry/white. (*Change colours:* Black)
Nickname: 'Mods'
Floodlights: No
Membership: £15
Programme: 20p (Editor: A. Clarke)
Local newspaper: Nottingham Evening Post
League: Notts, Lincs, Derbys 1
Final position (1987–88): Winners (promoted)
Competitions won: Notts, Lincs, Derbys Cup 1976, Notts Cup ×4, John Player Pennant Comp. ×3, Notts, Lincs, Derbys (Courage League) Division One Winners.

CHESTERFIELD

Stonegravels, Chesterfield. Tel: (0246) 332321.
Founded: 1920
President: T. Pass
Secretary: P.I. Jackson, 396 Old Road, Chesterfield Tel: (0246) 70112 (B), 56828 (H).
Fixtures Secretary: P. Lourie, 33 Robert Road, Sheffield 8. Tel((0742) 373580.
Club captain (1987–88): D. Bradley
Club captain (1988–89): C. McKee
No. of teams: Senior 4, Youth & Minis 4
Directions to Ground: A61 from Chesterfield Town Centre to Sheffield, 1 mile on left.
Ground capacity: Stand 100
Colours: Red white hoops. (*Change colours:* Black)
Floodlights: No
Membership: £15 Play, £5 Social
Local newspaper: Derbyshire Times
League: NLD 1
Final position (1987–88): Second
Playing record (1987–88): P 32, W 20, L 12, D 0, F 459, A 372.

SCUNTHORPE

Heglam Park, Ashby Road, Scunthorpe. Tel: 0724 843013.
Founded: 1929
President: Not elected yet
Chairman: G.A.S. Ray
Coach: Not elected yet
Secretary: A.C. Taylor, 49A Moorwell Road, Scunthorpe. Tel: 0724 866960.
Fixtures Secretary: P. Cleal, 18 Cheltenham Close. Tel: 0724 856801.
Club captain (1987–88): P. Hewitt
Club captain (1988–89): P. Hewitt
No. of teams: Senior 5, Youth & Minis 8
Directions to Ground: M181 – A11 to Queens Way Hotel – *Map available*
Clubhouse: 6 changing rooms etc – bar open every day.
Colours: Lincoln green. (*Change colours:* Royal blue)
Floodlights: Yes
Admission: Collect 10p
Membership: £15 – player (Senior). £5.00 – Member.
Programme: 20p (Editor: R. Wells)
Local newspaper: Scunthorpe Evening Telegraph
League: N.L.D. Div. 1
Final position (1987–88): 2nd
Playing record (1987–88): P 38, W 25, D 2, L 11, F 720, A 328.
Competitions won: Humberside Merit table, Lincs County '7's' Sept. 87, Lincolnshire Merit table, Clugston Cup Dec. 87, North Lincs. Cup April 87.

WEST BRIDGFORD

Stamford Road, West Bridgford, Nottingham. Tel: Nottingham 232506.
Founded: 1939
President: K. Grundy
Chairman: P. Garland
Coach: R. Studholme
Secretary: D. Sutton, 22 Vernon Avenue, Wilford Village, Nottingham NG11 7AE. Tel: Nottingham 818621.
Fixtures Secretary: J. Kimpson, 125 Rutland Road, West Bridgford, Nottingham. Tel: Nottingham 822157.
Club captain (1987–88): K. Howells
Club captain (1988–89): K. Howells
No. of teams: Senior 5, Youth & Minis 1
Directions to Ground: From town to Trent Bridge, follow Melton Mowbary Road after 2 sets of traffic lights, turn left 6th road on, onto Stamford Road.
Clubhouse: Full amenities + changing rooms.
Colours: Black shirts with red/gold stripe, black shorts/socks. (*Change colours:* Blue/yellow)
Floodlights: Yes
Membership: £17.50 Full, £5 Social
Local newspaper: Nottingham Evening Post
League: Notts, Lincs, Derbys 1
Final position (1987–88): 4th
Playing record (1987–88): P 33, W 20, L 13.

SOUTHWELL

Park Lane, Southwell, Notts. Tel: 0636 812576.
Founded: 1930
President: M. Elias
Chairman: B. Richmond
Coach: S. Butler
Secretary: M. Jones, 4 The Ridgeway, Farmsfield, Notts. Tel: 0623 883100.
Fixtures Secretary: D. Tinley, Middle Hey, Oxton Hill, Oxton, Southwell, Notts. Tel: 0602 655945.
Club captain (1987–88): D. Hunt
Club captain (1988–89): D. Hunt
No. of teams: Senior 5. Youth & Minis 4.
Directions to Ground: On the A612, just south of Southwell.
Ground capacity: 2,000
Colours: Maroon. (*Change colours:* Maroon, white, navy hoops)
Floodlights: Yes
Membership: £20
Local newspaper: Newark Advertiser
League: N.L.D. 1
Final position (1987–88): 4th
Playing record (1987–88): P 219, W 14, L 13, D 2.
Competitions won: 3 Counties Sevens Champions 1979, Colts County Champions 86–87.

WORKSOP

Stubbington Meadow, Stubbing lane, Worksop, Notts. Tel: 0909 484247.
Founded: 1898

Notts, Lincs & Derbys 1

Secretary: J.H. Gibson, 40 Church Walk, Worsop. Tel: 0909 487101.
Fixtures Secretary: N. Gordan, Craggs Lodge, Welbeck, Worksop. Tel: 0909 720516 (H & W).
League: N.L.D. 1
Final position (1987–88): 6th

KESTEVEN

Woodnook, Grantham, Lincs. Tel: 0476 64887.
Founded: 1947
Secretary: P.G. Woods, 18 Belton Grove, Grantham, Lincs. Tel: 0476 68611 (H) 0476 62424 (W).
League: N.L.D. 1
Final position (1987–88): 7th

GLOSSOP

Hargate Hill Lane, Charlesworth, Glossop. Tel: 04574 64553)
Founded: 1973
President: F. Stevenson
Chairman: B. Thompson
Coach: D. Fricker
Secretary: I. Beckett, 25 Croft Manor, Glossop SK13 8PP. Tel: 04574 64287).
Fixtures Secretary: D. Fricker, 62 Long Lane, Charlesworth, Glossop. Tel: 04574 64207
Club captain (1987–88): M. Kershaw
Club captain (1988–89): M. Kershaw
No. of teams: Senior 5.
Directions to Ground: Use A57 Manchester–Sheffield Road, take A627 to Marple, ground is 1 mile on right hand side.
Clubhouse: 4 separate changing rooms, bath, bar social area
Colours: Navy blue shirts
Floodlights: No
Membership: £25
Local newspaper: High Peak Courier
League: Notts, Lincs, Derbys 1
Final position (1987–88): 8th

MELLISH

Tel: 0602-266653.
Founded: 1931
President: F. Earnshaw
Chairman: M. Browne
Coach: M. Wrench
Secretary: P.A. Brook, 5 Grasmere Road, Begston, Nottingham. Tel: 0602-255553.
Fixtures Secretary: M. Fisher, 8 Lanceld Drive, Watnall, Nottingham. Tel: 0602-387933.
Club captain (1987–88): B. Nicholson
Club captain (1988–89): I. Nicholson
No. of teams: Senior 5, Youth & Minis 4
Directions to Ground: On B684.
Colours: Black, yellow, green
Floodlights: Yes
Membership: £20
Local newspaper: Evening Post
League: NLD 1
Final position (1987–88): 4th
Playing record (1987–88): P 34, W 14, D 1, L 19.
Competitions won: Notts City Cup winners '71, '72, '82. Notts Merit table '79, NLD 7's Champions '78.

BOSTON

Great Fen Road, Wyberton, Boston PE21 7PB. Tel: 0205 62683.
Founded: 1927
President: S.B. Julian
Chairman: S.B. Julian
Coach: J.D. Sneddon
Secretary: R.G. Clark, 41 Spilsby Road, Boston PE21 9NX. Tel: 0205 62040.
Fixtures Secretary: N.R. Burden, Halltoft Hall Lane, Algarkirk, Nr. Boston PE20 2HG. Tel: 0205 460845 (H), 0205 820747 (B).
Club captain (1987–88): P. McLeod
Club captain (1988–89): S.G. Dunlop
No. of teams: Senior 3
Directions to Ground: On the main Boston/Slehford Road about 3 miles from centre of Boston.
Ground capacity: More than enough.
Colours: Blue & white hoops. (*Change colours:* Red)
Nickname: Unknown
Floodlights: No
Membership: £17 p.a. Players
Local newspaper: Lincolnshire Standard
League: NLD 1
Final position (1987–88): 10th
Playing record (1987–88): P 36, W 15, L 19, D 2.
Competitions won: 1) Plowman Cup 15.9.87. 2) Lincolnshire County Cup 13.12.87.

GRIMSBY

Springfield Road, Grimsby. Tel: 0472-78594.
Founded: 1885
President: W. Boyers
Chairman: E. Macklam
Coach: A. Blair
Secretary: C.J. Byrom, 57 Langton Road, Holton-Le-Clay, Grimsby DN56 5BA. Tel: 0472-825190.
Fixtures Secretary: A. Blair, 7 Chadwell Springs, Waltham, Grimsby. Tel: 0472-827470.
Club captain (1987–88): R. Smith
Club captain (1988–89): R. Smith
No. of teams: Senior 3, Youth & Minis 2.
Directions to Ground: RT. at College of Further Education into Scartho Road, Scartho roundabout take Waltham Road – 600 yds RT in Springfield Road, 200 yds on right.
Ground capacity: 3–400
Clubhouse: Clubhouse, bar & changing rooms.
Colours: Royal Blue & white. (*Change colours:* Red & white)
Floodlights: No
Admission: N/A
Membership: £15 plus VAT.
Programme: Free (Editor: D. Foulkes)
Local newspaper: Grimsby Evening Telegraph.
League: Notts, Lincs & Derbys 1
Final position (1987–88): Bottom (relegated)
Competitions won: Runners up in Lincolnshire 7 a-side competition.

AMBER VALLEY

Palmer Moorwood Recreation Ground, Swanwick, Derbyshire. Tel: 0773 605072.
Founded: 1967
Secretary: S. Fox
League: N.L.D. 2
Final position (1987–88): 1st

EAST RETFORD

Water Board Ground, Ordsall Road, Retford. Tel: 0777 703243.
Founded: 1952
Secretary: M. Storey, 3 Bankside, Ordsall, Retford, Notts. Tel: Retford 706072 (H) Retford 707351 (W).
League: N.L.D. 2
Final position (1987–88): 2nd

MARKET RASEN

Willingham Road, Market Rasen. Tel: 0673 843162.
Founded: 1950
Secretary: B.N. Harper, Nongoby, Church Lane, Manby, Louth, Lincs LN11 8HL. Tel: 0507 82318 (H).
League: N.L.D. 2
Final position (1987–88): 3rd

SLEAFORD

East Road Ground, Sleaford, Lincs. Tel: Sleaford 0529 303335.
Founded: 1979
Secretary: W.E. Golland, c/o 15 Southgate, Sleaford, Lincs. Tel: 05295 228 (H) 0529 302271 (W).
League: N.L.D. 2
Final position (1987–88): 4th

SPALDING

St Thomas Road, Spalding, Lincs.
Founded: 1923
President: Donald Beecham
Chairman: Brian Stray
Coach: Robert Wishart
Secretary: Geoffrey Nichols, Hethersett House, Redmile Close, Pinchbeck, Spalding, Lincs. Tel: 0775 69897.
Fixtures Secretary: David Feuerhelm, The Cottage, School Lane, Bicker, Boston, Lincs. PE20 30W. Tel: 0775 820695.
Club captain (1987–88): John Constable
Club captain (1988–89): Martin Beecham
No. of teams: Senior 3, Youth & Minis 1
Directions to Ground: Spalding Grammar School Playing Fields, St Thomas's Road, Spalding.
Clubhouse: Spalding Sports Club Ltd (Rugby, Hockey and Cricket).
Colours: Maroon–navy hoops. (*Change Colours:* Green)
Floodlights: Yes. At Sir Halley Stewart Playing Field, Winfrey Avenue, Spalding.
Admission: No charge
Membership: Players £15.00, VPs £5.00, Students £5.00, Youth £2.00.
Local newspaper: Lincs Free Press
League: Notts Lincs Derbys 2
Final position (1987–88): 5th
Playing record (1987–88): P 38, W 23, D 2, L13 , F 719, A 339.
Competitions won: Evening Telegraph (Peterborough) Cup 1979.

KEYWORTH

Willoughby Lane, Widmerpool, Notts. Tel: 06077 5579.
Founded: 1976
Secretary: J.W. Bowker, 4 Malvern Road, West Brigford, Nottingham NG2 7DG. Tel: 0602 231437.
League: N.L.D. 2
Final position (1987–88): 6th

NOTTINGHAM CASUALS

Canal Side, Meadow Road, Beeston, Notts. Tel: (0602) 250135.
Founded: 1922
President: J.V. Grealy
Chairman: I. Lowndes
Coach: M. Boxshall
Secretary: A. Moll, 2 Egerton Drive, Stapleford, Nottingham NG9 8ME. Tel: (0602) 392005.
Fixtures Secretary: D. Smith
Club captain (1987–88): I. Lowndes
Club captain (1988–89): M. Boxshall
No. of teams: Senior 4
Directions to Ground: Approach Beeston on A6005 from Long Eaton. Go past Notts RFC on right, next traffic lights turn right. Follow this road until meet canal, go over canal bridge – 100 yds on right.
Colours: Maroon & white
Floodlights: Yes
Membership: £15
Local newspaper: Nottingham Evening Post
League: Notts, Lincs & Derbys 2
Final position (1987–88): 7th
Playing record (1987–88): P 33, W 13, D 1, L 19.

ILKESTON

Gallows Innfield, Ilkeston. Tel: 0602 323088.
Founded: 1926
Secretary: D.E. Wykes, 8 Carmen Close, Watnall, Nottingham. Tel: Nottingham 384307 (H) Nottingham 384093 (W).
League: N.L.D. 2
Final position (1987–88): 8th

NOTTINGHAMIANS

Adbolton Lane, West Bridgford, Nottinghamshire. Tel: (0602) 811372.
Founded: 1971 as an open club. [was Old Nottinghamians].
President: D. Cuum
Club Captain: P. Renshaw
Secretary: G. Barnes, 19 Main Street, Lowdham, Notts. Tel: (0602) 663847.
Fixtures Secretary: G. Bareford, 8 Osborne Close, Sandiacre, Notts. Tel: (0602) 391011.
Club captain (1987–88): P. Renshaw
Club captain (1988–89): P. Renshaw
No. of teams: Senior 4
Directions to Ground: Next to the National Water Sports Centre.
Colours: Purple/Black/White hoops. (*Change colours:* Purple)
Floodlights: No
Membership: £20
Local newspaper: Nottingham Evening Post
League: N/L/D 2
Final position (1987–88): 9th

DRONFIELD

Dronfield Woodhouse Sports Social Club, Carr Lane, Dronfield, Sheffield. Tel: 890913.
Secretary: A.M. Thomas, 11 Lings Lane, Wickersley, Rotheram, S. Yorks S66 0JP. Tel: Wicks 548135 (H) Roth 365537 (W).
League: N.L.D. 2
Final position (1987–88): 11th

NOTTINGHAMSHIRE POLICE

C/O Hugh Grundy, 6 Coopers Green, Wollaton, Nottingham NG8 2RP.
Founded: 1960
President: R. Hadfield
Chairman: C. Fox
Coach: P. McLaughlin
Secretary: H. Grundy, 6 Coopers Green, Wollaton, Nottingham NG8 2RP. Tel: 0602 289473.
Fixtures Secretary: M. Hewitt, 10 The Mount, Redhill, Nottingham NG5 8LU.
Club captain (1987–88): P. Bradshaw
Club captain (1988–89): P. Bradshaw
No. of teams: Senior 2.
Directions to Ground: Take A6005 from Nottingham–Long Eaton, turn into Station Road, over Beeston Railway Bridge. Follow road to canal, take small bridge over canal, turn left, ground 100 yds on right.
Clubhouse: Notts Casuals RFC. Canal Side Beeston.
Colours: Black shirt and shorts, green socks. Gold collar, cuffs, numbers. (*Change colours:* Gold)
Floodlights: No
Membership: £5
Local newspaper: Nottingham Evening Post
League: Notts, Lincs, Derbys Div 2
Final position (1987–88): 11th (relegated)
Competitions won: Regional Police 7-a-side.

NOTTS, LINCS, DERBYS 3

ALL SPARTANS

All Spartans R.U.F.C., Victor M Wilkes, 87 Bancroft Lane, Mansfield, Notts. Tel: Mansfield 647773.
Founded: 1980
Chairman: V. Wilkes
Coach: M. Revil
Secretary: G. Usher, 85 Sherwood Road, Rainworth, Mansfield, Notts. Tel: (0623) 797815.
Fixtures Secretary: V. Wilkes, 87 Bancroft Lane, Mansfield, Notts. Tel: Mansfield 647773.
Club captain (1987–88): J. Higgins
Club captain (1988–89): J. Higgins
No. of teams: Senior 2
Directions to Ground: Destination Sutton in Ashfield ground is on Sutton Lawn, off Station Road, Sutton Ashfield Show Ground.
Clubhouse: We use the Mansfield Hosiery Mills Sports Club on Sutton Road, Mansfield.
Colours: Navy blue broad amber hoop, black shorts, socks. (*Change colours:* Blue amber hoops)
Nickname: Spartans
Floodlights: No
Admission: None
Membership: £12.00 for Spartans, £3.00 for Hosiery Mills Sports Club.
Local newspaper: Mansfield Chad
League: N.L.D. 3
Final position (1987–88): First (promoted)
Playing record (1987–88): P 10, W 10 (League record)
Competitions won: N.L.D. Division 3 Notts Junior Shield Runners Up 1987.

LONG EATON

Club House, West Park. Tel 0602 460907.
Founded: 1961
President: M. Smith
Chairman: D Mackintosh
Coach: R. Burton
Secretary: S. Bradford, 9 Elm Avenue, Long Eaton, Notts. Tel: 0602 733533 (H) 0602 691300 (W).
Fixtures Secretary: A. Potter, 296 Bennett Street, Long Eaton, Notts. Tel: 0602 725932.
Club captain (1987–88): P. Podboraczynski
Club captain (1988–89): P. Podboraczynski
No. of teams: Senior 4. Youth & Minis 1.
Directions to Ground: J25 M1/A52 follow signs Long Eaton. Turn right at island, straight on next island, ground ½ mile on left.
Clubhouse: Bar (new)
Colours: Blue/white shorts. (*Colour change:* Black/white 2″ stripes)
Floodlights: No
Membership: £15
Local newspaper: Long Eaton Advertiser/Nottingham Evening Post
League: N.L.D. 3
Final position (1987–88): 2nd
Playing record (1987–88): P 34, W 15, L 19, F 459, A 631.
Competitions won: Derbyshire 7's Plate.

BELPER

Eyes Meadow, Duffield.
Founded: 1975
Chairman: P. Melhuish
Coach: M. Finn/J. Kenning
Secretary: M.A. Ryan, 6 Oakwood Drive, Oakwood, Derby. Tel: 0332 665377.
Fixtures Secretary: R. Morgan
Club captain (1987–88): A. Marshall
Club captain (1988–89): R. Parker
No. of teams: Senior 3.
Directions to Ground: Follow A6, north of Derby. At village of Duffield turn right, between Kennings Garage and Building Society. Follow signs.
Ground capacity: Open playing area.
Clubhouse: Duffield C.C. pavilion
Colours: Black/white hoops. (*Change colours:* All black)
Floodlights: No
Membership: £20
Local newspapers: Belper News/Derby Evening Telegraph
League: NLD3
Final position (1987–88): 3rd
Playing record (1987–88): P 31, W 18, D 1, L 12, F 406, A 333.
Competitions won: Semi-final Derbys Cup.

ASHFIELD SWANS

Ashfield School, Sutton Road, Kirkby-in-Ashfield, Notts. Tel: 0623 752008.
Founded: 1972
Secretary: S. Trainer, 14 King Street, Kirkby-in-Ashfield, Nots NG17 8AG. Tel: 0602 652341.
League: N.L.D. 3
Final position (1987–88): 4th

BOOTS ATHLETIC

Lady Bay, West Bridgford, Nottingham. Tel: 822392.
Founded: 1928
President: Arthur Bramham
Chairman: Brian Richmond
Coach: Neil Malik
Secretary: Nick Sleigh, 70 Chetwynd Road, Toton, Nottingham. Tel: 720918.
Fixtures Secretary: Tom Miller, 22 Promenade, Nottingham. Tel: 598053.
Club captain (1987–88): Trevor Sills
Club captain (1988–89): Trevor Sills
No. of teams: Senior 3
Directions to Ground: Follow signs from Nottingham A52 to Grantham. Turn right after Trent Bridge, left at next traffic lights.
Colours: Dark/light blue quarters. (*Change colours:* Maroon)
Floodlights: No
Membership: £3.50 p.a.
Local newspaper: Nottingham Evening Post
League: Notts, Lincs & Derbys 3
Final position (1987–88): 5th
Playing record (1987–88): P 31, W 17, D 3, L 11, F 276, A 282.
Competitions won: Nottinghamshire Junior Cup – 17th April 1988.

NKOB

Unfortunately no information available at the time of going to press.

GAINSBOROUGH

Rose Leisure Club, North Warren Road, Gainsborough, Lincs. Tel: 0427 2915.
Founded: 1974
Secretary: G.P. Taylor, 5 Wedgewood Road (Plot 106A), Kingswood, Doddington Park, Lincoln. Tel: 0522 688769 (H) 0522 513311 (W).
League: N.L.D. 3
Final position (1987–88): 7th

SKEGNESS

Wainfleet Road, Skegness. Tel: 0754.
Founded: 1950
President: G.R. Bell
Chairman: B.S. Major
Secretary: Alan Hawkes, South View Farm, East Keal, Spilsby. Tel: 0790 52788/52176.
Fixtures Secretary: B.V. Hill, 8 Tothby Lane, Alford. Tel: 052122544
Club captain (1987–88): S. Hatch
Club captain (1988–89): A. Archer
No. of teams: Senior 2
Directions to Ground: Boston/Wainfleet Road out of Skegness by Indoor Bowls.
Ground capacity: 2 pitches
Clubhouse: 2 changing, showers, toilets, kitchen, bar.
Colours: Blue & white hooped jerseys. (*Change colours:* Light blue)
Nickname: Seasiders
Floodlights: No
Membership: £9
Local newspaper: Skegness News & Lincs Standard.
League: N.L.D. (3)
Final position (1987–88): 7th
Playing record (1987–88): P 30, W 16, D 1, L 13.

ROLLS ROYCE

R.R. Rec. Society Ground, Merrill Way, Derby. Tel: 0352 249167.
Founded: 1943
Secretary: W.A. Cushion, 9 Brightstone Close, Alvaston, Derby DE2 0UB. Tel: 0332 756651 (H) 0332 249856 (W).
League: N.L.D. 3
Final position (1987–88): 9th

BAKEWELL

League: N.L.D. 3
Final position (1987–88): 10th

BINGHAM

Bingham Sports Centre, The Banks, Bingham. Tel: Bingham 38628.
Founded: 1971
Secretary: K.H. Bartsch, 14 Sherwood Grove, Bingham, Nottingham NG13 8RG. Tel: Bingham 39008 (H) 0533 663086 (W).
League: N.L.D. 3
Final position (1987–88): 11th (bottom)

ASHBOURNE

Founded: 1934
President: F. Bates
Chairman: P. King
Secretary: D. Shelton, 26 Belper Road, Ashbourne, Derbyshire. Tel: 0335 43579.
Fixtures Secretary: F. Bates, 5 Spencer Close, Ashbourne. Tel: 0335 42701 or 43440 after 6 p.m.
Club captain (1987–88): A. Keeling
Club captain (1988–89): A. Keeling
No. of teams: Senior 3. Youth 1.
Directions to Ground: Recreation Ground, Ashbourne – asky anybody.
Clubhouse: Council Pavilion
Colours: Old gold/dark blue. (*Change colours:* Royal blue)
Floodlights: No
Membership: £12.50
Local newspaper: Ashbourne News Telegraph
League: N.L.D. 4 West
Final position (1987–88): 1st
Competitions won: Abare league

HOPE VALLEY

Peak Hotel, Castleton, Derbyshire. Tel: 0433 20247.
Founded: 1979
President: J.E. Mason
Chairman: R. Gray
Coach: P. Holwell
Secretary: P. Mildenstein, 6 Gladstone Mews, Sheffield S10 3HS.
Fixtures Secretary: P. Mildenstein, as above.
Club captain (1987–88): M. Ellis
Club captain (1988–89): P. Gale
No. of teams: Senior 2.
Directions to Ground: A625 out of Sheffield to Castleton, after Peak Hotel turn right into Back Lane.
Ground capacity: 400
Clubhouse: Shower and change facilities
Colours: Purple/green/white. (*Change colours:* Green)
Nickname: "Valley"
Floodlights: No
Membership: £20
Local newspaper: Derbyshire Times/Star
League: N.L.D. 4 West
Final position (1987–88): 2nd
Competitions won: Runner-up N.L.D. Div 4 West

BUXTON

Fairfield Centre, Victoria Road, Fairfield, Buxton.
Founded: 1927
Secretary: K. Beevers, 40 Dovedale Crescent, Buxton, Derbyshire SK17 9BH. Tel: 0298 70884.
League: N.L.D. 4 West
Final position (1987–88): 3rd

MELBOURNE

Melbourne Recreation Ground, Cockshut Lane, Melbourne, Derby.
Founded: 1983
Secretary: J. Hesketh, "Surfs Up", The Common, Melbourne, Derby DE7 1DH. Tel: 03316 4507 (H).
League: N.L.D. 4 West
Final position (1987–88): 4th

LEESBROOK

Asterdale Club, Borrowash Road, Spondon, Derby. Tel: 668656.
Founded: 1978
President: L. Woodside
Chairman: M. Wilson
Coach: P. Swannick, J. Golding
Secretary: N. Buckler, 27 Wallaton Road, Chaddesden, Derby. Tel: 674470.
Fixtures Secretary: L. Woodside, 1 South Drive, Chaddesden, Derby. Tel: 673872.
Club captain (1987–88): L. Woodside
Club captain (1988–89): P. Albon
No. of teams: Senior 1
Directions to Ground: The A6005 from Derby to Nottingham, turn left opposite Bemrose Printing into Borrowash Road, Club on the right.
Clubhouse: Privately owned – Asterdale Club.
Colours: Emerald green, sky blue white and black. (*Change colours:* Black)
Floodlights: No
Membership: £20.00
Local newspaper: Derby Evening Telegraph
League: Nl & D 4 West
Final position (1987–88): Fourth

EAST LEAKE

Harry Carlton School. Tel: (EL 2956).
Founded: 1977/78
President: Colin Fearn
Chairman: Graham Hay
Coach: Tony Weston
Secretary: Tony Weston, 5 St Andrew Close, Gotham, Notts. Tel: (Nott 830813).
Fixtures Secretary: Alan Sharkey, 13 Eastham Road, Arnold, Nottingham. Tel: 205640.
Club captain (1987–88): Paul Cobbin
Club captain (1988–89): Paul Johnson
No. of teams: Senior 2
Directions to Ground: ¼ mile from centre of the village – East Leake Leisure Centre, off Lantern Lane.
Clubhouse: Nags Head Public House
Colours: Maroon & white hoops. (*Change colours:* Plain maroon shirts)
Floodlights: No
Membership: £5
Local newspaper: Loughborough Echo
League: Notts, Lincs, Derbys 4 West
Final position (1987–88): 6th
Playing record (1987–88): P 34, W 23, D 1, L 10, F 532, A 284.

TUPTON

Recreation Ground, North Side, Tupton, Chesterfield.
Founded: 1970
Secretary: B.A. Wakefield, 14 Redfern Street, Tupton, Derby.
League: N.L.D. 4 West
Final position (1987–88): 7th

BOLSOVER

Founded: 1982
President: Gerald Weeden
Chairman: Gerald Weeden
Coach: Clive Ponder
Secretary: Ken Dudhill, 32 Sandhills Road, Bolsover, Derbys S44 6EY. Tel: 0246-826738.
Fixtures Secretary: John Wright, 1 Oxcroft Lane, Bolsover, Derbys. Tel: 0246-826240.

Notts, Lincs, Derbys 4 West

Club captain (1987–88): Ian Richardson
Club captain (1988–89): Chris Smith
No. of teams: Senior 1
Directions to Ground: Bolsover School, Mooracre Lane, Bolsover.
Colours: Navy/white hoops, navy shorts.
Floodlights: No
Membership. £10 p.a. playing
Local newspaper: Derbyshire Times
League: NLD 4W
Final position (1987–88): 8th

WHITWELL

League: N.L.D. 4 West
Final position (1987–88): 9th (bottom)

NOTTS, LINCS, DERBYS 4 EAST

BARTON & DISTRICT

Mill Lane, Barrow-on-Humber, S. Humberside.
Founded: 1963
President: T. Binks
Chairman: R. Proctor
Secretary: T.P.R. Phipb, 16–18 Frances Street, Scunthorpe. Tel: 0724 847888.
Fixtures Secretary: K. Alldridge, 16 St James Road, Briyy. Tel: (0652) 53485.
Club captain (1987–88): M. Meeker
Club captain (1988–89): M. Meeker
No. of teams: Senior 3
Directions to Ground: Into Barrow from Barton right at mini roundabout, next right into Mill Lane.
Clubhouse: Bar/changing rooms
Colours: Red & white. (*Change colours:* Black & white)
Nickname: Superstars
Floodlights: No
Membership: £18
Local newspaper: Scunthorpe Evening Telegraph
League: Notts, Lincs & Derbys 4 East
Final position (1987–88): 1st (promoted)
Playing record (1987–88): P 31, W 24, L 6, D 1.
Competitions won: Lincs 7's Plate League.

MEDEN VALE

Welbeck Colliery Pitch, Meden Vale, Mansfield.
Founded: 1980
Secretary: M. Chicken, 121 Egmanton Road, Meden Vale, Mansfield. Tel: Mansfield 846291 (H) 0623 25577 (W).
League: N.L.D. 4 East
Final position (1987–88): 2nd

OLLERTON

Ollerton Rec. Centre, Whinney Lane, New OLlerton, Newark, Notts. Tel: 0623 862469.
Founded: 1983
Secretary: D.G. Price, 10 The Brambles, Walesby, Newark, Notts. Tel: 0623 860871 (H).
League: N.L.D. 4 East
Final position (1987–88): 3rd

YARBOROUGH BEE'S

Yarborough Sports Centre, Lincoln. Tel: 24228.
Founded: 1976
President: P. Mitchell
Chairman: H. Sampson
Coach: H. Sampson
Secretary: D. Stobie, 131 Newark Road, North Hykeham, Lincoln LN6 8QT. Tel: Linc. 689449.
Fixtures Secretary: R. Payne, Disney Place Hotel, Eastgate, Lincoln LN2 4AA. Tel: Linc. 38881.
Club captain (1987–88): Z. Gray
Club captain (1988–89): Z. Gray
No. of teams: Senior 1
Directions to Ground: A15 Uphill Lincoln, Yarborough Sports Centre.
Ground capacity: Sports Centre field.
Colours: Maroon/amber hoop's
Nickname: The Bee's
Floodlights: No
Membership: £10
Local newspaper: Linc's Echo
League: NLD East 4
Final position (1987–88): 3rd

CLEETHORPES

Taylors Avenue, Cleethorpes.
Founded: 1979
Chairman: C.S. Marks
Secretary: S. Regan, 75 Poplar Road, Cleethorpes. Tel: 0472 691285.
Fixtures Secretary: J. Walsham, 9 Queenmary Avenue, Cleethorpes. Tel: 0472 42628.
Club captain (1987–88): R. Benefer
Club captain (1988–89): M. Debnam
No. of teams: Senior 2
Colours: Blue yellow hoops
Floodlights: No
Membership: £2
Local newspaper: Grimsby Evening Telegraph
League: NLD 4 East
Final position (1987–88): 4th
Playing record (1987–88): P 30, W 16, D 2, L 12.

RAINWORTH

League: N.L.D. 4 East
Final position (1987–88): 6th

HARWORTH COLLIERY

Recreation ground, Scrooby Road, Bircotes.
Founded: 1986
Chairman: Bill Jackson
Coach: T. Wilkinson
Secretary: Chris Shail, 157 Scrooby Road, Bircotes, Doncaster DN11 8AD.
Fixtures Secretary: As above
Club captain (1987–88): Terry Wilkinson
Club captain (1988–89): Terry Wilkinson
No. of teams: Senior 1
Directions to Ground: 2 miles Sth of Bantry on A614, turn right to Bircotes ground ½ mile on left.
Colours: Royal blue & white
Floodlights: No
Admission: None
Membership: £5
Programme: 30p (Editor: Chris Shail)
Local newspaper: Worksop Guardian
League: NLD 4E
Final position (1987–88): Sixth

BOURNE

c/o The Nags Head, Market Place, Bourne, Lincs. Tel: 0778 422095.
Founded: 1987
President: A. Cooke
Chairman: R.I. Johnson
Secretary: A.D. Lock, The Nags Head, Market Place, Bourne. Tel: 0778 422095.
Fixtures Secretary: A. Rowe, 54 North Road, Bourne. Tel: 0778 424353.
Club captain (1987–88): R.E. Griffith
Club captain (1988–89): M. Hempstead
No. of teams: Senior 2
Directions to Ground: A151 from town centre – 1 mile left hand side – one field back.
Ground capacity: Unlimited
Clubhouse: At Nags Head
Colours: Navy/amber circlet
Floodlights: No
Admission: None
Membership: £15 playing
Local newspaper: Stamford & Rutland Mercury
League: Notts, Lincs & Derby 4 East
Final position (1987–88): 8th
Playing record (1987–88): Won eight lost the rest.

HORNCASTLE

St. Lawrence School, Bowl Alley Lane, Horncastle, Lincs. Tel: 06582/2365.
Founded: 1985
President: Philip Sharpe
Chairman: Bill Laing
Coach: Trevor Francis (RFU coach)
Secretary: Trevor Francis, 54 Langton Hill, Horncastle, Lincs LN9 5AH. Tel: 06582/2325.
Fixtures Secretary: Trevor Francis, 54 Langton Hill, Horncastle, Lincs LN9 5AH. Tel: 06582/2325.
Club captain (1987–88): Robin Parker
Club captain (1988–89): David Middlebrook
No. of teams: Senior 1
Directions to Ground: From traffic lights on the main Lincoln/Skegness road travel 200 yds towards Skegness; turn left onto Stanhope Road; 100 yds on the right is Bowl Alley Lane; ground 200 yds on the left.
Clubhouse: On premises of St. Lawrence School, but separate building.
Colours: Green/with inverted yellow 'V'.
Floodlights: No
Membership: £15
Local newspaper: Horncastle News & Horncastle Standard
League: Notts, Lincs, Derbys East 4
Final position (1987–88): 9th of 9
Playing record (1987–88): P 29, W 10, L 19.

STAFFORDSHIRE/WARWICKSHIRE LEAGUE

WHEREAS North Midlands and Notts., Lincs., and Derbys with their large leagues have direct promotion to the Midland 2 West and 2 East respectively, promotion to the former from the two small leagues of Staffordshire and Warwickshire is through a combined competition which was won by Bedworth, who had a clear margin in their favour ahead of Old Leamingtonians and Leek. The unlucky basement sides were Kenilworth and Handsworth.

TABLES 1987–88

STAFFS/WARWICKS

	P	W	D	L	F	A	Pts
Bedworth	10	8	1	1	173	49	17
O Leamingt's	10	6	1	3	120	84	13
Leek	10	6	1	3	90	84	13
Nuneat'n OE	10	6	0	4	106	99	12
O Longton's	10	5	1	4	121	100	11
Stoke OB	10	5	0	5	112	82	10
Newcastle	10	5	0	5	98	111	10
Willenhall	10	4	1	5	140	135	9
Stratford	10	4	0	6	126	102	8
Kenilworth	10	2	0	8	58	195	4
Handsworth	10	1	1	8	72	181	3

STAFFS/WARWICKS

BEDWORTH

Rectory Fields, Smarts Road, Bedworth, Warwicks. Tel: 0203 312025.
Founded: 1970
Secretary: Mrs A. Darlison, 44 Smarts Road, Bedworth CV 12 0SP.
League: Staffs/Warwicks
Final position (1987–88): 1st
Competitions won: Staffs/Warwicks

OLD LEAMINGTONIANS

The Crofts, Bericote Road, Leamington Spa. Tel: 0926 24991.
Founded: 1931
Secretary: E. Bayliss, 1 Puckerings Lane, Warwick. Tel: Warwick 495373 (H) Coventry 28381 (W).
League: Staffs/Warwicks
Final position (1987–88): 2nd
Playing record (1987–88): P 39, W 18, D 0, L 21, F 588, A 543.

LEEK

Strangman Street, Leek. Tel: 0538 383680.
Founded: 1923
Secretary: M.J. Clewes, 55 Westwood Park Drive, Leek, Stafs ST13 8NW. Tel: 0538 382922 (H) 0782 612669 (W).
League: Staffs/Warwicks
Final position (1987–88): 3rd
Playing record (1987–88): P 37, W 24, D 1, L 12, F 423, A 370.

NUNEATON OLD EDWARDIANS

Weddington Road, Nuneaton. Tel: 0203 386778.
Founded: 1910
President: S. Savage
Chairman: R.R. Arnold
Coach: J. Jones
Secretary: A.P. Betney, 8 Sunnyside, Hinckky. Tel: 0455 637515.
Fixtures Secretary: J. Sparkes, 140 Lutterworth Road, Nuneaton. Tel: 0203 326029.
Club captain (1987–88): M.A. Hall
Club captain (1988–89): M.A. Hall
No. of teams: Senior 5, Colts 1
Directions to Ground: On Weddington Road going North on left-hand side (Cricket ground).
Clubhouse: Large brick built structure containing clubroom, six changing rooms for rugby, 4 squash courts etc.
Colours: Red & white hoops. (*Change colours:* White)
Floodlights: No
Membership: £10
Local newspaper: Nuneaton Evening Tribune
League: Staffs/Warks
Final position (1987–88): 4th
Playing record (1987–88): P 34, W 23, L 11, F 507, A 339.

OLD LONGTONIAN

Roughcote Lane, Caverswall, Stoke-on-Trent. Tel: (0782) 39449.
Founded: 1953
President: M.J. Carson
Chairman: M. Hamer
Coach: S.R. Tams
Secretary: T.J. Keeling, Checkleybank Farmhouse, Checkley, Stoke-on-Trent. Tel: (0538) 722750.
Fixtures Secretary: J.R. Till, 174 Stallington Road, Blythe Bridge, Stoke-on-Trent. Tel: (0782) 395396.
Club captain (1987–88): J. Wainwright
Club captain (1988–89): R. Tams
No. of teams: Senior 4, Youth & Minis 3
Directions to Ground: Six miles from J14 (M6) & M1220 J15 (M6) just off A520 at Caverswall.
Clubhouse: 6 changing rooms, 2 clubhouse rooms, gym.
Colours: Black & amber. (*Change colours:* Black)
Floodlights: No
Admission: Free!
Membership: £25
Programme: Sponsored (Editor: M. Hamer)
Local newspaper: Evening Sentinel
League: Staffs/Warwicks
Final position (1987–88): 5th
Playing record (1987–88): P 34, W 22, D 2, L 10.
Competitions won: Leek Sevens – Heckle Shield.

STOKE OLD BOYS

Brookvale Avenue, Binley, Coventry. Tel: 0203 453631.
Founded: 1921
Secretary: B.V. Hopkins, 122 Stonebury Avenue, Eastern Green, Coventry CV5 7NX. Tel: 0203 460913 (H) 0203 452152 (W).
League: Staffs/Warwicks
Final position (1987–88): 6th

NEWCASTLE (STAFFS)

Lilleshall Road, Newcastle, Staffs. Tel: 0782 617042.
Founded: 1947
President: J. Whittaker
Chairman: A. Marsh
Coach: G. Radwell
Secretary: B. Conroy, 237 Fearns Avenue, Bradwell, Newcastle, Staffs. Tel: 0782 625771.
Fixtures Secretary: D. Westrup, 11 Henshall Drive, Sandbach, Cheshire. Tel: 0270 766538.
Club captain (1987–88): C. Ward
Club captain (1988–89): C. Ward
No. of teams: Senior 5. Youth & Minis 2.
Directions to Ground: Leave M6, Junction 15 to Newcastle. Turn left at 1st roundabout, over next roundabout, right at next roundabout, 2nd road on left.
Clubhouse: 4 changing room, ref., lounge, games room, gym.
Colours: Maroon, white hoops. (*Change colours:* All maroon)
Nickname: Castle
Floodlights: Partial. Will complete this season.
Membership: £17.50
Local newspaper: Evening Sentinel
League: Mids/Staffs, Warks.
Final position (1987–88): 5th
Playing record (1987–88): P 31, W 14, L 13, D 4.

WILLENHALL

Bognor Road, Essington, Staffs. Tel: 0922 405694.
Founded: 1963
President: W. Simkin
Chairman: A. Moore
Coach: E. Field
Secretary: E. Pugh, 9 Five-Fields Road, Willenhall, West Mids.
Fixtures Secretary: G. Aucott, 17 River Way, Wednesbury, West Mids. Tel: 021 556 0794.
Club captain (1987–88): G. Featherstone
Club captain (1988–89): R. Swift
No. of teams: 5 Seniors & Colts U 10, 14, 17.
Directions to Ground: Off Junction 1, M54. 300 yds towards Wolverhampton, left into Bognor Road, 1½ miles to club.
Ground capacity: 500
Colours: Maroon. (*Change colours:* Black)
Floodlights: Yes
Membership: £20 playing members
Local newspaper: Express & Star
League: Staffs/Warwicks
Final position (1987–88): 8th
Playing record (1987–88): Won 50% of all matches
Competitions won: Colts won Staffs Merit Table, beaten finalists in Staffs Cup, won 30 matches out of 34.

STRATFORD-ON-AVON

Pearcecroft, Loxley Road, Stratford-upon-Avon.
Founded: 1876
President: Dr. Holley
Chairman: R. Withers
Coach: Paul Gisbourne
Secretary: Ian Fathers, 61 Loxley Road, Stratford. Tel: (0789) 205715.
Club captain (1987–88): Chris "Ossie" Price
Club captain (1988–89): Paul Gisbourne
No. of teams: Senior 4, Youth & Minis 8/10

Directions to Ground: South of Clopton Bridge, along Tiddington Road, turn up Loxley Road, 400 yds on left.
Ground capacity: 2000. Stand, 200
Colours: Black & white hoops. White shorts. (*Change colours:* Black shirts)
Nickname: "The Bards"
Floodlights: Yes
Membership: £30 full membership
Local newspaper: Stratford Herald
League: Staff/Warks
Final position (1987–88): 8th
Playing record (1987–88): P 36, W 19, L 17.

KENILWORTH

Glasshouse Lane, Kenilworth. Tel: 0926 53945.
President: J.W. Lynes
Chairman: G. Jordan
Coach: R. Bennett
Secretary: L.J.S. Pendle, 24 Convent Close, Kenilworth, Warwicks. Tel: 0926 57168.
Fixtures Secretary: D. Davies, 33 Fishponds Road, Kenilworth, Warwicks. Tel: 0926 54824.
Club captain (1987–88): L. Sibley
Club captain (1988–89): R.J. Bulow
No. of teams: Senior 5, Youth & Minis 10
Directions to Ground: Travel down the main street in Kenilworth (from Clock Tower). Turn left at island into Buches Lane. This runs into Glasshouse Lane and the Club is on left.
Colours: Light blue shirts
Floodlights: No
Membership: £22.00 playing
Programme: Free
Local newspaper: Kenilworth Weekly News
League: Staffordshire/Warwickshire
Final position (1987–88): Relegated from Staffs/Warwicks.
Playing record (1987–88): P 38, W 12, L 26, D 0, F 438, A 686.

HANDSWORTH

A50 Birmingham Road, Walsall, West Midlands. Tel: 021-357-6427.
Founded: 1887
President: L. Still
Chairman: M. Dallison
Coach: G. Slevin
Secretary: A. Hardy, 6 Freemount Square, Great Barr, Birmingham B43 5QT. Tel: 021-358-6612 (H), 021-200-2266 (B).
Fixtures Secretary: L.M. Taylor, 44 Ashfurlong Crescent, Sutton Coldfield. Tel: 021-378-3530 (H), 92-36262 (W).
Club captain (1987–88): T. Cartwright
Club captain (1988–89): T. Cartwright
No. of teams: Senior 4, Youth & Minis 9
Directions to Ground: Junction 7, M6, take A34 to Walsall, adjacent to Bell Inn.
Ground capacity: 200+
Colours: Red and white hooped shirts, blue shorts. (*Change colours:* Blue and white shirts)
Floodlights: No
Membership: £20 playing, £5 social.
Local newspaper: Express and Star and Walsall Observer
League: Staffs/Warwickshire
Final position (1987–88): bottom Staffs/Warks League (relegated).
Playing record (1987–88): P 33, W 17, D 2, L 14, F 410, A 413.
Competitions won: 1986–87 Midshires Merit Table Winners.

A Japanese visitor to the Twickenham headquarters studies the memorial to the Second World War fallen – including Prince Obolensky, a famous try scorer against the All Blacks. Photo: C. Henry.

WARWICKSHIRE LEAGUES

WARWICKSHIRE had three leagues with a total of 32 clubs and there were no 100 percent records, although Keresley won the top league unbeaten, having drawn twice as they finished comfortably in front.

Manor Park only lost one match to take the second league title comfortably, whilst Coventrians won Warwickshire 3 with only one defeat from 10 games and a points total of 251, which gave them top place on points difference from Old Warwickians (second) and A.P. Lockheed. Coventry Tech lost all their games but gallantly completed their programme.

TABLES 1987–88

WARWICKSHIRE 1

	P	W	D	L	F	A	Pts
Keresley	10	8	2	0	198	63	18
Cov Welsh	10	7	1	2	146	68	15
O Coventrians	10	6	1	3	109	78	13
Trinity Guild	10	6	0	4	154	100	12
GEC Coventry	10	6	0	4	102	128	12
Broad St	10	5	1	4	148	94	11
Rugby St Andrews	10	5	1	4	121	124	11
Dunlop	10	4	1	5	114	124	9
O Wheatleyans	10	3	0	7	59	164	6
Atherstone	10	1	0	9	52	195	2
O Laurentians	10	0	1	9	60	125	1

WARWICKS 2

	P	W	D	L	F	A	Pts
Manor Park	10	9	0	1	143	63	18
Southam	10	7	0	3	171	73	14
Spartans	10	7	0	3	122	91	14
Cov Saracens	10	6	0	4	171	80	12
Earlsdon	10	6	0	4	110	129	12
Pinley	10	5	1	4	128	110	11
Standard	10	5	1	4	101	106	11
Silhillians	10	4	0	6	120	123	8
Harbury	10	4	0	6	68	143	8
Berks & B'sall	10	1	0	9	66	191	2
Rugby Welsh	10	0	0	10	47	138	0

WARWICKSHIRE 3

	P	W	D	L	F	A	Pts
Coventrians	9	8	0	1	251	54	16
O Warwickians	9	8	0	1	196	45	16
A P Lockheed	9	8	0	1	100	523	16
Shipston-on-Stour	9	4	1	4	127	69	9
Warwick	9	4	1	4	87	102	9
Alcester	9	3	1	5	75	144	7
Caludon Castle	9	3	1	5	91	195	7
Post Office	9	2	1	6	45	89	5
Shottery	9	2	1	6	82	132	5
Cov Tech	9	0	0	9	30	202	0

WARWICKSHIRE 1

KERESLEY

Burrow Hill Lane, Corley, Nr. Coventry. Tel: Fillongley 40082.
Founded: 1953
President: J. Radford
Chairman: J. Magee
Coach: R. Freemantle
Secretary: J. Frawley, 37 The Crescent, Keresley. Tel: Ker 7537.
Fixtures Secretary: B. Clements, 12 Cecily Road, Coventry. Tel: Cov. 501694.
Club captain (1987–88): M. Connor
Club captain (1988–89): R. Freemantle
No. of teams: Senior 5, Youth & Minis 6
Directions to Ground: Situated off the main Bennetts Road North, just past Keresley Village.
Clubhouse: 4 changing rooms, bar, upstairs lounge.
Colours: Royal Blue/scarlet/white. (*Change colours:* Dark blue/white)
Nickname: K's
Floodlights: No
Membership: £15.50 playing
Local newspaper: Coventry Evening Telegraph
League: Warks 1
Final position (1987–88): 1st
Playing record (1987–88): Warks Div 1.

COVENTRY WELSH

Burbages Lane, Exhall, Coventry. Tel. Cov 360303.
Founded: 1947
Secretary: M. Tainton, 96 Winfield Street, Rugby, Warks. Tel: 0788 2121 (W).
League: Warwicks 1
Final position (1987–88): 2nd

OLD COVENTRIANS

Tile Hill Lane, Coventry. Tel: Coventry 715273.
Founded: 1930
President: R.C. Richards
Chairman: J. Over
Coach: M. Reavell
Secretary: W.G. Wanley, 121 Maidavale Crescent, Coventry. Tel: 0203 412153.
Fixtures Secretary: N. Twaite, 43 Ivybridge Road, Coventry. Tel: ?203 416833.
Club captain (1987–88): M. Taylor
Club captain (1988–89): M. Taylor
No. of teams: Senior 4. Youth & Minis 2.
Directions to Ground: Junction of A45 (Coventry Bypass) and Tile Hill Lane.

Warwickshire 1

Colours: Black, red, gold. (*Change colours:* yellow)
Nickname: OC's
Floodlights: No
Membership: £12.50
Programme: (Editor, I. Locke)
Local newspaper: Coventry Evening Telegraph
League: Warwickshire 1
Final position (1987–88): 3rd
Playing record (1987–88): P 37, W 20, D 2, L 15, F 581, A 376.

TRINITY GUILD

Rowley Road, Coventry. Tel: Coventry 305928.
Founded: 1899
President: G. Bosworth
Chairman: R.W. Wormell
Coach: T. Dingley
Secretary: A.R. Medlock, 5 Bywater Close, Coventry CV3 6ND. Tel: 414215.
Fixtures Secretary: J. Morton, 63 Shirley Road, Coventry. Tel: 617128.
Club captain (1987–88): N. Mountford
Club captain (1988–89): T. Dingley
No. of teams: Senior 4, Youth & Minis 1
Directions to Ground: Rowley Road adjoins the island at A45 Willenham roundabout.
Ground capacity: 400–500. Stand, (small)
Clubhouse: All facilities.
Colours: Maroon, old gold & dark blue. (*Change colours:* Blue)
Floodlights: No
Membership: Varies according to status.
Local newspaper: Coventry Evening Telegraph
League: Warwicks 1
Final position (1987–88): 3rd
Playing record (1987–88): P 38, W 30, L 8.
Competitions won: Earlsdon 7's R.V. 87/88. County Minor Cup winners 1984.

GEC (COVENTRY)

Allard Way. Tel: 0203 451157.
Founded: 1925
President: A.G.W. Johnson
Chairman: R.V. Thomas
Coach: C. Rogers/R. Wood
Secretary: R.G. Everitt, 23 Bruntingthorpe Way, Binley, Coventry CV3 2GD.
Fixtures Secretary: A.G.W. Johnson, 21 Brookvale Avenue, Coventry.
Club captain (1987–88): M.J. Smith
Club captain (1988–89). P.J.A. Kelly
No. of teams: Senior 4
Directions to Ground: Off Allard Way, Copsewood, Coventry.
Colours: Red/blue/green hoops. (*Change colours:* Green/red)
Nickname: 'Gees'
Floodlights: No
Admission: Nil
Membership: £10 + social club fee.
Local newspaper: Coventry Evening Telegraph
League: Warks 1
Final position (1987–88): 5th
Playing record (1987–88): P 36, W 19, L 17.

BROADSTREET

Ivor Preece Field, Brandon Road, Coventry. Tel: 0203 451706 (Caretaker) 0203 453982 (Clubhouse).
Founded: 1929
President: E. Sheldon
Chairman: G. Watts
Coach: R. Skene
Secretary: C.J. McGintt, 14 Glendower Avenue, Whobexley, Coventry CV5 8BE. Tel: 0203 79261.
Fixtures Secretary: D. Wilkinson, 4 Court Leet, Binley Woods, Coventry. Tel: 0203 543548.
Club captain (1987–88): S. Buttriss
Club captain (1988–89): Buttriss
No. of teams: Senior 4. Youth & Minis 5.
Directions to Ground: Once in Coventry take sign to Brandon Village. Ground found at the Brandon Intersection of Coventry Eastern Bypass.
Colours: Red with green and white band. Navy shorts. (*Change colours:* White with green and red band. Navy shorts.)
Nickname: The Street
Floodlights: Training lights only.
Membership: £2.50
Local newspaper: Coventry Eveneing Telegraph
League: Warwickshire 1
Final position (1987–88): 5th

RUGBY ST ANDREWS

League: Warwicks 1
Final position (1987–88): 7th

DUNLOP

Burnaby Road, Coventry. Tel: TBA.
Founded: 1924
President: J.B. Roberts
Chairman: C.J. Shore
Coach: V. Townsley
Secretary: K.T. Davies, 8 Cheltenham Close, Bedworth, Warks. Tel: 490138.
Fixtures Secretary: B.P. Brown, 176 Sutton Avenue, Coventry. Tel: 461187.
Club captain (1987–88): J. Lilley
Club captain (1988–89): S. Ormsby
No. of teams: Senior 3, Youth 1
Directions to Ground: Holbrooks Area (North) of Coventry. Burnaby Road runs between Holbrook Lane and Beake Avenue.
Ground capacity: 700+
Clubhouse: Brick built, situated on Burnaby Road sports ground.
Colours: Black/amber hoops. (*Change colours:* Green)
Nickname: 'Dees'
Floodlights: No
Programme: Cup games only (Editor: K.T. Davies)
Local newspaper: Coventry Evening Telegraph
League: Warks 1
Final position (1987–88): 8th
Playing record (1987–88): P 30, W 12, D 2, L 16.

OLD WHEATLEYANS

Norman Place Road, Coventry. Tel: Keresley 4888.
Founded: 1929
President: K.S. Bailey
Chairman: A. Partridge
Secretary: R. Leigh, 8 Orchard Crescent, Coventry CV3 6HJ. Tel: 0203 501998.
Fixtures Secretary: D. Margetts, 2 Rochester Road, Coventry. Tel: 0203 72952.
Club captain (1987–88): D. Edwards
Club captain (1988–89): P. Routledge
No. of teams: Senior 4
Colours: Blue, maroon, gold
Nickname: Old Wheats
Floodlights: No
Membership: £27
Local newspaper: Coventry Evening Telegraph
League: Warwickshire 1
Final position (1987–88): 9th
Playing record (1987–88): P 35, W 18, D 0, L 17, F 368, A 426.

ATHERSTONE

Ratcliffe Road, Atherstone, Warwickshire. Tel: 0827 714934.
Founded: 1968
President: J. Stevenson
Chairman: D. Wetton
Coach: J. Burdett
Secretary: D. Boal, 74 South Street, Atherstone, Warks. Tel: 0827 713145.
Fixtures Secretary: K. Berry.
No. of teams: Senior 3. Youth & Minis 1.
Directions to Ground: Drive into Town Centre, turn at Midland Bank.
Colours: Black. (*Change colours:* Yellow)
Floodlights: No
Membership: £5
League: Warwickshire 1
Final position (1987–88): 10th

OLD LAURENTIANS

Lime Tree Avenue, Bilton, Rugby, Warwickshire. Tel: 0788 810855.
Founded: 1919
President: B. Ray
Chairman: J. Keenan
Coach: M. Warwick
Secretary: A. Simpson, 24 Cromwell Road, Rugby. Tel: 0788 565425.
Fixtures Secretary: R.R. Roberts, 261 Alwyn Road. Tel: 9788 810276.
Club captain (1987–88): J. Whittaker
Club captain (1988–89): S. Birch
No. of teams: Senior 4
Directions to Ground: Off Alwyn Road, Bilton, Rugby. (A4071).
Clubhouse: 1,000 sq ft.
Colours: Maroon/green & gold hoop. (*Change colours:* Blue/gold)
Nickname: O.L's
Floodlights: No
Membership: £20
Local newspaper: Rugby Advertiser
League: Warwick's 1
Final position (1987–88): Bottom I (relegated)
Playing record (1987–88): W 6, L 29, D 1.

WARWICKS 2

MANOR PARK

Griff & Coton Sports Club, Heath End Road, Nuneaton, Warks. Tel: 0203 386798.
Founded: 1961
President: A. Broomfield
Chairman: C. Taylor
Coach: M. Cooper
Secretary: M. Broomfield, 75 Hinckley Road, Burbage, Leics. Tel: 0455 633718.
Fixtures Secretary: T. Poole, 4 Cazlyle Close, Nuneaton, Warks. Tel: 0203 395494.
Club captain (1987–88): J. Jenkins
Club captain (1988–89): J. Jenkins
No. of teams: Senior 4
Directions to Ground: A444 Nun–Cov at roundabout follow signs for George Elliot Hospital, ground opposite.
Ground capacity: Two hundred
Clubhouse: Half share with cricket section of bar & changing rooms. Seperate from main sports club.
Colours: Red & Black hoops, black hose. (*Change colours:* Green)
Floodlights: No
Membership: Ten pounds
Local newspaper: Nuneaton Evening Tribune
League: Warks 2
Final position (1987–88): Top (promoted)
Playing record (1987–88): P 32, W 22, L 10, F 518, A 404.
Competitions won: Warks Div 2 87–88.

SOUTHAM

Kineton Road, Southam, Warks. Tel: 092681-3674 (H), 0203-410104 (B).
Founded: 1963
President: R. Jones
Chairman: A. Mitchell
Coach: T. Perkin
Secretary: M.S. Haville, 11 Banbury Road, Southam, Warks. Tel: 092681-4803.
Fixtures Secretary: L.T. Williams, 27 Hillyard Road, Southam, Warks. Tel: 092681-2194 (H), 092681-2560 (B).
Club captain (1987–88): D. Hazelwood
Club captain (1988–89): M. Harvey
No. of teams: Senior 4, Youth & Minis 1
Directions to Ground: Enter Southam and follow signs for Kineton/Industrial Estate continue past industrial estate, club 400 yds on right.
Ground capacity: 500
Clubhouse: 5 changing rooms.
Colours: White hoops on navy blue. (*Change colours:* Navy blue hoops on white)
Nickname: Dinosaurs
Floodlights: No
Membership: £15/annum
Local newspaper: Leamington Courier
League: Warks 2
Final position (1987–88): 2nd (promoted)
Playing record (1987–88): P 37, W 21, L 13, D 1, F 510, A 321.

SPARTANS

Coppice Lane, Middleton, Nr. Tamworth, Staffs. Tel: 021 308 5857.
Founded: 1960
President: Roger Green
Chairman: Graham Lloyd
Coach: Tim Rich & Julian Whiting
Secretary: Miss Sarah McGrory, 12 Russell Bank Road, Four Oaks, Sutton Coldfield, West Midlands B74 4RE. Tel: 021 353 7365.
Fixtures Secretary: Steve Owen, 98 The Brambling, Wilnecote, Tamworth, Staffordshire. Tel: Tamworth 281936.
Club captain (1987–88): Tim Rich
Club captain (1988–89): Tim Rich
No. of teams: Senior 4
Directions to Ground: By the junction of the A445 and Coppice Lane, ¼ mile on the Coleshill side of the A453 at Bassett's Pole.
Ground capacity: Loads
Clubhouse: Clubhouse incl. changing rooms/bar.
Colours: Black jerseys/black shorts. (*Change colours:* Red shirts, black shorts)
Floodlights: Yes, for training only
Membership: £25.00 VIP, £25.00 full playing, £5.00 social & ladies.
Local newspaper: Sutton Coldfield Observer, Sutton Coldfield News

Warwicks 2

League: Warwickshire 2
Final position (1987–88): 3rd
Playing record (1987–88): P 33, W 20, D 2, L 11, F 361, A 345.
Competitions won: 1985 Sutton Coldfield R.F.C. Invitation Sevens Winners.

COVENTRY SARACENS

Bredon Avenue, Binley, Coventry. Tel: 0203 453557.
Founded: 1979
Secretary: D.G. Robbins, 8 Loweswater Road, Ernsford Grange, Coventry, W. Mids CV3 3HJ. Tel: 0203 458851 (H) 092681 3232 (W).
League: Warwicks 2
Final position (1987–88): 4th

EARLSDON

Mitchell Avenue, Canley, Coventry. Tel: 0203 464467.
Founded: 1905
Secretary: P. Carnall, 3 Worsfold Close, Allersley, Coventry CV5 9FT. Tel: 0203 403390 (H) 0203 75521 (W).
League: Warwicks 2
Final position (1987–88): 5th

PINLEY

The Croft, Wyken Croft, Wyken, Coventry.
Founded: 1950
President: T. O'Niel
Chairman: C. Bottrill
Coach: M. Meade
Secretary: P. Williams, 26 Ferndale Road, Coventry CV3 2BG. Tel: 0203 543740.
Fixtures Secretary: J. Brady, 87 Ansty Road, Coventry. Tel: 0203 445264.
Club captain (1987–88): K. Ellis
Club captain (1988–89): A. Smith
No. of teams: Senior 3, Youth & Minis 2
Directions to Ground: M6 junc 2, A46 to City Centre for 1½ miles, Wyken Croft on right.
Clubhouse: Bar & changing facilities.
Colours: Black & red. (*Change colours:* Red)
Floodlights: No
Admission: Free
Membership: £6.00
Local newspaper: Coventry Evening Telegraph
League: Warks 2
Final position (1987–88): 3rd
Playing record (1987–88): P 31, W 18, D 4, L 9.

STANDARD

Tile Hill Lane, Canley, Coventry. Tel: 0203 75186.
Founded: 1931
Secretary: P.J. James, 27 Coniston Road, Coventry. Tel: 0203 77054.
League: Warwicks 2
Final position (1987–88): 7th

SILHILLIANS

Warwick Road, Copt Heath, Solihull. Tel: 05645 77680.
Founded: 1932
Secretary: P.G. Newby, 8 Ullenhall Road, Knowle, Solihull, W. Mids B92 8EF. Tel: 05645 79559 (H) 021 200 3111 (W).
League: Warwicks 2
Final position (1987–88): 8th

HARBURY

Waterloo Fields, Middle Road, Harbury, Leamington Spa, Warwickshire. Tel: 0926-613462.
Founded: 1962
President: John Bromley
Chairman: Ian Holroyd
Coach: Dyl Rogers
Secretary: Jerry Birkbeck, 22 Campion Terrace, Leamington Spa, Warwickshire CV32 4SX. Tel: 0926-24053.
Fixtures Secretary: Bob New, 139 Cubbington Road, Leamington. Tel: 0926-25915.
Club captain (1987–88): Pepe Pavel
Club captain (1988–89): Pepe Pavel
No. of teams: Senior 3, Youth & Minis 8
Directions to Ground: A425 & 250 from Leamington Spa to Fosse Way Junction, south 1½ miles beneath railway bridge, left turn to Harbury.
Ground capacity: 3 senior pitches, 5 permanent main pitches. (9.5 acres).
Clubhouse: Clubroom, lounge, showers, 4 changing rooms. Programme of expansion for 1988 in hand.
Colours: Red & white hoops and black shorts. (*Change colours:* Blue & white hoops)
Floodlights: No
Membership: £17
Local newspaper: Leamington Spa Courier (Sports Editor: Doug Hughes)
League: Warwickshire 2
Final position (1987–88): 9th
Playing record (1987–88): P 35, W 18, L 17, F 337, A 392.

BERKSWELL & BALSALL COMMON

Sports Heart of England School, Balsall Common, Warwickshire.
Founded: 1982
President: Dr M. Matthews
Chairman: J. Mayer
Coach: S. Staunton
Secretary: M.W. Shuter, 99 Kelsey Lane, Balsall Common, Coventry. Tel: Berkswell 34616.
Fixtures Secretary: L. Edwards, 22A Kenilworth Road. Tel: Berkswell 34119.
Club captain (1987–88): L. Edwards
No. of teams: Senior 1.
Directions to Ground: Heart of England School.
Colours: Red/black. (*Change colours:* Black/black)
Floodlights: No
Membership: £15
Local newspaper: Coventry Telegraph
League: Warwickshire 2
Final position (1987–88): 10th (relegated)

RUGBY WELSH

Alwyn Road, Old Bilton. Tel: 0788 65605.
Founded: 1936
Secretary: P. O'Neil, 140 Lytham Road, Rugby, Warwickshire CV22 7PH. Tel: 0788 815677.
Fixtures Secretary: R. Goodall, 17 Charles Street, Rugby, Warks. Tel: 0788 61483.
League: Warwicks 2
Final position (1987–88): 11th (bottom)

COVENTRIANS

Black Pad (off Yelverton Road), Radford, Coventry CV6 4NW. Tel: 0203-682885.
Founded: 1918
President: Trevor L. Lyon

Coach: M. Cowburn
Secretary: James Parke, 47 High Street, Ryton, Dunsmore, Nr. Coventry.
Fixtures Secretary: J.S. Daniell, 116 Mill Farm Park, Marston Jabbet, Nuneaton. Tel: 373470.
Club captain (1987–88): P.S. Brown
Club captain (1988–89): C. Flick
No. of teams: Senior 4, Youth 1
Directions to Ground: See attached map.
Ground capacity: 2 pitches – shanding only.
Clubhouse: 4 changing, showers, bar, lounge.
Colours: 1st R. Blue/white squares. 2/3/4 R. Blue.
Nickname: Covents
Floodlights: Training only
Admission: Nil
Membership: £10 per an.
Programme: Nil
Local newspaper: Coventry Evening Telegraph
League: War Div 3
Final position (1987–88): 1st (promoted)
Playing record (1987–88): P 34, W 26, L 8, F 701, A 280.
Competitions won: Warwick Div 3 (1987/88).

OLD WARWICKIAN

Hampton Road, Warwick. Tel: 0926 496295.
Founded: 1929
President: Nor Morris
Chairman: Paul Williams
Coach: Paul Williams
Secretary: Stef McMahon, 52 Cannon Close, Coventry. Tel: 0203 418489.
Fixtures Secretary: Bob Gregory, 8 Tuckwell Close, Stockton, Nr. Southam.
Club captain (1987–88): Rob McClean
Club captain (1988–89): Terry Bennett
No. of teams: Senior 4
Directions to Ground: Birmingham exit (A41) off A46 bypass into Warwick, turn right onto B4095. Hampton Road past Warwick racecourse (on right) ground ½ mile on right just after bridge over A46 bypass.
Clubhouse: Bar & 4 changing & refs room.
Colours: Maroon and white hoops. (*Change colours:* Royal blue)
Floodlights: No
Membership: £15
Local newspaper: Leamington Spa Courier, Warwick Advertiser, Coventry Evening Telegraph.
League: Warwickshire 3
Final position (1987–88): 1st
Playing record (1987–88): P 33, W 18, D 1, L 14, F 487, A 478.
Competitions won: League Warwickshire 3 1987/88 winners.

A.P. LOCKHEAD

Tackbrook Road, Leamington Spa, Warwicks. Tel: 0926 27000.
Founded: 1943
Secretary: M.J. Wilson, 63 St Helens Road, Leamington Spa, Warwicks CV31 3QG. Tel: 0926 28246 (H) 0926 27000 (W).
League: Warwicks 3
Final position (1987–88): 3rd

SHIPSTON ON STOUR

Mayo Road, Shipston on Stour, Warks.
Founded: 1963
President: Dr. G. Williams
Chairman: D. Leeson
Secretary: T. Carr, Top Farm, Froglands Lane, Cleeve Prior, Evesham, Worcs.
Fixtures Secretary: R. Hawkins, Washbrook, Ilmington, Nr. Shipston on Stour, Warks.
No. of teams: Senior 3
Directions to Ground: On the A34 on the north side of Shipston, turn into Badgers Crst. Take first left, then first right.
Ground capacity: 800
Clubhouse: Bar and changing facilities.
Colours: Black shorts and shirts. (*Change colours:* Yellow shirts)
Nickname: Rams
Floodlights: No
Admission: Nil
Membership: £5
Local newspaper: Evening Journal
League: Warks 3
Final position (1987–88): 3rd
Playing record (1987–88): P 28, W 12, L 13, D 3.

WARWICK

Warwick Sports Club, Hampton Road, Warwick. Tel: 0926 491569.
Founded: 1976
Secretary: J. Hardy, 36 Makepeace Avenue, Woodloes Park, Warwick. Tel: 0926 491788 (H) Stratford 204 242 (W).
League: Warwicks 3
Final position (1987–88): 5th

ALCESTER

Kings Laughton, Nr Alcester, Warwicks.
Founded: 1960
Secretary: M.J. Edwards, 8 Icknield Row, Alcester, Warwicks. Tel: 0789 764096 (H) 0789 762285 (W).
League: Warwicks 3
Final position (1987–88): 6th

CALUDON CASTLE

Caludon Castle School, Axholme Road, Coventry.
Founded: 1956
Secretary: N.R. Barker, 9 Hoylake Close, Whitestone, Nuneaton, Warks. Tel: 0203 386795 (H) 0203 450215 (W).
League: Warwicks 3
Final position (1987–88): 7th

COVENTRY POST OFFICE

Telepost Club, Northbrook Road, Coundon, Coventry. Tel: Keresley 2714.
Founded: 1982
President: W. Ward
Chairman: K.J. Tams
Coach: D. Morgan
Secretary: Miss Y. Graham, 251 Telfer Road, Radford, Coventry CV6 3DS. Tel: Cov. 598378.
Fixtures Secretary: T. Burnham, 80 Glendower Avenue, Coventry.
Club captain (1987–88): D. Morgan
Club captain (1988–89): I. Croston
No. of teams: Senior 2
Directions to Ground: Along Coundon Road from city

centre to 'Nugget Public House' first left, ground at bottom of hill.
Ground capacity: 200
Clubhouse: Sports & social club
Colours: Red & black hoops. (*Change colours:* Amber & red hoops)
Nickname: 'Cov Post'
Floodlights: Yes training only
Admission: N/A
Membership: £15
Programme: N/A
Local newspaper: Coventry Evening Telegraph
League: Warwickshire 3
Final position (1987–88): 8th
Playing record (1987–88): P 30, W 10, L 20.

SHOTTERY

League: Warwicks 3
Final position (1987–88): 9th

COVENTRY TECH.

Charter Avenue, Canley, Coventry. Tel: 0203 47133.
Founded: 1929
Secretary: N. Franklin, 42 Haynestone Road, Coundon, Coventry CV6 1GS. Tel: 0203 668706.
League: Warwicks 3
Final position (1987–88): 10th (bottom)

EAST MIDLANDS/LEICESTERSHIRE LEAGUE

THIS feeder league in the pyramid for Midlands 2 East was a desperately close affair with Stewart's & Lloyd's winning on points difference from Towcester thanks to a scoring effort which produced 213 in their 10 matches.

Poor Melton Mowbray were beaten in all their 10 games and go down. South Leicester finished in 10th place although they won three matches and played with spirit.

TABLES 1987–88

EAST MIDLANDS/LEICS

	P	W	D	L	F	A	Pts
Stewart & Lloyd	10	9	0	1	213	45	18
Towcestrians	10	9	0	1	153	37	18
Luton	10	6	0	4	70	85	12
Long Buckby	10	5	0	5	141	106	10
N'hampton Trin	10	5	0	5	107	75	10
Bedford Ath	10	5	0	5	92	120	10
Oadby Wygg	10	4	0	6	75	107	8
O N'hamptons	10	4	0	6	70	137	8
Sth Leicester	10	3	0	7	55	166	6
Melton Mowbray	10	0	0	10	70	178	0

EAST MIDLANDS/LEICS

STEWART & LLOYD

Occupation Road, Corby. Tel: 0536 202370.
Founded: 1936
Secretary: G. Seymour, 1 High Street, Gretton, Nr Corby, Northants. Tel: 0536 770415.
League: E.M.L.
Final position (1987–88): 1st
Competitions won: East Midlands/Leicestershire.

TOWCESTRIANS

Greens, Norton Road, Towcester. Tel: 0327 50141)
Founded: 1933
Secretary: T.C. Wilson, Preston Fields Farm, Preston Capes, Daventry, Northants NN11 6SZ. Tel: 032 736 667.
League: E.M.L.
Final position (1987–88): 2nd

LUTON

Wood Meadow, Rotherham Avenue, Farley Hill, Luton. Tel: 0582 203555.
Founded: 1931
Secretary: R. John, 37 Byron Crescent, Flitwick, Bedford MK45 1PY. Tel: 0525 716560 (H) 0582 573255 (W).
Fixtures Secretary: P. Godwin, Claydown Way, Slipend, Luton, Beds. Tel: 0582 418957.
League: E.M.2
Final position (1987–88): 3rd
Playing record (1987–88): P 31, W 14, D 1, L 16, F 283, A 331.

BUCKBY

Station Road, Long Buckby, Northampton.
Founded: 1875
President: G.G. Tebbitt
Chairman: P.K. Spokes
Coach: R. Pebody
Secretary: P.J. Osborne, Ashthorne, Teeton Road, Ravensthorpe, Northampton. Tel: N. 770772.
Fixtures Secretary: S. Ruddlesden, 37 Rockhill Road, Long Buckby. Tel: L.B. 842933.
Club captain (1987–88): D. Bennett
Club captain (1988–89): M. Dickens
No. of teams: Senior 5, Youth & Minis 8
Directions to Ground: From west via Daventry, from north down A5 or A45 or M1. From east via Market Harborough/Kettering. From South via Northampton or M1. (From centre of village 500 metres down Station Road)
Ground capacity: Standing for at least 1,000.
Clubhouse: Plenty of room, lårge bar, separate lounge.
Colours: Emerald green. (*Change colours:* White)
Floodlights: No
Membership: £1 (non players), £7.50 players.
Programme: Every 1st XV game (Editor: M. York)
Local newspaper: Weekly Express (Daventry), Chronicle and Echo (Northampton).
League: East Midlands/Leicestershire
Final position (1987–88): 4th
Playing record (1987–88): 1st XV P 21, L 14, D 2, F 626, A 419.
Competitions won: Northampton Alliance Cup (October 87).

NORTHAMPTON TRINITY

Abbey Street, Northampton.
Founded: 1960
President: G. Grimshaw
Chairman: H. Cooke
Coach: T.B.A.
Secretary: P.W. Collyer, 3 School Lane, Quinton, Northampton. Tel: 0604 863456.
Fixtures Secretary: I. Billson. Tel: 0604 880070.
Club captain (1987–88): H. Cooke
Club captain (1988–89): J. Sharpe
No. of teams: Senior 4, Youth 2
Directions to Ground: Next to Express Life Tower off Weedon Road Northampton.
Clubhouse: Adjacent to ground.
Colours: Em green red/white hoop
Floodlights: Yes
Membership: £18 playing
Programme: Free (Editor: P.W. Collyer)
Local newspaper: Chronicle & Echo
League: EM/Leics
Final position (1987–88): 5th

BEDFORD ATH

Putnoe Wood, Wentworth Drive, Bedford. Tel: 0234 50874.
Founded: 1908
Secretary: D.J. Clarke, 30 Kingsbrook Road, Beds MK42 0BH. Tel: 0234 215101 (H) 01 405 3411 (W).
Fixtures Secretary: J. Ross, 68 Avon Drive, Bedford. Tel: 0234 43151.
League: E.M.L.
Final position (1987–88): 6th
Playing record (1987–88): P 34, W 17, DS 1, L 16, F 457, A 409.

AYLESTONE ST JAMES

c/o Covert Lane, Scraptoft, Leicester.
Founded: 1902
President: Malcolm Webb
Chairman: Roger Price
Coach: Kingsley Harmer
Secretary: John Fenton, Nook Farm, Church Lane, Ratby, Leicester.
Fixtures Secretary: Richard Hickson, 12 Springdale Road, Thurmaston, Leicester. Tel: 693745.
Club captain (1987–88): Jim Mitchelson
Club captain (1988–89): Jim Mitchelson
No. of teams: Senior 5, Youth & Minis 1
Directions to Ground: A47 East of Leicester, T. lights Station Lane–Scraptoft to Scraptoft Church.
Clubhouse: Excellent bar & changing rooms.
Colours: Blue & white hoops. (*Change colours:* Red)
Nickname: Dimmies
Floodlights: Yes training
Admission: Donations welcomed
Membership: £20
Local newspaper: Leicester Mercury
League: East Mids/Leicester
Final position (1987–88): 5th
Playing record (1987–88): P 33, W 22, L 11.
Competitions won: County Cup semi-finalists 85/86, 87/88.

OADBY-WIGGESTONIAN

Wigston Road, Oadby, Leicester. Tel: 0533 714848.
Founded: 1888
President: Peter Bayley
Chairman: Martin Bromley
Secretary: John Fox, 4 Grafton Drive, Wigston, Leicester LE8 1WT
Fixtures Secretary: Neil Bromley, 38 wintersdale Road, Leicester. Tel: 0533 414856
Club captain (1987–88): John Rogerson
Club captain (1988–89): Neil Jones
No. of teams: Senior 5. Youth & Minis 5.
Directions to Ground: On A5096 between Oadby (A6) and Wigston (A50)
Clubhouse: Marvellous. Capacity 120, (five days).
Colours: White, black, gold hoops. (*Change colours:* White).
Floodlights: No
Membership: £10 non playing; £30 playing.
Local newspaper: Leicester Mercury
League: Leics/E. Mids
Final position (1987–88): 7th
Playing record (1987–88): P 30, W 17, L 13. F 295, A 305.

OLD NORTHAMPTONIANS

Biuing Road, Northampton. Tel: 0604 34045.
Founded: 1923
President: Headmaster
Chairman: P. Morris
Coach: M. Lee
Secretary: K. Newton, 73 Cavendish Drive, Langlands, Northampton.
Fixtures Secretary: A. Deathe, 11 Hallam Close, Moulton, Northampton.
Club captain (1987–88): A. Hodgson
Club captain (1988–89): A. Hodgson
No. of teams: Senior 4, Youth 1
Directions to Ground: Junction 15 M1 – off ring road signposted Kettering/Wellingboro
Colours: Cardinal navy & gold hoops
Nickname: The On's
Floodlights: Yes training only
Membership: £25.00

East Midlands/Leics

Local newspaper: Chronicle & Echo
League: East Mids/Leics
Final position (1987–88): 9th

SOUTH LEICESTER

Welford Road, Wigston, Leics. Tel: (0533) 882066.
Founded: 1919
President: F.L. Brewin
Chairman: J.E. Gunby
Secretary: R.P. Dowdall, 4 Bodmin Ave, Wigston, Leics. 885606.
Fixtures Secretary: S. Kirkpatrick, Horseweula, Wigston, Leicester.
Club captain (1987–88): G. Honeywell
Club captain (1988–89): R. Rayner
No. of teams: Senior 4, Youth & Minis 9 + Colts
Directions to Ground: Take Leicester ring road to A50 (Welfor Road). Travel through Wigston. Club is by final roundabout.
Clubhouse: Lounge, bar, six changing rooms, baths.
Colours: Green & white hoops.
Nickname: South
Floodlights: Partial
Membership: £35
Local newspaper: Leicester Mercury
League: E. Mids/Leic
Final position (1987–88): 10th

MELTON MOWBRAY

Sarby Road, Melton Mowbray. Tel: 0664 63342.
Founded: 1922
Secretary: R. Goldthorpe, 14 Kirk Hill, Bingham, Notts NG13 8FF. Tel: Bingham 37638 (H) Nottingham 419866 (W).
League: E.M.L.
Final position (1987–88): 11th (bottom)

EAST MIDLANDS LEAGUE

THERE were 31 clubs in the three East Midlands leagues with only Northampton Men's Own (10 wins and 308 points in the second league) and Bedford Quins (eight wins and 293 points in the bottom league) having perfect records.

Wellingborough finished top of the first league with three points in hand, as they drew one and lost one to finish clear of the high-scoring St. Neots team. Biggleswade had the same number of points as St. Neots and could challenge strongly in future.

TABLES 1987–88

EAST MIDLANDS 1

	P	W	D	L	F	A	Pts
Wellingboro	10	8	1	1	198	55	17
St Neots	10	7	0	3	210	107	14
Biggleswade	10	7	0	3	133	102	14
N'ton BBOB	10	6	1	3	114	79	13
N'Pton O Scts	10	5	0	5	117	101	10
Ampthill	10	5	0	5	129	122	10
Huntingdon	10	5	0	5	100	95	10
Daventry	10	4	0	6	82	152	8
Rushden	10	3	0	7	84	137	6
W'ingboro OG	10	3	0	7	79	156	6
Dunstablians	10	1	0	9	64	204	2

EAST MIDLANDS 2

	P	W	D	L	F	A	Pts
N'ton Mens O	10	9	0	0	308	63	20
Brackley	10	7	1	2	205	68	15
Corby	10	7	0	3	140	70	14
N'ton Casuals	10	7	0	3	146	101	14
St Ives	9	5	0	4	99	46	10
Oundle	10	4	0	6	86	154	8
Vauxhall	10	4	0	6	97	199	8
Cutler Hammer	10	3	1	6	68	134	7
Colworth H	9	3	0	6	74	155	6
O Wellburian	10	2	0	8	47	229	4
Deeping	10	1	0	9	83	131	2

EAST MIDLANDS 3

	P	W	D	L	F	A	Pts
Bedford Qns	8	8	0	0	292	34	16
Westwood	8	6	0	2	159	63	12
Bugbrooke	8	6	0	2	139	66	12
N'ton Hthns	8	5	0	3	65	75	10
Bedford Swifts	8	3	0	5	123	106	6
RAF Bedford	8	3	0	5	104	123	6
Potton	8	2	0	6	69	151	4
Bretton	8	2	0	6	37	284	4
Ramsey	8	1	0	7	69	155	2

WELLINGBOROUGH

Cut Throat Lane, Gt Doddington, Wellingborough. Tel: 0933 222260.
Founded: 1922
Secretary: T.W. Meyer, 43 Wilson Way, Earls Barton, Northampton NN6 0NZ. Tel: 0604 811151 (H) 0733 502001 (W).
Fixtures Secretary: M.R. Carter, 84 Eastfield Road, Wollaston, Northants.
League: East Mids 1
Final position (1987–88): 1st

ST. NEOTS

The Common, St. Neots, Cambs. Tel: 0480-74285.
Founded: 1936
President: V.J. Ibbett
Chairman: C. Owen
Coach: R. Binham
Secretary: D. Peppler, 18 Park Avenue, Little Paxton, St. Neots, Cambs.
Fixtures Secretary: M. Truswell, 13 Fydell Court, St. Neots, Cambs. Tel: 0480-74512.
Club captain (1987–88): T. Ibbett
Club captain (1988–89): T. Ibbett
No. of teams: Senior 4, Youth & Minis all age groups Colts to U7's.
Directions to Ground: East of A1, on St. Neots Common.
Clubhouse: New clubhouse and changing rooms adjacent to ground.
Colours: Light blue with dark blue hoop. (*Change colours:* Red)
Nickname: Saints
Floodlights: No
Membership: £17.50
Local newspaper: St. Neots Advertiser
League: East Midlands 1
Final position (1987–88): Second
Playing record (1987–88): P 38, W 23, L 11, D 4.
Competitions won: Huntingdon Floodlit Cup, Tring 7's.

BIGGLESWADE

Langford Road, Biggleswade. Tel: 0767-312463.
Founded: 1949
President: John Jordan
Chairman: Jack Chisholm
Coach: Mick Buck
Secretary: Mike Williams, 8 Laurel Way, Ickleford, Hitchin, Herts. Tel: 0462-54782 (H), 01-867-8478 (B).
Fixtures Secretary: Roy Caulfield, 76 Winston Crescent, Biggleswade. Tel: 0767-316106.
Club captain (1987–88): Joe Jordan
Club captain (1988–89): Grant Ingle
No. of teams: Senior 5, Youth & Minis 8
Directions to Ground: 1½ miles out of Biggleswade on A6001 Biggleswade to Henlow Road.
Clubhouse: Main clubroom + lounge bar. Above changing facilities + 4 squash courts, + tennis courts (2).
Colours: Navy with red hoop. (*Change colours:* Green)
Nickname: Biggy
Floodlights: Yes training only
Membership: £25 playing, £5 social
Local newspaper: Biggleswade Chronicle
League: East Midlands 1
Final position (1987–88): 3rd
Playing record (1987–88): P 34, W 17, D 3, L 14.
Competitions won: Colts – Beds Sevens.

NORTHAMPTON B.R.O.B.

St Andrews Mill, St Andrews Road, Northampton. Tel: 0604 32460.
Founded: 1933
Secretary: D.J. Room, c/o St Andrews Mill, St Andrews Road, Northampton. Tel: 0604 52658.
League: East Mids 1
Final position (1987–88): 4th

NORTHAMPTON OLD SCOUTS

Rushmore Road, Northampton. Tel: 0604 33639.
Founded: 1927
Secretary: D. Walsh, 14 Berry Close, Rothersthorpe, Northampton NN7 3JQ. Tel: 0604 831455, 0327 71100.
Fixtures Secretary: K.D. Shurville, 41 Churchill Avenue, Northampton. Tel: 0604 494374.
League: East Mids 1
Final position (1987–88): 5th

AMPTHILL & DISTRICT

Dillingham Park, Woburn Road, Ampthill, Bedford. Tel: 0525 403303.
Founded: 1951 (originally 1881)
President: R. Dillingham
Chairman: B. Clark
Coach: G. McElroy
Secretary: R.G. Churchill, The Bungalow, Park Gardens, Bletchley, Milton Keynes MK3 6HT.
Fixtures Secretary: P. New, 39 Station Road, Ampthill. Tel: 0525 404945.
Club captain (1987–88): G. Whitehall
Club captain (1988–89): P. Nouch
No. of teams: Senior 6. Youth & Minis 10.
Directions to Ground: West of Ampthill Town Centre, opposite Ampthill Park.
Ground capacity: Open
Clubhouse: Two storey, brick built.
Colours: Maroon/amber. (*Change colours:* Maroon)
Floodlights: No
Membership: £25 players. £6 non-players.
Local newspaper: Ampthill/Flitwick Times & Express. Tel: 0525 402511.
League: East Midlands 1
Final position (1987–88): 5th
Playing record (1987–88): P 30, W 15, L 15.
Competitions won: Colts Won Loughbro 7's.

HUNTINGDON

The Racecourse, Brampton, Huntingdon.
Founded: 1935
President: P.S. Onyett
Chairman: J.A. Woodward
Secretary: J.R. Bishop, 2 Willow Close, Lt. Paxton, Huntingdon. Tel: 0480 72468.
Fixtures Secretary: N.J. Whitsey, The Vines, Bridge Road, Broughton, Huntingdon. Tel: 0487 823159.
Club captain (1987–88): A. Bragg
Club captain (1988–89): A. Bragg
No. of teams: Senior 4, Youth & Minis 1
Directions to Ground: West of Huntingdon on the A604.
Colours: Emerald green shirts, blue shorts. (*Change colours:* Blue shirts)
Nickname: The Stags
Floodlights: Yes

East Midlands 1

Membership: £20
Local newspaper: Hunts Post
League: East Midlands 1
Final position (1987–88): 7th
Competitions won: Winner Royston Sevens. Winner Cambs County Colts Sevens.

DAVENTRY

Stefen Hill, London Road, Daventry, Northants. Tel: 0327 703802.
Founded: 1968
Secretary: D.W. Oakes, 47 Staverton Road, Daventry, Northants. Tel: 0327 72333 (H) 0327 703431 (W).
League: East Mids 1
Final position (1987–88): 8th

RUSHDEN AND HIGHAM

Manor Park, Bedford Road, Rushden, Northants. Tel: 0933 312071.
Founded: 1959
President: M. Wright
Chairman: B. Ward
Coach: R. John
Secretary: S. Miles, 9 Grange Road, Lt. Cransley, Kettering. Tel: 0604 235410 (B), 0536 790429 (H).
Fixtures Secretary: C. Stringer, 18 Paddocks Road, Rushden. Tel: 0933 58481 (H), 0536 85616 (B).
Club captain (1987–88): A. Mulcahy
Club captain (1988–89): G. Riding
No. of teams: Senior 4, Youth & Minis 6
Directions to Ground: By side of A6 (right from Bedford, left to Bedford)
Clubhouse: Clubhouse & changing rooms.
Colours: Black/white hoops. (*Change colours:* Yellow)
Floodlights: No
Membership: £20.00
Local newspaper: Evening Telegraph
League: E.M. 1
Final position (1987–88): 9th

Playing record (1987–88): P 38, W 31, L 17, D 0, F 472, A 423.
Competitions won: East Northants and East Midlands Champions 1983–84.

WELLINGBOROUGH OG

Sanders Road, Wellingborough. Tel: 0933 227231.
Founded: 1938
Secretary: R. Smart, 14 Hatton Avenue, Wellingborough. Tel: 0933 227231 (H) 09334 50477 (W).
League: East Mids 1
Final position (1987–88): 10th

DUNSTABLIANS

Bidwell Park, Houghton Regis, Dunstable, Beds LU5 6JP. Tel: 0582 866555.
Founded: 1948
President: Ross Barrington
Chairman: William Thorburn
Coach: Anthony Whittle
Secretary: Paul Freeman, 19 Preston Road, Toddington, Dunstable, Beds. Tel: 05255 4550.
Fixtures Secretary: David Marchant, 20 Yew Tree Close, Eaton, Bray.
Club captain (1987–88): Norman Cook
Club captain (1988–89): Martin Morris
No. of teams: Senior 4, Youth & Minis 6

Directions to Ground: Junction 12 M1, through Toddington, ground on 'S' bend, entering Houghton Regis.
Clubhouse: 2 bars, 6 changing rooms.
Colours: Red, silver & black. (*Change colours:* Black)
Nickname: None
Floodlights: Yes
Admission: Free
Membership: £17.25
Local newspaper: Dunstable Gazette
League: East Midlands 1
Final position (1987–88): Bottom (relegated)
Playing record (1987–88): P 36, W 10, D 0, L 26.
Competitions won: Stockwood Park 7's, Vauxhall 7's (1987).

EAST MIDLANDS 2

NORTHAMPTON MENS OWN

Stoke Road, Ashton, Northampton. Tel: 0604-862463.
Founded: 1922
President: James Attwood
Chairman: R. Bunting
Coach: John Wilson
Secretary: Dave Edwards, 1A Landcross Drive, Abington, Northampton NN3 3NA. Tel: 0604-28972.
Fixtures Secretary: Ernie Dalby, 39 Forest Road, Piddington, Northampton NN7 2DA. Tel: 0604-870609.
Club captain (1987–88): Andy Morris
Club captain (1988–89): Andy Morris
No. of teams: Senior 5, Youth & Minis 2
Directions to Ground: M1 junction 15, A508 to village of Roade, pass through to X roads, left 700 yds on right.
Ground capacity: 2000
Clubhouse: 6 changing rooms, 3 pitches, large car park, mainhall, lounge, committee room, kitchen.
Colours: White blue hoop. (*Change colours:* Blue)
Nickname: The Own
Floodlights: Yes for training
Membership: £12.50

Programme: 50p (Editor: T. Casserly)
Local newspaper: Northants Post, Chronicle & Echo.
League: East Midlands 2
Final position (1987–88): Winners (promoted)
Playing record (1987–88): P 34, W 30, D 2, L 2.
Competitions won: Northampton & District Alliance Paget Cup Winners (Season competition). Courage East Midlands Division II Winners. Lewis Shield 1986–87 Winners. Oceanic Cup 1986–87 Winners, Ball of &&&&& Chronicle & Echo twice 1987–88.

BRACKLEY

The Clubhouse, Pavillons Way, Brackley, Northants. Tel: 0280 700685.
President: D. Vernon
Chairman: J. Hartley
Coach: N. Johnson
Secretary: N. Hooper, Ingrams Cottage, Hinton in the Hedges, Brackley NN13 5NE. Tel: 0280 703563.
Fixtures Secretary: R. Grant, 1 The Square, Aynho, Oxon. Tel: Croughton 810819.
Club captain (1987–88): C. Page
Club captain (1988–89): C. Page
No. of teams: Senior 3

East Midlands 2

Directions to Ground: From Brackley take the Banbury Road, after ¼ mile turn left into Pavillons Way, Entrance to ground on left after ½ mile.
Colours: Blue shirts, black shorts. (*Change colours:* Red shirts, blue shorts)
Floodlights: No
Membership: £18
Local newspaper: Banbury Guardian
League: East Midlands 2
Final position (1987–88): 2nd

CORBY

Northern Park, Rockingham Road, Corby. Tel: 204466.
Founded: 1958
Secretary: A.G. Portman, 2 Teesdale Road, Corby, Northants NN17 1LN. Tel: 0536 69288 (H).
League: East Mids 2
Final position (1987–88): 3rd

NORTHAMPTON CASUALS

Rush Mills House, Bedford Road, Northampton. Tel: (0604) 36716.
Founded: 1922
President: M.D. Askew
Chairman: J.T. Wearing
Coach: T.B.A.
Secretary: T.B.A.
Fixtures Secretary: M.D. Askew, 60 Hinton Road, Kingsthorpe, Northampton. Tel: (0604) 846959.
Club captain (1987–88): P.D. Horrocks
Club captain (1988–89): P.D. Horrocks
No. of teams: Senior 4, Youth & Minis 6
Directions to Ground: From A45 ring road take A428 Bedford exit. Entrance to grounds is approx 500 yds on right from exit.
Clubhouse: Old house set in six acres of land.
Colours: Black with amber band. (*Change colours:* Yellow shirts/black shorts & socks.
Nickname: The 'K's'
Floodlights: No
Membership: £15.00
Local newspaper: Northampton Chronicle & Echo
League: E.M. 2
Final position (1987–88): 4th
Playing record (1987–88): P 34, W 17, D 0, L 17, F 413, A 491 = 50%.

ST IVES

St Ivo Outdoor Centre, Califor Road, St Ives, Cambs.
Founded: 1976
Secretary: P.A. Reeve, 7 Aragon Close, Buckden, Huntingdon, Cambs PE18 9TY. Tel: 0480 811272 (H) 0480 56181 (W).
League: East Mids 2
Final position (1987–88): 5th

OUNDLE

Occupation Road. Tel: 73101.
Founded: 1986
President: H.R.M. Adams
Chairman: G.J. Snelling
Coach: G.J. Snelling
Secretary: R. Smith, 6 Pheasants Way, Yaxley, Peterborough. Tel: 242344.
Fixtures Secretary: S. Davies, Lilac Cottage, Apethorpe, Peterborough. Tel: 078087 476.
Club captain (1987–88): G. Davies
Club captain (1988–89): T. Curtis
No. of teams: Senior 3, Youth & Minis 10
Directions to Ground: Peterborough end of Oundle – turn by garage – bear to right – goal posts ahead.
Colours: Black with red & white hoops.
Nickname: Owls
Floodlights: No
Membership: £1
Local newspaper: Evening Telegraph
League: E. Mid. 2
Final position (1987–88): 6th
Playing record (1987–88): P 30, W 10, D 1, L 19.
Competitions won: East Midlands U16 and U18 seven-a-side competition.

VAUXHALL

Brache Estate, Osborne Road, Luton. Tel: 0582 454785.
Founded: 1926
Secretary: K.I. Munn, 5 Stoneleigh Close, Bramingham Park, Luton, Beds. Tel: Luton 508781 (H) Luton 21122 (W).
League: East Mids 2
Final position (1987–88): 7th

CUTLER HAMMER

Bell End, High Street, Kempston. Tel: 0234/852499.
Founded: 1922
President: Ken Porter
Chairman: Barry Williams
Coach: Kevin Canning
Secretary: Will Hunt, 5 Vyne Close, Kempston, Beds. MN42 8RH.
Fixtures Secretary: Steve Porter, 9 The Briars, Kempston. Tel: 0234/853337.
Club captain (1987–88): Dave Robinson
Club captain (1988–89): Dave Robinson
No. of teams: Senior 3
Directions to Ground: Ask for the King William Pub in Kempston – we are 800 yds to west on corner on right.
Clubhouse: Bar, concert room – changing.
Colours: Black/red
Nickname: "Icranic"
Floodlights: No
Membership: £14 playing
Local newspaper: Beds Times – Bedford Journal
League: E. Mids 2
Final position (1987–88): 8th
Playing record (1987–88): P 30, W 16, L 10, D 4.
2Competitions won:

COLWORTH HOUSE

Unilever Research, Colworth House, Sharnbrook, Beds. Tel: (0234) 222221.
Founded: 1964
President: Dr D. Osborne
Chairman: S. Williamson
Coach: S. Batty
Secretary: S. Dyks, Unilever Research, Section 947, Colworth House, Sharnbrook, Beds.
Fixtures Secretary: J. Harris, Address as above, but Section 777.
Club captain (1987–88): B. Cowper
Club captain (1988–89): S. Dyks
No. of teams: Senior 3
Directions to Ground: Leave Rushden on A6 – Bedford, after 6 miles turn into Sharnbrook, at URL Colworth signs, follow sports field directions.
Clubhouse: Colworth House Sports and Social Club.
Colours: Emerald green/black. (*Change colours:* Red/ black)
Floodlights: No
Membership: Included in match fees (£3 per game) + £1 social club fee.

East Midlands 2

Local newspaper: Northants Evening Telegraph/ Bedfordshire Times.
League: E. Mid. 2
Final position (1987–88): 7th
Playing record (1987–88): P 32, W 12, D 0, L 20.

O. WELLINGBURIAN

Sports Ground, The Embankment, Wellingborough, Northants.
Founded: 1981
Secretary: R. Vaux, 11 Gilbey Close, Wellingborough, Northants. Tel: 0536 522641 (W).
League: East Mids 2
Final position (1987–88): 10th

DEEPINGS

Linchfield Road, Deeping St James, Peterborough. Tel: 0778/345228.
Founded: 1983
President: G.D. Cox
Chairman: D.K. Evans
Coach: C. Davies
Secretary: Brian Kirby, 14 Halfleet, Market Deeping, Peterborough PE6 8DB. Tel: 0778/343048.
Fixtures Secretary: Pete Ward, 14 Manor Way, Deeping St James, Peterborough. Tel: 0778/343489.
Club captain (1987–88): P. Fox
Club captain (1988–89): M. Whitehead
No. of teams: Senior 2, Youth 2
Directions to Ground: Spalding Road from Market Deeping take left turn just before footbridge over the road then immediately right through gate.
Clubhouse: Clubroom, 4 changing rooms.
Colours: Yellow green black hoops. (*Change colours:* White)
Floodlights: No
Membership: £15
Local newspaper: Peterboro Evening Telegraph, Stamford Mercury.
League: E.M. 3
Final position (1987–88): Relegated from E.M.2
Playing record (1987–88): P 28, W 10, L 18, D 0, F 223, A 340.

EAST MIDLANDS 3

BEDFORD QUINS

League: East Mids 3
Final position (1987–88): 1st

WESTWOOD

Founded: 1944
President: M.J. Mason
Chairman: R. Barnett
Secretary: M. Marjoram, 57 Uplands, Werrington, Peterborough PE4 5AF. Tel: 0733 77369.
Fixtures Secretary: M. Stevenson, 78 Apsley Way, Longthorpe, Peterborough. Tel: 261497.
Club captain (1987–88): R. Swinscoe
Club captain (1988–89): R. Swinscoe
No. of teams: Senior 3
Directions to Ground: Westfield Road, Peterborough, located at the rear of APV Baker Ltd.
Colours: Red/white hoops. (*Change colours:* Black)
Floodlights: No
League: E. Mids 2
Final position (1987–88): 2nd E. Mids III
Playing record (1987–88): P 34, W 20, D 1, L 13.

BUGBROOKE

Founded: 1976
Secretary: S.J. Vaughan, Orchard Flat, Hipwells, Upper Heyford, Northampton NN3 5DG. Tel: 0604 830513 (H) 0604 583105 (W).
League: East Mids 3
Final position (1987–88): 3rd

NORTHAMPTON H'TH'N

Race Course, Kettering Road, Northampton. Tel: 0604 31016.
Founded: 1920
Secretary: D.G. Hodgkinson, 26 Roe Road, Northampton NN1 4PJ. Tel: 0604 35758 (H) 01-247 5422 (W).
League: East Mids 3
Final position (1987–88): 4th

BEDFORD SWIFTS

Newnham Athletic Track, Barkers Lane, Bedford. Tel: 0234 54606.
Founded: 1950
President: M. Cotter
Chairman: J. Clark
Coach: E. Quinn
Secretary: T.N. Stewart, 64 Ravensden Road, Renhold, Bedford MK41 0JY. Tel: Bedford 771828.
Fixtures Secretary: S. davidson, 26 Thornton Street, Kempston, Bedford. Tel: Bedford 857529.
Club captain (1987–88): J. Clark
Club captain (1988–89): N. Hichliffe
No. of teams: Senior 4.
Directions to Ground: From A1 North and South follow A428 west towards Northampton/Birmingham. Follow signs left turn to Milton Keynes, Luton and M1 South. Ground 200 yards on left.
Clubhouse: Shared with Bedford Athletics Club.
Colours: Gold/royal blue striped. Navy shorts and socks. (*Change colours:* All gold shirts)
Nickname: Swifts
Floodlights: No
Membership: £15
Local newspaper: Bedfordshire Times
League: East Midlands 3
Final position (1987–88): 5th
Playing record (1987–88): P 28, W 15, L 10, D 3.

RAF BEDFORD

League: East Mids 3
Final position (1987–88): 6th

POTTON

League: East Mids 3
Final position (1987–88): 7th

BRETTON

Bretton Woods School, Bretton, Peterborough.
Founded: 1981
Secretary: Dr A.S. Dawson, 105 Alderemans Drive, Peterborough. Tel: 0733 46988.

League: East Mids 3
Final position (1987–88): 8th

RAMSEY

Ramsey Ailwyn School
Founded: 1978
President: I. Milne
Chairman: M. Proud
Secretary: M. Proud, 64 Ramsey Road, Warboys, Cambs. Tel: 0487 822951.
Fixtures Secretary: W. Hutchcraft, 9 Tunkers Lane, Bury, Ramsey. Tel: 812096.
Club captain (1987–88): A. Dawson
Club captain (1988–89): A. Dawson
No. of teams: Senior 1
Colours: Amber shirts
Nickname: Rams
Floodlights: No
Membership: £12
Local newspaper: Peterboro' Evening Telegraph
League: East Midlands 3
Final position (1987–88): Bottom
Playing record (1987–88): P 25, W 14, L 11.
Competitions won: None

LEICESTERSHIRE LEAGUES

LEICESTERSHIRE have many clubs in higher situations and could only muster 15 teams for their county leagues in two sections. Belgrave won all their eight matches in the top league, but New Parks only won the second league on points difference from Aylestonians. Oakham bravely completed their five fixtures and lost them all, conceding 164 points and scoring only 14.

TABLES 1987–88

LEICESTERSHIRE 1

	P	W	D	L	F	A	Pts
Belgrave	8	8	0	0	149	65	16
Coalville	8	7	0	1	134	63	14
O Bosworthians	8	5	0	3	150	88	10
Lutterworth	8	4	1	3	98	71	9
West Leics	8	3	1	4	82	140	7
Market Bros	8	3	0	5	78	80	6
Ibworth	8	3	0	5	45	97	6
O Ashbeians	8	1	0	7	83	126	2
Old Newtonians	8	1	0	7	73	162	2

LEICESTERSHIRE 2

	P	W	D	L	F	A	Pts
New Parks	5	4	0	1	86	32	8
Aylestonians	5	4	0	1	79	34	8
Anstey	5	3	0	2	95	65	6
Birstall	5	2	0	3	91	36	4
Burbage	5	2	0	3	49	83	4
Oakham	5	0	0	5	14	164	0

● *The tables are published from information supplied. Any queries should be directed to the appropriate league secretary*

LEICESTERSHIRE 1

BELGRAVE

Belgrave Pastures, Thurcaston Road, Leicester. Tel: Leics. 663033.
Founded: 1883
President: John Coupland
Chairman: Roger Broughton
Coach: John Coupland
Secretary: John Goddard, 16 Burstall Road, Birstall, Leics. Tel: 677383.
Fixtures Secretary: Bill Smith, 2 Elsadene Avenue, Leics. Tel: 681733.
Club captain (1987–88): Ian Parnell
Club captain (1988–89): Bob Kyley
No. of teams: Senior 4, 1 Colts
Directions to Ground: Abbey Lane/Thurcaston Road.
Clubhouse: All facilities.
Colours: Red & black hoops. (*Change colours:* Dark green)
Nickname: The Graves
Floodlights: No
Membership: £15 per year
Local newspaper: Leic's Mercury
League: Leics. Div. 1
Final position (1987–88): Top unbeaten (promoted)
Playing record (1987–88): P 33, W 28, D 1, L 4.
Competitions won: Leics Div. 1 champions.

COALVILLE

Memorial Ground, Broomleys Road. Tel: 812059.
Founded: 1902
Secretary: G.H. Gadsby, 172 Ashburton Road, Hugglescote, Leicester. Tel: 0530 31949 (H) 0530 61052 (W).
League: Leics 1
Final position (1987–88): 2nd

OLD BOSWORTHIANS

Hinckley Road, Leicester Forest East. Tel: 387136.
Founded: 1955
President: P. Penny
Chairman: M. Willcox
Coach: R. Merrick
Secretary: G.D. Spendlove-Mason, Croft House Farm, Newton Harcourt, Leicester LE8 0FN. Tel: Leic. 557803 (B), Great Glem 2965 (H).
Fixtures Secretary: C. Hughes, 97 Rosslyn Road, Whitick, Leic. Tel: Coalville 34493 (H), Lough 611011 X4102 (B).
Club captain (1987–88): R. Beason
Club captain (1988–89): J. Coulthurst

Leicestershire 1

No. of teams: Senior 4, Youth & Minis 3
Directions to Ground: Go West on the A47 out of Leicester, pass over M1, 1 mile on the right.
Ground capacity: 1,500
Clubhouse: 6 changing rooms, large clubroom and bar.
Colours: Navy shirt + shorts. (*Change colours:* Navy + sky blue hoops)
Nickname: Old Bos
Floodlights: No
Membership: £5
Local newspaper: Leicester Mercury
League: Leicestershire 1
Final position (1987–88): 4th
Playing record (1987–88): P 31, W 14, L 16, D 1, F 433, A 404.

LUTTERWORTH

Ashby Lane, Bitteswell, nr. Lutterworth.
Founded: 1873
President: M.J. Ross
Chairman: M.J. Ross
Coach: P. Donovan
Secretary: C. Hudson, Mason & Bowns Cottage, Ashby Parva, Lutterworth. Tel: 0455 209053.
Fixtures Secretary: C. Payne, Cawder Ghyll, Shawell, Lutterworth.
Club captain (1987–88): R. Tranter
Club captain (1988–89): R. Tranter
No. of teams: Senior 4, Youth & Minis 8
Directions to Ground: North from Lutterworth on A426 towards Leicester, approx 1½ miles out of Lutterworth. Left turn signposted ashby Parva. Ground at end of road approx 1 mile.
Ground capacity: Open
Clubhouse: Large main room, 4 changing rooms, baths and showers.
Colours: red, green and white hoops. (*Change colours:* Blue.)
Floodlights: No
Membership: 15 subscriptions
Programme: Free. Editor: M.J. Ross
Local newspaper: Swift Flash
League: Leics 1
Final position (1987–88): 4th
Playing record (1987–88): P 38, W 18, D 2, L 18. F 505, A 498.

WEST LEICESTER

78A Granby Street, Leicester LE1 1DJ. Tel: 0533-540634.
Founded: 1962
President: Barry Bell
Chairman: Don Dixon
Coach: John McHugh
Secretary: Richard Pittom, 98 Grace Road, Leicester LE2 8AZ. Tel: 0533 834373 (H), 0533 536725 (B).
Fixtures Secretary: George Bosworth, 33 Anglessey Road, South Wigston, Leicester. Tel: 0533 782905.
Club captain (1987–88): Mark Foster
Club captain (1988–89): Mark Foster
No. of teams: Senior 3
Directions to Ground: Western Park on the A47 on the west side of Leicester 2 miles from City centre.
Colours: Red shirts
Floodlights: No
Membership: £20 p/a
Local newspaper: Leicester Mercury
League: Leics. 1
Final position (1987–88): 5th
Playing record (1987–88): P 35, W 14, D 2, L 19, F 380, A 566.

MARKET BOSWORTH

Cadeby Lane, Cadeby, Nuneaton, Warks.
Founded: 1965
President: K.W. Coleman
Chairman: B. Godfrey
Coach: J. Brown
Secretary: M. Darlow, 8 Gwendoline Drive, Countesthorpe, Leicester LE8 3SE.
Fixtures Secretary: P. Spencer, 10 Beaumont Avenue, Hinckley, Leics.
Club captain (1987–88): P. Jarvis
Club captain (1988–89): S. Moore
No. of teams: Senior 3. Youth & Minis 7.
Directions to Ground: Take the road to Cadeby out of Market Bosworth for half a mile.
Clubhouse: Club room, kitchen, 4 changing rooms, shower, toilets. Brick with slate roof.
Colours: Royal blue/amber/white. (*Change colours:* Red)
Floodlights: Yes
Membership: £10
Local newspaper: Hinckey Times/Leicester Mercury
League: Leicestershire 1
Final position (1987–88): 6th
Playing record (1987–88): P 34, W 22, D 1, L 11.

KIBWORTH

Gores Lane, Mkt. Harborough. Tel: 0858-64210.
Founded: 1923
President: K.R.D. Wiggins
Chairman: J.B. Morris
Coach: R. Hall
Secretary: D.R. Coe, 114 Harborough Road, Desborough, Northants. Tel: 0536-761637.
Fixtures Secretary: H.J. Smith, 1 Elm Drive, Mkt. Harborough. Tel: 0858-63924.
Club captain (1987–88): C.M. Giles
Club captain (1988–89): C.M. Giles
No. of teams: Senior 4, Youth & Minis 6
Directions to Ground: Follow A6 signs through Mkt. Harborough to Kettering – Gores Lane is last turn left out of town at bottom of Clack Hill.
Clubhouse: Low beamed clubroom – typical "Olde" club style.
Colours: Black. (*Change colours:* Blue & white hoops)
Nickname: "Kibby"
Floodlights: No
Membership: Over 19 yrs £20.00
Local newspaper: Harborough Mail
League: Leicestershire Division One
Final position (1987–88): 6th
Playing record (1987–88): P 33, W 14, L 16, D 3.
Competitions won: Gartree Sevens Sept. 1987.

OLD ASHBEIANS

New Field, Lower Packington Road, Ashby de-la-Zouch, Leicestershire. Tel: 0530 413992.
Founded: 1949
President: D.E. Herbert, BA
Chairman: J. Little
Coach: I. Sharpe/T. Beales
Secretary: A. Porter, 26 Swallowdale, Thringstone, Leics. Tel: 0530 222137.
Fixtures Secretary: P. Clewes, 49 Lower Packington Road, Ashby-de-la-Zouch.
Club captain (1987–88): A. Jackson
Club captain (1988–89): A. Jackson
No. of teams: Senior 3. Youth & Minis 5.
Directions to Ground: South of Ashley, via Lower Packington Road, off A453.
Colours: Maroon & sky hoops.
Floodlights: No
Membership: £25
Local newspaper: Ashby Times
League: Midlands Leicestershire 1
Final position (1987–88): 8th

OLD NEWTONIANS

Hinckley Road (A47), Leicester Forest East, Leicester. Tel: (0533) 392389.
Founded: Originally 1904, re-formed 1928.
President: G.A. Clark
Chairman: J. Weir
Coach: P. Frost/G. Corns
Secretary: G.A. Clark250 Wigston Lane, Aylestone, Leicester LE2 8DH. Tel: (0533) 832309.
Fixtures Secretary: A. Massey, 314 Scraptoft Lane. Tel: (0533) 413928.
Club captain (1987–88): P. Frost
Club captain (1988–89): P. Frost
No. of teams: Senior 4
Directions to Ground: From Leicester along A47 towards Hinckley approx 1 mile past Red Cow Pub – towards Leicester from Hinckley A47 approx 1 mile past Bull's Head on right.
Colours: Navy with red/green/white central band. (*Change colours:* Red with navy/green/white central bands)
Nickname: "Newts"
Floodlights: No
Membership: £15
Local newspaper: Leicester Mercury
League: Leicestershire 1
Final position (1987–88): 9th
Playing record (1987–88): P 39, W 12, D 2, L 25, F 341, A 675.
Competitions won: Old Coventrians 'Sevens' winners 1969.

LEICESTERSHIRE 2

NEW PARKS

New Park Boys School, St Oswalds Road, New Parks, Leics. Tel: 0533 872115.
Secretary: J.P. Cluer, 50 Babingley Drive, Leics LE4 0HH. Tel: Leics 352457.
League: Leicestershire 2
Final position (1987–88): 1st

AYLESTONIANS

Knighton Lane East, Leicester. Tel: Leics 834899.
Founded: 1921
Secretary: K. Moffoot, 1 Eton Close, Knighton, Leicester LE2 3TZ. Tel: Leics 701177 (H) Coalville 813111 (W).
League: Leicestershire 2
Final position (1987–88): 2nd

ANSTEY

Link Road, Anstey, Leicester.
Founded: 1980
President: G. Dowling
Chairman: F. Johnson
Coach: G. Affleck
Secretary: T. Everley, 287 Leicester Road, Markfield, Leicester LE6 0RH. Tel: 0530 243458.
Fixtures Secretary: D. Worrall, 72A Forest Gate, Anstey, Leicester. Tel: 0533 351321.
Club captain (1987–88): P. Bower
Club captain (1988–89): R. Pearson
No. of teams: Senior 2, Minis 4
Directions to Ground: A50 from Leicester; right into Gynsill Lane, left into Anstey Lane and Village right in the Nook, left into link road, ground behind Anstey Martins School.
Colours: Black. (*Change colours:* Red)
Floodlights: No
Admission: Free
Membership: £15
Local newspaper: Leicester Mercury
League: Leicestershire 2
Final position (1987–88): 3rd
Playing record (1987–88): P 31, W 20, D 1, L 10, F 509, A 302.
Competitions won: October 1987 John Hill Trophy.

BIRSTALL COMMUNITY COLLEGE

Birstall Community College, Wanlip Lane, Birstall, Leics.
Founded: 1957
President: M. Cooper
Chairman: D. Sewart
Coach: M. Fisher
Secretary: R. Offley, 41 Town Green Street, Rothley, Leicestershire. Tel: 0533-2503.
Fixtures Secretary: J. Cross, 9 Foxglove Close, East Goscote, Leicestershire. Tel: 0533-601543.
Club captain (1987–88): J. Allen
Club captain (1988–89): B. Cox
No. of teams: Senior 3
Directions to Ground: Leicester North A6 trunk road, 3 miles Birstall Longslade/Stonehill School campus.
Ground capacity: School playing field (Open)
Clubhouse: Comm. Coll. lounge & bar.
Colours: Green, white & black hoops.
Nickname: "Greendogs"
Floodlights: No
Membership: Annual sub. £10 (playing member); £4 associate member.
Local newspaper: Leicester Mercury: Loughborough Echo.
League: Leics. 2
Final position (1987–88): 4th

BURBAGE

John Cleveland College, Butt Lane, Hinckley.
Founded: 1983
Secretary: J.R. Thomas, 15 Blenheim Close, Hinckley, Leics LE10 1TT. Tel: 0455 616321.
League: Leicestershire 2
Final position (1987–88): 5th

OAKHAM

Agricultural Showground, Barleythorne Road, Oakham, Rutland. Tel: 0572 4206.
Founded: 1923
Secretary: J.A. Williamson, 6 The Finches, Market Overton, Oakham, Leicester. Tel: 057283 780.
League: Leicestershire 2
Final position (1987–88): 6th (bottom)

Phoenix of Bucks/Oxon 2 feature giant lock Andy Lowes against Herts Division 2 team St Albans. Photo: Chris Roberts.

SOUTH WEST DIVISION

THE South West have a similar organisation to that of the North with two leading divisions followed by two strong regional leagues and then two tough combined leagues to feed them through the pyramid system. The counties then take over in their own right. In all there are 22 leagues.

Again, there are a number of traditional junior teams which have a great chance to shake up the stronger sides above them and there is also the prospect of Devon and Cornwall returning from the doldrums to a former position of strength. Redruth have started this process by winning South West 1.

Other clubs with a great chance of going all the way are now Berry Hill, High Wycombe and Matson. The status quo is about to badly disrupted by the new and brash challengers.

SOUTH WEST LEAGUES

THREE outstanding teams emerged from the season's campaigning with Redruth winning South West 1 to strengthen the Cornish hand in the Area League South. But they only managed to win on points difference from High Wycombe and there had been strong efforts by Maidenhead and Torquay Athletic behind them. At the foot of the table it was sad to see St. Ives in trouble with the luckless Bournemouth only winning one match.

In South West 2 Berry Hill won all their games and scored 290 points in the process, so they were out in front and also won the Rugby World & Post Junior Team of the Year award. Reading were their nearest challengers with Devonport Services in last place.

Newbury had the same number of match points but an inferior points difference as compared to Devon and Cornwall Constabulary and Henley and they filled 10th place as a result.

TABLES 1987–88

SOUTH-WEST 1

	P	W	D	L	F	A	Pts
Redruth	10	8	0	2	213	102	16
High Wycombe	10	8	0	2	157	89	16
Maidenhead	10	7	0	3	197	121	14
Torquay	10	7	0	3	156	117	14
Clifton	10	6	0	4	210	112	12
Taunton	10	4	1	5	99	122	9
Oxford	10	4	1	5	115	152	9
Weston	10	4	0	6	146	107	8
Bridgwater	10	3	0	7	98	154	6
St Ives	10	2	0	8	90	189	4
Bournemouth	10	1	0	9	63	280	2

SOUTH-WEST 2

	P	W	D	L	F	A	Pts
Berry Hill	10	10	0	0	290	102	20
Reading	10	7	1	2	146	75	15
Barnstaple	10	7	0	3	123	97	14
Brixham	10	5	0	5	142	135	10
Cinderford	10	5	0	5	135	145	10
Launceston	10	4	0	6	125	159	8
Abbey	10	4	0	6	94	148	8
D & C Const	10	3	1	6	126	175	7
Henley	10	3	1	6	109	164	7
Newbury	10	3	1	6	99	172	7
Devonport S	10	2	0	8	140	157	4

REDRUTH

The Recreation Ground, Redruth. Tel: Redruth (0209) 215520
Founded: 1875
President: J. Penberthy
Chairman: R. Peters
Coach: T.A. Pryor
Secretary: I. Horscroft, 6 Renryn Street, Redruth, Cornwall TR15 2SP. Tel: Redruth (0209) 215941
Fixtures Secretary: B. Mankee, 7 Victoria Street, Camborne. Tel: Camborne (0209) 713947
Club captain (1987–88): R. Tregoning
Club captain (1988–89): R. Tregoning
No. of teams: Senior 3. Youth & Minis 3
Ground capacity: 25,000. Stand 750
Clubhouse: Main and lounge bars
Colours: Red shirts/white shorts. (*Change colours*: Black shirts)
Nickname: Reds
Floodlights: No
Admission: £1
Membership: Vice President £12 per annum
Programme: 8 page
Local newspaper: West Briton
League: SW1
Final position (1987–88): Top (promoted)
Playing record (1987–88): P 38, W 28, D 3, L 7, F 973, A 344
Competitions won: Courage League, South West 1, Cornwall Knockout Cup

HIGH WYCOMBE

Kingsmead Road, High Wycombe, Bucks. Tel: 0494 24407
Founded: 1929
President: J.C. Rivett
Chairman: J. Cook
Coach: To be appointed
Secretary: D.H. Dickerson, 3 Talbot Avenue, High Wycombe HP13 5HG. Tel: 0494 32024 (H) & 0494 41211 (W)
Fixtures Secretary: T.G. Baker, 5 Orchard Way, Holmer Green, High Wycombe. Tel: 0494 713047
Club captain (1987–88): C. Field
Club captain (1988–89): C. Roddick
No. of teams: Senior 10, Youth & Minis 11
Directions to Ground: A40 from East – turn left into Station Road, Loudwater and right into Kingsmead Road. A40 from West – turn left into Abbey Barn Road and right into Kingsmead Road
Clubhouse: Two storey with all facilities
Colours: White/green/black hoops (*Change colours*: Black)
Floodlights: Yes
Membership: Life V.P. minimum £75, V.P. minimum £10, over 21 £18, 18–21 £8, under 18 & students £5
Programme: 50p (Editor: D.H. Dickerson
Local newspaper: Bucks Free Press
League: SW1
Final position (1987–88): Runners up
Playing record (1987–88): P 42, W 28, D 2, L 12, F 702, A 444
Competitions won: Trevor Thomas Cup

MAIDENHEAD

Braywick Playing Fields, Braywick Road, Maidenhead, Berks. Tel: 0628 29663.
Founded: 1922
Secretary: D.A. Bartley-Sams, Braywick Playing Fields, Maidenhead SL6 1BN. Tel: 0628 42749.
Fixtures Secretary: A.G. Cowen, 31 Furze Platt Road, Maidenhead, Berks. Tel: 0628 29327 (H), 0865 246681 (W).
No. of teams: Senior 4, Youth & Minis 11
Directions to Ground: From town centre take road to Windsor (A423); ground is 1 mile on left. From M4 take exit top Maidenhead Central, left at 1st roundabout. Ground is ½ mile on right.
Ground capacity: 2,000 +
Clubhouse: Main bar, changing rooms, etc.
Nickname: "Maids"
Floodlights: No
Admission: by programme
Programme: Donation (Editor: Secretary)
Local newspaper: Maidenhead Advertiser
League: South-West 1
Final position (1987–88): 3rd
Playing record (1987–88): P 34, W 26, D 1, L 7, F 754, A 348.

TORQUAY ATHLETIC

Recreation Ground, Sea Front, Torquay. Tel: 0803 23842
Founded: 1875
President: Bryan Lang
Chairman: Alan Partridge
Coach: Keith Hatter
Secretary: Ken Evans, 15 Broadstone Park Road, Torquay. Tel: 0803 606233
Fixtures Secretary: Malcolm Baker, "Trevaunance", Barton Hill Road, Torquay. Tel: 0803 36542
Club captain (1987–88): Kevin Butterworth
Club captain (1988–89): Kevin Butterworth
No. of teams: Senior 3, Colts 1, U16, U14, U12, U10 & Minis
Directions to Ground: Ground close to sea front Torquay, adjacent to Grand Hotel and railway station
Ground capacity: 5,000. Stand 400
Clubhouse: Main bar, Predisent's lounge, dining room, kitchen, toilets – North end of stand
Colours: Black & white hoops. (*Change colours*: Red)
Nickname: The 'Tics
Floodlights: No – training only
Admission: £1.25
Membership: £18 (£15 OAP). Playing member £15
Programme: 8 pages, 20p (Editor: Brian Cummings)
Local newspaper: Torbay Herald Express
League: SW1
Final position (1987–88): 5th
Playing record (1987–88): P 36, W 18, D 0, L 18, F 493, A 585
Competitions won: Devon Cup 1979

CLIFTON

Station Road, Cribbs Causeway, Henbury, Bristol BS10 7TT. Tel: 500445
Founded: 1872
President: G. Watson
Chairman: N. Golding
Coach: R. Jordan
Secretary: I. Carpenter, 62 Oakfield Road, Clifton, Bristol BS8 2BG. Tel: 741021.
Fixtures Secretary: B. Jordan, 17 Royal Close, Henbury, Bristol. Tel: 504723.
Club captain (1987–88): Neil Morgan
Club captain (1988–89): Neil Morgan
No. of teams: Senior 7. Youth & Minis 10.
Directions to Ground: Clifton junction of M5. Travel down Cribbs Causeway (dual carriageway). Club on right at bottom of Cribbs Causeway. Signposted from there.
Colours: Lavender and black. (*Change colours:* Yellow).
Floodlights: Yes
Membership: £30
Programme editor: B. Jordan and I. Carpenter
Local newspaper: Evening Post

League: SW1
Final position (1987–88): 3rd
Playing record (1987–88): P 39 W 22, L 17, D 0, F 616, A 617.

TAUNTON

Priory Park, Priory Bridge Road. Tel: 0823 275670
Founded: 1875
President: G. Babbage
Chairman: M. Newport
Coach: M. Taylor
Secretary: R. Farthing. Tel: 0823 257894/5
Fixtures Secretary: D. Ward, 9 Bridge Close, Taunton. Tel: 0823 335037
Club captain (1987–88): M. Reece
Club captain (1988–89): M. Reece
No. of teams: Senior 3. Youth & Minis 7
Directions to Ground: Take junction 25 for Taunton on the motorway. Travel under the motorway, past the Crest Hotel. Travel straight across three roundabouts into Priory Bridge Road, ground on the right.
Ground capacity: 5,000. Stand, 500
Clubhouse: Main bar, hall, lounge, changing rooms
Colours: Maroon/white/black hoops. (*Change colours*: Black)
Floodlights: Yes
Admission: £1
Membership: Patrons £17. Ground £12
Programme: 50p (Editor: Rodney Reed)
Local newspaper: County Gazette
League: SW1
Final position (1987–88): 8th
Playing record (1987–88): P 40, W 29, D 1, L 10, F 748, A 433
Competitions won: Bass South West Division 1985–86, County up 1985–86

OXFORD

Southern By Pass, North Hinksey, Oxford. Tel: 0865-243984.
Founded: 1909
President: B. Deane
Chairman: D. Bagnall
Coach: J. Gunter
Secretary: R. Martin, Pantiles, 22 Didcot Road, Long Wittenham, Oxon OX14 4PZ. Tel: 086730-7528.
Fixtures Secretary: R. Whitfield, 3 Henwood Drive, Wootton, Boars Hill, Oxford. Tel: 0865-739136.
Club captain (1987–88): P. Maton
Club captain (1988–89): R. Davies
No. of teams: Senior 3, Youth & Minis 1
Directions to Ground: Turn left at North Hinksey off A34 going South towards Abingdon.
Ground capacity: Stand, 150
Clubhouse: Main bar, lounge, hall, 2 squash courts.
Colours: Green, black, silver. (*Change colours:* Green)
Floodlights: Yes
Membership: £16
Programme: 25p (Editor: R. Tyrrell
Local newspaper: Oxford Mail
League: South-West 1
Final position (1987–88): 6th
Playing record (1987–88): W 16, L 12, D 2.
Competitions won: Oxfordshire County Cup 20/3/88. Oxford RFC Courage Floodlit Cup 29/3/88.

WESTON SUPER MARE

Clubhouse, The Recreation Ground, Drove Road, Weston Super Mare.
Founded: 1875
President: Dr. G.W.J. Papworth
Chairman: R.C. Crocker
Coach: G. Redmond
Secretary: J.N. Brentnall, 37 The Boulevard, Weston Super Mare BS23 1PK. Tel: 0272 829625 (H) & 0934 413535 (W)
Fixtures Secretary: C. Hope, 9 Brighton Road, Weston Super Mare. Tel: 0934 22921
Club captain (1987–88): P. Tinchnell
Club captain (1988–89): P. Tincknell
No. of teams: Senior 3. Youth & Minis 5
Directions to Ground: Ground is situated adjoining the railway station, close to the centre of town
Ground capacity: 3,000. Stand, 600
Clubhouse: Large clubhouse, committee room, lounge bar, skittle alley
Colours: Royal blue. (*Change colours*: Red)
Floodlights: Yes
Admission: £1
Membership: £18
Programme: 10p (Editor: Secretary)
Local newspaper: Weston Super Mare Mercury
League: SW1
Final position (1987–88): 7th
Playing record (1987–88): P 43, W 19, D 1, L 23, F 770, A 580

BRIDGWATER & ALBION

Broadway, Bridgwater, Somerset. Tel: 0278 423900.
President: J. Taylor
Chairman: R. Chidgey
Coach: T. Self
Secretary: T. Self, 51a Wembdon Rise, Bridgwater, Somerset TA6 3NF. Tel: 0278-450081 (H), 0278-455622 (W).
Fixtures Secretary: A. Pomeroy, "Hafod-y-Gam", Newton Road, North Petherton, Somerset TA6 6SN. Tel: 0278-662181 (H), 0278 455631 (B).
Club captain (1987–88): P. Burne
Club captain (1988–89): A. Harris
No of teams: Senior 3. Youth & Minis 5.
Directions to Ground: From M5 follow A38 through town to roundabout junction A38/A39. Follow A39. Entrance immediately on the left.
Ground capacity: 2000. Stand, 600.
Colours: Yellow, black & amber. (*Change colours:* Green.)
Floodlights: Yes.
Admission: £1.00
Membership: £17.50
Programme: 20p. (Editor: M. Derrick)
Local newspaper: Bridgwater Mercury
League: South-West 1
Final position (1987–88): 9th
Playing record (1987–88): P 28, W 13, D 1, L 14, F 428, A 379.

ST. IVES

Alexandra Road, St. Ives, Cornwall. Tel: 0736 795346
Founded: 1887
President: E.M. Trewhella
Chairman: N.A. Simpson
Coach: J. Trevorrow & J. Cocking
Secretary: M. Gee, "Suhaili", 7 Hellesvean Close, St. Ives TR26 2HQ. Tel: 0736 797168
Fixtures Secretary: M. Gee, as Secretary
Club captain (1987–88): T. Bassett
Club captain (1988–89): To be appointed
No. of teams: Senior 3.
Directions to Ground: From A30 take coach route/holiday route to St. Ives via B3311 & B3306, turn left at first mini roundabout
Ground capacity: 5,000. Stand (when erected) 200
Clubhouse: 4 bars – open every night. Tel: 0736 795346
Colours: Navy & white shorts. (*Change colours*: White with navy hoop)

South West 1

Nickname: The Hakes
Floodlights: Yes
Admission: 80p
Membership: £10
Programme: 10p (Editor: Secretary – M. Gee)
Local newspaper: St. Ives Times & Echo
League: SW1
Final position (1987–88): 10th
Playing record (1987–88): P 36, W 19, D 1, L 16
Competitions won: Cornwall Knockout Cup Winners – 1969, 1970, 1971, 1979, 1981, 1982, 1986

BOURNEMOUTH

Kinson Park Road, Northbourne, Bournemouth. Tel: 0202 573089 or 0202 571352
Founded: 1893
President: A.J. Thorne
Chairman: N.R.E. Yeoman
Coach: J. Read
Secretary: R.G.S. Llewellyn, Argyle Chambers, Fir Vale Road, Bournemouth
Fixtures Secretary: J. Arthur, 62 Iddlesleigh Road, Bournemouth. Tel: 0202 292676 (H) & 0202 687424 (W)
Club captain (1987–88): R. Clayton
Club captain (1988–89): R. Clayton
No. of teams: Senior 7. Youth & Minis 5
Directions to Ground: North of Bournemouth – heading to Ferndown – off The New Road, Northbourne
Stand capacity: 100
Clubhouse: 2 bars, skittle alley, function/tea room, 2 squash courts & 9 changing rooms, etc
Colours: Yellow & black (*Change colours*: Red)
Floodlights: No – next year
Admission: Nil
Membership: Playing members senior £25. Non-playing members £10
Programme: 50p (Editor: N.R.E. Yeoman)
Local newspaper: Bournemouth Evening Echo & Streetlife
League: SW1
Final position (1987–88): Bottom (relegated)
Playing record (1987–88): P 27, W 8, D 1, L 18, F 249, A 526

SOUTH-WEST 2

BERRY HILL

Lakers Road, Berry Hill, Coleford, Glos GL16 7LY. Tel: Dean (0594) 33295
Founded: 1889
President: R.W. Jenkins
Chairman: R. Powell
Coach: T.B.A.
Secretary: T.J. Baldwin, Hill Brink, Joyford Hill, Coleford, Glos GL16 7AH. Tel: 0594 32539
Fixtures Secretary: G.R. Goddard, 71A Cheltenham Road, Gloucester. Tel: 0454 306749
Club captain (1987–88): John Evans
Club captain (1988–89): Jeff Powell
No. of teams: Senior 5. Youth 1. Minis 6
Directions to Ground: Follow directions to nearest town Coleford, then the road signs for Berry Hill
Ground capacity: 2,000
Clubhouse: Lakers Road, Berry Hill
Colours: Black & amber (*Change colours*: Red & white)
Floodlights: Yes
Admission: Under £1
Membership: Players £5. Social £2
Programme: Free. (Editor: J. Belcher, Club's Publicity Officer)
Local newspaper: Forest of Dean Newspapers
League: SW2
Final position (1987–88): Winners
Playing record (1987–88): P 36, W 27, L 8, D 1, F 775, A 399
Competitions won: Winners Courage League South West Division II, Rugby World Junior Club of the Year, runners up Gloucestershire County Cup

READING (formerly Berkshire Wanderers)

Holme Park, Sonning Lane, Sonning, Reading RG4 0ST. Tel: 0734 696592 and 690030.
Founded: 1898
President: Gordon Richens
Chairman: Graham Ethelston
Coach: Jeff Owen
Secretary: Mike Wickson, 21 Lunds Farm Road, Woodley, Reading RG5 4PZ.
Fixtures Secretary: Bob Pendleton, 1 Greencroft Gardens, Reading. Tel: 0734 580014.
Club captain (1987–88): Ian Turrell
Club captain (1988–89): Ian Turrell
No. of teams: Senior 6. Youth & Minis 6.
Directions to Ground: Signposted from A4 about two miles east of Reading.
Ground capacity: 500. Stand, 120.
Clubhouse: 2 bars, hall, 2 squash courts, weights room, 6 changing rooms.
Colours: Myrtle and white hoops, blue shorts. (*Change colours:* Blue shirts).
Floodlights: Yes, training only
Membership: £8.30 p month (playing member)
Programme: Home games 50p. (Editor: Graham Lyke)
Local newspaper: Reading Chronicle, Reading Evening Post
League: SW2
Final position (1987–88): 2nd in SW2
Playing record (1987–88): P 31, W 26, L 4, D1. F 627, A 243.
Competitions won: 1987/88. Promotion from SW2, Berkshire Cup Champions, Southern Merit Table Champions 1986/7, JP Cup Third Round, Southert Merit Table Champions, RW&P Junior Club of Year 1985/86, Berkshire Cup Champions.

BARNSTAPLE

Pottington Road, Barnstaple. Tel: B'ple 45627
Founded: 1877
President: F.C. Passmore
Chairman: E. Parsley
Coach: Tony Stevens
Secretary: B.C. Williams, 'The Mews', Whiddon Park, Landkey Road, Barnstaple. Tel: 79289. Ex 329LA.
Fixtures Secretary: A. Wasley, 39 St Mary's Road, Barnstaple. Tel: 71553.
Club captain (1987–88): Ian Innes
Club captain (1988–89): Ian Innes
No. of teams: Senior 3. Youth & Minis 5.
Directions to Ground: From town square follow Braunton signs. Turn left into Pottington Road at traffic lights in Rolle Street.
Ground capacity: 3000–4000. Stand, 500.
Clubhouse: 2 bars, dining room, kitchen.
Colours: Red shirts, white shorts. (*Change colours:* White or brown).
Nickname: 1st XV – Chiefs

Abbey youngsters (l to r) Nick Hammond, Chris Hayter, Huw Jones, Mark Rennell, Jame Beddoe, Liam Corbett. Photo: Steve Templeman.

Floodlights: No
Admission: £1
Membership: £10 playing, £10 VP.
Programme: 20p. (Editor: B.C. Williams)
Local newspaper: N. Devon Journal
League: SW2
Final position (1987–88): 3rd
Playing record (1987–88): P 33, W 17, D 1, L 15. F 509, A 458.
Competitions won: Devon RFU Colts Cup Winners 1984–88

BRIXHAM

Astley Park. Tel: 0803882162
Founded: 1874
President: E. Crow, FCA
Coach: David Wiggins
Secretary: Bob Houston, "St. Cloud", Cliff Park Road, Gooderington, Paignton. Tel. 0803 550427 (H) & 0392 52155 (B)
Rugby Secretary: Danny Irvine, BEM, 1 Great Rea Road, Brixham TQ5 9SW. Tel: 0803 882219 (H) & 08043 2337 (B)
Club captain (1987–88): Sean Irvine
Club captain (1988–89): Sean Irvine
No. of teams: Senior 5. Youth & Minis 4
Directions to Ground: Follow road signs pointing to Torbay, on entering town turn right at traffic lights at Bolton Cross, follow Bolton Street for about 400m then turn left up Rea Barn Hill
Ground capacity: 5,000. Stand 300
Clubhouse: Two storey building incorporating main bar area, lounge bar, players bar and reception room, dressing rooms
Colours: Black with 6″ white band. (*Change colours*: white/red or orange)
Nickname: The Fishermen
Floodlights: Yes
Admission: First XV £1. Junior matches 50p
Membership: Players £10. Members £6
Programme: Included in admission. (Editor: Norman Marler)
Local newspaper: Western Morning News, Sunday Independent/Herald Express
Free newpaper: The Weekender & Brixham News
League: SW2
Final position (1987–88): 4th
Playing record (1987–88): P 40, W 30, D 0, L 10, F 812, A 429

CINDERFORD

Recreation Ground, Dockham Road, Glos. Tel: 0594 22673
Founded: 1886
President: R.H. Beavis
Chairman: K. Morse
Coach: D. Hargreaves
Secretary: Mrs M. Beavis, 5 Abbots Road, Cinderford, Glos. Tel: 0594 23779
Fixtures Secretary: J. Gazzard, 1 Wedgewood Crescent, Cinderford. Tel: 0594 22333
Club captain (1987–88): P. Crowell
Club captain (1988–89): D. Richards
No. of teams: Senior 4. Youth & Minis 4
Directions to Ground: Bus station at the centre of the town.
Ground capacity: 4,000. Stand 300
Clubhouse: Licensed – open weekdays
Colours: Red, black & amber (*Change colours*: Red)
Nickname: Cindy
Floodlights: Yes
Admission: £1
Membership: £5
Programme: £1 (Editor: Mr. N. Wilce)
Local newspaper: 3 Forest of Dean Newspaper
League: SW2
Final position (1987–88): 4th
Playing record (1987–88): P 39, W 23, D 1, L 15, F 677, A 405
Competitions won: Runners up Drybrook 7's, Quarter Finals City Cup, Won Pernod Attack Award

LAUNCESTON

Polson, Launceston, Cornwall. Tel: 0566 3406.
Founded: 194[illegible]
Patron: R. Williams
President: Reverend Martin James
Chairman: D. Baker
Coach: Ian Davies
Secretary: S. Towers, 7 Trecarn Close, Launceston. Tel: 0566 5447.
Fixtures Secretary: M.D. Yeo, White Row, Lewdown, Okehampton. Tel: Lewdown 83230.
No. of teams: Senior 3, Youth & Minis 6
Clubhouse: 4 changing rooms, 2 bars.
Colours: Black
Floodlights: Yes
Admission: £1
Membership: £10
Programme: £1
Local newspaper: Cornish & Devon Post
League: South-West 2
Final position (1987–88): 6th
Competitions won: Runners up Cornwall Cup.

ABBEY

Roschill, Peppard Road, Emmer Green, Reading, Berks. Tel: Reading (0734) 722881
Founded: 1956
President: A. Young
Chairman: M. Lee
Coach: M. Probyn
Secretary: P. Loveridge, 1 Clifton Park Road, Caversham, Reading, Berks. Tel: (0734) 477427
Fixtures Secretary: P. Carroll, 24 Harrogate Road, Caversham, Reading, Berks. Tel: (0734) 482257
Club captain (1987–88): A. Kilford
Club captain (1988–89): A. Lester
No. of teams: Senior 6. Youth & Minis 9
Directions to Ground: From Reading town centre follow signs to Peppard and Sonning Common, Club on left after 2/3 miles
Colours: Navy blue with white & green hoops
Floodlights: Yes
Membership: £20 (seniors)
Local newspaper: Reading Chronicle & Evening Post
League: SW2
Final position (1987–88): 7th
Playing record (1987–88): P 37, W 15, D 1, L 21, F 468, A 572

DEVON & CORNWALL POLICE

Middlemead, Exeter. Tel: 52101
Founded: 1971
President: D. Elliott QPM
Chairman: J. Essery
Coach: P. Angove
Secretary: E. Evans, Westwood House, 33 Buttercombe Close, Ogwell Cross, Newton Abbot, Devon TQ12 6AJ. Tel: 0626 56858
Fixtures Secretary: C. Hucker, Tywardreath Police Station. Tel. 072681 2262
Club captain (1987–88): I. Main
Club captain (1988–89): I. Main
No. of teams: Senior 1
Directions to Ground: M5 to Exeter – follow signs to city centre. Ground is 1 mile from M5

Ground capacity: 200
Colours: Black/white hoops/black shorts (*Change colours*: Green)
Nickname: D & C
Floodlights: No
Admission: 50p
Membership: £12
Programme: 20p (Editor: Secretary)
Local newspaper: Western Morning News
League: SW2
Final position (1987–88): 8th
Playing record (1987–88): P 43, W 22, D 1, L 21, F 731, A 675
Competitions won: Runners up National Police Cup 1987/88, Devon Sevens 1981

HENLEY

Dry Leas, Marlow Road, Henley-on-Thames. Tel: 0491 574499
Founded: 1930
President: S.W. Lewington
Chairman: N.P. North
Coach: G. Horner
Secretary: D.A. Trower, 60 Makins Road, Henley-on Thames, Oxon. Tel: 0491 572862
Fixtures Secretary: A.W. Cooke, 86 Makins Road, Henley-on-Thames. Tel: 0491 575789
Club captain (1987–88): A. Hooper
Club captain (1988–89): M. Poulson
No. of teams: Senior 6. Youth & Minis 9
Directions to Ground: 100 yds on left hand side from the mini roundabout/junction of A4155 & A423
Clubhouse: Bar, kitchen, toilets
Colours: Green/gold & blue hoop shirts, blue shorts, green socks. (*Change colours*: Dark green)
Floodlights: No
Membership: Players £20
Programme: 50p
Local newspaper: Henley Standard
League: SW2
Final position (1987–88): 9th
Playing record (1987–88): P 34, W 12, D 2, L 20, F 482 A 496
Competitions won: Pernod Trophy as top try scorers in Oxfordshire Cup

NEWBURY

The Clubhouse, Newtown Road Ground, Pinchington Lane, Newbury RG14 7HB. Tel: Newbury 40103
President: R. Tucker
Chairman: G. Wickens
Coach: E. Butler
Secretary: L. Sugden, Brook Cottage, Boxford, Newbury. Tel: Boxford 607
Fixtures Secretary: A. Boyer, 11 Christopher Court, Boundary Road, Newbury. Tel: Newbury 40574
Club captain (1987–88): G. Brown
Club captain (1988–89): R. King
No. of teams: Senior 5. Youth & Minis 7
Directions to Ground: Pinchington Lane off A34 (South of Newbury)
Clubhouse: Bars, dressing rooms
Colours: Dark & light blue. (*Change colours*: Red)
Floodlights: No
Admission: 50p includes programme
Membership: £5
Programme: (Editor: A. Boyer)
Local newspaper: Newbury Weekly News
League: SW2
Final position (1987–88): 10th

DEVONPORT SERVICES

The Rectory Field, Devenport, Devon. Tel: 0752 51065.
Founded: 1919
Secretary: Sub. Lt. Rob Nairn, R.N., The P.T. Office H.M.S. Drake, Devenport, Plymouth. Tel: 0752 555306 (W).
League: South-West 2
Final position (1987–88): 11th
Playing record (1987–88): P 29, W 17, L 12, F 500, A 388.

WESTERN COUNTIES LEAGUE

MATSON drew one and won the rest of their 10 matches and easily won this League which feeds South West 2. Gordon League, in spite of their John Player Cup successes, could not match that league form and Sidmouth were just not good enough to keep their place finishing last with the Avon and Somerset Constabulary just one place above them.

Matson's 343 points should be a warning to their opponents next season.

TABLES 1987–88

WESTERN COUNTIES

	P	W	D	L	F	A	Pts
Matson	10	9	1	0	343	58	19
Gordon Lge	10	6	2	2	213	80	14
Clevedon	10	6	1	3	150	118	13
Truro	10	6	0	4	111	178	12
O Redcliffs	10	5	0	5	144	138	10
Newquay Hor	10	4	1	5	107	160	9
Okehampton	10	3	2	5	103	127	8
Cirencester	10	4	0	6	76	124	8
Tiverton	10	3	1	6	74	121	7
Av & Som Con	10	3	0	7	79	193	6
Sidmouth	10	2	0	8	79	182	4

MATSON

Redwell Road, Matson, Gloucester. Tel: 28963
Founded: 1957
President: H. Jones
Chairman: T. Loader
Coach: R. Hayes
Secretary: G. Locke, 39 Oxmoor, Abbeydale, Glos. Tel: 419587 (H) & 712802 (W)
Fixtures Secretary: C.J. Maton, 57 The Richmonds, Gloucester. Tel: 504563
Club captain (1987–88): R.W. Correia
Club captain (1988–89): R.W. Correia
No. of teams: Senior 4
Colours: Black/white (*Change colours*: Black/white hoops
Floodlights: No
Admission: Free
Membership: £5
Local newspaper: The Citizen
League: Western Counties
Final position (1987–88): 1st (promoted)
Playing record (1987–88): L 2
Competitions won: North Gloucester Combination Cup 7–3 against Gordon League, Western Counties Courage Club Championship

GORDON LEAGUE

Hempstead Lane, Gloucester. Tel: 303434
Founded: 1888
President: Mayor of Gloucester
Chairman: John Emery
Coach: Peul Red
Secretary: John Wakefield, 1 Berry Lawn, Wheatway, Gloucester
Fixtures Secretary: Howard Williams, 62 Escourt Road, Gloucester. Tel: 20913
Club captain (1987–88): Steven Artus
Club captain (1988–89): Steven Artus
No. of teams: Senior 5. Junior 17s 1
Directions to Ground: Map supplied to visiting teams
Ground capacity: 1,500. Stand 150
Clubhouse: A new clubhouse to be completed by November 1988
Colours: White with red sash (*Change colours*: Red)
Nickname: The League
Floodlights: Yes. Training only
Admission: League games only 50p
Membership: £10
Programme: With entry. (Sports editor: Terry Phillips)
Local newspaper: The Citizen
League: Western Counties
Final position (1987–88): 2nd
Playing record (1987–88): P 40, W 32
Competitions won: Local Combination Cup, approx 17 times; County Cup, 3 times; Local Sevens, 15 times,;County Under 15s, 3 times; Last 16 John Player, twice

CLEVEDON

Coleridge Vale Playing Fields, Clevedon, Avon. Tel 0272 877772
Founded: 1921
President: O.R.L. Taylor
Chairman: R.W.J. Newton
Coach: H. Jones
Secretary: R.G. Legge, 2 Kingston Avenue, Clevedon. Avon
Fixtures Secretary: O.R.L. Taylor, 40 Ash Hayes Drive, Naksea, Bristol.
Club captain (1987–88): D. Smith
Club captain (1988–89): D. Hussey
No. of teams: Senior 4. Youth & Minis 7
Directions to Ground: M5, junction 20, first and second roundabout, leave at 12-o'clock roadway junction. At lights turn left, take next left, take second left. Ground can be seen in front of you
Colours: Royal blue/gold hoops (*Change colours*: *Royal blue)*
Floodlights: No
Membership: £3 non-playing. £13.50 playing (senior)
Programme: 50p (Editor: Sue Davis)
Local newspaper: Clevedon Mercury
League: Western Counties
Final position (1987–88): Joint 2nd
Playing record (1987–88): P 35, W 22, D 2, L 11, F 733, A 380
Competitions won: Bristol Combination Sevens

TRURO

St Clements Hill, Truro, Cornwall. Tel: 0872 74750.
Founded: 1920
Secretary: W. Austin, 5 Valley Close, Highertown, Truro. Tel: 0872 40150 (H). 0872 71591 (W).
Fixtures Secretary:
League: Western Counties
Final position (1987–88): 4th
Playing record (1987–88): P 35, W 19, D 1, L 15. F 552, A 533.

OLD REDCLIFFIANS

Stockwood Road, Brislington, Bristol. Tel: 0272 778501
Founded: 1918
President: A.A. Johnson
Chairman: K. Warren
Coach: M. Fry
Secretary: V. Heybyrne, 34 Bristol Road, Winterbourne, Bristol BS17 1RG. Tel: 0454 775547
Fixtures Secretary: R. Yandell, 5 High Street, Portbury, Bristol. Tel: Pill 3444
Club captain (1987–88): G. Cox
Club captain (1988–89): L. Yandell
No. of teams: Senior 5. Youth & Minis 5
Directions to Ground: Take the main Bath road from Britsol to Brislington, turn right into Stockwood Lan at last traffic lights leaving Brislington, ground situated approx ½ mile on right of lane
Clubhouse: 60′ × 30′ building adjacent to changing accommodation and 1st team pitch
Colours: Red & black hoops (*Change colours*: Blue & white hoops)
Nickname: Old Reds
Floodlights: Yes. Training only
Membership: £5 annually plus £1.50 match fees
Programme: 50p (Editor: G. Sibley)
Local newspaper: Western Daily Press & Evening Post
League: Western Counties
Final position (1987–88): 5th
Playing record (1987–88): P 32, W 18, L 14, F 505, A 362
Competitions won: Imperial Sevens, Sept 87

NEWQUAY HORNETS

Newquay Sports Centre, Tretherras Road, Newquay, Cornwall. Tel: 0637 875533
Founded: 1933
President: R.R. Edwards
Chairman: S.J. Dunn
Coach: F. Barnett
Secretary: R.T. Delbridge, "Thurso", Cubert, Newquay TR8 5HB. Tel: 0637 830441

Fixtures Secretary: C.R. Roberts, 18 St. Annes Road, Newquay. Tel: 0637 874568
Club captain (1987–88): R. Pryor
Club captain (1988–89): S. Taylor
No. of teams: Senior 3. Youth & Minis 2
Directions to Ground: Turn left on the main route into the town. The Sports Centre is sign posted
Clubhouse: Owned by Newquay Sports Centre Ltd
Colours: Green & white hoops (*Change colours*: Blue)
Floodlights: Training lights only
Admission: 50p last season
Membership: £20
Programme: As admission (Editor: K. Platton)
Local newspaper: Cornish Guardian
League: Western Counties
Final position (1987–88): 6th
Playing record (1987–88): P 36, W 17, D 1, L 18, F 484, A 517, 48.6%

OKEHAMPTON

Oaklands Showfield, Okehampton. Tel: 2508
Founded: 1884
President: Eric Chowings
Chairman: Russ Thomas
Coach: Ray Westlake
Secretary: Ted Cann, 11 Exeter Road, Okehampton. Tel: 2759
Fixtures Secretary: Bryan Hucker, The Brackens, South Zeal, Okehampton. Tel: 840428
Club captain (1987–88): Robert Barkwell
Club captain (1988–89): Nick Holliday
No. of teams: Senior 3. Youth & Minis 3
Directions to Ground: Hatherleigh Road, Okehampton
Ground capacity: 2,500. Stand 250
Clubhouse: Bar, dining area
Colours: Maroon/amber hoops (*Change colours*: Plain maroon)
Nickname: The Okes
Floodlights: No
Admission: League games £1
Membership: Players sub. £7.50 senior. £5 junior
Programme: £1 (Editor: Eddie Hawkins. Tel: 2473)
Local newspaper: Okehampton Times
League: Western Counties
Final position (1987–88): 7th
Playing record (1987–88): P 37, W 21, D 3, L 13
Competitions won: Bass Devon Cup finalists, April 26th, 1988

CIRENCESTER

The Whiteway, Cirencester, Gloucestershire. Tel: 0285 4435.
Founded: 1948
Secretary: P.M. Davies, 1 Sawyers Close, Minety, Malmesbury, Wilts. Tel: 0666 860482 (H). 0285 4875 (W).
League: Western Counties
Final position (1987–88): 8th
Playing record (1987–88): P 36, W 25, D 1, L 10. F 496, A 290.

TIVERTON

Coronation Field, Bolham Road, Tiverton. Tel: 252271
Founded: 1868
President: G. Burt
Chairman: S. Andrews
Coach: D. Lewis
Secretary: M. Heard, 6 Norwood Road, Tiverton. Tel: 258600
Fixtures Secretary: K. Sutton, 42 Belmont Road, Tiverton.
Club captain (1987–88): P. Cole
Club captain (1988–89): P. Cole
No. of teams: Senior 3. Youth & Minis 4
Directions to Ground: Junction 27 on M5, drive to end of Link Road for N. Devon. Club on left
Stand capacity: 200
Clubhouse: 2 bars, multi-gym, etc
Colours: Light & dark blue hoop. (*Change colours*: Yellow)
Nickname: Tivvy
Floodlights: Yes
Admission: 50p
Membership: Non-players £3. Players £2.50
Programme: 50p (Editor: G. Bulley)
Local newspaper: Tiverton Gazette
League: Western Counties
Final position (1987–88): 9th
Playing record (1987–88): P 39, W 16, L 21, D 2, F 478, A 566

AVON & SOMERSET CONSTABULARY

Kings Weston Sports Ground, Napier Miles Road, Kings Weston, Bristol. Tel: 0272 828307.
Founded: 1935
Secretary: B. Gardiner, "Hillsley", Bleadon Road, Bleadon, Weston-Super-Mare, Avon. Tel: 0934 812020 (H). 0934 25411 (W).
League: Western Counties
Final position (1987–88): 10th

SIDMOUTH

Blackmore Field. Tel: 03955 6816.
Founded: 1884
President: B.K. Thomas
Chairman: D. Marchant
Secretary: D.R. Salter, 5 Barrington Mead, Sidmouth. Tel: 03955 3678.
Fixtures Secretary: T. O'Brien, 2 Rivulet Cottages, Sidford, Sidmouth. Tel: 03955 77403.
Club captain (1987–88): R. Smith
Club captain (1988–89): R. Smith
No. of teams: Senior 3. Youth & Minis 4.
Directions to Ground: From A3052 (M5) follow signs to town centre to Station Road. left to Heydons Lane.
Stand capacity: 150
Clubhouse: 2 bars
Colours: Green. (*Change colours:* Navy blue).
Floodlights: No
Admission: 40p
Membership: £10 players
Local newspaper: Sidmouth Herald
League: Western League
Final position (1987–88): 11th
Playing record (1987–88): P 42, W 19, D 1, L 22. F 625, A 694.
Competitions won: Devon Merit Table A 1985–86.

SOUTHERN COUNTIES

A REALLY tough competition ended with the old boys team Redingensians taking the top spot although they were beaten twice, as were Swindon who drew one into the bargain and failed by a single point. There were also strong efforts from Wimborne and Marlow.

The unlucky basement teams were Oxford Marathon and Bracknell who lost all their games.

TABLES 1987–88

SOUTHERN COUNTIES

	P	W	D	L	F	A	Pts
Redingensian	10	8	0	2	159	80	16
Swindon	10	7	1	2	162	66	15
Wimborne	10	7	0	3	175	95	14
Marlow	10	7	0	3	135	78	14
Oxford OB	10	6	0	4	142	82	12
Aylesbury	10	5	1	4	156	110	11
Banbury	19	4	1	4	129	111	9
Windsor	10	3	2	5	86	144	8
Bletchley	10	3	0	7	76	176	6
Oxford Mara	10	1	1	8	66	257	3
Bracknell	9	1	1	9	63	150	0

SOUTHERN COUNTRIES

REDINGENSIAN

Old Bath Road, Sonning, Reading. Tel: 0734 695259.
Founded: 1924
Secretary: J.H. Cook, 95 Century Court, Grove End Road, London N.W.8. Tel: 01-289-1887 (H), 01-638-1282 (B).
Directions to Ground: On A410 Maidenhead turn right at Sonning.
League: Southern Counties
Final position (1987–88): 1st (promoted)
Playing record (1987–88): P 31, W 18, D 1, L 12, F 458, A 311.

SWINDON

Greenbridge Road, Swindon. Tel: 0793 21148
Founded: 1895
President: R. Nash
Chairman: I.I. Pantzig
Coach: L. Morgan
Secretary: W.M. Hillybro, 12 Fitzroy Road, Swindon. Tel: 611925.
Fixtures Secretary: H. Evans, The Close, High Street, Warborough, Swindon. Tel: 790432.
Club captain (1987–88): I. Binfiold
Club captain (1988–89): T. Brant
No. of teams: Senior 4.
Directions to Ground: Greenbridge Road off Darcan Way – by W.H. Smith Distribution Centre.
Clubhouse: 2/3 bars and hall.
Colours: Blue, amber shirts. (*Change colours:* Cherry, white hoops).
Floodlights: Yes, training only
Membership: £25 rugby, £5 social
Local newspaper: Evening Advertiser
League: Southern Counties
Final position (1987–88): 2nd
Playing record (1987–88): P 35, W 27, D 1, L 7.
Competitions won: Dorset & Wilts Cup 1st and 2nd XV. (March 1988). Dorset & Wilts 1st Team Cup also won in 1984 and 1986.

WIMBORNE

Leigh park, Wimborne, Dorset. Tel: 0202 882602.
Founded: 1950
President: T. Gill
Chairman: D. Mitchell
Coach: B. Maidment
Secretary: G. Emery, 4 River Close, Wimborne. Tel: 0202 888830.
Fixtures Secretary: D. Beck, 112 Old Wareham Road, Corfe Mullen, Dorset. Tel: 0202 693205.
No. of teams: Senior 6. Youth & Minis 6.
Directions to Ground: Approach Wimborne on A31 from East. 1 m from town centre turn left into Gordon Road, ground 100 yds ahead.
Ground capacity: More than adequate!
Clubhouse: Two bars, next to pitches.
Colours: Black. (*Change colours:* Black, white hoops).
Floodlights: No
Membership: £28
Local newspaper: Evening Echo
League: Southern Counties
Final position (1987–88): 3rd
Playing record (1987–88): W 22, L 8, D 2.
Competitions won: D&W Cup Holders 1979 and 1982.

MARLOW

Riverwoods Drive, Marlow, Bucks. Tel: 06284 3911.
Founded: 1948
Secretary: R.J. Gates, "St. Jasual", Wheeler End Common, High Wycombe, Bucks. Tel: 0494 881089 (H), 0494 450171 (B).
Fixtures Secretary: A. Sanderson, 26 Dedmere Court, Marlow, Bucks. Tel: Marlow 71731 (H).
Local newspaper: Bucks Free Press
League: Southern Counties
Final position (1987–88): 4th
Playing record (1987–88): P 31, W 24, L 7, F 469, A 259.
Competitions won: Won Bucks County Cup and qualify for Pilkington Cup.

Marlow RFC

OXFORD OLD BOYS

Marston Ferry Road, Marston, Oxford. Tel: 0865 52813.
Founded: 1963
Secretary: A.J. Hand, 1 Cavendish Road, Oxford OX3 7AR. Tel: 0865 510542 (H & B).
Fixtures Secretary: T. Jarman, 14 Bicester Road, Long Crendon, Aylesbury, Bucks. HP18 9BP. Tel: 0844 208545.
League: Southern Counties
Final position (1987–88): 5th
Playing record (1987–88): P 36, W 15, D 3, L 18, F 358, A 347.

AYLESBURY

Ostlers Field, Brookend, Weston Turville, Aylesbury, Bucks. Tel: 0296 61 2556.
Founded: 1931
President: G.V. Cowen
Chairman: T. Palm
Coach: M. Poste
Secretary: R.J. Langdon, Ivy Cottage, Halton Village, Aylesbury, HP22 5NS. Tel: 0296 622572.
Fixtures Secretary: D. Furby, Yew Tree Cottage, Stockaway, Weedon, Aylesbury. Tel: 0296 641289.
Club captain (1987–88): G. Charlier
Club captain (1988–89): H. Stone
No of teams: Senior 6. Youth & Minis 11
Directions to ground: On north side of road between Weston Turville and Aston Clinton. South by Aylesbury.
Ground capacity: 2000. Stand, 300.
Clubhouse: Large clubroom and 2 bars.
Colours: Magenta & black. (*Change colours:* White.)
Nickname: Ducks
Floodlights: No.
Membership: £25.
Local newspaper: Buck Herald
League: Southern Counties 1
Final position (1987–88): 6th
Playing record (1987–88): P 27, W 13, D 3, L 11, F 349, A 266.

BANBURY

Oxford Road, Banbury, Oxon. Tel: Banbury 3862.
Founded: 1925
President: J.W. Briggs
Chairman: B.J. Nichols
Coach: John Brodley
Secretary: M. Thomas, 24 Poplars Road, Chacombe, Banbury, Oxon. Tel: Banbury 711582.
Fixtures Secretary: T. Humphreys. Tel: (0295) 75330.
Club captain (1987–88): M. Court
Club captain (1988–89): M. Court
No. of teams: Senior 5, Youth 4, Minis 3
Directions to Ground: 1 mile South of Banbury Cross on A41 Oxford Road.
Clubhouse: Bar/lounge, 5 changing rooms.
Colours: Dark blue white hoops. (*Change colours:* Dark blue)
Floodlights: No
Membership: Players £19.00
Programme: Yes Free (Editor: C. Hayes)
Local newspaper: Banbury Guardian
League: Southern Counties
Final position (1987–88): 7th
Playing record (1987–88): P 32, W 18, D 1, L 13, F 477, A 365.

WINDSOR

Home Park, Datches Road, Windsor, Berks
Founded: 1922
President: Bob Deeley
Chairman: Willy Beckett
Coach: Chris Unwin
Secretary: Martin Unsworth, 7 Fairlight Avenue, Windsor, Berks. Tel: 0753 855555 (W)
Fixtures Secretary: Bill Manger, 127 Springfield Road, Windsor, Berks. Tel: 0753 869943
Club captain (1987–88): A.J. Dingley
Club captain (1988–89): A.J. Dingley
No. of teams: Senior 6. Youth & Minis 10. Vets 1
Directions to Ground: M4, junction 6, Windsor, Riverside Station
Ground capacity: 3,000+
Clubhouse: 2 clubhouses, two bars, five changing rooms, two baths, showers
Colours: Green/gold/maroon/black quarters (*Change colours*: Green/black/red hoops)
Nickname: W's
Floodlights: No
Membership: £25
Programme: 10p
Local newspaper: Windsor & Eton Express
League: Southern Counties
Final position (1987–88): 8th
Playing record (1987–88): P 31, W 11, D 3, L 17, F 443, A 519

BLETCHLEY

Manor Fields, Bletchley, Milton Keynes, Bucks. Tel: Milton Keynes 72298
Founded: 1946/47
President: Norman Anderson
Chairman: Paul Isherwood
Coach: David Lyon
Secretary: Frank Taylor, 57 South Lawne, Bletchley. Tel: Milton Keynes 640077
Fixtures Secretary: Richard Jackaman, 62 Quantock Crescent, Emerson Valley. Tel: Milton Keynes 501186
Club captain (1987–88): Alban Turney
Club captain (1988–89): Tim Rawles
No. of teams: Senior 4
Directions to Ground: On reaching Bletchley, Milton Keynes, aim for Fenny Stratford on Watling Street (A4146). Turn off into Aylesbury Street. Take first left after mini-roundabout into Sycamore Avenue. Proceed over bridge to ground
Stand capacity: 30
Clubhouse: Bletchley Sports Club, Manor Fields, Bletchley. 3 pitches, 2 bars, 2 dressing rooms
Colours: Burgundy & white (*Change colours*: White)
Floodlights: No. But being arranged for next season
Membership: £20

Tristan Scott-Evans, Windsor wing – 1987–88. Photo: Chris Roberts.

Windsor of Southern Counties face Abbotstonians seconds fielding a front-row of Micky Judge (left), Bruce Jack and Micky Crawshaw. Jack was at Eton College and is from South Africa. Photo: Chris Roberts.

Southern Counties

Programme: Yes. Price t.b.a. (Editor: Paul Isherwood)
Local newspaper: Citizen, Mirror & Herald
League: Southern Counties
Final position (1987–88): 9th
Playing record (1987–88): P 33, W 14, L 19
Competitions won: Bucks Cup 1984 & 1985, North Bucks Shield Holders

OXFORD MARATHON

Horspath Road, Cowley, Oxford. Tel: Oxford 775765
Founded: 1948
President: W.G. Franklin
Chairman: K. Hearn
Coach: G. Williams
Secretary: A.W.G. Barson, 97 Oxford Road, Garsington, Oxford OX9 9AD. Tel: 086 736540
Fixtures Secretary: R. Reynolds, 2 The Orchard, Badswell Lane, Appleton, Abingdon, Oxon. Tel: 0865 863765
Club captain (1987–88): J. Warrell
Club captain (1988–89): G. Williams
No. of teams: Senior 4. Youth & Minis 1
Directions to Ground: Oxford Ring Road to Cowley. Look for Horspath Road 400 yds from roundabout
Clubhouse: Members' bar, main hall
Colours: Navy with amber hoops (*Change colours*: Red)
Nickname: Maras
Floodlights: Yes. For training
Membership: £15
Local newspaper: Oxford Mail
League: Southern Counties
Final position (1987–88): 10th
Playing record (1987–88): P 31, W 13, D 2, L 16, F 349, A 581
Competitions won: Oxon Cup Semi-Finalists

BRACKNELL

Lily Hill, London Road, Bracknell. Tel: 0344 424013
Founded: 1955
President: J.R. Dance
Chairman: M. Dixon
Coach: G. Parsons
Secretary: A. Gooch, 15 Denmark Road, Reading. Tel: 0734 872306
Fixtures Secretary: N. Featherstone, 25 Claverdon, Bracknell. Tel: 0344 422471
Club captain (1987–88): B. Price
Club captain (1988–89): C. Vaal
No. of teams: Senior 8. Youth & Minis 9
Colours: Green/gold/black. (*Change colours*: Black)
Floodlights: No
Membership: Players £12
Programme: 20p
Local newspaper: Post & Mail
League: Southern Counties
Final position: 11th (relegated)
Playing record (1987–88): P 33, W 11, L 22

GLOUCESTER/SOMERSET LEAGUE

THE Western Counties League place from this section goes to Avon Old Boys, who finished two points clear of John Horton's Combe Down. The latter played one game less but the top men had scored more than 300 points and some kind of miracle would have been needed from the Somerset team to have overtaken them. They did have the consolation of winning their county cup and qualify for the Pilkington Cup this coming season. Down in the basement Tredworth and St. Brendans were out on their own although both put up a brave show.

TABLES 1987–88

GLOUCESTER/SOMERSET

	P	W	D	L	F	A	Pts
Avon OB	10	9	0	1	304	90	18
Combe Down	9	8	0	1	178	85	16
Coney Hill	10	7	0	3	193	89	14
Whitehall	10	7	0	3	196	104	14
Cleve	10	4	1	5	146	127	9
Keynsham	10	4	1	5	137	118	9
Midsomer Norton	10	4	0	6	151	171	8
Gordano	10	4	0	6	85	133	8
Minehead	10	3	0	7	94	197	6
Tredworth	9	2	0	7	38	154	4
St Brendans	10	1	0	9	76	330	2

AVONMOUTH OBs

King George Field, Barracks Lane, Avonmouth. Tel: 0272 829093
Founded: 1897
President: A.W. Baker
Chairman: I.W. Bees
Coach: G. Luker
Secretary: G.L. Rees, 403 Pertway, Shirehampton, Bristol. Tel: 0272 822360
Fixtures Secretary: M. Rowlands, 400 Portway, Shirehampton. Tel: 0272 824235
Club captain (1987–88): D. Hone
Club captain (1988–89): R. Thayer
No. of teams: Senior 5. Youth 4. Minis 1
Directions to Ground: Exit M5 junction, take immediate left turn at exit, roundabout then second left (opposite shops), continue for 200 yds
Ground capacity: 2,000
Clubhouse: Double storey brick construction with car park (at ground)
Colours: Black with red hoop (*Change colours*: Cherry & white hoops)
Nickname: Bacon Porkers
Floodlights: No
Membership: £15 per annum
Programme: To be determined
Local newspaper: Bristol Evening Post
League: Gloucester/Somerset
Final position (1987–88): Champions Div 1. Gloucester/Somerset League
Playing record (1987–88): P 30, W 23, D 1, L 6
Competitions won: Bristol & District Combination Cup, 1972–3, 83–84, 86–87, 87–88; Gloucester-Somerset Lg Div 1, 1978–88; Bristol & District 7's, 1985–86; Bristol Evening Post Merit Table Champions 1975–76, 85–85, 85–86, 86–87

COMBE DOWN

Holly's Corner, North Road, Combe Down, Bath. Tel: 832075
Founded: 1896
President: Pat Payton
Chairman: Roger Hillman
Coach: Simon Jones
Secretary: Peter Langley, 7 Ivy Grove, Bath. Tel: 318431
Fixtures Secretary: Wyn Bailey, 3 Keels Hill, Peasedown St. John, Nr. Bath. Tel: 34845
Club captain (1987–88): Simon Jones
Club captain (1988–89): Bob Gay
No. of teams: Senior 3. Youth & Minis 2
Ground capacity: 1,000. Stand, 150
Clubhouse: Bar and lounge with skittle alley
Colours: Black & amber (*Change colours*: Yellow)
Floodlights: Yes
Admission: Collection (Cup games £1)
Membership: £10
Programme: Cup matches only (Editor: John Heal)
Local newspaper: Bath Chronicle
League: GOS/SOM
Final position (1987–88): 2nd
Playing record (1987–88): P 34, W 30, L 4
Competitions won: Somerset Cup, 1988; Bath Combination Cup, 1985, 1986; Bath Sevens (7); Bath Combination Sevens (5); Bruggen (Germany) Sevens, 1988; Unbeaten 1st XV 1931, 1952

CONEY HILL

Tel: 306239
Founded: 1949
President: T. Brinkworth
Chairman: J. Barnett
Coach: W. Hall
Secretary: K. Stokes, 1 Stamway Road, Coney Hill, Glos. Tel: 410899
Fixtures Secretary: B. Dix, Coney Hill. Tel: 306239
Club captain (1987–88): M. Lock
Club captain (1988–89): P. Mansel
No. of teams: Senior 4
Ground capacity: Open
Colours: Amber & black
Floodlights: No
Membership: £8 players. £3 supporters
Local newspaper: Citizen
League: GLOS/SOM
Final position (1987–88): 3rd

WHITEHALL

Speedwell Recreation Ground, Foundry Lane, Speedwell, Bristol. Tel: 0272 659636.
Founded: 1931
President: C. Scott
Chairman: T. Hickey
Coach: M. Tomlin
Secretary: D. Weaver, 27 Nevalan Drive, St George, Bristol BS5 8TT. Tel: 0272 607988.
Fixtures Secretary: A. Ferguson, 8 Stonleigh Road, Knowle, Bristol. Tel: 0272 772898.
Club captain (1987–88): M. Hickey
Club captain (1988–89): M. Hickey
No. of teams: Senior 5. Youth & Minis 3.
Directions to Ground: Off M32 m'way at Fishponds junction, left alongside park, left at roundabout to lights. Turn right, follow signs for Fishponds Trading Estate.
Colours: Myrtle (dark green) and gold. (*Change colours:* Red, gold and black hoops).
Nickname: Whites
Floodlights: No
Membership: £15
Local newspaper: Bristol Evening Post
League: Gloucester/Somerset
Final position (1987–88): 4th
Playing record (1987–88): P 35, W 26, L 9, D 0. F 633, A 327.

CLEVE

Bromley Heath Road, Downend
Founded: 1922
President: E.B. Reakes
Chairman: J. Tasker
Coach: G. Beer
Secretary: R. Pocock, 44 Spring Hill, Kingswood, Bristol. Tel: 611079
Fixtures Secretary: R.T. Reed, 58 Keys Avenue, Horefield, Bristol. Tel: 690258
Club captain (1987–88): T. Doyle
No. of teams: Senior 4. Youth & Minis 4
Directions to Ground: Off M4 to the M32, come off roundabout to Kingswood. The ground is 1 mile on right hand side
Clubhouse: Player bar, dance hall, 4 changing rooms
Colours: Maroon (*Chance colours*: Orange)
Floodlights: Yes
Membership: £15
Local newspaper: Observer
League: GOS/SOM
Final position (1987–88): 7th

KEYNSHAM

The Crown Fields, Bristol Road, Keynsham, Bristol. Tel: 0272 867879
Founded: 1923

President: D.E. Cockbaine
Chairman: R. Palmer
Coach: A.K. Weaden
Secretary: D.G. Courtier, 105 Lays Drive, Keynsham, Bristol BS18 2LD. Tel: 0272 865771
Fixtures Secretary: A.J. Oxenham, 54 Rock Road, Keynsham, Bristol. Tel: 0272 867334
Club captain (1987–88): J. Clark
Club captain (1988–89): J. Clark
No. of teams: Senior 5. Youth & Minis 9
Directions to Ground: From Bristol follow A4 to Keynsham. From Bath follow A4 to Keynsham. Through town centre and follow signs to Bristol
Clubhouse: At above ground address
Colours: Amber/black
Floodlights: No
Local newspaper: Keynsham Weekly Chronicle, Bristol Evening Post
League: Gos/Som
Final position (1987–88): 6th
Playing record (1987–88): P 39, W 21, D 4, L 14
Competitions won: Somerset Cup Winners 1982, Bristol Combination Cup Winners 1982

MIDSOMER NORTON

Norton Down Playing Field, Midsomer Norton. Tel: 0761 412827
Founded: 1936
President: D. Lyons
Chairman: R. Ladd
Coach: P. Helps
Secretary: M. Carter, 16 Redfield Road, Midsomer Norton. Tel: 0761 418745 (H) & 0225 314400 (W)
Fixtures Secretary: N. Carter, 6 Riding Barn Hill, Wick, Bristol
Club captain (1987–88): J. Barnes
Club captain (1988–89): S. Pratt
No. of teams: Senior 6. Youth & Minis 6
Directions to Ground: 1 mile off A367 on B3139
Clubhouse: Licensed clubroom, 6 dressing rooms, 2 shower rooms
Colours: Scarlet (*Change colours*: Cherry & white)
Floodlights: Yes. Training standard
Membership: £18
Local newspaper: Somerset Guardian
League: GLOS/SOM
Playing record (1987–88): P 35, W 15, D 2, L 18, F 584, A 628
Competitions won: Somerset Knockout Cup 1980

GORDANO

Caswell Lane, Portbury, Bristol. Tel: 0272 8813486.
Founded: 1970
Secretary: M.H. Pritchard, 32 Drakes Way, portishead, Bristol BS20 9XA. Tel: 0272 845893 (H). 0272 266091. Extn. 248 (W).
League: Gloucester/Somerset
Final position (1987–88): 8th

MINEHEAD BARBARIANS

Tom Stewart Field, Ellicombe, Minehead. Tel: 0643 5662
Founded: 1946
President: Malcolm Appleton
Chairman: David Bodley
Coach: James Waterman
Secretary: Malcolm Parslow, Ladbrook, The Holloway, Minehead TA24 5PB. Tel: 0643 2101 (H) & 0272 876726 (W)
Fixtures Secretary: Mike Turner, 4 Wristland Road, Watchet TA4. Tel: 0984 31170
Club captain (1987–88): John Baker
Club captain (1988–89): Tim Campbell
No. of teams: Senior 3. Youth & Minis 6
Directions to Ground: Beside A39, ½ mile before Minehead from Williton turn off at roundabout signed Ellicombe
Clubhouse: Modern building, changing rooms, showers, 2 bars, hall, function room
Colours: Black & white hoops (*Change colours*: Red or Blue)
Floodlights: No
Local newspaper: West Somerset Free Press, Williton
League: GLOS/SOM
Final position (1987–88): 9th
Playing record (1987–88): P 34, W 18, D 2, L 14

TREDWORTH

The Lannett, King Edwards Avenue, Gloucester.
Founded: 1904
Secretary: R.E. Bowhett, Kingston House, 5 Landsown road, Gloucester GL1 3IW. Tel: 0452 593893.
Fixtures Secretary: 1904
League: Gloucester/Somerset
Final position (1987–88): 10th

ST. BRENDANS OLD BOYS

Northway, Filton, Bristol. Tel: Bristol 692793
Founded: 1929
President: M. Titcomb
Chairman: M. Witts
Coaches: J. Knight/F. Piekarski
Secretary: J. Franklin, 49 Farm Road, Milton, Weston-Super-Mare, Avon BS22 8BE. Tel: Weston-Super-Mare 27926
Fixtures Secretary: M. Mohan, 76 Upper Cranbrook Road, Bristol BS6 7UP. Tel: Bristol 420694
Club captain (1987–88): G. Davies
Club captain (1988–89): G. Davies
No. of teams: Senior 4. Youth & Minis 7
Directions to Ground: Off A38 south of junction 17 with M5
Clubhouse: 200 capacity
Colours: Maroon/old gold hoops (*Change colours*: Maroon)
Nickname: Saints
Floodlights: No
Membership: Playing/weekly/associate/donation
Local newspaper: Bristol Evening Post/Western Daily Press
League: GLOS/SOM
Final position (1987–88): Last (relegated)
Playing record (1987–88): P 31, W 5, D 2, L 23, F 180, A 360

DEVON/CORNWALL LEAGUE

A CLOSE 'three-horse-race' ended with Crediton taking the honours on points difference from Exmouth with Cornwall's Penryn a point further behind. The bottom clubs were Newton Abbot, who lost all their ten games, and St. Austell, who played bravely but were not quite good enough.

TABLES 1987–88

DEVON/CORNWALL

	P	W	D	L	F	A	Pts
Crediton	10	9	0	1	232	65	18
Exmouth	10	9	0	1	187	64	18
Penryn	10	8	1	1	191	67	17
Penzance Newlyn	10	7	1	3	166	111	13
Falmouth	10	6	0	4	110	140	12
Paignton	10	5	0	5	156	157	10
Teignmouth	10	4	0	6	112	176	8
Bideford	10	3	0	7	160	153	6
Hayle	10	2	1	7	107	157	5
St Austell	10	1	1	8	69	193	3
Newton Abbott	10	0	0	10	31	238	0

DEVON/CORNWALL

CREDITON

Blagdon, Exhibition Road. Tel: 03632 2784
Founded: 1878
President: J.C. Hayes
Chairman: H.W. Wadsworth
Coach: T. Crocker
Secretary: P.H. Gibbings, Enfield House, Threshers, Crediton
Fixtures Secretary: Capt. K.S. Pitt, RN (Retd), Tannery Farm, Bow. Tel: 03633 230
Club captain (1987–88): J.W. May
Club captain (1988–89): M.J. Leyman
No. of teams: Senior 3. Youth & Minis 5
Directions to Ground: M5, A377 Exeter–Crediton. Ground on A3072 (Crediton–Tiverton Road)
Ground capacity: 1,200. Stand, 250
Clubhouse: Two storey, changing room, showers (lower floor); bar & lounge/diner (upper)
Colours: Black & amber. (*Change colours*: Amber)
Nickname: Kirton
Floodlights: No
Admission: 50p–£1
Membership: £8
Programme: Club Advertiser 50p (Editor: J.C. Hayes)
Local newspaper: Express & Echo, Western Morning News
League: Western Counties
Final position (1987–88): Top of Cornwall & Devon League
Playing record (1987–88): W 25, D 0, L 10, F 614, A 307
Competitions won: Devon Senior Cup 1897, Devon Junior Cup 1947, Havill Plate 1985, Cornwall & Devon League 1987–88

EXMOUTH

Imperial Recreation Ground, Royal Avenue, Exmouth, Devon. Tel: 0395 263665.
Founded: 1873
Secretary: B.Cornall, 40 Lawn Road, Exmouth EX8 1QJ. Tel: 03952 75332 (H). 03952 72344 (W).
League: Devon/Cornwall
Final position (1987–88): 2nd
Playing record (1987–88): P 37, W 24, L 13. F 824, A 403.

PENRYN

The Memorial Ground, Kernick Road, Penryn, Cornwall
Founded: 1872
President: C. Vanstone
Chairman: Dr D. Shier
Coach: D. Thomas
Secretary: Mrs S.A. Head, 8a Lambs Lane, Falmouth, Cornwall. Tel: 0326 319811.
Fixtures Secretary: K. Loft, 6 Belle Vue, Penryn, Cornwall. Tel: 0326 72862.
Club captain (1987–88): M. Smith
Club captain (1988–89): TBA
No. of teams: Senior 2. Youth & Minis 8.
Directions to Ground: From Truro keep to Falmouth signs, at Treluswell turn off for Penryn. (A39) up through town towards industrial estate. Well sign posted.
Ground capacity: 10,000. Stand, 400.
Clubhouse: 2 bars plus changing rooms
Colours: Red, black. (*Change colours:* Black).
Nickname: The Borough
Floodlights: No
Admission: 80p
Membership: VP £10, Ordinary £3.50, OAP £2
Programme: 20p. (Editor: Club Secretary)
Local newspaper: Falmouth Packet, West Briton & Leader
League: Devon/Cornwall
Final position (1987–88): Joint 2nd
Playing record (1987–88): P 38, W 27, D 1, L 10. F 668, A 309.
Competitions won: Plate Cup in Cornwal County 7's.

PENZANCE & NEWLYN

Alexandra Road, Penzance, Cornwall. Tel: 0736 64227
Founded: 1945
President: Alvin Williams

Chairman: Cecil Dunn
Coach: Paul Greaves
Secretary: Phil Western, "Kimberley", 9 Fore Street, Madron, Penzance, Cornwall TR20 8SL. Tel: 0736 61602
Fixtures Secretary: Keith Stirling, 4 Leckinnick Terrace, Penzance. Tel: 0736 67796
Club captain (1987–88): Gary Dawe
Club captain (1988–89): Dave Elliott
No. of teams: Senior 2. Youth & Minis 7
Directions to Ground: Take Harbour Road on entering Penzance, go along Promenade and turn right at roundabout by Beachfield Hotel
Ground capacity: 6,000. Stand, 700
Clubhouse: Open every evening & lunchtime, weekends and bank holidays
Colours: Black/red/white (*Change colours*: Black)
Nickname: The Pirates
Floodlights: Yes
Admission: 70p
Membership: £12 (including social membership)
Programme: 10p (Editor: Phil Westren)
Local newspaper: The Cornishman
League: Devon & Cornwall
Final position (1987–88): 4th
Playing record (1987–88): P 39, W 20, D 2, L 17
Competitions won: Cornwall Knockout Cup 1976

FALMOUTH

Dracaena Avenue. Tel. 31130/316924
Founded: 1873
President: B.F. Smales
Chairman: P. Tierney
Coach: P. Smith
Secretary: E. Nicholls, 4 Elm Grove Cottages, Arwenack Avenue, Falmouth. Tel: 314618
Fixtures Secretary: D. Chatterton, 5 Treworder Road, Truro, Cornwall. Tel: 72970
Club captain (1987–88): S.C. Wills
Club captain (1988–89): N. Blight
No. of teams: Senior 2. Colt 1 & Mini Rugby
Directions to Ground: Main road into Falmouth, along Dracaena Avenue. Ground at end of avenue
Ground capacity: 8,000-10,000. Stand, 600
Clubhouse: Two bars, general facilities
Colours: Black & white (*Change colours*: Red & navy blue)
Floodlights: No
Admission: 80p
Membership: £7
Local newspaper: Falmouth Packet
League: Devon & Cornwall
Final position (1987–88): 5th
Playing record (1987–88): P 40, W 11, D 1, L 28, F 318, A 955

PAIGNTON

Queens Park, Paignton. Tel: 0803 557715
Founded: 1873
President: T. Ward
Chairman: M. Bagge
Coaches: N. Thomas/N. Harries
Secretary: K.A.P. Ferris, 128 Torquay Road, Paignton. Tel: 0803 526532
Fixtures Secretary: G. Platt, 72 Osney Crescent, Paignton. Tel: 521646
Club captain (1987–88): A. Baker
Club captain (1988–89): A. Baker
No. of teams: Senior 2. Youth & Minis 4
Directions to Ground: Town centre, Paignton
Ground capacity: 3,000. Stand, 50
Clubhouse: Under stand, bar, lounge
Colours: Red/white (*Change colours*: Blue)
Nickname: Cherries
Floodlights: Yes
Admission: £1 and 50p
Membership: £10
Programme: 10p (Editor: Chairman)
Local newspaper: Herald Express
League: Devon & Cornwall
Final position (1987–88): 6th
Playing record (1987–88): P 35, W 10, L 25, F 384, A 576

TEIGNMOUTH

Lower Bitton Sportsground, Bitton Park Road, Teignmouth. Tel: 06267 4714
Founded: 1874
President: J.E. Rowland
Chairman: A.S. Norsworthy
Coach: D. Attwell
Secretary: Mrs M.O. Powell, Leyden, 6 Fourth Avenue, Teignmouth, Devon TQ14 9DR. Tel: 06267 4950
Fixtures Secretary: R. Loveridge, 59 Second Avenue, Teignmouth. Tel: 06267 5891
Club captain (1987–88): Graham Pattison
No. of teams: Senior 3 Youth & Minis 2
Directions to Ground: Coming from Exeter Road, go past park in Bitton Road, turn sharp left at Newsmag, just before Talbot Pub
Ground capacity: approx. 500. Stand, approx 100
Clubhouse: Bar opens daily at 7.30pm. Weekends & lunchtimes as well.
Colours: Red, white and black hoops (*Change colours*: Black shirts, white shorts)
Nickname: Teigns
Floodlights: Yes
Admission: 50p
Membership: To be reviewed at AGM
Programme: 50p (Editor: Committee)
Local newspaper: Teignmouth News & Teignmouth Post
League: Devon & Cornwall
Final position (1987–88): 7th
Playing record (1987–88): P 36, W 13, D 0, L 23, F 363, A 724
Competitions won: Havill Plate Shield 1986-87

BIDEFORD

King George's Field, Bideford, Devon. Tel: 02372 74049
Founded: 1926
President: G. Woolf
Chairman: H. Jones
Coach: R. Harris
Secretary: B.A. Ridd, Higher Benton, Bratton Fleming, Devon. Tel: Brayford 298
Fixtures Secretary: R. Ovenell, Meadow Farm, Langtree, Devon. Tel: Langtree 232
Club captain (1987–88): R. Scambler
Club captain (1988–89): N. Giddy
No. of teams: Senior 3. Youth & Minis 4
Directions to Ground: Right over Bideford Old Bridge, right again, follow bank past Kingsley Statue
Ground capacity: 2,000. Stand, 250
Clubhouse: Lounge, members' bars, 3 changing rooms
Colours: Red & white hoops (*Change colours*: Blue & white hoops or White)
Nickname: Biddy
Floodlights: Yes
Admission: 50p
Membership: £15
Programme: Free. Adverts and teams. (Editors: Club Chairman & Secretary)
Local newspaper: North Devon Journal
League: Cornwall & Devon
Final position (1987–88): 8th
Playing record (1987–88): P 31, W 10, L 21, F 449, A 560

HAYLE

Memorial Park, Hayle, Cornwall. Tel: 0736 753320
Founded: 1877
President: Lt. Cdr. R. Coombe
Chairman: M. Trathen
Coach: T.B.A.
Secretary: P.M. Yendell, Fairview Cottage, Goldsithney, Nr. Penzance. Tel: 0736 710955
Fixtures Secretary: M. Doney, 2 Bohelland Way, Penryn, Cornwall. Tel: 0326 77370
Club captain (1987–88): F. Partridge
Club captain (1988–89): B. Gibson
No. of teams: Senior 2. Youth & Minis 1
Directions to Ground: Eastern side of Hayle – adjoining A30
Ground capacity: 1,000+
Clubhouse: Lounge bar, large functions bar
Colours: Green/black/white
Nickname: Lions
Floodlights: Yes
Admission: 80p
Membership: Playing £10. Non-playing £3
Programme: Included in admission
Local newspaper: Cornishman
League: Devon & Cornwall
Final position (1987–88): 9th
Playing record (1987–88): P 32, W 7, D 2, L 23, F 303, A 675

ST. AUSTELL

Tregorrick Lane, St. Austell (new ground – telephone and clubhouse to be installed soon)
Founded: July 1963
President: Ivor Price
Chairman: Chris Owen
Coach: To be appointed
Secretary: Peter Bishop, 57 Stannary Road, Stenalees, St. Austell. Tel: 851 036
Fixtures Secretary: Ms Julie Old, 66 Polgrean Place, St. Blazey. Tel: Par 7073
Club captain (1987–88): Rob Daniels
Club captain (1988–89): Rob Daniels
No. of teams: Senior 2. Youth & Minis 1
Directions to Ground: Main road (A390) Plymouth to Truro, by-pass to St. Austell, turn left onto Porthpean Road, then second right into Tregorrick Lane
Stand capacity: 400
Clubhouse: 2 bars, dining room, snooker, pool, committee, kitchen, 2 bedroomed steward's flat, sportshall, sauna & weight training, etc
Colours: Red & white 4″ hoops (*Change colours*: Dark & light blue 4″ hoops)
Nickname: Saints
Floodlights: Yes to two pitches
Membership: £10 players
Local newspaper: Cornish Guardian & Independent
League: Devon & Cornwall
Final position (1987–88): 10th (relegated)
Playing record (1987–88): P 27, W 3, D 1, L 23, F 168, A 658

NEWTON ABBOT

"Rackerhayes" Kingsteignton Road, Newton Abbot. Tel: 0626 54150
Founded: 1873
President: W.J.C. Watts
Chairman: R.S. Burgin
Coach: C. Pomeroy
Secretary: Roy Baker, 44 The Avenue, Newton Abbot. Tel: 0626 61390
Fixtures Secretary: David Aggett, 6 Norman Close, Highweek, Newton Abbot. Tel: 0626 52427
Club captain (1987–88): Mark Beavis
Club captain (1988–89): Mark Beavis
No. of teams: Senior 3. Youth & Minis 5
Directions to Ground: From Exeter A38 to Newton Abbot. Approx 20 mins. Ground immediately opposite Newton Abbot Racecourse
Ground capacity: 1,500. Stand, 150
Clubhouse: Large main hall and bar, lounge bar, kitchan and dining room
Colours: White jersey & shorts/black stockings (*Change colours*: Amber/maroon/black hoops)
Nickname: All Whites
Floodlights: No
Admission: £1
Membership: £16 player. £5 non-player
Local newspaper: Mid-Devon Advertiser and Torbay Herald & Express
League: Devon
Final position (1987–88): Bottom of Cornwall/Devon
Playing record (1987–88): P 39, W 3, D 1, L 35, F 267, A 719
Competitions won: Devon Senior Cup 1923, 1924, 1927

GLOUCESTERSHIRE LEAGUES

GLOUCESTERSHIRE has always been a strong county in rugby terms and they managed to produce four leagues consisting of 44 clubs. Only Old Bristolians in the third league had a perfect record and their 10 victories were hard won as they only scored 157 points and conceded 60.

Spartans in winning the top league lost only one match and scored 275 points and North Bristol in winning the second section won all but one game, drawing the other, but they had to work hard for their victories.

The fourth league was also a very hard fought affair with Smiths edging out Old Elizabethans by a single point. A draw in the one case and extra defeat for the old boys side made all the difference, but both will play in better company next season.

Only Bristol Saracens in the top league lost all their games, which is a testimony to the even standards in the competition.

TABLES 1987–88

GLOUCESTERSHIRE 1

	P	W	D	L	F	A	Pts
Spartans	10	9	0	1	275	61	18
Dings Crusad	10	9	0	1	153	65	18
Drybrook	10	6	0	4	181	95	12
Longlevens	10	6	0	4	124	133	12
O Patesians	10	5	1	4	152	112	11
O Colstonian	10	5	1	4	75	112	11
St Mary's OB	10	4	1	5	92	112	9
Widden	10	4	1	5	92	112	9
Bream	10	2	1	7	109	154	5
Cheltenham N	10	2	0	8	71	146	4
Bristol Sara	**10**	**0**	**0**	**10**	**41**	**273**	**0**

GLOUCESTERSHIRE 2

	P	W	D	L	F	A	Pts
N Bristol	10	9	1	0	148	54	19
Saintbridge	10	7	2	1	159	69	16
Ashley Down	10	6	2	2	189	93	14
Chelt Sara	10	6	1	3	120	79	13
Cotham Park	10	5	1	4	120	124	11
O Cryptians	10	4	1	5	95	160	9
Barton Hill	10	4	0	6	87	102	8
Chelt'ham CS	10	3	1	6	87	123	7
Brockworth	10	3	0	7	147	130	6
Dursley	10	3	0	7	90	180	6
Cainscross	10	0	1	9	42	170	1

GLOUCESTERSHIRE 3

	P	W	D	L	F	A	Pts
O Bristolian	10	10	0	0	157	60	20
Gloster OB	10	9	0	1	352	43	18
Chipping Sod	10	8	0	2	173	91	16
Frampton Cot	10	6	0	4	176	115	12
Thornbury	10	4	1	5	127	131	9
Kingswood	10	4	0	6	73	161	8
Tewsbury	10	3	0	7	94	168	6
Chosen Hill	10	3	0	7	73	188	6
Painswick	10	3	0	7	101	226	6
Gloster CS	10	2	1	7	79	154	5
Bishopston	10	2	0	8	99	167	4

GLOUCESTERSHIRE 4

	P	W	D	L	F	A	Pts
Smiths	10	8	1	1	125	82	17
O Elizabeth	10	8	0	2	136	63	16
Bristol Tels	10	7	0	3	162	66	14
Broad Plain	10	6	1	3	121	76	13
All Blues	10	6	1	3	133	94	13
Aretians	10	6	0	4	88	76	12
BAC	10	5	0	5	138	99	10
Hucclecote	10	4	0	6	99	78	8
Newent	10	2	1	7	73	137	5
O Cothamians	10	0	1	9	46	160	1
Minchin'ton	10	0	1	9	36	226	1

GLOUCESTERSHIRE 1

SPARTANS

St. Catherines Meadow, Cattle Market Complex, St. Oswald Road, Gloucester. Tel: 410552
Founded: 1927
President: Colin Teague
Chairman: David Fowke
Coach: Bobby Fowke
Secretary: S. Martin, 130 Oxford Road, Gloucester. Tel: 26340
Fixtures Secretary: Steven Lodge, 61 Armscroft Road, Gloucester. Tel: 305515
Club captain (1987–88): Gary Brown
Club captain (1988–89): Phillip Brown
No. of teams: Senior 4. Youth 2. Minis 1
Directions to Ground: Ask for Cattle Market, use road between Cattle Market & Public House, all the way down, then turn left
Clubhouse: Large dance hall & bar, lounge, 4 dressing rooms, showers and bath
Colours: Red shirts, black shorts. (*Change colours*: Green)
Nickname: Sparts
Floodlights: No
Membership: £10
Local newspaper: Citizen
League: GLOS1
Final position (1987–88): 1st (promoted)
Playing record (1987–88): P 35, W 30, L 0, F 1051, A 251
Competitions won: Div. 1 Gloucester County League

DINGS CRUSADERS

Landseer Avenue, Lockleaze, Bristol. Tel: 0272 691367
Founded: 1897
President: Graham Backep
Chairman: Floyd Waters
Coach: Bob Beynon
Secretary: Graham Troote, 50 Kipling Road, Filton, Bristol BS7 0QR. Tel: 0272 694141
Fixtures Secretary: Terry Webb, 50 Monks Park Avenue, Horfield, BS7 0UH. Tel: 0272 692749
Club captain (1987–88): Stephen Lloyd
Club captain (1988–89): Stephen Lloyd
No. of teams: Senior 5. Youth & Minis 3–4
Directions to Ground: M32, Filton, Filton Avenue, Lockleaze, Landseer Avenue
Stand capacity: 25
Clubhouse: Bar, food, gym
Colours: Royal blue & black
Floodlights: Yes
Membership: £10
Local newspaper: Evening Post
League: GLOS1
Final position (1987–88): 2nd
Playing record (1987–88): P 37, W 32, D 1, L 4, F 658, A 261

DRYBROOK

The Mannings Ground, High Street, Drybrook, Glos. Tel: Dean (0594) 542595
Founded: 1893
President: Rev. C. Davies
Chairman: A.J. Tate
Coach: P. Jones
Secretary: C.J. Hale, The Cross, Drybrook, Glos. Tel: Dean 543138
Fixtures Secretary: A.P. Mason, 29 Carisbrook Road, Mitcheldean, Glos. Tel: Dean 543948
Club captain (1987–88): C. Tingle
Club captain (1988–89): A. Miles
No. of teams: Senior 4. Youth & Minis 4
Directions to Ground: A40 from Gloucester, turn right to Huntley, then to Mitcheldean, then to Drybrook
Colours: Green with one black hoop. (*Change colours*: Black and white hoops)
Floodlights: No
Membership: £3.50 per annum
Local newspaper: Dean Forest Mercury
League: GLOS1
Final position (1987–88): 3rd
Playing record (1987–88): P 33, W 22, D 1, L 10, F 806, A 249

LONGLEVENS

Clubhouse, Longford Lane, Longlevens, Glos. Tel: 0452 306880
Founded: 1954
President: J.E. Humphris
Chairman: K.D. Hending
Secretary: C.F. Dunford, 66 Estcourt Road, Glos. Tel: 0452 22795 (H) & 0452 411666 (W)
Fixtures Secretary: M.J. Dunford, 66 Estcourt Road, Glos. Tel: 0452 22795
Club captain (1987–88): C. Jones
Club captain (1988–89): J. Norman
No. of teams: Senior 4. Youth & Minis 5. Colts 1
Colours: Red (*Change colours*: Blue)
Nickname: Levens
Floodlights: Yes. For training only
Membership: £5
Local newspaper: The Citizen & Gloucester Journal
League: GLOS1
Final position (1987–88): Equal 3rd
Competitions won: NGC Senior Cup 1961; NGC Junior Cup on 3 occasions, Gloucestershire Colts Cup 1986/87 & 1987/88, Under 17 County Cup on 3 occasions & Under 15 County Cup on 3 occasions

OLD PATESIANS

Everest Road, Leckhampton, Cheltenham. Tel: 0242 524633
Founded: 1913
President: Rev. D.G. Powell
Chairman: D. Harper
Coach: To be appointed
Secretary: M.J. Richards, 8 The Lawns, Gotherington, Cheltenham. Tel: 0242 672758
Fixtures Secretary: G. Hughes-Jones, "Hillside", Undercliff Avenue, Leckhampton, Cheltenham. Tel: 0242 34623
Club captain (1987–88): D. Kingscott
Club captain (1988–89): P. Morris
No. of teams: Senior 5. Youth & Minis 3
Directions to Ground: One mile off A40 along Old Bath Road, South Cheltenham.
Clubhouse: Salubrious
Colours: Magenta/white/navy
Nickname: Old Pats
Floodlights: No
Admission: You must be joking!
Membership: £12
Local newspaper: Gloucestershire Echo
League: GLOS1
Final position (1987–88): 5th, Div. 1
Playing record (1987–88): P 33, W 20, D 2, L 11
Competitions won: Cheltenham & District 7s

OLD COLSTONIANS

New Road, Stoke, Gifford, Bristol BS12 6QW. Tel: 0272 690009.
Founded: 1902
Chairman: M. Humphries
Coach: S. Lewis
Secretary: D. Muir, 1 Samian Way, Stoke Gifford, Bristol BS12 6UQ. Tel: 0272 791688.
Fixtures Secretary: I. Parks, 4 Woodmans Vale, Chipping Sodbury, Bristol BS12 6UQ. Tel: 0454 311080.
Club captain (1987–88): S. Pomphrey
Club captain (1988–89): S. Pomphrey
No. of teams: Senior 4. Youth & Minis 3.
Directions to Ground: (From M3) follow signs to Parkway Station. Ground is on left side of new road next to Filton High School.
Colours: Blue, black and old gold hoops.
Floodlights: No
Membership: £15
Local newspaper: Western Daily Press/Bristol Evening Post
League: Gloucester 1
Final position (1987–88): 6th
Playing record (1987–88): P 32, W 16, L 14, D 2. F 420, A 431.
Competitions won: Chipping Sodbury Floodlit Cup 1984/5. Imperial Sevens 1980/1.

ST MARY'S OLD BOYS

Woodlands Lane, Almondsbury, Bristol. Tel: 0454 612349.
Founded: 1898
Secretary: Mrs L. Collins, 46B Asheley Road, Bristol B56 5NT. Tel: 0272 49879.
League: Gloucestershire 1
Final position (1987–88): 7th

WIDDEN OLD BOYS

Memorial Ground, Tuffley Avenue, Gloucester. Tel: 0452 34080.
Founded: 1922
Secretary: A. Lane, 13 tuffley Avenue, Gloucester GL1 5LS. Tel: 9452 504226.
League: Gloucestershire 1
Final position (1987–88): 8th

BREAM

High Street, Bream, Near Lydney, Gloucestershire. Tel: 0594 562320.
Founded: 1878
Secretary: J. Grail, 31 Highbury Road, Bream, Near Lydney, Gloucestershire GL15 6EF. Tel: Dean 562737 (H). dean 562320 (W).
League: Gloucestershire 1
Final position (1987–88): 9th

CHELTENHAM NORTH

Stoke Road, Bishops Cleeve. Tel: 0242 675968
Founded: 1905
President: P.K. Wheatley
Chairman: A. Rodgers
Coach: L. Dick
Secretary: A.D. Page, 22 Fairfield Avenue, Leckhamtpon, Cheltenham. Tel: 0242 515633
Fixtures Secretary: R.A. Jones, 8 Brookvale Drive, Charlton Kings, Cheltenham
Club captain (1987–88): S. Gourlay
Club captain (1988–89): S. Gourlay
No. of teams: Senior 4
Directions to Ground: Take A435 out of Cheltenham to Bishops Cleeve and take road to Stoke Orchard, on right 1 mile
Ground capacity: 500
Clubhouse: Use of social club in Cheltenham, 377 High Street
Colours: Red & black. (*Change colours*: Black or yellow)
Floodlights: Semi training purposes (need cash for more)
Membership: £10
Local newspaper: Gloucestershire Echo
League: GLOS1
Final position (1987–88): Bottom but one, Div. 1
Playing record (1987–88): P 32, W 12, D 4, L 16
Competitions won: Cheltenham Senior & Junior Combination Cup Final Winners

BRISTOL SARACENS

Bakewell Memorial Ground, Station Road, Henbury, Bristol. Tel: 0272 500037.
Founded: 1896
Secretary: A.S. Swash, 71 Falcondale Road, Westbury on Tryan, Bristol. Tel: 0272 629047 (H). 0272 506666 (W).
League: Gloucestershire 1
Final position (1987–88): 11th (relegated)

GLOUCESTERSHIRE 2

NORTH BRISTOL

Oaklands, Almondsbury, Bristol. Tel: 0454 612740
Founded: 1933
President: C.H. Hill
Chairman: K. Rendell
Coach: D. Martin
Secretary: C.H. Hill, 7 Keinton Walk, Henbury, Bristol BS10 7EE. Tel: 0272 508123 (H)
Fixtures Secretary: E. Payne, 3 Welland Road, Keynsham, Bristol. Tel: 0272 864432
Club captain (1987–88): Steve Arthur
Club captain (1988–89): John Harris
No. of teams: Senior 5. Youth 2
Directions to Ground: Junction 16 on M5
Clubhouse: Brick building, changing 6 teams, club room, lounge, treatment room. Car park for 100 cars
Colours: Red & light blue hoops. (*Change colours*: Light green)
Nickname: North
Floodlights: Yes. Two pitches
Membership: £10 plus £2 per game
Local newspaper: Bristol Evening Post & Gloucestershire Gazette
League: GOS2
Final position (1987–88): 1st
Playing record (1987–88): P 37, W 22, L 12, D 3
Competitions won: League Gloucestershire Div. 2 Chipping Sodbury Floodlit Competition

SAINTBRIDGE

Saintbridge Sports Centre, Painswick Road, Gloucester, Tel: Glos 303768.
Founded: 1937
President: J. Smith
Chairman: M. Slatter
Coach: A. Locke
Secretary: S. Fritchley, 7 Saintbridge Close, Gloucester GL4 9QN. Tel: Glos 22690.
Fixtures Secretary: S. Slatter, 40 Eagle Way, Heron Park, Gloucester. Tel: Glos 411142.
Club captain (1987–88): P. Jordan
Club captain (1988–89): J. Roberts
No. of teams: Senior 4. Youth & Minis 6.
Directions to Ground: At Saintbridge Sports Centre
Clubhouse: Changing rooms, 3 bars.
Colours: Navy blue, royal blue, gold rings.
Floodlights: No
Membership: £10
Local newspaper: Citizen
League: Gloucestershire 2
Final position (1987–88): 2nd (promoted)
Playing record (1987–88): P 33, W 22, L 14, D 2.

ASHLEYDOWN OLD BOYS

121 Cheltenham Road, Bristol. Tel: 0272 40887.
Founded: 1921
Secretary: J.D. Bennett, 307 Ashley Down Road, Bristol BS7 9BG. Tel: 0272 43734 (H). 0272 797366 (W).
League: Gloucestershire 2
Final position (1987–88): 3rd

CHELTENHAM SARACENS

Swindon Road, Cheltenham, Glos.
Founded: 1975
Chairman: H. Attwood

Gloucestershire 2

Coach: K. Holland
Secretary: C. Wheeler, c/o Bredon School, Pull Court, Bushley, nr. Tewksbury, Glos. Tel: 0684 294119 (H), 0684 293156 (W).
Fixtures Secretary: W.R. Dickenson, Flat 8, Scoriton House, 16 Pitville Crescent, Cheltenham, Glos. Tel: 0242 572178.
Club captain (1987–88): A. Parker
Club captain (1988–89): D. Walsh
No. of teams: Senior 4. Youth & Minis 1.
Clubhouse: Not at ground, in town centre
Colours: Blue with gold circlet.
Nickname: Saras
Floodlights: No
Membership: £7
Local newspaper: Glos Echo
League: Gloucestershire 2
Final position (1987–88): 4th

COTHAM PARK

Beggar Book Lane, Failand, Bristol.
Founded: 1901
Secretary: J. Crocker, Grove House, Tennessee Grove, Henleaze, Bristol. Tel: 0272 424885 (H). 0272 292227 (W).
League: Gloucestershire 2
Final position (1987–88): 5th

OLD CRYPTIANS

Memorial Ground, Gloucester. Tel: 0452 20052.
Founded: 1925
Secretary: S.A.F. robinson, 32 Denham Close, Tuffley, Gloucester. Tel: 0452 424849 (H). 0451 21751 (W).
League: Gloucestershire 2
Final position (1987–88): 6th

BARTON HILL

Duncombe Lane, Speedwell, Bristol. Tel: 0272
Founded: 1908
President: Jim Pruett
Chairman: Don Blackmore
Secretary: Andy Coles, 169 Wick Road, Brislington, Bristol
Fixtures Secretary: Paul Uppington, 18 Eaton Close, Fishponds, Bristol. Tel: 650340
Club captain (1987–88): Alan Knowlson
Club captain (1988–89): Andy (Cosy) Powell
No. of teams: Senior 4. Youth & Minis 3. Colts 1
Directions to Ground: Follow signs for Fishponds when leaving M32
Colours: White with cherry band
Nickname: The Barts
Floodlights: No
Membership: £10
Local newspaper: Bristol Evening Post
League: GLOS2
Final position (1987–88): 4th

CHELTENHAM CIVIL SERVICE

Civil Service Sports Ground, Tewkesbury Road, Cheltenham, Glos. Tel: 0242 680424
Founded: 1947
President: B.W. Collins
Chairman: D. Townsend
Coach: P. Beard
Secretary: B.F. Didlick, 66A Clarence Street, Cheltenham. Tel: 0242 221491, Ext 2479 (W)
Fixtures Secretary: M.J. Wallace, 96 Beeches Road, Charlton King, Cheltenham. Tel: 0242 528715 (H)
Club captain (1987–88): N. Evans
Club captain (1988–89): N. Evans
No. of teams: Senior 4. Youth & Minis 1
Directions to Ground: About 2 miles from centre of Cheltenham on main Cheltenham to Tewkesbury Road (A4019)
Clubhouse: Shared clubhouse at Civil Service Sports Ground
Colours: Navy blue. (*Change colours*: Red)
Floodlights: No
Membership: £5
Local newspaper: Gloucestershire Echo
League: GLOS2
Final position (1987–88): 8th
Playing record (1987–88): P 34, W 15, L 17, F 523, A 426
Competitions won: Cheltenham Combination Cup 1973, 1976, 1982; Cheltenham Combination Sevens 1967, 1973

BROCKWORTH

Mill Lane, Brockworth, Gloucester
Founded: 1975
President: B. Mitchell
Chairman: S. Hickey
Coach: B. Isom
Secretary: Mrs J. Farrington, 6 Westfield Avenue, Brockworth, Gloucester. Tel: Glos 500500 (daytime only)
Fixtures Secretary: J. Ford, Pomona, St. Georges Road, Brockworth, Gloucester
Club captain (1987–88): P. Holden
Club captain (1988–89): G. Wetson
No. of teams: Senior 3. Youth & Minis 1
Directions to Ground: Turn left at lights by Flying Machine Pub (coming from Glos), straight over roundabout, first left, second left (at top of hill)
Clubhouse: Large function room and bar, changing rooms, shower
Colours: Black with white V. (*Change colours*: Black & white hoops)
Nickname: The Badgers
Floodlights: No
Membership: £12
Local newspaper: The Citizen
League: GLOS2
Final position (1987–88): 9th

DURSLEY

Stinchcombe Stragglers, Dursley. Tel: 3693
Founded: 1953
President: Jack Heaven
Chairman: Geof Reynolds
Coach: Stuart Freeman
Secretary: John Darlaston, Windrush, Field Lane, Dursley, Glos GU1 6JF. Tel: 0453 3135
Fixtures Secretary: Dave Weeks, Dursley. Tel: 0453 89850
Club captain (1987–88): Rob Phillips
Club captain (1988–89): Kevin Tudor
No. of teams: Senior 3. Youth & Minis 1
Directions to Ground: From Dursley, direction Wotton-U-Edge to Stinchcombe
Clubhouse: Bar, 4 changing rooms, club room, kitchen
Colours: Maroon & amber. (*Change colours*: Navy blue or Yellow)
Floodlights: Only training
Membership: £15
Local newspaper: Dursley Gazette
League: GLOS3
Final position (1987–88): 10th
Playing record (1987–88): P 35, W 12, D 3, L 20, F 415, A 673

CAINSCROSS

Victory Park, Cainscross, Stroud, Gloucestershire. Tel: 04536 6707.
Founded: 1894
Secretary: S. Mynett, 118 Orchard Road. Ebley, Stroud, Gloucestershire GL5 4UA. Tel: 045382 2566 (H).
League: Gloucestershire 2
Final position (1987–88): 11th

GLOUCESTERSHIRE 3

OLD BRISTOLIANS

Memorial Playing Field, Failand, Bristol. Tel: 0272 392137
Founded: 1925
President: Garth Morris
Chairman: Mac Coveney
Coach: Garth Morris
Secretary: Nick Noble, 7 North Street, Nailsea, Bristol. Tel: 0272 856070
Fixtures Secretary: Richard Potterton, 35 Concorde Drive, Westbury-on-Trym, Bristol. Tel: 505104
Club captain (1987–88): Ray Jones
Club captain (1988–89): Ray Jones
No. of teams: Senior 4. Youth 1
Directions to Ground: Off Beggar Bush Lane near Redwood Lodge Country Club
Clubhouse: One bar, 6 changing rooms, 2 rugby pitches & 3 hockey, 2 cricket pitches in summer
Colours: Maroon/amber/green hoops (*Change colours*: Maroon)
Nickname: OBs
Floodlights: On training pitch only
Membership: £25
Local newspaper: Bristol Evening Post
League: GLOS3
Final position (1987–88): Winners of GOS3 Div
Playing record (1987–88): P 33, W 15, D 1, L 17
Competitions won: Winners of Gloucester Div. 3 (unbeaten in League)

GLOUCESTER OLD BOYS

Horton Road, Gloucester. Tel: 0452 302390
Founded: 1904
President: G.A. Roberts
Chairman: A. Sinclair
Secretary: Norman P. Partridge, 17 Armscroft Place, Barnwood, Gloucester
Fixtures Secretary: R. Mansell, 24 Kingsholm Square, Gloucester. Tel: 0452 303055
Club captain (1987–88): P. Wickenden
Club captain (1988–89): R. Ellis
No. of teams: Senior 3
Directions to Ground: From centre of Gloucester out on London Road turn right into Horton Road (approx 2 miles)
Clubhouse: 2 bars, 3 changing rooms
Colours: Claret/gold/navy hoops
Nickname: Bs
Floodlights: No
Membership: Players £10 per annum, £2 per match
Local newspaper: Citizen
League: GOS3
Final position (1987–88): 2nd

CHIPPING SODBURY

The Ridings, Chipping Sodbury. Tel: 312852
Founded: 1952
President: H. Price
Chairman: M. Woodward
Coach: P. Hill
Secretary: R. Tucker, 46 Lilliput Avenue, Chipping Sodbury. Tel: 312724
Fixtures Secretary: D. Greenaway, 110 Melrose Avenue, Yate. Tel: 316980
Club captain (1987–88): R. Perry
Club captain (1988–89): C. Edgar
No. of teams: Senior 4. Youth & Minis 1
Directions to Ground: Off Wickwal Road, Chipping Sodbury
Colours: Black. (*Change colours*: Green)
Floodlights: Yes
Membership: £17.50 per annum
Local newspaper: The Gazette, Dursley
League: GLOS3
Final position (1987–88): 3rd

FRAMPTON COTTERELL

School Road, Frampton Cotterell, Bristol. Tel: Winterbourne 772947.
Founded: 1973
Secretary: J. Lynett, 32 Rockside Gardens, Frampton Cotterell, Bristol BS17 2HL. Tel: 0454 775241 (H). 0454 291587 (W).
League: Gloucestershire 3
Final position (1987–88): 4th

THORNBURY

Coopers Farm, Newton, Rockhampton Road, Thornbury. Tel: Thornbury (0454) 412096
Founded: 1963
President: C. Barrington
Chairman: D. Williams
Coach: G. Davies
Secretary: G. Dykes, 42 Maple Avenue,Thornbury. Tel: 415451
Fixtures Secretary: M. Carling, 57 Ashgrove, Thornbury. Tel: 415083
Club captain (1987–88): S. Whittingham
Club captain (1988–89): K. Rivers
No. of teams: Senior 5. Youth & Minis 5
Directions to Ground: 1½ miles north of Thornbury on Rockhampton Road
Clubhouse: 2 bars, function room
Colours: Amber & black hoops. (*Change colours*: Blue or Red)
Nickname: Thorns
Floodlights: No
Local newspaper: Gazette & Evening Post
League: GLOS3
Final position (1987–88): 6th
Playing record (1987–88): P 41, W 19, D 2, L 20, F 544, A 566

KINGSWOOD

Church Avenue Playing Field, London Road, Warmley, Bristol.
Founded: 1954

Gloucestershire 3

Secretary: P.A. Jones, 23 Christchurch Avenue, Downend, Bristol BS16 5TG. Tel: 0272 572140 (H). 0272 276241. Extn. 3036 (W).
League: Gloucestershire 3
Final position (1987–88): 6th

TEWKESBURY

64A High Street, Tewkesbury, Gloucestershire. Tel: 0684 294364.
Founded: 1955
Secretary: M.J. Slatter, Cleeve Cottage, Bushley, Tewkesbury, Gloucestershire. Tel: 0684 294364.
League: Gloucestershire 3
Final position (1987–88): 7th

CHOSEN HILL F.P.

Brookfield Road, Churchdown, Glos
Founded: 1971
President: A. Laycock
Chairman: A. Nield
Coach: K. Claridge
Secretary: M.F. Reid, 212 Cheltenham Road East, Churchdown, Glos
Fixtures Secretary: I. Yeates, 20 Westover Court, Churchdown, Glos. Tel: 0452 713502
Club captain (1987–88): D. MacRae
No. of teams: Senior 3. Colts 1
Directions to Ground: Situated between Gloucester and Cheltenham. Head for Churchdown Village, clubhouse adjacent to M5 motorway bridge
Clubhouse: Dressing rooms, bar, pitches adjacent to club
Colours: Myrtle green & white. (*Change colours*: White)
Floodlights: Training lights
Membership: £10 per annum
Local newspaper: The Citizen & The Echo
League: GLOS3
Final position (1987–88): 8th
Playing record (1987–88): P 28, W 11, L 17

PAINSWICK

Painswick or Broadham Field, Stroud Road, Painswick, Glos.
Founded: 1872
Secretary: K. Maybank, 3 Fielden Road, Abbeydale, Gloucestershire GL4 9EN. Tel: 0452 500544 (H). 04536 6321. Extn. 267 (W).
League: Gloucestershire 3
Final position (1987–88): 9th

GLOUCESTERSHIRE

Estcourt Road, Gloucestershire. Tel: 0452 28317.
Founded: 1945
Secretary: A.J. Apperley, 327b Stroud Road, Gloucester G24 0AY. Tel: 0452 28733 (H). 0452 21521. Extn. 2554 (W).
League: Gloucestershire 3
Final position (1987–88): 10th

BISHOPSTON

Bonnington Walk, Lockleaze, Bristol. Tel: 691916
Founded: 1894
President: T.R. Dowell
Chairman: R. Burge
Secretary: D.G.J. Hockley, 21 Pinewood Close, Westbury-on-Trym, Bristol. Tel: 623509
Fixtures Secretary: S. Oakley, 389 Soundwell Road, Bristol BS15. Tel: 600658
Club captain (1987–88): M. Golesworthy
Club captain (1988–89): S. Oakley
No. of teams: Senior 4. Youth & Minis 1
Directions to Ground: M4/M5 interchange into A38 Gloucester Road, left into Toronto Road at lights, straight across Filton Avenue, left past railway bridge
Clubhouse: Licensed clubhouse
Colours: Red with black hoop. (*Change colours*: Black & white hoops)
Nickname: Bish
Floodlights: No
Membership: £10
Local newspaper: Bristol Evening Post
League: GLOS3
Final position (1987–88): Bottom
Playing record (1987–88): P 33, W 7, D 2, L 24, F 282, A 561

GLOUCESTERSHIRE 4

SMITHS (INDUSTRIES)

The Newlands, Evesham Road, Bishops Cleeve, Cheltenham. Tel: 0242 67 2752
Founded: 1952
President: J.H. Sykes
Chairman: R.W. Ellis
Coach: J. Moore
Secretary: G.D. Owen, 79 Station Road, Bishops Cleeve, Cheltenham. Tel: 0242 67 6345
Fixtures Secretary: R. Brennan, Driftwood, Shutter Lane, Gotherington, Cheltenham. Tel: 0242 67 3902
Club captain (1987–88): P. Crossland
Club captain (1988–89): P. Crossland
No. of teams: Senior 4
Directions to Ground: 2 miles north of Cheltenham on A435
Ground capacity: Open Sports Field
Clubhouse: Smiths Industries Sports and Social Club
Colours: White with blue hoop. (*Change colours*: Blue with white hoop
Floodlights: No
Membership: £10
Local newspaper: Gloucestershire Echo
League: GLOS3
Final position (1987–88): 1st in GOS4
Playing record (1987–88): P 36, W 21, D 1, L 14

OLD ELIZABETHANS

Severn Road, Hallen, Bristol
Founded: 1932
Secretary: A.J.B. Forster, 16 Ramsey Road, Horfield, Bristol BS7 0JF. Tel: 0272 519964 (H). 0272 666961 (W).
League: Gloucestershire 4
Final position (1987–88): 2nd

BRISTOL TELEPHONE AREA

British Telecom Sports Ground, Stockwood Lane, Stockwood, Bristol. Tel: 0272 891776
Founded: 1961
President: B.J. Woollet
Chairman: S. Clarke
Coach: S. O'Reilly
Secretary: S.W. Partridge, 103 Hungerford Road, Brislington, Bristol BS4 5HE. Tel: 0272-721980 (H). 0272-296368 (W).
Fixtures Secretary: S. Robbins, 46 Holly Close, Speedwell, Bristol BS5 7XR. Tel: 0272-650979 (H)
Club Captain (1987–88): A. Weymouth
Club Captain (1988–89): S. O'Reilly
No. of teams: Senior 3
Directions to ground: Follow A37 (Wells Road) for approx 4 miles from city centre. Turn left at Black Lion Pub in Whitchurch Village. Ground is approx ½ mile on right.
Clubhouse: One bar, home and away changing rooms, showers and bath, hot food.
Colours: Red, white and blue hoops. (*Change colours:* Maroon.)
Nickname: Phones or Teles
Floodlights: Yes. Training only.
Membership: £10 per annum
Local newspaper: Bristol Evening Post
League: Gloucester 4
Final position (1987–88): 3rd
Playing record (1987–88): P 32, W 21, D 0, L 11.

BROAD PLAIN

Clement St. Easton, Bristol BS2 9EQ. Tel: 0272 552782
Founded: 1909
President: J. Shean
Chairman: A. McCarthy
Coach: B. Davies
Secretary: I. Gregory, 7 Luxton St. Easton, Bristol. Tel:0272 540706
Fixtures Secretary: J. Daveridge, 115 Ravenhill Road, Knowle, Bristol. 0272 771823
Club captain (1987–88): Steve Hucker
Club captain (1988–89): John White
No. of teams: Senior 3. Youth & Minis 2
Directions to Ground: Bonnington Walk, Lockleaze, off Filton Avenue, Bristol
Clubhouse: Broad Plain Rugby Social Club situated in central Bristol
Colours: Blue/maroon/gold. (*Change colours*: Maroon)
Nickname: Plainers
Floodlights: Yes. Portable
Membership: £5 + weekly subscription
Local newspaper: Evening Post
League: GLOS4
Final position (1987–88): 4th
Playing record (1987–88): P 33, W 20, D 1, L 12

GLOUCESTER ALL BLUES

The Oxlease, Gloucester, Glos.
Secretary: G.J. Redding, 28 Knowles Road, Tredworth, Gloucester, Glos.
League: Gloucestershire 4
Final position (1987–88): 5th

ARETIANS

The Clubhouse, Station Road, Little Stoke, Bristol. Tel: Almonsbury 621004.
Founded: 1961
President: M. Dart
Chairman: C. Luton
Coach: R. Solomans
Secretary: P. Pritchard, 25 Kelstoke Road, Stoke Bishop, Bristol. Tel: 0272 683595.
Fixtures Secretary: D. Bowles, 52 Alma Court, Alma Vale Road, Clifton, Bristol. Tel: 0272 733675.
Club captain (1987–88): P. Josham
Club captain (1988–89): K. Hazleldine
No. of teams: Senior 4. Youth & Minis 4.
Directions to Ground: At BAC/Rolls Royce flyover on A38 (Filton) take Yate Road, Gipsy Patch Lane, first left.
Clubhouse: 2 bars, dining facilities, 4 changing rooms, weight/multigym
Colours: Black. (*Change colours:* blue, white hoops
Floodlights: Planned for season 89/90
Membership: £20
Local newspaper: Bristol Evening Post
League: Gloucester 4
Final position (1987–88): 4th

BRISTOL AEROPLANE (BAC)

Sports Pavilion, Southmead Road, Filton, Bristol. Tel: 0272 692507.
Founded: 1921
Secretary: M. Bremner, 98 Worthing Road, Patchway, Bristol. Tel: 0272 697264 (H). 0272 693831. Extn. 3225 (W).
League: Gloucestershire 4
Final position (1987–88): 7th

HUCCLECOTE OLD BOYS

Pinehalt Club, 160 Hucclecote Road, Gloucester. Tel: 0452 66474.
Founded: 1970
Secretary: J.E. Ring, 9 Conway Road, Hucclecote, Gloucester GL3 9PD.
League: Gloucestershire 4
Final position (1987–88): 8th

NEWENT

Watery Lane, Newent, Glos. Tel: 0531 821517.
Founded: 1970
President: M. Poole
Chairman: R. Everest
Secretary: R. Randall, 2 Court Cottages, Little Witcombe, Gloucester.
Fixtures Secretary: D. Nottingham, Belmont Annex, Glebe Road, Newent. Tel: Glos 821798.
Club captain (1987–88): R. Smith
Club captain (1988–89): S. Turner
No. of teams: Senior 3. Youth & Minis 2.
Directions to Ground: A40 through Gloucester, follow signs to Newent (Ross Road).
Clubhouse: Capacity 100.
Colours: Green and gold. (*Change colours:* Gold and green).
Floodlights: No
Local newspaper: Citizen
League: Gloucestershire 4
Final position (1987–88): 7th
Playing record (1987–88): P 34, W 6, D 3, L 25.

OLD COTHAMIANS

New Pavilion, Northway, Filton Combination Ground, Filton, Bristol. Tel: 0272 790260
Founded: 1924
President: D. Pratton
Chairman: J. Pinches
Secretary: B. Meredith, 44 Bayham Road, Knowle, Bristol. Tel: 771509
Fixtures Secretary: J. Pinches, 135 Sefton Park Road, Bristol 7
Club captain (1987–88): G. Parker
Club captain (1988–89): K. Hannam
No. of teams: Senior 2
Directions to Ground: Off A38 from Gloucester to Bristol at Filton Aerodrome
Colours: Green/mauve/white. (*Change colours*: Green)
Nickname: Old Cots
Floodlights: No
Membership: £10
Local newspaper: Evening Post
League: GLOS4
Final position (1987–88): 11th
Playing record (1987–88): P 32, W 4, D 1, L 27

MINCHINHAMPTON

The Ram, Minchinhampton, Near Stroud, Gloucestershire. Tel: 0453 886051.
Founded: 1982
Secretary: Simon Young, The Crest, Windmill Road, Stroud, Glos. Tel: 0453 882323.
League: Gloucestershire 4
Final position (1987–88): 11th

DEVON LEAGUES

THE three Devon leagues embrace 27 clubs and the only section which produced runaway winners was at the top where Exeter Saracens had an outstanding campaign and won all 10 matches. Their closest challengers were Plymouth Civil Service, but they were beaten twice. The unfortunate Ilfracombe failed to avoid defeat in any of their games, but Prince Rock fought hard to escape the indignity of the other bottom placing – in vain.

DHSOB won Devon 2A from Victoria by virtue of a draw and defeat as opposed to the second placed side's two losses, but down at the bottom Plympton lost all seven games played and Tamar Saracens only managed to win once in eight outings.

In Devon 2B Cullompton were the first side to win a league in the whole Courage competition, but they ended with one defeat from six games – enough to keep them clear of Dartmouth. The last team – North Tawton – escaped a whitwash by drawing with fifth placed Topsham.

TABLES 1987–88

DEVON 1

	P	W	D	L	F	A	Pts
Exeter Saracens	10	10	0	0	207	66	20
Plymouth C Serv	10	8	0	2	167	95	16
Ivybridge	9	7	0	2	191	73	14
Totnes	10	6	1	3	148	113	13
Honiton	10	5	1	4	153	139	11
South Molton	10	4	1	5	159	97	9
Kingsbridge	10	3	1	6	90	150	7
Plymouth Argaum	10	3	1	6	123	224	7
Old Technicians	9	3	0	6	66	116	6
Prince Rock	10	1	3	6	62	151	5
Ilfracombe	10	0	0	10	46	188	0

DEVON 2A

	P	W	D	L	F	A	Pts
DHSOB	8	6	1	1	152	51	13
Victoria	8	6	0	2	94	42	12
Jesters	8	6	0	2	56	32	12
Plymouth YM	8	4	1	3	65	63	9
OPO	7	3	2	2	81	41	8
OPM	8	4	0	4	112	123	8
St Columba	8	3	0	5	78	97	6
Tamar Sara	8	1	0	7	47	123	2
Plymouth	7	0	0	7	37	150	0

DEVON 2B

	P	W	D	L	F	A	Pts
Cullompton	6	5	0	1	92	38	10
Dartmouth	6	4	0	2	134	59	8
Tavistock	6	4	0	2	94	36	8
Salcombe	6	4	0	2	94	71	8
Topsham	6	2	1	3	74	86	5
Withycombe	6	1	0	5	16	100	2
North Taunton	6	0	1	5	30	144	1

EXETER SARACENS

County Showground, Whipton, Exeter. Tel: 0392 66993
Founded: 1953
President: D. Mortimore
Chairman: G. King
Coach: G. Jones
Secretary: R. Buchanan, 72 Sylvan Road, Pennsylvania, Exeter. Tel: 0392 30804 (H) & 0392 33641 (W)
Fixtures Secretary: P. Blackmore, 1 Vieux Close, Behind Hayes, Otterton, Budleigh Salterton. Tel: Colaton Raleigh 6777 (H) & Exmouth 264373 (W)
Club captain (1987–88): M. Flavin
Club captain (1988–89): M. Flavin
No. of teams: Senior 4. Youth & Minis 8
Directions to Ground: From city centre take Pinhoe Road. At Whipton shops turn left into Summer Lane, under railway bridge, ground on right
Ground capacity: 2,000+. Stand, 200
Clubhouse: Brick building, adjoining pitch. Bar, kitchen, changing rooms
Colours: Red shirts, black shorts. (*Change colours*: Black shirts with red/white hoop)
Nickname: Sarries
Floodlights: Training lights
Admission: Free. £1 Cup games
Membership: £10 per annum
Programme: Not regular (Editor: N. Leech – Vice Capt)
Local newspaper: Express & Echo
League: Devon 1
Final position (1987–88): Champions, (promoted)
Playing record (1987–88): P 31, W 25, D 0, L 6, F 482, A 287
Competitions won: Courage League, Devon Div. 1

PLYMOUTH CIVIL SERVICE

C.S.S.A., Beacon Down, Recreation Road, Peverell, Plymouth
Founded: 1928
President: T. Butler
Chairman: M. Welsfor
Coach: R. Jewell
Secretary: C. Travers, 54 Salisbury Road, St. Judes, Plymouth. Tel: 662420
Fixtures Secretary: S. Brown, 1 Westways Close, Staddiscombe, Plymouth
Club captain (1987–88): B. Attis
Club captain (1988–89): B. Attis
No. of teams: Senior 2
Directions to Ground: Best to phone secretary
Clubhouse: Civil Service Club (2,000 capacity)
Colours: Red & white hoops. (*Change colours*: Red/black)
Floodlights: No
Membership: £10
Local newspaper: Evening Herald
League: Devon 1
Final position (1987–88): 3rd
Playing record (1987–88): P 34, W 30, L 4 (2nd – P 35, W 35)
Competitions won: R.N.E.C. Cup, Pedrick Cup, Lockie Cup, Ellis Cup, Haville Plate, Combination 7s

IVYBRIDGE

Cross in Hand, Exeter Road, Ivybridge, Devon. Tel: 0752 894392.
Founded: 1975
Secretary: T.P. Trigg, 129 Blackford Road, Ivybridge, Devon PL21 0AE. Tel: 0752 894381 (H). 0752 229259 (W).
League: Devon 1
Final position (1987–88): 3rd
Playing record (1987–88): P 41, W 34, D 1, L 6. F 1011, A 349.

TOTNES

Borough Park, Totnes. Tel: 86374
Founded: 1889
President: B. Perring
Chairman: C. Taylor
Coach: C. Williamson
Secretary: Miss J. Pantry, 50 Punchards Down, Follaton, Totnes, Devon. Tel: 864581
Fixtures Secretary: R. Lang, 42 The Carrions, Totnes. Tel: 864516
Club captain (1987–88): A. Pearson
Club captain (1988–89): A. Pearson
No. of teams: Senior 2. Youth & Minis 2
Directions to Ground: Adjacent to Totnes railway station
Clubhouse: Full bar, food, changing facilities
Colours: Blue & white
Nickname: Blues
Floodlights: No
Membership: £10 players. £5 social
Local newspaper: Totnes Times
League: Devon 1
Final position (1987–88): 4th
Playing record (1987–88): W 19, D 3, L 18, F 635, A 588
Competitions won: Local Derby, Paignton v. Totnes, January 1988

HONITON

All Hallows Playing Fields, Honiton, Devon. Tel: 0404 41239
Founded: 1883
President: G.J. George
Chairman: G. Brown
Coach: N. Huggett
Secretary: J. Rice, 2 Fouracres Close, Offwell, Honiton, Devon. Tel: Wilmington 492
Fixtures Secretary: K. Clark, Millhouse, Mill Hayes, Stockland, Honiton, Devon. Tel: Stockland 249
Club captain (1987–88): D. Meadows
Club captain (1988–89): D. McGrath
No. of teams: Senior 2. Youth & Minis 2
Directions to Ground: Behind church, Honiton High Street, near swimming pool/community college and sports hall
Clubhouse: Changing rooms and bar
Colours: Red/amber/black. (*Change colours*: Yellow shirts)
Floodlights: No. Not yet
Admission: Donations
Membership: £10
Local newspaper: Honiton Pulman & East Devon News
League: Devon 1
Final position (1987–88): 4th
Playing record (1987–88): P 34, W 12, D 2, L 20, F 473, A 541

SOUTH MOLTON

Furze Bray, Station Road, South Molton, Devon. Tel: 07695 2024.
Founded: 1935
Secretary: P. Snow, 4 Gwythers, South Molton, Devon EX36 4AZ. Tel: 07695 3027 (H), 07695 3204 (W).

Devon 1

Fixtures Secretary: R.H. Holmes, "Woods", Ash Mill, Bishops Nympton, North Devon.
League: Devon 1
Final position (1987–88): 6th

KINGSBRIDGE

High House, Kingsbridge, Devon. Tel: 0548 2051.
Founded: 1889
Secretary: P. Edwards, 8 Camperdown Road, Salcombe, Devon.
League: Devon 1
Final position (1987–88): 7th

PLYMOUTH ARGUAM

Bickley Down Road, Roborough, Plymouth, Devon. Tel: 06752 772156.
Founded: 1887
Secretary: M. Pike, 24 Frensham Avenue, Glenholt, Plymouth, Devon. Tel: 0752 341493.
League: Devon 1
Final position (1987–88): 8th

OLD TECHNICIANS

Weston Mill, Ferndale Road, Weston Mill, Plymouth. Tel: 0752 363352
Founded: 1932
President: K. Slater
Chairman: R. Ninnis
Coach: R. Hancock
Secretary: D.K.G. Mills, Sunnyview, 9 Glenholt Road, Glenholt, Plymouth PL6 7JA. Tel: 0752 783776
Fixtures Secretary: As Hon. Sec.
Club captain (1987–88): T. Williams
Club captain (1988–89): S. Matts
No. of teams: Senior 4
Directions to Ground: A38 to Plymouth take St. Budeaux bypass to Weston Mill
Colours: Black with white circlet. (*Change colours*: Red)
Nickname: Techs
Floodlights: No
Membership: £6.50
Local newspaper: Evening Herald
League: Deven 1
Final position (1987–88): 9th
Playing record (1987–88): P 33, W 22, D 1, L 10, F 460, A 346
Competitions won: Eddie Jones Plate (runners up Plymouth Combination, Lockie Cup), Havil Plate runners up (Devon RFU Cup)

PRINCE ROCK

Founded: 1964
President: D. Bishop
Chairman: L. Perkin
Coach: R. Perkin
Secretary: R.M. Hibbs, 23 Lydcot Walk, Eggbuckland, Plymouth, Devon. Tel: 0752 780184
Fixtures Secretary: L. Fowden, 1 Hayes Road, Oreston, Plymouth. Tel: 0752 405018
Club captain (1987–88): G. Weight
Club captain (1988–89): G. Weight
No. of teams: Senior 2
Directions to Ground: A38 Marsh Mills roundabout, keep to A 38 until next junction for Tavistock A386, 1½ miles on right hand side, Seaton Barracks
Clubhouse: British Telecom Sports Bar, Manadon Roundabout, Plymouth
Colours: Amber shirts, white shorts
Nickname: Rockeys
Floodlights: No
Membership: £10
Local newspaper: Plymouth Evening Herald
League: Devon 1
Final position (1987–88): 10th
Competitions won: Prince Rock 7s Tournament

ILFRACOMBE

Brimlands, Ilfracombe. Tel: 0271 64249
Founded: 1887
President: R.C. Beer
Chairman: A. Beer
Coach: P. Coats and R.C. Beer
Secretary: Janet Kift, Highcroft, Shaftsboro, Lee, Ilfracombe. Tel: 0271 62797.
Fixtures Secretary: J. Williams, 5 Castle Hill Villas. Tel: 0271 65198.
Club captain (1987–88): N. Ellis
Club captain (1988–89): D. Hutchings
No. of teams: Senior 1. Youth & Minis 3.
Directions to Ground: 1½ miles from town centre on Combe Martin road (above harbour).
Clubhouse: Bar, kitchen, dining room, changing rooms, 3 showers, loos.
Colours: blue and white. (*Change colours:* White).
Floodlights: No
Admission: Pass round hat
Membership: £7.50
Programme: only on cup matches 50p
Local newspaper: North Devon Journal
League: Devon 1
Final position (1987–88): 11th
Competitions won: U14 County Festival

DEVON 2A

DEVONPORT HIGH SCHOOL OLD BOYS

Devonport High School for Boys, Paradise Road, Millbridge, Plymouth
Founded: 1927
President: Peck, M.A.
Chairman: G.K. Simpson
Coach: Club Captain
Secretary: Brian Sherrell, 50 Highclere Gardens, Roborough, Plymouth. Tel: 0752 706594
Fixtures Secretary: G.K. Simpson, 108 Pattinson Drive, Mainstone, Plymouth. Tel: 707432
Club captain (1987–88): A. Cunningham
Club captain (1988–89): W.S. Lapthorne
No. of teams: Senior 1
Directions to Ground: From Plymouth College of Further Education turn right into Paradise Road towards Millbridge, the school is 300 yds on the right
Ground capacity: 500
Clubhouse: Exmouth Road Social Club
Colours: Green/black/white – irregular hoops. (*Change colours*: Myrtle/green with white collars)
Floodlights: No
Membership: £20
Local newspaper: Western Evening Herald
League: Devon 2A
Final position (1987–88): 1st (promoted)
Playing record (1987–88): P 35, W 21, D 3, L 11, F 561, A 411
Competitions won: Devon Div. 2A

VICTORIA

27 Hooe Road, Hooe, Plymstock, Plymouth, Devon. Tel: 0752 405196
Founded: 1981
President: Barry John
Chairman: Ray Purchase
Coach: Jim Lacey
Secretary: Jean M. Pardy, 25 Longacre, Woodford, Plympton, Devon PL7 4RQ. Tel: 0752 344081
Fixtures Secretary: As above. Tel: 0752 344081
Club captain (1987–88): Jim Lacey
Club captain (1988–89): Jim Lacey
No. of teams: Senior 2
Directions to Ground: King George V Playing Fields, Standerhayes Road, Elburton, Plymouth
Clubhouse: Courage Public House (Victoria Inn)
Colours: Black. (*Change colours*: Red)
Nickname: The Vic
Floodlights: No
Membership: £15
Local newspaper: Western Evening Herald
League: Devon 2A
Final position (1987–88): 2nd
Playing record (1987–88): P 38, W 26, D 3, L 9
Competitions won: 1984 – Salcombe 7s, 1983 – Victoria 7s

JESTERS

Marsh Meadow, Lower Leigham, Plym Valley, Plymouth
Founded: 1953
Chairman: M. Edwards
Coach: R. Ellis
Secretary: K. McLaren, 7 Downham Gardens, Tamerton Foliot, Plymouth. Tel: 706531
Fixtures Secretary: J. Gillan, Bassitt House, Hatch Green, Gunnislake, Cornwall. Tel: Tavistock 332919
Club captain (1987–88): D. Williams
Club captain (1988–89): M. Pascoe
No. of teams: Senior 2
Colours: White/red/black/gold quarters. (*Change colours*: Black & white hoops)
Floodlights: No
Membership: £10 per annum
Local newspaper: Plymouth Evening Herald
League: Devon 2A
Final position (1987–88): 3rd

PLYMOUTH YMCA

Burrington School, Honicknowle, Plymouth
Founded: 1910
President: D. Libbey
Chairman: D. Padfield
Coach: A. Pyle
Secretary: Mrs J. Pyle, 5 Dudley Road, Plympton, Plymouth. Tel: 345853
Fixtures Secretary: S. Briggs, 16 Holland Road, Peverel, Plymouth. Tel: 261663
Club captain (1987–88): J. Lee
Club captain (1988–89): J. Lee
No. of teams: Senior 1
Colours: Black with red hoop
Floodlights: No
Local newspaper: Western Evening Herald & Sunday Independent
League: Devon 2A
Final position (1987–88): 4th
Playing record (1987–88): P 29, W 16, D 1, L 12, F 394, A 318

OLD PUBLIC OAKS

King George V Playing Field (Council hired) at Elburton, Plymouth
Founded: 1927
President: W.E. Jones
Chairman: T. Crocker
Coach: D. Birchall
Secretary: Dave Barrett, 77 Vaughan Close, St. Boniface Park, Plymouth, Devon PL2 3QP. Tel: 0752 702412
Fixtures Secretary: Graham Mathews, 25 Colwill Road, Mainstone, Plymouth. Tel: 0752 707363
Club captain (1987–88): S. Philpott
Club captain (1988–89): K. Potter
No. of teams: Juniors 2
Directions to Ground: Take Plymstock Road, left at roundabout
Clubhouse: Socialise at R.A.F.A Club, Mutley, Plymouth
Colours: Dark green/gold – unequal hoops. (*Change colours*: Emerald)
Nickname: The Oaks
Floodlights: No
Membership: £15 per annum
Local newspaper: Western Evening Herald
League: Devon 2A
Final position (1987–88): 4th
Competitions won: R.N.E.C. Cup 1967, Lockie Cup 1959 & 1967, Pedrick Cup 1983, Roy Ellis Trophy 1983

OLD PLYMOTHIAN & MANNAMEADIAN

Bickleigh Down Lane, Roborough, Plymouth
Founded: 1926
President: F.J. Jeffery
Chairman: E.C. Keast
Secretary: S.A. Adams, 7 Stanlake Close, Church Road, Saltash, Cornwall. Tel: 07555 5219
Fixtures Secretary: G.A. Wesley, 33 Church Road, Plymstock, Plymouth. Tel: 0752 408526
Club captain (1987–88): C. Furnival
Club captain (1988–89): C. Furival
No. of teams: Senior 1
Directions to Ground: A386 from Plymouth towards Tavistock, turn right at Roborough sign, immediate second left and follow lane to clubhouse
Ground capacity: 200
Clubhouse: Bar, dining area (capacity 150)
Colours: Claret/blue hoops. (*Change colours*: Red)
Nickname: OPMs
Floodlights: No
Membership: £10 per annum
Local newspaper: Western Evening Herald, Western Morning News & Sunday Indepenent
League: Devon 2A
Final position (1987–88): 5th
Playing record (1987–88): P 34, W 23, D 1, L 10

ST COLUMBA

Defiance Field, Torpoint, Devon.
Founded: 1927
Secretary: P.C. Summers, 112 Rochford Crescent, Ernesette, Plymouth PL5 2Q.Tel: 0752 362785 (H), 0752 552986 (W).
League: Devon 2A
Final position (1987–88): 7th

TAMAR SARACENS

Tamar Valley Sports & Social Club, Ernesette, Plymouth, Devon. Tel: 0752 363080.
Founded: 1973

Devon 2A

Secretary: C. Knight, 87 Flam Stead Crescent, Kings Tamerton, Plymouth, Devon. Tel: 0752 369875 (H). 0752 665384 (W).
League: Devon 2A
Final position (1987–88): 7th

PLYMPTON

Founded: 1977
Secretary: D. St. John Smith, 4 The Old Priory, Marbet Road, Plympton, Plymouth PL7 3QS. Tel: 0752 333298.
League: Devon 2A
Final position (1987–88): 9th

DEVON 2B

CULLOMPTON

Stafford Park, Knowle Lane, Cullompton, Devon. Tel: 0884 32480
Founded: 1892
President: Lester Neale
Chairman: Ian Wood
Coach: John Robinson
Secretary: Tony Lindsell, Kirkdale, Stoneyford, Cullompton. Tel: 0884 38884
Fixtures Secretary: Terry Radmore, Rull House, Ashill. Tel: 0884 40817
Club captain (1987–88): M. Dyke
Club captain (1988–89): P. Sanders
No. of teams: Senior 3. Youth & Minis 1
Directions to Ground: Tiverton side of Cullompton
Clubhouse: New clubhouse opening Dec/Jan 88/89
Colours: Red & black hoops.(*Change colours*: Blue)
Floodlights: Yes
Admission: Free
Membership: £10
Local newspaper: Cullompton & District New and Exeter Express & Echo
League: Devon 2B
Final position (1987–88): League Winners
Playing record (1987–88): P 32, W 18, D 2, L 12
Competitions won: Devon Junior Cup 1952, Courage League Devon 2B 1987/88

DARTMOUTH

Dartmouth Community College, Milton Lane, Dartmouth, Devon. Tel: 08043 3994.
Founded: 1952
Secretary: Ms J. Evans, 58A Victoria Road, Dartmouth, Devon TD6 9DZ. Tel: 08043 3311 (H). 08043 4921 (W).
League: Devon 2B
Final position (1987–88): 2nd

TAVISTOCK

Mary Tavy Playing Fields, Tavistock, Devon
Founded: 1971
President: W. Oliver
Chairman: R. Watson
Coach: K. Oliver
Secretary: J. Lawson, 4 Mount Ford, Tavistock, Devon PL19 8EB.
Fixtures Secretary: C. Sutton, 121 Plymouth Road, Tavistock, Devon.
Club captain (1987–88): J. Wakem
Club captain (1988–89): J. Wakem
No. of teams: Senior 2. Youth & Minis 6.
Directions to Ground: Alongside main road in centre of Mary Tavy Village, 3 miles east of Tavistock on A386.
Ground capacity: 300+
Clubhouse: Being built 88/89.
Colours: red shirts, black shorts, red socks. (*Change colours:* Black shirts).
Floodlights: No
Membership: Social £3
Local newspaper: Tavistock Times and Gazette
League: Devon 2B
Final position (1987–88): 3rd
Playing record (1987–88): P 42, W 21, D 5, L 16.

SALCOMBE

Twomeads, Camperdown Road, Salcombe, South Devon. Tel: 054884 2639.
Founded: 1888
Secretary: G.S. McCormack, Dorset House, Devon Road, Salcombe, South Devon.
League: Devon 2B
Final position (1987–88): 4th

TOPSHAM

Bonfire Field, Exeter Road, Topsham, Exeter
Founded: Re-founded 1982
President: Paul Pirongs
Chairman: Clive Pascoe
Coach: Peter Scott
Secretary: Geoffrey Hogg, 22 Newcourt Road, Topsham, Exeter, Devon. Tel: 4129
Fixtures Secretary: Paul Pirongs, Dutch Ho, The Strand, Topsham. Tel: 7347
Club captain (1987–88): Jerry Alford
Club captain (1988–89): Jerry Alford
No. of teams: Senior 3
Directions to Ground: Bonfire Field on left as you drive into Topsham from Exeter, just before Pretty's Garage
Clubhouse: Wooden ex-Army hut under construction at present!
Colours: Dark & light blue hoops. (*Change colours*: Red)
Floodlights: No
Membership: £15 per annum
Local newspaper: Express & Echo (daily), Exmouth Journal (weekly)
League: Devon 2B
Final position (1987–88): 5th
Playing record (1987–88): P 34, W 14, D 2, L 18, F 523, A 560

WITHYCOMBE

Rugby, Football & Recreation Club, Raleigh Park, Hulham Road, Exmouth, Devon. Tel: 0395 266762
Founded: 1924
President: Mrs Joan Rowsell-Pryce
Chairman: R.E. Jones
Secretary: D.M. Josey, 2 Larch Close, Marley Gardens, Exmouth, Devon EX8 5NQ. Tel: 0395 275038
Fixtures Secretary: D.J. Field, "The Bishop Blaize", The Quay, Exeter, Devon. Tel: 0392 214499
Club captain (1987–88): C. Locke
Club captain (1988–89): H. Symons
No. of teams: Senior 2
Directions to Ground: From Exeter, M5 junction 30, take A376 to Exmouth at box junction *before* first traffic lights, turn left into Hulham Road. Ground is 200 yds on right (on bend)
Ground capacity: 2,000. Stand, 50

Clubhouse: Clubroom, lounge, large changing rooms, cloakrooms, weights room
Colours: Emerald green & black hoops. (*Change colours*: Yellow)
Nickname: The Withies
Floodlights: No
Admission: Free. (Collection)
Membership: £5
Local newspaper: Exmouth Journal & Exmouth Herald
League: Devon 2B
Final position (1987–88): 6th (of 7)
Playing record (1987–88): P 34, W 8, L 26, F 224, A 656
Competitions won: Crediton 7s 1974, Withycombe 7s 1982

NORTH TAWTON

Butts Barton Street, North Tawton, Devon
Founded: 1885
President: J. Avery
Chairman: M. Thwaites
Coach: M. Thwaites
Secretary: Mrs G.M. Hoggins, The Old Forge, North Street, North Tawton. Tel: 983 782 516
Fixtures Secretary: Mark Roach, The Dell, Brightly Road, Okehampton. Tel: Okehampton 4186
Club captain (1987–88): M. Roach
Club captain (1988–89): R. Tidball
No. of teams: Senior 2
Ground capacity: 250
Clubhouse: Two changing rooms & bar area
Colours: Black & amber hoops. (*Change colours*: Amber)
Nickname: Tawts
Floodlights: No
Membership: £10
Local newspaper: Express & Echo
League: Devon 2B
Final position (1987–88): Bottom
Playing record (1987–88): P 32, W 10, D 2, L 20

BUCKS/OXON LEAGUES

TWO divisions made up the Bucks/Oxon leagues – one of 12 clubs and the other of 10. It was very stoutly contested with Slough predominant in the top league where they drew once in 11 games and won the rest to finish three points clear of Bicester. Down in the basement Didcot and Abingdon finished well adrift of the others, although neither was whitewashed and both played gallantly. Abingdon's defence needed tightening, but Didcot usually lost by respectable scores.

Drifters just finished top of an exciting second section and their 203 points were a most praiseworthy testimonial to enterprising play. Three teams finished a point behind with Milton Keynes enjoying a superior points difference to Olney and Wheatley.

Chesham at the foot of the table had a wretched time losing all nine games and conceding 357 points.

TABLES 1987–88

BUCKS/OXON 1

	P	W	D	L	F	A	Pts
Slough	11	10	1	0	162	61	21
Bicester	11	9	0	2	210	78	18
Chiltern	11	7	0	4	169	85	14
Littlemore	11	6	1	4	134	124	13
Grove	11	5	1	5	157	99	11
Beaconsfield	11	5	1	5	108	112	11
Chinnor	11	5	1	5	89	109	11
Pennanians	11	4	1	6	115	128	9
Witney	11	4	1	6	91	113	9
Buckingham	11	4	0	7	119	175	8
Abingdon	11	2	0	9	67	241	4
Didcot	11	1	1	9	56	152	3

BUCKS/OXON 2

	P	W	D	L	F	A	Pts
Drifters	9	7	1	1	203	51	15
Milt Keynes	9	7	0	2	168	56	14
Olney	9	7	0	2	158	54	14
Wheatley	9	7	0	2	144	63	14
Phoenix	9	5	1	3	143	78	11
Cholsey	9	4	0	5	78	122	8
Gosford AB	9	3	0	6	111	123	6
Chipping Ntn	9	2	0	7	87	114	4
Harwell	9	2	0	7	116	223	4
Chesham	9	0	0	9	33	357	0

SLOUGH

Upton Court Park, Slough, Berks. Tel: Slough 22107.
Founded: 1928
Secretary: S. Webb, 8 Chestnut Avenue, Wokingham, Berks RG11 2UU. Tel 0734 784040 (H) 0344 86666 (W).
Fixtures Secretary: M. Carter, 65 Wavell Road, Maidenhead, Berks. Tel: 0628 25640.
League: Bucks/Oxon 1
Final position (1987–88): 1st (promoted)
Playing record (1987–88): P 36, W 19, D 2, L 15, F 400, A 388.

BICESTER

Oxford Road, Bicester, Oxon.
Founded: 1948
Secretary: B. Tomlin, 12 Mill Lane, Croughton, Nr Brackley, Northants. Tel: 0869 810124 (H) 0869 810311 (W).
Fixtures Secretary: G. Davies, 166 Barty Avenue, Bicester, Oxon. Tel: 0869 241993.
League: Bucks/Oxon 1
Final position (1987–88): 2nd

CHILTERN

Weedon Lane, Amersham, Bucks. Tel: 02403 725161.
Founded: 1924
President: B. Arrib
Chairman: S. Griffiths
Coach: E. Planken-Bichler
Secretary: P. Jalland, Greenhaven, 20 Green Lane, Chesham Bois, Bucks. Tel: 02403 725588.
Fixtures Secretary: R. Cook, Twitchell's Cottages, Twitchell's Lane, Jordans, Bucks. Tel: Chalfon St Giles 5051.
Club captain (1987–88): M. Watson
Club captain (1988–89): A. Pegley
No. of teams: Senior 7. Youth & Minis 20+.
Directions to Ground: Left at first roundabout after "Boot & Slipper" on Amersham → Chesham Road, 2nd left into Weedon Lane.
Ground capacity: 2000
Colours: Claret and white hoops. (**Change colours:** TBC)
Nickname: Chiltern Welsh
Floodlights: Yes
Membership: £30
Local newspaper: Bucks Examiner
League: Bucks/Oxon 1
Final position (1987–88): 3rd
Playing record (1987–88): P 30, W 17, D 2, L 11.

LITTLEMORE

Peers School, Littlemore, Oxford. Tel: 0865 715776.
Founded: 1978
Secretary: C. Bowler, Hillside, Elm Drive, Garsington, Oxon. Tel: 086 736 766.
League: Bucks/Oxon 1
Final position (1987–88): 4th

GROVE

Grove Recreation Ground, Cane Lane, Grove. Tel: 02357 67041.
Founded: 1972
President: E.A. Prosser
Chairman: D.R. Williams
Coach: M. Brewster
Secretary: S. Hopkins, 35 Mill Road, Abingdon. Tel: 0235 32273.
Fixtures Secretary: A. Davies, 23 Cameron Avenue, Abingdon. Tel: 0235 33568.
Club captain (1987–88): A. Blow
Club captain (1988–89): B. Hallam
No. of teams: Senior 4. Youth & Minis 2.
Directions to Ground: Main road from Oxford to Wantage. Take 2nd Grove turn second left into Cane Lane. Ground on left 200 yds.
Colours: Red, white, blue.
Floodlights: No
Membership: £15
Local newspaper: Wantage Herald
League: Bucks/Oxon 1
Final position (1987–88): 4th

BEACONSFIELD

Oak Lodge Meadow, Windsor End. Tel: 04946 3783
Founded: 1953
President: N. Hickman
Chairman: A. Batty
Coach: M. Wood
Secretary: P. Badman, Southways, Burket Crescent, Beaconsfield. Tel: 04946 0000
Fixtures Secretary: A. Batty, 43 Lakes Lane, Beaconsfield. Tel: 04946 3471
Club captain (1987–88): S. Wall
Club captain (1988–89): S. Wall
No. of teams: Senior 6. Youth & Minis 10
Directions to Ground: From M40 follow signs to Beaconsfield, turn left in centre of town
Colours: Green/yellow. (*Change colours*: Blue/white)
Floodlights: Yes
Membership: £36 playing
Local newspaper: Bucks Advertiser
League: Bucks & Oxon 1
Final position (1987–88): 6th
Playing record (1987–88): P 32, W 14, D 1, L 17

CHINNOR

Kingsey Road, Thame, Oxon. Tel: Thame 3735.
Founded: 1963
President: J.E. Slinger
Chairman: N.K. Robinson
Secretary: N. Gardham, 5 Emmington, Nr Chinnor, Oxon.
Fixtures Secretary: N.K. Robinson, Pathways, 10 The Rise, Kingston Blount, Oxon. Tel: KB 53428.
Club captain (1987–88): B. Evans
Club captain (1988–89): B. Evans
No. of teams: Senior 6. Youth & Minis 8.
Directions to Ground: Proceed to Thame and take the Kingsey Road signred for Princes Risborough. Club is located on the Thame ring road.
Colours: Black and white hoops. (*Change colours:* All white)
Floodlights: No
Membership: Playing £25, Vice President £20.
Local newspaper: Oxford Mail, Thame & Risborough Gazette
League: Bucks/Oxon 1
Final position (1987–88): 5th
Playing record (1987–88): W 15, L 10, D 1, F 398, A 220.
Competitions won: Oxfordshire County Cup Winners, 1977; Oxfordshire County Colts Cup Winners, 1982, 1984, 1985.

PENNANIANS

Farnham Park Sports Field, Farnham Royal, Bucks. Tel: 028 14 6252
Founded: No
President: Bob Gaskell
Chairman: Richard Thomas
Coach: Dick Thomas
Secretary: Martin Bartlett, 14 Adam Close, Baughurst, Hants RG26 5HG. Tel: 07356 2867
Fixtures Secretary: Dave Watson, 40 St. Andrews Way, Cippenham, Slough, Berks. Tel: 06286 66098
Club captain (1987–88): Wally Rota
Club captain (1988–89): Nigel Pyefinch
No. of teams: Senior 4
Directions to Ground: From M4, exit 6, towards Beaconsfield A355, through Farnhan Royal, 200 yds turn right into Farnham Park
Clubhouse: Built ourselves 1979, presently extending
Colours: Black/white. (*Change colours*: White with two 2″ black bands thro chest)
Nickname: Penns
Floodlights: No
Membership: £25
Local newspaper: Slough Express & Slough Observer
League: Bucks & Oxon 1
Final position (1987–88): 7th

WITNEY

Harley Road, Witney, Oxon. Tel: 0993 71043.
Secretary: S. Miles, 12 Farmers Close, Witney, Oxon. Tel: 0993 4063.
Fixtures Secretary: R. Mountford, 26 Crecy Walk, Woodstock, Oxford. Tel: 0993 812389.
League: Bucks/Oxon 1
Final position (1987–88): 9th

BUCKINGHAM

Moreton Road, Buckingham, Bucks. Tel: 0280 815474
Founded: 1933
President: R.A. Smith
Chairman: E. Curtis
Coach: C. Martin
Secretary: F.M. Gemmell, 22 Elmfields Gate, Winslow, Bucks. Tel: 0296 714640 (H) & 0296 393123, Ext 2388 (W)
Fixtures Secretary: F.A.W. Smith, 10 Mare Leys, Buckingham. Tel: 0280 815634
Club captain (1987–88): S. Ward
Club captain (1988–89): J. Evershed
No. of teams: Senior 4. Youth & Minis 6
Directions to Ground: From centre of Buckingham (Market Square) follow A413 to Towcester and ground is on left on edge of town, one mile from town centre
Colours: Green/white hoops. (*Change colours*: Black)
Floodlights: No
Membership: £25 players
Local newspaper: Buckingham Advertiser
League: Bucks & Oxon 1
Final position (1987–88): 10th
Playing record (1987–88): P 37, W 13, D 0, L 24

ABINGDON

Southern Sports Park, Lambrick Way, Abingdon, Oxon.
Founded: 1930s
President: G. Dimond
Chairman: R. Simpson
Secretary: K. Sykes, 24 Segsbury Road, Wantage, Oxon OX12 9XP. Tel: 02357 69320.
Fixtures Secretary: T. Soden, 22 Oxford Road, Dorchester. Tel: Oxford 341171.
Club captain (1987–88): N. Crossley
Club captain (1988–89): N. Crossley
No. of teams: Senior 3.
Clubhouse: Being built
Colours: Green/yellow hoops. (*Change colours:* Green)
Floodlights: No
Membership: £15
Local newspaper: Abingdon Herald
League: Bucks/Oxon 1
Final position (1987–88): 11th

DIDCOT

The Park, Park Road, Didcot, Oxon.
Founded: 1955
Secretary: J. Kilzzynski, 46 Slade Road, Didcot, Oxon OX11 7AT. Tel: 0235 815582.
League: Bucks/Oxon 1
Final position (1987–88): 12th (relegated)

BUCKS/OXON 2

DRIFTERS

Farnham Common Sports Club, One Pin Lane, Farnham Common, Bucks. Tel: Farnham Common 4190.
Founded: 1963
Secretary: P. Southernden, 1 Hatches Lane, Great Kingshill, High Wycombe, Bucks HP15 6DZ. Tel: 0494 715782 (H) 02814 5834 (W).
League: Bucks & Oxon 2
Final position (1987–88): 1st (promoted)

MILTON KEYNES (formerly Wolverton)

Field Lane, Greenleys, Milton Keynes, Bucks. Tel: 0908 313858.
Founded: 1895
Secretary: W.P. Jones, 47 Green Lane, Wolverton, Milton Keynes, Bucks. Tel: 0908 311906.
League: Bucks & Oxon 2
Final position (1987–88): 2nd

OLNEY

Recreation Ground, East Street, Olney. Tel: 0234 712880.
Founded: 1877
President: L.E. Fairey
Chairman: A.B. Howkins
Coach: A. Carter
Secretary: S.J. Parkin, West View Farm, Olney, Bucks.
Fixtures Secretary: R. Taylor, 24 Elmlea Drive, Olney, Bucks.
Club captain (1987–88): R.E.G. Morel
Club captain (1988–89): R.E.G. Morel
No. of teams: Senior 5.
Directions to Ground: Entering Olney from Newport Pagnell turn right at Market Square then left into East Street. Approx 400 yards turn right into Recretion Ground car park.
Colours: Cerise & french grey. (*Change colours:* Blue)

Drifters – 1987–88 Bucks/Oxon 2 Champions. Back (l to r): Chris Pritchard, Nice, Morris, Carling, Hughes, Gates, Rawson, Burgess, O'Brien, Sandbrook, Paulin, Furness (T/judge); Front: Kemp, Hawes, Cess Pritchard (Capt.), Spellman, Gillingham. Photo: Chris Roberts.

Wimborne "No 8" at the break with his scrum half in support in their 16–0 victory at Slough . Photo: Chris Roberts.

Slough (1987–88 Bucks/Oxon Division 1 champions) face a tough Southern Counties baptism against Wimborne in the new season. Their centre Dave Clark (with ball) seems to have run out of support. Photo: Chris Roberts.

Drifters v Chesham (Bucks/Oxon 2). John Hewes (Drifters) scores five tries in this encounter and lays claim to the title of the fastest wing in the Windsor–Slough area. Photo: Chris Roberts.

Phoenix – still in Bucks/Oxon Division 2 this season. Photo: Chris Roberts.

Pennanians face Drifters in a friendly – this season it will be for Bucks/Oxon Division 1 points. Penns' scrum-half Keith Manning about to fling out a pass and start his backs moving. Photo: Chris Roberts.

Floodlights: Yes (training)
Membership: Playing members £10
Programme: Yes (Editor: D. Coltman)
Local newspaper: Milton Keynes Citizen & Milton Keynes Herald
League: Bucks & Oxon 2
Final position (1987–88): 3rd
Playing record (1987–88): P 39, W 17, L 22.

WHEATLEY

Founded: 1971
Secretary: B. Axford, 24 Waterperry, Oxford OX9 1LB. Tel: 08447 860.
League: Bucks & Oxon 2
Final position (1987–88): 4th

PHOENIX

Institute Road, Taplow, Bucks. Tel: 06286 64319
Founded: 1963
President: Peter Carr
Chairman: Steve Rafferty
Coach: Tom Fisher
Secretary: Steve Marsden, 15 Boulters Court, Maidenhead. Tel: 0628 27025
Fixtures Secretary: Steve Turner, 20 Balmoral Close, Cippenham, Berks. Tel: 06286 61660
Club captain (1987–88): Steve Turner
Club captain (1988–89): Steve Turner
No. of teams: Senior 4
Directions to Ground: M4 exit junction 7, A4 head towards Maidenhead, over crossroads, over roundabout, next right, first left after bridge
Clubhouse: As ground
Colours: Red/black. (*Change colours*: Black)
Floodlights: No. Training lights only
Membership: £20
Local newspaper: Slough Express, Slough Observer, Maidenhead Advertiser
League: Bucks & Oxon 2
Final position (1987–88): 5th
Playing record (1987–88): P 33, W 17, D 2, L 14

CHOLSEY

Hithercroft Road, Wallingford, Oxon. Tel: 0491 35044.
Founded: 1967
Secretary: D.W. Haynes, 20 Hambleden Drive, Wallingford, Oxon OX10 0PQ. Tel: 0491 35578 (H) 0727 26766 (W).
Fixtures Secretary: R. Hodgson, 11 Anthony Hill Road, RAF Benson, Wallingford, Oxon. Tel: 0491 39975.
League: Bucks & Oxon 2
Final position (1987–88): 6th

GOSFORD ALL BLACKS

Lanford lane, Kidlington, Oxford. Tel: Kidlington 3994.
Founded: 1956
Secretary: P. Willars, 'Stonelee', 15 Spindlers, Kidlington, Oxford OX5 2YP. Tel: 08675 6077 (H) 0865 721306 (W).
League: Bucks & Oxon 2
Final position (1987–88): 7th

CHIPPING NORTON

Greystones, Burford Road, Chipping Norton, Oxon. Tel: Chipping Norton 3968.
Founded: 1975
Secretary: D.P. Soper, 133 Walterbush Road, Chipping Norton, Oxon OX7 5DQ.
League: Bucks & Oxon 2
Final position (1987–88): 8th

HARWELL

Social Club, A.E.R.E. Harwell, Chiltern, Oxon. Tel: 0235 834331
Founded: 1947
President: B.A. Arnold
Chairman: P. Browning
Coach: G. Daluzveiria
Secretary: C. Bartlett, 66 Upthorpe Drive, Wantage, Oxon. Tel: Wantage 67596
Fixtures Secretary: B.L. Flanders, Old Cross House, Coscote, Didcot, Oxon OX11 0NP. Tel: 0235 816523
Club captain (1987–88): C. Mason
Club captain (1988–89): N. Cook
No. of teams: Senior 3
Directions to Ground: A4130 main gate A.E.R.E. Harwell, just off A34 mid-way between Oxford and Newbury
Clubhouse: Social club, 3 bars, dining hall, games room, air hall, etc
Colours: Navy/light blue/white hoops. (*Change colours*: Blue)
Floodlights: No
Membership: £15
Local newspaper: Didcot Herald & Oxford Mail
League: Bucks & Oxon 2
Playing record (1987–88): P 34, W 7, D 1, L 26, F 372, A 809

CHESHAM

Chess Valley Sports & Leisure Association, The Moor, Chesham, Bucks.
Founded: 1981
Secretary: K. Bagley, 27 Rothschild Avenue, Aston Clinton, Aylesbury, Bucks HP22 5LY. Tel: Aylesbury 630831 (H) 0494 782066 (W).
League: Bucks & Oxon 2
Final position (1987–88): 12th

Feltham at Phoenix in an early season battle. Can Phoenix scrum-half Pat Thomas escape the attentions of the Feltham flankers, who look ready to pounce? Photos: Chris Roberts.

Pennanians powerhouse – 1987–88. Peter Bailey (left) smuggles the ball out against Phoenix. Chris Shelley receives. Photo: Chris Roberts.

BERKS/DORSET/WILTS LEAGUES

THE three southern counties had two leagues involving 22 clubs but they had a top section of 10 sides with the rest in the second.

The top league proved to be a thrilling contest between Swanage and Wareham and Devizes with the Dorset team winning on points difference after both had lost just one match.

Hungerford, who bravely soldiered on through a torrid first season of competition, lost all nine games and conceded a massive 428 points, but Marlborough in ninth place could blame their position on a poor defence which left them below Aldermaston on points difference.

Chippenham won the lower section after a tense struggle with Corsham; both lost a single match, but Chippenham had a superior points difference. At the foot of the league Swindon College fought gallantly and were consoled by one victory.

TABLES 1987–88

BERKS/DORSET/WILTS 1

	P	W	D	L	F	A	Pts
Swanage & W	9	8	0	1	266	31	16
Devizes	9	8	0	1	254	72	16
Dorchester	9	7	0	2	108	42	14
Sherborne	9	6	0	3	160	34	12
Weymouth	9	6	0	3	198	79	12
Wootton Bas	9	3	0	6	174	141	6
Reme A'bfld	9	3	0	6	117	155	6
Aldermaston	9	2	0	7	64	180	4
Marlborough	9	2	0	7	57	258	4
Hungerford	9	0	0	9	22	428	0

BERKS/DORSET/WILTS 2

	P	W	D	L	F	A	Pts
Chippenham	11	10	0	1	302	74	20
Corsham	11	10	0	1	265	52	20
Puddleton	11	8	0	3	176	82	16
Supermarine	11	8	0	3	128	108	16
N Dorset	11	7	0	4	232	84	14
Lychett Min	11	5	0	6	170	143	10
Poole	11	5	0	6	147	142	10
Oakmedians	11	4	0	7	86	166	8
Trowbridge	11	3	0	8	91	220	6
Bradford	11	3	0	8	84	216	6
Minety	11	2	0	9	70	193	4
Swindon Col	11	1	0	10	49	320	2

BERKS/DORSET/WILTS 1

SWANAGE & WAREHAM

Bestwall, Wareham, Dorset. Tel: 09295 2224
Founded: 1953
President: J.R. Procter
Chairman: J. Woolley
Coach: R. Croom
Secretary: J.M. Hopkins, 'Sospan', Greenclose Lane, Leigh, Wimborne, Dorset BH21 2AL. Tel: 0202 886804
Fixtures Secretary: As Secretary above
Club captain (1987–88): M. Perry
Club captain (1988–89): J. Strange
No. of teams: Senior 4. Youth & Minis 6
Directions to Ground: A351 from North and East, A352 from West, to traffic lights in town centre, turn into East Street, proceed to the end, ground on the left
Ground capacity: 1,000 approx
Clubhouse: Clubroom, President's bar, kitchen, 6 changing rooms, showers, toilets (male and female)
Colours: Maroon
Nickname: Swans
Floodlights: No
Membership: £20 senior players
Local newspaper: Evening Echo, Bournemouth
League: Berks, Dorset & Wilts 1
Final position (1987–88): 1st
Playing record (1987–88): P 34, W 22, D 2, L 10, F 662, A 325
Competitions won: 1st XV: Berks, Dorset & Wilts Champions 1988, Winners Dorset & Wilts Plate 1988, Winners Lytchett Minster RFC 7s 1988. Colts: Winners Dorset & Wilts Knockout Cup 1986 and 1988, Winners Dorset & Wilts 7s 1987

DEVIZES

Sports Club, London Road, Devizes, Wilts. Tel: Devizes 3763.
Founded: 1931
Secretary: M.J. Maundrell, Manor House, Calstone, Calne, Wilts. Tel: Calne 812373.
League: Berks/Dorset/Wilts 1
Final position (1987–88): 2nd
Playing record (1987–88): P 31, W 23, D 2, L 6. F 718, A 273.

DORCHESTER

Weymouth Avenue, Dorchester, Dorset. Tel: 0305 65692
Founded: 1934
President: E. Mills
Chairman: N. Jones
Secretary: G. Meyers, 12 Manor Road, Dorchester DT1 2AU. Tel: 0305 66343 (H) & 0305 64774 (W)
Fixtures Secretary: H. Meyers, 28 Victoria Road, Dorchester. Tel: 0305 65877
Club captain (1987–88): E. Taylor
Club captain (1988–89): E. Taylor
No. of teams: Senior 3. Youth & Minis 6
Directions to Ground: Take the Weymouth Road out of Dorchester. The ground is the last sports field on left hand side
Clubhouse: Bar, hall, kitchens
Colours: Green & white hoops. (*Change colours*: Red)
Floodlights: No
Membership: £15

Local newspaper: Dorset Evening Echo
League: Berks/Dorset/Wilts 1
Final position (1987–88): 3rd
Playing record (1987–88): P 30, W 21, L 9, F 480, A 230

SHERBORNE

The Terrace, Sherbourne, Dorset
Founded: 1980
Secretary: A. Fall, 18 Manor Close, Bradford Abbas, Dorset. Tel: Yeovil 25747 (H). Sherbourne 813122 (W).
League: Berks/Dorset/Wilts 1
Final position (1987–88): 4th

WEYMOUTH

Monmouth Avenue, Weymouth, Dorset DT3 5HZ. Tel: Weymouth 778889
Founded: 1872
President: W.M.C. Whittle, JP
Chairman: J.H. Parker
Coach: P. Absolom
Secretary: G. Barber, 23 Purbeck Close, Weymouth. Tel: 778531
Fixtures Secretary: R.E. Foyle, 12 Powys Close, Dorchester. Tel: 66144
Club captain (1987–88): H. Mason
Club captain (1988–89): H. Mason
No. of teams: Senior 4. Youth & Minis 2
Directions to Ground: Down Dorchester Road, straight across roundabout on Ring Cross railway bridge, next left at Olds Garage
Clubhouse: One year old, 4 changing rooms plus usual facilities
Colours: Light blue/navy
Nickname: Sea Horses
Floodlights: No
Membership: £15 per annum
Local newspaper: Dorset Evening Echo
League: Berks, Dorset & Wilts 1
Final position (1987–88): 4th
Playing record (1987–88): P 34, W 25, D 0, L 9, F 633, A 363

WOOTTON BASSETT

Rylands Field, Stoneover Lane, Wootton Bassett, Wilts. Tel: 0793 851425.
Founded: 1971
Secretary: H. Keith, 25 Briars Close, Wootton Bassett, wilts. Tel: 0793 850985 (H). 0793 615601 (W).
Fixtures Secretary: J. Brierly, 1 Forsey Close, Lyncroft, Swindon, Wilts. Tel: 0793 722908.
League: Berks/Dorset/Wilts 1
Final position (1987–88): 6th

REME (ARBORFIELD)

Garrison Sports Club, School of Electronic Engineering, Arborfield, Reading, Berks. Tel: 0734 760421. Extn. 344.
Secretary: Capt. d.R. Prowse, School of Electronic Engineering, Arborfield, Reading, Berks. Tel: 0734 410105 (H). 0374 760421. Extn. 2341 (W).
League: Berks/Dorset/Wilts 1
Final position (1987–88): 7th

ALDERMASTON

Aldermaston Recreational Society, Awe Aldermaston, Reading, Berks RG7 4PR. Tel: 07356 411, Ext 7614
Founded: 1954
Chairman: Derek Griggs
Coach: Ian Titley
Secretary: Dr. David McGinnes, 11 Rowan Close, Tadley, Hants RG26 6RP. Tel: 07356 3213
Fixtures Secretary: Arthur Cuss, 153 Winchester Road, Basingstoke. Tel: Basinstoke (0256) 24129
Club captain (1987–88): Paul Gelliot
Club captain (1988–89): Terry Francis
No. of teams: Senior 4. Youth & Minis 1
Colours: Scarlet. (*Change colours*: White)
Floodlights: No
Local newspaper: Basingstoke & North Hampshire Gazette
League: Berks, Dorset & Wilts 1
Final position (1987–88): 8th
Playing record (1987–88): P 9, W 2, L 7 (League only)

MARLBOROUGH

The Commcn, Marlborough, Wilst. Tel: 0672 54717.
Founded: 1967
Secretary: N.P. Ludlow, 10 Sawden Close, Hungerford, Berks RG17 0LB. Tel: 0488 82159 (H). 0488 83334 (W).
Fixtures Secretary: A. Thomas, 2 Dando Drive, Marlborough, Wilts. Tel: 0672 52296.
League: Berks, Dorset and Wilts/1
Final position (1987–88): 9th

HUNGERFORD

50 High Street, Hungerford, Berks.
Founded: 1986
Secretary: C. Dowse, 38 Dunn Crescent, Kintbury, Near Newbury, Berks. Tel: 0488 58896.
No. of teams: Senior 1
Directions to Ground: Ground is near cricket club off Bulpitt Lane.
Ground capacity: Considerable (all standing).
Clubhouse: Cricket club.
Floodlights: No
Local newspaper: Newbury Weekly News
League: Berks/Dorset/Wilts 1
Final position (1987–88): 10th

BERKS/DORSET/WILTS 2

CHIPPENHAM

Birch Grove, Chippenham. Tel: 0249 656390
Founded: 1929
President: G. Fathers
Chairman: R. Turvey
Coach: M. Coombs
Secretary: J. Wakefield, 46 Langley Road, Chippenham. Tel: 0249 651677 (H) & 0272 617248 (W)
Fixtures Secretary: G. Millard, 11 Murray Walk, Melksham, Wilts. Tel: 702469
Club captain (1987–88): M. Prangle
Club captain (1988–89): M. Prangle
No. of teams: Senior 4. Youth & Minis 3
Directions to Ground: Out of Chippenham, take the B4069 road to Lyneham, opposite "Westinghouse" Factory gates, turn left into Birch Grove
Ground capacity: 300 approx
Clubhouse: Clubroom, lounge, changing rooms, showers, kitchen
Colours: Black & white hoops. (*Change colours*: Red)
Floodlights: Yes. For training only

Membership: Players £15. Social £5
Local newspaper: Chippenham News, Wiltshire Gazette & Herald
League: Berks, Dorset & Wilts 2
Final position (1987–88): 1st (promoted)
Playing record (1987–88): P 33, W 23, D 0, L 10
Competitions won: Winners Berks, Dorset & Wilts Div. 2

CORSHAM

Corsham Sports Club House, Station Road, Corsham, Wilts SN13 9LU. Tel: 0249 713929
Founded: 1964
President: J. Wiltshire
Chairman: P. Kaljusko
Coach: M. Lye
Secretary: F.T. Trahair, MBE, 5 Penleigh Close, Corsham, Wilts SN13 9LE. Tel: 0249 714468
Fixtures Secretary: K. Jones, Staple Cottage, Sandridge Park, Melksham. Tel: 705597
Club captain (1987–88): John Beazer
Club captain (1988–89): John Beazer
No. of teams: Senior 1. Youth 2
Directions to Ground: Lacock Road, ⅓ mile east of Methuen Arms Hotel, Corsham
Ground capacity: 500
Colours: Red/white
Floodlights: No
Membership: £10 per annum
Programme: Commence 1988/89 season. (Editor: S. McDonald)
Local newspaper: Bath Chronicle
League: Berks, Dorset & Wilts 2
Final position (1987–88): 2nd (promoted Div. 1)
Playing record (1987–88): P 32, W 17, D 2, L 12, F 518, A 317
Competitions won: Promoted from Div. 2 to Div. 1 of Dorset & Wilts

PUDDLETOWN

Greenfields, Piddlehinton, Dorset. Tel: Puddletown 0305 848808.
Founded: 1974
President: Sir D. Spicer MP
Chairman: E. Durey, MBE, RE
Coach: I. J. Ring
Secretary: A.R. Foot, Bookham Farm, Buckland Newton, Dorchester. Tel: 03005 511.
Fixtures Secretary: P. Smeeth. Tel: 03004 310.
Club captain (1987–88): J. Brown
Club captain (1988–89): P. Talbot
No. of teams: Senior 2
Directions to Ground: Off B3143 4 miles from Dorchester, 1 mile from Piddlehinton.
Colours: Red shirts, black shorts. (*Change colours:* White shirts, black shorts).
Floodlights: No
Membership: £17
Programme: £1.50. (Editor: D.H.J. Foot)
Local newspaper: Dorset Evening Echo
League: Berks/Dorset/Wilts 2
Final position (1987–88): 3rd
Playing record (1987–88): P 29, W 23, L 6.

SUPERMARINE

Highworth Road, Stratton St Margaret, Swindon, Wilts. Tel: 0793 824828.
Secretary: P.L. Ferris, 22 Read Street, Swindon, Wilts. Tel: 0793 613119 (H). 0793 28291 (W).
League: Berks/Dorset/Wilts 2
Final position (1987–88): 4th

NORTH DORSET

Slaughterhouse Lane, Wyke, Gillingham, Dorset. Tel: 07476 2748.
Founded: 1951
Secretary: N. Porthecary, 71 Sylvan Way, Gillingham, Dorset. Tel: 07476 4658 (H). 07476 4141 (W).
League: Berks/Dorset/Wilts 2
Final position (1987–88): 5th

LYTCHETT MINSTER OLD BOYS

Lytchett Minster School, Lytchett Minster, Dorset.
Secretary: G. Glover, 14 Birchdale Road, Highland Park, Wimborne, Dorset. Tel: 0202 886489 (H). 0202 622143 (W).
League: Berks, Dorset, Wilts 2
Final position (1987–88): 6th

POOLE

Turlin Moor, Hamworthy, Poole
Founded: 1963
Chairman: R. Knight
Coach: D. Hadfield
Secretary: J. Wateridge, 8 Harness Close, Wimborne, Dorset BH21 2UF. Tel: 0202 889105.
Fixtures Secretary: G. Sellars, 18 Plantation Road, Poole. Tel: 0202 69247.
Club captain (1987–88): I. Appleton
Club captain (1988–89): I. Appleton
No. of teams: Senior 3. Youth & Minis 6.
Directions to Ground: On A350 Blandford to Poole, turn right after Sherry & Haycock.
Colours: Amber and blue hoops. (*Change colours:* Blue).
Nickname: Dolphins
Floodlights: No
Membership: £15
Local newspaper: Bournemouth Evening Echo
League: Berks/Dorset/Wilts 2
Final position (1987–88): 7th
Playing record (1987–88): W 12, D 1, L 17. F 377, A 389.

OAKMEDIANS

White Farm, Ensbury Park, Slades Farm Road, Bournemouth, Dorset.
Founded: 1963
Secretary: Miss S. Bennett, 63 Stewart Road, Charminster, Bournemouth, Dorset. Tel: 0202 36757 (H), 0202 572271. Extn. 255 (W).
League: Berks/Dorset/Wilts 2
Final position (1987–88): 8th

TROWBRIDGE

Green Lane, Ashton Park, Trowbridge, Wilts. Tel: 02214 61389.
Founded: 1931
Secretary: P. Riddiford, Pepperacre Lane, Hilperton Road, Trowbridge, wilts. Tel: 02214 3764 (H).
Fixtures Secretary: A.J. Taylor, 71 Clarendon Avenue, Trowbridge, Wilts. Tel: 02214 68208.
League: Berks/Dorset/Wilts 2
Final position (1987–88): 9th

BRADFORD ON AVON

Founded: 1982
Secretary: J.W. Brockbank, 17 Whitehill, Bradford or Avon, Wilts. Tel: 02216 3803 (H). 02216 3911 (W).
League: Berks, Dorset, Wilts 2
Final position (1987–88): 10th

MINETY

The Playing Fields, Silver Street, Minety, Wilts. Tel: 0666 860802.
Founded: 1972
Secretary: C. Comport, 46 Risingham Mead, Westlea, Swindon, Wilts. Tel: 0793 874762 (H). 0666 824077 (W).
League: Berks/Dorset/Wilts 2
Final position (1987–88): 11th

SWINDON COLLEGE

Merton Fields, Merton Avenue, Swindon, Wilts.
Founded: 1964
Secretary: I. McHenry, 37 Weedon Road, Stratton, St. Margaret, Swindon, Wilts SN3 4EG. Tel: 0793 828954 (H). 0793 616161. Extn. 2912 (W).
League: Berks/Dorset/Wilts 2
Final position (1987–88): 12th

SOMERSET LEAGUES

SOMERSET had 33 clubs in their leagues and these were divided into three divisions of 12, 11 and 10 teams, which produced some hot competition. Old Culverhaysians won the top section although both they and Frome lost only one match, but the East Somerset side spoiled their record with two draws. Oldfield Old Boys and Walcott Old Boys also did well here, but at the bottom of the table Wellington languished without a single point and Crewkerne were also isolated even though they won two games.

St. Bernadette's won Somerset 2 with only one loss in 11 games and they were closely followed by Bristol Harlequins. At the foot of the table were Cheddar Valley with one win to their credit, but Chard were unlucky to finish one place above them after winning four matches; their points difference was inferior to Stothert and Bath O.E.

Avonvale dropped just one point in Somerset 3, which left them clear of Westland, who were also unbeaten but drew two games. Wincanton with a single point were last.

TABLES 1987–88

SOMERSET 1

	P	W	D	L	F	A	Pts
O Culverhays	11	10	0	1	205	77	20
Frome	11	8	2	1	200	47	18
Oldfield OB	11	8	0	3	235	101	16
Walcott OB	11	8	0	3	223	126	16
O Sulians	11	6	2	3	151	94	14
N Petherton	11	4	2	5	121	94	10
Yatton	11	4	1	6	149	158	9
Burnham	11	4	1	6	78	140	9
Hornets	11	4	0	7	136	149	8
Yeovil	11	4	0	7	108	144	8
Crewkerne	11	2	0	9	58	218	4
Wellington	11	0	0	11	39	355	0

SOMERSET 2

	P	W	D	L	F	A	Pts
St Bernadet	10	9	0	1	160	72	18
Bristol Harl	10	7	2	1	209	62	16
Avon	10	6	1	3	120	102	13
Blagdon	10	5	0	5	140	156	10
Wells	10	4	1	5	132	112	9
Winscombe	10	4	1	5	85	89	9
Imperial	10	4	1	5	84	121	9
Stothert & P	10	4	0	6	70	81	8
Bath OE	10	4	0	6	126	148	8
Chard	10	4	0	6	99	150	8
Cheddar Val	10	1	0	9	67	199	2

SOMERSET 3

	P	W	D	L	F	A	Pts
Avonvale	9	8	1	0	221	45	17
Westland	9	7	2	0	135	58	16
Backwell	9	5	0	4	213	92	10
Tor	9	5	0	4	152	100	10
O Ashtonians	9	5	0	4	144	118	10
Morganians	9	5	0	4	113	89	10
Chew Valley	9	3	2	4	163	99	8
Bath CS	9	3	0	6	103	166	6
Castle Cary	9	9	2	7	62	142	2
Wincanton	9	0	1	8	43	440	1

OLD CULVERHAYSIANS

Old Fosse Road, Bath. Tel: 0225 832081
Founded: 1959
President: A. Bond
Chairman: M. Cooper
Coach: R. Barnfield
Secretary: T. Shore, 54 Edgeworth Road, Kingsway, Bath. Tel: 0225 29979
Fixtures Secretary: R. Barnfield, 72 Edgeworth Road, Bath. Tel: 0225 330122
Club captain (1987–88): D. Gimson
Club captain (1988–89): D. Gimson
No. of teams: Senior 3. Youth & Minis 6
Directions to Ground: From Bristol, take Combe Down Road, turn left by "Clarks" Factory. From Radstock turn left just as you enter city boundary
Ground capacity: 1,000
Clubhouse: Good sized with bar, kitchen, hall, changing rooms, showers, etc
Colours: Black. (*Change colours*: Amber)
Nickname: Old Cs or Cs
Floodlights: No
Membership: £5
Local newspaper: Bath & Wilts Evening Chronicle and Bristol Evening Post
League: SOM1
Final position (1987–88): Top (promoted)
Playing record (1987–88): P 30, W 27, L 3, F 428, A 167
Competitions won: SOM1 leaders, Bath 7s runners up, Somerset Cup 1987, Bath Combination Cup

FROME

Showground, Frome. Tel: 0373 65382
Founded: 1883
President: P. Quick
Chairman: J. Twigger
Coach: D. Fuszard
Secretary: D. Rose, 140 High Street, Chapmanslade, Wilts. Tel: Chapmanslade 647
Fixtures Secretary: P. Lovatt, Bath Arms, Horningsham, Wilts. Tel: Maiden Bradley 308
Club captain (1987–88): D.J. Kelly
Club captain (1988–89): D.J. Kelly
No. of teams: Senior 4. Youth & Minis 6
Directions to Ground: On Bath Road from Frome take lane (Gypsy Lane) opposite Mendip Hotel, ground approx ½ mile on left
Clubhouse: On Frome showground, large bar room, lounge, function room, kitchen, showers, changing rooms, toilets, large car park
Colours: Red/white/black hoops. (*Change colours*: Red/black hoops)
Floodlights: No
Membership: £10 non-players, £12 players
Programme: To be decided (Editor: A. Lund)
Local newspaper: Somerset Standard
League: SOM1
Final position (1987–88): Runners up (promoted)
Playing record (1987–88): P 36, W 29, D 2, L 5
Competitions won: ARC 15-a-side competition

OLDFIELD OLD BOYS

Tel: Bath 310464 (club) or 834135 (ground)
Founded: 1951
President: D.R. Green
Chairman: E.A. Sweet
Coach: C. Lilley
Secretary: S.J. Godwin, 12 Lime Grove Gardens, Bath. Tel: 318612
Fixtures Secretary: B. Quintin, 10 Gordon Road, Peasdown, Nr. Bath. Tel: Radstock 33308
Club captain (1987–88): S. Withey
Club captain (1988–89): C. Lilley
No. of teams: Senior 4. Youth & Minis 6
Directions to Ground: Follow signs for the University then ask for Shaft Road, Combe Down.
Ground capacity: 500
Clubhouse: Lower Bristol Road, Bath
Colours: Maroon/gold hoops. (*Change colours*: Maroon)
Nickname: Oldfields
Floodlights: Yes. Part
Admission: 50p Cup games
Membership: £10 players. £3 non-players
Local newspaper: Bath & Wilts Evening Chronical
League: SOM1
Final position (1987–88): 3rd
Playing record (1987–88): P 36, W 28, D 1, L 7
Competitions won: Wooton Basset 7s, Avon RFC 7s, Somerset U17 Cup

WALCOT OLD BOYS

Albert Field, Lansdown, Bath. Tel: Bath 330199
Founded: 1882
President: M. Greensides
Chairman: B.T. Wheatley
Coach: B.T. Wheatley
Secretary: K. Jones, 14 Canterbury Road, Oldfield Park, Bath. Tel: Bath 27045
Fixtures Secretary: J.F. Gifford, 131 Lymore Avenue, Oldfield Park, Bath. Tel: Bath 28524
Club captain (1987–88): R. Hookway
Club captain (1988–89): M. Brown
No. of teams: Senior 4. Youth & Minis 1
Directions to Ground: Out of city centre, Lansdown Road, Lansdown
Clubhouse: New clubhouse 1988
Colours: Black/white. (*Change colours*: Red)
Floodlights: No
Membership: £5
Local newspaper: Bath & Wilts Evening Chronicle
League: SOM1
Final position (1987–88): 4th
Playing record (1987–88): P 34, W 20, D 1, L 13, F 636, A 421

OLD SULIANS

Lansdown Road, Bath, Avon. Tel. 0225 310201
Founded: 1926
President: J. Trude
Chairman: P. Beach
Coach: J. Wrigley
Secretary: A. Slee, 8 Heathfield Close, Weston, Bath. Tel: 0225 317256
Fixtures Secretary: M. Bailey, 32 Napier Road, Weston, Bath. Tel 0225 314060
Club captain (1987–88): M. Self
Club captain (1988–89): M. Self
No. of teams: Senior 3. Youth & Minis 1
Directions to Ground: From centre of City, take London Road to Lansdown Raod, travel up hill for 2 miles approx, pass M.O.D. buildings, ground on left, 100 yds
Ground capacity: 500–750
Clubhouse: Large showers, 2 large changing rooms, referees room, bar & clubromm
Colours: Red band on blue. (*Change colours*: Green or White)
Nickname: Sus
Floodlights: Training purposes only
Membership: £7
Local newspaper: Bath & Wilts Evening Chronicle
League: SOM1
Final position (1987–88): 5th

Playing record (1987–88): P 32, W 23, D 3, L 6, F 580, A 252
Competitions won: Bath Combination 2nd XV Cup, April 1988

NORTH PETHERTON

Beggars Brook, North Petherton, Somerset. Tel: 0278 663028.
Founded: 1893
Secretary: R. Foster, 19 Hyde Park Avenue, North Petherton, Bridgwater, Somerset. Tel: 0278 662964 (H), 0278 422432 (B).
League: South-West Somerset 1
Final position (1987–88): 6th

YATTON

North End Road, Yatton. Tel: 832085.
Founded: 1968
President: Roy Screen
Chairman: Tony Leigh
Coach: Arthur Parsons
Secretary: Graham Goodhind, 8 Binhay Road, Yatton BS19 4HD. Tel: Yatton 835434.
Fixtures Secretary: Richard Scott, 13 Beech Road, Yatton. Tel: 832949.
Club captain (1987–88): Andy Burrell
Club captain (1988–89): Jonathan Crew
No. of teams: Senior 4, Youth & Minis 5
Directions to Ground: J20 (M5) left at r'bout, left to Yatton at next roundabout.
Ground capacity: 300
Colours: Black & amber. (*Change colours:* Green)
Floodlights: No
Admission: Free
Membership: £15.00
Local newspaper: Weston Mercury
League: Somerset 1
Final position (1987–88): 6th
Playing record (1987–88): P 35, W 22, D 2, L 11.

BURNHAM ON SEA

B.A.S.C. Ground, Stoddens Road, Burnham On Sea. Tel: 0278 788355.
Founded: Reformed 1947
President: F. Cross
Chairman: Michael O'Farrell
Coach: Graham Watts
Secretary: Christopher Garner, Brendon Cottage, Church Road, East Brent, Somerset. Tel: 0278 760787.
Fixtures Secretary: Gareth Berry, 86 Burnham Road, Highbridge, Burnham On Sea.
Club captain (1987–88): Peter Gaylard
Club captain (1988–89): Peter Gaylard
No. of teams: Senior 4, Youth & Minis 1
Directions to Ground: Junction 22, M5 motorway follow signs to B.A.S.C. Sportsground.
Ground capacity: One stand plus touchline barrier,capacity for thousands. Stand, 120.
Clubhouse: Two storey changing facilities downstairs– bar/clubroom upstairs – balcony overlooking main pitch.
Colours: Royal blue & white hoops, white shorts. (*Change colours:* Royal blue)
Floodlights: Yes training lights
Admission: None. Via programme.
Membership: £20
Programme: At least 50p (Editor: John Clist/Michael O'Farrell)
Local newspaper: Burnham & Highbridge Weekly News
League: Somerset 1
Final position (1987–88): 8th – 12 in league
Playing record (1987–88): P 35, W 19, D 3, L 13, F 543, A 364.
Competitions won: None

HORNETS

Hutton Moor. Tel: 0934-21433.
Founded: 1962
President: F.L.P. Costeloe
Chairman: D.A. Pollard
Coach: C. Reeves
Secretary: B.A. Collard, 8 Wayside, Worle, Weston-S-Mare, Avon. Tel: 0934-22570.
Fixtures Secretary: F. Toman, 5 Southmead Road, W-S-M. Tel: 0934-419715.
Club captain (1987–88): N. Mager
Club captain (1988–89): N. Mager
No. of teams: Senior 5, Youth & Minis 10
Directions to Ground: Follow Main Road into Weston turn left traffic lights at Mac's Garage over bridge ground on left foot of bridge.
Ground capacity: Open
Clubhouse: New clubhouse built 1988
Colours: Black/amber. (*Change colours:* Amber)
Floodlights: No
Membership: £15
Local newspaper: Evening Post/Weston Mercury
League: Somerset 1
Final position (1987–88): 7th

YEOVIL

Johnson Park, Yeovil, Somerset. Tel: 0935 74433
Founded: 1875
President: G. Habberfield
Chairman: V.J. Jenkins
Coach: G. Richards
Secretary: R.E. Johnson, 55 Westbourne Grove, Yeovil, Somerset BA20 2DG. Tel: 0935 28458
Fixtures Secretary: C. Brock, 2 Rustywell, Yeovil. Tel: 0935 79186
Club captain (1987–88): A. Jarvis
Club captain (1988–89): A. Jarvis
No. of teams: Senior 2. Youth & Minis 2
Directions to Ground: Off A37 (Ilchester Road) Yeovil, turning off near Picketty Witch PH
Ground capacity: 2,000 approx
Clubhouse: As above
Colours: Blue/yellow hoops. (*Change colours*: White)
Floodlights: Yes
Admission: Free. (Ground collection)
Membership: £12 (membership paid by club). £3 (match fees)
Local newspaper: Somerset Star & Western Gazette
League: SOM1
Final position (1987–88): 9th
Playing record (1987–88): P 41, W 18, D 2, L 22, F 498, A 455

CREWKERNE

Henhays, Crewkerne, Somerset. Tel: 0460 76422
Founded: Re-formed 1975
President: P. MacCready
Chairman: J. Williams
Coach: G. Cooper
Secretary: C. MacDonald, 8 Sycamore Drive, Crewkerne, Somerset. Tel: 0460 76136 (H) or 0460 75685 (W)
Fixtures Secretary: J. Davies, Old School House, Drimpton, Beaminster, Dorset. Tel: 0308 68388
Club captain (1987–88): T. Boyer
Club captain (1988–89): T. Boyer
No. of teams: Senior 2. Youth & Minis 1
Directions to Ground: Directly adjoining the main car park centre of town
Clubhouse: Shared with other sports clubs

Colours: Scarlet & black hoops. (*Change colours*: Cambridge blue)
Floodlights: No
Admission: Free
Membership: Various types
Local newspaper: Western Gazette
League: SOM1
Final position (1987–88): 11th
Playing record (1987–88): P 38, W 22, L 16, F 570, A 560

WELLINGTON

The Athletic Ground, Corams Lane, Wellington. Tel: 3758
Founded: 1874
President: G.E. Sprague
Chairman: G.P. Dyke
Coach: D. Hughes
Secretary: B.K. Colman, Meadowside, Mangle Street, Wellington TA21 8BG
Fixtures Secretary: G.R. Vickery, 7 Seymour Street, Wellington. Tel: 4695
Club captain (1987–88): A.W. Terry
Club captain (1988–89): A.W. Terry
No. of teams: Senior 3. Youth & Minis 5
Directions to Ground: Next to sports centre
Ground capacity: 3,000+
Clubhouse: 2 bars (200 capacity)
Colours: Red/black. (*Change colours*: Blue)
Floodlights: No
Admission: Donation
Membership: £10
Local newspaper: Wellington Weekly News
League: SOM1
Final position (1987–88): 12th (relegated)
Playing record (1987–88): P 33, W 4, D 3, L 26, F 168, A 814

SOMERSET 2

ST. BERNADETTES OLD BOYS

Hengrove Park, Bamfield, Whitchurch, Bristol. Tel: 0272 891500
Founded: 1964
President: James Gallagher
Chairman: Trevor Woore
Secretary: Sean Broad, 25 Blakeney Road, Patchway, Bristol BS12 5LY. Tel: 0272 698031
Fixtures Secretary: Brian Murphy, 4 Rookery Way, Whitchurch, Bristol BS14 0DT. Tel: 0272 837702
Club captain (1987–88): Kevin Crehan
Club captain (1988–89): Kevin Crehan
No. of teams: Senior 4. Youth & Minis 2
Directions to Ground: Hartcliffe Way. Past W.D. & H.O. Wills to major roundabout, follow signs for Whitchurch Sports Centre, turn left past Harvey's Wine Merchants into Bamfield Clubhouse situated ¼ mile on left hand side by bus lay-by
Clubhouse: Lounge bar, showers, 3 changing rooms (1 large, 2 medium), catering facilities
Colours: Green & blue hoops. (*Change colours*: Red)
Nickname: The Lords of Lourdes
Floodlights: No
Membership: £10
Local newspaper: Bristol Evening Post
League: SOM2
Final position (1987–88): 1st (promoted)
Competitions won: Bristol 7s 1973/74

BRISTOL HARLEQUINS

Broomhill Road, Brislington, Bristol. Tel: 0272 721650.
Founded: 1926
President: V. Sidoli
Chairman: S. Croot
Coach: R. Hobbs
Secretary: P.J. Broome, 1 Ketch Road, Bristol B53 5DQ. Tel: 0272 713815 (H), 0272 266031, Extn 364 (W).
Fixtures Secretary: E. Morrison, 4 Lowbourne, Whitchurch, Bristol. Tel: 0272 832580.
Club captain (1987–88): S. Mason
Club captain (1988–89): S. Mason
No. of teams: Senior 4. Youth & Minis 1.
Directions to Ground: From A4 (Bath) turn right into Emery Road, then 1st right into Broomhill Road, 3rd entrance on right.
Colours: Blue, black and white.
Nickname: Quins
Floodlights: No
Membership: £10
Local newspaper: Bristol Evening Post
League: Somerset 2
Final position (1987–88): 2nd (promoted)
Competitions won: Runners-up Somerset Div 2, winners Bristol Combination Knockout Plate Competition

AVON

Hicks Field, London Road East, Bath, Avon. Tel: 0225 852446.
Founded: 1925
Secretary: M.J. Sawyer, 29 Mayfield Road, Bath, Somerset. Tel: 0225 26264 (H), 0225 331304 (B).
League: Somerset 2
Final position (1987–88): 3rd

BLAGDON

Somerset
Founded: 1958
President: A. Addicott
Chairman: D. Slinn
Coach: M. Badger
Secretary: N. Williams, 16 Stockton Close, Whitchurch, Bristol
Fixtures Secretary: W. Fitzpatrick, 2 The Linxs, Cheddar
Club captain (1987–88): I. Simmonds
Club captain (1988–89): I. Simmonds
No. of teams: Senior 3
Directions to Ground: Located on A365 at Blagdon, between Bath and Weston-Super-Mare
Clubhouse: Village Club
Colours: Green. (*Change colours*: Blue
Floodlights: Yes
Membership: £5
Local newspaper: Evening Post
League: SOM1
Final position (1987–88): 4th

WELLS

The Portway, Wells. Tel: 0749 72823 (call box)
Founded: 1876 (inaugural)
President: R.D. Draper
Chairman: T. Western
Coach: J. Askew
Secretary: M.F.P. Dennis, 2 Bilbury Lane, Glastonbury, Somerset. Tel: 34625

Fixtures Secretary: R. McCarthey, 26 Elm Close, Wells. Tel: 77582
Club captain (1987–88): J. Taylor
Club captain (1988–89): R. Norman
No. of teams: Senior 3. Youth & Minis 4
Directions to Ground: Weston-Super-Mare Road from Wells (A371), signed through housing estate to club
Ground capacity: 2 pitches on site, one in reserve
Clubhouse: Extensive changing facilities, comfortable club room
Colours: Black & white hoops. (*Change colours*: Mid blue)
Floodlights: Yes. Training
Admission: (Collection)
Membership: £5
Local newspaper: Wells Journal & Weston Gazette (Yeovil)
League: SOM3
Final position (1987–88): 5th

WINSCOMBE

Longfield Recreation Ground, Winscombe, Avon. Tel: Winscombe 2720
Founded: 1962
President: S. Hart
Chairman: G. New
Secretary: M. Ford, Emley Fm, Burrington, Bristol. Tel: 0934 833394
Fixtures Secretary: A. Ellis, 30 Wimblestone Road, Winscombe. Tel: 3087
Club captain (1987–88): E. Ford
Club captain (1988–89): M. Badger
No. of teams: Senior 3. Youth & Minis 3
Directions to Ground: Take A38 South 10 miles out of Bristol, turn right in Sidcot signposted Winscombe. Take left turn on sharp right bend, turn first right into rec.
Clubhouse: Property of Winscombe Cricket Club. No revenue to RFC
Colours: Black. (*Change colours*: Red)
Floodlights: No
Membership: £20
Local newspaper: Weston Mercury
League: SOM2
Final position (1987–88): 5th
Playing record (1987–88): P 34, W 15, D 1, L 18
Competitions won: Battscombe Quarry, Cheddar 7s Cup

IMPERIAL (BRISTOL)

Imperial Athletic Ground, West Town Lane, Knowle, Bristol. Tel: 0272 777210 & 776659.
Founded: 1905
Secretary: H.F. Walton, 1 Rushmoor Grove, Backwell, Bristol BS19 3BW. Tel: 027583 3405 (H), 0272 641111 X 2641 (B).
League: Somerset 2
Final position (1987–88): 7th

STOTHERT & PITT

Newton-St-Loe, Bath. Tel: Bath 25569
Founded: 1906
Chairman: I. Guy
Coach: G. Tugwell
Secretary: R.V. Garraway, 2 Westfield Park South, Lower Weston, Bath BA1 3HT. Tel: Bath 316863
Fixtures Secretary: B. Gibbs, 114 Newton Road, Bath. Tel: Bath 330455
Club captain (1987–88): R. Saunders
Club captain (1988–89): T. Humphries
No. of teams: Senior 3
Directions to Ground: Bristol side of Bath, situated on A4 road
Ground capacity: 200
Clubhouse: Changing rooms, showers & bar
Colours: Blue/black/amber. (*Change colours*: Blue)
Nickname: Cranes
Floodlights: No
Membership: £6
Local newspaper: Bath & Wilts Evening Chronicle
League: SOM2
Final position (1987–88): 6th
Playing record (1987–88): P 33, W 16, D 1, L 16

BATH OLD EDWARDIANS

King Edward's School, Playing Fields, Bathampton, Bath.
Founded: 1926
Secretary: N.P. Cox, 49 Fint Avenue, Bath, Avon. Tel: 0225 20652 (H), 0225 62675 (B).
League: Somerset 2
Final position (1987–38): 9th

CHARD

Ground Park Road, Chard, Somerset. Tel: Chard (04606) 2495
Founded: 1878
President: R.W. Morgan
Chairman: G. Hughes
Secretary: A.S. Walker, Merryfield House, Ilton, Somerset. Tel: 51601.
Fixtures Secretary: D. Mumby
Directions to Ground: off Chard High Street
Ground capacity: 1000
Clubhouse: Yes.
Colours: Red, black, gold. (*Change colours*: Red.)
Floodlights: No.
Membership: £20.
League: Somerset 2
Final position (1987–88): 10th
Competitions won: John Player Cup, April 1988.

CHEDDAR VALLEY

Sharpham Road, Cheddar, Somerset. Tel: 0934 743623.
Founded: 1963
Secretary: E.M. Roberts, 1 Brimridge Road, Winscombe, Avon. Tel: 093 484 372 (H), 0272 333179 (B).
League: Somerset 2
Final position (1987–88): 11th

AVONVALE

Bathford Playing Fields, Bathford, Bath, Avon. Tel: 0225 858295
Founded: 1883
President: G. Atchison
Chairman: M. Stanton
Coach: B. Crouch
Secretary: P. Kilmister, 33 West Park Road, Corsham. Tel: 0249 712906
Fixtures Secretary: S. Vowles, 25 Mills Road, Melksham. Tel: 0225 708699
Club captain (1987–88): A. Ball
Club captain (1988–89): A. Ball
No. of teams: Senior 3. Youth & Minis 1
Directions to Ground: From Bath, take A4 London Road to Bathford, fork right at the roundabout towards Bradford on Avon, fork left at "The Crown", turn left opposite "The Inn"
Clubhouse: Built 1971, extended changing rooms 1986
Colours: Navy blue & white. (*Change colours*: Red)
Nickname: The Vale
Floodlights: No
Membership: £2
Local newspaper: Bath & West Evening Chronicle
League: SOM3
Final position (1987–88): 1st
Playing record (1987–88): P 32, W 22, D 2, L 8, F 630, A 241
Competitions won: Somerset Div. 3 Champions 1987/88

WESTLAND

Westland Sports & Social Club, Westbourne Close, Yeovil, Somerset. Tel: 400 74297.
Founded: 1954
President: P. Holland
Chairman: D. Thompson
Secretary: K. Biggin, 121 Mudford Road, Yeovil. Tel: Yeo 73731.
Fixtures Secretary: T. Newby, The Knoll, Preston Road, Yeovil. Tel: Yeo 21822.
Club captain (1987–88): H. Williams
Club captain (1988–89): S. Kitto
No. of teams: Senior 3. Youth & Minis 3.
Directions to Ground: Follow Taunton signs out of Yeovil, rugby ground at Bunford Lane can be easily seen.
Floodlights: Yes, training only
Membership: £5
Local newspaper: Western Gazette
League: Somerset 3
Final position (1987–88): 2nd
Playing record (1987–88): P 33, W 15, D 3, L 11.

BACKWELL

Winton Rugby Sports Centre, Winton Meadow, Nailsea, Bristol.
Founded: 1972
Secretary: P. Smallman, 15 Silverlow Road, Nailsea, Bristol. Tel: Nailsea 851953 (H), 854338 (B).
League: Somerset 3
Final position (1987–88): 3rd

TOR

Wirrall Park, Glastonbury, Somerset. Tel: 0458 31360
Founded: 1954
President: D. Sparks
Chairman: B. Harbinson
Secretary: J. Whittock, Shapwick Manor, Shapwick, Bridgwater
Fixtures Secretary: K. Elver, 170 Strode Road, Street. Tel: 0458 47284
Club captain (1987–88): J. Marshfield
Club captain (1988–89): J. Morse
No. of teams: Senior 2. Youth & Minis 6
Directions to Ground: On main A39 between Street and Glastonbury
Clubhouse: Wooden building, 2 changing rooms & bar area
Colours: Maroon
Floodlights: No
Admission: Donation
Membership: Non-players £7. Players £11.50
Local newspaper: Central Somerset Gazette
League: SOM3
Final position (1987–88): 4th
Playing record (1987–88): P 30, W 15, D 2, L 13

OLD ASHTONIANS

Ashton Park School, Blackmore Lane, Bower Ashton, Bristol. Tel: 0272 28385.
Founded: 1963
Secretary: M. Cox, "Lyndale", Wick Road, Brislington, Bristol BS4 4HV. Tel: 0272 773025 (H), 0272 731191 (B).
League: Somerset 3
Final position (1987–88): 5th

MORGANIANS

Chedroy Lane, Bridgwater. Tel: 423434
Founded: 1923
President: S.W. Vinecombe
Chairman: G.P. Bohot
Secretary: D.C. Presdee, 66 Woodbury Road, Bridgwater. Tel: 451366
Fixtures Secretary: D. Bryant, 14 Norfolk Close, Bridgwater. Tel: 427411
Club captain (1987–88): M. Derewicz
No. of teams: Senior 2
Directions to Ground: A39 out of Bridgwater, first right over motorway bridge
Clubhouse: Hall, lounge, skittle alley, 2 changing rooms, shower/bath block
Colours: Navy with red & gold bands. (*Change colours*: Red
Nickname: Morgs
Floodlights: No
Membership: £12
Local newspaper: Bridgwater Mercury
League: SOM3
Final position (1987–88): 6th
Playing record (1987–88): P 35, W 14, D 1, L 20

CHEW VALLEY OLD BOYS

Founded: 1968
Secretary: P. Nichols, 1 Lye Mead, Winford, Bristol BS18 8AV. Tel: 027 5872168 (H), 0272 500001 (B).
League: Somerset 3
Final position (1987–88): 7th

BATH CIVIL SERVICE

CS Club, Claverton Down, Bath. Tel: 0225 832403.
Founded: 1947
President: W. Chippendale
Chairman: C. Trout
Coach: R. McCullough

Somerset 3

Secretary: B. Clough, Linsley House, Beechen Cliff Road, Bath. Tel: 0225 319697.
Fixtures Secretary: B. Clough, as above.
Club captain (1987–88): A. Pike
Club captain (1988–89): A. Pike
No. of teams: Seniors 3.
Directions to Ground: From M4 take the main A36 to Bath, then follow signs to Bath until sign for A367 Exeter and Combe Down. Follow A367 past the University and ground on left.
Colours: Navy blue, cardinal red and gold. (*Change colours:* red).
Floodlights: No
Membership: £12 playing, £1 non-playing
Local newspaper: Bath Evening Chronicle
League: Somerset 3
Final position (1987–88): 7th
Playing record (1987–88): P 31, W 9, L 22.

CASTLE CARY

Brookhouse Field, Alhampton, Castle Cary, Somerset.
Founded: 1888
President: B.J. Crossfield
Chairman: B. Knock
Coach: J. Cranmer
Secretary: Mrs M.J. Armson, Brookhampton Cott, North Cadbury, Yeovil, Somerset. Tel: N.CAD 40648.
Fixtures Secretary: C. Watts, 15 Woodford Green, Ansford, Castle Cary, Somerset. Tel: C/Cary 50162.
Club captain (1987–88): J. Montgomery
Club captain (1988–89): N. Knight
No. of teams: Senior 2
Directions to Ground: 1 mile North of Castle Cary on A371 to Shepton Mallet.
Clubhouse: Full facilities
Colours: Red & black
Floodlights: No
Membership: £17.50 playing member
Local newspaper: Western Gazette, Yeovil
League: Somerset 3
Final position (1987–88): 9th
Playing record (1987–88): P 33, W 14, L 16, D 3.

WINCANTON

Hale Farm, Cocklington, Wincanton, Somerset.
Secretary: B.M. Watts, Coneygore, 60 Greenway Close, Wincanton, Somerset. Tel: 0963 33244 (H), 0963 33800 X 8334 (B).
League: Somerset 3
Final position (1987–88): 10th

CORNWALL LEAGUES

CORNWALL had a strong top division of 11 clubs, but their lower division comprised only five – a mere 16 clubs in all with another five in the Devon/Cornwall league, two in the Western League and another five in the two main South West divisions. Camborne, of course, play in Area League South. So the county is short of clubs in proper competition.

The top league was won by unbeaten Illogan Park, who drew just one game and won a Rugby World & Post monthly junior award. Wadebridge gave them a tough time and finished two points adrift, but at the foot of the table Stithians lost all matches and St. Just managed just one victory over their fellow-strugglers.

Competition in the tiny second section was fierce with Veor ending a point clear of Lankelly and Redruth GSOB and Roseland only one point further away from them. R.A.F. St. Mawgan gained only one point but their actual point differential showed that with luck they could have won a few matches and challenged for honours. They scored 16 points and conceded only 21.

TABLES 1987–88

CORNWALL 1

	P	W	D	L	F	A	Pts
Illogan Park	10	9	1	0	163	61	19
Wadebridge	10	8	1	1	200	89	17
Saltash	10	7	2	1	171	85	16
Helston	10	6	0	4	166	80	12
Liskeard	10	5	1	4	129	87	11
Bude	10	4	2	4	105	90	10
St Agnes	10	4	1	5	131	120	9
Bodmin	10	4	0	6	128	126	8
Redruth Alb	10	3	0	7	93	154	6
St Just	10	1	0	9	41	310	2
Stithians	10	0	0	10	49	174	0

CORNWALL 1

	P	W	D	L	F	A	Pts
Veor	4	3	0	1	34	19	6
Lankelly	4	2	1	1	37	39	5
Redruth GSOB	4	2	0	2	41	25	4
Roseland	4	2	0	2	21	45	4
RAF S Mawgan	4	0	1	3	16	21	1

● *The tables are published from information supplied. Any queries should be directed to the appropriate league secretary*

ILLOGEN PARK

Paynters Lane End, Illogan, Redruth, Cornwall.
Founded: 1967
Chairman: T. May
Coach: T. May
Secretary: I. Collett, Paynters Lane End, Illogan, Redruth, Cornwall.
Fixtures Secretary: G. Nicholls, 3 Railway Villas, Barncoose, Redruth, Cornwall.
Team secretary: B. Sullivan
Club captain (1987–88): M. Downing
Club captain (1988–89): M. Downing
Clubhouse: Good facilities.
Colours: Yellow shirts, one thick blacck hoop. Black shorts.
Nickname: "Park"
Floodlights: No
Local newspaper: The Cornishman
League: Cornwall 1
Final position (1987–88): 1st
Playing record (1987–88): P 38, W 28, D 4, L 6. F650, A280.
Competitions won: Rugby World & Post Junior Club of the Month March 1988.

WADEBRIDGE CAMELS

Bodieve, Wadebridge, Cornwall
Founded: 1955
President: Peter Richards
Chairman: Mike Howells
Coach: Brian Stevens
Secretary: John Owen, 5 Valley View, Wadebridge. Tel: 020 881 3453.
Fixtures Secretary: Mike Richards, 115 Egloshayle Road, Wadebridge, Cornwall. Tel: 020 881 2519.
Club captain (1987–88): Chris Taylor
Club captain (1988–89): Chris Taylor
No. of teams: Senior 2.
Directions to Ground: Northern side of Wadebridge (Cornwall), adjacent to Wadebridge FC.
Ground capacity: Touchline perimeter.
Clubhouse: Basic only, at present
Colours: Chocolate and gold.
Nickname: Camels
Floodlights: Yes, training only.
Membership: £8 players.
Programme: Free to members and VPs. (Editor: Tim Hitchman)
Local newspaper: Cornish Guardian
League: Cornwall 1
Final position (1987–88): 2nd
Playing record (1987–88): W 26, D 1, L 13. F 617, A 376.
Competitions won: Launceston Floodlit competition. J & B Rare Whisky & Rugby Ball, also 74 cans of beer from Courage for 74–3 win in league.

SALTASH

Moorlands Lane, Saltash, Cornwall. Tel: 7227
Founded: 1969
President: E.J. Jackett
Chairman: R.A. Dickerson
Coach: M. Thomas
Secretary: W.T. Ryan, 15 Fairmead Mews, Saltash, Cornwall. Tel: 075 55 3565
Fixtures Secretary: M.S. Charlick, 23 Plymtree Drive, Plympton, Plymouth. Tel: 0752 339186
Club captain (1987–88): N. Skinnard
Club captain (1988–89): J. Greiner
No. of teams: Senior 3. Youth & Minis 1
Directions to Ground: Cross Tamar Bridge, go through town centre, bear right at top to traffic lights, turn left, then second right at the Ploughboy Inn
Ground capacity: Public park
Colours: Red/black/gold. (*Change colours*: Red or maroon)
Nickname: Ashes
Floodlights: No
Membership: £7.50 players. £2 social
Local newspaper: Western Evening Herald & Cornish Times
League: Cornwall 1
Final position (1987–88): 3rd
Playing record (1987–88): P 38, W 19, D 4, L 15, F 578, A 503
Competitions won: Junior Merit Table Champions 1987/88, R. Ellis Knockout Cup (Plymouth Combination)

HELSTON

Clodgey Lane, Helston. Tel: 0326 573423
Founded: 1964
President: R.G.W. Sanders
Chairman: D.W. Wearne
Coach: J.C.C. Muirhead
Secretary: P.R.A. Collins, 'Chyreen', Cadgwith, Helston. Tel: 0326 290754 (H), 0290 712941 (W).
Fixtures Secretary: Mrs B.A. Davis, 8 Penrose Road, Helston. Tel: 0326 563744 (H), 0209 215620 (W).
Club captain (1987–88): D. Lockwood
Club captain (1988–89): R.S. Yelland
No. of teams: Senior 2. Youth & Minis 5.
Directions to Ground: Off Clodgey Lane, opposite Glenhaven Caravan Park at Helston Cricket Club entrance.
Clubhouse: Helston Cricket Club Pavillion, Clodgey Lane, Helston.
Colours: Navy and white hoops. (*Change colours:* Green and blue hoops).
Floodlights: No
Membership: £7
Local newspaper: Helston Packet/West Briton
League: Cornwall 1
Final position (1987–88): 4th
Playing record (1987–88): P 34, W 19, D 0, L 15. F 535, A 398.
Competitions won: 1988 Cornwall Plate Competition Cup

LISKEARD

Lux Park, Liskeard, Cornwall. Tel: 0579 42665
Founded: 1956
President: J.W.W. Smith
Chairman: Robin Stephens
Coach: Chris Hocking
Secretary: Geoff Collings, Little Polscoe, Lostwithiel. Tel: 0208 873201.
Fixtures Secretary: Geoff Collings. As above.
Club captain (1987–88): Tony Patten
Club captain (1988–89): Ian Strang
No. of teams: Senior 3. Youth & Minis 7.
Directions to Ground: Leave A38 to A 390 follow signs to Liskeard Sports Centre.
Clubhouse: Shared Liskeard Sports Club.
Colours: Red and black hoops. (*Change colours:* black).
Floodlights: No
Membership: £10 playing, £12 VP
Local newspaper: Cornish Times, Western Morning News
League: Cornwall 2
Final position (1987–88): 5th
Playing record (1987–88): P 35, W 22, D 1, L 12.

BUDE

Bencoolen Meadow, Bude. Tel: 4795
Founded: 1966
President: G.J. Woodward
Chairman: P. Tilzey
Coach: E. Gent
Secretary: C.R. Woodward, 24 St Marwenne Close, Marhamchurch, Bude. Tel: 0288 85750.
Fixtures Secretary: J. Boundy, Linhays, Butterbearex, Bridgerule, Devon.
Club captain (1987–88): P. Cholwill
Club captain (1988–89): M. Fry
No. of teams: Senior 2. Youth & Minis 1.
Directions to Ground: Main road into Bude turn left at bottom of hill, then first right.
Clubhouse: Bar plus changing rooms.
Colours: Maroon and blue hoops.
Floodlights: No
Membership: £120 (full life membership) £5 social membership
Local newspaper: Bude & Stratton Post
League: Cornwall 1
Final position (1987–88): 6th

ST. AGNES

Ground: Wheal Butson, St. Agnes
Clubhouse: Enys Park, St. Agnes. Tel: 0872 553673
Founded: 1972
President: G. Jones
Chairman: M. Watts
Coach: G. Gibson
Secretary: P. Carson, 22 Polstain Road, Threemilestone, Truro. Tel: 0872 75479
Fixtures Secretary: M. Watts, Trevalunace Point Hotel, St. Agnes. Tel: 0872 553275
Club captain (1987–88): M. Boeck
Club captain (1988–89): C. Blackmore
No. of teams: Senior 2
Directions to Ground: Proceed through St. Agnes Village to the St. Agnes Hotel, turn left, carry on for ½ mile and take right fork. Enys Park is a short way along on the right
Clubhouse: Shared facility with St. Agnes Sports Club. 4 changing rooms & bar area
Colours: Red & black hoops. (*Change colours*: Blue)
Nickname: Chiefs (1st team)
Floodlights: No
Membership: £10
Local newspaper: West Briton & West Briton Argus
League: Cornwall Combination 1
Final position (1987–88): 7th
Playing record (1987–88): P 32, W 15, D 3, L 14

BODMIN

Cliffden Park, Bodmin, Cornwall.
Founded: 1969
Secretary: A. Cornish, 7 Whitestone Crescent, Bodmin, Cornwall. Tel: Bodmin 2174.
League: Cornwall 1
Final position (1987–88): 8th
Playing record (1987–88): P 38, W 13, D 1, L 24. F 465, A 560.

REDRUTH ALBANY

2 Station Hill, Redruth, Cornwall. Tel: 0209 216945
Founded: 1928/29
President: N.J. Goldsworthy
Chairman: N. Barnes
Coach: C. Instance
Secretary: W.J. Rogers, "Pencoys", Roskear, Camborne, Cornwall. Tel: 0209 714102
Fixtures Secretary: C. Johns, "Colaine", Strawberry Lane, Redruth. Tel: 0209 218886
Club captain (1987–88): Alan Mitchell
Club captain (1988–89): Alan Mitchell
No. of teams: Senior 2. Youth & Minis 1
Directions to Ground: ½ mile in a south-westerly direction from the centre of Redruth
Clubhouse: 2 bars
Colours: Royal blue. (*Change colours*: Blue & white squares)
Floodlights: Yes. Partial
Membership: £6
Local newspaper: Camborne & Redruth Packet
League: Cornwall 1
Final position (1987–88): 7th
Playing record (1987–88): P 42, W 27, D 1, L 14

ST JUST

Turnpike Road, Treyeseal, St Just in Penwith, Cornwall. Tel: 0736 788593.
Founded: 1967
Secretary: R. Warren, Sheldon, Tredavoe Lane, Newlyn, Cornwall TR18 5DN. Tel: 0736 62986 (H).
Local newspaper: The Cornishman
League: Cornwall 1
Final position (1987–88): 10th
Playing record (1987–88): P 37, W 11, D 1, L 24. F 332, A 879.

STITHIANS

Stithians, Truro, Cornwall
Founded: 1890
Secretary: N. Plummer, New Road, Stithians, Truro, Cornwall.
Local newspaper: The Cornishman
League: Cornwall 1
Final position (1987–88): 11th (relegated)
Playing record (1987–88): P 33, W 13, L 20. F 352, A 457.

VEOR

Whealgerry, Cliff View Road, Camborne, Cornwall
Founded: 1969
President: R. Goldby
Chairman: J. Mankee
Coach: T. Bassett
Secretary: N.J. Barber, JP, 86 Dolcoath Road, Camborne, Cornwall TR14 8RP. Tel: 0209 710593
Fixtures Secretary: P. Pascoe, 18 Condurrow Road, Beacon, Camborne. Tel: 0209 716535
Club captain (1987–88): P. Jewell/D. Andrew
Club captain (1988–89): To be appointed
No. of teams: Senior 1
Directions to Ground: Turn off A30 Camborne & Redruth bypass at Camborne signpost and follow sign to Camborne, turn right at traffic lights, at bottom of hill turn right again (just before pedestrian crossing), follow this road for approx ½ mile, then turn right at crossroads after T.A. centre. Ground is 100 yds on right hand side, next to school
Clubhouse: Red Jackets Inn, Trevenson Street, Camborne
Colours: Black with amber V.(*Change colours*: Amber shirts, black shorts
Nickname: Gerrymen
Floodlights: No
Membership: £5 per annum
Local newspaper: Camborne & Redruth Packet
League: Cornwall 2
Final position (1987–88): Winners
Playing record (1987–88): P 32, W 14, D 2, L 16, F 416, A 402

LANKELLY-FOWEY

Lankelly Farm, Fowey. Tel: 072-683 3350
Founded: 1968
President: J.W. Lewis
Chairman: C.S. Biggs
Coach: B. Monk
Secretary: J.W. Lewis, 62 Esplanade, Fowey, Cornwall PL23 1FA. Tel: 972-683 3464.
Fixtures Secretary: N. Dennis, 38 Allen Vale, Gypsy Lane, Liskeard. Tel: 0579 47678
No. of teams: Senior 1
Directions to Ground: Turn right into Lankelly Lane at entrance to Fowey opposite Cotswold Garage.
Clubhouse: Penlee Hotel, Fowey
Colours: Navy Blue. (*Change colours:* Yellow.)
Nickname: Kelly
Floodlights: No
Admission: Collection
Membership: £10
Local newspaper: Cornish Guardian & Cornish Times
League: Cornwall 2
Final position (1987–88): Runners-up
Playing record (1987–88): P 31, W 12, D 5, L 14.

REDRUTH GS OBs

Clijan Croft, Redruth. Tel: 216586
Founded: 1958
President: Mrs. Joan Meneer
Chairman: Ewart Thomas
Coach: K.P. Bawden/A. Parsons
Secretary: A.P. Lay, 27 Bosvean Road, Shortlanesend, Truro, Cornwall
Fixtures Secretary: Alan Wetheralt. Tel: 213995
Club captain (1987–88): David Teague
Club captain (1988–89): Nigel Mitchell
No. of teams: Senior 1
Directions to Ground: From Redruth centre follow signs to Falmouth, after ½ mile go over traffic lights at Trefusis Arms. Ground on right after 300 yds down Wheal Trefusis
Clubhouse: Newish, Council (Kerrier) owned
Colours: Red/black. (*Change colours*: Green)
Nickname: Old Boys
Floodlights: No
Local newspaper: Falmouth/Redruth Packet
League: Cornwall 2
Final position (1987–88): 3rd

ROSELAND

Philleigh, Truro, Cornwall. Tel: 0872 58254
Founded: 1971
President: D.L. Sinnot
Chairman: D. Thomas
Coach: R. Grove
Secretary: C.R. Thomas, Parton Vrane, Gerrans, Portscatho, Cornwall TR2 5ET. Tel: 0872 58495
Fixtures Secretary: C.J. Trerise, Omega, Blackwater, Truro, Cornwall. Tel: 0872 560248
Club captain (1987–88): H. Stobart
Club captain (1988–89): H. Stobart
No. of teams: Senior 1
Directions to Ground: Follow sings from Truro for St. Mawes, then Philleigh
Clubhouse: Roseland Inn
Colours: Navy & scarlet
Floodlights: No
Membership: £5 per annum
League: Cornwall 2
Final position (1987–88): 4th

RAF ST. MAWGAN

RAF St. Mawgan, Newquay, Cornwall. Tel: Newquay 872201
President: Wg. Cdr. Spalding
Chairman: Flt. Lt. Aunger
Secretary: Sac. C. Palmer, RAF St. Mawgan
Fixtures Secretary: Cpl. Cheadle, RAF St. Mawgan
Club captain (1987–88): Cpl. Barraclough
Club captain (1988–89): Sac. Blanken
No. of teams: Senior 1
Directions to Ground: On RAF St. Mawgan Station itself
Colours: Light/dark blue hoop. (*Change colours*: Red/blue/yellow hoops)
Floodlights: No
Membership: £5
Local newspaper: Cornish Guardian
League: Cornwall 2
Final position (1987–88): 5th

London's Simon Smith hauls down South-West's Simon Halliday on 13th December 1986, but the West Country men win. Photo: Colorsport.

London's Ken Moss takes a pass from Mark Rigby against the North, who win and are also the 1986–87 champions. Photo: Colorsport.

LONDON DIVISION

THE London Division has no less than 31 leagues starting with a top division (London 1), followed by two regionally based second divisions and a further four geographically selected third divisions. The leagues are then organised below that level by counties, which have leagues of various sizes.

Eastern Counties are the largest of the latter groupings with five major divisions and more to come? Hertfordshire with only 15 clubs completing their programmes are the smallest.

The John Player Cup gave an indication about the strength of so-called junior clubs in the division and it will be interesting to see how Ealing, the London 1 champions, fare at a stronger level. Others to watch in the future are Ruislip, the Sussex club Lewes, Ipswich, North Walsham and Basingstoke. Bancrofts in Eastern Counties 5 scored a massive 447 points but if they were to progress upwards without any kind of hindrance it would take them something like six years just to reach the top divisional leagues. They surely have the patience for that.

LONDON LEAGUES

A TOTAL of seven leagues are coverd by the 'London' heading starting with London 1, which was won comfortably by the ambitious Ealing club, who lost but one match and finished four points clear of Ruislip. Lewes maintained a good challenge from Sussex and Ipswich from Suffolk – neither place a rugby hotbed. Upper Clapton at the foot of the table were out of their depth, but Esher, who have excellent club facilities, were unlucky to go down with them owing to an inferior points difference as compared to United Services, Portsmouth, who rallied late in the campaign.

North Walsham won London 2N by a single point in a most hotly contested league from Grasshoppers; it was a great pity that West London Institute, which has a number of good players, withdrew during the campaign. This left St. Mary's Hospital, who managed a draw only in the fixtures, at the foot of the table with a score of '−1', the result of a rules breach! It was, needless to say, one of the lowest scores of any team in the whole organisation nationally. Hertford were the other basement side owing to an inferior points difference to Old Albanians and Old Merchant Taylors.

Basingstoke were also pushed to win their league – London 2S – again on points difference from Old Mid Whitgiftians and the two basement sides were Portsmouth and Old Juddians.

The four third leagues produced some good winners in Barking (NE), Bishops Stortford (NW), Tunbridge Wells (SE) and Purley (SW). All were at least one point clear of the main challengers, although none were unbeaten. Bishops Stortford had a fine season overall and won a Rugby World & Post Junior Club of the Month award.

The basement sides were Brentwood and Bury St. Edmunds (NE), Twickenham and Old Paulines (NW), Gillingham Anchorian and Canterbury (SE) and Warlingham and the luckless Trojans (SW). Only Twickenham (on points difference from Bacavians) and Warlingham (for the same reason from Guy's Hospital) could be counted as unlucky.

TABLES 1987–88

LONDON 1

	P	W	D	L	F	A	Pts
Ealing	s10	9	0	1	198	60	18
Ruislip	10	7	0	3	182	68	14
Lewes	10	6	0	4	120	87	12
Ipswich	10	6	0	4	97	103	12
O.Gayton's	10	5	0	5	99	122	10
Dartfordians	10	5	0	5	90	159	10
Sutton & Epsom	10	4	1	5	108	110	9
Guildford & God	10	4	0	5	100	104	8
US Portsm'th	10	3	1	6	100	128	7
Esher	10	3	1	6	68	133	7
Upr Clapton	10	1	1	8	53	141	3

LONDON 2N

	P	W	D	L	F	A	Pts
N Walsham	9	7	0	2	180	72	14
Grasshoppers	9	6	1	2	134	121	13
Norwich	9	6	0	3	109	63	12
Cheshunt	9	5	1	3	160	93	11
Thurrock	9	5	1	3	118	59	11
Woodford	9	5	0	4	135	104	10
O. Albanians	9	2	2	5	94	121	6
Old Merchant Taylors	9	2	2	5	112	167	6
Hertford	9	2	2	5	47	112	6
St Marys Hospital**	9	0	1	8	46	223	−1

West London Institute withdrawn – all results void
***2 points deducted – breach of rules*

LONDON 2S

	P	W	D	L	F	A	Pts
Basingstoke	10	8	0	2	253	89	16
Old Mid Whitgiftians	10	8	0	2	176	113	16
Worthing	10	7	0	3	171	117	14
Camberley	10	7	0	3	139	122	14
Old Alleynian	10	6	0	4	157	80	12
Gravesend	10	5	0	5	97	180	12
Old Brockleians	10	4	0	6	100	137	8
K.C.S. O.B.	10	3	1	6	108	187	7
Old Reigatian	10	3	0	7	71	133	6
Portsmouth	10	2	1	7	98	142	5
Old Juddian	10	1	0	9	123	193	2

LONDON 3 NE

	P	W	D	L	F	A	Pts
Barking	10	8	1	1	204	61	17
Eton Manor	10	8	0	2	171	76	16
West Norfolk	10	6	1	3	115	108	13
Colchester	10	6	0	4	126	94	12
Old Westcliffians	10	5	2	3	149	118	12
Chingford	10	5	0	5	117	96	10
Ipswich YMCA	10	4	0	6	100	122	8
Saffron Walden	10	4	0	6	91	117	8
Old Cantabrigian	10	4	0	6	99	130	8
Brentwood	10	2	0	8	75	196	4
Bury St. Edmunds	10	1	0	9	61	190	2

LONDON 3 NW

	P	W	D	L	F	A	Pts
Bishops Stortford	10	9	0	1	192	72	18
Hendon	10	8	0	2	166	89	16
Letchworth	10	7	1	2	120	76	15
Tabard	10	7	1	2	104	87	15
Fullerians	10	6	0	4	159	98	12
Old Kingsburian	10	5	0	5	169	115	10
Mill Hill	10	4	1	5	107	104	9
Harrow	10	2	1	7	77	156	5
Bacavians	10	2	0	8	70	140	4
Twickenham	10	2	0	8	47	177	4
Old Paulines	10	1	0	9	65	162	2

LONDON 3 SE

	P	W	D	L	F	A	Pts
Tunbridge Wells	10	7	2	1	169	106	16
Beckenham	10	7	1	2	106	77	15
Old Colfeians	10	6	1	3	148	115	13
Westcombe Park	10	5	2	3	149	77	12
Crawley	10	5	0	5	116	108	10
Horsham	10	5	0	5	104	123	10
East Grinstead	10	4	1	5	109	99	9
Old Dunstonian	10	4	15	95	113	9	
Old Beccehamians	10	4	0	6	84	110	8
Gillingham Anchorian	10	3	1	6	78	122	7
Canterbury	10	0	1	9	59	177	1

LONDON 3 SW

	P	W	D	L	F	A	Pts
Purley	10	9	0	1	228	67	18
Alton	10	7	0	3	187	96	14
Old Walcountians	10	7	0	3	133	102	14
Eastleigh	10	6	0	4	170	95	12
Old Emanuel	10	6	0	4	133	106	12
Jersey	10	5	0	5	168	121	10
Old Whitgiftians	10	5	0	5	90	117	10
Winchester**	10	4	0	6	126	142	8
Guy's Hospital	10	3	0	7	149	161	6
Warlingham	10	3	0	7	102	165	6
Trojans	10	0	0	10	43	369	0

***12 match points deducted – ineligible player.*

EALING

Berkeley Avenue, Greenford, Middlesex. Tel(01-422-0868.
Founded: 1871
Secretary: C.R. Benjamin, "Kenilworth", 30 Woodville Road, Ealing, London W5. Tel: 01-997-5967 (H), 01-507-5167 (B).
Fixtures Secretary: P. Monteith, 65 Pinner Hill Road, Pinner, Middlesex. Tel: 01-429-3009 (H), 01-638-1001 (B).
Colts Secretary: W. Taylor, 435 Whitton Avenue, West Greenford, Middlesex. Tel: 01-864-6542 (H).
League: London 1
Final position (1987–88): 1st
Playing record (1987–88): P 32, W 27, L 5, F 712, A 206.

RUISLIP

Herlwyn Fields, West End Road, Ruislip, Middlesex. Tel: 0895 633102.
Founded: 1936
Secretary: S. Westfallen, 4 Upper Hill Rise, Chorleywood, Rickmansworth, Herts. WD3 2NU. Tel: 0923 774012 (H).
Fixtures Secretary: G. Sykes, 11 Ivy Close, Eastcote, Pinner, Middlesex. Tel: 01-866-5430.
Colts Secretary: M. Gravestock, 177B Swakeleys Road, Ickenham, Middlesex UB10 8DN.
League: London 2
Final position (1987–88): 2nd
Playing record (1987–88): P 39, W 29, L 10, F 721, A 314.
Competitions won: Reached 3rd round – John Player Cup.

LEWES

5 Cleve Terrace, Lewes, E. Sussex BN7 1JJ. Tel: 0378-72588.
Founded: 1930
President: R.B. Rees
Chairman: G. Thompson
Coach: Terry Powell
Secretary: Phil Clark, 5 Cleve Terrace, Lewes, E Sussex BN7 1JJ
Fixtures Secretary: Ken Gordon, Lynsted, Coopers Green, Uckfield, E. Sussex
Club captain (1987–88): Nic Hanson
Club captain (1988–89): Paul Taylor
No. of teams: Senior 5. Youth & Minis 4.
Colours: Blue and White Hoops
Nickname: None
Floodlights: No
Membership: £20
Local newspaper: Sussex Express
League: London I
Final position (1987–88): 3rd
Competitions won: Sussex Cup Winners: 1972, 1974, 1975, 1977, 1978, 1979, 1981, 1985, 1987

IPSWICH

Valley Road, Ipswich, Suffolk.
Founded: 1870
Secretary: N. Farthing, 72 Orford Street, Ipswich, Suffolk. Tel: 0473 53677 (H), 0473 213221 (W).
League: London 1
Final position (1987–88): 4th
Playing record (1987–88): P 27, W 16, L 11, F 409, A 321.

OLD GAYTONIANS

South Vale, Sudbury Hill, Harrow, Middx. Tel: 01-423 4133.
Founded: 1934
President: J.W. Carroll
Chairman: J.H. Rigby
Secretary: A. Pusher, 9 Paynesfield Road, Bushey Heath, Herts WD2 1PQ. Tel: 01-950 2956.
Fixtures Secretary: J. Brake, 14 Foxes Way, Warwick, Warwickshire CV3 468X. Tel: 0926 494408.
Club captain (1987–88): D. Maxted
Club captain (1988–89): S. Rigby
No. of teams: Senior 5. Youth & Minis 1.
Directions to Ground: Piccadilly Line to Sudbury Hill Station. Turn left. Ground in road opposite the 'Rising Sun'. By road: South Vale is a turning off Greenford Road (A4127). Opposite the Rising Sun.
Colours: White jerseys with broad band of light blue, chocolate and green; white shorts. (*Change colours:* Dark green)
Floodlights: No
Membership: £26.50
Local newspaper: Harlow Observer
League: London 1
Final position (1987–88): 5th
Playing record (1987–88): P 32, W 18, L 13, D 1, F 512, A 419.
Competitions won: Middx Agar Cup 1980, 1981, 1982, 1983, 1985, 1986; Berks 7's Plate 1987, 1988; Hertford Floodlit 7's 1982, 1983, 1984.

DARTFORDIANS

Bourne End, Bexley, Kent. Tel: Crayford 524176.
Founded: 1924
Secretary: D. Stilling, 2 Brookfield, Kemsing, Near Sevenoaks, Kent TN15 6SQ. Tel: Otford 4468 (H), 01-629-4509 (B).
Fixtures Secretary: D. Rapley, 11 Felhampton Road, New Eltham, London SE19. Tel: 01-857-6198.
League: London 1
Final position (1987–88): 6th
Playing record (1987–88): P 27, W 12, D 1, L 14, F 265, A 363.

SUTTON & EPSOM

Cuddington Court, Rugby Lane, West Drive, Cheam, Surrey. Tel: 01-642 0280.
Founded: 1881
President: B.A. Moore
Coach: C. Marshall
Secretary: I.C. Evans, 29 Dorling Drive, Epsom, Surrey KT17 3BH. Tel. 01-393 8949 (H). 01 247 7666 (W).
Fixtures Secretary: R.E.G. Canes, 5 Shirley Road, Wallington, Surrey. Tel: 01-647 7464.
Club captain (1987–88): D. Steel
Club captain (1988–89): R. Cheall
No. of teams: Senior 8. Youth & Minis 10.
Directions to Ground: Convenient to M25 and A3, near Ewell Bypass.
Ground capacity: c. 2000. Stand, c. 400.
Clubhouse: 2 bars
Colours: Black & white hoops, black shorts & socks. (*Change colours:* Light blue)
Floodlights: Yes
Membership: Playing £40; Non-playing £15; Life £75; U21 £25; U18 £20; Family £10; Lady £1.
Programme: Editor, I.P. Smith.
Local newspapers: Epsom & Ewell Herald, Sutton Herald
League: London 1
Final position (1987–88): 6th

Playing record (1987–88): P 32, W 14, D 3, L 15.
Competitions won: Surrey Cup 1983/4; Surrey Veterans Cup 1985/6, 1986/7; Surrey Colts Cup 1986/7; Numerous 7's competitions.

GUILDFORD & GODALMING

Broadwater, Guildford Road, Godalming, Surrey. Tel: 048-68-6199
Founded: 1922
President: G.S. Howell
Chairman: J. Vivian
Coach: A. Roberts
Secretary: A.W. Bird, The Old Barn, Hog's Hill, Fernhurst, Haslemere, Surrey. Tel: 0428-53359
Fixtures Secretary: L. Bodill, 11 Briarway, Burpham, Guildford. Tel: 570580.
Club captain (1987–88): A.C. Sacha
Club captain (1988–89): A.C. Sacha
No. of teams: Senior 6. Youth & Minis 10.
Directions to Ground: A3100 Guildford to Godalming Road. 3 miles.
Ground capacity: 1,000
Colours: Green & white hoops
Change colours: Red or blue
Nickname: G & G
Floodlights: No
Membership: Players £30. Non-players £17.50.
Programme: 20p
Local newspaper: Surrey Advertiser
League: London I
Final position (1987–88): 8th
Playing record (1987–88): P37, W22, L15, F538, A364
Competitions won: Surrey Cup Runners-up

UNITED SERVICES PORTSMOUTH

Burnaby Road, Portsmouth, Hants. Tel: 0705 825394.
Founded: 1882
Secretary: Lt. D. Seal, R.N., Wardroom, HMS Collingwood, Fareham, Hants. Tel: 0705 822351 Ex 85705 (W).
Fixtures Secretary: Lt. Cdr. N.J. Stone, R.N., Supply Officer, HMS Warrior, Northwood, Middlesex. Tel: 09274 2161 Ex 390 (W).
League: London 1
Final position (1987–88): 9th
Playing record (1987–88): P 29, W 10, D 1, L 18, F 340, A 432.

ESHER

369 Molesey Road, Hersham, Surrey
Founded: 1924
President: A.R. Prentice
Chairman: B.J. Holland
Coach: E. Collins
Secretary: A.R. Till, 25 Motspur Park, New Malden, Surrey KT3 6PS. Tel: 01-942-1380(H)
Fixtures Secretary: J. Inverdale, 37 Borough Road, Kingston on Thames, Surrey. Tel: 01-546-6342
Club captain (1987–88): P. Stevens
Club captain (1988–89): P. Wogan
No. of teams: Senior 8. Youth & Minis 6.
Directions to Ground: 369 Molesey Road near Hersham BR Station – Walton-on-Thames – 15 mins from M25.
Ground capacity: 2000
Clubhouse: Excellent clubhouse with bars and changing rooms.
Colours: Black & amber (*Change colours*: White)
Floodlights: Yes
Admission: Varies
Membership: £30 full playing
Programme: Varies
Local newspaper: Surrey Herald, Surrey Comet
League: London 25
Final position (1987–88): Relegated from London Div I.
Playing record (1987–88): W13, D2, L21.

UPPER CLAPTON

The Clubhouse, Upland Road, Thornwood Common, nr Epping, Essex. Tel: 0378-72588
Founded: 1879
President: Mike Maskell
Coach: Alan Birkbeck
Secretary: David Miller, 13 Rushfield, Sawbridgeworth, Herts CM211 9NF. Tel: 9279-724849
Fixtures Secretary: Roger Barnett, 9 Church Hill, Loughton, Essex. Tel: 01-508-8856
Club captain (1987–88): Andy Miller
Club captain (1988–89): Jim O'Shea
No. of teams: Senior 5. Youth & Minis 3.
Directions to Ground: Take M11 north to Junction 7 (Harlow exit). Turn south to Epping on B1393 (old A11). Approx 1 mile, upland road on right. Signposted Epping Green, Just before Texaco Petrol Station.
Ground capacity: 500 plus
Clubhouse: Large clubhouse (300 capacity). Changing facilities for 8 teams. Plunge bath and 12 showers, large bar.
Colours: Red & white. 7″ hoops
Change colours: All white.
Nickname: The Club
Floodlights: No
Membership: £30 players, £7 non-players
Local newspaper: Guardian Gazette
League: London 1
Final position (1987–88): Last (relegated)
Playing record (1987–88): P32, W15, D1, L16, F350, A420
Competitions won: Essex 7-a-Side winners 9 times, Essex Cup Winners twice.

LONDON 2N

NORTH WALSHAM

Norwich Road, Slotton, North Walsham, Norfolk. Tel: 069 269416.
Founded: 1962
Secretary: J.P. Kefford, 93 Onley Street, Norwich, Norfolk NR2 2EA. Tel: 0603 661943 (H), 0603 660202. Extn 7762 (W)
Fixtures Secretary: J. Hodges, Church View, Town Street, Hickling, Norfolk. Tel: Hickling 318.
League: London 2N
Final position (1987–88): 1st (promoted)
Playing record (1987–88): P 36, W 28, D 1, L 7. F 797, A 263.
Competitions won: 1st London 2N 1987–88

GRASSHOPPERS

MacFarlane Sports Ground
Founded: 1950
Secretary: G. Neve, 59 Meadow Road, Hanworth, Middx. Tel: 01-898 9388 (H), 01-741 2849 (W).
Fixtures Secretary: P. Welsh, 56 Crane Way, Whitton, Middx. Tel: 01-894 0446.
League: London 2N
Final position (1987–88): 2nd
Playing record (1987–88): P 24, W 17, D 2, L 5. F 342, A 227.

NORWICH

Beeston Hythe, North Walsham Road, Norwich.
Founded: 1885
Secretary: C.T. Gillham, Daynes Hill & Perks, Paston House, Princes Street, Norwich NR3 1BD. Tel: 0603 58439 (H), 0603 660241 (W).
Fixtures Secretary: K.E.G. Searle, Mardon House, Ashby St Mary, Norwich NR14 7BJ. Tel: Thurton 364 (H), 0603 53786 (W).
League: London 2N
Final position (1987–88): 3rd
Playing record (1987–88): P 31, W 23, L 8. F 623, A 210.

NORTH CHESHUNT

Founded: 1952
Secretary: R.S. Boulton, Cobweb Cottage, 9 Brickendon Lane, Brickendon, Herts. Tel: 099 286 483.
Fixtures Secretary: C. Garside, 14 Walton Road, Ware, Herts SG12 9PF. Tel: 0920 2968.
League: London 2N
Final position (1987–88): 4th
Playing record (1987–88): P 31, W 22, D 1, L 8. F 825, A 292.
Competitions won: Finalists in Benidorm Sevens

THURROCK

"Oakfield", Long Lane, Grays, Essex. Tel: 0375 374877.
Founded: 1928
Secretary: D.H. Evans, 29 Mayfields, Connaught Avenue, Grays, Essex. Tel: 0375 379571 (W).
League: London 2N
Final position (1987–88): 5th
Playing record (1987–88): P 30, W 18, D 2, L 10. F 466, A 244

WOODFORD

Highams, Woodford High Road, Woodford Green, Essex. Tel: 01-504-6764.
Founded: 1926
President: H.H. Colley
Chairman: E.J. Beck
Coach: P. Lees
Secretary: N. Savage, 35D Grange Court, Gordon Road, South Woodford, London E18 1DN. Tel: 01-506-0640 (H), 01-405-8400 (W).
Fixtures Secretary: N. Hooper, Sheepcots Cottage, Clavering, Saffron Walden, Essex CB11 4SJ.
Club captain (1987–88): P.R. Christey
Club captain (1988–89): P. Grindley
No. of teams: Senior 7, Youth & Minis 10
Directions to Ground: Woodford Tube Station North via Snakes Lane to Woodford High Road thence right for 500 yards. Club entrance on right.
Ground capacity: Stand, 250
Clubhouse: 1926 wooden with slightly "Run Down" character.
Colours: White, lavender & black. (*Change colours:* Purple)
Floodlights: Yes training purposes only.
Admission: Free
Membership: £34.50 before 20.8.88 for playing members.
Local newspaper: Gazette
League: London 2 North
Final position (1987–88): Sixth
Playing record (1987–88): P 33, W 11, L 21, D 1, F 387, A 446.
Competitions won: Runners-up in the Essex Cup Final.

OLD ALBANIANS

Beech Bottom, Old Harpenden Road, St Albans, Herts. Tel: Club House: St.A. 64476
Steward: St.A. 52082
Founded: 1922
President: I.F. Jennings
Coach: R. Stewart
Secretary: P. Lipscomb, 35 Gurney Court Road, St. Albans Herts. Tel: St. A. 63621
Fixtures Secretary: D. Verdon, 9 Bucknalls Lane, Garston, Herts. Garston 679471
Club captain (1987–88): H. Harrison
Club captain (1988–89): J. Hibberd
No. of teams: Senior 5. Youth & Minis 5.
Directions to Ground: 1 mile from centre of St Albans on A1081 towards Luton, 150 yards from the Ancient Briton Public House.
Ground capacity: 3 pitches and cricket square
Clubhouse: Single storey, 5 changing rooms, baths and showers.
Colours: Red, blue and gold hooped shirts
Nickname: O.AS
Floodlights: Yes, training only.
Membership: £28 members, £12 students, Colts free, V.P.s £10
Programme: 20p (Editor: P. Brazier)
Local newspaper: Herts Advertiser
League: London North 2
Final position (1987–88): 6th
Playing record (1987–88): P 34, W 15, L 16 D 3.

OLD MERCHANT TAYLORS

Durrants, Lincoln Drive, Croxley Green, Rickmansworth, Herts. Tel: 0923 773014.
Founded: 1882
Secretary: M. Foster, 16 New Road, Croxley Green, Rickmansworth, Herts. Tel: 0923 775793 (H), 0923 45951 (W).
Fixtures Secretary: G.W. Shilling, The Lodge, Wellingrove, Woodcock Hill, Rickmansworth, Herts. Tel: 0923 774506.
League: London 2N
Final position (1987–88): 8th
Playing record (1987–88): P 37, W 20, D 3, L 14. F 582, A 410.

HERTFORD

"Highfields", Hoe Lane, Ware, Herts SG12 9NZ. Tel: 0920 2975
Founded: 1931
President: Mr J.R.H. Creasey
Chairman: Mr J.S. Atkinson
Coach: Mr P. (Peter) Cadle
Secretary: Mr J. (John) Beard, 251 Ware Road, Hertford, AL1 1NG. Tel: 0992 589135 (H): 0727 35504 (B)
Fixtures Secretary: Mr I.B.K. (Ian) Kennedy, 211 High Road, Broxbourne, Herts EN10 6PZX. Tel: 0992 463135
Club captain (1987–88): Mr N. (Nick) Brooking

London 2N

Club captain (1988–89): Mr G. (Graeme) Walters
No. of teams: Senior 7. Youth & Minis 9.
Directions to Ground: From London A10, come off at A414 junction signposted Harlow/Chelmsford. At Stansted roundabout turn immediately left onto B1502. Ground in Hoe Lane, 3 miles on right. From the west take A414 to Hertford. At Gallows Hill roundabout take b1502 and ground is in Hoe Lane, 500 yards on left.
Ground capacity: 500
Clubhouse: 2 bars, kitchen and catering faciliites, function room for dining and/or dancing, committee room, bath/showers, 2 squash courts, 5 pitches, adequate parking.
Colours: Black, royal blue and gold (*Change colours:* Light blue)
Floodlights: Yes
Admission: 30p
Membership: £30, Non-playing membership £5
Programme: 8 pages, 30p. (Editor: Mr I.B.K. (Ian) Kennedy)
Local newspaper: Hertfordshire Mercury; "This Week" (free sheet inc. Rugby Report)
League: Londfon 2 North
Final position (1987–88): 9th
Playing record (1987–88): 1st XV Home Leage Games – P 34, W 10, D 4, L 20, 321 F. 424 A.
Full Club Playing Record in 1987–88 – P 226, W 137, D 14, L 75. Pts for 3,469; Pts Against 2,116
Competitions won: Winners Herts 7s Tournament 1951; 1959; 1961. Winners Herts Colts Cup 1987. Winners Hertford RFC Leda Floodlit Cup Comp 1987

ST MARY'S HOSPITAL

St Mary's Hospital Medical School, Norfolk Place, Paddington, London W2.
Founded: 1866
President: Dr. G.V. Strong, FFARCS
Secretary: R.A.L.Young, FRCS, West Middlesex Hospital, Twickenham Road, Middlesex
Fixtures Secretary: A. Sim, FRCS, St Mary's Hospital, Praed Street, London W2
Club captain (1987–88): A. Taylor
Club captain (1988–89): A. Ellery
No. of teams: Senior 4.
Directions to Ground: St Mary's Hospital Athletic Ground, Udney Park Road, Teddington.
Clubhouse: Tel: 01-088-3100
Colours: Blue and white
Floodlights: No
Membership: Post Graduate Subscription £10 p.a.
League: London North 3
Final position (1987–88): 10th (London N2)
Competitions won: 1987 seven Counties Merit Table 7-a-Sides. 1988 United Hospitals Challenge Cup.

WEST LONDON INSTITUTE

Borough Road, Isleworth, Middlesex TW7 5DV
Founded: 1891
President: Dr J.E. Kane
Chairman: F. Jamieson
Coach: Jon Atkin
Administrator & Fixtures Secretary: John Hunter, Head 07 P.E. A2 WLIHE, X 2937.
Club captain (1987–88): Paul Tappin
Club captain (1988–89): John Keohane
No. of teams: Senior 3.
Directions to Ground: Beside the Great West Road in Osterley/Isleworth – on A2
Ground capacity: 300
Clubhouse: S.U. facilities
Colours: Chocolate, black and white
Nickname: The Bees
Floodlights: Yes, training only
Membership: £10
Local newspaper: Middlesex Chronicle
League: London 2N
Final position (1987–88): Withdrawn
Competitions won: British Colleges Cup 1987–88

LONDON 2S

BASINGSTOKE

Down Grange, Pack Lane, Basingstoke, Hants. Tel: 0256 23308.
Founded: 1948
Secretary: D.A. Williams, 150A Pack Lane, Kempshott, Basingstoke, Hants RG22 5HR. Tel: 0256 58667 (H), 0256 51821 (W).
League: London 2S
Final position (1987–88): 1st (Promoted)
Playing record (1987–88): P 34, W 24, L 10. F 786, A 365.
Competitions won: London 3S

OLD MID-WHITGIFTIAN

The Clubhouse, Lime Meadow Avenue, Sanderstead, Surrey. Tel: 01-657 2014
President: Mike Scott
Chairman: Chris Nunn
Coach: Colin Parrish
Secretary: Jeremy Glynne-Jones, 33 The Bridle Road, Purley, surrey CR2 3JB. Tel: 01-660 4188
Fixtures Secretary: Andy Hillburn, 47a Foxearth Road, Selsdon. Tel: 01-657 1825
Club captain (1987–88): John Carey
Club captain (1988–89): John Carey
No. of teams: Senior 4. Youth 1.
Directions to Ground: To Sanderstead roundabout head towards Selsdon and take 1st turning on right follow Onslow Gardens until reaching Lime Meadow Avenue (Onslow Gardens)
Ground capacity: 1000
Clubhouse: Members bar and large club bar. Full size snooker table.
Colours: Dark blue. (*Change colours:* Green)
Nickname: Midwives
Floodlights: No
Membership: £45
Local newspaper: Croydon Advertiser
League: London 2
Final position (1987–88): 2nd
Playing record (1987–88): P 30, W 26, L 4.
Competitions won: Surrey Cup 1984/85 and 87/88. Club Merit Table (several times). Surrey Cup (Colts) 1983/84.

WORTHING

The Rugby Park, Roundstone Lane, Angmering, West Sussex. Tel: 0903 784706.
Founded: 1920
Secretary: B. Vincent, 29 St Botolphs Road, Worthing, West Sussex. Tel: Worthing 206516.
Fixtures Secretary: C. Saint, 39 Arlington Avenue, Worthing, West Sussex. Tel: Worthing 505534.
League: London 2S

London 2S

Final position (1987–88): 3rd
Playing record (1987–88): P 31, W 21, L 10. F 675, A 322.
Competitions won: Sussex County Cup, Winners Qualify for Pilkington Cup 1988–89.

CAMBERLEY

Watchetts Park Road, Camberley, Surrey
Founded: 1931
Secretary: J.E. Cozens, Mead House, Eversley Cross, Hants. Tel: 0734 730303.
League: London 2S
Final position (1987–88): 4th
Playing record (1987–88): P 36, W 22, D 2, L 12. F 681, A 399.

OLD ALLEYNIAN

Dulwich Common, London SE21. Tel: 01-693 2402.
Founded: 1898
President: A. Verity, Master of Dulwich College
Chairman: E.S.J. Sutton
Coach: Peter Ashworth
Secretary: Robert Crow, 13 Gable Court, Lawrie Park Avenue, Sydenham, London SE26 6HR. Tel: 01-778 2868
Fixtures Secretary: R. Jackman, 28 Kingsfield Avenue, N. Harrow, HZ2 6AT. Tel: 01-423 8600
Club captain (1987–88): D. Llewellyn
Club captain (1988–89): P. Ashworth
No. of teams: Senior 6.

Directions to Ground: On South Circular, opposite Dulwich Park.

Colours: Dark blue/Light Blue/Black. (*Change colours:* White)
Floodlights: No
Membership: £37.50 if over 25 (Dulwich College Old Boys only)
Local newspaper: South London Press
League: London South 2
Final position (1987–88): 5th
Playing record (1987–88): P36, W27, D2, L7
Competitions won: Playing record includes Tour of Bermuda ("International" won 23–0) with a record of P5, W5, D0, L0.

GRAVESEND

The Rectory Field, Miltown Road, Gravesend, Kent. Tel: 0474 53480.
Founded: 1921
Secretary: J. Moore, 375A Singlewell Road, Gravesend DA11 7RL. Tel: 0474 62998 (H), 0474 534840 (W).
Fixtures Secretary: J. Gorman, 4 The Downage, Gravesend, Kent. Tel: 0474 355559.
League: London 3S
Final position (1987–88): 6th
Playing record (1987–88): P 39, W 24, L 15. F 618, A 552.

OLD BROCKLEIANS

Eltham Palace Road, London SE9. Tel: 01-850-8650
Founded: 1924
President: A. Gearing
Chairman: A. Gearing
Secretary: R. Ellery, 13 Peacock Gardens, Selsdon CR2 8TE. Tel: 657-7973
Fixtures Secretary: G. Wright, 3 Birling Avenue, Bearsted, Maidstone ME14 4DG. Tel: 0622 38396
Club captain (1987–88): S. Freeman-Haynes
Club captain (1988–89): R. Cox
No. of teams: Senior 5. Youth & Minis 1.
Directions to Ground: Near Junction A2–A21, South Circular Road (M25 exit 4)
Clubhouse: Cosy
Colours: Chocolate, emerald and old gold
Nickname: "Brocks"
Floodlights: Yes, training only
Membership: £25 pa
Local newspaper: Kentish Times
League: London S 2
Final position (1987–88): 7th

KCS OLD BOYS

Near Robin Hood Gate, Richmond Park, SW15. Tel: 01-546 5461.
Founded: 1907
President: J.D.E. Hamilton
Chairman: T.B.A.
Secretary: M.E. Bruce, 40 Prince's Road, Kington-upon-Thames, Surrey KT2 6AZ. Tel: 01-549 5118.
Fixtures Secretary: A.B. Todd, 5 Wendover Drive, New Malden, Surrey KT3 5RN. Tel: 01-942 0048 (H)
Club captain (1987–88): K.T. Parrack
Club captain (1988–89): R. Shinn
No. of teams: Senior 5.
Directions to Ground: A3 from Putney. Ground on left past Robin Hood Roundabout.
Clubhouse: Primitive
Colours: Red/navy blue/old gold
Floodlights: No
Membership: £20
League: London 2S
Final position (1987–88): 8th
Playing record (1987–88): P 28, W 11, D 1, L 16, F 345, A 440.

OLD REIGATIAN

Park Lane, Reigate. Tel: 0737 245634.
Founded: 1927
President: J. Hamlyn
Chairman: J. Rowlands
Secretary: A. Walker, 43 Yorke Road, Reigate, Surrey RH2 9HH
Fixtures Secretary: K. Ireland, 36 Barrow Green Road, Oxted, Surrey.
Club captain (1987–88): D. Payton
Club captain (1988–89): I. Kirk
No. of teams: Senior 6.
Directions to Ground: Enter Reigate Town 1 way system on A25 and go thorugh centre of twon. At west end turn left into Park Lane.
Ground capacity: 1000
Colours: Green/Blue hoops
Nickname: OR's
Floodlights: No
Admission: Nil
Membership: £30
Local newspaper: Surrey Mirror
League: London 2 South
Final position (1987–88): 9th
Playing record (1987–88): P 27, W 8, D 1, L 18, F 254 A 356

PORTSMOUTH

Rugby Camp, Copnor Road, Hilsea, Portsmouth. Tel: 0705 660610
Founded: 1886
Secretary: A.W. Megarry, 10 Garden Lane, Southsea PO5 3DP. Tel: 0705 826904 (H), 0705 822411 (W).
League: London 2S
Final position (1987–88): 10th
Playing record (1987–88): P 26, W 15, D 1, L 10. F 678, A 440.

OLD JUDDIANS

The Slade, Tonbridge, Kent TN9 1HR. Tel: Tonbridge 358548.
Founded: 1928
President: K. Starling
Chairman: C. Wickham
Coach: J. Hams
Secretary: S. Davey, moving to new address before season begins.
Fixtures Secretary: A.B. Russell, 28 Whistler Road, Tonbridge. Tel: Tonbridge 355582.
Club captain (1987–88): M. Hogwood
Club captain (1988–89): S. Rees
No. of teams: Senior 5
Directions to Ground: OJRFC play on Tonbridge sports ground. Turn from Tonbridge High Street into Castle Street (opposite Rose & Crown Hotel); bear right, left and right again; take next LH turn into The Slade; fork right at end into OJRFC clubhouse car park.
Ground capacity: As many as can crowd the touchline
Clubhouse: Clubhouse, The Slade, Tonbridge, Kent TN9 1HR. Tel: 358548.
Colours: Claret and Light Blue Hoops (*Change colours:* Usually plain red)
Nickname: The Js
Floodlights: No.
Membership: £30 (playing); £15 (non-playing)
Local newspaper: Kent and Sussex Courier
League: London 2 South
Final position (1987–88): 11th in London Two (South)
Playing record (1987–88): P 27, W 15, D 0, L 12 499–356
Competitions won: Try Pernod Attack Winners of Kent Section 1985/6 and 1986/7; Cornwallis Trophy Winners (7s) – 1986/87.

LONDON 3 NE

BARKING

104 South Park Drive, Ilford, Essex. Tel: 01-590 3144.
Founded: 1931
Secretary: J. Marner, 231 Wilmington Gardens, Barking, Essex. Tel: 01-373 0120 (H), 0708 858252 (W).
League: London 3NE
Final position (1987–88): 1st (promoted)
Playing record (1987–88): P 34, W 25, D 1, L 8. F 697, A 323.

ETON MANOR

Eton Manor RFC, The Clubhouse, Sidmouth Road, Leyton E10
Founded: 1928
Chairman: Frank Overland
Coach: Kevin Bevan
Secretary: Jim Slough, 112 Copenhagen Place E14 7DE. Tel: 01-987 7216
Fixtures Secretary: Martin Scott, 24 Preston Drive, Wanstead, E11.
Club captain (1987–88): Gary Wood
Club captain (1988–89): Grant Mansfield
No. of teams: Senior 4. Youth & Minis Yes.
Directions to Ground: The Eastway Sports Centre, Quarter Mile Lane, Leyton E10. (Hackney Marsh)
Clubhouse: Licensed. Away from playing area.
Colours: Dark blue/light blue hoop. (*Change colours:* Green)
Nickname: The Manor
Floodlights: No.
Membership: £20
Local newspaper: Newhaven Recorder
League: London NE3
Final position (1987–88): 2nd
Playing record (1987–88): P 36, W 29, L 7.
Competitions won: Hackney 15-A-Side Knockout Sept 1987; Middlesex 7s Prelims at Saracens. Essex 7s. The Essex Cup 1985.

WEST NORFOLK

Founded: 1923
Secretary: M. Ballman, 47 Queens Avenue, Kings Lynn, Norfolk. Tel: 0533 763483.
League: London 3NE
Final position (1987–88): 3rd

COLCHESTER

Mill Road, Mile End, Colchester, Essex CO4 5JF. Tel: 0206-851610
Founded: 1925
President: Don Reid
Chairman: Tim Wright
Coach: Paddy Smith
Secretary: Ron Hatch, 99 Ernest Road, Wivenhoe, Esse, CO7 9LJ. 0206-22-3548.
Fixtures Secretary: John Roberts, 5 Spencer Close, Maldon, Essex. Tel: Maldon 54043.
Club captain (1987–88): Richard Parker
Club captain (1988–89): Clive Bentley
No. of teams: Senior 6. Youth & Minis 11.
Directions to Ground: A12 from London, Colchester turn-off to Station; A134 as far as "Dog & Pheasant", turn right into Mill Road, club on left after ¾ mile.
Clubhouse: 2 storey, 6 changing rooms.
Colours: Black. (*Change colours:* Red & gold hoops)
Floodlights: Yes.
Admission: Free.
Membership: £25
Programme: Free. (Editor: Gino Debiase)
Local newspaper: Essex Standard
League: London NE3
Final position (1987–88): 4th
Playing record (1987–88): W 20; D1; L9; F 440; A 259

OLD WESTCLIFFIANS

"The Gables", Aviation Way, Southend-on-Sea, Essex SS2 6UN
Founded: 1922
President: M.W. Turner
Chairman: A.J. Gardner
Coach: Vacant
Secretary: N.J. Crowe, 68 Leighton Avenue, Leigh-on-Sea, Essex SS9 1QA. Tel: 0702-711647
Fixtures Secretary: I. Dudley, 105 Eversley Road, Benfleet, Essex. Tel: 0268-794112
Club captain (1987–88): A. Myles
Club captain (1988–89): J.P. Rafferty
No. of teams: Senior 5. Youth & Minis 3.
Directions to Ground: A127 to Southend. Left at Kent Elms Corner, right into Snares Lanes, right at junction into East Woodbury Lane, 4th left into Aviation Way, carry on to sharp right bend, ground 50 yds on left.
Clubhouse: Two bars, two squash courts, mini gymnasium.

Colours: Maroon and gold.
Nickname: WES (others unprintable)
Floodlights: Training lights only.
Membership: £30 (£5 Colts)
Programme: Free on league days. (Editor: C. Sharples/ N. Crowe/G. Sawyer)
Local newspaper: Southend Evening Echo
League: London 3NE
Final position (1987–88): 5th
Playing record (1987–88): P 35, W 16, D 4, L 15, F 482, A 429.
Competitions won: Essex Sevens 1957, 1964–5–6–7, 1969, 1970, 1973. O. Gaytonians sevens 1956, 1974–5. O. Colfeians Sevens 1974–5. O. Haberdashers Sevens 1956, 1973. North London Floodlit Sevens 1976. Barnet Sevens 1969, Basildon Floodlit Sevens 1988.

CHINGFORD

Lea Valley Playing Fields, Waltham Way, Chingford E4. Tel: 01-529 4879
Founded: 1928
President: Howard Hartley
Coach: Steve Slowick
Secretary: Jeff Carratt, 24 Alpha Road, Chingford E4 6TB. Tel: 01-524 2005
Fixtures Secretary: Raz Hales, 24 Moreland Way, London E4
Club captain (1987–88): Richard Gaze
Club captain (1988–89): Ian Rabey
No. of teams: Senior 4. Youth & Minis 6.
Directions to Ground: Turn off North Circular Road (A406) by B & Q Warehouse (A1009 – Chingford). Ground ½ mile along on left (next to golf driving range).
Ground capacity: Unlimited – playing fields
Clubhouse: One large bar, hall, kitchen, showers, refs room, medical room, large changing room with 2 separate team rooms.
Colours: Black jersey, blue and white hoops, white shorts, blue socks. (*Change colours:* Red and black hooped shirts)
Nickname: "Ching"
Floodlights: Only for training
Membership: £20
Local newspaper: Waltham Forest Guardian
League: London 3NE
Final position (1987- 88): 6th
Playing record (1987–88): P 29, W 14, D 1, L 14, F 388 A 302
Competitions won: 1987/88 Runners-Up Essex Colts; Runners-Up in Benidorm International 7s, Cheshunt 7s, Winners – Essex 7s Plate

IPSWICH YMCA

The Street, Rushmnere, Ipswich
Founded: 1926
President: D.L. Sanders
Chairman: R. Hood
Coach: A. Clarke
Secretary: S. Thorn, 78 Sandringham Close, Stoke Park, Ipswich IP2 9DH. Tel: Ipswich 683413
Fixtures Secretary: S. Byam, 20 Oak Hill Lane, Ipswich.
Club captain (1987–88): K. King
Club captain (1988–89): D. Smith
No. of teams: Senior 4. Youth & Minis 1.
Directions to Ground: Take turning off Ipswich bypass for Rushmere, go through village, pass church. YMCA sports ground on right.
Clubhouse: New pavilion and bar to be built.
Colours: Gold and maroon hoops.
Floodlights: Yes, for training
Membership: £30
Local newspaper: Ipswich Evening Star; East Anglian Daily Times
League: London 3 NE
Final position (1987–88): 7th
Playing record (1987–88): P 26, W 13, L 12, D 1.

SAFFRON WALDEN

Springate, Henham, Nr Bishops Stortford, Herts. Tel: 0279 850791.
Founded: 1963
Secretary: M.P. Curtis, New Barn Farm, Lindsell, Near Great Dunnmow, Essex. Tel: 037 184 461.
League: London 3NE
Final position (1987–88): 8th

OLD CANTABRIGIAN

Sedley Taylor Road, Cambridge CB2 2PW. Tel: 0223 213061.
Founded: 1945
President: C.W. Gifford
Chairman: G.C. Cresswell
Coach: M.C. Cracknell
Secretary: B.J. Wakefield, The Old Manse, 27 High Street, Ramsey, Huntingdon, Cambs PE17 1AE. Tel: 0487 812146 (H), 01-822 2737 (W).
Fixtures Secretary: A.L. Winbey, 40 Ellison Lane, Hardwick, Cambridge CB3 7QA. Tel: 0954 210122.
Club captain (1987–88): S. Brear
Club captain (1988–89): M.C. Cracknell
No. of teams: Senior 5.
Clubhouse: Open fire, bar, lounge, kitchen.
Colours: Navy blue with white hoops. (*Change colours:* yellow)
Nickname: Cantabs
Floodlights: No
Membership: £20 playing
Programme: Editor, D.C. Rattenbury
Local newspaper: Cambridge Evening News
League: London Div.3NE
Final position (1987–88): 9th
Playing record (1987–88): P 33, W 16, L 15, D 2, F 312, A 371.
Competitions won: Cambs Invitation Sevens 1987–88.

BRENTWOOD

Ingrave Road, Brentwood. Tel: 0277 210267.
Founded: 1935
President: Mike Fleming
Chairman: Tony Broom
Coach: Scott Milne
Secretary: Clive Gildersleeves, 19 Further Meadwo, Writtle, Essex CM1 3LE. Tel: 0245-420679.
Fixtures Secretary: Clive Gower, 11 The Oaks, Gt Burstead CM11 2RP.
Club captain (1987–88): Andy Joselyn
Club captain (1988–89): Peter Cook
No. of teams: Senior 5. Youth & Minis 8.
Directions to Ground: Leave A12 taking A1023 to Brentwood. Follow A1023 past "Eagle & Child". Turn left into Middleton Hall Lane then left at lights into Ingrave Road. Ground (King George Field) is ½ mile right after railway crossing.
Ground capacity: 4 pitches. Spectators standing only.
Colours: Maroon, grey, white.
Floodlights: No.
Membership: £40
Local newspaper: Brentwood Gazette
League: London 3 NE
Final position (1987–88): 10th (out of 11)
Playing record (1987–88): P 35, W 9, D 2, L 24. F 368, A 767

BURY ST EDMUNDS

The Haberden, Southgate Green, Bury St Edmunds. Tel: 0284 753920
Founded: 1923
President: R. Scruby
Chairman: R.C. Fenner
Coach: Vacant
Secretary: R.S. Lawson, c/o 81A Guildhall Street, Bury St Edmunds
Fixtures Secretary: R. Lion, 2 The Gardens, Bury Road, Beyton, Bury St Edmunds.
Club captain (1987–88): R.S. Lawson
Club captain (1988–89): C. Hayner
No. of teams: Senior 5. Youth & Minis 5.
Directions to Ground: A45 to Bury St Edmunds East. Follow directions to Town Ground 400 yards on right opposite Cramphorn's Garden Centre
Clubhouse: New. 5 changing rooms, bar area/ committee room.
Colours: Green (*Change colours:* Yellow)
Floodlights: Yes
Membership: £25
Programme: Free (Editor R.C. Fenner)
Local newspaper: Bury Free Press
League: London NE3
Final position (1987–88): Last
Playing record (1987–88): P 38, W 10, L 27, D 1.

LONDON 3 NW

BISHOPS STORTFORD

Silverleys, Hadham Road, Bishops Stortford, Herts. Tel: 0279 52092.
Founded: 1920
Secretary: D.H. Fuller, Grimwade House, Bishops Stortford College, Maze Green Road, Bishops Stortford, Herts. Tel: 0279 54226.
League: London 3NW
Final position (1987–88): 1st (promoted)
Playing record (1987–88): P 29, W 22, D 2, L 5. F 635, A 232.
Competitions won: Rugby World & Post Team of the Month

HENDON

Copthall Playing Fields, Great North Way, Hendon. Tel: 01-203 1737.
Founded: 1932
Secretary: I.C. Panting, 38 Birbeck Road, Mill Hill, London NW7 4AA. Tel: 01-906 2809 (H), 0707 51141. Extn. 256 (W)
Fixtures Secretary: R.J. Brown, 27 Norcot Close, Dunstable, Beds. Tel: 0582 699276. Tel: 0582 699276.
League: London 3NW
Final position (1987–88): 2nd
Playing record (1987–88): P 30, W 21, D 1, L 9. F 434, A 325.

LETCHWORTH GARDEN CITY

Baldock Road, Letchworth, Herts. Tel: 0462 682554.
Founded: 1924
Secretary: B. Jones, 131 Wilbury Road, Letchworth SG6 4JG. Tel: 0462 676412.
Fixtures Secretary: C.L. Priestly, 88 Cowslip Hill, Letchworth, Herts. Tel: 0462 686768.
League: London 3NW
Final position (1987–88): 3rd
Playing record (1987–88): P 35, W 17, D 3, L 15. F 482, A 369.

TABARD

Cobden Hill, Radlett, Herts. Tel: 09274 5561
Founded: 1951
President: W. Fullerlove
Chairman: B. Brennan
Coach: I. Jones
Secretary: R. Hopçroft, 100 Manor Road, Barton-le-Clay, Beds MK45 4NS
Fixtures Secretary: C. Carmichael, 10 Chandos Road, Borehamwood, Herts. Tel: 01-953 9006
Club captain (1987–88): R. Welsh
Club captain (1988–89): T. Smithers
No. of teams: Senior 4. Youth & Minis 1.
Directions to Ground: Off the A5, opposite 'Cat & Fiddle' PH in Radlett.
Colours: Broad yellow band, edged red. (*Change colours:* Various (to suit)
Nickname: 'Tabs'
Floodlights: No
Admission: Free
Membership: £20
Local newspaper: Herts Advertiser
League: London NW3
Final position (1987–88): 4th
Playing record (1987–88): P 30, W 21, L 8, D1.
Competitions won: Winners Herts Presidents Cup 20/3/88

FULLERIANS

Conningsby Drive, (Off Parkside Drive), Watford, Herts. Tel: (0923) 224483
Founded: 1925
President: R.E. Seymour
Chairman: J. Vain
Coach: R. Gravestock
Secretary: P. Ramsbottom, 17 Raglan Gardens, Oxhey, Watford, Herts. Tel: (0923) 37905.
Fixtures Secretary: J. Ayres, 9 Church Grove, Little Chalfont, Bucks. Tel: (02404) 3266.
Club captain (1987–88): R. Gravestock
Club captain (1988–89): S. Craze
No. of teams: Senior 6. Youth & Minis 1.
Directions to Ground: South off A411, North West of Watford, into Langley Way. Turn right at end into Conningsby Drive.
Colours: Black, red, green hoops
Nickname: "Fullers"
Floodlights: No.
Membership: £40
Local newspaper: Watford Observer
League: London NW3
Final position (1987–88): 5th
Playing record (1987–88): P 32, W 18, D1, L 13, F 466, A 333

KINGSBURIANS

Northwich Park Pavilion, The Fairway, Kenton, Middx.
Founded: 1961
Chairman: Dave Hollings
Coach: Brian Jones
Secretary: Ian Kitchen, 6 Bankside Downs, Chorleywood Road, Rickmansworth, Herts. Tel: 0923-779520 (H). 01-499 1001 (W).
Fixtures Secretary: Bruce Bland, 10 Clitheroe Avenue, Rayners Lane, Harrow, Middx. Tel: 01-868 5244 (H); 01-204 4442 (W).

London 3 NW

1st XV captain (1987–88): James Mitchell
1st XV captain (1988–89): Warren Jones
No. of teams: Senior 4.
Directions to Ground: East of Watford Road (A404). Behind Northwick Park Hospital, Harrow College and Northwick Park Tube Station.
Colours: Black and amber hoops. (*Change colours:* All black
Nickname: Kings
Floodlights: Yes, training only.
Membership: £18 full membership
Local newspaper: Harrow Observer
League: London 3 NW
Final position (1987–88): 6th
Playing record (1987–88): P 27, W 15, D 2, L 10, F 440, A 296.
Competitions won: Final stages of Middlesex 7-A-Side in 1984.

MILL HILL

Page Street, Mill Hill, London NW7. Tel: 91-293 0685.
Founded: 1937
Secretary: A.P. Hall, 39 Thorpe Road, St. Albans, Herts. Tel: 0727 68075 (H), 01-372 5671 (W).
Fixtures Secretary: P. Braddock, 43 Winstre Road, Borehamwood, Herts. Tel: 01-953 6500 (H).
Colts secretary: D. Munro, 193 Woodcote Avenue, Mill Hill, London NW7.
League: London 3NW
Final position (1987–88): 7th
Playing record (1987–88): P 25, W 10, D 2, L 33. F 304, A 334.

HARROW

Grovefield Wood Lane, Stanmore, Middx. Tel: 01-954 2615.
Founded: 1891
Secretary: A. Wheeler, 55 Whippendell Road, Watford, Herts. Tel: 0923 228184 (H). 01-954 2311. Extn 4123 (W)
Fixtures Secretary: P.R. Pope, 16 Kenilworth Drive, Croxley Green, Herts. Tel: Watford 41504 (H)
League: London 3NW
Final position (1987–88): 8th
Playing record (1987–88): P 36, W 15, D 1, L 20. F 385, A 556.

BACAVIANS

Bragbury House, Bragbury End, Stevenage, Herts. Tel: 0438 812985
Founded: 1958
President: Mr. G. Walker
Chairman: Mr. G. Hamilton
Coach: To be appointed
Secretary: H. Crompton, 22 York Road, Stevenage, Herts SG1 4HE. Tel: 0438-354904.
Fixtures Secretary: F. McCarthy, 10 Lismore, Stevenage. Tel: 0438-316372.
Club captain (1987–88): F. Richardson
Club captain (1988–89): F. Richardson
No. of teams: Senior 6. Youth & Minis 1.
Directions to Ground: From A1(M) Stevenage South East follow A602 towards Hertford. Ground on left hand side just past golf course.
Clubhouse: Large sports and social club
Colours: Green shirts with amber hoop, white shorts, green socks. (*Change colours:* Blue shirts, white shorts, green socks.
Floodlights: No
Admission: Free
Membership: £19
Local newspaper: North Herts Gazette, Stevenage Comet
League: London 3NW
Final position (1987–88): 9th

TWICKENHAM

'Parkfields', South Road, Hampton, Middlesex. Tel: 01-979 2427
Founded: 1867
President: Peter Harvey
Chairman: Peter Harvey
Coach: John Bailey
Secretary: Simon Weathers, 41 Silver Crescent, London W4 5SF. Tel: 01-747 1127.
Fixtures Secretary: Ray Bairstow, 20 Tudor Avenue, Hampton. Tel: 01-979 1401.
Club captain (1987–88): Ian Wallis
Club captain (1988–89): Ray Dudman (ex Harlequins & Barbarians)
No. of teams: Senior 6. Youth & Minis 10. Note: Colts – Saturdays; U16 down – Sundays.
Directions to Ground: On request (they are not simple!)
Ground capacity: 100,000 all standing!
Clubhouse: Beer, food and hot water.
Colours: Red and black irregular hoops. (*Change colours:* light blue)
Floodlights: Yes, training only.
Admission: Free.
Membership: £20
Programme: 12 page glossy, 50p (Editor: David Lawrenson (Sunday Times)
Local newspaper: Middlesex Chronicle/Richmond & Twickenham Times
League: London 3NW
Final position (1987–88): 10th (relegated)
Playing record (1987–88): P 32, W 7, D 0, L 25, F 326, A 484.
Competitions won: Twickenham Centenary Sevens 1984/85; Twickenham XV-A-Side Tournament 1984; Mini-Rugby honours include age group wins in Middlesex County Festival, London Irish Festival and Winchester.

OLD PAULINES

Speer Road, Thames Ditton, Surrey. Tel: 01 398 1858.
Founded: 1871
Secretary: J.R. Goode, 6 Sandringham Court, Arragon Road, Twickenham, Middx. Tel: 01-891 4597 (H), 01-482 8851 (W).
Fixtures Secretary: B.M. Jones, 27 Montrose Avenue, Whitton, Twickenham, Middlesex. Tel: 01-898 6408.
League: London 3NW
Final position (1987–88): 11th
Playing record (1987–88): P 29, W 8, D 2, L 19. F 227, A 386.

TUNBRIDGE WELLS

St. Mark's, Frant Road, Tunbridge Wells, Kent. Tel: 0892-27448.
Founded: 1933
President: J. Theobald
Chairman: M. Greenslade
Coach: A.D. Moxon/T. O'Brien
Secretary: R.J.H. Clarke, 4 Wallace Close, Tunbridge Wells, Kent TN2 5HW.
Fixtures Secretary: K. Bassi, 12 Richardson Road, Tunbridge Wells. Tel: 0892-28542 (H), 0892-515720 (B).
Club captain (1988–89): F.J. Delves
No. of teams: Senior 6, Youth & Minis 8
Directions to Ground: Proceed to the Pantiles roundabout and take the A signposted Eastbourne. 1¼ miles top of hill, ground on left 50 yds from Forest Road intersection.
Clubhouse: Two-storey brick built – 1983.
Colours: Royal blue & white hoops – white shorts – royal blue socks.
Floodlights: No
Membership: £5
Programme: Free (Editor: P. Price)
Local newspaper: Kent & Sussex Courier
League: London 2SE
Final position (1987–88): 1st in London Div.3 South-East.
Playing record (1987–88): P 34, W 26, D 2, F 666, A 273.
Competitions won: Champions of London Div. 3SE Courage League, Winners Medway 5th VII a side. U10's Kent Mini Champions.

BECKENHAM

Balmoral Avenue, Elmers End, Beckenham, Kent. Tel: 01-650 7176.
Founded: 1894
President: L. Pinn
Chairman: L. Pinn
Coach: M. Parker
Secretary: W.G. Sumner, 19 Lakeside, Wickham Road, Beckenham, Kent BR3 2LX.
Fixtures Secretary: J.J. Arger, 15 Thatcher Road, Staplehurst, Kent TN12 0ND.
Club captain (1987–88): P. Slattery
Club captain (1988–89): P. Slattery
No. of teams: Senior 3. Youth & Minis 3.
Directions to Ground: Club entrance in Balmoral Avenue which runs between Eden Park Avenue and A214 Upper Elmers End Road. Turn off Croydon Road A222 into either road.
Ground capacity: 3 rugby pitches/1 soccer pitch and training area. Stand, 250
Clubhouse: Tea room, bar, lounge bar, kitchen, 2 baths, 6 showers, 6 changing rooms.
Colours: Royal blue and old gold. (*Change colours:* Brown/purple
Floodlights: Yes, for training only
Admission: None
Membership: £30
Programme: 1st matches. (Editor: C. Stevens, 49 Harlescott Road, SE15 3DA. Tel: 01-732 9790)
Local newspaper: Beckenham Times (Kentish Times) and Beckenham Advertiser/Bromley Advertiser
League: London 3SE
Final position (1987–88): 2nd
Playing record (1987–88): P 33, W 24, D 1, L 8, F 548, A 249
Competitions won: Kentish Times Sevens and Runners Up. The preliminary rounds of the Middlesex Seven-A-Side competition are played on the Beckenham RFC ground every year.

OLD COLFEIANS

Horn Park, Eltham Road, Lee, SE12. Tel: 01-852 1181
Founded: 1928
President: Pat Paynter
Chairman: Martin Wale
Coach: Andy Smith
Secretary: Dia Andrew. Tel: 01-851 1973.
Fixtures Secretary: John Nunn, 27 Westmount Road, Eltham, London SE9 2JB. Tel: 01-850 1853.
Club captain (1987–88): Clive Reffell
Club captain (1988–89): Martin Fenner
No. of teams: Senior 5. Youth 1 (U19).
Directions to Ground: On Eltham road, (A20). 400 metres from Lee Green and 600 metres from intersection of A20 with the A205 (South Circular Road)
Ground capacity: 1000
Clubhouse: 8 changing rooms, 3 bars, 2 squash courts.
Colours: Blue, black, maroon and old gold bands. (*Change colours:* Scarlet)
Nickname: O.C's
Floodlights: Yes. Part pitch, training only.
Admission: Free
Membership: £40 including Old Colfeian Association Membership
Local newspaper: Kentish Mercury & Kentish Times
League: London 3SE
Final position (1987–88): 3rd
Playing record (1987–88): P 37, W 20, D 2, L 15

WESTCOMBE PARK

Craven Road, Orpington, Kent BR6 7RT. Tel: 0689 26422.
Founded: 1904
President: J.E. Yeates
Chairman: M. Payne
Coach: C. Gouveia
Secretary: R.I. Taylor, 24 Pinchbeck Road, Green Street Green, Orpington, Kent BR6 6DR. Tel: 0689 55052.
Fixtures Secretary: P. Pinner, 67 Cloonmore Avenue, Orpington, Kent BR6 9LG. Tel: 0689 51747.
Club captain (1987–88): M. Scott
Club captain (1988–89): F. Thompson
No. of teams: Senior 6. Youth & Minis 11.
Directions to Ground: From Court Road, Orpington (Bypass) turn into Avelon Road (Fire Station). Craven Road off Avelon Road.
Ground capacity: Yet to be tested.
Clubhouse: Single storey building of great charm.
Colours: Navy & white hoops, navy shorts. (*Change colours:* Scarlet with navy collar/cuffs)
Nickname: 'Combe
Floodlights: For training only
Admission: Nil
Membership: £25 (£35 if not paid before 1st Nov)
Programme: 1st XV have only (Editor: S. Robinson)
Local newspaper: Kentish Times
League: London 3SE
Final position (1987–88): 4th
Playing record (1987–88): P 32, W 22, D 3, L 7, F 496, A 231.
Competitions won: Kent Colts Cup Winners; Kent County Colts Sevens 1987/88; Courage Floodlit Cup 1987/88; Winners at Gravesend RFC.

CRAWLEY

West Green, Crawley, Sussex. Tel: 0293 33995
Founded: 1923, refounded 1950
President: B. Roberts
Chairman: D. Jenn
Coach: H. Townsend
Secretary: G. Pye, "Grangeways", Kerves Lane, Horsham, Sussex RH13 6ET. Tel: 0403 63979
Fixtures Secretary: K. Stokes, 1 Rivermead, Ifield Green, Ifield, Crawley, Sussex. Tel: 0293 547118
No. of teams: Senior 5. Youth & Minis 8.
Directions to Ground: Crawley exit onM23, follow A23 on bypass round town and turn left at roundabout signposted for hospital. Ground is 100 metres on left.
Colours: Maroon & sky blue hoops. (*Change colours:* blue and yellow hoops.
Nickname: "Bricklayers"
Floodlights: Yes
Admission: £1 with programme
Membership: £25 for players
Programme: £1 including admission. (Editor: H. Townsend)
Local newspaper: Crawley Observer and Crawley News
League: London 3SE
Final position (1987–88): 5th
Playing record (1987–88): P 27, W 16, L 22. F 489, A 272.
Competitions won: Beaten finalists in Sussex Cup.

HORSHAM

Coolhurst, Hammer Pond Road, Horsham, Sussex. Tel: 0403 65027.
Founded: 1928
Secretary: C. Wright, 119 Comprons Lane, Horsham, West Sussex RH13 5NZ. Tel: 0403 57427 (H), 0403 44742 (W).
Fixtures Secretary: G. Curtis, The Bungalow, Church Road, Mannings Heath, West Sussex. Tel: Horsham 68262 (H).
League: London 3SE
Final position (1987–88): 6th
Playing record (1987–88): P 32, W 20, L 12. F 472, A 387.
Competitions won:

EAST GRINSTEAD

Saint Hill Road, East Grinstead, W. Sussex. Tel: 0342 22338.
Founded: 1929
President: J.R.P. Price
Chairman: A.D. Harris
Coach: N. Penn
Secretary: C.S.L. Williams, Woodhurst, Lewes Road, East Grinstead. Tel: 0342 25690.
Fixtures Secretary: R.P. Russell, 1 Rose Cottages, Plaistow Street, Lingfield, Sy. Tel: 0342 834648.
No. of teams: Senior 5, Youth & Minis 6
Directions to Ground: Saint Hill on minor road to Horsted Keynes, from B2110 Turners Hill Road.
Ground capacity: 3 pitches & training area.
Clubhouse: Main club room, bars, kitchen, 7 changing rooms, showers etc.
Colours: Blue with broad white hoop.
Nickname: G's
Floodlights: No
Admission: None
Membership: £36
Local newspaper: Courier
League: London 3SE
Final position (1987–88): 5th
Playing record (1987–88): P 9, W 4, D 1, L 4, F 109, A 92.
Competitions won: 1981/2 Sussex Cup. 1987 Midds 7 plate.

OLD DUNSTONIAN

St Dunstan's lane, Langley Park, Beckenham, Kent. Tel: 01-650 1779.
Founded: 1903
President: S.D. Kelly
Coach: R. Bodenham
Secretary: N.A. Rogers, "Aboyne", Pickhurst Lane, West Wickham, Kent BR4 0HN. Tel: 01-402 3064 (H) 01-379 7383 (W).
Fixtures Secretary: P.W. France Esq., 5 The Mead, West Wickham, Kent. Tel: 01-776 0872 (H) 01-261 3368 (W).
Club captain (1987–88): K. McNally
Club captain (1988–89): H.G. Evans
No. of teams: Senior 6.
Directions to Ground: St. Dunstan's Lane or Hawksbrook Lane off Wickham Way, Beckenham, Kent.
Ground capacity: 2000
Clubhouse: 6 changing rooms, showers/bath, 3 bars, hall & kitchen, 2 car parks.
Colours: Navy blue and white. (*Change colours:* Navy blue and pink quarters)
Nickname: Pink Elephants
Floodlights: Training only.
Membership: £30 (playing); £10 (honorary).
Local newspaper: Beckenham Journal/Bromley & Kentish Times
League: London 3SE
Final position (1987–88): 8th
Playing record (1987–88): P 33, W 15, D 2, L 16, F 408, A 434.
Competitions won: Kent Sevens 1970; Kent Cup Finalists 1927, 1977; Colfeians Sevens Plate 1970, 1972, 1978, 1981.

OLD BECCEHAMIAN

Sparrows Den, Corkscrew Hill, West Wickham, Kent. Tel: 01-777 8105
Founded: 1933
President: Ian Douglas
Chairman: Ian Douglas
Coach: Ron Beveridge
Secretary: W. Gault, 45 bushey Way, Beckenham, Kent. Tel: 01-650 2994.
Fixtures Secretary: David Skidmore, 16 Surrey Road, West Wickham, Kent. Tel: 01-777 4287.
Club captain (1987–88): David Adkins
Club captain (1988–89): Les Simpson
No. of teams: Senior 7. Youth & Minis 12.
Directions to Ground: Near Croydon/Bromley – Junction A2022 and A232
Ground capacity: Lots
Colours: Maroon, black, silver hoops. (*Change colours:* Maroon)
Floodlights: No
Membership: £20 p.a. + match fee
Programme: Varies. (Editor: contact Hon. Sec.)
Local newspaper: Kentish Times Group – Croydon Advertiser Group
League: London 3SE
Final position (1987–88): 9th
Playing record (1987–88): P 27, W 13, D 1, L 13. F 302, A 277
Competitions won: Last 8 at twickenham 7's. Lost to Maidstone 19–12 in 4th Round Kent Cup.

GILLINGHAM ANCHORIANS

Darland Avenue, Gillingham, Kent. Tel: Medway (0634) 51495.
Founded: 1928
President: A.T.J. Harrington
Chairman: M. Masters

Coach: R.D. Fisher
Secretary: J.C.B. Jennings, 49 Marshall Road, Rainham, Gillingham, Kent ME8 0AW. Tel: Medway (0634) 33431.
Fixtures Secretary: B. Barker, 16 The Covert, Walderslade, Chatham, Kent ME5 9JJ. Tel: Medway (0634) 684064.
Club captain (1987–88): C. Heather
Club captain (1988–89): C. Heather
No. of teams: Senior 6. Youth 1.
Directions to Ground: Darland Avenue joins the A2 at the Star Public House in Gillingham
Colours: Purple, black and silver (*Change colours:* Dark blue)
Nickname: Anchs
Floodlights: In near future
Membership: £15 + £5 association sub.
Local newspaper: Chatham, Rochester and Gillingham News; Evening Post.
League: SE3
Playing record (1987–88): P 34, W 12, D 1, L 21, F 396, A 539.
Competitions won: Canterbury 7's 1987, 1988; 7's: Kent, Dover, Canterbury, Brighton and Worthing 1985/86.

CANTERBURY

Merton Lane, Canterbury. Tel: 0227 68958
Founded: 1929
President: David Hallwood
Chairman: Dickie Ovenden
Coach: T.B.A.
Secretary: Steve Uglon, 98 Whitstable Road, Canterbury. Tel: 0227 61657
Fixtures Secretary: Eddy Hardy, Gentil Knight, Shipman Avenue, Canterbury. Tel: 0227 65891
Club captain (1987–88): Paul Coakley
Club captain (1988–89): Dave Pearson
No. of teams: Senior 6. Youth & Minis 8.
Directions to Ground: Enter Canterbury on A2, follow ring road to 4th roundabout – take 3rd exit (Old Dover Road), proceed over traffic lights, after 3/5 mile turn right on B2068, after 9/10 mile, turnright. Do not cross over by-pass.
Ground capacity: 1000. Stand 200
Clubhouse: Single storey, clubroom with bar/kitchen, VPs bar, large changing.
Colours: Black/amber hoops. (*Change colours:* White or red, white, blue hoops
Floodlights: Yes
Membership: £20 sub, £2.50 match fee
Programme: 25p. (Editor: Mike Inlester. Tel: 0227 450426)
Local newspaper: Kentish Gazette
League: London SE3
Final position (1987–88): Last (relegated)
Playing record (1987–88): P 32, W 8, L 21, D 3.
Competitions won: Kent Cup 1975, Masterbrew Floodlit 1983/1986, various sevens.

LONDON 3 SW

PURLEY

Parsons Pightle, Old Coulsdon, Surrey. Tel: Downland 53042
Founded: 1926
President: Mansel H.T. Barnes
Coach: Not yet appointed
Secretary: Ian Martin, 41 Court Road, Caterham, Surrey. Tel: Caterham 48509.
Fixtures Secretary: Jean Hayes, 27a High Street, Caterham. Tel: Caterham 43597.
Club captain (1987–88): D. Bannister
Club captain (1988–89): B. Johnson
No. of teams: Senior 6. Youth & Minis 1.
Directions to Ground: 600 yards past Tudor Rose, Coulsdon Road, the only pub on right hand side going towards Caterham.
Colours: Black and white. (*Change colours:* Green and white.)
Floodlights: No
Membership: £30
Local newspaper: Surrey/Croydon Advertiser
League: London 3SW
Final position (1987–88): 1st (Promoted)
Playing record (1987–88): P 28, W 23, L 5, F 632, A 251.
Competitions won: London SWIII, Old Caterhamian 7's, Reigate XV-A-Side, Evergreen Cup.

ALTON

Anstey Park, Alton, Hampshire. Tel: 0420 82076.
Founded: 1924
Secretary: T. Mills, 15 Hawthorns, Alton, Hampshire. Tel: 0420 84978 (H), 0420 23456 (W).
League: London 3SW
Final position (1987–88): 2nd
Playing record (1987–88): P 25, W 19, L 6. F 505, A 230.

OLD WALCOUNTIANS

The Clockhouse Ground, Carshalton Road, Woodmansterne, Surrey. Tel: 07373-54348
Founded: 1927
President: W.J. Ireland
Chairman: G. Ranson
Coach: B. Jones
Secretary: G. Jones, 3 Braemar Avenue, Purley CR2 0QA. Tel: 01-660 7892 (H); 01-680 2638 (W)
Fixtures Secretary: R. McDowell, 56 Hillside Gardens, Wallington, Surrey. Tel: 01-669 6801
Club captain (1987–88): N. Smith
Club captain (1988–89): N. Smith
No. of teams: Senior 6. Youth & Minis 1.
Directions to Ground: Off A2022 Purley–Banstead Road.
Colours: Blue, black, gold hoops. (*Change colours:* Red.
Floodlights: Yes, training only
Admission: Free
Membership: £35 pa players. £15 social.
Programme: (Editor: G. Jones on special matches only)
Local newspaper: Croydon Advertiser Group
League: London 3SW
Final position (1987–88): 2nd
Competitions won: C.L.O.B. Merit Table, Surrey County COUTS Cup

EASTLEIGH

Bishopstoke Playing Fields. Tel: 0703-641312.
Founded: 1931
President: W.H.J. Saffery
Chairman: E.T. Lynch
Coach: R. Millard
Secretary: J.W. Trevarthen-Jordan, 67 Atherley Road, southampton SO1 5DT. Tel: 0703-226939.

Fixtures Secretary: J.S. Sneezum, Bursledon Lodge, Salterns Lane, Old Bursledon, Soton SP3 8DH. Tel: Bursledon (042121) 2286.
Club captain (1987–88): C. Rennison
Club captain (1988–89): C. Rennison
No. of teams: Senior 4. Youth & Minis 4.
Directions to Ground: Leave M27 at exis no 6. Join one-way system in centre of Eastleigh leaving by Bishopstoke Road, B3037 over railway bridge. Ground ½ mile on left.
Colours: Black, amber, red
Floodlights: No
Membership: VP £10, PM £20, N-PM £3.
Local newspaper: Eastleigh Weekly News
League: London 3SW
Final position (1987–88): 4th

OLD EMANUEL

Blagdon's, New Maldon, Surrey. Tel: 01-942 3857
Founded: 1910
President: Gordon Dear
Chairman: Vic Dodds
Secretary: Ian Blair, 28 Hunters Road, Chessington, Surrey KT9 1RV. Tel: 01-397 1272.
Fixtures Secretary: John Monkhouse, 26 Oriental Road, Woking, surrey GU22 7AN. Tel: 04862-64114.
Club captain (1987–88): Brian Cassidy
Club captain (1988–89): Brian Cassidy
No. of teams: Senior 4.
Directions to Ground: Shannon Corner, New Maldfen on London-bound slip road of A3
Ground capacity: 1500
Clubhouse: Two bars, dining facilities.
Colours: White. (*Change colours:* Royal Blue).
Floodlights: No
Membership: Varies from £2 – £25.
Programme: Free mostly. (Editor: John Evans)
Local newspaper: Surrey Comet
League: London 3SW
Final position (1987–88): 5th
Playing record (1987–88): P 32, W 22, D 2, L 8. F 533. A 373.

JERSEY

Airport Road, St. Peter. Tel: 0534 42255.
Founded: 1879
Secretary: D.J. Bigmore, Midland Farm, Augres, Trinity, Jersey. Tel: 0534 610455 (H), 0534 35244 (W).
League: London 3SW
Final position (1987–88): 6th

OLD WHITGIFTIANS

Croham Manor Road, South Croydon, Surrey, CR2 7BG. Tel: 01-688 3248/01-686 2127.
Founded: 1876 as North Park Whitgift Football Club. Reformed as OWRFC 1901.
President: John Jacobson
Chairman: Michael Spanswick
Coach: Colin Parrish
Secretary: Geoff Austin, Flat 8, Nicoll Court, 48 Nicoll Road, Harlesden, London NW10 9AD. Tel: 01-965 0498 (H). 01-761 1911 (W).
Fixtures Secretary: 1st XV – Andrew Stone, 86 Greenacres, Oxted, Surrey RH8 0PB. Tel: Oxted (088371) 2857 (H). 01-683 1161 (W). Other XVs – David Caygill, 5 Redwood Close, Kenley, Surrey CR2 5DA. Tel: 01-660 9646 (H). 01-491 8687 Ext 4502 (W).
Club captain (1987–88): Andy Collis
Club captain (1988–89): Nigel Cooper
No. of teams: Senior 4. Minis 3.
Directions to Ground: From South Croydon BR Station, turn right down steps into Croham Road and turn left. Ground is ½ mile on right. Bus 64 from West Croydon passes ground.
Ground capacity: Not known. Stand 25 (open seating on clubhouse roof).
Clubhouse: Well appointed club house on ground.
Colours: Red, black & blue hooped shirts, white shorts. (*Change colours:* all white.)
Floodlights: No
Admission: Voluntary. Donation box only.
Membership: Playing £50, non-playing £22
Programme: 12 pages, 25p. (Editor: Geoff Austin)
Local newspaper: Croydon Advertiser
League: London 3SW
Final position (1987–88): 7th
Playing record (1987–88): P 36, W 16, D 1, L 19, F 335. A 479.
Competitions won: Surrey Cup: Winners 1905. Runners-up 1977. Surrey Sevens: Winners 1949, 1970. Runners-up 1955, 1960, 1963, 1965, 1977. Note: The Old Whitgiftians also hold the record number of *consecutive* appearances in the Final Rounds of the Middlesex Sevens at Twickenham for a junior club – 6 (1961–6)

WINCHESTER

Beverley Meads, Barham Road, Copse Hill, Wimbledon, London SW19. Tel: 01-946 3156.
Founded: 1929
Secretary: P. Walder, Pedlars Cottage, Gunville Hill, Winterslow, Salisbury, Wilts SP5 1PJ. Tel: 0980 862315 (H), 0722 26128 (W).
Fixtures Secretary: D. Walters, "Conkers", The Pastures, Kingsworthy, Winchester, Hants. Tel: 0962 880659 (H)
League: London 3SW
Final position (1987–88): 8th
Playing record (1987–88): P 33, W 12, D 1, L 20. F 462, A 509.

GUY'S HOSPITAL

Boland House, Guy's Hospital, London SE1 9RT. Tel: 01-407 7600 Extn. 3118/3119.
Founded: 1843
President: Dr T. Gibson, MD, FRCP
Chairman: Dr T. Gibson, MD, FRCP
Secretary: Dr M. Martin, MBBS, c/o Rugby Club, Boland House, Guys Hospital, London SE1 9RT. Tel: 01-407 7600 Extn 3118/3119.
Fixtures Secretary: G. Ryan, Boland House, Guys Hospital, London SE1 9RT. Tel: 01-407 7600 Extn 3118/3119.
Club captain (1987–88): C. Beardmore
Club captain (1988–89): W. Llewellyn
No. of teams: Senior 4. Youth & Minis 0.
Directions to Ground: Guy's Hospital Clubs Union Ground, Honor Oak Park, London SE23 1NW. British Rail – Honor Oak or Crofton Park. Buses 36A, 141, 171.
Ground capacity: 5,000. Stand 1000.
Colours: Navy blue and gold hoops. (*Change colours:* Navy blue)
Floodlights: No
League: London 3SW
Final position (1987–88): 9th
Playing record (1987–88): P 28, W 11, D 0, L 17

WARLINGHAM

Maunsey Green, Limpsfield Road, Warlingham, Surrey. Tel: 08832 2825.
Founded: 1922
Secretary: J.L. Desbottes, 167 Hillbury Road, Sanderstead, South Croydon, Surrey. Tel: 01-657 7628 (H), 01-686 5611. Extn 234 (W)
League: London 3SW
Final position (1987–88): 10th
Playing record (1987–88): P 34, W 14, D 1, L 19. F 462, A 509.

TROJANS

Stoneham Park, Stoneham Lane, Eastleigh, Hants. Tel: 0703 612400.
Founded: 1874
Secretary: J.W.J. Mist, Westbury House, 14 Bellvue Road, Southampton SO1 2AY. Tel: 0703 583450 (H), 9793 332844 (W).
Fixtures Secretary: C. Holt, 338 Hill Lane, Southampton SO1 2PM. Tel: 0703 35711 (W).
League: London 3SW
Final position (1987–88): 11th

SURREY LEAGUES

SURREY started their programme with an 11-team first division, two second leagues of 12 clubs each, and a third league – with 13 clubs. However, the top legue was thrown into some confusion by the withdrawal during the campaign of St. Thomas's Hospital, who nevertheless did compete in the Hospitals Cup.

Unbeaten Old Guildfordians – with only one point dropped – were good winners of the top league from Dorking, who were two points adrift. John Fisher Old Boys were last from Old Cranleighans, who presumably keep their place in the division.

Effingham, who had a marvellous season and dropped only one league point, won Surrey 2A by three points from Wimbledon, with Shene Old Grammarians and Chobham in the last two places, whilst Merton with a perfect record went one better than Effingham in taking the 2B title by a clear four points from Mitchan. Old Bevonians and Old Epsomians filled the last two positions, although neither had played badly.

Surrey 3 was a benefit league for Harrodians, who won all their 11 matches and scored a massive 373 points. Thc Law Society and Reigate and Redhill finished five points behind, whilst at the bottom Lightwater failed to win a game and Racal Decca also finished pointless having lost two for a rules violation. Further chaos was caused to this division when Oxted caught the London 'withdrawal symptoms' and failed to complete their fixtures.

TABLES 1987–88

SURREY 1

	P	W	D	L	F	A	Pts
O Guilfordians	9	8	1	0	199	37	17
Dorking	9	7	1	1	141	54	15
Old Blues	9	5	2	2	128	80	12
Old Rutlishian	9	6	0	3	95	103	12
Cranleigh	9	4	2	3			10
O Wimbledonians	9	4	1	4	87	72	9
Old Tiffians	9	2	2	5	109	116	6
O Surbitonians	9	1	2	6	51	139	4
O Cranleighans	9	1	1	7	53	191	3
John Fisher OB's	9	1	0	8	73	151	2

St Thomas Hospital (withdrawn – all matches void

SURREY 2A

	P	W	D	L	F	A	Pts
Effingham	11	10	1	0	201	80	21
Wimbledon	11	9	0	2	216	93	18
Raynes Park	11	8	0	3	227	67	16
Univer'y Vandals	11	61	4	193	129	13	
Old Freemans	11	6	0	5	163	119	12
Kingston	11	41	6	1104158		9	
Charing X/West Hospital	11	4	0	7	144	140	8
Old Haleyburians	10	5	0	5	97	129	8
Old Reedonians	10	4	0	6		150	7
Chobham	11	2	0	9			4
Shene OG's	11	2	1	10	74	255	2

***2 championship points deducted – breach of rules*

SURREY 2B

	P	W	D	L	F	A	Pts
Merton	11	11	0	0	227	46	22
Mitcham	11	9	0	2	243	42	18
O Pelhamians	11	7	0	4	101	60	14
O Wandsworth's	11	6	1	4	150	83	13
Old Joohnians	11	61	4	144	125	13	
Bee Old Boys	11	6	0	5	117	124	12
Kings Coll Hos	11	5	2	4	110	158	12
Shirley Wand	11	4	1	6	129	117	9
O Suttonians	11	3	3	5	111	133	9
Chipstead	11	2	1	8	51	208	5
Old Epsomians	11	2	0	9	40	221	4
Old Bevonians	11	0	1	10	62	174	1

SURREY 3

	P	W	D	L	F	A	Pts
Harrodians	11	11	0	0	373	46	22
Law Society	11	8	1	2	242	55	17
Reigate & Redhill	11	8	1	2	226	77	17
Surrey Police	11	8	0	3	275	102	16
Old Croydonians	11	6	0	5	186	98	12
Battersea Ironsides	11	5	0	6	164	147	10
London Fire Bde	11	5	0	6	109	182	10
Haslemere	11	5	0	6	58	196	10
BBC	11	4	0	7	129	180	8
Old Caterhamians	11	4	0	7	129	180	8
Racal Decca**	11	1	0	10	74	364	0
Lightwater	11	0	0	11	35	379	0

Oxted (withdrawn – all matches void)

***2 championship points deducted – rule violation*

OLD GUILDFORDIANS

Pavilion, Stoke Park, London Road, Guildford, Surrey
Founded: 1931
President: J. Daniels MA
Chairman: Dr D. Keir
Coach: P. Townsend/J. Allen
Secretary: I. Newton, 36 Ambleside Road, Lightwater, Surrey GU18 5TA. Tel: 0276 74367 (H), 01-270 8214 (W).
Fixtures Secretary: G. Hills, 28 Bannister Close, Wheeler Lane, Witley, Surrey. Tel: Wormley 4337.
Club captain (1987–88): A. Harding
Club captain (1988–89): P. Townsend
No. of teams: Senior 5. Youth & Minis 1.
Directions to Ground: Take London Road from centre of Guildford towards A3. Pavilion is at north end of Stoke Park close to old "AA" roundabout, about 5 minutes from town centre. Whilst new clubhouse under construction matches will be played at "Urnfield" Downs Road, Guildford. Directions from T. Maguire Tel: 0483 36514 (H).
Clubhouse: New clubhouse under construction (following destruction of old clubhouse by fire). Due for completion in second half of season.
Colours: Shirts green with narrow maroon and white hoops. Shorts white, socks red.
Nickname: OGs
Floodlights: No
Membership: £5
Local newspaper: Surrey Advertiser
League: London 3SW
Final position (1987–88): Winners Surrey Div 1
Playing record (1987–88): P 31, W 27, L 3, D 1.
Competitions won: 1987/88 Surrey Div 1, D. Alleynians 7-A-Side, Lensbury Seven-A-Side, Digne (France) International Seven-A-side Tournament.

DORKING

The Pavilion, Big Field, Kiln Lane, Brockham, Surrey. Tel: Betchworth 3928
Founded: 1921
President: A.E. Clatworthy
Chairman: John Milner
Secretary: Robert Brigham, 12 Clyde Road, Sutton SM1 2RR. Tel: 01-661 0338 (H), 01-661 0321 (W).
Fixtures Secretary: James Beardmore, 7 Riverside Dorking. Tel: 036 884049 (H), 0306 885055 (W).
Club captain (1987–88): A.W. Longley
Club captain (1988–89): J.A. Evans
No. of teams: Senior 5. Youth & Minis 5.
Directions to Ground: Take sighposted road to Brockham off A25 between Dorking and Reigate (Dorking 1½ miles). Ground on right.
Colours: Red and white hoops, blue shorts. (*Change colours:* Blue)
Floodlights: No
Membership: £25 + VAT
Local newspaper: Dorking Advertiser
League: Surrey 1
Final position (1987–88): 2nd
Playing record (1987–88): P 36, W 30, D 2, L 4. F 639, A 190
Competitions won: 1987/88 U11's Warlingham Festival and Dorking Festival. U16's Dorking 7's. Kingston Centenary.

OLD BLUES

Arthur Road, Motspur Park, Surrey. Tel: 01-542 1361.
Founded: 1873
President: J. Watt, DSO, MC
Chairman: A.J. Cosedge
Secretary: M. Lyne, 1 Essex Court, Temple, London EC4Y 9AL. Tel: 01-673 0998 (H) 01-583 7759 (W).
Fixtures Secretary: M. Fagan, 107 Stapleton Hall Road, London N4 4RH. Tel: 01-341 3631 (H) 01-387 3340 (W).
Club captain (1987–88): T.S. Hackshaw
Club captain (1988–89): J. Simpson
No. of teams: Senior 4.
Directions to Ground: A3 from London, exit S.P. Worcester Park. 1st left to Motspur Park, 2nd right after Station into Arthur Road. Ground at end.
Ground capacity: 500
Clubhouse: Homely
Colours: Navy, maroon, old gold. (*Change colours:* Yellow)
Floodlights: No
Membership: Player £40 (Student + UB40 £15); Non Player £10.
League: Surrey 1
Final position (1987–88): 3rd
Playing record (1987–88): P 31, W 24, D 2, L 5, F 549, A 264.
Competitions won: Lost in the mists of time.

OLD RUTLISHIANS

The Clubhouse, Poplar Road, Merton, London SW19. Tel: 01-542 3678.
Founded: 1923
Secretary: W.H. Griffin, 68 Love Lane, Morden, Surrey SM4 6LP. Tel: 01-644 9299 (H), 01-405 4377. Extn. 2517 (W)
Fixtures Secretary: S.A. Bryant, 418 Kingston Road, London SW20 8LL. Tel: 01-543 9629.
March Secretary: P.D. Milne, 4 Oakleigh Court, Bond Road, Tolworth, Surbiton, Surrey. Tel: 01-560 3100. Extn. 261
League: Surrey 1
Final position (1987–88): 4th
Playing record (1987–88): P 28, W 15, L 13. F 325, A 388.

CRANLEIGH

Wildwood Lane, Craneleigh, Surrey. Tel: 0483 275843.
Founded: 1967
Secretary: Dr B.J. Squire, 18 Homewood, The Ridgway, Cranleigh, Surrey GU6 7Hg. Tel: 0483 275843.
League: Surrey 1
Final position (1987–88): 5th
Playing record (1987–88): P 28, W 19, D 3, L 6. F 407, A 227.

OLD WIMBLEDONIANS

104 Cottenham Park Road, West Wimbledon. Tel: 01-879 0700.
Founded: 1923
Secretary: D. Laundy, 39 Parkside Gardens, Wimbledon, London SW19. Tel: 01-946 8541 (H), 01-947 8621 (W).
Fixtures Secretary: H. Groenen, 58 Southway, Raynes Park, London SW20.
League: Surrey 1
Final position (1987–88): 6th
Playing record (1987–88): P 32, W 17, D 1, L 14. F 400, A 372.

OLD TIFFINIANS

Grist Memorial Ground, Summer Road, East Molesey, Surrey. Tel: 01-398 1391.
Founded: 1924
Secretary: B.A. Bench, 70 Trinity Road, Wimbledon, London sW19., Tel: 01-543 1645 (H), 01-549 9222 (W).
Fixtures Secretary: R.G. Kirkwood, 63 Shaftesbury Avenue, Strawberry Hill, Twickenham, Middlesex. Tel: 01-898 1767.
League: Surrey 1
Final position (1987–88): 7th
Playing record (1987–88): P 27, W 11, D 2, L 14. F 292, A 340.

OLD SURBITONIANS

Fairmile Lane, Cobham, Surrey
Founded: 1930
Secretary: I. Johnson, 15 Mossfield, Cobham, Surrey KT11 1PF. Tel: 0932 68202 (H). 0932 66664 (W).
Fixtures Secretary: J. Role, 22 Langton Road, East Molesey, Surrey KT8 0HX. Tel: 01-979 9431 (H). 01-583 6520 (W).
League: Surrey 1
Final position (1987–88): 8th
Playing record (1987–88): P 32, W 8, D 4, L 20. F 289, A 427.

OLD CRANLEIGHANS

OC Ground, Portsmouth Road, Thames Ditton, Surrey. Tel: 01-398 3092.
Founded: 1928
President: D. Stephen
Chairman: T. Hill
Coach: TBA
Secretary: A. Williams, St. Michaels Road, Ashwood Road, Woking Surrey. Tel: 438 0663.
Fixtures Secretary: J. Rossare, Bank of England, NC2 New Change, London EC4M 9AA. Tel: 01-601 4444. Extn 3010.
Club captain (1987–88): Richard Durrance
Club captain (1988–89): Mark Lynn
No. of teams: Senior 4.
Directions to Ground: A3 from London to Guildford take Claygate exit to Esher (Scilly Isles Roundabout). Take 3rd exit Portsmouth Road to iron railway bridge. Turn left onto private road.
Ground capacity: 2000. Stand 200.
Colours: Blue, gold, white
Nickname: The OC Boys
Floodlights: Yes
Membership: £35
Local newspaper: Surrey Comet
League: Surrey 1
Final position (1987–88): 7th
Competitions won: Truman Merit Table Winners 83/84

JOHN FISHER OLD BOYS

198 Limpsfield Road, Hamsey Green, Warlingham, Surry. Tel: 08832 5149.
Founded: 1959
President: T. King (Headmaster of John Fisher School)
Chairman: Bryan Whicher
Secretary: Niel Kenny, 20 Leith Road, Epsom, Surrey KT17 1DA. Tel: 03727 40831 (H). 01-582 5344 (W).
Fixtures Secretary: Tim Walkden, 24 Hyde Road, Sanderstead. Tel: 01-651 4686.
Club captain (1987–88): Steve Brown
Club captain (1988–89): Richard Wood
No. of teams: Senior 4.
Directions to Ground: Take the A2022, which is the first left on the Godstone Road after Purley railway station. Continue on the A2022 to the first roundabout. Turn right at the roundabout into the Limpsfield Road. The ground is approx 1 mile down on the right hand side.
Colours: Royal blue, white, gold hoops. (*Change colours:* Gold)
Floodlights: No
Membership: £23.50
Local newspaper: Croydon Advertiser
League: Surrey 1
Final position (1987–88): Relegated from Surrey 1
Playing record (1987–88): P 30, W 12, D 1, L 17
Competitions won: CLOB Merit Table Winners 1982/83 and 1986/87 (Surrey Division)

ST THOMAS'S HOSPITAL

St Thomas's House, Lambeth Palace Road, London.
Founded: 1863
President: Dr A.J. Wing, MA, DM, FRCP
Coach: Mr B. Collison FBCC(Hons), CL
Secretary: J.F. Hopkisson, St Thomas's House, Lambeth Palace Road.
Fixtures Secretary: Dr A.J. Wing, MA, DM, FRCP
Club captain (1987–88): Mr G.L. Bayley
Club captain (1988–89): Mr M.C. Solan
No. of teams: Senior 2.
Directions to Ground: By train: 30 mins from Waterloo – 3 minute walk from Cobham Station via private path. By road: from London A3 to Esher. Approx 1½ miles past Esher turn down Fairmile Lane (on left) signposted Stoke D'Artenon. Turn left onto A245 over railway bridge on right.
Ground capacity: Stand 150
Colours: Red, white, blue hoops, 3 inch bands. (*Change colours:* White)
Floodlights: No
League: Surrey 2A
Final position (1987–88): Bottom 1A – due to failure to play in one game, all points deducted.
Competitions won: University of London Cup 1987–88. National Medical Schools Sevens 1987–88.

SURREY 2 A

EFFINGHAM

Brown's Lane, Effingham, Surrey. Tel: Bookham 58845.
Founded: 1966
President: D. Hughes-Hallet
Chairman: G. Hill
Coach: D. Wilkinson
Secretary: N.J. Webster, 'Glenside' 154 Connaught Road, Brookwood, Woking, Surrey GU24 0AL. Tel: Brookwood 80477 (H), 0483 757555 Ext 2511 (W).
Fixtures Secretary: Ed Newton, 42 Milner Road, Kingston-Upon-Thames, Surrey. Tel: 01-549 8213.
Club captain (1987–88): N. Firth
Club captain (1988–89): N. Firth
No. of teams: Senior 5, Youth & Minis 10
Directions to Ground: By car, The A246 between Guildford and Leatherhead. Entrance from Browns Lane 100 yards on Leatherhead side of Effingham traffic lights.
Clubhouse: Have recently built our own clubroom and bar.
Colours: Green and gold hoops. (*Change colours:* Yellow)

Floodlights: Yes (Training only)
Membership: £25
Local newspaper: Leatherhead Advertiser
League: Surrey 2A
Final position (1987–88): Top of Surrey 2A
Playing record (1987–88): P 32, W 28, D 3, L 1, F 643, A 207.
Competitions won: Courage League Surrey 2A.

WIMBLEDON

Beverley Meads, Barham Road, Copse Hill, Wimbledon. Tel: 01-946 3156.
Founded: 1865
Secretary: A. Blows, 121 Stoneleigh Park Road, Ewell, Surrey KT19 0RF. Tel: 01-393 7416 (H). 01-828 9777 (W).
Fixtures Secretary: B. Thomas, 10 Sycamore Lodge, Gipsy Lane, Barnes, London SW15. Tel: 01-878 6088.
League: Surrey 2A
Final position (1987–88): 2nd
Playing record (1987–88): P 25, W 14, D 1, L 10. F 399, A 294.

RAYNES PARK

Taunton Avenue, West Barnes Lane, Raynes Park, London SW20. Tel: 01-946 8385.
Founded: 1923
Secretary: M.C. Sayer, 15 Gale Close, Hampton, Middlesex, TW12 2AP. Tel: 01-941 5752 (H). 01-549 8763 (W).
League: Surrey 2A
Final position (1987–88): 3rd
Playing record (1987–88): P 28, W 17, D 1, L 10. F 454, A 259.
Competitions won:

UNIVERSITY VANDALS

Brown Acres, Tow Path, Walton-on-Thames, Surrey. Tel: 0932 29610.
Founded: 1932
Secretary: A. Dudman, 21 Crescent Road, Long Cottage, Shepperton, Middx. Tel: Walton-on-Thames 28655 (H), Weybridge 45522. Extn. 5269 (W).
League: Surrey 2A
Final position (1987–88): 4th
Playing record (1987–88): P 26, W 166 D 3, L 7. F 464, A 265.

OLD FREEMANS

Ashtead Park, Ashstead, Surrey. Tel: Ashtead 74158
Founded: 1931
President: N.H. Barnett
Chairman: J.G. Wild
Coach: H. Carter
Secretary: J.A.V. Maddock, Beech Cottage, Elms Drive, Leatherhead, Surrey. Tel: L'head (0372) 373148
Fixtures Secretary: J.M. Mason, 30 Ryefield Road, Upper Norwood, SE19 3QU. Tel: 01-771 5815.
Club captain (1987–88): R. Cox
Club captain (1988–89): M.F. Sims
No. of teams: Senior 5. Youth 1
Directions to Ground: In the grounds of the City of London Freemen's School, Ashtead Park, Ashtead, Surrey.
Clubhouse: Licenced!
Colours: Shirts dark blue, maroon and gold. Shorts dark blue. (*Change colours:* Gold).
Floodlights: Yes, training only.
Membership: £20
Local newspaper: Leatherhead Advertiser
League: Surrey 2A
Final position (1987–88): 5th
Playing record (1987–88): P 31, W 19, D 1, L 11. F 580, A 330.

KINGSTON

The Clubhouse, King Edward Recreation Ground, Hook Road, Kingston, Surrey
Founded: 1887
President: J. Dove
Chairman: P. Stovell
Coach: G. Pickering/A. Hardy
Secretary: D. Wills, Brookwood, Weare Street, Ockley, Surrey RH5 5NA. Tel: 0306-79222.
Fixtures Secretary: I. Ockendon, 88 Charter Ct, Lindon Grove, New Malden, Surrey. Tel: 01-949 5828.
Club captain (1987–88): I. Barnes
Club captain (1988–89): I. Barnes
No. of teams: Senior 4. Youth & Minis 8.
Directions to Ground: Turn off A3 at Hook Underpass towards Chessington. Ground 200 yds on right.
Clubhouse: 2 bars, kitchen, showers, 4 changing rooms.
Colours: Marron and white hoops, blue shorts. (*Change colours:* black shirts, amber collar/cuffs.
Floodlights: Yes
Membership: £25
Local newspaper: Surrey Advertiser
League: Surrey 2A
Final position (1987–88): 6th
Playing record (1987–88): P 31, W 14, L 17.

CHARING CROSS AND WESTMINSTER HOSPITALS

CXW Athletics Union, Stoke D'Abernon, Cobham, Surrey. Tel: 0932 62013.
Founded: 1984
Secretary: The Hon. Secretary, Westminster Medical School, Horseferry Road, London, SW1P 2AR. Tel: 01-828 9811. Extn. 2289 (W)
League: Surrey 2A
Final position (1987–88): 7th

OLD HAILEYBURIANS AND ISC

27 Ruxley Lane, Kingston Road, Ewell, Surrey. Tel: 01-393 3901.
Founded: 1903
Secretary: P.J.F. Whyte, 49 Wandsworth Common, Westside London SW18 2EE. Tel: 01-874 4745 (H), 01-930 7571 (W).
Fixtures Secretary: S.N. Hill, Willowtree Cottage, Early Dene, Sunninghill, Berks. Tel: 01-390 5646.
League: Surrey 2A
Final position (1987–88): 8th

OLD REEDONIANS

Whiteley Village, Burwood Road, Walton, Surrey. Tel: 09328 49616.
Founded: 1931
Chairman: C. Mortimore
Secretary: S. Bailey, 12 Annett Road, Walton, Surrey KT12 2JR. Tel: 0932 231130.
Fixtures Secretary: D. McElhiney, Bradfords, Ireton Avenue, Walton, Surrey. Tel: 0932 227632.
Club captain (1987–88): H. Rigg
Acting Club captain (1988–89): R. Deans
No. of teams: Senior 4.
Directions to Ground: A3 to Cobham, Surrey. Turn off at intersection towards Byfleet, turn right into Seven

Hills Road and right into Burwood Road. Club house on left hand side.
Ground capacity: 200 cars and 200/400 spectators.
Clubhouse: Small club, 4 changing rooms, bath, shower, bar and dining area.
Colours: Red, white, light blue, dark blue.
Nickname: OR's
Floodlights: Yes
Membership: £20
Programme: Editor: George Spinks
Local newspaper: Esher News
League: Surrey 2A
Final position (1987–88): 8th
Playing record (1987–88): P 10, W 3, D 1, L 6, F 66, A 149.

CHOBHAM

Windsor Road, Chobham, Surrey. Tel: Chobham 8616.
Founded: 1968
Secretary: A. White-Aldworth, Jacks Furlong, 22 Commonfields, West End, Woking, Surrey. Tel: Chobham 8375 (H), 01-437 6977 (W).
Fixtures Secretary: M. Smith, Woodhurst, Cold Harbour Lane, Pyrford, Woking, Surrey. Tel: Byfleet 48889.
League: Surrey 2A
Final position (1987–88): 10th

SHENE OLD GRAMMARIANS

Queen Elizabeth Walk, Barnes. Tel: 01-876 2059
Founded: 1962
President: Bill Holmes
Chairman: Brian Clymer
Coach: J. Thomson
Secretary: R. Church, 44 South Street, Epsom, Surrey KT18 7PQ. Tel: Epsom 40907.
Fixtures Secretary: N. Russell, 1 Winterton Court, Hampton Wick. Tel: 943-0270
Club captain (1987–88): peter Buckerfield
Club captain (1988–89): Martin Smith
No. of teams: Senior 2.
Directions to Ground: South over Hammersmith bridge to "The Red Lion" Public House, turn left down side road.
Clubhouse: Changing rooms, bar and food.
Colours: Sky blue. (*Change colours:* Red.)
Floodlights: No.
Membership: £15
Local newspaper: Richmond Informer
League: Surrey 3
Playing record (1987–88): P 27, W 11, D 1, L 15.

SURREY 2 B

MERTON

Faversham Road, Morden. Tel: 01-648 3239.
Founded: 1957
Secretary: M. Flood, 29 Parsons Field Road, Banstead, Surrey. Tel: 01-247 4321 (W).
Fixtures Secretary: A.P. Rees, 40 Braxted Park, Streatham, London SW16. Tel: 01-764 6014.
Colts secretary: K. Phelps, 99 Tennyson Avenue, New Malden, Surrey. Tel: 01-942 8035.
League: Surrey 2B
Final position (1987–88): 1st (Promoted)

MITCHAM

Wandle Valley Hospital Grounds, Middleton Road, Carshalton, Surrey. Tel: 648 4626
Founded: 1934
President: Richard King
Chairman: Ian McCluskey
Coach: Vacant
Secretary: Mike Kelly, 47 Brookfield Avenue, Sutton, Surrey. Tel: 641 4720.
Fixtures Secretary: Garry Ashburn, 142 Northwood Road, Thornton Heath, Surrey. Tel: 771-0791.
Club captain (1987–88): Stan Fisher
No. of teams: Senior 4. Youth & Minis 6.
Directions to Ground: Turn left out of Mitcham Junction Station and then right at Goat pub. Ground is on the left (entrance to Wandle Valley Hospital).
Clubhouse: Since July 1987 we have been on a month to month basis with local Health Authority that own our ground. It is in the process of being sold off for redevelopment. Once this is finalised we will be without a home and no where to go.
Colours: Green and lavender hoops. (*Change colours:* Green shirts, white shorts).
Nickname: Mitcham Midgets
Floodlights: Yes training only.
Membership: £30
Local newspaper: South London News/Mitcham Guardian
League: Surrey 2B
Final position (1987–88): 2nd
Playing record (1987–88): P 31, W 16, D 2, L 13, F 420, A 298

OLD PELHAMIANS

Poulter Park, Bishopsford Road, Mitcham, London. Tel: 01-648 3755.
Founded: 1969
Secretary: M. Dines, Floor 1, 44 Chatsworth Avenue, Wimbledon Chase, London SW20. Tel: 01-549 3840 (H), 01-836 9975 (W), 06284 75881 (W).
League: Surrey 2B
Final position (1987–88): 3rd

WANDSWORTHIANS

The Memorial Ground, Woodstock Lane South, Chessington, Surrey KT9 10F. Tel: 01-398 3720
Founded: 1929
President: David Pollard
Chairman: John Saunders
Coach: Terry Mackie
Secretary: Elizabeth Morris, 29 Mullens House, Chartfield avenue, Putney, SW15 6DA. Tel: 01-788 5738.
Fixtures Secretary: Martin Smith, 612 Khama Road, Tooting, London SW17 0EN. Tel: 01-767 3957
Club captain (1987–88): Robert Andrew
Club captain (1988–89): Andy Archer
No. of teams: Senior 4.
Directions to Ground: A3 take Claygate turn-off. Adjacent to Surbiton golf club.
Clubhouse: Bar and changing facilities.
Colours: Maroon, white and gold
Floodlights: No
Membership: £30
Local newspaper: Surrey Comet
League: Surrey 2B
Final position (1987–88): 4th
Playing record (1987–88): P 30, W 19, D 1, L 10. F 414, A 256.

OLD JOHNIANS

Oaken Lane, Claygate, Surrey
Founded: 1960
Secretary: S. Dunford, 4 Old Lane, Cobham, Surrey. Tel: 04865 51 93.
League: Surrey 2B
Final position (1987–88): 5th

BEC OLD BOYS

Openview Sports Club, Openview Road, London SW18. Tel: 01-874 5411
Founded: 1930
Secretary: R. Bigchen, 28 Woodland Road, Thornton Heath, Surrey. Tel: 01-832 2363 (W).
Fixtures Secretary: S. Skrzynski, 54 Moffat Road, Thornton Heath, Surrey. Tel: 01-771 0205 (H). 01-370 0771 (W).
League: Surrey 2B
Final position (1987–88): 6th
Playing record (1987–88): P 32, W 20, D 3, L 9. F 482, A 282.

KING'S COLLEGE HOSPITAL

KCH Playing Fields, Dog Kennel Hill, East Dulwich. Tel: 01-274 3976.
Founded: 1869
Secretary: A. Padgett, KCHS Students Union, King's College Hospital, Denmark Hill, London SE5. Tel: 01-274 6222 Extn. 2059.
League: Surrey 2B
Final position (1987–88): 7th

SHIRLEY WANDERERS

Kentgate, Addington Road, West Wickham, Kent. Tel: 01-777 5298.
Founded: 1956
Secretary: A. Goddard, 11 Lancaster Close, Bromley, Kent. Tel: 01-290 5147 (H). 01-729 4616 (W).
Fixtures Secretary: G. Jeffcoats, 96 Woodlands Way, West Wickham, Kent. Tel: 01-777 5146.
League: Surrey 2B
Final position (1987–88): 8th

OLD SUTTONIANS

Walsh Pavilion, Priesthill Playing Fields, Banstead Road, Ewell, Surrey. Tel: 01-393 7427.
Founded: 1970
Secretary: S. Williams, 16 Highfields, Sutton Common Road, Sutton, Surrey SM2 3HW. Tel: 01-641 4618.
League: Surrey 2B
Final position (1987–88): 9th

CHIPSTEAD

The Heads, High Road, Chipstead, Surrey. Tel: 07375 53035
Founded: 1959
President: Colin Vaughan
Chairman: David Barber
Secretary: Peter Thornton
Fixtures Secretary: Peter Sidebotham. Tel: 07373 56314
No. of teams: Senior 4. Youth & Minis 8.
Colours: Blue/gold. (*Change colours:* Black).
Nickname: Chips
Floodlights: No
Membership: £30
League: Surrey 2B

OLD EPSOMIAN

The Big Field Pavilion, Kiln Lane, Brockham, Betchworth, Surrey. Tel: Betchworth 073784 3942
Founded: 1963
President: Dr C.A. Hill
Chairman: I. Stewart-Hunter
Secretary: D.C. Kingham, Posterns Farm, Henfold Lane, south Holmwood, Dorking, Surrey, RH5 4NX. Tel: Dorking (0306) 888184
Fixtures Secretary: I. Stewart-Hunter, 25 Manor Road, Teddington, Middlesex.
Club captain (1987–88): S. Burgess
Club captain (1988–89): S. Burgess
No. of teams: Senior 3
Directions to Ground: A 25 from Dorking Eastbound for 2 miles, right towards Brockham, after 800 yards turn left. Ground is on left.
Colours: Navy blue shirts, white shorts. (*Change colours:* Navy blue & white narrow hoops).
Floodlights: No
Membership: £25 playing, £6 non-playing and students
League: Surrey 2B
Final position (1987–88): 11th
Playing record (1987–88): P 26, W 7, D 2, L 17.

OLD BEVONIANS

Ballard Coombe, Robin Hood Way, Kingston Vale, London SW15 3QX. Tel: 01-942 2907
Founded: 1970
President: David Philp
Chairman: Colin Caddy
Coach: Bob Rosall
Secretary: Ian Sedgley, 227 Kings Road, Kingston upon Thames, Surrey. Tel: 01-541 3610.
Fixtures Secretary: Trevor Trout, 20 Cleveland Road, New Malden, Surrey. Tel: 01-949 7850
Club captain (1987–88): Michael Drye
Club captain (1988–89): Paul O'Conner
No. of teams: Senior 3.
Directions to Ground: A3 Londonbound. Take 1st left after Coombe Lane flyover into service road. Ground on left. A3 esherbound turn right towards Kingston along Kingston Hill and take first left into Robin Hood Lane. At end turnleft then right into service road. Ground on right.
Clubhouse: 2 changing rooms, showers, bar and large lounge. Opened 1982.
Colours: Yellow, black, green hoops. Black shorts and socks. (*Change colours:* Yellow shirts).
Floodlights: Yes training only
Membership: £30 playing, £5 associate
Local newspaper: Surrey Comet
League: Surrey 3
Final position (1987–88): Bottom Surrey 2B
Playing record (1987–88): P 29, W 8, D 1, L 20, F 225. A 453.

HARRODIANS

Mill Lodge, Lonsdale Road, Barnes, London SW13 9QN. Tel: 01-748 5535.
Founded: 1912
President: Richard O'Rourke
Chairman: Paul Kirby
Coach: James Connolly
Secretary: Paul Kirby, 53 Stanhope Gardens, London SW7 5RF
Fixtures Secretary: Jeff Ellis, 12A Evelyn Road, London W4. Tel: 01-629 6290 (W).
Club captain (1987–88): David Williams
Club captain (1988–89): Peter Walker
No. of teams: Senior 3. Vets. 1.
Directions to Ground: Over Hammersmith Bridge into Barnes, take second right into Lonsdale Road, ¾ mile on left.
Clubhouse: Mixed sports/social club.
Colours: Green/gold hoops, white shorts, green & gold socks. (*Change colours:* Black jerseys, black shorts).
Nickname: "The Store"
Floodlights: No. (Training lights only)
Admission: Free
Membership: Strictly by invitation only.
Programme: Surrey Cup Only. (Editor: Hon. Sec.)
Local newspaper: Richmond & Twickenham Times
League: From 1988–89 Surrey 3
Final position (1987–88): Won Div 3 (Promoted)
Playing record (1987–88): P 11, W 11, D 0, L 0, F 373, A 46. League points 22.
Competitions won: League Champions Season 87–88. Surrey Div 3..

LAW SOCIETY

c/o Old Wimbledonians, Cricket Club, Clayton Road, Hook, Surrey. Tel: 01-397 1962.
Founded: 1964
Secretary: A. Singy, 61 Ferntower Road, London N5 2JE. Tel: 01-226 8654 (H), 01-600 0808 (W).
Fixtures Secretary: J.G. Smith, 55 Turney Road, London SE21 8AB. Tel: 01-733 8828 (H), 01-229 9361 (W).
League: Surrey 3
Final position (1987–88): 2nd

REIGATE & REDHILL

Eric Hodgkins Memorial Ground, Colley Lane, Reigate, Surey. Tel: Reigate 221110
Founded: 1934
President: Mike Tobitt
Chairman: Brian St John Hall
Coach: Tony Leonard
Secretary: Ann St John Hall, 62 Nutley Lane, Reigate. Tel: 245938.
Fixtures Secretary: Mary Rawlings, Maesdown, 3 Brightlands Road. Tel: Reigate 247444.
Club captain (1987–88): R.A.F. Mattar
Club captain (1988–89): Terry Boardman
No. of teams: Senior 4.
Directions to Ground: From Dorking A25 turn into Colley Lane opposite Black Horse Inn.
Clubhouse: Rebuilt 1986 following fire.
Colours: Royal Blue. (*Change colours:* Red).
Floodlights: No
Membership: £30
Local newspaper: Surrey Mirror
League: Surrey 3
Final position (1987–88): 3rd
Playing record (1987–88): P 32, W 14, D 1, L 17. F512, A 364.

SURREY POLICE

Police HQ, Sandy Lane, Guildford. Tel: 0483 571212.
Founded: 1963
President: N/A
Chairman: Supt Brian Roberts
Coach: PC Gary Steadman
Secretary: C/I Shane Burrows, 4 Junewood Close, Woodham, Weybridge, Surrey. Tel: 09323 44607.
Fixtures Secretary: DC Bob Miller. Tel: Ashtead 78486.
Club captain (1987–88): Gary Steadman
Club captain (1988–89): Paul Palmer
No. of teams: Senior 3.
Directions to Ground: From Guildford on A3100 turn right at Ship P/H then ¼ mile on left.
Clubhouse: At Police HQ.
Colours: All black, red socks. (*Change colours:* Blue shirts).
Floodlights: No
Local newspaper: Surrey Herald/Guildford Advertiser
League: Surrey 3
Final position (1987–88): 4th
Competitions won: British Airways Invitation Sevens September 1987

OLD CROYDONIANS

Layhams Road, Keston, Bromley, Kent. Tel: 0959 73409.
Founded: 1924
Secretary: J. Matthews, 12 Birdwood Close, Selsdon, Croydon CA2 8QG. Tel: 01-621 1010. (W)
League: Surrey 3
Final position (1987–88): 5th
Playing record (1987–88): P 31, W 15, L 16. F 367, A 321.

BATTERSEA IRONSIDES

Burntwood Lane, London SW17. Tel: 01-874 9913
Founded: 1943
President: J. Dickeson
Chairman: D. Wright
Secretary: M.P. Tanner, 38 Victory Road, Wimbledon SW19. Tel: 01-540 5784.
Fixtures Secretary: T. O'Shea, 37 Headington Road, London SW18.
Club captain (1987–88): N. Leslie-Miller
No. of teams: Senior 4. Youth & Minis 2.
Directions to Ground: BR to Earlsfield Station. Turn left out of station in Magdalen road. Openview 3rd right ground at end on left.
Colours: Emerald green with white band.
Floodlights: No
Membership: £20
Local newspaper: Wandsworth Borough News/ Wimbledon Borough News
League: Surrey 3
Final position (1987–88): 6th

LONDON FIRE BRIGADE

Banstead Road, Ewell, Surrey. Tel: 01-394 1946. 01 393 0046.
Founded: 1947
President: G. Clarkson, Chief Officer
Chairman: B. Barklamb
Coach: TBA
Secretary: C. Down, 14 St Botolph Road, Northfleet, Kent DA11 8ES. Tel: 0474 363410.

Fixtures Secretary: B. Barklamb, 24 Northcroft Road, West Ewell, Surrey.
Club captain (1987–88): I. Brunning
Club captain (1988–89): I. Brunning
No. of teams: Senior 3.
Colours: Flame, ember, charcoal. (*Change colours:* Red).
Floodlights: No
League: Surrey 3
Final position (1987–88): 7th

HAZLEMERE

Sports Ground, Woolmer Hill, Haslemere, Surrey. Tel: Haslemere 3072.
Founded: 1953
President: John Pearce
Chairman: David Mussell
Coach: Guy Dinnoodie
Secretary: T.B.A., c/o 44 Hoggs Mead, Petersfield, Hants. Tel: 61776.
Fixtures Secretary: Mrs C. Brodie, Mallaig House, Passfield, Liphook, Hants. Tel: Passfield 481.
Club captain (1987–88): Guy Dinnoodie
Club captain (1988–89): Alan Mathens
No. of teams: Senior 2. Youth & Minis Several.
Directions to Ground: A3 south to Hindhead traffic lights. Continue for 1 mile approx. at start of dual carriageway turn left. 400 yards on turnleft. Ground 200 yards on left.
Clubhouse: Timber
Colours: Royal blue and white hoops. (*Change colours:* Plain blue).
Nickname: 'Mere
Floodlights: Yes (Training 8, no halogen)
Membership: £15
Local newspaper: Haslemere Herald
League: Surrey 3
Final position (1987–88): Joint 6th

BRITISH BROADCASTING CORPORATION

Motspur Park, Surrey
Founded: 1924
Secretary: A. Pigott, 58 Charlmont Road, London SW17 9AH. Tel: 01-4161265 (H), 01-832 7400 (W).
Fixtures Secretary: A. James, 85 Cromwell Road, London SW19 8LF. Tel: 01-540 6070 (H), 01-831 7400 (W)
League: Surrey 3
Final position (1987–88): 9th

OLD CATERHAMIANS

Park Avenue, Caterham, Surrey. Tel: 0883 43488.
Founded: 1928
Secretary: S. Verral, 10 Hillacre, Underwood Road, Caterham, Surrey. Tel: 0883 47211 (H), 01-480 7200. Extn. 3233 (W)
Fixtures Secretary: A. Manby, 25 Littl Roke Avenue, Kenley, Surrey. Tel: 01-668 7621.
League: Surrey 3
Final position (1987–88): 10th
Playing record (1987–88): P 28, W 12, D 1, L 15. F 254, A 372.

RACAL DECCA

Racal Decca Sports & Social Club, Kingston Road, Tolworth, Surrey. Tel: 01-337 0519.
Founded: 1978
Secretary: N. Charter, 155 Ellerdine Road, Hounslow, Middlesex TW3 2PU. Tel: 0932 228851. Extn. 3486 (W).
League: Surrey 3
Final position (1987–88): 11th

LIGHTWATER

Lightwater Leisure Centre, The Avenue, Lightwater, Surrey.
Founded: 1975
President: J.D. Barnett
Chairman: J.D. Barnett
Coach: J. Russell
Secretary: A. Sharp, 65 Cedar Close, Bagshot, Surrey GU19 5AB. Tel: 0276-72994.
Fixtures Secretary: M. Hobson.
Club captain (1987–88): M. Butler
Club captain (1988–89): D. Garrett
No. of teams: Senior 2
Directions to Ground: Junction 3 off M3 – head towards Guildford – first right off dual carriageway – 2nd right up Avenue.
Ground capacity: 500
Clubhouse: Modern bar
Colours: White/green quarters. (*Change colours:* Blue)
Nickname: "Arseholes"
Floodlights: No
Membership: £20
Local newspaper: Camberley News
League: Surrey 3
Final position (1987–88): Bottom
Playing record (1987–88): P 22, W 4, L 18.

OXTED

Hoskins Arms, Oxted. Tel: 0883-71
Founded: 1984
President: Martin Turner
Chairman: C. Evamy and P Budge
Secretary: G.A. Metcalfe, Staffend, Icehouse Wood, Oxted. Tel: 0883 714609.
Fixtures Secretary: N. Newton, 18 Bradbourne Road, Sevenoaks. Tel: 0732 453198.
Club captain (1987–88): R. Peed
Club captain (1988–89): R. Peed
No. of teams: Senior 2.
Directions to Ground: From A25 turn south on to Woodhurst Lane proceed 1½ miles through Holland. Ground on right opposite Diamond Inn.
Clubhouse: Not yet built. Marley building 2000 sq ft ordered to be constructed July–Sept 1988.
Colours: White jersey, red hoop. Blue shorts, red stockings.
Floodlights: No.
Membership: Full playing members £20. Non-playing and Juniors £7.
Local newspaper: Surrey Mirror
League: Surrey 4
Final position (1987–88): Surrey 3 – 13th
Playing record (1987–88): P 21, w 4, D 0, L 17. F 143, A 373.

HAMPSHIRE LEAGUE

HAMPSHIRE started the campaign with 22 clubs evenly split into two leagues, but IBM were another to suffer from the 'London Illness' and withdrew from the second section.

The top section was comfortably won by Gosport, who still dropped three points in the process. Southampton were second with Millbrook and Isle of Wight putting in strong challenges. There was a bizarre situation at the foot of the table with four teams having six points from three wins – Tottonians, Fareham Heathens, Petersfield and New Milton. The latter two had the worst points differences – although it was not a very pronounced situation.

Fordingbridge and Guernsey were separated by only one point in Hampshire 2, but at the foot of the table the unfortunate Nomads lost all their games, scoring only nine points and conceding 264. They deserve great praise for sticking it out and not giving up.

TABLES 1987–88

HAMPSHIRE 1

	P	W	D	L	F	A	Pts
Gosport	10	8	1	1	147	55	17
Southampton	10	7	0	3	158	72	14
Millbrook	10	6	1	3	182	89	13
Isle of Wight	10	6	0	4	109	106	12
Esso	10	5	0	5	129	115	10
Sandown & Shanklin	10	5	0	5	129	115	10
Rushmoor	10	5	0	5	87	101	10
Tottonians	10	3	0	7	68	119	6
Fareham Heath's	10	3	0	7	75	137	6
Petersfield	10	3	0	7	70	156	6
New Milton	10	3	0	7	64	165	6

HAMPSHIRE

	P	W	D	L	F	A	Pts
Fordingbridge	9	8	0	1	219	75	16
Guernsey	9	7	1	1	181	62	15
Romsey	9	6	1	2	147	57	13
Waterlooville	9	6	0	3	125	98	12
Andover**	8	4	0	4	123	117	8
Overton	9	4	0	5	63	92	8
Pegasus**	8	3	0	5	68	120	6
Ventnor**	8	2	0	6	70	79	4
Ellingham	9	2	0	7	97	138	4
Nomads**	8	0	0	8	9	264	0

IBM withdrawn – all matches void

HAMPSHIRE 1

GOSPORT & FAREHAM

Gosport Park, Park Road, Gosport, Hants. Tel: 0705 589852.
Founded: 1946
Secretary: M.T. Edwards, 30 Meadow Walk, Gosport, Hants. Tel: 0329 283084 (H), 0329 224189 (W).
Fixtures secretary: K. O'Toole, 20 Rowalian Avenue, Gosport, Hants. Tel: 0705 587926.**League:** Hampshire 1
Final position (1987–88): 1st (promoted)
Playing record (1987–88): P 27, W 17, D 1, L 9. F 445, A 357.

SOUTHAMPTON

Test Playing Fields, Millbrook, Southampton. Tel: 0703 737777.
Founded: 1964
Secretary: S. Edge, 15 Bangor Road, Shirley, Southampton. Tel: 0703 786758.
League: Hampshire 1
Final position (1987–88): 2nd

MILLBROOK

WSSC, Redbridge Lane, Nursling, Southampton. Tel: 0703 739759.
Founded: 1971
Secretary: T. Allan, 3 Willow Close, Hedge End, Southampton. Tel: 048 92 87337.
League: Hampshire 1
Final position (1987–88): 3rd

ISLE OF WIGHT

Tel: Wootton 0983-883240
Founded: 1924
President: C. Bawdon
Chairman: M. Farr
Coach: D. Hoyle
Secretary: A. Cargen, 114 Station Road, Wootton, IOW. Tel: 0983-883537.
Fixtures Secretary: D. Wessom, Flat 3, Egremont E. Hill Road, Ryde.
Club captain (1987–88): D. Ricketts
Club captain (1988–89): R. Jones
No. of teams: Senior 1.
Directions to Ground: No 1 bus from Ryde Esplanade
Clubhouse: Clubhouse changing rooms
Colours: Blue/gold
Floodlights: No
Membership: £20
Local newspaper: IOW County Press
League: Hants 1
Final position (1987–88): 4th

ESSO (FAWLEY)

Recreation Club, Long Lane, Holbury, Hants. Tel: 0703 893570.
Founded: 1935
Secretary: J.E. Toombs, 16 Hayley Close, Hythe, Hants. Tel: 0703 895450.
League: Hampshire 1
Final position (1987–88): 5th

SANDOWN & SHANKLIN

The Clubhouse, The Fairway, Lake, near Sandown, IOW. Tel: 0983 404707.
Founded: 1961
Secretary: R.W. Simpson, Verandah Cottage, The Close, Sea Grove Bay, Seaview, IOW, PO34 5BT. Tel: 0983 613317 (H), 0983 616228 (W).
League: Hampshire 1
Final position (1987–88): 6th

RUSHMOOR (Farnborough)

Tile Barn Close, Farnborough, Hants. Tel: 0252 5427501.
Founded: 1915
Secretary: P.L. Davies, 8 Thirlmere Walk, Camberley, Surrey GU15 1RG. Tel: 0276 61298 (H), 0276 24676 (W).
League: Hampshire 1
Final position (1987–88): 7th

TOTTONIANS

c/o Totton College, Water Lane, Totton, Southampton, Hants.
Founded: 1960
President: Mr. K. Johnson
Chairman: Mr A. Woodhouse
Secretary: Mr I. Hutchings, Edhendor, Winsor Road, Winsor, Southampton.
Club captain (1987–88): Mr M. Townsend
Club captain (1988–89): Mr M. Townsend
No. of teams: Senior 3. Youth & Minis 5.
Directions to Ground: M27 Junction 3. Turn south M271. Sign post Totton. In Totton take the Ringwood Road, turn right at Calmore Road, water Lane on right (college on corner).
Clubhouse: King George 5th Playing Fields
Colours: Green, black, white hoops.
Floodlights: No
Membership: £18
Local newspaper: Southend Evening Echo
League: Hants 1
Final position (1987–88): 9th

FAREHAM HEATHENS

Cams Alders Sports Ground, Highfield Avenue, Fareham, Hants. Tel: 0329 221793.
Founded: 1975
President: G. Neighbour
Chairman: M. Blow
Coach: R. Evans
Secretary: R. Botham, 5 The Copse, Oakmount Park, Chandlers Ford, Hants. Tel: 0703 2162489.
Fixtures Secretary: C. Turner, 4 Warberton Avenue, Portsmouth, Hants. Tel: 0705 370139.
Club captain (1987–88): Jim Black
Club captain (1988–89): Jim Black
No. of teams: Senior 5.
Directions to Ground: Take A27 from Fareham town centre towards Southampton. Cross roundabout by Fareham railway station. Take 2nd left then right into Highfield Avenue.
Clubhouse: Council owned. Own bar, four changing rooms.
Colours: Red and black. (*Change colours:* Green, black).
Nickname: The Heathens
Floodlights: No
Membership: £10
Local newspaper: Solent Reporter
League: Hants 1
Final position (1987–88): 7th
Playing record (1987–88): P 28, W 12, D 0, L 16. F 281, A 352.

PETERSFIELD

Penn's Place, Durford Road, Petersfield, Hants GU31 4EX. Tel: 0730 64588
Founded: 1927
President: A.E.D. Sayer
Chairman: C.J.M. Fairley
Coach: C. Howarth
Secretary: J.L. Holden, 1 Heathermount, Stoney Bottom, Grayshott, Hindhead, Surrey GU26 6UN.
Fixtures Secretary: D. Pafford, 15 Mansvid Avenue, E. Cosham, Portsmouth PO6 2LX.
Club captain (1987–88): J. Ray
Club captain (1988–89): M. Longley
No. of teams: Senior 4. Youth & Minis 5.
Directions to Ground: From A3 in Petersfield town centre, follow signs for Sports Centre.
Clubhouse: Wrecked by hurricane, being rebuilt (finish 2/89)
Colours: Red with a white hoop. (*Change colours:* Blue or white).
Floodlights: Yes, training only
Membership: £30 seniors, £10 colts, £7.50 minis. (reductions if paid early)
Local newspaper: Petersfield Herald, East Hants Post.
League: Hants 1
Final position (1987–88): 10th (relegated)
Playing record (1987–88): P 32, W 13, L 19. F 366, A 502.

NEW MILTON & DISTRICT

Ashley Sports Ground, New Milton, Hants. Tel: 0425 610401.
Founded: 1925
Secretary: D. Conacher, 31 Ambleside Road, Lymington, Hants. Tel: 0590 77179 (H), 0703 778115 (W).
League: Hampshire 1
Final position (1987–88): 11th

FORDINGBRIDGE

Recreation Ground, Fordinbridge, Hants. Tel: 0425 52047.
Founded: October 1983
President: S. Howard
Chairman: M. Noke
Secretary: S. Godden, 157 Station Road, Fordinbridge, Hants SP6 1DF. Tel: 0425 54069
Fixtures Secretary: J. Trim, "Trees", Fryern Court Road, Fordingbridge, Hants. Tel: 0425 55156.
No. of teams: Senior 2. Minis 1.
Directions to Ground: Recreation Ground, Ringwood Road, Fordingbridge.
Clubhouse: Mixed sports club.
Colours: Sky blue. (*Change colours:* Black).
Floodlights: No
Membership: £12.50
Local newspaper: Fordingbridge Journal
League: Hants 2
Final position (1987–88): Top (promoted)
Playing record (1987–88): P 33, W 22, L 11.
Competitions won: Hants Div 2 League. Promoted to Div 1.

GUERNSEY

PO Box 181, Footes Lane, St Peter Port, Guernsey. Tel: 0481-54590.
Founded: 1928
President: M.K. Duquemin
Chairman: B.A. Mansell
Coach: J. Good
Secretary: D.J. Christopher, PO Box 181.
Fixtures Secretary: M. Boot, Gorey Villa Private Hotel, Route Des Coutoures, St. Sampsons. Tel: 44377.
Club captain (1987–88): M. Petit
Club captain (1988–89): D. Wadley
No. of teams: Senior 3. Youth & Minis 2.
Ground capacity: 1000
Clubhouse: Club address above.
Colours: Green. (*Change colours:* Blue.
Floodlights: No
Membership: £15
Local newspaper: Guernsey Evening Press
League: Hants 2
Final position (1987–88): 2nd
Playing record (1987–88): P 22, W 15, D 0, L 7.
Competitions won: Siam Cup 23 april 1988 (Annual game v Jersey)

ROMSEY

The Sports Centre, Romsey, Hants. Tel: 0794 515503.
Secretary: J.H. Wilkinson, Lisle House, Church Lane, easton, Hants. Tel: 096278 484 (H), 0264 51844 (W).
League: Hampshire 2
Final position (1987–88): 3rd

WATERLOOVILLE

Rowlands Avenue, Waterlooville, Hants.
Founded: 1981
Secretary: I. Halmer, 19 Jodrell Close, Horndean, Hants. Tel: 0705 595216 (H), 0705 327311 (W).
League: Hampshire 2
Final position (1987–88): 4th

ANDOVER

Goodship Park, Southway, Walworth Industrial Estate, Andover. Tel: 0264 61578.
Founded: 1959
Secretary: J.M. Howcroft, 12a Hanson Road, Andover, SP10 3HL. Tel: 0264 5461 (H).
League: Hampshire 2
Final position (1987–88): 5th

OVERTON

Town Meadow, High Street, Overton, Hants.
Founded: 1971
Secretary: P.J. ??, 8 the Greenways, St Johns Road, Oakley, near Basingstoke, Hants. Tel: 0256 780874 (H).
League: Hampshire 2
Final position (1987–88): 6th

PEGASUS

c/o P.S.S.C., Lansing Bagnall, Kingsclere Road, Basingstoke, Hants.
Founded: 1972
President: T. Ham
Chairman: D.J. Hine
Coach: D. Morris
Secretary: D. Pink, 68 Millard Close, Oakridge, Basingstoke. Tel: 0256 63416.
Fixtures Secretary: A. Wheatley, 3 Loveridge Close, Basingstoke, Hants.
Club captain (1987–88): A. Wheatley
No. of teams: Senior 1, Youth & Minis 1
Directions to Ground: 3 miles West of Basingstoke on A30 towards London Lansing Sports Ground on left turn left at Red Lion Pub.
Ground capacity: As many as we can get.
Clubhouse: Lansing Bagnall Sports and Social Club.
Colours: Sky/navy quarters. (*Change colours:* Red)
Nickname: "Pigs"
Floodlights: No
Membership: £5.00 per season
Local newspaper: Basingstoke Gazette
League: Hampshire 2
Final position (1987–88): 6th
Playing record (1987–88): P 27, W 16, L 11, F 411, A 303.
Competitions won: Nil

VENTNOR

Watcombe Bottom, Whitwell Road, Ventnor.
Founded: 1936
Secretary: R. Bayliss, Medina House, Church road, Northwood, Cowes, Isle of Wight. Tel: 0983 298448 (H), 0983 525121 (W).
League: Hampshire 2
Final position (1987–88): 8th

ELLINGHAM

Picket Post, Ringwood, Hants. Tel: 04254 6668.
Founded: 1966
Secretary: H. Neale, Plas Bryn Carw, Harthill Drove, Redlynch, Salisbury, Wilts. Tel: 0725 21621 (H), 0703 778115 (W).
League: Hampshire 2
Final position (1987–88): 9th

Hampshire 2

NOMADS

The Sailing Club, Eastern Road, Portsmouth.
Founded: 1978
Secretary: P. England, 47 Westbourne Road, Copnor, Portsmouth PO2 7LB. Tel: 0705 695889.
League: Hampshire 2
Final position (1987–88): 10th

IBM

IBM, Havant. Tel: 0705 486363
Founded: 1968
Chairman: Peter Walmsley
Secretary: Robert Carr, 2 Kenilworth Villas, Kenilworth Road, Southsea, Hants PO9 2PQ. Tel: 0705 824433.
Fixtures Secretary: Colin Nightingale, 17 Matthews Close, Bedhampton, Hants PO9 3NJ. Tel: 0705 4500s00.
Club captain (1987–88): C. Nightingale
Club captain (1988–89): P. Brooks
No. of teams: Senior 1.
Directions to Ground: A27 Havant into IBM on south side of A27.
Clubhouse: IBM (South Hants) Clubhouse
Colours: Green & Black Hoops. (*Change colours:* Blue with yellow band).
Floodlights: No.
Membership: £7
Local newspaper: Evening News (Portsmouth)
League: Hants 2
Final position (1987–88): Withdrawn

EASTERN COUNTIES LEAGUE

THE major Eastern Counties leagues consisted of a top four embracing 11 clubs each and a fifth section of a dozen teams, all of whom completed their fixtures. Metropolitan Police, Chigwell, dropped only one point in the top group and that was their margin of success over second placed Cambridge, who lost just one game and were themselves a point clear of Romford & Gidea Park. In contrast Thetford lost all their games, but it took points difference to leave Shelford and Redbridge clear of Ely in 10th spot.

Basildon – with two draws as the only blemish on their record – won Eastern Counties 2 from Canvey Island, but there was no argument about the basement where Diss (one win) and Ilford Wanderers (all 10 matches lost) were isolated.

Old Edwardians dropped just one point in the third group leaving South Woodham Ferrers to take second place (five points away) on points difference from Holt and Newmarket. Last were Southwold, who lost all their games, and next to them were Lakenham-Hewett, whose points difference (but not their scoring power) was inferior to that of Harwich & Dovercourt.

In Eastern Counties 4 two points separated Campion, Old Bealonians and Stowmarket with the first two going up. Campion scored a massive 421 points. Rayleigh were one of three teams who lost two points for rules breaches and finished last with Clacton – on points differential from Mayfield Old Boys – in 10th place.

Eastern Counties 5 produced the season's best league performance – from Bancrofts, who won 11 matches and scored 447 points. Old Brentwoods also did well in this group to finish second after losing only to the champions and London Hospital, with only two defeats, also did well. In contrast Orwell lost all 11 games – but they deserve credit for staying the course and not withdrawing like some others did. Sawston – on points differential from Norwich Union – were the other basement team after winning three matches.

TABLES 1987–88

EASTERN COUNTIES 1

	P	W	D	L	F	A	Pts
Met Police, Chigwell	10	9	1	0	157	62	19
Cambridge	10	9	0	1	223	72	18
Romford & Gidea Park	10	8	1	1	167	46	17
Harlow	10	6	0	4	322	110	12
Rochford	10	5	0	5	99	87	10
Lowestoft & Yarmouth	10	4	0	6	100	129	8
Crusaders	10	4	0	6	99	174	8
Shelford	10	3	0	7	111	150	6
Redbridge	10	3	0	7	102	175	6
Ely	10	3	0	7	69	202	6
Thetford	10	0	0	10	45	292	0

EASTERN COUNTIES 2

	P	W	D	L	F	A	Pts
Basildon	10	8	2	0	189	66	18
Canvey Island	10	8	0	2	140	107	16
Chelmsford	10	7	0	3	168	98	14
P.L.A.	10	5	3	2	105	90	13
Braintree	10	5	2	3	132	115	12
Upminster	10	4	2	4	99	94	10
Wanstead	10	5	0	5	87	117	10
Woodbridge	10	4	1	5	137	144	9
East London	10	3	0	7	92	85	6
Diss	10	1	0	9	65	171	0

EASTERN COUNTIES 3

	P	W	D	L	F	A	Pts
O Edwardians	10	9	1	0	320	74	19
S. Woodham Ferrers	10	7	0	3	184	76	14
Holt	10	7	0	3	148	87	14
Newmarket	10	7	0	3	125	64	14
Maldon	10	6	0	4	163	102	12
Wymondham	10	4	90	6	142	125	8
Beccles	10	4	0	6	48	152	7
Wisbech	103	1	6	48	152	7	
Harwich & Dovercourt	10	3	0	7	83	145	6
Lakenham-Hewett	10	3	0	7	99	179	6
Southwold	10	0	0	10	48	330	0

EASTERN COUNTIES 4

	P	W	D	L	F	A	Pts
Campion	10	9	0	1	421	34	18
Old Bealonians	10	8	1	1	211	60	17
Stowmarket	10	8	0	2	170	81	16
O Palmerians	10	6	1	3	171	123	13
Gothic**	10	6	0	4	169	137	10
Fakenham	10	5	0	5	78	167	10
Felixstowe	10	3	1	6	141	165	7
NELPOB	10	2	1	7	56	251	5
Mayf'd OB*	9	3	0	6	121	184	4
Clacton	10	2	0	8	98	182	4
Rayleigh**	9	0	0	9	19	271	2

***2 championship points deducted – breach of rules.*

EASTERN COUNTIES 5

	P	W	D	L	F	A	Pts
Bancrofts	11	11	0	0	447	35	22
O Brentwoods	11	10	0	1	327	80	20
London Hospital	11	9	0	2	408	75	18
Dereham	11	6	1	4	242	226	13
March	11	6	0	5	171	202	12
Haverhill	11	5	0	6	154	144	10
Thurston	11	4	1	6	135	189	9
Loughton	11	4	0	7	156	199	8
Swaffham	11	4	0	7	136	192	8
Norwich Union	11	3	0	8	106	263	6
Sawston	11	3	0	8	86	307	6
Orwell	11	0	0	11	42	498	0

●*The tables are published from information supplied. Any queries should be directed to the appropriate league secretary*

EASTERN COUNTIES 1

METROPOLITAN POLICE CHIGWELL RFC

Metropolitan Police Sports Club, Chigwell Hall, Chigwell Road, Chigwell, Essex. Tel: 01-500 2735
Founded: 1943
President: Commissioner of Police
Chairman: M. Lawrence
Coach: C. Sutherland
Secretary: P.J. Ingham, 68 Gelsthorpe Road, Collier Row, Romford, Essex. Tel: 0708 28582
Fixtures Secretary: J. Harding, 30 Buxton House, Buxton Drive, London E11. Tel: 01-489 2991
Club captain (1987–88): K. Truscott
Club captain (1988–89): C. Burnell
No. of teams: Senior 3.
Directions to Ground: By tube to Chigwell. Out of station, turn right. Grounds 1 mile on left. 1 mile from M11 in Chigwell village.
Clubhouse: Police sports club.
Colours: Royal blue. (*Change colours:* Red)
Nickname: Chigwell Piggeries
Floodlights: No
Membership: Closed
Programme: Free. (Editor: C. Burnell)
Local newspaper: Romford Recorder/Ilford Gazette
League: Eastern Counties 1
Final position (1987–88): Champions
Playing record (1987–88): P 37, W 21, D 3, L 13. League P 10, D 1, L 0.
Competitions won: Essex Cup Winners 1970. Champions Eastern Counties League 1 1987–88.

CAMBRIDGE

Granchester Road, Cambridge
Founded: 1923
President: John Ashley
Chairman: David Beck
Coach: Russell Jones
Secretary: David Martin, 45 York Street, Cambridge. Tel: 0223 314705.
Fixtures Secretary: Alan Curtis, Kendal Lodge, Coton, Cambridge.
Club captain (1987–88): Stuart Gibbons
Club captain (1988–89): Kenny Isbister
No. of teams: Senior 5.
Directions to Ground: Take junction 12 off of M11 to towards Cambridge about one mile – turn right into Grantchester Road.
Ground capacity: 3000 if need be
Clubhouse: 5 changing rooms, large bar, lounge bar, 2 large baths, 8 showers.
Colours: Blood & sand. (*Change colours:* Cambridge blue
Floodlights: No
Membership: £23
Local newspaper: Cambridge Evening News
League: Eastern Counties 1
Final position (1987–88): 2nd
Playing record (1987–88): P 29, W 22, D 1, L 6. F 490, A 240.
Competitions won: Cambridgeshire Cup, December 87.

ROMFORD & GIDEA PARK

Crow Lane, Romford, Essex
Founded: 1930
Secretary: J.E. Howland, 1 Bush Elms Road, Romford, Essex RM11 1LR. Tel: Hornchurch 47305 (H). Wickford 61252 (W).
Fixtures Secretary: K. Parry, 112 London Road, Brentwood, Essex. Tel: Brentwood 224881.
League: Eastern Counties 1
Final position (1987–88): 3rd
Playing record (1987–88): P 32, W 23, D 2, L 7. F 482, A 211.

HARLOW

Elizabeth Way, Harlow. Tel: 0279 29750
Founded: 1955
President: R. Bracewell
Chairman: M. Ryland
Coach: R. Harris
Secretary: A. Price, 111 Chapel Fields, Harlow. Tel: 0279 418043.
Fixtures Secretary: J. Pendleton, 29 Priory Court, Harlow. Tel: 0279 39265.
Club captain (1987–88): J. Lewis
Club captain (1988–89): S. Cook
No. of teams: Senior 6. Youth & Minis 5.
Directions to Ground: Left at ski-slope roundabout when approaching from town centre, ½ mile on the right.
Ground capacity: 400
Clubhouse: Bar, dining room, lounge area, committee room.
Colours: Red. (*Change colours:* Green)
Nickname: The Rams
Floodlights: Yes. Training only at present.
Membership: £30
Local newspaper: Harlow Gazette
League: E. Counties 1
Final position (1987–88): 4th
Playing record (1987–88): P 39, W 23, D 4, L 12. F 994, A 452.
Competitions won: E. Counties Merit Table (1), D. Counties Div 3 (1), Brentwood Silver Ball (2), Thurrock Floodlit Competition (1), Essex Sevens (2), Hertford Sevens (2), Saffron Walden Sevens (1).

ROCHFORD HUNDRED

Founded: 1962
Secretary: S. Wakefield, 54 Henry Road, Chelmsford, Essex CM1 1RG. Tel: 0245 266168 (H), 0702 541581 (W).
League: Eastern Counties 1
Final position (1987–88): 5th

LOWESTOFT & YARMOUTH

Gunton Park, Long Lane, Carlton, Lowestoft, Suffolk. Tel: 0502 730260.
Founded: 1879
Secretary: I.G. Walker, 45 Marlborough Green Crescent, Martham, Norfolk NR29 4TL. Tel: Great Yarmouth 740456.
League: Eastern Counties 1
Final position (1987–88): 6th

CRUSADERS

Beckhythe, Little Melton, Norwich, Norfolk. Tel: (0603) 811157.
Founded: 1962
President: Brian Wilde
Chairman: Clive Hall
Coach: Ray Marsh
Secretary: David Austin, 3 Albury Walk, Eaton, Norwich.
Fixtures Secretary: David Williams, 6 St. Johns Close, Great Horsett, Norwich.
Club captain (1987–88): David Larson
Club captain (1988–89): Alan Smith
No. of teams: Senior 4, Youth 1
Directions to Ground: Old A11 to Norwich turn right to Colney going from Norwich towards Wynandham, first left, first right, next left, after ½ mile, turn left and ground is 200 yards down on your right hand side.
Ground capacity: 400
Clubhouse: One brick built clubhouse with complete bar and changing facilities. Floodlit training.
Colours: Green & yellow. (*Change colours:* Red)
Nickname: Crus
Floodlights: No
Membership: £25
Local newspaper: Eastern Daily Press
League: Eastern Counties 1
Final position (1987–88): 7th
Playing record (1987–88): P 32, W 16, L 16.
Competitions won: 2nd XV won Norfolk league Div. 3

SHELFORD

Davey Field, Cambridge Road, Gt. Shelford, Cambridge
Founded: 1933
President: R.A.F. Martin
Coach: T. Cadman
Secretary: K.L. Thopias, 169 Mill Road, Cambridge. Tel: 243157.
Fixtures Secretary: John Brown, 65 Eversden Road, Harlton.
Club captain (1987–88): Peter Kennedy
Club captain (1988–89): Peter Kennedy
No. of teams: Senior 4. Youth & Minis 1.
Directions to Ground: Leave M11 exit 11.
Colours: Maroon & white hoops.
Floodlights: Yes
Membership: £20
Local newspaper: Cambridge Evening News
League: Eastern Counties 1
Final position (1987–88): 8th

REDBRIDGE

Founded: 1952
Secretary: M.D. Hornby, 22 Washington Avenue, Laindon West, Basildon, Essex. Tel: Basildon 41430.
League: Eastern Counties 1
Final position (1987–88): 9th

ELY

Downham Road, Ely, Cambs. Tel: 0353 66 2156
Founded: 1967
President: Paul Leach
Chairman: Terry Moore
Coach: Terry Moore
Secretary: Peter Honess, 50 West End, Ely, Cambs CB6 3AY. Tel: 0353 663042.
Fixtures Secretary: Andy Emery, 51 Mudenhall Road, Littleport, Ely. Tel: Bunt Fen 224.
Club captain (1987–88): Ian O'Donnell
Club captain (1988–89): Chris Hughes
No. of teams: Senior 4. Youth & Minis 6. 1 womens team.

Directions to Ground: Turn off the A10 at the Little Downham/Ely staggered junction (A10 Ely bypass). 1st left. (Ground and club house very visible from A10 Ely bypass).
Ground capacity: 1000+
Clubhouse: Two storey brick and tile building. Lounge and main bar. Changing rooms (6) overlooking 3 pitches. Squash club (2 courts).
Colours: Black and gold hoops.
Floodlights: No
Membership: £25
Local newspaper: Ely Standard, Cambridge Evening News
League: Eastern Counties 1
Final position (1987–88): Bottom (relegated)
Playing record (1987–88): P 32, W 12, L 19, D 1.

THETFORD

Two Mile Bottom, Mundford Road, Thetford, Norfolk. Tel: 0842 5176.
Founded: 1959
Secretary: T. Tumath, Gael Cottage, The Avenue, Brookville, Norfolk IP26 4RF. Tel: 0366 728633 (H). 0842 819769 (W).
League: Eastern Counties 1
Final position (1987–88): 11th (relegated)

EASTERN COUNTIES 2

BASILDON

The Clubhouse, Gardiner Close, Basildon, Essex. Tel: 0268 3136
Founded: 1955
President: O.J. Knott
Chairman: S. Nash
Secretary: N. Searle, Address as above.
Fixtures Secretary: D. Dunn, 73 Brackendale Avenue, Pitsea, Essex. Tel: 0268 554657.
Club captain (1987–88): D. Terrell
Club captain (1988–89): D. Terrell
No. of teams: Senior 5. Youth & Minis 4.
Directions to Ground: Take A132 turning off the A127 in direction of Basildon. At first roundabout turnright. Proceed to a set of traffic lights, turn right into Gardiners Lane South. First left into Gardiners Close and then right at the bottom of the road.
Clubhouse: Recently extended bar and clubhouse, with 4 changing rooms and showers.
Colours: Bottle green with two white hoops.
Floodlights: Yes
Membership: £25 full membership
Local newspaper: Evening Echo
League: Eastern Counties Div 1
Final position (1987–88): Top of Eastern Counties Div 2
Playing record (1987–88): P 35, W 21, D 3, L 11
Competitions won: Eastern Counties Div 2, Brentwood Silver Ball

CANVEY ISLAND

Tewkes Creek, Dovervett Road, Canvey Island, Essex. Tel: 0268 681881.
Founded: 1970
Secretary: K. Bennett, 1D Arcadia Road, Canvey Island, Essex SS8 7SP. Tel: 0268 684544.
League: Eastern Counties 2
Final position (1987–88): 2nd

CHELMSFORD

Coronation Park, Timsons Lane, Chelmsford. Tel: 0245 261159.
Founded: 1920
President: R.C. Gamrie, JP
Chairman: Colin Ash
Coach: Andy Green
Secretary: John Bacon, Nutwood, Hopping Jacks Lane, Danbury, Essex CM3 4PQ. Tel: 0245 41 4660 (H), 0376 500600 (W)
Fixtures Secretary: Ian Stuart, 49 Hillside Grove, Chelmsford, Essex. Tel: 0245 352790.
Club captain (1987–88): Nicky Pilgrim
Club captain (1988–89): Nicky Pilgrim
No. of teams: Senior 5. Youth & Minis 6.
Ground capacity: 1000
Clubhouse: The Pavilion, Timsons Lane, Springfield, Chelmsford.
Colours: Navy Blue. (*Change colours:* Claret
Nickname: Sausages
Floodlights: No
Membership: £25
Local newspaper: Essex Chronicle
League: Eastern counties 2
Final position (1987–88): 3rd
Playing record (1987–88): P 33, W 14, D 1, L 18. F 395. A 441.

PORT OF LONDON AUTHORITY

PLA Sports Social Club, The Drive, Ilford, Essex. Tel: 01-554 3276.
Founded: 1875
Secretary: A.C. Guest, 57 Shaftsbury Road, Forest Gate, London E7. Tel: 01-471 7571.
Fixtures Secretary: D.I. Westbrook, 91 Ashurst Avenue, Thorpe Bay, Essex. Tel: 0702 582440 (H). 01-497 7272 (W).
League: Eastern Counties 2
Final position (1987–88): 4th
Playing record (1987–88): P 25, W 15, D 5, L 5. F 382, A 182.

BRAINTREE

Recreation Field, Tabor Avenue, Braintree, Essex. Tel: Braintree 22282.
Founded: 5th
Secretary: P. Carter, 11 Orchard Avenue, Halstead, Essex. Tel: Halstead 473977 (H), Halstead 477261 (W).
League: Eastern Counties 2
Final position (1987–88): 5th

UPMINSTER

Hall Lane Playing Fields, Upminster, Essex. Tel: 04022 20320.
Founded: 1964
Secretary: D. Hope, 115A Corbets Tey Road, Upminster, Essex RM14 2AA. Tel: 04022 24526 (H). 01-377 0660 (W).
League: Eastern Counties 2
Final position (1987–88): 6th

WANSTEAD

Roding Lane North, Woodford Bridge, Ilford, Essex. Tel: 01-550 1561.
Founded: 1892
Secretary: G. Reeves, 105 Kingswood Road, Ilford, Essex IG3 8UB.
Fixtures Secretary: P. Jacobs, 10 Clayside, Chigwell, Essex. Tel: 01-591 0891 (H). 01-588 0078 (W).
League: Eastern Counties 2
Final position (1987–88): 7th
Playing record (1987–88): P 20, W 10, D 2, L 8. F 178, A 191.

WOODBRIDGE

Hatchley Barn, Bromeswell, Woodbridge, Suffolk. Tel: 0394 460630
Founded: 1969
President: Michael G. Lubbock
Chairman: Michael G. Lubbock
Coach: Roger Coombs
Secretary: David M. Neal, Bradtiere Lodge, Spring Lane, Wickham Mkt, Woodbridge, Suffolk IP13 0SH. Tel: 0728-746442 (H), 03943-2263 (W).
Fixtures Secretary: Christopher Steward, 5 Norfolk Crescent, Framlingham, Woodbridge, Suffolk. Tel: 0728 723061 (H).
Club captain (1987–88): John Cummings
Club captain (1988–89): John Cummings
No. of teams: Senior 4. Youth & Minis 3.
Directions to Ground: North or South on A 12, take B1084 Orford Road. Pass Woodbridge Golf Club, ground ½ mile on right hand side.
Clubhouse: Modern, centrally heated brick and tile building.
Colours: Sky blue
Floodlights: Yes
Membership: £1 pa for players
Local newspaper: East Anglian Daily Times
League: E Counties 2
Final position (1987–88): 7th
Playing record (1987–88): P 37, W 25, L 12.
Competitions won: Suffolk Merit Table 87–88. Colts Seasons Cup 1987–88.

EAST LONDON

Clubhouse and ground, Holland Road, West Ham, London E15. Tel: 01-474 6761.
Founded: 1950
President: Not filled since death of first president
Chairman: O.N. Evans
Coach: T.B.A.
Secretary: R.H. James, 84 Forest Approach, Woodford Green, Essex. Tel: 01-504 1477.
Fixtures Secretary: A. Oldaker, 154 Amery Gardens, Romford, Essex. Tel: 0708 762900.
Club captain (1987–88): Ray Gladman
Club captain (1988–89): Ray Gladman
No. of teams: Senior 6. Youth & Minis 2.
Directions to Ground: From West Ham Tube Station (District Line) turn left into Memorial Avenue, follow to end, turn right into Holland Road and club faces you.
Colours: Maroon and navy. (*Change colours:* Grey).
Floodlights: Yes, training only
Membership: £25 (includes squash)
Local newspaper: Newham Recorder and Stratford Press
League: Eastern counties 2
Final position (1987–88): 8th
Playing record (1987–88): P 29, W 7, D 1, L 21, F272, A 394.

DISS

Bellrope Lane, Roydon, Diss, Norfolk. Tel: 0379 642891.
Founded: 1958
President: B.A.C. Gaze
Chairman: T.J. Childerhouse
Coach: K.J. Davies/H Lind
Secretary: S.R.W. Smith, 10 Waveney Road, Diss, Norfolk. Tel: 0379 651108 (H), 0379 651931 (W).
Fixtures Secretary: P. Whetter, 35 Fair Green, Diss. Tel: 0379 642077
Club captain (1987–88): S.D. Middleton
Club captain (1988–89): T. Baldwin
No. of teams: Senior 5. Youth & Minis 7.
Directions to Ground: Travelling west on a1066 from diss, proceed through Roydon, turn right opposite White Hart PH. Club on left.
Colours: Royal Blue/White (*Change colours:* Blue, white hoops/pink
Floodlights: Yes, training only.
Membership: £25 playing membership
Local newspaper: Diss Express/Eastern Daily Press
League: Eastern Counties 2
Final position (1987–88): 9th
Competitions won: Norwich 7's. Plate Comp May 1988

ILFORD WANDERERS

Forest Road, Barkingside, Essex. Tel: 01-500 4622.
Founded: 1896
President: Dr B. Cronin
Chairman: L.T.G. Kirwan
Secretary: T. Kneeshaw, 103 Kinfauns Road, Goodmayes, Ilford, Essex. IG3 9QJ. Tel: 01-599 3505 (H). 01-534 7601 (W).
Fixtures Secretary: J. Dixon. Tel: 0245 414968
Club captain (1987–88): S. Stuckey
Club captain (1988–89): T. Gunyon
No. of teams: Senior 5. Youth & Minis 1.
Directions to Ground: Central line to Hainault Station. 5 mins walk from Ilford. Bus 150 or 247 to Hainault.
Clubhouse: Excellent facilities.
Colours: Red, green, white.
Nickname: Wanderers
Floodlights: Yes training area only.
Membership: £30
Local newspaper: Recorder
League: Eastern Counties 2
Final position (1987–88): 11th (relegated)
Playing record (1987–88): P 27, w 4, D 2, L 21. F 232, A 491.

OLD EDWARDIANS

Westlands Playing Fields, London Road, Romford, Essex.
Founded: 1967
Secretary: P.J. Hensher, 108 Stanley Avenue, Gidea Park, Romford, Essex. Tel: Romford 64429 (H). 01-593 7621 (W).
League: Eastern Counties 3
Final position (1987–88): 1st (promoted)
Playing record (1987–88): P 27, W 21, D 2, L 4. F 675, A 232.

SOUTH WOODHAM FERRERS

Founded: 1981
Secretary: P. Burgess, "Forelands", 203A North Drive, Maylandsea, Chelmsford, Essex. Tel: 0261 742342 (H). 07089 861122 (W).
League: Eastern Counties 3
Final position (1987–88): 2nd

HOLT

Bridge Road, High Kelling, Holt, Norfolk. Tel: 0263 712191.
Founded: 1961
President: Canon D. Maurice
Chairman: Ian MacBrayne
Secretary: M.D. Bush, The Warren, Sir Williams Lane, Aylsham, Norwich NR11 6Aw. Tel: 0263 732051.
Fixtures Secretary: R. Harrison, Hall Farm, Metton, Norwich. Tel: 0263 761255.
Club captain (1987–88): R.K. Day
Club captain (1988–89): R.K. Day
No. of teams: Senior 4. Youth 3.
Directions to Ground: Approx 1½ miles from Holt on Cromer Road, A148.
Clubhouse: Single storey brick building with pitched roof.
Colours: Black shirts, shorts and socks. (*Change colours:* White shirts, black shorts and socks.
Nickname: The Owls
Floodlights: No (not at present)
Membership: £20 per year playing members plus weekly match fees
Local newspaper: Eastern Daily Press & North Norfolk News
League: Eastern Counties 3
Final position (1987–88): 3rd
Playing record (1987–88): P 34, W 20, D 2, L 12. F 567, A 333.
Competitions won: 1976 Norfolk Cup Winners. Winners of various 7s tournaments.

NEWMARKET & DISTRICT

Scaltback Middle School, Elizabeth Avenue, Newmarket, Suffolk. Tel: 0638 663082.
Founded: 1956
Secretary: M. Wiltshire, 60 Drinkwater Close, Newmarket, Suffolk. Tel: 0638 660221 (H). 0638 662345 (W).
League: Eastern Counties 3
Final position (1987–88): 4th

MALDON

Drapers Farm Sports Club, Drapers Chase, Goldhanger Road, Heybridge, Maldon, Essex. Tel: 0621 52152.
Founded: 1947
Secretary: N. Meadows, 23 Cedar Avenue, Tiptree, Maldon, Essex. Tel: 0621 818030 (H).
League: Eastern Counties 3
Final position (1987–88): 5th

WYMONDHAM

Tutles Lane East, Wymondham, Norfolk. Tel: 0953 607332.
Founded: 1971
President: J. Meen
Chairman: D. Shaw
Coach: J. Kelly
Secretary: M. Warren, 67 Hawkes Lane, Bracon Ash, Norfolk NR14 8EN. Tel: 0508 70669.
Fixtures Secretary: S. Good, 9 Poplar Way, Attleborough, Norfolk. Tel: 0953 453006.
Club captain (1987–88): C. Dinneen
Club captain (1988–89): C. Dinneen
No. of teams: Senior 3. Youth & Minis 7.
Directions to Ground: A11 to north of Wymondham. Turn off roundabout sign post Dereham. Straight over second roundabout, 400 yards on right.
Colours: Black and red. (*Change colours:* Black.
Floodlights: No
Membership: £30
Local newspaper: Eastern Daily Press
League: Eastern Counties 3
Final position (1987–88): 5th
Playing record (1987–88): P 30, W 17, D 0, L 13. F 475, A 309.

BECCLES

Beef Meadow, Common Lane, Beccles. Tel: 712016.
Founded: 1966
President: J. Hipperson
Chairman: I. Johnstone
Secretary: W.J. Wells, Cliff Cottage, Pudding Moor, Eccles, Suffolk. Tel: 715509.
Fixtures Secretary: D. Smith, 17 Scales Street, Bungay. Tel: 2234.
Club captain (1987–88): M. Penney
Club captain (1988–89): N. Beese
No. of teams: Senior 3. 4 Youth & 3 Minis.
Directions to Ground: Turn to Beccles on bypass – pass station over railway line, turn left into Common Lane.
Clubhouse: Council owned, shared
Colours: Emerald green.
Floodlights: No
Membership: £17
Local newspaper: Beccles & Bungay Journal – Eastern Daily Press.
League: Eastern Counties 3
Final position (1987–88): 4th
Playing record (1987–88): P 29, W 16, D 1, L 12

WISBECH

Chapel Road, Wisbech. Tel: 0945 63666
Founded: 1947
President: Gordon Timm
Chairman: Tony Maris
Coach: David Debson
Secretary: Peter Sheldrick, 36 Tavistock Road. Tel: 63829.

Eastern Counties 3

Fixtures Secretary: Mick Woods, 2 Anderson Close. Tel: 581091
No. of teams: Senior 3. Youth & Minis 1.
Directions to Ground: 100 yards from Old Bridge, Town Centre.
Clubhouse: Ex stables.
Colours: Red shirts, blue shorts. (*Change colours:* Green.
Floodlights: Yes
Membership: £25
Local newspaper: Wisbech Standard/Fenland Advertiser
League: Eastern Counties 3
Final position (1987–88): 7th
Playing record (1987–88): P 35, W 14, L 21.

HARWICH & DOVERCOURT

The Pavilion, Low Road Playing Fields, Dovercourt, Suffolk. Tel: 0255 506571.
Secretary: G. Brazier, 10 Main Road, Great Oakley, Harwich, Essex. CO12 5AZ. Tel: 0255 886233 (H). 0255 428231 (W).
League: Eastern Counties 3
Final position (1987–88): 9th

LAKENHAM-HEWETT

Tel: 0508 78826
Founded: 1962
President: R. Jenkinson
Chairman: B. Ridgeway
Coach: R. Rowley
Secretary: M. Chapman, 94 Muriel Road, Norwich NR2 3NZ. Tel: Norwich 58437.
Fixtures Secretary: B. Ridgeway, 130 Abinger Way, Norwich, Norfolk. Tel: Norwich 53076.
Club captain (1987–88): A. Pullinger
Club captain (1988–89): G. Brown
No. of teams: Senior 3. Youth & Minis 2.
Directions to Ground: Take A140 out of Norwich. After 3 miles turn right onto B1113. Clubhouse 1½ miles on right before Swardeston.
Clubhouse: Clubhouse/Three large size pitches.
Colours: Red shirts, stockings, white shorts.
Floodlights: No
Membership: £25
Local newspaper: Eastern Evening News
League: Eastern Counties 3
Final position (1987–88): 10th
Playing record (1987–88): P 33, W 16, L 16, D 1.

SOUTHWOLD

The Pavilion, The Common, Southwodl, Suffolk.
Founded: 1964/65
President: A.P. Kelk
Chairman: R. Middleditch
Coach: R. Excell
Secretary: A.S. Toone, 17 Portesh Close, Saxon Fields, Carlton Colville, Lowestoft, Suffolk. Tel: Lowestoft 515649.
Fixtures Secretary: R. Stephenson, Woodside Farm, Holton, Halesworth, Suffolk. Tel: Halesworth 722907.
Club captain (1987–88): R. Temple
Club captain (1988–89): R. Temple
No. of teams: Senior 3. Youth & Minis 1.
Directions to Ground: Turn right at Kings Head Hotel and proceed straight towards water tower.
Colours: Black, old gold hoop. (*Change colours:* Maroon).
Floodlights: No
Membership: £15 (players). Vice-Presidents £10
Local newspaper: Lowestoft Journal
League: EC 4
Final position (1987–88): Bottom Div 3
Playing record (1987–88): P 60, W 26, D 3, L 31. (Club)
Competitions won: suffolk Knockout (Chadacre Cup) Plate Winners 1985/86, 1987/88

EASTERN COUNTIES 4

CAMPION

Clubhouse, Cottons Park, Cottons Approach, Romford, Essex. Tel: 0708 753209
Founded: 1977
President: Dr Rowbottom
Chairman: Peter O'Brien
Coach: Danny McCarthy
Secretary: Kelvin Wilson, 290 Southend Arterial Road, Hornchurch, Essex RM11 2SG.. Tel: 04024 70587.
Fixtures Secretary: Kevin Marmion, 132 Warley Hill, Brentwood, Essex CM14 5HB. Tel: 0277 211148.
Club captain (1987–88): Kevin O'Neill
Club captain (1988–89): Kevin O'Neill
No. of teams: Senior 4.
Directions to Ground: From Gallows Corner (junction A127 and A12) proceed towards London. turn right at 3rd set lights. Right into Marks Road. First left into Cottons Approach.
Clubhouse: Recently refurbished.
Colours: Red and black hoops. (*Change colours:* Sky blue).
Floodlights: No
Membership: £30
Local newspaper: Romford Recorder
League: EC4
Final position (1987–88): Winners (promoted)
Playing record (1987–88): P 32, W 23, D 1, L 8. F 956, A 319.
Competitions won: County Clubs 7's at Twickenham.

OLD BEALONIONS RFC

Clubhouse, Wards Road, Ilford, Essex. Ground, Beal High School, Woodford Bridge Road, Redbridge.
Founded: 1964
Chairman: J. Sims
Coach: P. Morrison
Secretary: M.P. March, 22 Londview Gardens, Marden Ash, Ongar, Essex CM5 9EG.
Fixtures Secretary: M. Venables. Tel: 04027 24824.
Club captain (1987–88): S. Lewis
Club captain (1988–89): P. Morrison
No. of teams: Senior 3.
Directions to Ground: M11 to Redbridge, A12 to Gants Hiull. A4306 from gants Hill and ground is in Woodford, Bridge Road, about 2 miles from Gants Hill.
Colours: Scarlet. (*Change colours:* Red,yellow and black hoops.
Floodlights: No
Membership: Open to old boys and by invitation.
Local newspaper: Ilford Recorder
League: Eastern Counties 3
Final position (1987–88): 2nd in EC4.
Playing record (1987–88): P 30, W 17, L 12, D 1. F 445, A 358.

STOWMARKET

Chilton Field Sports Club, Chilton Way, Stowmarket, Suffolk.
Founded: 1962
President: R. Cresswell
Chairman: As above
Coach: C. Manning
Secretary: V.J. Franklin, 46 Finborough Road, Stowmarket. Tel: 0449 676607
Fixtures Secretary: G. Wright, Jeda, Station Road, Bacton, Stowmarket. Tel: 0449 781866.
Club captain (1987–88): P. Relf
Club captain (1988–89): P. Relf
No. of teams: Senior 3.
Directions to Ground: From town centre traffic lights follow sign to Mid-Suffolk Leisure Centre, approx ½ mile turn right into Onehouse Road, follow road past high school, turn right into Chilton Way.
Clubhouse: Club room, 4 changing rooms, opening August 1988
Colours: Navy with one red hoop and two small white hoops. (*Change colours:* Yellow and black hoops).
Nickname: Vultures
Floodlights: No
Membership: £15
Local newspaper: East Anglian Daily Times
League: EC4
Final position (1987–88): 3rd
Playing record (1987–88): P 29, W 18, L 10, D 1. F 472, A 292.

OLD PALMERIANS

c/o Palmers College, Grays, Essex. Tel: 0385 370121.
Founded: 1977
President: A.K. Smetham
Chairman: P. Clarke
Coach: E. McNuley
Secretary: R.O. Heapy, 48 Nutberry Avenue, Grays, Essex RM16 2TL. Tel: 0375 379359.
Fixtures Secretary: A.J. Marr, 38 Whitehall Lane, Grays, Essex. Tel: 0375 375346.
Club captain (1987–88): N. Flack
Club captain (1988–89): A. Bayliss
No. of teams: Senior 3. Youth & Minis run by college.
Directions to Ground: M25 junctions 30/31. A13 Eastbound. 1st turnoff Grays. 1st roundabout, 2nd exit Lodge Lane to Chadwell St Mary. 1st roundabout 3 exit Woodview. Bear left at fork. College on right next to traffic lights.
Clubhouse: c/o St Thomas's Social Club, East Thurrock Road, Grays.
Colours: Sky/Navy. (*Change colours:* Black).
Floodlights: Yes, training only
Membership: £12
Local newspaper: Thurrock Gazette
League: Eastern Counties 4
Final position (1987–88): 4th

GOTHIC

Earlham School, Earlham, Norwich. Tel: 0603 51611.
Founded: 1979
Secretary: T. Stubbs, 94 Dover Street, Norwich. Tel: 0603 611370 (H).
League: Eastern Counties 4
Final position (1987–88): 5th

FAKENHAM

Fakenham High School, Field Lane, Fakenham, Suffollk.
Founded: 1982
Secretary: T.E. Bishop, 1 Hall Staithe, Fakenham, Norfolk. Tel: 0328 4818 (H). 0328 2545 82238 (W).
League: Eastern Counties 4
Final position (1987–88): 6th

FELIXSTOWE

Coronation Ground, Mill Lane, Felixstowe, Suffolk. Tel: 0394 270150.
Founded: 1930
Secretary: D. Jones, 114 High Road, Trinley St Mary, Near Ipswich. Tel: 0394 278202 (H). 0473 227399 (W).
League: Eastern Counties 4
Final position (1987–88): 7th

NORTH EAST LONDON POLYTECHNIC OLD BOYS

High view, Lambourne Road, Chigwell, Essex. Tel: 01-500 8574.
Founded: 1938
Secretary: J. Hagger, 189 Marston Avenue, Dagenham, Essex RM10 7LP. Tel: 01-592 6301 (H). 01-526 1671 (W).
League: Eastern Counties 4
Final position (1987–88): 8th

MAYFIELD OLD BOYS

Whitbread Sports Ground, Durham Avenue, Buckhurst Hill, Essex.
Founded: 1971
President: P. Harvey
Chairman: B. Jones
Secretary: Mrs P. Willcocks, 59 Felbrigge Road, Ilford, Essex IG3 8DN. Tel: 01 599-6672.
Fixtures Secretary: J. Holland, 72 Park Avenue, Barking, Essex. Tel: 01 591-0410.
Club captain (1987–88): J. Holland
Club captain (1988–89): M. Feild
No. of teams: Senior 2
Directions to Ground: North Circular to Charlie Browns roundabout Chigwell Road to Snakes Lane East Prospect Road to Durham Avenue.
Ground capacity: Plenty of standing room.
Clubhouse: We use local pub.
Colours: Green & white hoops.
Nickname: The Feild
Floodlights: No
Membership: £20.00
Local newspaper: Ilford Recorder
League: Eastern Counties 4
Final position (1987–88): 9th

CLACTON

Valley Road, Clacton on Sea. Tel: 421602
Founded: 1935
President: Lou Wood
Chairman: Tony Cook
Coach: Ian Turner
Secretary: Graham Barney, c/o Clubhouse, Valley Road, Clacton.
Fixtures Secretary: Chris White, 87 Old Road, Frinton-on-Sea. Tel: 71884.
Club captain (1987–88): Trevor Moore
Club captain (1988–89): Mark Pickett
No. of teams: Senior 3. Youth & Minis 1/2.

Directions to Ground: Ask for ambulance station, Valley Road, Clacton. Ground and clubhouse opposite.
Colours: Maroon shirts, blue shorts.
Floodlights: No
Membership: £15
Local newspaper: East Essex Gazette
League: Eastern Counties 4
Final position (1987–88): 10th/11th
Playing record (1987–88): P 33, W 14, L 17, D 2.

RAYLEIGH WYVERNS

St John Fisher Playing Fields, Little Wheatleys Chase, Rayleigh, Essex.
Founded: 1971
Secretary: T. March, 8 Hambra Avenue, Rayleigh, Essex SS6 9NJ. 0628-771908 (H); Brentwood 219131 (W).
Colours: Scarlet, Emerald, Black.
League: Eastern Counties 4
Final position (1987–88): 11th

EASTERN COUNTIES 5

BANCROFT

Buckhurst Way, Buckhurst Hill, Essex. Tel: 01-594 0429.
Founded: 1894
Secretary: S.B. Thirsk, 4 Bentley Way, Woodford Green, Essex IG8 0SE. Tel: 01-504 1468 (H). 0378 561111 (W).
League: Eastern Counties 5
Final position (1987–88): 1st (promoted)
Playing record (1987–88): P 30, W 25, D 1, L 4. F 713, A 180.

OLD BRENTWOODS

Ashwells Road, Kelvedon Hatch, Brentwood, Essex. Tel: 0277 74070
Founded: 1967
President: G.N. Kingston
Chairman: D.J. Oldham
Coach: G. Waite
Secretary: T.M.B. Kerrigan, c/o 20 Wormwood Street, London EC21 M1RQ. Tel: 0277 223045 (H), 01-588 4303 (W).
Fixtures Secretary: D.K. Hatton, 13 Regent Square, Bruce Road, London E3 3HQ.Tel: 01-981 0421.
Club captain (1987–88): M.T. Wheeler
Club captain (1988–89): M.T. Wheeler
No. of teams: Senior 3
Directions to Ground: From Brentwood Town Centre take Ongar Road for approx 2 miles. Ashwells Road is on right hand side.
Clubhouse: Built 1978. 2 squash courts, 3 tennis courts, 2 rugby pitches, 4 soccer pitches, 1 cricket square.
Colours: Dark/light blue hoops.
Floodlights: No
Membership: £35
Local newspaper: Brentwood Gazette
League: Eastern Counties 5
Final position (1987–88): EC 5th – 2nd
Playing record (1987–88): P 31, W 21, D 1, L 9. F 626, A 322.

THE LONDON HOSPITAL

Wadham Road, Hale End, Walthamstow, London.
Founded: 1865
President: Dr C. Barnes
Secretary: S. Curry, London Hospital Clubs Union, Stepney Way, Whitechapel, London E1 2AD.
Fixtures Secretary: P. Jameson. See Secretary.
Club captain (1987–88): T. Crosby
Club captain (1988–89): D. Baker
No. of teams: Senior 3.
Directions to Ground: 150 yards down Wadham Road, on the left hand carriageway from the Crooked Billet (on N Circular Road).
Colours: Blue/White chequers. (*Change colours:* Blue/white hoops).
Nickname: The London
Floodlights: No
League: Eastern Counties 5
Final position (1987–88): 3rd
Playing record (1987–88): P 35, W 20, D 4, L 11.
Competitions won: United Hospitals VIIs. United Hospitals A Cup both '87–'88.

DEREHAM

Moorgate, Dereham, Norfolk
Founded: 1974
President: I. Walker
Chairman: P. Corham
Coach: J. Vaughan
Secretary: W. Parfitt, 41 Windmill Avenue, Dereham, Norfolk. Tel: (0362) 693450.
Fixtures Secretary: L. Grauwiler, Daleview House, Dereham Road, Scarning, Dereham, Norfolk. Tel: (0362) 694141.
Club captain (1987–88): R. Drew
Club captain (1988–89): F. Savage
No. of teams: Senior 2. Youth & Minis 1.
Directions to Ground: Dereham turning off A47 through Moorgate Housing Estate.
Colours: Maroon, black, white. (*Change colours:* Pale blue
Floodlights: No
Membership: £20 playing member
Local newspaper: Dereham & Fakenham Times
League: Eastern Counties 5
Final position (1987–88): 4th
Playing record (1987–88): P 31, W 18, D 2, L 11. F 529, A 448.

MARCH

BRSA Field, Elm Road, March, Cambridge.
Founded: 1968
Secretary: D. Odlin, 4 Willow Drive, March, Cambridgeshire. Tel: 0354 52312 (H). 0354 51627 (W).
League: Eastern Counties 5
Final position (1987–88): 5th

HAVERHILL

Castle Playing Fields, Haverhill, Suffolk. Tel: 0440 702871.
Founded: 1964 (25th this season)
President: D. Nicholas
Chairman: K. Bond
Coach: A Hope, P. Marper, P. Raffell, R. Green
Secretary: K. Ager, 40 Chapple Drive, Haverhill, Suffolk CB9 0DW. Tel: 706796.
Fixtures Secretary: R. Green, 1 Pakenham Place, Haverhill, Suffolk CB9 0JA. Tel: (0440) 704710.
Club captain (1987–88): A. Hope
Club captain (1988–89): K. Pullen
No. of teams: Senior 2. Youth 1.
Directions to Ground: Through main High Street, up Comps Road and 5th on right, School Lane, top of School Lane.
Clubhouse: Wooden clubhouse, bar, showers and changing rooms.
Colours: Maroon and blue hoops.
Floodlights: No
Membership: £20 playing, £5 colts.
Local newspaper: Haverhill Echo
League: Eastern Counties 5
Final position (1987–88): 6th
Playing record (1987–88): P 27, W 15, L 11, D 1.

THURSTON

Thurston Upper School, Thurston, Bury St Edmonds, Suffolk.
Founded: 1973
Secretary: R. Tully, Seletar, Hepworth Road, Stanton, Bury St Edmonds, Suffolk. Tel: 0359 50160 (H).
Fixtures Secretary: R. Wyatt, Stone Cottage, The Green, Beyton, Suffolk. Tel: 0359 70410 (H).
League: Eastern Counties 5
Final position (1987–88): 7th

LOUGHTON

Hornbeam Road, Buckhurst Hill, Essex. Tel: 01-504 0064.
Founded: 1955
President: Malcolm Wallace
Chairman: Laurie Grace
Coach: Chris Parker
Secretary: Chris Palmer, 'Elmcroft', Coppice Row, Theydon Bois, Epping, Essex CM16 7ER.
Fixtures Secretary: Brian Westley, 30 The Avenue, St Pauls Cray, Orpington, Kent. Tel: 01-302 0755.
Club captain (1987–88): Matthew Baldwin
Club captain (1988–89): Michael Corker
No. of teams: Senior 3.
Directions to Ground: Squirrels Lane off Hornbeam Road which is opposite the Monkhams Pub in Buckhurst Way, Buckhurst Hill.
Clubhouse: Bar and clubroom with dance floor, weights room, 2 large changing rooms, showers, etc.
Colours: White with black and green. (*Change colours:* Green.
Nickname: Louts
Floodlights: Np
Membership: £25 pa (Playing Seniors)
Local newspaper: West Essex Gazette
League: Eastern Counties 5
Final position (1987–88): 5th
Playing record (1987–88): P 27, W 11, L 14, D 2. F 370, A 454.

SWAFFHAM

North Pickenham Road, Swaffham, Norfolk.
Founded: 1981
Secretary: D. Routledge, Mardle Bank, London Road, Swaffham, Norfolk PE37 7DH. Tel: 0760 22401 (H). 0760 21480 (W).
League: Eastern Counties 5
Final position (1987–88): 9th

NORWICH UNION

School Lane, Whitefarm Lane, Off Harvey Lane, Thorpe, Norfolk.
Founded: 1885
Secretary: D.K. Johnson, c/o Norwich Union (CSYS L3 Department), Surrey Street, Norwich NR1 2NG. Tel: 0603 496322 (H), 0603 683870 (W).
League: Eastern Counties 5
Final position (1987–88): 10th

SAWSTON

Sawston Village College, Sawston, Cambridge. Tel: 0223 836615
Founded: 1978
President: J. Marven
Chairman: M.P. Tomlinson
Coach: G. McMillan
Secretary: Ms K. Elbrow, 5 Rawlyn Close, Cambridge CB5 8NN. Tel: (0223) 244486
Fixtures Secretary: D. Cox, 9 Westmoore Avenue, Sawston, Cambridge. Tel: Cambridge (0223) 836011.
Club captain (1987–88): S. Cox
Club captain (1988–89): S. Cox
No. of teams: Senior 2.
Directions to Ground: Sawston High Street, turn left down New Road, college on right. Ground and clubhouse on the edge of playing fields.
Clubhouse: Brick built.
Colours: Navy, black with one white stripe. (*Change colours:* Red/white hoops.
Nickname: "Qupnis Hora Temulenti!"
Floodlights: No
Admission: Free
Membership: £15
Local newspaper: Sawston Reporter, Cambridge Evening News.
League: Eastern Counties 5
Final position (1987–88): 10th
Playing record (1987–88): P 32, W 16, L 15, D 1.

ORWELL

Gainsborough Sports Centre, Manyon Road, Ipswich, Suffolk. Tel: 0473 713088.
Founded: 1964
President: B. Kinsey
Chairman: P. Gardner
Coach: S. Bevan
Secretary: R. Knowles, Felixstowe 284350
Fixtures Secretary: D. Botwright, 12 Vermont Road, Ipswich, Suffolk. Tel: 0473 215866.
Club captain (1987–88): M. Ferguson
Club captain (1988–89): M. Ferguson
No. of teams: Seniors 2.
Directions to Ground: A45 bypass to Felixstowe. 1st left after Orwell Bridge. Follow signs to airport.
Colours: Red, black. (*Change colours:* Black, red.
Floodlights: No
Membership: £15
Local newspaper: Evening Star
League: Eastern Counties 6
Final position (1987–88): Bottom
Playing record (1987–88): P 29, W 7, D 2, L 20.

MIDDLESEX LEAGUES

MIDDLESEX started with four leagues, which consisted of 11, 12, 11 and 12 clubs respectively, the latter two being geographically selected groups, which saw the southern section spoiled by the withdrawal of Brunel University and St. Mary's College.

Finchley, who also won the Middlesex County Cup, took the top honours after dropping only three points. Staines were their nearest challengers – three points behind. Orleans F.P. and Old Millhillians won two matches each, which left them isolated at the foot of the table.

Middlesex 2 was a 'one-horse-race' with Old Abbotstonians, another club which own a Rugby World & Post junior award, winning all 11 matches. Centaurs in second place were eight points behind! The very unlucky bottom teams were Pinner & Grammarians and Antlers, who both ended the campaign with seven points; in most leagues that would have left them safe.

Haringay had a perfect record of 10 wins and won Middlesex 3N from Wembley who lost two games. Enfield Old Grammarians (only two points) and luckless Kodak (none at all) propped up the table.

The depleted Middlesex 3S, with its two student teams deserting during the season, saw Hammersmith & Fulham drop three points but still finish two ahead of C.A.V. in second place. Old Isleworthians were a brave third. Meadhurst (four points) and Hayes (one less) ended up in the last two places, but this is misleading information.

TABLES 1987–88

MIDDLESEX 1

	P	W	D	L	F	A	Pts
Finchley	10	8	1	1	130	38	17
Staines	10	7	0	3	129	87	14
O Haberdashers	10	6	0	4	110	77	14
Sudbury Court	10	6	0	4	110	77	12
Uxbridge	10	6	0	4	78	91	12
Lensbury	10	5	0	5	114	89	10
London NZ	10	4	1	5	114	123	9
Hampstead	10	4	0	6	115	152	8
Old Meadonians	10	3	0	7	82	105	6
Orleans FP	10	2	0	8	65	131	4
Old Millhillians	10	2	0	8	63	130	4

MIDDLESEX 2

	P	W	D	L	F	A	Pts
Old Abbotsonians	11	11	0	0	19	63	22
Centaurs	11	7	0	4	209	116	14
Civil Service	11	6	0	5	167	106	12
Hackney	11	5	2	4	136	101	12
O Hamptonians	11	6	0	5	104	106	12
Richmond Thamesians	11	6	0	5	104	106	12
Barclays Bank	11	4	1	6	90	124	9
St. Bart's Hos	11	4	1	6	90	124	9
London Cornish	11	4	0	7	127	218	8
Osterley	11	4	0	7	147	218	8
Antlers	11	3	1	83	156	7	
Pinner & Grammarians	11	3	1	7	54	158	7

MIDDLESEX 3N

	P	W	D	L	F	A	Pts
Haringey	10	10	0	0	279	35	20
Wembley	10	8	0	2	202	50	16
O Tottonians	10	6	1	3	168	85	13
Belsize Park	10	6	1	3	123	103	13
O Grammarians	10	6	0	4	182	75	12
Roxeth Man OB	10	5	0	5	99	88	0
UCS OB	10	5	0	5	99	88	10
Old Ignatians	10	4	0	6	101	106	8
ST and C	10	2	0	8	70	235	4
Enfield O Gram	10	1	0	9	41	245	2
Kodak	10	0	0	10	28	351	0

MIDDLESEX 3S

	P	W	D	L	F	A	Pts
Hammersmith & Fulham	9	7	1	1	163	73	15
CAV	9	6	1	2	82	57	13
O Isleworthians	9	6	0	3	109	77	12
Quintin	9	5	1	3	94	81	11
Bank of England	9	4	1	4	98	53	9
O Actonians	9	4	1	4	88	84	9
London French	9	4	0	5	1342	102	8
Feltham	9	3	0	6	54	117	6
Meadhurst	9	2	0	7	64	127	6
Hayes	9	1	1	7	22	135	3

Brunel University withdrawn – all results void
St. Mary's College withdrawn – all redults void

FINCHLEY

Summers Lane, Finchley, London N12. Tel: 01-445 3746
Founded: 1925
President: S.F. Beard
Chairman: N. Heasman
Coach: G. Edwards
Secretary: S. Clough, 91 Arcadian Gardens, London N22. Tel: 888 6526
Fixtures Secretary: J. Devlin, 35 Richmond Road, New Barnet.
Club captain (1987–88): P. Kamara
Club captain (1988–89): L. Gibbons
No. of teams: Senior 5. Youth & Minis 1.
Directions to Ground: Turn off North Circular (A406) at High Road, North Finchley heading north, take 1st first right. Club 200 yards on right.
Ground capacity: 2000. Stand, 400.
Colours: Red and white hoops. (*Change colours:* Navy blue).
Nickname: Finches
Floodlights: No
Admission: Free
Membership: £25
Programme: 30p
Local newspaper: Finchley Times
League: Middlesex 1
Final position (1987–88): Winner Middx. 1
Playing record (1987–88): P 33, W 24, D 1, L 8. F 473, A 242.
Competitions won: Winner Middx Cup, winner Middx League 1, Winner Agar Cup, Winner Hendon Sevens.

STAINES

"The Reeves", Feltham Hill Road, Hanworth, Middx TW13 7NB. Tel: 01-890 3051.
Founded: 1926
President: E.J. de Vail
Chairman: W. Lee
Coach: R. Pettifer
Secretary: G.M. Clark, 38 Shepherds Close, Shepperton, Middx. TW17 9AL. Tel: 0932 242045.
Fixtures Secretary: E.J. de Vail, 94 Groveley Road, Sunbury-on-Thames, Middx. Tel: 01-890 6643.
Club captain (1987–88): Kevin Jones
Club captain (1988–89): Chris Smith
No. of teams: Senior 7. Youth 7 & Minis 5.
Directions to Ground: The Club is situated off A316. Turn left just past Jobs Dairy – ground is on the left.
Ground capacity: 5 pitches
Clubhouse: New – 10 changing rooms
Colours: Red and blue hoops. (*Change colours:* Blue
Nickname: Swans
Floodlights: Yes
Membership: £28
Programme: Free. (Editor: David Hoade)
Local newspaper: Staines & Egham
League: Middx. 1
Final position (1987–88): 2nd
Playing record (1987–88): P 321, W 14, D 3, L 14. F 371, A 415.
Competitions won: Numerous 7s competitions in the early 1970s.

OLD HABERDASHERS

Croxdale Road, Theobald Street, Boreham Wood, Herts WD6 4PY. Tel: 01-953-1987
Founded: 1903
Secretary: M. Tappin, 10 Woodway, Holtspur, Beaconsfield, Bucks HP9 1DH. Tel: 04946-2459 (H); 01-440-8260 (W).
Fixtures Secretary: J.J. Hansom, 77 Loom Lane, Radlett, Herts. Tel: 09276-6836 (H); 01-953 2178 (W).
Colours: Blue, white, magenta.
League: Middlesex 1
Final position (1987–88): 3rd

SUDBURY COURT

The Pavilion, East Lane, North Wembley, Middx. Tel: 01-904 8485
Founded: 1958
President: M.G. Leftley
Chairman: P. Wilkinson
Coach: A. Lewis
Secretary: D.P. Gray, 33 Northwick Park Road, Harrow, Middx. Tel: 01-4237 4155.
Fixtures Secretary: D. Keeling, 17 Nunnery Lane, Luton, Beds. Tel: 0582 507602.
Club captain (1987–88): M. Broderick
Club captain (1988–89): R. Thompson
No. of teams: Senior 5
Directions to Ground: Train to North Wembley station, turn left on leaving and ground is 600 yards on left. Or train to Sudbury Town station and No 245 bus to East Lane School. Ground is opposite bus stop.
Clubhouse: 4 changing rooms, modern bath and shower facilities, 2 bars.
Colours: Dark blue, red and white. (*Change colours:* Yellow).
Floodlights: Yes, training only.
Membership: £15 players, £9 non players
Local newspaper: Weekly Observer
League: Middx. 1
Final position (1987–88): 4th
Playing record (1987–88): P 35, W 17, D 2, L 16. F 479, A 368.

UXBRIDGE

Belfry Avenue, Harefield, Middlesex. Tel: 089 582 3281.
Founded: 1948
Secretary: C. Webb, 124 Whitby Road, South Ruislip, Middlesex HA4 9DR. Tel: Ruislip 631746 (H), 01-864 5373. Extn. 4309 (W)
League: Middlesex 1
Final position (1987–88): 5th
Playing record (1987–88): P 37, W 23, D 2, L 12. F 371, A 311.

LENSBURY

Founded: 1920
Secretary: R.G. Golding, 1 Christchurch Avenue, Teddington, Middlesex TW11 9AB. Tel: 01-977 4014 (H), 01-934 5272 (W).
Fixtures Secretary: P. Stovald, 6 The Paddock, The Drive, Godalming, Surrey GU7 1XD. Tel: Godalming 23150 (H), 01-637 8575 (W).
League: Middlesex 1
Final position (1987–88): 6th
Playing record (1987–88): P 21, W 14, L 7. F 443, A 202.

LONDON NEW ZEALAND

St Pauls Playing Fields, Jersey Road, Osterley, Middlesex. Tel: 577 6420.
Founded: 1926
President: E. Sturmer

Coach: R. Francis
Secretary: Mrs W. Whitechurch
Fixtures Secretary: R. Peacock, Oakwell, Downlea Common, High Wycombe. Tel: 0494 448157.
Club captain (1987–88): J. White
Club captain (1988–89): J. White
No. of teams: Senior 1, Youth & Minis 1
Directions to Ground: Follow A4 Greatwestern Road, follow signs to Osterley Park House, turn left/South at entrance Down Jersey Road. Rugby ground ½ mile on right Jersey Road Osterley.
Colours: Black. (*Change colours:* White)
Floodlights: Yes
Admission: No cost
Membership: £10.00
Programme: None
Local newspaper: U.K. New Zealand News
League: Middlesex 1
Final position (1987–88): 5th
Playing record (1987–88): P 29, W 12, L 14, D 3.

HAMPSTEAD

Tel: 01-458 6512
Founded: 1968
President: M.P.L. Flynn
Chairman: S.J. Loffler
Coach: T. Skyrme
Secretary: S.J. Loffler, 29 Kingsley Way, London N2 0EH. Tel: 01-458 6512 (H), 01-759 4822 (W).
Fixtures Secretary: T. Harrison, 26C Thames Road, Strand on the Green, London W4. Tel: 01-747 5028 (H), 01-581 3817 (W).
Club captain (1987–88): O. Jenkins
Club captain (1988–89): O. Jenkins
No. of teams: Senior 6.
Directions to Ground: Hampstead Way, Heath Extension, Hampstead Garden Suburb, London NW11.
Clubhouse: The Washington, Englands Lane, Hampstead NW3.
Colours: Gold, white and claret. (*Change colours:* Yellow).
Floodlights: No.
Membership: £25
Local newspaper: Hampstead & Highgate Gazette
League: Middx 1
Final position (1987–88): 7th
Playing record (1987–88): P 34, W 14, L 18, D 2.

OLD MEADONIANS

Riverside Lands, Chiswick, London W4. Tel: 01-994 6956.
Founded: 1958
Secretary: T.D. Smith, 2 Sandford cottages, Kingsclere, Newbury, Berks. Tel: 0635 298231 (H), 9628 39255 (W).
Fixtures Secretary: R. Willingace, Fairmile Farm Cottage, Denbyrd, Cobham, Surrey. Tel: 0932 66927 (H). 0932 45599 (W).
League: Middlesex 1
Final position (1987–88): 9th
Playing record (1987–88): P 36, W 17, D 3, L 16. F 369, A 380.

ORLEANS FORMER PUPILS

Orleans Park, Richmond Road, Twickenham. Tel: 01-892-5743.
Founded: 1963
President: D. Davidson
Chairman: P. Tanner
Coach: J. Doyle
Secretary: A. Squire, 3 Lyndhurst Avenue, Twickenham, Middx. Tel: 01-894-4100.
Fixtures Secretary: P. Tanner, 81 Twining Avenue, Twickenham. Tel: 01-898-3976.
Club captain (1987–88): H. Formella
Club captain (1988–89): H. Formella
No. of teams: Senior 3
Directions to Ground: From Twickenham station turn left to traffic lights. Turn left along Richmond Road. Past Orleans Sch on right, entrance to club before Crown Public House.
Colours: Maroon, gold, white hoops
Floodlights: No
Membership: £25
Local newspaper: Richmond & Twick. Times
League: Middx 1
Playing record (1987–88): P 29, W 12, D 1, L 16, F 296. A 318.

OLD MILLHILLIANS

Headstone Lane, Harrow, Middlesex. Tel: 01-428 2281.
Founded: 1878
Secretary: M. Leon, Wild Acre, Bushfield Road, Bovingdon, Hemel Hempstead, Herts HP3 0DR. Tel: 0442 833665.
Fixtures Secretary: D. Roddala, 1 The Chestnuts, Walton-on-Thames, Surrey K12 1EE. Tel: 0932 20318.
League: Middlesex 1
Final position (1987–88): 11th (relegated)
Playing record (1987–88): P 31, W 8, L 23. F 248, A 506.

OLD ABBOTSTONIANS

Gainsborough Road, Pole Hill Open Spaces, Hillingdon, Middlesex. Tel: 01-845 1452.
Founded: 1957
Chairman: G. Jackson
Coach: D. Harper
Secretary: G.J. Brotesta, 2 Denecroft Crescent, Hillingdon, Middlesex UB10 9HU. Tel: (0875) 71100. 01-798 7045.
Fixtures Secretary: D. Wiggins, 49 Pethworth Gows, Hillingdon. Tel: (0895) 51585.
Club captain (1987–88): M. Wray
Club captain (1988–89): D. Harper
No. of teams: Senior 4. Youth 1 & Vets. 1.
Directions to Ground: Gainsborough Road, Hayes, Middlesex.
Ground capacity: Open fields
Colours: Red and blue hoops. (*Change colours:* Blue)
Nickname: Abbots
Floodlights: No
Membership: £20
Local newspaper: Hillingdon Gazette
League: Middlesex 2
Final position (1987–88): 1st
Playing record (1987–88): W 26, D 1, L 5.
Competitions won: Reached Semi Finals of Middlesex Cup. Won Junior Club of the Month award and Rugby ??? ???. Won Midsdlesex League 2.

CENTAURS

Gower Road, Syon Lane, Isleworth, Middlesex. Tel: 01-560 4500.
Founded: 1923
Secretary: R. Charon, 54A Sydney Road, Twickenham, middlesex tW12 1JR. Tel: 01-891 0951 (H). 01-379 3385 (W).
Fixtures Secretary: P. Astbury, 32 Kneller Gardens, Isleworth, Middlesex. Tel: 01-898 5372 (H). 01-725 2313/5 (W).
League: Middlesex 2
Final position (1987–88): 2nd
Playing record (1987–88): P 33, W 18, D 2, L 14. F 497, A 374.

CIVIL SERVICE

Dukes Meadows, Riverside Drive, Chiswick, London W4
Founded: 1922
Secretary: N.G. Alway, 14 Freshford Street, London SW18 3TF. Tel: 01-946 3082 (H), 01-836 8333 (W).
Press Officer: M.G. Power. Tel: 0234 214225
Directions to Ground: On main road from Chiswick Roundabout to Richmond.
Colours: White shirts, blue shorts.
League: Middlesex 2
Final position (1987–88): 3rd
Playing record (1987–88): P 20, W 7, D 1, L 12. F 199, A 268.

HACKNEY

Spring Hill Ground, Spring Hill, Hackney, London. Tel: 01-806 5289
Secretary: A. Leader, 4 Wilbury Way, London N18. Tel: 01-803 9413 (W)
League: Middlesex 2.
Final position (1987–88): 4th

OLD HAMPTONIANS

Dean Road, Hampton, Middx.
Founded: 1957
President: The Headmaster of Hampton School, G. Able
Chairman: J. Wells
Coach: TBA
Secretary: J.R. Bugler, 3 Walpole Place, Teddington, Middx. Tel: 01-977 1380.
Fixtures Secretary: R. Hudson, 29 Undine Road, Clippers Quay, London E14. Tel: 01-538 0773.
Club captain (1987–88): R. Severn
Club captain (1988–89): D. Jacob
No. of teams: Senior 3.
Directions to Ground: Coming west from London on the A316 turn left at 'Apex Corner' on to the A312. After approx ¾ mile turn right into Hanworth Road, travel past 3 schools and turn right into Dean Road. Club entrance is on the right.
Colours: Black, gold, silver hoops. (*Change colours:* Plain dark blue).
Floodlights: No
Membership: £225
Local newspaper: Richmond & Twickenham Times, Middx Chromicle, Surrey Comet
League: Middx 2
Final position (1987–88): 5th
Playing record (1987–88): P 31, W 14, L 13, D 4. F 365, A 343.

RICHMOND THAMESIANS

Richmond College, Egerton Row, Twickenham, Middlesex.
Founded: 1962
Secretary: K.J. Patrick, 65 Surbiton Court, St Andrews Square, Richmond, Surrey KT6 4ED.
League: Middlesex 2
Final position (1987–88): 6th

BARCLAYS BANK

Park View Road, Ealing, London W5 2JF
Founded: 1921
President: D.C. Mann
Chairman: D. Hooper
Secretary: B.D. Stevenson, 89 Oyster Lane, Byfleet, Surrey KT14 7JF. Tel: 09323-44937.
Fixtures Secretary: D.M. Bevan-Jones, 23 Cypress Avenue, Whitton, Middx. Tel: 01-898 4107.
Club captain (1987–88): D.J.J. Lavery
Club captain (1988–89): D.J.J. Lavery
No. of teams: Senior 5.
Directions to Ground: Off the North Circular on the western side of Hanger Lane.
Clubhouse: Adjacent to pitches
Colours: Maroon with gold and silver band. (*Change colours:* Navy blue).
Floodlights: No
Membership: Closed Club. Barclays staff only.
League: Middx. Div II.
Final position (1987–88): k7th
Playing record (1987–88): P 36, W 13, D 2, L 21. F 356 A 536.
Competitions won: Champion bank, Inter-Bank 7-A-Side Champions (both 1987/88)

ST BART'S HOSPITAL

West Smithfield, London EC1
Founded: 1873
President: J. Gilmore
Secretary: G.C. Cloud, Medical College, St Barts Hospital, Charterhouse Square, London EC1. Tel: 01-987 5129.
Fixtures Secretary: G.C. Cloud. As above.
Club captain (1987–88): M. Wood
Club captain (1988–89): D. Clarke
No. of teams: Senior 1.
Directions to Ground: Perry Street, Foxbury, Chislehurst, Kent. (By train from London Bridge).
Ground capacity: Fair. Stand 2–300.
Clubhouse: Bar & dining facilities and changing rooms for 6–4 teams.
Colours: Black and white. (*Change colours:* White and black).
Nickname: Barts
Floodlights: No
League: Middlesex 2
Final position (1987–88): 7th
Playing record (1987–88): P 23, W 10, D 1, L 12.
Competitions won: Winners Norwich 7's

LONDON CORNISH

Richardson Evans, Memorial Ground, Roehampton Vale, Kingston-on-Thames, Surrey. Tel: 01-778 3638.
Secretary: S. Lang, 12 Albert Road, Hampton Hill, Middlesex TW123 1LB. Tel: 01-941 0234 (H), 01-874 3922 (W).
League: Middlesex 2
Final position (1987–88): 9th
Playing record (1987–88): P 23, W 11, D 1, L 11. F 284 A 320.

OSTERLEY

Tentelow Lane, Norwood Green, Southall, Middlesex. Tel: 01-574 3774.
Founded: 1922
Secretary: D.R. Shepherd, 34 Chandos Avenue, Ealing, London W5. Tel: 01-847 2759 (H), 01-560 5151 (W).
Fixtures Secretary: J. Green, 92 Roxborough Avenue, Isleworth, Middlesex. Tel: 01-568 5557.
League: Middlesex 2
Final position (1987–88): 10th
Playing record (1987–88): P 36, W 17, D 2, L 17. F 452, A 560.

ANTLERS

Bushy Park, Teddington, Middlesex. Tel: 01-977 4989.
Founded: 1966
Chairman: S. Croft
Coach: T. O'Connor
Secretary: P.J. Woolgar, 114 Elgin Avenue, Ashford, Middlesex. Tel: 0784 259734.
Fixtures Secretary: R. Bromfield, 104 Station Road, Hampton, Middx. Tel: 01-979 5635
Club captain (1987–88): R. Jones
Club captain (1988–89): P. Rattenbury
No. of teams: Senior 4.
Colours: Dark blue. (*Change colours:* Various).
Floodlights: No
Membership: £20
Local newspaper: Richmond & Twickenham times
League: Middx. 2
Final position (1987–88): 11th (relegated)

PINNER & GRAMMARIANS

Shaftsbury Playing Fields, Grimsdyke Road, Harch End, Pinner, Middlesex. Tel: 01-428 3136.
Founded: 1934
Secretary: D. Hiles, 31 Lulworth Close, South Harrow, Middlesex HA2 9NR. Tel: 01-864 0787 (H), 01-954 0671 (W).
League: Middlesex 2
Final position (1987–88): 12th
Playing record (1987–88): P 27, W 8, D 4, L 15. F 157, A 334.

MIDDLESEX 3N

HARINGAY

New River Sports Centre, White Hart Lane, Wood Green, London N22 5QW. Tel: 01-889 9981.
Founded: 1963
Chairman: Ken Williams
Coach: Alan Richards/Mike Brock
Secretary: Glynne Jones, 44 Park Hall Road, E. Finchley, London N2 9PX. Tel: 01-883 8091 (H).
Fixtures Secretary: Colin Field, 53 Brookside South, East Barnet, Herts EN4 8LJ. Tel: 01-368 4383 (H), 01-340 1771 (W).
Club captain (1987–88): Charles Henderson
Club captain (1988–89): Lyndon Morris
No. of teams: Senior 5.
Directions to Ground: A406 (N. Circular Road) to junction with A10 (Gt. Cambridge Road) A10 in direction of Central London. White Hart Lane 6th right, ground ½ mile.
Ground capacity: 2,000 +
Clubhouse: Under Athletics Spectator Stand.
Colours: Green, scarlet, white.
Nickname: The Rhinos
Floodlights: No
Membership: £20
Newsletter: (Editor: Secretary – runs weekly newsletter Rhino Rumblings).
Local newspaper: The Hornsey Journal, Tottenham Lane, N8.
League: Middlesex 3 North
Final position (1987–88): 1st
Playing record (1987–88): W 19, D 1, L 8. F 480, A 228.
Competitions won: Middlex Div 3 North Championship

WEMBLEY LM

Broadfields, Headstone Lane, North Harrow, Middlesex. Tel: 01-428 0286.
Founded: 1927
Secretary: Mrs N. Conlon, 62 Canterbury Road, Croxley Green, Herts. Tel: 0923 39640 (H).
League: Middlesex 3N
Final position (1987–88): 2nd
Playing record (1987–88): P 23, W 12, D 1, L 10. F 342, A 242.

OLD TOTTONIANS

Tottenham School, Selby Road, London N17.
Founded: 1931
Secretary: T.W. De La Salle, 25 Penton Drive, Cheshunt, Herts EN8 9RS. Tel: 0992 38492 (H). 0494 444816 (W).
League: Middlesex 3N
Final position (1987–88): 3rd
Playing record (1987–88): P 25, W 11, D 1, L 13. F 313, A 316.

BELSIZE PARK

c/o Belsize Tavern, Belsize Lane, London NW3.
Founded: 1972
President: John Connelly
Chairman: Giles Lenton
Secretary: Keiran Ryan, Flat 6, Eton Garages, Eton Avenue, London NW3 4PE.
Fixtures Secretary: Brian East, 17 waterlow Road, London NI9 5NJ. Tel: 01-272 5686 (H), 01-485 4100. Extn 287 (W).
Club captain (1987–88): frank Sampong
Club captain (1988–89): John Roche
No. of teams: Senior 3.
Directions to Ground: Copthall Stadium, Copthall Playing Fields, Barnet.
Colours: Black and lavender. (*Change colours:* Red and blue).
Floodlights: No
Membership: £17
Local newspaper: Hampstead & Highgate Express
League: Middlesex 3 (N)
Final position (1987–88): 4th
Playing record (1987–88): P 27, W 15, L 11, D 1. F 332, A 377.
Competitions won:

OLD GRAMMARIANS

Ground: Queen Street, Tottenham, London N17.
Clubhouse: Corner of Manor Road/Denmark Street, Tottenham, London N.2. Tel: 01-898 7697.
Founded: 1929
President: K. McGuinness
Coach: D. Kaplan
Secretary: B. Calderwood, 17 Birch Crescent, Aylesford, Kent ME20 7QE. Tel: 0622 78350.
Fixtures Secretary: M. Holt, 64 Chandos Road, London N2 9AP. Tel: 01-883 4016.
Club captain (1987–88): J. Wing
Club captain (1988–89): J. Wing
No. of teams: Senior 4
Directions to Ground: Queen St, Tottenham, N 17. Off White Hart Lane, N17. approached via Great Cambridge Road (A10)/High Road (A1010)
Clubhouse: Situated at Corner of Manor Road/ Denmark Street, Tottenham N17. Tel: 01-808 7697.
Colours: Navy, light blue, red.
Floodlights: No
Membership: £25
Local newspaper: Hornsey Journal
League: Middlesex 3N
Final position (1987–88): 5th
Playing record (1987–88): P 29, W 17, D 1, L 11. F 373, A 238.

ROXETH MANOR OLD BOYS

Polytechnic of North London Sports Ground, Honey Pot Lane, Stanmore, Middx HA7 1AR. Tel: 01-952 1893
Founded: 1961
President: Dennis Holliday
Chairman: Roger Meek
Secretary: Rad Stone, 50 Browning Way, Heston, Middx TW5 9BE. Tel: 01-570 6781.
Fixtures Secretary: Phil Noot, 18 Glebe Road, Chalfont St Peter, Bucks. Tel: 0753 886702.
Club captain (1987–88): Laurence Seabridge
Club captain (1988–89): Lawrence Seabridge
No. of teams: Senior 5.
Directions to Ground: Close to A4140 – Marsh Lane – Stanmore.
Colours: Black. (*Change colours:* Amber).
Floodlights: No
Membership: £15
Local newspaper: Harrow Gazette
League: Middx N3
Final position (1987–88): 6th
Playing record (1987–88): P 28, W 12, L 16. F 353, A 338

UCS OLD BOYS

UCS Playing Fields, Ranulf Road, London NW2. Tel: 01-452 4337.
Founded: 1892
Secretary: A.G.B. Paterson, 29 Nicholas Way, Northwood, Middlesex HA6 2TR. Tel: 09274 21417 (H). 01-260 7242 (W).
Fixtures Secretary: T. Bebroft, 14 Batchworth Lane, Northwood, Middlesex. Tel: 09274 24602 (H). 01-935 9978 (W).
League: Middlesex 3N
Final position (1987–88): 7th
Playing record (1987–88): P 32, W 14, D 2, L 16. F 311, A 395.

ENFIELD IGNATIANS

The Clubhouse, Donkey Lane, Enfield, Middx. Tel: 01-363 2877.
Founded: 1951
Chairman: K.G. Jones
Coach: J. Cooper
Secretary: D. Wills, 81 Eastbrook Road, Waltham Abbey, Essex. Tel: 0992 715541.
Fixtures Secretary: T. Ryan, 72 Gt Bushey Drive, Totteridge, London N20. Tel: 01-445 5372.
Club captain (1987–88): P. Poulain
Club captain (1988–89): T. Fenn
No. of teams: Senior 4.
Directions to Ground: South of M25 on A20 at Queen Elizabeth Stadium.
Clubhouse: Own clubhouse, bar and changing facilities.
Colours: Gold and blue. (*Change colours:* Red).
Nickname: Old I's
Floodlights: Yes
Membership: £25 season
Local newspaper: Enfield Gazette
League: Middx. 3N
Final position (1987–88): 6th
Playing record (1987–88): P 29, W 11, D 1, L 17. F 439, A 400.

STC (NEW SOUTHGATE)

Oakleigh Road, New Southgate, London N11. Tel: 01-368 1234.
Founded: 1927

Secretary: D. Hockey, 107 Hazelwood Lane, Palmers Green, London N13 5HQ. Tel: 01-882 5080 (H). 01-606 7321 (W).
League: Middlesex 3N
Final position (1987–88): 9th

ENFIELD OLD GRAMMARIANS

Enfield Grammar School (Lower), Parsonage Lane, Enfield, Middx.
Founded: 1981
Secretary: P. Carroll, 1 The Alders, Winchmore Hill, London N21. Tel: 01-360-3800 (H); 01-623-9661 (W).
League: Middlesex 3N
Final position (1987–88): 10th

KODAK

c/o K.R.S. Kodak Ltd, Harrow, Middlesex, HA1 4TY.
Founded: 1937
President: M. Simmonds
Chairman: J. Davis
Coach: P. Childs
Secretary: D. Jackson, 82 Langley Way, Watford, Herts WD1 3EF.
Fixtures Secretary: P. Summers, 63 Ridge Lea, Hemel Hempstead, Herts.
Club captain (1987–88): B. Haynes
Club captain (1988–89): P. Childs
No. of teams: Senior 2.
Directions to Ground: Rayners Lane (LT) H1 bus to "Goodwill" Public House. Ground 200 yards along Harrow View on left. Bakerloo line to Headstone Lane, left outside station.
Ground capacity: 200
Clubhouse: Excellent bar and showers and restaurant.
Colours: Gold and green. (*Change colours:* Green and gold or blue).
Floodlights: Yes, partial.
Membership: £25
Local newspaper: Harrow Observer, Watford Observer and Watford Review
League: Middlesex 3N
Final position (1987–88): Bottom Middx 3N.

MIDDLESEX 3S

HAMMERSMITH & FULHAM

Hurlingham Stadium, Hurlingham Park, London SW6. Tel: 01-736 5186
Founded: 1978
President: Cliff Morgan
Chairman: Terry Alleyne
Coach: Dave Higgins
Secretary: Chris Cuthbertson, 17 Wheatsheaf Wharf, Wheatsheaf Lane, London SW6 6LS. Tel: 01-381 5064 (H), 0252 875075 (W).
Club captain (1987–88): Tony Richards
Club captain (1988–89): Tony Richards
No. of teams: Seniors 4.
Directions to Ground: From Hammersmith Broadway take the Fulham Palace Road (A219) towards Putney Bridge. Just before the bridge turn left at the traffic lights into the New Kings road (A308). Take the first right, under the railway bridge, into Hurlingham Road. The ground is 300 yards on the right.
Ground capacity: 4000. Stand, 3000.
Clubhouse: No clubhouse. Use the Alma pub in Parsons Green Lane, London SW6.
Colours: Red shirt with two white and one blue band. (*Change colours:* Sky blue or white).
Nickname: The Hammers
Floodlights: No
Membership: £20
Local newspaper: Fulham Chronicle
League: Middlesex 2
Final position (1987–88): Winners Middlesex 3S.
Playing record (1987–88): P 30, W 17, L 11, D 1. F 490, A 353.
Competitions won: Winners Middlesex League Three (South)

NORTHOLT (formerly CAV)

Lord Halsbury Sports and Social Club, Lord Halsbury Playing Fields, Eastcote Lane, Northolt, Middx. Tel: 01-841 1296.
Founded: 1960
President: T. Lynham
Chairman: S. Knight
Coach: A. Ross
Secretary: C. Nicholl, 20B Northolt Avenue, Ruislip, Middx, MA4 6ST
Fixtures Secretary: G. Payne, 16 Brackenbridge Drive, St Ruislip.
Club captain (1987–88): D. Rutherford
Club captain (1988–89): M. Cooke
No. of teams: Senior 4.
Directions to Ground: From A40 Target Roundabout take A312 (Church Road) towards Harrow. Turndown Eastcote Lane (4th left). follow road till Islip Manor School and Abbot Close. Take the driveway between the school and railway line. Clubhouse at end of this driveway.
Clubhouse: Use private sports and social club's facilities.
Colours: royal/Light blue hoops. (*Change colours:* White).
Floodlights: No
Membership: £30
Local newspaper: Greenford & Northolt Gazette or Ealing Gazette
League: Middx 3S
Final position (1987–88): 2nd
Playing record (1987–88): P 28, W 18, D 3, L 7.
Competitions won: 2nd in Middx Div 3 Sth

OLD ISLEWORTHIANS

Wood Lane, Isleworth, Middlesex. Tel: 01-560 7949.
Founded: 1957
Secretary: K. Tighe, 40 Douglas Lane, Wraysbury, Berks. Tel: 078481 2622 (H), 01-626 0566. Extn. 3417 (W).
League: Middlesex 3S
Final position (1987–88): 3rd

QUINTIN (formerly Polytechnic)

Hartington Road, Chiswick, London W4.
Founded: 1885
Secretary: N. Smith, 16 Church Road, Acton, London W3 8PP. Tel: 01-991 5614 (H). 01-242 9050. Extn. 3582 (W).
League: Middlesex 3S
Final position (1987–88): 4th

BANK OF ENGLAND

Tel: 01-876 8417
Founded: 1908
Chairman: R.M. Beales
Coach: R Gomm (N. Spaven, T. Barker)
Secretary: B.S. Brown, 62 Gilpin Avenue, East Sheen, SW14. Tel: 01-878 3396.
Fixtures Secretary: S.L. Williams, c/o Bank of England, Threadneedle Street, London EC12 R8AH. Tel: 01-601 4444.
Club captain (1987–88): B.S. Brown
Club captain (1988–89): S. Tregoning
No. of teams: Senior 3.
Directions to ground: Waterloo to Barnes (BR) – to Priory Lane, past Rosslyn Park rFC and 200 yards on right.
Clubhouse: 2 bars, restaurant, 15 changing rooms, plungebaths, gym and pool.
Colours: Old gold, blue and white. (*Change colours:* white).
Nickname: "House"
Floodlights: No
Membership: Employers facilities – private
League: Middx 3 South
Final position (1987–88): 5th
Playing record (1987–88): P 30, W 16, D 3, L 11. F 418, A 344
Competitions won: Interbank Junior 7s, Interbank Senior 7s Plate May 1988

OLD ACTONIANS

Gunnersbury Drive, London W5. Tel: 01-567 4556.
Founded: 1968
Secretary: A. Hart, 60 St Mary's Road, Harlesden, London NW10 4AX. Tel: 01-961 7578 (H), 01-353 8000. Extn. 4088 (W)
League: Middlesex 3S
Final position (1987–88): 6th

LONDON FRENCH

Prince Georges Playing Fields, Bushey Road, Raynes Park, London SW20.
Founded: 1959
Secretary: A. James, 8 Beaumont Crescent, West Kensington, London W14 9PE. Tel: 01-385 7132 (H), 01-629 8191 (W).
League: Middlesex 3S
Final position (1987–88): 7th

FELTHAM (formerly Old Twickenham)

Hanworth Park, Park Road, Hanworth, Middlesex. Tel: 01-894 3609.
Founded: 1947
Secretary: A.D. Keen, 80 worple Road, Staines, Middlesex. Tel: 0784 53035 (H), 01-560 1234. Extn. 3380 (W).
Fixtures Secretary: R. Brewer, 23 Chaucer Road, Ashford, Middlesex TW15 2QU. Tel: 07842 46044.
League: Middlesex 3S
Final position (1987–88): 8th

MEADHURST

Meadhurst Club, Sunbury-on-Thames, Middx. Tel: 09327 63502.
Founded: 1952/53
President: R. Malpas
Chairman: R. Corbett
Coach: T. Fearn
Secretary: J. Norley, BP Research Centre, Chertsey Road, Sunbury-on-Thames, Middx TW16 7LN. Tel: 09327 64038 (W).
Fixtures Secretary: K. wills, 30 Waldemar Avenue, Ealing, London W13 9PY. Tel: 01-965 6031 (W).
Club captain (1987–88): R. Mountford
Club captain (1988–89): I. Somerville
No. of teams: Senior 3. Youth & Minis 0.
Directions to Ground: From Richmond (A316) or Kingston (A308) to Sunbury Cross roundabout. Exit along A308 to Staines. In ¼ mile turn right at lights by Shears pub into Cadbury Road. Continue for ½ mile. Club is on right just beyond lights.
Ground capacity: 200
Clubhouse: Large bar area/restaurant. Own ground. 10 changing rooms and showers. (2 pitches)
Colours: Green. (*Change colours:* Maroon).
Floodlights: No
Membership: Closed club
Local newspaper: Staines Informer
League: Middlesex 3 South
Final position (1987–88): 9th
Playing record (1987–88): P 27, W 13, L 14. F 331, A 322.
Competitions won: Oil Company 7s April 1988

HAYES (MIDDX)

Grosvenor Playing Field, Kingshill Avenue, Hayes, Middx. Tel: 01-845 4963
Founded: 1965
President: B. Kelly
Chairman: B.E. Nash
Coach: G. Humphrey
Secretary: M.R. Hall, 2 Fulwood Close, Church Road, Hayes, Middx. Tel: 01-573 7133.
Fixtures Secretary: J. Green, 23 Lambourne Court, Uxbridge. Tel: 0895 71410.
Club captain (1987–88): A. Wilkes
Club captain (1988–89): J. Lamport
No. of teams: Senior 3. Youth & Minis 2.
Directions to Ground: From London via the A40 (Western Avenue) turn off at Target. Proceed down Church Road to roundabout. Cross over heading for Hayes. Turn right at first set traffic lights (Kingshill Avenue). Ground 1 mile on right.
Clubhouse: Clubhouse, includes 2 bars, large function hall plus members bar. Size 30m × 13m. Separate building 6 changing rooms/showers.
Colours: Navy. (*Change colours:* Yellow with blue band).
Floodlights: Yes, training lights.
Membership: £15

Middlesex 3S

Local newspaper: Hayes Gazette
League: Middx 4
Final position (1987–88): 9th
Playing record (1987–88): P 26, W 12, D 2, L 16.

BRUNEL UNIVERSITY

University Playing Fields, Kingston Lane, Uxbridge, Middx. Tel: Uxbridge 360558 35955.
Founded: 1959
Secretary: Hon. Secretary, RFC, Brunel University, Kingston Lane, Uxbridge, Middlesex. Tel: Uxbridge 39125.
League: Middlesex 3S
Final position (1987–88): Withdrew.

ST MARY'S COLLEGE

St Mary's College, Twickenham, Middx. Tel: 01-892 3308 & 01/977 2009.
Founded: 1913
Secretary: Hon. Secretary, St Mary's College, Strawberry Hill, Twickenham, Middlesex. Tel: 01-892 0992.
League: Middlesex 3s
Final position (1987–88): Withdrew

Feltham 1988–89. Middlesex challengers. Photo: Chris Roberts.

KENT LEAGUES

KENT did not suffer from any withdrawals, probably because their only student team (Thames Polytechnic) took a responsible attitude to the competition. Their four leagues consisted of two with 11 clubs each and two more of nine each. The competition was mostly tight and exciting.

Charlton Park and Erith fought out the top group with the former drawing only one match and giving their rivals their only defeat for a single point success. Old Shootershillians lost all their games to finish last, but Sevenoaks had a superior points difference over National Westminster Bank, who thus took 10th place even though they won three matches.

Kent 2 was won by Betteshanger who lost a solitary game and finished two points clear of Snowdown and Folkestone; the former were second on points difference. Metropolitan Police (Hayes) and Orpington failed to win any of the nine games they played and did not meet each other, preferring to share last place.

New Ash Green won all eight games in Kent 3 to finish four points ahead of Linton and Vigo with the former taking second place – on points! Bexley (all games lost) and Cranbrook (two wins) were the bottom two clubs.

Old Williamsonians won Kent 4 by a single point from Old Olavians, who lost the match between the two leaders. Williamsonians dropped just one point to third placed STC Footscray, who maintained a strong challenge throughout. Lordswood were another brave basement side with all eight games lost and 302 points conceded, but they did complete their fixtures and all honour to them for that.

TABLES 1987–88

KENT 1

	P	W	D	L	F	A	Pts
Charlton Park	10	9	1	0	266	57	19
Erith	10	9	0	1	234	78	18
Medway	10	6	1	3	151	94	13
Park House	10	6	0	4	151	126	12
Thanet Wanderers	10	6	0	4	151	126	12
Bromley	10	4	0	6	132	128	8
Tonbridge	10	3	2	5	84	131	8
O Elthamians	10	3	1	6	88	112	7
Sevenoaks	10	3	0	7	83	301	6
Nat West Bank	10	3	0	7	83	301	6
O Shootershill's	10	0	0	10	57	179	0

KENT 2

	P	W	D	L	F	A	Pts
Betteshanger	10	9	0	1	211	81	18
Snowdowns	10	8	0	2	191	75	16
Folkestone	10	8	0	2	182	104	16
Dover	10	7	0	3	197	133	14
Ashford	10	6	0	4	208	114	12
Greenwich	10	5	0	5	114	109	10
Midland Bank	10	5	0	5	136	153	10
Lloyds Bank	10	4	0	6	138	154	8
Thames Poly	10	2	0	8	104	223	4
Met Police Hayes	9	0	0	9	78	202	0
Orpington	9	0	0	9	43	254	0

KENT 3

	P	W	D	L	F	A	Pts
New Ash Green	8	8	0	0	156	34	16
Linton	8	6	0	2	154	83	12
Vigo	8	6	0	2	103	30	12
Sittingbourne	8	4	1	3	65	58	9
Deal Wanderers	8	3	2	3	68	72	8
O Gravesend's	8	3	0	5	70	86	6
Sheppey	8	2	1	5	58	79	5
Cranbrook	8	1	2	5	52	90	4
Bexley	8	0	0	8	22	236	0

KENT 4

	P	W	D	L	F	A	Pts
O Williamsonians	8	7	1	0	153	28	15
O Olavians	8	7	0	1	145	18	14
STC Footscray	8	6	1	1	70	26	13
Edenbridge	8	4	0	4	69	58	8
Darenth Valley	8	3	0	5	103	51	6
Univ of Kent	8	3	0	5	100	74	6
Whitstable	8	3	0	5	122	113	6
East Peckham	8	2	0	6	55	169	4
Lordswood	8	0	0	8	22	302	0

● *The tables are published from information supplied. Any queries should be directed to the appropriate league secretary*

CHARLTON PARK

Appenhall Sports Ground, Footscray Road, Eltham, SE9. Tel: 01-850 0408.
Founded: 1893
President: Peter Budd
Chairman: Andy Potts
Coach: David Collen
Secretary: Dennis Attwood, 6 Somerset Gardens, St Johns, Lewisham, London SE13 7SY.
Fixtures Secretary: Roger Foxon, 245 McLeod Road, Abbeywood, SE2 0XJ. Tel: 01-311 9580 (Day).
Club captain (1987–88): A. Penfold
Club captain (1988–89): A. Penfold
No. of teams: Senior 5. Youth & Minis 1.
Directions to Ground: Entrance at junction of Footscray Road, Southend Crescent, Eltham, London SE9.
Clubhouse: At ground, large new.
Colours: Red, white. (*Change colours:* Navy.
Floodlights: No
Membership: £30
Programme: (Editor: John Hughes)
Local newspaper: SE London Mercury, Kentish Times
League: London SE3
Final position (1987–88): Won Kent Div I
Playing record (1987–88): P 31, W 22, D 2, L 7. F 736, A 252
Competitions won: Gained promotion from Kent Division I to London SE3. Two players, M. Haynes and N. Whitter, gained County Rep Honours.

ERITH

Northumberland Playing Fields, Sussex Road, Erith. Tel: erith 32295.
Founded: 1927
President: P.T. Green
Chairman: N. Button
Coach: S. Northage
Secretary: J.N. McConville, 18 Buxton Road, Erith. Tel: (0322) 337064.
Fixtures Secretary: B. Fielder, 50 Holmesdale Hill, South Darenth, Kent. Tel: Farningham 864574
Club captain (1987–88): S. Northage
Club captain (1988–89): S. Button
No. of teams: Senior 4. Youth & Minis 5.
Directions to Ground: Turn off Bexley Road, Erith into Brook Street. Left at Duchess of Kent.
Clubhouse: Bar and facilities for approx. 150
Colours: D. blue and L. blue hoops. (*Change colours:* Maroon).
Floodlights: Yes, training only
Membership: Playing £18
Local newspaper: Kentish Times
League: Kent 1
Final position (1987–88): 2nd
Playing record (1987–88): P 32, W 20, D 2, L 10. F 466, A 269

MEDWAY

Priestfields, Rochester, Kent. Tel: 0634 47737.
Founded: 1931
Secretary: R. Doyle, 57 Wheatcorft Grove, Rainham, Kent ME9 4JE. Tel: 0634 387934 (H), 01-870 3568 (W).
League: Kent 1
Final position (1987–88): 3rd

PARK HOUSE F.C.

Barnet Wood Road, Hayes, Kent. Tel: 01-462 3157
Founded: 1883
President: John W. Peasley
Coach: Pat McCarthy
Secretary: John Gross, 85 Murrey Avenue, Bromley, Kent. Tel: 01-464 6456.
Fixtures Secretary: James McGarey, 5 Pondfield Road, Hayes, Kent. Tel: 01-462 1130
Club captain (1987–88): S.D. Jefferies
Club captain (1988–89): A. Wakefield
No. of teams: Senior 6. Youth & Minis 4.
Directions to Ground: Turn off A26 signposted Biggin Hill. Turn right into Barnet Wood Road, Ground on left.
Ground capacity: 4 pitches
Clubhouse: Brick built, bar and 6 changing rooms.
Colours: Red and black. (*Change colours:* Black.)
Floodlights: No.
Membership: £35
Local newspaper: Kentish Times
League: Kent 1
Final position (1987–88): 3rd
Playing record (1987–88): P 34, W 13, d 1, L 11. F 548, A 322.
Competitions won: Kent County 7's PWITE

THANET WANDERERS

St Peters Recreation Ground, Callis Court Road, Broadstairs, Kent. Tel: Thanet (0843) 61499.
Founded: 1886
President: r.T. Mercer
Chairman: P.J. Hawkins
Coach: A. Williamson
Secretary: J.A. Challinor, 124 Dumpton Park Drive, Ramsgate, Kent. Tel: Thanet (0843) 595712.
Fixtures Secretary: P.J. Hawkins, 51 Park Road, Ramsgate, Kent. Tel: Thanet (0843) 593142.
Club captain (1987–88): J. Sowden
Club captain (1988–89): T. Carlier
No. of teams: Senior 6. Youth & Minis 4.
Directions to Ground: Follow sign post for Broadstairs. Club house is sign posted off St Peters Park Road.
Clubhouse: On ground, one bar, small lounge area.
Colours: Blue, black and yellow. (*Change colours:* Royal blue).
Nickname: Wanderers
Floodlights: Yes, training only.
Membership: playing member £20, VP £10.
Local newspaper: Isle of Thanet Gazette
League: Kent 1
Final position (1987–88): 5th
Playing record (1987–88): P 29, W 21, D 4, L 4.

BROMLEY

Barnet Wood Road, Hayes, Bromley, Kent. Tel: 01-462 3430
Founded: 1886
President: D.J. Davies
Chairman: J.T.A. Bromage
Coach: E.C. Millar
Secretary: R.R. Thomas, 118 Ravensbourne Avenue, Shortlands, Bromley BR2 0AX. Tel: 01-460 2816 (H), 01-460 4661 (W).
Fixtures Secretary: J.T.A. Bromage, 4 Sunningdale Road, Bickley, Bromley. Tel: 01-467 4375 (H), 01-403 1171 (W).
No. of teams: Senior 6, Youth & Minis 6.
Directions to Ground: see London A–Z
Clubhouse: Small and perfectly formed.
Colours: Black and amber. (*Change colours:* Black or gold).
Floodlights: No.
Membership: £40
Local newspaper: Kentish Times
League: Kent 1
Final position (1987–88): 5th or 6th
Playing record (1987–88): P 31, W 13, L 17, D 1. F 373, A 395.

TONBRIDGE

The Clubhouse, Avebury Avenue, Tonbridge, Kent. Tel: 0732 350067.
Founded: 1904
Secretary: M. Grasby, 29 Fairview Close, Hilltop, Tonbridge, Kent.
Fixtures Secretary: D. Carver, 50 Pennington Place, Southborough, Tunbridge Wells, Kent. Tel: 0892 43736.
Colts secretary: M. Pankhurst, 4 Turner Road, Tonbridge, Kent TN10 4AH. Tel: 0732 358430.
League: Kent 1
Final position (1987–88): 7th
Playing record (1987–88): P 29, W 10, D 2, L 17. F 344, A 363.

OLD ELTHAMIANS

"Foxbury", Perry Street, Chislehurst, Kent. Tel: 01-467 1296.
Founded: 1911
Secretary: M. Tinner, 19 Badgers Copse, Orpington, Kent. Tel: 0689 75917.
League: Kent 1
Final position (1987–88): 8th

SEVENOAKS

Knole Paddock, Plymouth Drive, Sevenoaks, Kent. Tel: 0732 452027.
Founded: 1925
Secretary: A. Townsend, 50A Foxgrove Road, Beckenham, Kent. Tel: 01-658 7703.
Fixtures Secretary: H. Pearl, 10 Barnfield Road, Riverhead, Sevenoaks, Kent. Tel: 0732 451641.
League: Kent 1
Final position (1987–88): 9th
Playing record (1987–88): P 31, W 10, D 1, L 20. F 264, A 580.

NATIONAL WESTMINSTER BANK

Copers Cope Road, Beckenham, Kent. Tel: 01-650 4559.
Founded: 1886
Secretary: I.J. Wilkinson, c/o NWB Plc, Bloomsbury Way, London WC1A 2TS. Tel: 01-405 7386 (W).
Fixtures Secretary: D. Otway, 161 Brompton Road, London SW3 1QU. Tel: 01-589 6641.
League: Kent 1
Final position (1987–88): 10th
Playing record (1987–88): P 28, W 6, L 22. F 255, A 746.

OLD SHOOTERSHILLIANS

72 Footscray Road, Eltham, Kent. Tel: 01-850 9500.
Founded: 1929
Secretary: G. Luckraft, 98 Chapel Market, London N1. Tel: 01-278 6256 (H). 01-242 5363 (W).
League: Kent 1
Final position (1987–88): 11th (relegated)

KENT 2

BETTESHANGER C.W.

Welfare Ground, St Richards Road, Mill Hill, Deal, Kent.
Founded: 1948
Secretary: J.K. Ashley, 14 Peak Drive, Eastry, Kent. Tel: 0304 611561 (H), 0304 613311 (W).
League: Kent 2
Final position (1987–88): 1st (promoted)

SNOWDOWN COLLIERY

Welfare Ground, Aylesham. Tel: 0304 840278.
Founded: 1931
President: L. Kingston
Chairman: C. Owen
Coach: Lester Powell
Secretary: E.J. Sullivan, 4 Burgess Road, Aylesham, Canterbury, Kent. Tel: 0304 840052.
Fixtures Secretary: Les Powell. Tel: 0304 840103.
Club captain (1987–88): R. Hadfield
Club captain (1988–89): R. Hadfield
No. of teams: Senior 4. Youth & Minis 1.
Directions to Ground: Take left turning off A2 approx ½ way between Canterbury and Dover, 1 mile further on.
Clubhouse: Small Clubhouse
Colours: Red and blue hoops. (*Change colours:* Black).
Floodlights: No
Membership: Players £10, non-players £4.
Local newspaper: Dover Express
League: Kent 2
Final position (1987–88): 2nd
Playing record (1987–88): P 31, W 26, L 4, D 1.
Competitions won: Master Brew Trophy (Canterbury RFC Flloodlight Cup).

FOLKESTONE

New Burlington Field, Bargrove, Newington, Folkestone, Kent CT18 8BM. Tel: 0303 66887
Founded: 1974
President: Alan Frew
Chairman: John Kidson
Coach: Jim Nixon
Secretary: Paul Barber, 1 Ethelburga Drive, Lyminge, Kent CT18 8JJ. Tel: 0303 863036.
Fixtures Secretary: Dave Gilbert, 113 Surrenden Road, Folkestone CT19 4AC. Tel: 0303 76640.
Club captain (1987–88): Anton Phillips
Club captain (1988–89): Anton Phillips
No. of teams: Senior 4. Youth & Minis 8.
Directions to Ground: Take exit 12 on M20 and follow signs to Newington. After 1·2 miles take 1st turning at roundabout to Hythe. Ground ½ mile on right.
Ground capacity: 2000
Clubhouse: Opened June 1988 after Eurotunnel took over possession of previous clubhouse.
Colours: Green. (*Change colours:* Green and white hoops.
Floodlights: Fundraising for them at present.
Membership: £21 players, £15 non-player, £5 social
Programme: Only on cup days. 20p. (Editor: D. Gilbert)
Local newspaper: Folkestone Herald
League: Kent 2
Final position (1987–88): 3rd
Playing record (1987–88): P 33, W 20, D 1, L 12. F 469, A 325.
Competitions won: Kent Sevens Competition April 1988. Runners up Canterbury Sevens – April 1988. Runners Up Kent Colts Sevens – April 1988. Winners East Kent Colts League – 1988.

DOVER

The Pavilion, The Big Field, Brockham, Betchworth, Surrey. Tel: 973794 3928.
Founded: 1925
Secretary: R. Brigham, 12 Clyde Road, Sutton, Surrey SM1 2RR. Tel: 01-661 0338. 01-661 0321 (W).
Fixtures Secretary: I. Beardmore, 7 Riverside, Dorking, Surrey RH4 1PR. Tel: 0306 884049 (H). 0306 885055 (W).
League: Kent 2
Final position (1987–88): 4th
Playing record (1987–88): P 26, W 13, L 13.

ASHFORD

Kinneys Field, Canterbury Road, Ashford, Kent. Tel: 0233 24693.
Founded: 1885
Secretary: M.R. Briscall, "Applegarth", Singleton Road, Great Chart, Ashford, Kent TN23 3BB. Tel: 0233 26052 (H), 0732 845845 (W).
Fixtures Secretary: D.D. Skewson, 21 Tadworth Road, Kennington, Ashford, Kent TN24 9JT. Tel: 0233 26052 (H), 0233 812761 (W).
League: Kent 2
Final position (1987–88): 5th
Playing record (1987–88): P 35, W 15, L 20. F 464, A 426.

GREENWICH (formerly Bloomfield & Lewisham)

Old Mill Road, Plumpstead Common, Plumpstead, London SE18. Tel: 01-854 8637.
Founded: 1986
Secretary: D.J. Bennett, 318 Plumpstead High Street, Plumpstead, London SE18. Tel: 01-854 0898 (H), 0322 332612. Extn. 22 (W)
League: Kent 2
Final position (1987–88): 6th
Playing record (1987–88): P 29, W 18, D 1, L 10. F 421, A 252.

MIDLAND BANK

Lennard Road, New Beckenham, Kent. Tel: 01-778 6885
Founded: 1911
President: J.A. Brooks
Secretary: C.J. Rouse, 59 Crantock Road, SE6. Tel: 01-698 4527.
Fixtures Secretary: J.R.D. Hayhow, Five Trees, 36 Holbrook Lane, Chislehurst BR7 6PF. Tel: 01-467 3314.
Club captain (1987–88): P.R. Ayling
Club captain (1988–89): P.R. Ayling
No. of teams: Senior 4.
Directions to Ground: Adjoining New Beckenham Railway Station.
Colours: Green shirts, navy blue shorts. (*Change colours:* Red shirts).
Nickname: City
Floodlights: No
League: Kent 2
Final position (1987–88): 7th
Playing record (1987–88): P 29, W 16, L 12, D 1. F 449, A 337.

LLOYDS BANK

Lloyds Bank Sports Club, Copers Cope Road, Beckenham, Kent. Tel: 01-658 3818.
Founded: 1913
Secretary: D.E. Perry, 83 Glanfield Road, Beckenham, Kent BR3 3JT. Tel: 01-652 7214.
Fixtures Secretary: T.D. Gaston, 8 Linden Close, Chelsfield, Kent BR6 6JJ. Tel: Farnborough 57552 (H). 01-283 1000. Extn. 3361 (W).
League: Kent 2
Final position (1987–88): 8th
Playing record (1987–88): P 32, W 12, D 1, L 19. F 404, A 470.

THAMES POLYTECHNIC

Kidbrooke Lane, Eltham, London SE9 6TA.
Founded: 1937
President: P. Arscott
Chairman: M. Doveston
Coach: K. Shaw
Secretary: J. Baker, 26 Capel Place, Wilmington, Kent DA2 7PU. Tel: 0322 28162
Fixtures Secretary: G. Miller, 85 Earlshall Road, Eltham, London SE9. Tel: 01-850 2794.
Club captain (1987–88): A. Galloway
Club captain (1988–89): C. Wilson
No. of teams: Senior 4
Directions to Ground: Kidbrooke Lane, Eltham, London SE9 (adjacent to S. Circular Road, Westhorne Avenue)
Colours: Red, green, gold.
Floodlights: No
Membership: £30
Local newspaper: Kentish Times
League: Kent 2
Final position (1987–88): 9th (relegated)
Playing record (1987–88): P 28, W 8, D 0, L 20.

METROPOLITAN POLICE (HAYES)

The Warren, Croydon Road, Hayes Common, Kent. Tel: 01-462 1266.
Founded: 1948
Chairman: M. McCawly
Secretary: J.A. Early, 30 The Crescent, West Wickham, Kent. Tel: 01-777 6828
Fixtures Secretary: N. Yeo, 32 Abbotsbury Road, Hayes, Kent. Tel: 01-462 5782.
Club captain (1987–88): B. O'Rourke
Club captain (1988–89): B. O'Rourke
No. of teams: Senior 3.
Directions to Ground: A21 Bromley to Farnborough. Turn right into Croydon Road. Ground 1 mile on right.
Clubhouse: Police Sports Club
Colours: Sky Blue. (*Change colours:* Maroon).
Floodlights: No
Membership: Any Police Officer
Local newspaper: Kentish Times
League: Kent 2
Final position (1987–88): Bottom (relegated)

COURAGE CLUBS CHAMPIONSHIP

ORPINGTON

Hoblingwell Wood Recreation Ground, St Pauls Cray, Kent. Tel: 0689 23913.
Founded: 1969
President: John Hawkins
Chairman: Roland Payn
Secretary: Ross Campbell, 42 Barncroft Drive, Hempstead, Kent ME7 6TJ.
Fixtures Secretary: Warwick Marriner, 23 Partridge Drive, Orpington, Kent.
Club captain (1987–88): Tom Foster
Club captain (1988–89): Gary O'Day
No. of teams: Senior 3.
Directions to Ground: A224 turn off at Leesons Hill. Turn right into Chipperfield Road, left into Petersham Drive, right into Leesons Way.
Ground capacity: Unlimited. Stand, 30.
Clubhouse: Est. 1921 – closed 1939. Re-established 1969
Colours: Black and amber hoops. (*Change colours:* Black).
Nickname: "Ton" or "Buffs"
Floodlights: Yes, training lights.
Membership: £20
Local newspaper: Orpington Kentish Times
League: Kent 2
Final position (1987–88): Bottom
Playing record (1987–88): P 9, L 9

KENT 3

NEW ASH GREEN

Punch Croft, New Ash Green, Dartford, Kent. Tel: 0474 874660.
Founded: 1974
Secretary: L. Ellard, 9 Lambardes, New Ash Green, Near Dartford, Kent DA3 H8X. Tel: 0474 873924 (H).
League: Kent 3
Final position (1987–88): 1st (Promoted)
Playing record (1987–88): P 30, W 19, D 1, L 10. F 409, A 279.

LINTON RFC

Founded: 1977
President: Jack Williams
Chairman: Dave Enston
Coach: Norman Bateman
Secretary: Bob Wilson, 7 Westwood Road, Loose, Maidstone, Kent ME15 6BB. Tel: 0622 44468.
Fixtures Secretary: Dave Enston, 47 Hornbeam Close, Larkfield, Maidstone ME20 6LZ. Tel: 0732 842666.
Club captain (1987–88): Ken Harrison
Club captain (1988–89): Nigel Baker
No. of teams: Senior 4.
Directions to Ground: Mote Road, Maidstone and into Mote Park. Follow directions for 'the Pavilion' which overlooks the lake.
Clubhouse: After match hospitality at the "British Queen" public house.
Colours: Red shirt, black shorts, red socks. (*Change colours:* Blue shirts).
Nickname: The "Bulls" after name of the public house we first used.
Floodlights: No
Membership: £20 (1987/88)
Programme: Weekly newsletter. (Editor: Martin Cox)
Local newspaper: Kent Messenger
League: Kent 3
Final position (1987–88): 2nd (promoted)
Playing record (1987–88): P 29, W 17, L 11, D 1. F 414, A 370.
Competitions won: New Ash Green 7's, winnters 1981, 2 and 83: Kent 7's Plate Winners 1981: West Kent 7s Winners 1982: Sheppey 7's Winners 1981: Canterbury 7's Plate 1987.

VIGO

Swanswood Field, Harvel Road, Harvel, Kent. Tel: 0732 823830.
Founded: 1969
Secretary: J. Jarman, 21 Grove Park Avenue, Sittingbourne, Kent. Tel: 0795 77249 (H), 0795 77291 (W).
Fixtures Secretary: J. Taylor, Sandon, Burnt House Lane, Hawley, Dartford, Kent. Tel: Dartford 27363 (H). 01-320 1920 (W).
League: Kent 3
Final position (1987–88): 3rd
Playing record (1987–88): P 30, W 18, D 2, L 10. F 406, A 264.

SITTINGBOURNE

c/o Bowaters Sports Pavilion, Gore Court Road, Sittingbourne. Tel: 0795-77047.
Founded: 1977
President: F. Garwood
Chairman: S. Tatton
Coach: A. Ogden
Secretary: G.O. Langlands, 102 Staplehurst Road, Sittingbourne. Tel: 0795-28486.
Fixtures Secretary: J. Regan, 13 Heather Close, Sittingbourne. Tel: 0795-74356.
Club captain (1987–88): G.J. West
Club captain (1988–89): G. Collins
No. of teams: Senior 4, Youth & Minis 6
Directions to Ground: From London, into town on A2, follow small one way system "Town Centre" on rejoining main A2, 1st right, Park Road, follow round, Club on left.
Colours: Blue and amber. (*Change colours:* Blue and amber reversed)
Floodlights: No
Membership: £14
Local newspaper: East Kent Gazette
League: Kent 3
Playing record (1987–88): P 29, W 18, L 10, D 1, F 326, A 265.
Competitions won: Orpington 15 competition. Guernsey 15 competition.

DEAL WANDERERS

North Deal Playing Field, Western Road, Deal, Kent.
Founded: 1958
Secretary: A. Bewley, 22 William Pitt Avenue, Deal, Kent. Tel: 0304 367909 (H).
League: Kent 3
Final position (1987–88): 5th

OLD GRAVESENDIANS

Fleetway Sports Ground, Parrock Street, Gravesend, Kent. Tel: 0474 65503.
Founded: 1925
Secretary: J. Oxtoby, 43 The Old Yews, Longfield, Gravesend, Kent.
League: Kent 3
Final position (1987–88): 6th

SHEPPEY

Lower Road, Minster, Sheerness, Kent. Tel: 0795 872082
Founded: 1892
President: Ken Cooper
Chairman: Richard Barson
Coach: John Clayton
Secretary: Linda Neal, 16 New Road, Minster, Sheerness, Kent ME12 3PX. Tel: 0795 873983.
Fixtures Secretary: Gerry Lawson, Merba, Minster Drive, Minster, Sheerness, Kent. Tel: 0795 876363.
Club captain (1987–88): Mike Wells
Club captain (1988–89): Mike Wells
No. of teams: Senior 4. Youth & Minis 2.
Directions to Ground: A249 to Sheerness. Once on the Island take 2nd exit at roundabout. ½ mile on left side.
Clubhouse: Single storey.
Colours: White with single red hoop. (*Change colours:* Black).
Floodlights: No
Membership: £15
Local newspaper: Sheerness Times Guardian
League: Kent 3
Final position (1987–88): 7th

CRANBROOK

Tomlin Ground, Angley Road, Cranbrook, Kent. Tel: 0580 712777
Founded: .
President: M.I. McMinnies
Chairman: D.C. McMinnies
Secretary: D.L.J. Davies, Beeches Station Road, Staplehurst, Kent TN12 0QG. Tel: 0580 891448.
Fixtures Secretary: M. Fitzsimons, 32 Jaggard Way, Staplehurst. Tel: 0580 891178.
Club captain (1987–88): T. Claridge
Club captain (1988–89): A. Alison
No. of teams: Senior 4. Youth & Minis 4.
Directions to Ground: North side of Cranbrook bypass on A229.
Clubhouse: Licensed.
Colours: Magenta/white. (*Change colours:* White).
Nickname: Cranes
Floodlights: No
Membership: £0.50
Local newspaper: Kent & Sussex Courier
League: Kent 3
Final position (1987–88): 7th
Playing record (1987–88): P 30, W 3, D 2, L 25

BEXLEY

Thanet Road, Bexley, Kent. Tel: 0322 56198
Founded: 1957
President: The Rt. Hon. edward Heath, MBE, MP
Chairman: A. Hammond
Coach: J. Brunton
Secretary: K. Rutter, 19 Lakeside Close, Sidcup, Kent DA15 9PW. Tel: 01-304 5453.
Fixtures Secretary: A. Suter, 1 Oak Road, Stone, Dartford. Tel: 0322 78707.
Club captain (1987–88): N. Bodycomb
Club captain (1988–89): J. Butler
No. of teams: Senior 4.
Directions to Ground: Take Black Prince interchange on A2, 2nd exit on roundabout. Ground on right.
Colours: Royal blue and white hoop shirts, blue shorts, blue stockings with white tops.
Nickname: Hermits
Floodlights: No
Membership: £16
Local newspaper: Kentish Times
League: Kent 3
Final position (1987–88): 9th (relegated)
Playing record (1987–88): P 26, W 3, D 1, L 22. F 134, A 542.

KENT 4

OLD WILLIAMSONIANS

Maidstone Road, Rochester, Kent.
Founded: 1930
Secretary: R. Hoskin, Halden Court, Ashford Road, High Halden, Kent TN26 3BP. Tel: 023385 504 (H). 01-623 2323 (W).
League: Kent 4
Final position (1987–88): 1st (promoted)
Playing record (1987–88): P 29, W 15, D 2, L 12.
Competitions won: Promotion from Kent 4

OLD OLAVIANS

Goddington Lane, Orpington. Tel: 0689 30744.
Founded: 1952
President: F.D. Coulson
Chairman: G.S. Snelgrove
Secretary: C.N. Hudson, 50 Badgers Copse, Tower Road, Orpington. Tel: 0689 75065.
Fixtures Secretary: J. Michalis, 16 Ashley Gardens, Orpington. Tel: 0689 56664.
Club captain (1987–88): P. Hinton
Club captain (1988–89): P. Hinton
No. of teams: Senior 4.
Directions to Ground: From War Memorial roundabout at end of Orpington High Street along Sevenoaks Road and third turning on left. Ground is at St Olaves School up this road.
Colours: Purple, black and white.
Floodlights: No
Membership: £8.50
Local newspaper: Orpington Times
League: Kent 4
Final position (1987–88): Kent 4 2nd place

STC FOOTSCRAY (formerly Standard Kolster)

Maidstone Road, Sidcup, Kent. Tel: 01-300 3333.
Founded: 1967
Secretary: A.C. Delord, 19 Lamorbey Close, Sidcup, Kent DA15 8BA. Tel: 01-300 0369 (H), 01-632 5459 (W).
League: Kent 4
Final position (1987–88): 3rd

EDENBRIDGE

Lingfield Road Recreation Ground, Edenbridge, Kent.
Founded: 1977
Chairman: Ross Davies
Secretary: Terry Daking, 21 Brookfield, Four Elms, Kent.
Fixtures Secretary: Ron Mitchell, Amberly Crouch House Road, Edenbridge, Kent.
Club captain (1987–88): James Walker
Club captain (1988–89): James Walker
No. of teams: Senior 3. Youth & Minis 1.
Directions to Ground: Once in the High Street turndown Stangrove Road, left into Crouch House Road, right at Pound Green Pitch on the left.

Clubhouse: Very good – newly built
Colours: Yellow/black hoops. (*Change colours:* Red).
Nickname: The Bridge
Floodlights: No
Membership: £25
Local newspaper: Edenbridge Courier
League: Kent 4
Final position (1987–88): 4th
Competitions won: Plate Competition Dover 7s

DARENTH VALLEY

Five Bells, Eynsford, Kent DA4 0AB
Founded: 1977
President: David Kerr
Chairman: Ian Macknelly
Secretary: George Macknelly, 68 Saint Martins Drive, Eynsford, Kent DA4 0EZ.
Fixtures Secretary: David Wilson, 26 Ashen Drive, Dartford, Kent DA1 3UI. Tel: 0322 70781.
Club captain (1987–88): Steve Wood
Club captain (1988–89): Steve Wood
No. of teams: Senior 2
Directions to Ground: Seeking permanent home ground. Home features 88/9 at Hextable School. Go to centre of Hextable and then down College Road to Egerton Avenue.
Colours: Black – white V in front. (2nd XV black and white hoops).
Nickname: Valley
Floodlights: No
Membership: Players £20 for season + £3 a game.
Local newspaper: Kent Newspapers – Swanley & Dartford
League: Kent 4
Final position (1987–88): 5th
Playing record (1987–88): P 28, W 13, D 4, L 11. F 377, A 244.

KENT UNIVERSITY

Sports Federation, Sports Centre, UKC, Canterbury CT2 7NL. Tel: 0227 68027
Founded: 1967
Chairman: Alistair McCurheon
Secretary: Graham Letley, Vacation telephone no 01-650 8957.
Fixtures Secretary: as above.
Club captain (1987–88): Mike McCarthy
Club captain (1988–89): Robbie Collins
No. of teams: Senior 3
Directions to Ground: Follow directions to Canterbury off the A2. Don't go into Canterbury but turn left by Bernie/Beefeater restaurant on first roundabout, follow directions to university.
Clubhouse: Tel: 0227 453060.
Colours: Red and blue hoops. (*Change colours:* Black strip).
Floodlights: No
Membership: £5
Local newspaper: Kentish Gazette
League: Kent 4
Final position (1987–88): 6th

WHITSTABLE

c/o Hon. Sec.
Founded: 1981
President: T.R. Crowther
Chairman: P.A. Todd
Coach: D. Dickey
Secretary: Miss D. Perkins, 85a Tankerton Road, Tankerton, Whitstable, Kent CT5 2AJ. Tel: 0227 276843.
Fixtures Secretary: A.J. Cunningham, "Punch", Harbour Street, Whitstable, Kent CT5 1AG. Tel: 0227 264755
Club captain (1987–88): D. Thompson
Club captain (1988–89): P. Sparrow
No. of teams: Senior 3. Youth & Minis/Juniors 5.
Directions to Ground: Ground Church Street Playing Fields. From M2 onto Thanet Way (A299) take 1st left after 2nd roundabout, playing fields on left. From Thanet take 2nd right after Chestfield roundabout, playingfields on left.
Clubhouse: None, we use Cricket Club in Belmont Road or Whitstable Sports Centre for changing.
Colours: Blue-white hoops.
Floodlights: No
Membership: £15 players, £10 VPs
Local newspaper: Whitstable Times
League: Kent 4
Final position (1987–88): 7th

EAST PECKHAM

pippins Road, East Peckham, Tonbridge, Kent.
Founded: 1977
President: C.J. Chown
Chairman: K.N.C. Masters
Coach: A.N. Bodle
Secretary: M.J. Bull, 10 Leney Road, Wateringbury, Kent. Tel: 0622 812386 (H)
Fixtures Secretary: P.S. Tucker, 31 Medway Meadows, East Peckham, Kent. Tel: 0622 871994.
Club captain (1987–88): P.S. Tucker
Club captain (1988–89): P.K. Rucklidge
No. of teams: Senior 2.
Directions to Ground: From A20, take B2016 signposted Paddock Wood. Turn right onto B2015, turn right into Old Road by Rose & Crown, take fourth right into Bramley Road, and first left is Pippin Road.
Colours: Red, white and blue quarters. Blue shorts, white socks. (*Change colours:* Red shirts).
Nickname: The Villagers
Floodlights: Yes
Membership: £30 full
Programme: 50p. (Editor: A.N. Bodle)
Local newspaper: Kent Messenger, Kent & Sussex Courier
League: Kent 4
Final position (1987–88): 8th
Playing record (1987–88): P 29, W 9, L 20. F 250, A 450.

LORDSWOOD

Club Secretary: M. Brand, 26 Gould Road, Lordswood, Chatham, Kent.
League: Kent 4
Final position (1987–88): 9th

HERTFORDSHIRE LEAGUES

HERTFORDSHIRE started the campaign with two leagues – each of eight clubs. But the disease, mostly suffered by students' teams, saw Hatfield Polytechnic withdraw during the season leaving the second group sadly depleted.

The top league had a thrilling finish with Hemel Hempstead, Old Elizabethans, Barnet and Old Verulamians all winning five matches, but the first two took the top places on points difference. Tring lost all their games and finished last with Stevenage – despite two wins – in seventh place.

Hertfordshire 2 was also a close affair with Old Ashmolians and Royston each winning five and losing one. The Old Ashmolians had a better goal difference and took top place. East Herts College lost all their matches, but unlike their fellow students they 'stayed the course', which was most praiseworthy.

TABLES 1987–88

HERTFORDSHIRE 1

	P	W	D	L	F	A	Pts
Hemel Hempstead	7	5	0	2	124	5	10
O Elizabethans	7	5	0	2	79	53	10
Barnet	7	5	0	2	85	68	10
Old Verulamians	7	5	0	2	78	63	10
Welwyn	7	3	0	4	83	69	6
Harpenden	7	3	0	4	91	83	6
Stevenage	7	2	0	5	62	82	4
Tring	7	0	0	7	39	174	0

HERTFORDSHIRE 2

	P	W	D	L	F	A	Pts
O Ashmolians	6	5	0	1	95	43	10
Royston	6	5	0	1	64	41	10
St. Albans	6	4	0	2	90	54	8
Hitchin	6	3	0	3	49	82	6
Watford	6	3	0	3	49	82	6
Datchworth	6	1	0	5	33	82	2
East Herts Coll	6	0	0	6	19	87	0

Hatfield Poly withdrawn – all matches void

HERTFORDSHIRE 1

HEMEL HEMPSTEAD (CAMELOT)

Chaulden Lane, Hemel Hempstead, Herts. Tel: 0442 3408.
Founded: 1951
President: Ray Fisher
Chairman: Joe Weed
Coach: Gwyn Williams
Secretary: John Clapham, 49 Brook Court, Watling Street, Radlett, Herts WD7 7JA. Tel: Radlett 2104.
Fixtures Secretary: Adrian Wakefield, 18 Recotry Close, Slapton, Leighton Buzzard, Beds. Tel: 0525 221375.
Club captain (1987–88): Harry Pinner
Club captain (1988–89): Tony Impey
No. of teams: Senior 6. Youth & Minis 3.
Directions to Ground: On A41 by Railway Station turn off A41 at roundabout into Fishery Road. Proceed to small roundabout turn left into Northridge Way. Chaulden Lane is 250 yards on the left.
Ground capacity: 2000
Clubhouse: Main clubroom, kitchen, Camelot bar room, toilets, bar and bar store. 8 changing rooms, referees room and 2 shower blocks.
Colours: Royal blue with white hoop. (*Change colours:* Maroon or red).
Nickname: Camelot (name of old club)
Floodlights: Yes, training only
Membership: £25 players, £12.50 non-players
Local newspaper: Hemel Hempstead Herald, also Review
League: London N/W3
Final position (1987–88): 1st in Herts Div I
Playing record (1987–88): P 32, W 22, L 10. F 480, A 250.

OLD ELIZABETHANS (BARNET)

Gipsy Corner, Mays Lane, Barnet. Tel: 01-449 9481
Founded: 1935
President: R.D. Parker
Chairman: P.G. Yates
Coach: I. Whitefield
Secretary: N.A. Ward, 82 Barnet Road, Potters Bar, Herts. Tel: 0707 58066.
Fixtures Secretary: B.J. Fuller, 109 Margaret Road, New Barnet, Herts. Tel: 01-449 0590.
Club captain (1987–88): K. Watt
Club captain (1988–89): K. Watt
No. of teams: Senior 4. Youth 1.
Directions to Ground: From A1 take A411 towards Barnet Ground on left 1 mile.
Colours: Light and dark blue hooped shirts.
Nickname: O.E's
Floodlights: Yes, training only.
Membership: £22.50
Local newspaper: Barnet Press
League: Herts 1
Final position (1987–88): 2nd
Playing record (1987–88): P 28, W 19, D 1, L 8. F 355, A 210.

BARNET

Byng Road, Barnet, Herts. Tel: 01-449 0040.
Founded: 1919
Secretary: C.J. Pool, 24 Firs Walk, Tewin Wood, Welwyn, Herts. Tel: 0438 79469 (H). 01-609 8004 (W)

Hertfordshire 1

Fixtures Secretary: P. Glenister, 47 Bury Lane, Codicore, Herts. Tel: 0438 820692.
League: Hertfordshire 1
Final position (1987–88): 3rd
Playing record (1987–88): P 31, W 20, D 2, L 9. F 398, A 311.

OLD VERULAMIAN

Cotlands Wick, N. Orbital Road, St. Albans. Tel: 0727 22929.
Founded: 1948
President: Douglas V. Hobbs
Chairman: Alan Radford
Coach: Ian Minto
Secretary: Stuart R.A. Mather, 18 Allandale, St Albans. Tel: 0727 32785.
Fixtures Secretary: H. Grey, 48 Parkfield Cres, Kimpton. Tel: 832714.
Club captain (1987–88): S. Rickard
Club captain (1988–89): K. Taylor
No. of teams: Senior 5. Youth & Minis 2.
Directions to Ground: Off North Orbital Road, St Albans.
Colours: Royal Blue, Gold V. (*Change colours:* Red).
Nickname: O.V.'s
Floodlights: No
Membership: Varies
League: Herts 1
Final position (1987–88): Lost on points diff. 2nd.
Playing record (1987–88): P 31, W 21, L 7, D 3.

WELWYN

Handside Playing Fields, Hobbs Way, Welwyn Garden City, Herts. Tel: 0707 329116
Founded: 1931
President: K. Chivers
Chairman: D.G. Harris
Secretary: T.M. Sargeant, 67 Woodhall Lane, Welwyn Garden City, Herts. Tel: 0707 331186.
Fixtures Secretary: N. Aldridge, 147 Cole Green Lane, Welwyn Garden City, Herts. Tel: 0707 321012.
Club captain (1987–88): P. Emsden
Club captain (1988–89): P. Emsden
No. of teams: Senior 5. Youth & Minis 6.
Directions to Ground: Turn off Parkway (Centre of WGC) into Turnore Dale. Left into Colgrove, right into Hobbs Way.
Colours: Maroon and white hoops. (*Change colours:* Black shirts).
Floodlights: No
Membership: £17 Players, £7.50 students, £3.50 under 18, £5.75 non-players.
Local newspaper: Welwyn & Hatfield Times
League: Herts 1
Final position (1987–88): 5th
Playing record (1987–88): P 30, W 20, D 0, L 10. F 395, A 248.

HARPENDEN

Harpenden 460711
Founded: 1921
President: Vivian Jenkins (Wales, Barbarians, Sunday Times)
Chairman: Dick White
Coach: D. James
Secretary: Mike Ball, 9 ??? Drive, Redbourn, Herts. Tel: Redbourn 2097.
Fixtures Secretary: K. Duffy/G. Dignum, Redbourn Road, Harpenden, Herts.
Club captain (1987–88): A. Crick
Club captain (1988–89): A. Crick
No. of teams: Senior 5. Youth & Minis 8.
Directions to Ground: M25 St Albans and either A1081 or A5 to Redbourn Road, Harpenden.
Ground capacity: 2000. Stand 200–300.
Clubhouse: Two tiered, main bar.
Colours: Brown and white. (*Change colours:* White and brown).
Floodlights: Yes
Membership: £5 minimum
Local newspaper: S Harpenden Herald and Harpenden Review
League: Herts 1
Final position (1987–88): 4th
Playing record (1987–88): P 35, W 17, D 1, L 17. F 497, A 492.
Competitions won: Herts 7s Winners of Plate, 1986/7, 1987/8.

STEVENAGE

North Road, Old Town, Stevenage, Herts. Tel: 0438 359788.
Founded: 1955
Secretary: M. Curtin, 212 Chertsey Rise, Stevenage, Herts ST2 9JD. Tel: 0438 359605 (H), 0438 312981 (W).
Fixtures Secretary: B. Howe, 53 Robertson Close, Turnford, Herts. Tel: 0992 445061 (H), 01-804 8100 (W).
League: Hertfordshire 1
Final position (1987–88): 7th

TRING

Pendley, Cow Lane, Tring, Herts. Tel: Tring 5710.
Founded: 1965
President: S. Wallis
Chairman: C. Armstrong
Coach: M. Walters
Secretary: K. Boniface, 36 Millview Road, Tring. Tel: Tring 5053.
Fixtures Secretary: D. Clarke, 39 Chiltern Way, Tring. Tel: Tring 3753
Club captain (1987–88): M. Fountain
Club captain (1988–89): M. Fountain
No. of teams: Senior 5. Youth & Minis 9.
Directions to Ground: Cow Lane off A41 south side of Tring.
Clubhouse: New clubhouse opened 1986.
Colours: Black and gold hoops. (*Change colours:* Black).
Floodlights: No
Membership: £25 Playing, £5 Social
Local newspaper: Tring & Berkhamsted Gazette
League: Herts 1
Final position (1987–88): Bottom

OLD ASHMOLEANS

Ashmole School, Burleigh Gardens, Southgate N14. Tel: 01-368 4984 (Sports Hall)
Founded: 1961
President: A. Seagroatt
Coach: D. Perks
Secretary: J. Byrne, 85a Burford Gardens, Palmers Green, London N13 4LR. Tel: 01-886 5995.
Fixtures Secretary: N. Harper, 77b Holdenhurst Avenue, Finchley N12 0HY. Tel: 01-346 9940.
Club captain (1987–88): F. Colborne
Club captain (1988–89): N. Harper
No. of teams: Senior 3.
Directions to Ground: At the roundabout at Southgate underground station turn into Ashfield Parade, bear right into Burleigh Gardens. School first left.
Clubhouse: Share with local tennis club.
Colours: Scarlet/Emerald Hoops. (*Change colours:* Black).
Floodlights: Yes, training only.
Membership: £25 playing member
Local newspaper: Barnet Press
League: Herts 2
Final position (1987–88): P 24, W 14, D 0, L 10. F 330, A 220.
Playing record (1987–88): Hertfordshire League II Winners
Competitions won:

ROYSTON

Royston Sporting Club, Therfield Road, Royston, Herts. Tel: 0763 43613.
Founded: 1961
Secretary: S.G. Bristow, 28 Dryden Crescent, Stevenage, Herts. Tel: 0438 316331 (W).
League: Hertfordshire 2
Final position (1987–88): 2nd
Playing record (1987–88): P 22, W 14, L 8. F 264, A 196.

ST ALBANS

Boggymead Spring, Oaklands Lane, Smallford, St. Albans, Herts. Tel: 0727 69945.
Secretary: P.N. Cuneen, 13 Heath Road, St. Albans, Herts. Tel: 0727 65173 (H), 0727 40932 (W).
League: Hertfordshire 2
Final position (1987–88): 3rd

HITCHIN

King George V Fields, Old Hale Way, Hitchen, Herts. Tel: Hitchen 32679.
Founded: 1954
President: H. Sanderson
Chairman: J. Drew
Coach: G. Collings
Secretary: C. McDonald, 9 Claymore Drive, Ickleford, Hitchin, Herts. Tel: Hitchin 55595.
Fixtures Secretary: J. Humphries, 32 West Hill, Hitchin, Herts. Tel: Hitchin 32994.
Club captain (1987–88): A. Taylor
Club captain (1988–89): P. Newman
No. of teams: Senior 5. Youth 1.
Directions to Ground: At Angels Reply PH on A600 north side of Hitchin, turninto Bearton Road. Second left into Old Hale Way. Turn into ground by phone box.
Colours: Maroon and white shorts. (*Change colours:* Blue with red band).
Nickname: Hedgehogs
Floodlights: No
Membership: £22
Local newspaper: Gazette, Comet, Herald
League: Herts 2
Final position (1987–88): 4th
Playing record (1987–88): P 33, W 19, D 1, L 13. F 482, A 291.
Competitions won: Biggleswade 3rd XV, Coarse Rugby, Over 35 Hitchen

WATFORD

Knutsford Playing Fields, Radlett Road, Watford, Herts. Tel: 0923 43292.
Founded: 1973
Secretary: R.S. Tatford, 73 Buttermere Place, Linden Lea, Leavesden, Watford, Herts WD1 7DW. Tel: 0923 661088 (H). 0582 420613 (W).
League: Hertfordshire 2
Final position (1987–88): 5th

DATCHWORTH

Datchworth Green, Datchworth, Herts. Tel: 0438 812490.
Founded: 1969
Secretary: M. Davis, 31 Green Lanes, Hatfield, Garden Village, Herts AL10 9JH. Tel: 07042 61434.
League: Hertfordshire 2
Final position (1987–88): 6th
Playing record (1987–88): P 32, W 20, D 1, L 11. F 474, A 209.

EAST HERTS COLLEGE

East Herts College, Turnford, Near Broxbourne, Herts.
Founded: 1963
Secretary: E. J. Towner, 6 Bushby Avenue, Broxbourne, Herts EN10 6QE. Tel: 0992 461753 (H), 01-803 8946. Extn. 53 (W).
League: Hertfordshire 2
Final position (1987–88): 7th

HATFIELD POLYTECHNIC

Hatfield Polytechnic, Balls Park, Hertford. Tel: 0992 558451. Extn 287.
Founded: 1957
President: D. Evans
Chairman: N. Cowieson
Secretary: S. Maywood, c/o Hatfield Polytechnic, S.U., PO Box 109, Hatfield, Herts.
Fixtures Secretary: G.A. Cherry, Hatfield Polytechnic, Balls Park, Hertford. Tel: Hertford 0992 558451, Extn 287.
Club captain (1987–88): J. Wennel
Club captain (1988–89): M. Llewellyn
No. of teams: Senior 3.
Directions to Ground: From the A1 on the south side of Hatfield, follow signs for A1001 (Welham Green). Ground and pavilion in Southway.
Clubhouse: Changing rooms and showers only.
Colours: Black/white. (*Change colours:* Black or blue).
Floodlights: No
Membership: £5 students
Local newspaper: Welwyn & Hatfield Times
League: Herts 2
Final position (1987–88): Withdrew
Playing record (1987–88): 1987. SEETech 7-A-Side, 1988 BPSA 7-A-Side, 1988 Cheshunt 7-A-Side, SEETech & BPSA Plate Cups
Competitions won:

SUSSEX LEAGUES

SUSSEX mustered three leagues of 11, nine and eight teams respectively, but the second league had its fixtures disrupted by the withdrawal of yet another student side.

This, however, did not effect the superb form of Bognor who won all 10 matches in Sussex 1 and finished six points clear of Chichester in second place. Someone must be last and Hastings & Bexhill were the unlucky ones although they won three games. Sussex Police earned one more point but still ended in 10th place.

The abbreviated Sussex 2 saw Uckfield win all seven matches and score a massive 252 points in the process. Hellingly were three points behind in second place, whilst the bottom spot was taken by Azurians, who did manage one win.

Pulborough in Sussex 3 also won all seven games to finish two points clear of Brighton Polytechnic, who along with Sussex University (Sussex 2) did complete all their fixtures. Ditchling (with just one point) were in last place with Newick a point better off.

TABLES 1987–88

SUSSEX 1

	P	W	D	L	F	A	Pts
Bognor	10	10	0	0	195	44	20
Chichester	10	7	0	3	146	103	14
Eastbourne	10	5	1	4	121	10	
Seaford	10	5	0	5	129	121	10
Burgess Hill	10	4	1	5	69	94	9
Crowborough	10	4	1	5	82	131	9
Hove	10	4	0	6	156	97	8
Haywards Heath	10	4	0	6	76	119	8
Brighton	10	4	0	6	76	119	8
Sussex Police	10	3	1	6	83	199	7
Hastings & Bexhill	10	3	0	7	107	164	6

SUSSEX 2

	P	W	D	L	F	A	Pts
Uckfield	7	7	0	0	252	25	14
Hellingly	7	5	1	1	127	48	11
St Francis	7	4	0	3	47	45	8
Heathfield	7	3	0	4	96	89	6
Plumpton	7	3	0	4	102	178	6
Brit Caledonian	7	2	0	5	58	91	4
Sussex Univ	7	2	1	4	103	83	3
Azurians	7	1	0	6	8	228	2

(W.I.S.H.E. void)

SUSSEX 3

	P	W	D	L	F	A	Pts
Pulborough	7	7	0	0	189	22	14
Brighton Poly	7	6	0	1	141	55	12
Midhurst**	6	4	0	2	103	28	8
Robin Hood**	6	3	1	2	81	50	7
Arun**	6	2	0	4	42	107	4
Sunallon	7	2	0	5	35	132	4
Newick**	6	1	0	5	33	152	2
Ditchling	7	0	1	6	40	118	1

***Matches not played – Rule 10(c) applies.*

●*The tables are published from information supplied. Any queries should be directed to the appropriate league secretary*

SUSSEX 1

BOGNOR

Nyewood Lane, Bognor Regis
Founded: 1964
President: P.G. Mead
Chairman: C.P. Geo Ghegan
Coach: TBA
Secretary: J.M. Eley, 23 Ilex Way, Middleton-on-Sea, West Sussex PO22 6PQ.
Fixtures Secretary: d. Dency, 39 Careton Avenue, Rose Green, Bognor Regis. Tel: 0243 266185.
Club captain (1987–88): T. Upton
Club captain (1988–89): R. Hine
No. of teams: Senior 4. Youth & Minis 5.
Directions to Ground: Turn off A259 chichester Road into Hawthorn Road, through lights, ground 400 m on left.
Clubhouse: Large, upstairs bar, 3 squash courts built in.
Colours: Purple, white, green hoops. (*Change colours:* Green).
Floodlights: Yes, training standard.
Membership: £25 senior
Programme: One standard programme for leage home matches, free.
Local newspaper: Bognor Oberver, Bognor Post.
League: Sussex 1
Final position (1987–88): Winners
Playing record (1987–88): P 29, W 19, l 10. F 476, A 270.
Competitions won: Sussex Div 1 Champions

CHICHESTER

Oaklands Park, Wellington Road, Chichester, West Sussex. Tel: Chichester 779820.
Founded: 1927
Secretary: S. Hill, Tidewell Cottage, Selsey, Near Chichester, West Sussex. Tel: 0234 602 598 (H), 0243 781000 (W).

League: Sussex 1
Final position (1987–88): 2nd
Playing record (1987–88): P 32, W 20, L 12. F 514, A 419.

EASTBOURNE

Park Avenue, Hampden Park, Eastbourne, Sussex. Tel: Eastbourne 503076.
Founded: 1928
Secretary: Millard Hall, Flat 1, 14 Dittons Road, Eastbourne, sussex BN2 1DW. Tel: 0323 33380.
Fixtures Secretary: N. Creasey, 177 Seaside, Eastbourne, Sussex. Tel: 0323 648727.
League: Sussex 1
Final position (1987–88): 3rd

SEAFORD

Salts Recreation Ground, Esplanade, Seaford, Sussex. Tel: 0273 892355.
Founded: 1938
President: R.L. Hayes
Chairman: C. Hill
Coach: D. Cleaton
Secretary: E.A. Pugh, Shottery, 19 Chyngton Road, Seaford, Sussex. Tel: 0323 892020.
Fixtures Secretary: C. Cole, 32 Park Drive Close, Newhaven, Sussex. Tel: 0275 516388.
Club captain (1987–88): R. Debil
Club captain (1988–89): R. Debil
No. of teams: Senior 3. Youth & Minis 1.
Directions to Ground: Drive along Seaford sea front.
Colours: Scarlet.
Floodlights: No
Membership: £15 playing, £2 non-playing
Local newspaper: Sussex Express
League: Sussex 1
Final position (1987–88): 4th

BURGESS HILL

Poveys Close, Burgess Hill, Sussex.
Founded: 1962
Secretary: I.T. Churchill, 23 Dunstall Farm Road, Burgess Hill, West Sussex RM15 8AX. Tel: Burgess Hill 46700 (H), Burgess Hill 5432 (W).
League: Sussex 1
Final position (1987–88): 5th

CROWBOROUGH

Steel Cross, Crowborough, Sussex. Tel: 08926 4832.
Founded: 1937
Secretary: M.C. Clarke, 7 Cold Harbour Close, Crowborough, East Sussex. Tel: 08926 61026 (H). 01-488 3200, Extn. 6276 (W).
Fixtures Secretary: G.D. Pratt, Sherlocks Cottage, Motts Hill, Crowbridge, Tunbridge wells, Kent. Tel: 0892 76603 (H), 0892 29551 (W).
League: Sussex 1
Final position (1987–88): 6th

HOVE

Hove Park, Hove, East Sussex
Founded: 1933
Secretary: D.L. Huyton, 54 Berriedale Avenue, Hove, East Sussex. Tel: 0273 771924 (H), 01-382 5368 (W).
Fixtures Secretary: M. Richardson, 6 Wayside, Westdene, Brighton BN1 5HL. Tel: 0273 500512.
League: Sussex 1
Final position (1987–88): 7th
Playing record (1987–88): P 26, W 14, D 1, L 11. F 441, A 280.

HAYWARDS HEATH

Whiteman's Green, Cuckfield, Haywards Heath, Sussex. Tel: 0444 413950.
Founded: 1958
Secretary: D. Goodger, 22 By-Sunte, Lindfield, Haywards Heath, Sussex. Tel: 0444 414829 (H), 0444 459122. Extn. 320 (W)
Fixtures Secretary: J.K. Eden, Church Road, Scayneshill, Haywards Heath, Sussex. Tel: 0444 486221 (H).
League: Sussex 1
Final position (1987–88): 8th

BRIGHTON

Horsdean, Vale Avenue, Patcham, Brighton. Tel: 0273 506995
Founded: 1868
President: P.J. Wardlee
Chairman: D.T.C. Malby
Coach: M. Avery
Secretary: A.J. Bradley, 5 The Drive, Hove, E. Sussex BN3 3JE. Tel: 0273 205959.
Fixtures Secretary: C. Salter, 35 High Beech Lane, Haywards Heath. Tel: HH 458623.
Club captain (1987–88): Don Rees
Club captain (1988–89): Peter Thomson
No. of teams: Senior 6. Youth & Minis 1.
Directions to Ground: Follow A23 to Patcham lights at Borough boundary. Turn left and go over hill, ground on left.
Ground capacity: 500
Clubhouse: Built 1968
Colours: Royal blue with crest, blue shorts, red socks. (*Change colours:* Red shirts).
Floodlights: Yes
Membership: £24
Local newspaper: Evening Argus
League: Sussex 1
Final position (1987–88): 9th
Playing record (1987–88): P 38, W 16, D 2, L 20.

SUSSEX POLICE

Brighton RFC, Horsdean Vale Avenue, Brighton, Sussex.
Founded: 1968
Secretary: Det. Insp G. Randle, Police Station, Chichester, Sussex. Tel: 0903 784468 (H). 0243 784433. Extn. 223 (W).
League: Sussex 1
Final position (1987–88): 10th

HASTINGS & BEXHILL

The Polegrove, Brockely Road, Bexhill-on-Sea, Sussex. Tel: 0424 210224.
Founded: 1924
Secretary: J.A. Northern, 19 Fearon Road, Hastings, East Sussex TN34 2DL. Tel: 0424 421161 (H), 0424 439190 (W).
Fixtures Secretary: R. Hamilton, 1 Bluestone Close, Wishing Tree Road, St. Leonard-on-Sea, East Sussex. Tel: 0424 219224.
League: Sussex 1
Final position (1987–88): 11th (relegated)
Playing record (1987–88): P 34, W 14, D 1, L 19. F 404, A 503.

UCKFIELD

r/o Barley Mow, Eatbourne Road, Uckfield, East sussex. Tel: Framfield 664
Founded: 1967
President: Ray Martin
Chairman: Brian Evan Cook
Coach: Brian York
Secretary: Chris Sandus, 4 Princes Close, West Park, Uckfield, East Sussex. Tel: TBA
Fixtures Secretary: Ian Poole, 9 Keld Avenue, Uckfield. Tel: Uckfield 61151
Club captain (1987–88): Adrian Evans
Club captain (1988–89): Adrian Evans
No. of teams: Senior 4. Youth & Minis 4.
Directions to Ground: Approx 1 mile south of Uckfield town on A22 to Eastbourne. Behind Barley Mow public house.
Clubhouse: Single storey, 1 changing room and showers. Food hall and bar.
Colours: Amber with purple band. (*Change colours:* Black with amber and purple band).
Floodlights: Yes
Membership: £20
Local newspaper: Uckfield Courier
League: Sussex 2
Final position (1987–88): 1st (promoted)
Playing record (1987–88): 1st XV P 27, W 17, D 2, L 8. F 464, A 186. League P 8, W 8. F 267, A 28.
Competitions won: Promoted from Sussex division 2 to Sussex division 1.

HELLINGLY

Founded: 1972
President: John Westwood
Chairman: Peter Watkins
Coach: John Nicholas
Secretary: Steve Wennington. Tel: 0323 845469.
Fixtures Secretary: Tim Bowler. Tel: 0323 845838.
Club captain (1987–88): R. Francis
Club captain (1988–89): R. Francis
No. of teams: Senior 2. Youth & Minis 0.
Directions to Ground: Opposite White Hart pub. Recreation Ground – Horsebridge.
Clubhouse: At recreation ground.
Colours: Black/amber
Nickname: The Loonies
Floodlights: Yes, training only
Membership: £3
Local newspaper: Hailsham Gazette
League: Sussex 2
Final position (1987–88): 2nd Div 2
Playing record (1987–88): W 14, L 12, D 2.
Competitions won: 2nd in Sussex Div 2 and promoted to Div 1.

ST FRANCIS

Broadfield Playing Fields, Rathlin Road, Broadfield, Crawley, Sussex.
Founded: 1961
Secretary: G.T. Hill, 31 Albany Road, West Green. Crawley, West Sussex. Tel: 0293 33492 (H), 0293 510001 (W).
League: Sussex 2
Final position (1987–88): 3rd

HEATHFIELD & WALDRON

c/o Blackboys Inn, Blackboys, East Sussex.
Founded: 1980
Secretary: S.D. Leney, Mill Cottage, Cross-in-Hand, Heathfield, East Sussex. Tel: 04352 6401 (H), 0273 28833 (W).
League: Sussex 2
Final position (1987–88): 4th

PLUMPTON

Plumpton Race Course, Plumpton, Sussex
Founded: 1967
President: R.A. Ford
Chairman: C. Hills
Coach: M. Slade
Secretary: G. Medhurst, Townsend Cottage, Plumpton Lane, Plumpton, Lewes, Sussex. Tel: 9273 890055
Fixtures Secretary: D. Beale, Rock Cottages, Lindfield Farm, North Chailet, Sussex. Tel: Newick 3074.
Club captain (1987–88): P. Cragg
Club captain (1988–89): M. Johnston
No. of teams: Senior 1.
Directions to Ground: Plumpton racecourse, opposite Plumpton railway station.
Colours: Maroon with gold hoops.
Floodlights: No
Membership: £10
Local newspaper: Mid Sussex Times
League: Sussex 2
Final position (1987–88): 5th
Playing record (1987–88): P 39, W 28, D 1, L 10
Competitions won: Plumpton RFC, Sevens Tournament

BRITISH CALEDONIAN/ WINGSPAN

Wingspan Sports & Social Club, Caledonian House, Betts Way, Crawley, Sussex. Tel: 0293 546477.
Founded: 1972
Secretary: M. Crawford, 15 Payne Close, Pound Hill, Crawley, Sussex. Tel: 0293 885812 (H), 0293 27890, Extn. 2197 (W).
League: Sussex 2
Final position (1987–88): 6th

SUSSEX UNIVERSITY

Tel: Brighton 678155
Founded: 1963
President: To be appointed
Chairman: To be appointed
Coach: To be appointed
Secretary: Dean Lythgoe, 32 Guildford Road, Brighton. Tel: 600637.
Fixtures Secretary: Dean Lythgoe, as above.
Club captain (1987–88): Robert Pearce
Club captain (1988–89): Dominic Cotton
No. of teams: Senior 3. Youth & Minis 3.
Directions to Ground: Brighton – follow A27 to Lewes, for 3 miles. Take exit to University of Sussex – pitches at Sports Pavilion.
Stand capacity: 100
Clubhouse: Bar, TV room, aftermatch food by arrangement.
Colours: Blue/red hoops. (*Change colours:* Red/white hoops).
Nickname: Dalai Lamas

Floodlights: No
Membership: £7
Local newspaper: Brighton Evening Argus
League: Sussex 2
Final position (1987–88): 7th
Playing record (1987–88): P 27, W 12, D 2, L 13
Competitions won: Utrecht Challenge Cup

AZURIANS

Palatine Park, Palatine Road, Worthing, Sussex.
Founded: 1927
Secretary: C. Spratt, 61 Tarrant Street, Arundel, Sussex. Tel: Arundel 8836812 (H). Worthing 34343 (W).
Fixtures Secretary: D. Rogers, 69 Cokehamland, Sompting, Worthing, Sussex. Tel: Worthing 750877.
League: Sussex 2
Final position (1987–88): 8th

SUSSEX 3

PULBOROUGH

Rectory Field, Pulborough, Sussex. Tel: Pul 3020
Founded: 1968
President: James North
Chairman: John Mason
Coach: Clive Coulson
Secretary: Charles Francis, Greyfriars Farm, Storrington, Sussex, RH20 1ER. Tel: Stor. 2648
Fixtures Secretary: Jo Mercer, 14 Cousins Way, Pulborough. Tel: Pul 5168
Club captain (1987–88): John Scrase
Club captain (1988–89): Andrew McKinnon
No. of teams: Senior 3. Youth & Minis 6.
Directions to Ground: Rectory Lane, Pulborough. Off A29
Clubhouse: Joint Sports Club
Colours: Black and white hoops.
Floodlights: Yes
Membership: £15
Local newspaper: West Sussex County Times
League: Sussex 3
Final position (1987–88): 1st
Playing record (1987–88): P 29, W 22, L 7. F 529, A 168
Competitions won: Courage League Div 3, Sussex

BRIGHTON POLYTECHNIC

Founded: 1966
Secretary: K. Harrison, c/o Falmer Students Union Office, Brighton Poly., Sussex. Tel: 0273 671057.
League: Sussex 3
Final position (1987–88): 2nd

MIDHURST

The Ruins, Cowdray Park, Midhurst, Sussex.
Founded: 1981
Secretary: L.S. Lloyd, 4 Guillards Oak, Midhurst, West Sussex GU29 9JZ. Tel: 073081 2025 (H).
League: Sussex 3
Final position (1987–88): 3rd

ROBIN HOOD

"Robin Hood", Little Western Street, Brighton.
Founded: 1981
President: B. Hayes
Chairman: J. Taylor
Coach: R. Mullan
Secretary: P. Guy, 14 Leicester villas, Hove, E. Sussex. Tel: 0273 416858.
Fixtures Secretary: R. Mullan, c/o Club Secretary (temporary)
Club captain (1987–88): R. Mullan
Club captain (1988–89): R. Mullan
No. of teams: Senior 1
Directions to Ground: Brighton and Hove Sixth Form College on A27, entrance in dyke Road off A27 near "7 Dials".
Clubhouse: Robin Hood PH
Colours: Black and green quarters. (*Change colours:* Green and white hoops)
Nickname: "The Hoods"
Floodlights: No
Membership: £5
Local newspaper: Evening Argus
League: Sussex 3
Final position (1987–88): 4th
Playing record (1987–88): P 7, W 3, D 1, L 3 (League only)

ARUN

Littlehampton School, Hill Road, Littlehampton, Sussex.
League: Sussex 3
Final position (1987–88): 5th

SUNALLON RFC

North Heath Lane, Horsham, W. Sussex
Founded: 1971
Chairman: D.W. Fowler
Coach: I. Howard
Secretary: B.R. Lewis, 2 Wain End, Wimblehurst Park, Horsham, W. Sussex RH12 4TQ.
Fixtures Secretary: B.R. Lewis, as above.
Club captain (1987–88): S. Davis
Club captain (1988–89): S. Davis
No. of teams: Senior 1
Directions to Ground: From A24, take Warnham Road, second left into Wimblehurst Road, leading into North Heath Lane.
Clubhouse: Large, two bars, 6 dressing rooms.
Colours: Yellow and blue. (*Change colours:* Blue).
Nickname: Sun
Floodlights: No
Membership: £9.60
Local newspaper: West Sussex County Times
League: Sussex Div 3
Final position (1987–88): 5th
Playing record (1987–88): P 27, W 13, L 13, D 1. F 322, A 375.

NEWICK

Rear of Crown Inn, Church Road, Newick, Lewes, E. Sussex BN8 4JX. Tel: Newick (082572) 3293
Founded: 1965
President: D.L. Manwaring-Robertson
Chairman: P. Burnie
Coach: C. Briggs
Secretary: G.H. Major, 19 Oldaker Road, Newick, Lewes, E. Sussex BN8 4LN.
Fixtures Secretary: M. Barling, 80 Ditchling Road, Brighton, E. Sussex. Tel: Brighton 687110

Club captain (1987–88): M. Raffray
Club captain (1988–89): C. Briggs
No. of teams: Senior 1
Directions to Ground: Turn south off A272 in centre of village, keep left at the Bull Inn, into Church Road. The Crown Inn is 200 yards on right.
Clubhouse: At rear of Crown Inn.
Colours: Maroon and navy blue hoops
Floodlights: No
Membership: £15
Local newspaper: Mid Sussex Times
League: Sussex 3
Final position (1987–88): 6th
Playing record (1987–88): P 23, W 12, L 11

DITCHLING

Lewes Road, Ditchling, Sussex. Tel: Hassocks 3423.
Founded: 1962
President: Godfrey Harker
Chairman: Brian Griffiths
Coach: Bob Plummer
Secretary: Adam Godfrey, 82 Clarence Road, Horsham. Tel: 58604.
Fixtures Secretary: Kevin Rickard, 66 Ferndale Road, Burgess Hill. Tel: B/Hill 44505.
Club captain (1987–88): Steven Booth
Club captain (1988–89): TBA
No. of teams: Senior 2
Directions to Ground: From the cross roads head east, about ½ mile on left hand side.
Clubhouse: Pavillion with ample showers and bar, lounge and kitchen facilities.
Colours: Green/white shorts.
Nickname: Mothers
Floodlights: Yes
Admission: £2.50
Membership: £15
Local newspaper: Mid Sussex Times
League: Sussex 3
Final position (1987–88): Bottom

London's top sides – Wasps and Harlequins battle in the John Player Cup semi-final – won by Quins in extra-time (20–16). Quins' Edwards is brought down by Wasps's Pinnegar. Photo: Colorsport.

Wasps v Harlequins – John Player Cup semi-final. Quins' Adrian Thompson squares up to a tackle from Simon Smith (Wasps' no. 14). Photo: Colorsport.

COURAGE
CLUBS CHAMPIONSHIP
RESULTS 1987–88

NATIONAL DIVISIONS

DIV.	FIXTURE	RESULT
Sat. September 5		
1	Nottingham v Moseley	21–12
2	Headingley v Saracens	3–12
Sat. September 12		
1	Leicester v Bath	24–13
1	Gloucester v Coventry	39–3
1	Sale v Nottingham	3–17
2	London Irish v Bedford	12–12
2	Liverpool St. Helens v Gosforth	15–10
2	Saracens v London Welsh	7–23
3	Vale of Lune v Exeter	27–3
3	Plymouth Albion v Sheffield	43–7
Sat. September 19		
1	Bath v Moseley	14–0
2	Northampton v Richmond	3–16
2	Rosslyn Park v Gosforth	14–3
2	London Scottish v Headingley	6–22
3	Birmingham v Met Police	3–22
3	Sheffield v Fylde	13–12
3	Maidstone v Vale of Lune	14–16
Sat. September 26		
1	Bristol v Gloucester	16–21
1	Coventry v Sale	24–19
1	Harlequins v Leicester	9–12
1	Nottingham v Orrell	12–12
2	Rosslyn Park v London Welsh	16–15
Wed. September 30		
1	Coventry v Nottingham	15–20
2	Bedford v London Welsh	6–6
Sat. October 3		
1	Leicester v Coventry	32–16
1	Sale v Moseley	15–19
2	London Welsh v Richmond	22–26
2	London Scottish v Northampton	50–3
3	Birmingham v Vale of Lune	15–42
3	Fylde v Exeter	48–13
3	West Hartlepool v Sheffield	25–10
Sat. October 10		
1	Moseley v Orrell	28–10
1	Bristol v Wasps	12–12
2	Bedford v Blackheath	6–0
2	Headingley v Gosforth	26–7
2	London Irish v Saracens	9–27
2	Rosslyn Park v London Scottish	15–6
3	Met Police v Fylde	9–23
3	Sheffield v Maidstone	10–3
3	West Hartlepool v Morley	23–3
3	Plymouth Albion v Wakefield	16–12

DIV	FIXTURE	RESULT
Sat. October 17		
1	Bath v Bristol	15–9
1	Waterloo v Nottingham	10–9
2	London Scottish v Blackheath	18–9
2	Liverpool St. Helens v London Irish	14–0
3	Birmingham v Plymouth Albion	3–46
3	Morley v Fylde	13–38
3	Wakefield v Maidstone	23–9
3	Nuneaton v Met Police	7–12
Sat. October 24		
1	Bristol v Sale	37–3
1	Moseley v Coventry	26–3
1	Gloucester v Nottingham	17–9
2	Headingley v Rosslyn Park	12–12
3	Sheffield v Met Police	13–6
Wed. October 28		
2	Rosslyn Park v London Irish	20–3
Sat. October 31		
1	Nottingham v Bristol	3–16
1	Waterloo v Gloucester	16–6
2	London Irish v London Scottish	3–6
3	Birmingham v Wakefield	3–50
3	Exeter v West Hartlepool	6–18
3	Plymouth Albion v Fylde	33–17
3	Met Police v Maidstone	9–6
Sat. November 7		
1	Orrell v Sale	19–0
2	Gosforth v Richmond	12–10
2	Headingley v Blackheath	21–9
3	Fylde v Birmingham	68–7
3	Exeter v Wakefield	19–29
3	Maidstone v Nuneaton	9–3
3	Met Polie v Plymouth Albion	25 18
3	Vale of Lune v W Hartlepool	12–21
Sat. November 14		
1	Wasps v Bath	19–15
1	Orrell v Bristol	13–25
1	Nottingham v Leicester	13–22
2	Richmond v Liverpool St. Helens	3–13
3	Sheffield v Birmingham	34–0
Sat. November 21		
1	Coventry v Bath	9–9
1	Leicester v Wasps	12–9
2	Richmond v London Scottish	9–6
2	Bedford v Northampton	17–16
3	Sheffield v Met Police	Void
3	Nuneaton v Morley	21–6
1	Harlequins v Gloucester	9–9

Sat. November 28

1	Moseley v Leicester	3–21
1	Wasps v Nottingham	17–9
3	Met Police v Morley	26–12

Tue. December 1

1	Gloucester v Bath	9–16

Sat, December 5

1	Leicester v Gloucester	Off
2	Bedford v Gosforth	16–25
2	Saracens v Liverpool St. Helens	10–13
3	Morley v Birmingham	23–3
3	Wakefield v Nuneaton	33–3
3	W Hartlepool v Plymouth Albion	19–10

Sat. December 12

1	Bath v Waterloo	10–17
1	Bristol v Moseley	21–10
2	Rosslyn Park v Richmond	20–12
2	Northampton v London Irish	15–13
2	Saracens v Gosforth	7–7
3	Vale of Lune v Morley	25–19

Sat. December 19

1	Leicester v Bristol	15–10
2	Blackheath v Richmond	3–4
2	Liverpool St. Helens v Rosslyn Park	3–13
2	London Welsh v London Irish	6–13
3	Fylde v Vale of Lune	12–14
3	Exeter v Plymouth Albion	9–18
3	Wakefield v Sheffield	41–0

Fri. January 1

1	Gloucester v Moseley	18–12

Sat, January 2

1	Wasps v Harlequins	17–16
1	Waterloo v Sale	29–13
2	Rosslyn Park v Blackheath	14–8
2	Northampton v London Welsh	14–16
3	Birmingham v Nuneaton	3–3
3	Maidstone v Exeter	23–9
3	Met Police v W Hartlepool	6–22

Sat. January 9

2	London Irish v Richmond	17–15
2	Liverpool St. Helens v Blackheath	15–0
2	London Scottish v Gosforth	13–8
3	Maidstone v Birmingham	18–3
3	Nuneaton v Fylde	13–18
3	Plymouth Albion v Morley	24–0

Sat. January 16

2	London Welsh v Liverpool St. Helens	10–27

Sun. January 17

2	Blackheath v Northampton	19–12

Sat. January 30

2	Bedford v Rosslyn Park	15–3
3	Vale of Lune v Nuneaton	6–3

Fri. February 5

1	Moseley v Wasps	19–12

Sat. February 6

1	Richmond v Headingley	14–13
3	Birmingham v W Hartlepool	6–43

Sun. February 7

1	Coventry v Waterloo	15–10
1	Harlequins v Orrell	6–12
2	Blackheath v London Irish	12–16
2	Saracens v Northampton	22–6

Sat. February 13

2	Headingley v Bedford	7–13
1	Glouceser v Wasps	13–24
3	Met Police v Wakefield	6–7

Sat. February 20

1	Orrell v Leicester	30–6
2	Bedford v London Scottish	21–9
2	Gosforth v London Irish	14–2
3	Morley v Exeter	10–10

Sun. February 21

2	Saracens v Rosslyn Park	6–6

Sat. February 27

3	Plymouth Albion v Maidstone	45–11
3	Wakefield v Vale of Lune	32–12
1	Harlequins v Waterloo	37–4
2	Gosforth v Blackheath	26–8

Fri. March 4

1	Exeter v Met Police	4–3

Sat. March 5

1	Moseley v Harlequins	11–32
2	London Irish v Headingley	12–32
3	Morley v Sheffield	7–12

Sat. March 12

1	Sale v Wasps	6–14
2	Blackheath v London Welsh	22–7
2	Northampton v Rosslyn Park	0–22
3	Nuneaton v Exeter	9–11
3	Maidstone v Fylde	16–18
3	Vale of Lune v Met Police	Off
3	Morley v Wakefield	7–38

Sat. March 19

1	Coventry v Harlequins	12–15
1	Orrell v Gloucester	9–13
2	London Welsh v Headingley	10–18
3	Sheffield v Nuneaton	15–9
3	Wakefield v W Hartlepool	16–12

Sun. March 20

2	Saracens v Bedford	33–4

Wed. March 23

2	Blackheath v Saracens	12–48

Sat. March 26

1	Leicester v Sale	42–15
2	Liverpool St. Helens v Headingley	6–6
3	Exeter v Birmingham	32–0
3	Fylde v Wakefield	3–23
3	W Hartlepool v Maidstone	12–10
3	Nuneaton v Plymouth Albion	9–7
2	Richmond v Bedford	28–25
1	Bath v Orrell	23–18

Wed. March 30

2	Saracens v London Scottish	34–0

Sat. April 2

1	Waterloo v Wasps	13–22
3	Maidstone v Morley	15–0
1	Harlequins v Nottingham	34–8

Mon. April 4

1	Leicester v Waterloo	39–15

Thur. April 7

3	Sheffield v Vale of Lune	8–3

Sat. April 9

1	Bath v Harlequins	21–9

Wed. April 13

2	London Welsh v London Scottish	24–24

Thu. April 14

2	Richmond v Saracens	3–22

Sat. April 16

1	Orrell v Waterloo	30–6
1	Gloucester v Sale	61–7
2	Headingley v Northampton	38–3
2	Liverpool St. Helens v London Scottish	10–3
3	Fylde v W Hartlepool	12–17
3	Vale of Lune v Plymouth Albion	13–16

Sat. April 23

1	Coventry v Bristol	25–3
2	Gosforth v London Welsh	12–14
2	Northamtpon v Liverpool St. Helens	9–13
3	W Hartlepool v Nuneaton	37–14
3	Exeter v Sheffield	12–12
1	Harlequins v Sale	66–0

Tue. April 26

1	Moseley v Waterloo	27–3

Sat. April 30

1	Bristol v Waterloo	Off
1	Coventry v Orrell	11–24
2	Bedford v Liverpool St. Helens	33–25
1	Sale v Bath	17–46
1	Harlequins v Bristol	28–22

Wasps attack as they beat Bath with Ellison about to pass to Bates (left) with Bath's controversial scrum-half Richard Hill failing to intervene. Photo: Chris Roberts.

COURAGE
CLUBS CHAMPIONSHIP

RESULTS 1987–88

AREA LEAGUES

North Sat. September 12

Birkenhead Park v Broughton Park	7–6
Roundhay v Northern	0–0
Rugby v Lichfield	24–12
Solihull v Durham City	24–0
Stourbridge v Derby	21–4

South Sat. September 12

Askeans v Camborne	14–0
Southend v Salisbury	9–4
Streatham Croydon v Lydney	10–20
Stroud v Havant	9–7
Sudbury v Cheltenham	23–6

North Sat. September 19

Derby v Birkenhead Park	11–16
Durham City v Stourbridge	30–12
Lichfield v Solihull	18–13
Northern v Rugby	17–27
Preston Grasshoppers v Roundhay	6–6

South, Sat. September 19

Cheltenham v Askeans	3–20
Havant v Sudbury	14–10
Lydney v Stroud	24–3
Salisbury v Streatham Croydon	28–4
Sidcup v Southend	20–3

North Sat. October 3

Birkenhead Park v Durham City	9–26
Broughton Park v Derby	19–6
Rugby v Preston Grasshoppers	24–12
Solihull v Northern	7–16
Stourbridge v Lichfield	9–6

South, Sat. October 3

Askeans v Havant	14–3
Camborne v Cheltenham	17–6
Streatham Croydon v Sidcup	6–16
Stroud v Salisbury	19–10
Sudbury v Lydney	23–14

North, Sat. October 10

Durham City v Broughton Park	4–0
Lichfield v Birkenhead Park	27–0
Northern v Stourbridge	16–10
Preston Grasshoppers v Solihull	31–9
Rounday v Rugby	4–8

South, Sat. October 10

Havant v Camborne	6–7
Lydney v Askeans	25–3
Salisbury v Sudbury	10–0
Sidcup v Stroud	12–8
Southend v Streatham Croydon	3–0

North, Sat. October 17

Birkenhead Park v Northern	10–21
Broughton Park v Lichfield	23–9
Derby v Durham City	–
Solihull v Roundhay	0–12
Stourbridge v Preston Grasshoppers	26–15

South, Sat. October 17

Askeans v Salisbury	17–12
Camborne v Lydney	23–13
Cheltenham v Havant	11–15
Stroud v Southend	10–16
Sudbury v Sidcup	12–12

North, Sat. October 31

Lichfield v Derby	11–7
Northern v Broughton Park	15–13
Preston Grasshoppers v Birkenhead Park	24–17
Roundhay v Stourbridge	16–3
Rugby v Solihull	21–3

South, Sat. October 31

Lydney v Cheltenham	26–12
Salisbury v Camborne	6–6
Sidcup v Askeans	3–3
Streatham Croydon v Stroud	9–15
Southend v Sudbury	10–3

North, Sat. November 7

Birkenhead Park v Roundday	16–28
Broughton Park v Preston Grasshoppers	24–12
Derby v Northern	9–14
Durham City v Lichfield	23–15
Stourbridge v Rugby	11–0

South, Sat. November 7

Askeans v Southend	13–4
Camborne v Sidcup	19–19
Cheltenham v Salisbury	16–12
Havant v Lydney	19–11
Sudbury v Streatham Croydon	19–3

South, Sat. December 5

Southend v Camborne	6–18

North, Sat. January 2

Northern v Durham City	3–12
Preston Grasshoppers v Derby	22–10
Roundhay v Broughton Park	20–6
Rugby v Birkenhead Park	20–0
Solihull v Stourbridge	9–21

South, Sat. January 2

Salisbury v Havant	3–17

Sidcup v Cheltenham	17–3
Streatham Croydon v Askeans	9–18
Stroud v Sudbury	11–10

North, Sat. January 9

Birkenhead Park v Solihull	28–3
Broughton Park v Rugby	16–20
Derby v Roundhay	6–12
Durham City v Preston Grasshoppers	12–10
Lichfield v Northern	27–9

South, Sat. January 9

Askeans v Stroud	23–9
Camborne v Streatham Croydon	10–8
Cheltenham v Southend	15–0
Havant v Sidcup	6–10
Lydney v Salisbury	10–0

North, Sat. March 12

Preston Grasshoppers v Lichfield	19–15
Roundhay v Durham City	6–12
Rugby v Derby	28–16
Solihull v Broughton Park	7–14
Stourbridge v Birkenhead Park	13–14

South, Sat. March 12

Sidcup v Lydney	6–9
Southend v Havant	12–4
Streatham Croydon v Cheltenham	6–19
Stroud v Camborne	31–9
Sudbury v Askeans	15–16

North, Sat. March 26

Broughton Park v Stourbridge	20–6
Derby v Solihull	34–8
Durham City v Rugby	9–12
Lichfield v Roundhay	10–27
Northern v Preston Grasshoppers	6–22

South, Sat. March 26

Camborne v Sudbury	10–10
Cheltenham v Stroud	4–16
Havant v Streatham Croydon	25–15
Lydney v Southend	21–0
Salisbury v Sidcup	9–15

JOHN PLAYER SPECIAL CUP
RESULTS 1987–88

1st ROUND
Played on Saturday 26th September 1987

Askeans v London Irish	10–12
Bedford v Barker's Butts	35–4
Berry Hill v Salisbury	12–0
Devonport Services v Maidenhead	11–12
Dixonians v Droitwich	21–6
Ealing v Southend	10–9
Fylde v Hartlepool Rovers	30–9
Gordon League v Chiltern	44–7
Leighton Buzzard v Derby	10–7
Letchworth v Blackheath	0–26
Lichfield v Vipers	31–3
London Scottish v Sudbury	9–3
Nuneaton v Aspatria	4–43
Lewes v Havant	16–13
Old Alleynians v Maidstone	12–0
Oxford v Camborne	14–0
Redruth v Old Culverhaysians	26–9
Tynedale v Vale of Lune	16–15
Wakefield v Morley	22–0
Widnes v Birkenhead Park	4–3

2nd ROUND
Played on Saturday, 24th October 1987

Berry Hill v Lewes	35–9
Dixonians v Aspatria	3–53
Gordon League v Oxford	19–16
Leighton Buzzard v Bedford	6–24
Lichfield v Widnes	31–3
London Irish v Ealing	13–10
Maidenhead v Old Alleynians	13–3
Redruth v Blackheath *(after extra time)*	9–13
Tynedale v London Scottish	11–9
Wakefield v Fylde	24–21

3rd ROUND
Played on Saturday, 23rd January 1988

Aspatria v Wasps	6–13
Bedford v Bristol	4–21
Gloucester v Orrell	19–9
Gordon League v Headingley	10–0
Harlequins v Maidenhead	40–0
London Irish v Sale	3–16
London Welsh v Berry Hill	10–13
Plymouth Albion v Northampton	14–7
Richmond v Liverpool-St. Helens	10–6
Rosslyn Park v Leicester	0–15
Ruislip v Gosforth	10–13
Saracens v Blackheath	15–3
Waterloo v Nottingham	19–6

Played on Saturday, 30th January 1988

Coventry v Tynedale	7–6
Lichfield v Bath	3–43
Wakefield v Moseley	4–14

4th ROUND
Played on Saturday, 13th February 1988

Berry Hill v Harlequins	4–17
Bristol v Richmond	34–0
Coventry v Sale	0–13
Gloucester v Wasps	13–24
Gordon League v Waterloo	9–11
Leicester v Bath	6–13
Mosley v Gosforth	33–9
Plymouth Albion v Saracens	14–6

5th ROUND
Played on Saturday, 27th February 1988

Harlequins v Waterloo	37–4
Moseley v Bath	4–3
Plymouth Albion v Wasps	4–26
Sale v Bristol	15–19

SEMI-FINALS
Played on Saturday, 26th May 1988

Moseley v Bristol	6–34
Wasps v Harlequins *(after extra time)*	16–20

FINAL
Played on Saturday, 30th April 1988 at Twickenham

Harlequins v Bristol	28–22

The cup semi-final. Someone has to miss the big day. Wasps' and Quins' forwards at a line-out. Photo: Colorsport.

Never mind the ball, get on with the game! Action from the John Player Cup Final, a great exhibition of the game in reality. Photo: Colorsport.

COUNTY CUPS RESULTS 1987/88

NORTH

Cheshire: Winnington Park 16 Birkenhead Park 11
Cumbria: Aspatria 12 Cockermouth 10
Durham: Durham City 18 Stockton 12
Lancashire: Orrell 23 Liverpool St. Helens 6
Northumberland: Tynedale 13 Gosforth 6
Yorkshire: Headingley 21 Wakefield 9

MIDLANDS

Derbyshire: Derby 25 Matlock 15 (aet)*
East Midlands: Stockwood Park 17 Leighton Buzzard 15
Leicestershire: Stoneygate 13 Hinckley 6
Lincolnshire: Boston 12 Lincoln 6*
North Midlands: Hereford 22 Bromsgrove 10
Nottinghamshire: Newark 18 Southwell 6*
Notts., Lincs. & Derbys: Newark 20 Matlock 12
Staffordshire: Wolverhampton 12 Stoke 6
Warwickshire: Rugby 61 Stoke Old Boys 0

SOUTH-WEST

Berkshire: Reading 9 Maidenhead 7
Buckinghamshire: Marlow 15 High Wycombe 13
Cornwall: redruth 9 Launceston 7
Devon: Plymouth Albion 32 Okehampton 6
Dorset & Wilts: Swindon 8 Salisbury 3
Gloucestershire: Lydney 13 Berry Hill 7
Oxfordshire: Oxford 15 Banbury 9
Somerset: Combe Down 25 Old Culverhaysians 12

LONDON

Eastern Counties: Sudbury 12 North Walsham 0
Hampshire: Havant 14 Basingstoke 12
Hertfordshire: tabard 14 Cheshutn 13
Kent: Maidstone 29 Blackheath 0 (after 12–12 draw)
Middlesex: Finchley 9 Old Merchant Taylors 8
Surrey: Old Mid-Whitgiftians 19 Guildford & Godalming 0
Sussex: Worthing 12 Crawley 6

**These winners do not automatically qualify for the John Player Special cup in 1988–89.*

Maidstone's No 8 on a blind-side break which led to his side's first try in their 37–15 Pilkington Cup win at Marlow this season. Captain Andy Cushing (with beard) is in support. Photo: Chris Roberts.

SEVEN-A-SIDE COMPETITIONS RESULTS 1987/88

OXFORDSHIRE

Sunday, 17 April 1988, Iffley Road, Oxford

Bristol 28 Richmond 12

Rosslyn Park (sponsored by Wimpey Homes)

Wednesday, 20th April 1988

London Scottish 36 President's VII 0

Surrey

Sunday, 24 April 1988, Dorking

Harlequins 22 Blackheath 6

Middlesex

Saturday, 7th May 1988, Twickenham

Harlequins 20, Bristol 18

London Scottish appear to be outnumbered in the 1987 Middlesex Sevens by Rosslyn Park, but they have possession so what next? Photo Colorsport.

OTHER RESULTS 1987/88

TOSHIBA COUNTY CHAMPIONSHIP

SEMI FINALS:

Lancashire v Gloucestershire 11–6
(at Vale of Lune)

Warwickshire v Surrey 31–19
(at Coventry)

FINAL:

Landashire v Warwickshire 23–18
(at Twickenham)

DIVISIONAL CHAMPIONSHIP

North v London (*Otley*) 13–0
South-West v Midlands (*Bristol*) 12–9
South-West v North (*Torquay*) 13–15
Midlands v London (*Leicester*) 25–9
Midlands v North (*Northampton*) 15–23
London v South-West (*Imber Court*) 6–3

Table

	P	W	L	F	A	Pts
North	3	3	51	28	6	
Midlands	3	1	2	49	44	2
South-West	3	1	2	28	30	2
London	3	1	2	15	41	2

UNIVERSITY MATCH

(*at Twickenham*)
Oxford v Cambridge 10–15

INTER-SERVICES CHAMPIONSHIP

(*all at Twickenham*)
Royal Navy v The Army 3–35
Royal Navy v Royal Air Force 7–10
The Army v Royal Air Force 26–3

KNOCK-OUT CUP

Results of finals to date

1972	Gloucester v Moseley	17–6
1973	Coventry v Bristol	27–15
1974	Coventry v London Scottish	26–6
1975	Bedford v Rosslyn Park	28–12
1976	Gosforth v Rosslyn Park	23–14
1977	Gosforth v Waterloo	27–11
1978	Gloucester v Leicester	6–3
1979	Leicester v Moseley	15–12
1980	Leicester v London Irish	21–9
1981	Leicester v Gosforth	22–15
1982	Gloucester v Moseley (Title shared)	12–12
1983	Bristol v Leicester	28–22
1984	Bath v Bristol	10–9
1985	Bath v London Welsh	24–15
1986	Bath v Wasps	25–17
1987	Bath v Wasps	19–12
1988	Harlequins v Bristol	28–22

Sale's promising Simon Tipping. Photo: Colorsport.

ENGLAND'S INTERNATIONAL RESULTS 1988

FIVE NATIONS

v **France** Paris	L	9–10
v **Wales** Twickenham	L	3–11
v **Scotland** Murrayfield	W	9–6
v **Ireland** Twickenham	W	35–3

OTHER MATCHES

v **Ireland** Dublin (*Millennium Match*)	W	21–10
v **Australia** Brisbane (*1st Test*)	L	16–22
v **Australia** Sydney	L	8–28
v **Fiji** Suva	W	25–12

Overall record: Played 7, won 4, lost 3, points for 126, against 102.

Other Five Nations Results:

Ireland v Scotland (*Dublin*)	22–18
Scotland v France (*Murrayfield*)	23–12
France v Ireland (*Paris*)	25–6
Wales v Scotland (*Cardiff*)	25–20
Ireland v Wales (*Dublin*)	9–12
Wales v France (*Cardiff*)	9–10

FINAL FIVE NATIONS TABLE

	P	W	L	F	A	Pts
Wales	4	3	1	57	42	6
France	4	3	1	57	47	6
England	4	2	2	56	30	4
Scotland	4	1	3	67	68	2
Ireland	4	1	3	40	90	2

Five Nations Appearances: *Backs:* J. Webb (Bristol) F, W, S, I; M. Harrison (Wakefield) F (capt), W (capt); R. Underwood (Leicester/RAF) F,W,S.I; C.Oti (Cambridge University) S, I; W. Carling (Durham University/Harlequins) F,W,S,I; K. Simms (Wasps) F,W, S; Halliday (Bath) S,I, L; Cusworth (Leicester) F,W, R; Andrew (Wasps) S.I, N; Melville (Wasps) F,W,S; (capt),I(capt), R. Harding (Bristol) I (rep). *Forwards*: P. Rendall (Wasps) F,W,S,I; B. Moore (Nottingham) F,W,S.E; J. Probyn (Wasps) F,W,S,I; W. Dooley (Fylde) F,W,S.I; J. Orwin (Bedford) F,W.S.I; M. Skinner (Harlequins) F,W,S,I; P. Winterbottom (Headingley) F,W,S; G. Rees (Nottingham) S (rep),I; D. Richards (Leicester) F,W,S,I.

Team v Ireland in Dublin Millennium Match: Webb; J. Bentley (Sale), Carling, Halliday, Underwood; Andrew, Harding; Rendall, Moore, Probyn, Orwin (capt), Dooley, Skinner, Rees, D. Egerton (Bath). Replacement: G. Chilcott (Bath) for Rendall.

Five Nations Scorers: Webb (7 pens, 1 con.) 23 points, Oti (3 tries) 12 points, Underwood (2 tries) 8 points, Andrew (3 cons.) 6 points, Rees (1 try) 4 points, Cusworth (1 drop) 3 points. N.B. Webb (3 pens., 2 cons.) 13 points, Underwood (1 try) and Harding (1 try) scored for England in the Millennium Match.

Hoping to take London Scottish up Gavin Hastings does his stuff for Scotland. Brother Scott meanwhile stays in Scotland with Watsonians (he is the one in the background). Photo: Colorsport.

Fran Cotton – and without the mud. The Sale prop was a regular in the 70s for England and the British Isles. Photo: Colorsport.

Wayne Shelford needs all his remaining energy to lift 'The Bledesloe Cup' which 'The All Blacks' retained by beating Australia twice and drawing the third of a three match series. Photo: Associated Press.

ONLY GENUINE FOOTBALLERS NEED APPLY

by Terry O'Connor *(Daily Mail).*

PROVIDING the significance of what happened in New Zealand, and to a lesser extent Australia, this summer is fully understood, then rugby is about to change dramatically and produce the most exciting brand of football played in the world.

This was the message which emerged from New Zealand where Wales were torn to shreds by a genuine 15 man game when it was often difficult to differentiate between backs and forwards.

Encouraged by sharing the Five Nations championship with France and winning the Triple Crown, the Welsh team arrived believing they had an outside chance of winning, although haunted by the 49–6 World Cup defeat against the All Blacks in 1987.

Following a month's tour they returned home with only two victories from eight matches and two more humiliating test defeats when conceding 18 tries and more than a 100 points. Even afterwards few of the players, let alone travelling officials, seemed aware of the reasons for the slaughter.

Jonathan Davies, captain of Wales in the second test – he was the third tour skipper which indicates the toll of injuries – believed the main reason for the difference between the two teams was that many of their opponents receive individual sponsorship.

What escaped so many was that New Zealand had changed the game of rugby radically by including 15 footballers, all of whom ran and handled the ball which ensured attacks could be sustained. In contrast the Welsh forwards plodded from scrum to scrum hoping to create a static game, but found themselves forced to defend against driving forwards and straight running backs. Poor Wales had no answer, nor would any of the other home countries. By

'All Black' Sean Fitzpatrick is caught by Wales centre John Devereux (No 13) during the First Test at Lancaster Park, Christchurch.

Above: John Kirwan "the thinker". Photo: Bob Thomas

Right: 'the actionman'. Photo: Mark Leed.

building a team around genuine footballers New Zealand have swept aside the idea that they could be beaten by a team keeping play tight and creating pressure with downfield kicks.

Let Hart explain: 'I wanted to get away from a game where the forwards dominated with backs used just as supporters. This meant that I needed forwards who were not just satisfied with scrummaging, line-outs and rucks, but wanted to be out in the open handling.

'The first major step forward was to replace those who were not capable of performing these duties. I had always advocated that training should be performed by all players working together, rather than separating the forwards and backs. This way it was easy to find out forwards who were unable to cope with a running game.

'This meant finding new men and if necessary helping them improve physically. Also I insist that backs must acquire forward skills so they stay on their feet and retain possession until help arrives.'

As Auckland provided nearly two thirds of the players in New Zealands's World Cup winning squad, their influence became decisive regarding the play of the national teams.

New Zealand have always been renowned for their back row play and today in Wayne Shelford, Michael Jones and Alan Whetton they have a combination which rates with the best. Shelford and Jones would challenge for places in the all time team.

Second row man Gary Whetton has always excelled in open play and he is now supported by a front row of Steve McDowell, Sean Fitzpatrick and Richard Loe who contributed to the destruction of Wales with their running and handling ability.

Many European observers sneered at the standard of back play produced by this current All Black team and suggested that only that fabulous wing John Kirwan would make a Lions back division. These critics missed the point.

New Zealand have always put the emphasis on team rather than individual play. They do not encourage players to do their own thing as in Britain, but instead concentrate on producing a winning combination. Results indicate they are right, but I do not think individual talent should be stifled.

As far as back play is concerned it would be wrong to try to imitate the All Blacks, but their method of changing the line of attack frequently should be considerd. Any touring Welshman would testify that it is very effective.

Before the first New Zealand–Wales test this year skipper Shelford was asked whether he

feared his opponents scrummaging. He looked puzzled by the question as the thought had never entered his head. Quickly he came back with a significant remark: 'To me scrummaging is five seconds' concentration'.

This is the crux of the matter. Until the home countries escape from an obsession with tight play and belief that the scrum is all important, there is no chance of challenging the type of rugby now being played in the southern hemisphere.

The cost of allowing the forwards to gain control has been horrific. Once the Lions were renowned for producing the world's best backs and regularly proved this during tours to New Zealand and South Africa.

When coaching was introduced to these islands in the late 1960s the accent moved to forward play where there was a weakness. Fortunately sufficient quality backs had been left over from the old system to sustain two brilliant Lions tours which helped produce test victories in New Zealand (1971) and South Africa (1977).

After this the forwards took over and consequently back play has declined. Starved of possession the backs have been unable to develop the skills needed against top defences. It almost reached breaking point during the successful England tour of Australia this year when the backs and forwards were blaming each other for the test defeats.

If any of the home countries are to have a realistic chance of challenging for the World Cup in 1991, then forwards and backs must train together and only all-rounders should be considered at representative level. This means selectors must change their way of thinking and many established players forced out.

Also those aspiring to play at international level must be prepared to train at least six times a week like club athletes and swimmers. This might mean providing extra perks like other countries, but the game can remain amateur. The principle of no payment for performing is rigidly enforced.

Above: Robert Norster blocked out by McDowell Fitzpatrick and Shelford!

Left: Wales scrum half Jonathan Griffiths v All Blacks.

Richard Lee (Bath). Photo: Mike Brett

SOMEONE HAS TO BE BOTTOM

by Huw Richards

'SOMEONE has to be bottom', pointed out an Armthorpe Rovers player after they'd suffered yet another league defeat last season.

Rovers, based in a pit village on the edge of Doncaster, were in the position to know. They finished last season bottom not only of Yorkshire Six, but of the whole 1128 club, 106 division system.

Their status may not be as clearcut as Leicester's. But measured by distance from the top there's no lower division than Yorkshire Six. Even if champions Sheffield Oaks go on winning promotion every year they'll take twelve more seasons to reach the top.

Armthorpe were unequivocally bottom of this Division 14. A record of played 10, lost 10, for 52 against 438 left little room for doubt.

They have seen better days. Rovers were part of rugby's great grassroots boom in the 1960s. Former Hartlepool Rover Stuart Robinson, now President, founded the club in 1968, giving them his old club's name and colours. In the 1970s they ran three teams and had years of great local success. Decline began six years ago when an ambitious player broke away to form Markham RFC, named after the local pit and playing a few hundred yards away. Both clubs now run one side – with Markham finishing two places higher in the same division. Yorkshire Two club Doncaster, withfive sides and impressive clubhouse facilities, play half a mile away.

Armthorpe reckon their council-owned pitch is the best in Yorkshire: 'Don't ask me why, but it's always playable – even in snow', says secretary Barry Jones, another 1968 survivor. It is a quarter mile trudge from the changing room. De facto clubhouse is the nearby Tadcaster Arms pub – venue for pre-match selection meetings.

Barry Jones knew what to expect when he was persuaded to apply to the league. He says: 'It was against my better judgment. I knew we'd have a hard time. We don't play many other first teams. The league matches us with some clubs whose second and third teams were already on our fixture lists'.

The pre-Christmas matches lived down to expectations: 'We must have cost Courage a hell of a lot', says coach and number eight Tony McNally. Three of their first four opponents claimed the sponsor's pints for points offer of beer for teams scoring more than 50. In six games pre-Christmas they conceded 294 points, scoring 35 themselves.

Training sessions were ended by dark nights – they can't get a gym and the council charged them for training on their pitch.

Less resilient sides might have given up – several of the league's 1128 starters failed to make it to the finish line last year.

But Armthorpe came through the batterings with robust good spirits: 'The lads turn up for league games knowing they're going to lose, but it makes no difference to their attitude. The week after we lost 83–0 to Sheffield Oaks we still had 27 players at training', says Jones.

The rare narrow defeats were hailed as triumphs: 'Anyone would think we'd won and they'd lost to look round the pub after we held Maltby to 25–16', he says.

The trip to middle of the table Stocksbridge in mid-March, their penultimate league game, showed their spirit. On a pitch high above the little South Yorkshire steel town, surrounded by dry stone walls and watched by nine men and a dog they took on an older, heavier side on a muddy, uneven, blizzardswept pitch.

They started well and scrum-half Terry Cook – known as TC1 to distinguish him from outside-half Terry Cook – predictably TC2 – dropped a superb 35 yard goal. Jonathan Davies would have been proud of it, but the referee contentiously ruled the ball hadn't touched the ground before being struck. Many struggling sides would promptly have disintegrated, but Armthorpe went on stretching their opponents.

But one look at the line-out showed why they had struggled all season. Missing their highly-promising 17 year old lock David Copeland they had hardly a forward over six feet and were dwarfed by Stocksbridge, no giants themselves.

Ever since the Markham split took most of their experienced players they've been a young side. At a level where experience can count for a great deal they were giving away several years a man. Only two players are over 25, most 21 or under. Prop and match secretary Andy Pym, 21, is one of the most experienced players. The miners who might have provided some compensating physical presence are few and far between since the local industry declined – half of the team are out of work.

Nobody thought it one of their better performances. But they battled on in the worsening blizzard to make Stocksbridge fight all the way for a 19–0 win. 'It may have looked awful, but it was great to play in. The marvellous thing about these lads is they always try for 80 minutes. They're at their best when they're behind. It's only when we get a little ahead, like last week against Market Rasen 3rds, that you get arguments. All they lack is experience and a bit of height and power', said McNally.

Stocksbridge were pleased with two more league points. But nobody walking into their clubhouse without knowing the result would have guessed that the amiably noisy group of lads packed round a bar table were the losers: 'Some of the things we try come off, some don't. But we always enjoy it', says winger Mark Cook.

They're happily ironic about their league position: 'Someone's got to be bottom – come back in a couple of years time when we're playing Leicester', says skipper Steve Christian – known as "Shirley" since his team-mates decided that an unfortunate hairdo had left him looking like Shirley Temple or second from the bottom', retorts a good-humoured voice of realism from somewhere in the group.

'The league doesn't mean a great deal to us, but we don't regret joining. Now we've taken it on we've no intention of dropping out although we've no illusions about improving dramatically', says Jones.

Encouraged by their relative improvement in the second half of the season they'll be starting again in Yorkshire Six this year, hoping they can at least claim their first league win.

Losers matter. The Tour de France cycle race, most demanding of all sporting events, awards its backmarker the "Lanterne Rouge" – recognition that to finish at all is an achievement. Skijumper Eddie Edwards – before the hype took over – and the Jamaican bobsleighers won admiration for their cheerful efforts in the Winter Olympics. And Armthorpe as much as Leicester have shown the value of rugby's brave new competitive world.

Proclamations that taking part is what matters are ten a penny in rugby, as in other amateur sports. Here for once is a team that really practises that ideal.

THE TOP 30
by Peter Jackson

Eddie Saunders, the former Coventry wing who helped Rugby win promotion to the Third Division, outscored every other English player in the senior game last season to finish with 39 tries.

Despite his record-breaking flourish, Saunders would almost certainly have been a long way behind Mark Preston had the England B wing not turned professional last March by which time he had run in 35 tries for Fylde, Lancashire and England B.

Another Fylde player, Steve Burnage, outpointed every one in England, as well as Scotland and Wales. His total of 390 took the Orrell stand-off ahead of Rugby's Chris Howard and Dusty Hare who would probably have topped 400 but for an injury which forced him to miss Leicester's closing matches.

He resumes next season within reach of raising his world points record to a staggering 7,000 since starting his career with Nottingham.

Eddie Saunders. Photo: Ray Andrews.

TRIES

Eddie Saunders *(Rugby)*	39
Mark Preston* *(Fylde)*	35
Brendan Hanavan *(Fylde)*	28
David Fairclough *(Sheffield)*	27
Jim Breeze *(Gloucester)*	25
Peter Cooley *(Waterloo)*	25
Owen Evans *(West Hartlepool)*	24
Steve Walklin *(Plymouth Albion/Bath)*	23
Barry Evans *(Leicester)*	22
Gerry Ainscough *(Orrell)*	20
Jeremy Guscott *(Bath)*	20
Kevin Norris *(Plymouth Albion)*	20
Ian Russel *(Plymouth Albion)*	20
Peter Robinson *(West Hartlepool)*	20
Steve Brown *(Broughton Park)*	20
Rory Underwood *(Leicester)*	19
Tony Swift *(Bath)*	19
Frank Packman *(Northampton)*	19
Garry Walker *(Roundhay)*	19
Jez Swarbrick *(Preston Grasshoppers)*	19
John Carr *(Bristol)*	18
David Walker *(Gosforth)*	18
Ray Bowers *(Wakefield)*	18
Paul Shillingford *(Moseley)*	18
John Bentley *(Sale)*	17
David Scully *(Wakefield)*	17
David Wadham *(Birkenhead Park)*	17
Paul Alston *(Northampton)*	16
John Lilley *(Wakefield)*	16
Ian Ralston *(Vale of Lune)*	16
Jimmy Wilde *(Broughton Park)*	16
Tony Clarke *(Morley)*	16

* Now playing Rugby League

Figures restricted to club, cup representative and international to the end of the domestic season 1987/88.

POINTS: TOP 30

	Total	Tries	Cons	Pens	Drops
Steve Burnage *(Fylde)*	390	12	78	59	3
Chris Howard *(Rugby)*	385	13	87	53	0
Dusty Hare *(Leicester)*	374	1	74	71	3
Steve Kerry *(Preston Grhprs)*	341	12	43	61	8
Ray Adamson *(Wakefield)*	336	8	77	50	0
Jon Webb *(Bristol)*	325	9	68	51	0
Ian Aitchison *(Waterloo)*	319	8	46	48	17
Gerry Ainscough *(Orrell)*	304	20	46	42	2
Kevin O'Brien *(Broughton Pk)*	303	5	59	55	0
Simon Hodgkinson *(Nottingham)*	301	3	35	69	4
Garry Walker *(Rounday)*	285	19	46	39	0
Andy Higgin *(Vale of Lune)*	279	4	43	52	7
David Johnson *(Gosforth)*	279	1	37	57	10
Martin Livesey *(Plymouth Alb)*	253	2	55	44	1
John Stabler *(West Hartlepool)*	229	3	35	47	2
Andy Finnie *(Bedford)*	228	1	37	45	5
John Graves *(Rosslyn Park)*	225	6	39	41	0
Graham Jenion *(Sale)*	198	5	32	38	0
Mark Appleson *(Headingley)*	191	11	21	35	0
John Lilley *(Wakefield)*	205	16	27	29	0
Stuart Barnes *(Bath)*	184	6	26	30	6
Simon Smith *(Richmond)*	181				
Rob Andrew *(Wasps)*	154	8	19	23	0
Stuart Thresher *(Harlequins)*	146	8	33	16	0
Dave Wadham *(Birkenhead Park)*	142	17	7	20	0
Simon Hogg *(Bristol)*	141	8	14	21	6
Tim Smith *(Gloucester)*	141	4	31	21	0
John Goodwin *(Moseley)*	135	15	15	15	0
Nick Stringer *(Wasps)*	135	1	22	29	0
Ben Rudling *(Saracens)*	134	1	14	34	0

Strange but true!

ENGLAND, who have beaten New Zealand on three occasions and have possibly the best home countries record against them, have the only unfavourable record of the same four nations in matches against Australia, having lost eight of the 13 games played against them. Ireland share the series at six wins apiece against the Wallabies, and both Scotland and Wales have favourable balances.

COURAGE CLUBS CHAMPIONSHIP

FIXTURES 1988/89

DIVISIONS 1, 2 and 3

Sat 10th September (Week 2)
1 Bristol v Orrell
1 Gloucester v Moseley
1 Harlequins v Bath
1 Leicester v Wasps
1 Rosslyn Park v Nottingham
1 Waterloo v Liverpool St Helens
2 Gosforth v Bedford
2 Headingley v Saracens
2 London Irish v Coventry
2 London Scottish v Northampton
2 London Welsh v Blackheath
2 Sale v Richmond
3 Exeter v Sheffield
3 Fylde v Askcans
3 Maidstone v Nuneaton
3 Met Police v West Harlepool
3 Plymouth v Wakefield
3 Rugby v Vale of Lune

Sat 24th September (Week 4)
1 Bath v Gloucester
1 Liverpool St Helens v Leicester
1 Moseley v Rosslyn Park
1 Nottingham v Bristol
1 Wasps v Harlequins
1 Orrell v Waterloo
2 Bedford v London Scottish
2 Blackheath v Gosforth
2 Coventry v Sale
2 Northampton v Headingley
2 Richmond v London Welsh
2 Saracens v London Irish
3 Askeans v Exeter
3 Nuneaton v Fylde
3 Sheffield v Rugby
3 Vale of Lune v Plymouth
3 Wakefield v Met Police
3 West Hartlepool v Maidstone

Sat 8th October (Week 6)
1 Bristol v Moseley
1 Gloucester v Wasps
1 Harlequins v Liverpool St Helens
1 Leicester v Orrell
1 Rosslyn Park v Bath
1 Waterloo v Nottingham
2 Gosforth v Richmond
2 Headingley v Bedford
2 London Irish v Northampton
2 London Scottish v Blackheath
2 London Welsh v Coventry
2 Sale v Saracens
3 Exeter v Nuneaton
3 Fylde v West Hartlepool
3 Maidstone v Wakefield
3 Met Police v Vale of Lune
3 Plymouth v Sheffield
3 Rugby v Askeans

Sat 22nd October (Week 8)
1 Bath v Bristol
1 Liverpool St Helens v Gloucester
1 Moseley v Waterloo
1 Nottingham v Leicester
1 Orrell v Harlequins
1 Wasps v Rosslyn Park
2 Bedford v London Irish
2 Blackheath v Headingley
2 Coventry v Gosforth
2 Northampton v Sale
2 Richmond v London Scottish
2 Saracens v London Welsh
3 Askeans v Plymouth
3 Nuneaton v Rugby
3 Sheffield v Met Police
3 Vale of Lune v Maidstone
3 Wakefield v Fylde
3 West Hartlepool v Exeter

Sat 12th November (Week 10)
1 Bristol v Harlequins
1 Moseley v Bath
1 Nottingham v Wasps
1 Orrell v Liverpool St Helens
1 Rosslyn Park v Gloucester
1 Waterloo v Leicester
2 Bedford v Coventry
2 Blackheath v Richmond
2 Gosforth v London Welsh
2 Headingley v London Irish
2 London Scottish v Sale
2 Northampton v Saracens
3 Askeans v Wakefield
3 Exeter v Met Police
3 Fylde v Maidstone
3 Nuneaton v West Hartlepool
3 Rugby v Plymouth
3 Sheffield v Vale of Lune

Sat 19th November (Week 11)
1 Bath v Orrell
1 Gloucester v Bristol

1 Harlequins v Waterloo
1 Leicester v Rosslyn Park
1 Liverpool St Helens v Nottingham
1 Wasps v Moseley
2 Coventry v Blackheath
2 London Irish v Gosforth
2 London Welsh v London Scottish
2 Richmond v Northampton
2 Sale v Headingley
2 Saracens v Bedford
3 Maidstone v Exeter
3 Met Police v Rugby
3 Plymouth v Fylde
3 Vale of Lune v Askeans
3 Wakefield v Nuneaton
3 West Hartlepool v Sheffield

Sat 26th November (Week 12)
1 Bath v Wasps
1 Leicester v Harlequins
1 Moseley v Liverpool St Helens
1 Orrell v Nottingham
1 Rosslyn Park v Bristol
1 Waterloo v Gloucester
2 Blackheath v Saracens
2 Gosforth v London Scottish
2 Headingley v London Welsh
2 London Irish v Sale
2 Northampton v Bedford
2 Richmond v Coventry
3 Fylde v Exeter
3 Nuneaton v Vale of Lune
3 Rugby v Maidstone
3 Sheffield v Askeans
3 Plymouth v Met Police
3 West Hartlepool v Wakefield

Sat 14th January (Week 18)
1 Bristol v Waterloo
1 Gloucester v Leicester
1 Liverpool St Helens v Bath
1 Nottingham v Moseley
1 Orrell v Wasps
1 Rosslyn Park v Harlequins
2 Bedford v Richmond
2 Gosfroth v Headingley
2 London Scottish v London Irish
2 London Welsh v Sale
2 Northampton v Blacheath
2 Saracens v Coventry
3 Askeans v West Hartlepool
3 Exeter v Plymouth
3 Fylde v Rugby
3 Maidstone v Met Police
3 Sheffield v Nuneton
3 Vale of Lune v Wakfield

Sat 11th March (Week 26)
1 Bath v Nottingham
1 Harlequins v Gloucester
1 Leicester v Bristol
1 Moseley v Orrell
1 Wasps v Liverpool St Helens
1 Waterloo v Rosslyn Park
2 Blackheath v Bedford
2 Coventry v Northampton
2 Headingley v London Scottish
2 London Irish v London Welsh
2 Richmond v Saracens
2 Sale v Gosforth
3 Met Police v Fylde
3 Nuneaton v Askeans
3 Plymouth v Maidstone
3 Rugby v Exeter
3 Wakefield v Sheffield
3 West Hartlepool v Vale of Lune

Sat 8th April (Week 30)
1 Bath v Waterloo
1 Liverpool St Helens v Rosslyn Park
1 Moseley v Leicester
1 Nottingham v Harlequins
1 Orrell v Gloucester
1 Wasps v Bristol
2 Bedford v London Welsh
2 Blackheath v Sale
2 Coventry v Headingley
2 Northampton v Gosforth
2 Richmond v London Irish
2 Saracens v London Scottish
3 Askeans v Met Police
3 Nuneaton v Plymouth
3 Sheffield v Maidstone
3 Vale of Lune v Fylde
3 Wakefield v Exeter
3 West Hartlepool v Rugby

Sat 22nd April (Week 32)
1 Bristol v Liverpool St Helens
1 Gloucester v Nottingham
1 Harlequins v Moseley
1 Leicester v Bath
1 Rosslyn Park v Orrell
1 Waterloo v Wasps
2 Gosforth v Saracens
2 Headingley v Richmond
2 London Irish v Blackheath
2 London Scottish v Coventry
2 London Welsh v Northampton
2 Sale v Bedford
3 Exeter v Vale of Lune
3 Fylde v Sheffield
3 Maidstone v Askeans

AREA LEAGUE NORTH

Sat 10th September (Week 2)
Broughton Park v Birmingham
Northern v Roundhay
Lichfield v Stoke
Durham City v Winnington Park
Morley v Stourbridge

Sat 24th September (Week 4)
Birmingham v Morley
Stourbridge v Durham City
Winnington Park v Lichfield
Stoke v Northern
Roundhay v Preston Grasshoppers

Sat 8th October (Week 6)
Durham City v Birmingham
Morley v Broughton Park
Preston Grasshoppers v Stoke
Northern v Winnington Park
Lichfield v Stourbridge

Sat 22nd October (Week 8)
Broughton Park v Durham City
Birmingham v Lichfield
Stourbridge v Northern
Winnington Park v Preston Grasshoppers
Stoke v Roundhay

Sat 12th November (Week 10)
Northern v Birmingham
Lichfield v Broughton Park
Durham City v Morley
Roundhay v Winnington Park
Preston Grasshoppers v Stourbridge

Sat 19th November (Week 11)
Morley v Lichfield
Broughton Park v Northern
Birmingham v Preston Grasshoppers
Stourbridge v Roundhay
Winnington Park v Stoke

Sat 26th November (Week 12)
Roundhay v Birmingham
Preston Grasshoppers v Broughton Park
Northern v Morley
Lichfield v Durham City
Stoke v Stourbridge

Sat 14th January (Week 18)
Durham City v Northern
Morley v Preston Grasshoppers
Broughton Park v Roundhay
Birmingham v Stoke
Stourbridge v Winnington Park

Sat 11th March (Week 26)
Winnington Park v Birmingham
Stoke v Broughton Park
Rounday v Morley
Preston Grasshoppers v Durham City
Northern v Lichfield

Sat 8th April (Week 30)
Lichfield v Preston Grasshoppers
Durham City v Roundhay
Morley v Stoke
Broughton Park v Winnington Park
Birmingham v Stourbridge

Sat 22nd April (Week 32)
Stourbridge v Broughton Park
Winnington Park v Morley
Stoke v Durham City
Roundhay v Lichfield
Preston Grasshoppers v Northern

AREA LEAGUE SOUTH

Sat 10th September (Week 2)
Camborne v Ealing
Salisbury v Southend
Lydney v Redruth
Havant v Stroud
Cheltenham v Sudbury

Sat 24th September (Week 4)
Ealing v Cheltenham
Sudbury v Havant
Stroud v Lydney
Redruth v Salisbury
Southend v Sidcup

Sat 8th October (Week 6)
Havant v Ealing
Sidcup v Redruth
Salisbury v Stroud
Cheltenham v Camborne
Lydney v Sudbury

Sat 22nd October (Week 8)
Camborne v Havant
Ealing v Lydney
Sudbury v Salisbury
Stroud v Sidcup
Redruth v Southend

Sat 12th November (Week 10)
Salisbury v Ealing
Lydney v Camborne
Havant v Cheltenham
Southend v Stroud
Sidcup v Sudbury

Sat 19th November (Week 11)
Cheltenham v Lydney
Camborne v Salisbury
Ealing v Sidcup
Sudbury v Southend
Stroud v Redruth

Sat 26th November (Week 12)
Southend v Ealing
Sidcup v Camborne
Salisbury v Cheltenham
Lydney v Havant
Redruth v Sudbury

Sat 14th January (Week 18)
Havant v Salisbury
Cheltenham v Sidcup
Camborne v Southend
Ealing v Redruth
Sudbury v Stroud

Sat 11th March (Week 26)
Stroud v Ealing
Redruth v Camborne
Southend v Cheltenham
Sidcup v Havant
Salisbury v Lydney

Sat 8th April (Week 30)
Lydney v Sidcup
Havant v Southend
Cheltenham v Redruth
Camborne v Stroud
Ealing v Sudbury

Sat 22nd April (Week 32)
Sudbury v Camborne
Stroud v Cheltenham
Redruth v Havant
Southend v Lydney
Sidcup v Salisbury

NORTH DIVISION ONE

Sat 10th September (Week 2)
Wigton v Hull & ER
Aspatria v Harrogate
Hartlepool Rovers v West Park
Tynedale v Otley
Kendal v Halifax

Sat 24th September (Week 4)
Hull & ER v Kendal
Halifax v Tynedale
Otley v Hartlepool Rovers
West Park v Aspatria
Harrogate v Birkenhead Park

Sat 8th October (Week 6)
Tynedale v Hull & ER
Kendal v Wigton
Birkenhead Park v West Park
Aspatria v Otley
Hartlepool Rovers v Halifax

Sat 22nd October (Week 8)
Wigton v Tynedale
Hull & ER v Hartlepool Rovers
Halifax v Aspatria
Otley v Birkenhead Park
West Park v Harrogate

Sat 12th November (Week 10)
Aspatria v Hull & ER
Hartlepool Rovers v Wigton
Tynedale v Kendal
Harrogate v Otley
Birkenhead Park v Halifax

Sat 19th November (Week 11)
Kendal v Hartlepool Rovers
Wigton v Aspatria
Hull & ER v Birkenhead Park
Halifax v Harrogate
Otley v West Park

Sat 26th November (Week 12)
Harrogate v Hull & ER
Birkenhead Park v Wigton
Aspatria v Kendal
Hartlepool Rovers v Tynedale
West Park v Halifax

Sat 14th January (Week 18)
Tynedale v Aspatria
Kendal v Birkenhead Park
Wigton v Harrogate
Hull & ER v West Park
Halifax v Otley

Sat 11th March (Week 26)
Otley v Hull & ER
West Park v Wigton
Harrogate v Kendal
Birkenhead Park v Tynedale
Aspatria v Hartlepool Rovers

Sat 8th April (Week 30)
Hartlepool Rovers v Birkenhead Park
Tynedale v Harrogate
Kendal v West Park
Wigton v Otley
Hull & ER v Halifax

Sat 22nd April (Week 32)
Halifax v Wigton
Otley v Kendal
West Park v Tynedale
Harrogate v Hartlepool Rovers
Birkenhead Park v Aspatria

NORTH DIVISION TWO

Sat 10th September (Week 2)
Davenport v Alnwick
Bradford & Bingley v Middlesbrough
Widnes v New Brigthon
Sandal v Carlisle
Lymm v Huddersfield

Sat 24th September (Week 4)
Alnwick v Lymm
Huddersfield v Sandal
Carlisle v Widnes
New Brighton v Bradford & Bingley
Middlesbrough v Wharfedale

Sat 8th October (Week 6)
Sandal v Alnwick
Lymm v Davenport
Wharfedale v New Brighton
Bradford & Bingley v Carlisle
Widnes v Huddersfield

Sat 22nd October (Week 8)
Davenport v Sandal

Alnwick v Widnes
Huddersfield v Bradford & Bingley
Carlisle v Wharfedale
New Brighton v Middlesbrough

Sat 12th November (Week 10)
Bradford & Bingley v Alnwick
Widnes v Davenport
Sandal v Lymm
Middlesbrough v Carlisle
Wharfedale v Huddersfield

Sat 19th November (Week 11)
Lymm v Widnes
Davenport v Bradford & Bingley
Alnwick v Wharfedale
Huddersfield v Middlesbrough
Carlisle v New Brighton

Sat 26th November (Week 12)
Middlesbrough v Alnwick
Wharfedale v Davenport
Bradford & Bingley v Lymm
Widnes v Sandal
New Brighton v Huddersfield

hSat 14th January (Week 18)
Sandal v Bradford & Bingley
Lymm v Wharfedale
Davenport v Middlesbrough
Alnwick v New Brighton
Huddersfield v Carlisle

Sat 8th April (Week 30)
Widnes v Wharfedale
Sandal v Middlesbrough
Lymm v New Brighton
Davenpot v Carlisle
Alnwick v Huddersfield

Sat 22nd April (Week 32)
Huddersfield v Davenport
Carlisle v Lymm
New Brighton v Sandal
Middlesbrough v Widnes
Wharfedale v Bradford & Bingley

NORTH WEST DIVISION ONE

Sat 10th September (Week 2)
Sandbach v Egremont
Wirral v Sedgley Park
Chester v Wilmslow
Wigan v Rochdale
Manchester v Caldy

Sat 24th September (Week 4)
Egremont v Manchester
Caldy v Wigan
Rochdale v Chester
Wilmslow v Wirral
Sedgley Park v Mid-Cheshire College

Sat 8th October (Week 6)
Wigan v Egremont
Manchester v Sandbach
Mid-Cheshire College v Wilmslow
Wirral v Rochdale
Chester v Caldy

Sat 22nd October (Week 8)
Sandbach v Wigan
Egremont v Chester
Caldy v Wirral
Rochdale v Mid-Cheshire College
Wilmslow v Sedgley Park

Sat 12th November (Week 10)
Wirral v Egremont
Chester v Sandbach
Wigan v Manchester
Sedgley Park v Rochdale
Mid-Cheshire College v Caldy

Sat 19th November (Week 11)
Manchester v Chester
Sandbach v Wirral
Egremont v Mid-Chesire College
Caldy v Sedgley Park
Rochdale v Wilmslow

Sat 26th November (Week 12)
Sedgley Park v Egremont
Mid-Cheshire College v Sandbach
Wirral v Manchester
Chester v Wigan
Wilmslow v Caldy

Sat 14th January (Week 18)
Wigan v Wirral
Manchester v Mid-Cheshire College
Sandbach v Sedgley Park
Egremont v Wilmslow
Caldy v Rochdale

Sat 11th March (Week 26)
Rochdale v Egremont
Wilmslow v Sandbach
Sedgley Park v Manchester
Mid-Cheshire College v Wigan
Wirral v Chester

Sat 8th April (Week 30)
Chester v Mid-Cheshire College
Wigan v Sedgley Park
Manchester v Wilmslow
Sandbach v Rochdale
Egremont v Caldy

Sat 22nd April (Week 32)
Caldy v Sandbach
Rochdale v Manchester
Wilmslow v Wigan
Sedgley Park v Chester
Mid-Cheshire College v Wirral

NORTH WEST DIVISION ONE

Sat 10th September (Week 2)
Burnage v Macclesfield
Cockermouth v Blackburn
Penrith v Old Aldwinians
Workington v Leigh
Netherall v Southport

Sat 24th September (Week 4)
Macclesfield v Netherall
Southport v Workington
Leigh v Penrith
Old Aldwinians v Cockermouth
Blackburn v Merseyside Police

Sat 8th October (Week 6)
Workington v Macclesfield
Netherall v Burnage
Merseyside Police v Old Aldwinians
Cockermouth v Leigh
Penrith v Southport

Sat 22nd October (Week 8)
Burnage v Workington
Macclesfield v Penrith
Southport v Cockermouth
Leigh v Merseyside Police
Old Aldwinians v Blackburn

Sat 12th November (Week 10)
Cockermouth v Macclesfield
Penrith v Burnage
Workington v Netherall
Blackburn v Leigh
Merseyside Police v Southport

Sat 19th November (Week 11)
Netherall v Penrith
Burnage v Cockermouth
Macclesfield v Merseyside Police
Southport v Blackburn
Leigh v Old Aldwinians

Sat 26th November (Week 12)
Blackburn v Macclesfield
Merseyside Police v Burnage
Cockermouth v Nerthall
Penrith v Workington
Old Aldwinians v Southport

Sat 14th January (Week 18)
Workington v Cockermouth
Netherall v Merseyside Police
Burnage v Blackburn
Macclesfield v Old Aldwinians
Southport v Leigh

Sat 11th March (Week 26)
Leigh v Macclesfield
Old Aldwinians v Burnage
Blackburn v Netherall
Merseyside Police v Workington
Cockermouth v Penrith

Sat 8th April (Week 30)
Penrith v Merseyside Police
Workington v Blackburn
Netherall v Old Aldwinians
Burnage v Leigh
Macclesfield v Southport

Sat 22nd April (Week 32)
Southport v Burnage
Leigh v Netherall
Old Aldwinians v Workington
Blackburn v Penrith
Merseyside Police v Cockermouth

NW/DIVISION EAST NORTH ONE

Sat 10th September (Week 2)
Toc H v Vickers
Flettwood v Littleborough
Eccles v Moresby
Windermere v Heaton Moor
De la Salle v Oldham

Sat 24th September (Week 4)
Vickers v De la Salle
Oldham v Windermere
Heaton Moor v Eccles
Moresby v Fleetwood
Littleborough v Furness

Sat 8th October (Week 6)
Windermere v Vickers
De la Salle v Tock H
Furness v Moresby
Fleetwood v Heaton Moor
Eccles v Oldham

St 22nd October (Week 8)
Toc H v Windermere
Vickers v Eccles
Oldham v Fleetwood
Heaton Moor v Furness
Moresby v Littleborough

Sat 12th November (Week 10)
Fleetwood v Vickers
Eccles v Toc H
Windermere v De la Salle
Littleborough v Heaton Moor
Furness v Oldham

Sat 19th November (Week 11)
De la Salle v Eccles
Toc H v Fleetwood
Vickers v Furness
Oldham v Littleborough
Heaton Moor v Moresby

Sat 26th November (Week 12)
Littleborough v Vickers
Furness v Toc H
Fleetwood v De la Salle
Eccles v Windermere
Moresby v Oldham

Sat 14th January (Week 18)
Windermere v Fleetwood
De la Salle v Furness
Toc H v Littleborough
Vickers v Moresby
Oldham v Heaton Moor

Sat 11th March (Week 26)
Heaton Moor v Vickers
Moresby v Toc H
Littleborough v De la Salle
Furness v Windermere
Fleetwood v Eccles

Sat 8th April (Week 30)
Eccles v Furness
Windermere v Littleborough
De la Salle v Moresby
Toc H v Heaton Moor
Vickers v Oldham

Sat 22nd April (Week 32)
Oldham v Toc H
Heaton Moor v De la Salle
Moresby v Windermere
Littleborough v Eccles
Furness v Fleetwood

NW/DIVISION EAST ONE

Sat 10th September (Week 2)
Calder Vale v Ashton on Mersey
Old Bedians v Metrovick
Kersal v Crewe & Nantwich
Colne & Nelson v Congleton
Metrovick v Old Salians

Sat 8th October (Week 6)
Colne & Nelson v Ashton on Mesey
Bolton v Calder Vale
Old Salians v Crewe & Nantwich
Old Bedians v Congleton
Kersal v Tyldesley

Sat 22nd October (Week 8)
Calder Vale v Colne & Nelson
Ashton on Mersey v Kersal
Tyldesley v Old Bedians
Congleton v Old Salians
Crewe & Nantwich v Metrovick

Sat 12th November (Week 10)
Old Bedians v Ashton on Mersey
Kersal v Calder Vale
Colne & Nelson v Bolton
Metrovick v Congleton
Old Salians v Tyldesley

Sat 19th November (Week 11)
Bolton v Kersal
Calder Vale v Old Bedians
Ashton on Mersey v Old Salians
Tyldesley v Metrovick
Congleton v Crewe & Nantwich

Sat 26th November (Week 12)
Metrovick v Ashton on Mersey
Old Salians v Calder Vale
Old Bedians v Bolton
Kersal v Colne & Nelson
Crewe & Nantwich v Tyldesley

Sat 14th January (Week 18)
Colne & Nelson v Old Bedians
Bolton v Old Salians
Calder v Metrovick
Ashton on Mersey v Crewe & Nantwich
Tyldesley v Congleton

Sat 11th March (Week 26)
Congleton v Ashton on Mersey
Crewe & Nantwich v Calder Vale
Metrovick v Bolton
Old Salians v Colne & Nelson
Old Bedians v Kersal

Sat 8th April (Week 30)
Kersal v Old Salians
Colne & Nelson v Metrovick
Bolton v Crew & Nantwich
Calder Vale v Congleton
Ashton on Mersey v Tyldesley

Sat 22nd April (Week 32)
Tyldesley v Calder Vale
Congleton v Bolton
Crewe & Nantwich v Colne & Nelson
Metrovick v Kersal
Old Salians v Old Bedians

NW DIVISION EAST TWO

Sat 10th September (Week 2)
Broughton v Bowden
North Manchester v Grt Manchester FS
Ashton under Lyne v Oldham College
Chorley v Agecroft
Bury v Manchester YMCA
Dukinfield v Marple

Sat 24th September (Week 4)
Marple v Broughton
Bowden v Bury
Manchester YMCA v Chorley
Agecroft v Ashton under Lyne
Oldham College v North Manchester
Grt Manchester FS v Dukinfield

Sat 8th October (Week 6)
Chorley v Bowden
Bury v Broughton
Dukinfield v Oldham College
North Manchester v Agecroft
Ashton under Lyne v Manchester YMCA
Grt Manchester FS v Marple

Sat 22nd October (Week 8)
Marple v Bury
Broughton v Chorley
Bowden v Ashton under Lyne
Manchester YMCA v North Manchester
Agecroft v Dukinfield
Oldham Collge v Grt Manchester FS

Sat 12th November (Week 10)
North Manchester v Bowden
Ashton under Lyne v Broughton
Chorley v Bury
Grt Manchester FS v Agecroft
Dukinfield v Manchester YMCA
Oldham College v Marple

Sat 19th November (Week 11)
Marple v Chorley
Bury v Ashton under Lyne
Broughton v North Manchester
Bowden v Dukinfield
Manchester YMCA v Grt Manchester FS
Agecroft v Oldham College

Sat 26th November (Week 12)
Grt Manchester FS v Bowden
Dukinfield v Broughton
North Manchester v Bury
Ashton under Lyne v Chorley
Oldham College v Manchester YMCA
Agecroft v Marple

Sat 14th January (Week 18)
Marple v Ashton under Lyne
Chorely v North Manchester
Bury v Dukinfield
Broughton v Grt Manchester FS
Bowden v Oldham College
Manchester YMCA v Agecroft

Sat 11th March (Week 26)
Agecroft v Bowden
Oldham College v Broughton
Grt Manchester FS v Bury
Dukinfield v Chorley
North Manchester v Ashton under Lyne
Manchester YMCA v Marple

Sat 8th April (Week 30)
Marple v North Manchester
Ahston under Lyne v Dukinfield
Chorley v Grt Manchester FS
Bury v Oldham College
Broughton v Agecroft
Bowden v Manchester YMCA

Sat 22nd April (Week 32)
Manchester YMCA v Broughton
Agecroft v Bury
Oldham College v Chorley
Grt Manchester FS v Ashton under Lyne
Dukinfield v North Manchester
Bowden v Marple

NW DIVISION NORTH ONE

Sat 10th September (Week 2)
Kirkby Lonsdale v Rossendale
Keswick v St Benedicts
Creighton v Thornton Cleveleys
Carnforth v British Steel

Sat 24th September (Week 4)
British Steel v Creighton
Thornton Clevelsy v Keswick
St Benedicts v Kirkby Lonsdale
Rossendale v Millom

Sat 8th October (Week 6)
Carnforth v Blackpool
Millom v St Benedicts
Kirkby Lonsdale v Thornton Cleveleys
Keswick v British Steel

Sat 22nd October (Week 8)
Blackpool v Creighton
British Steel v Kirkby Lonsdale
Thornton Cleveleys v Millom
St Beneicts v Rossendale

Sat 12th November (Week 10)
Keswick v Blackpool
Creighton v Camforth
Rossendal v Thornton Cleveleys
Millom v British Steel

Sat 19th November (Week 11)
Carnforth v Keswick
Blackpool v Kirkby Lonsdale
British Steel v Rossendale
Thornton Cleveleys v St Benedicts

Sat 26th November (Week 12)
Millom v Blackpool
Kirkby Lonsdale v Carnforth
Keswick v Creighton
St Benedicts v British Steel

Sat 14th January (Week 18)
Creighton v Kirkby Lonsdale
Carnforth v Millom
Blackpool v Rossendale
British Steel v Thornton Cleveleys

Sat 11th March (Week 26)
St Benedicts v Blackpool
Rossendale v Carnforth
Millom v Creighton
Kirkby Lonsdale v Keswick

Sat 8th April (Week 30)
Keswick v Millom
Creighton v Rossendale
Carnforth v St Benedicts
Blackpool v Thornton Cleveleys

Sat 22nd April (Week 32)
British Steel v Blackpool
Thornton Cleveleys v Carnforth
St Benedicts v Creighton
Rossendale v Keswick
Millom v Kirkby Lonsdale

NW DIVISION NORTH TWO

Sat 10th September (Week 2)
Smith Bros v Upper Eden

Sat 24th September (Week 4)
Ambleside v Clietheroe
Upper Eden v Whitehaven

Sat 8th October (Week 8)
Lancaster Moor Hosp v Ambleside

Sat 22nd October (Week 8)
Ambleside v Silloth

Sat 12th November (Week 10)
Smith Bros v Ambleside
Lancaster Moor Hosp v Clitheroe

Sat 19th November (Week 11)
Clitheroe v Silloth
Ambleside v Whitehaven

Sat 26th November (Week 12)
Upper Eden v Ambleside
Smith Bros v Clitheroe
Silloth v Lancaster Moor Hosp

Sat 14th January (Week 18)
Lancaster Moor Hosp v Smith Bros
Clitheroe v Whitehaven

Sat 11th March (Week 26)
Upper Eden v Clitheroe
Whitehaven v Lancaster Moor Hosp
Smith Bros v Silloth

Sat 8th April (Wek 30)
Silloth v Whitehaven
Lancaster Moor Hosp v Upper Eden

Sat 22nd April (Week 32)
Upper Eden v Silloth
Whitehaven ve Smith Bros

NW DIVISION WEST ONE

Sat 10th September (Week 2)
Birchfield v Aspull
Old Isto nians v Ormskirk
Warrington v Old parkonians
Liverpool Collegiate OB v St Edwards OB
Newton le Willows v Douglas (IOM)

Sat 24th September (Week 4)
Aspull b Newton le Willows
Douglas (IOM) v Liverpool Collegiate OB
St Edwards OB v Warrington
Old Parkonians v Old Istonians
Ormskirk v Ruskin Park

Sat 8th October (Week 6)
Liverpool Collegiate OB v Aspull
Newton le Willows v Birchfield
Ruskin Park v Old Parkonians
Old Istonians v St Edwards OB
Warrington v Douglas (IOM)

Sat 22nd October (Week 8)
Birchfield v Liverpool Collegiate OB
Aspull v Warrington
Douglas (IOM) v Old Istonians
St Edwards OB v Ruskin Park
Old Parkonians v Ormskirk

Sat 12th November (Week 10)
Old Istonians v Aspull
Warrington v Birchfield
Liverpool Collegiate OB v Newton le Willows
Ormskirk v St Edwards OB
Ruskin Park v Douglas (IOM)

Sat 19th November (Week 11)
Newton le Willows v Warrington
Birchfield v Old Istonians
Aspull v Ruskin Park
Douglas (IOM) v Ormskirk
St Edwards OB v Old Parkonians

Sat 26th November (Week 12)
Ormskirk v Aspull
Ruskin Park v Birchfield
Old Istonians v Newton le Willows
Warrington v Liverpool Collegiate OB
Old Parkonians b Douglas (OIM)

Sat 14th January (Week 18)
Liverpool Collegiate OB v Old Istonians
Newton le Willows v Ruskin Park
Birchfield v Ormskirk
Aspull v Old Parkonians
Douglas (IOM) v St Edwards OB

Sat 11th March (Week 26)
St Edwards OB v Aspull
Olk Parkonians v Birchfield
Ormskirk v Neton le Willows
Ruskin Park v Liverpool Collegiate OB
Old Istonians v Warrington

Sat 8th April (Week 30)
Warrington v Ruskin Park
Liverpool Collegiate OB v Ormskirk
Newton le Willows v Old Parkonians
Birchfield v St Edwards OB
Aspull v Douglas (IOM)

Sat 22nd April (Week 32)
Douglas (IOM) v Birchfield
St Edwards OB v Newton le Willows
Old Parkonians v Liverpool Collegiate OB
Ormskirk v Warrington
Ruskin Park v Old Istonians

COURAGE
CLUBS CHAMPIONSHIP

NW DIVISION WEST TWO

Sat 10th September (Week 2)
South Liverpool v Chester College
Port Sunlight v Sefton
Old Anselmians v Eagle
Old Rockferrians v Vulcan
Hightown v Halton

Sat 24th September (Week 4)
Chester College v Hightown
Halton v Old Rockferrians
Vulcan v Old Anselmians
Eagle v Port Sunlight
Sefton v Oldershaw

Sat 8th October (Week 6)
Old Rockferrians v Chester College
Hightown v South Liverpool
Oldershaw v Eagle
Port Sunlight v Vulcan
Old Anselmians v Halton

Sat 22nd October (Week 8)
South Liverpool v Old Rockferrians
Chester College v Old Anselmians
Halton v Port Sunlight
Vulcan v Oldershaw
Eagle v Sefton

Sat 12th November (Week 10)
Port Sunlight v Chester College
Old Anselmians v South Liverpool
Old Rockferrians v Hightown
Sefton v Vulcan
Oldershaw v Halton

Sat 19th November (Week 11)
Hightown v Old Anselmians
South Liverpool v Port Sunlight
Chester College v Oldershaw
Halton v Sefton
Vulcan v Eagle

Sat 26th November (Week 12)
Sefton v Chester College
Oldershaw v South Liverpool
Port Sunlight v Hihtown
Old Rockferrians v Old Anselmians
Eagle v Halton

Sat 14th January (Week 18)
Old Rockferrians v Port Sunlight
Hightown v Oldershaw
South Liverpool v Sefton
Chester College v Eagle
Halton v Vulcan

Sat 11th March (Week 26)
Vulcan v Chester College
Eagle v South Liverpool
Sefton v Hightown
Oldershaw v Old Rockferrians
Port Sunlight v Old Anselmians

Sat 8th April (Week 30)
Old Anselmians v Oldershaw
Old Rockferrians v Sefton
Hightown v Eagle
South Liverpool v Vulcan
Chester College v Halton

Sat 22nd April (Week 32)
Halton v South Liverpool
Vulcan v Hightown
Eagle v Old Rockferrians
Sefton v Old Anselmians
Oldershaw v Port Sunlight

NW DIVISION WEST THREE

Sat 10th September (Week 2)
St Mary's OB v Lucas
Hoylake v Prescot Rainhill
Helsby v Shell Stanlow
Wallasey v Wigan College
Burtonwood v Mossley Hill
Gentlemen of Moore v Shell Carrington

Sat 8th October (Week 6)
Wallasey v Lucas
Burtonwood v St Mary's OB
Gentlemen of Moore v Shell Stanlow
Hoylake v Wigan College
Helsby v Mossley Hill
Prescot Rainhill v Shell Carrington

Sat 12th November (Week 10)
Hoylake v Lucas
Helsby v St Mary's OB
Wallasey v Burtonwood
Prescot Rainhill v Wigan College
Gentlemen of Moore v Mossley Hill
Shell Stanlow v Shell Carrington

Sat 19th November (Week 11)
Shell Carrington v Wallasey
Burtonwood v Helsby
St Mary's OB v Hoylake
Lucas v Gentlemen of Moore
Mossley Hill v Prescot Rainhill
Wigan College v Shell Stanlow

Sat 26th November (Week 12)
Prescot Rainhill v Lucas
Gentlemen of Moore v St Mary's OB
Hoylake v Burtonwwod
Helsby v Wallasey
Shell Stanlow v Mossley Hill
Wigan College v Shell Carrington

Sat 14th January (Week 18)
Shell Carrington v Helsby
Wallasey v Hoylake
Burtonwood v Gentlemen of Moore
St Mary's OB v Prescot Rainhill
Lucas v Shell Stanlow
Mossley Hill v Wigan College

Sat 11th March (Week 26)
Wigan College v Lucas
Shell Stanlow v St Mary's OB
Prescot Rainhill v Burtonwood
Gentlemen of Moore v Wallasey
Hoylake v Helsby
Mossley Hill v Shell Carrington

Sat 8th April (Week 30)
Shell Carrington v Hoylake
Helsby v Gentlemen of Moore
Wallasey v Prescot Rainhill
Burtonwood v Shell Stanlow
St Mary's OB v Wigan Tech
Lucas v Mossley Hill

Sat 22nd April (Week 32)
Mossley Hill v St Mary's OB
Wigan College v Burtonwood
Shell Stanlow v Wallasey
Prescot Rainhill v Helsby
Gentlemen of Moore v Hoylake
Lucas v Shell Carrington

NORTH EAST DIVISION ONE

Sat 10th September (Week 2)
Gateshell Fell v Blaydon
Old Brodleians v Novocastrians
Morpeth v Rotherham
Stockton v Keighley
Westoe v Thornesians

Sat 24th September (Week 4)
Blaydon v Westoe
Thronesians v Stockton
Keighley v Morpeth
Rotherham v Old Brodleians
Novocastrians v Old Crossleyians

Sat 8th October (Week 6)
Stockton v Blaydon
Westoe v Gateshead Fell
Old Crossleyians v Rotherham
Old Brodleians v Keighley
Morpeth v Thornensians

Sat 22nd October (Week 8)
Gateshead Fell v Stockton
Blaydon v Morpeth
Thornensians v Old Brodleians
Keighley v Old Crossleyians
Rotherham v Novocastrians

Sat 12th November (Week 10)
Old Brodleians v Blaydon
Morpeth v Gateshead Fell
Stockton v Westoe
Novocastians v Keighley
Old Crossleyians v Thornensians

Sat 19th November (Week 11)
Westoe v Morpeth
Gateshead Fell v Old Brodleians
Blaydon v Old Crossleyians
Thornensians v Novocastrians
Keighley v Rotherham

Sat 26th November (Week 12)
Novocastrians v Blaydon
Old Crossleyians v Gateshead Fell
Old Brodleians v Westoe
Morpeth v Stockton
Rotherham v Thornensians

Sat 14th January (Week 18)
Stockton v Old Brodleians
Westoe v Old Crossleyians
Gateshead Fell v Novocastrians
Blaydon v Rotherham
Thornensians v Keighley

Sat 11th March (Week 26)
Keighley v Blaydon
Rotherham v Gateshead Fell
Novocastrians v Westoe
Old Crossleyinas v Stockton
Old Brodleians v Morpeth

Sat 8th April (Week 30)
Morpeth v Old Crossleyians
Stockton v Novocastrians
Westoe v Rotherham
Gateshead Fell v Keighley
Blaydon v Thornensians

Sat 22nd April (Week 32)
Thornensians v Gateshead Fell
Keighley v Westoe
Rotherham v Stockton
Novocastrians v Morpeth
Old Crossleyians v Old Brodleians

NORTH EAST DIVISION TWO

Sat 10th September (Week 2)
Beverley v Newcastle University
Old Hymerians v Pontefract
Ripon v Ryton
Selby v Blyth
Roundhegians v York

Sat 24th September (Week 4)
Newcastle University v Roundhegians
York v Selby
Blyth v Ripon
Ryton v Old Hymerians
Pontefract v Pocklington

Sat 8th October (Week 6)
Selby v Newcastle University
Roundhegians v Beverley
Pocklington v Ryton
Old Hymerians v Blyth
Ripon v York

Sat 12th November (Week 10)
Old Hymerians v Newcastle University
Ripon v Beverley
Selby v Roundhegians
Pontefract v Blyth
Pockoington v York

Sat 19th November (Week 11)
Roundhegians v Ripon
Beverley v Old Hymerians
Newcastle University v Pocklington
York v Pontefract
Blyth v Ryton

Sat 26th November (Week 12)
Pontefract v Newcastle University
Pocklington v Beverley
Old Hymerians v Roundhegians
Ripon v Selby
Ryton v York

Sat 14th January (Week 18)
Selby v Old Hymerians
Roundhegians v Pocklington
Beverley v Pontefract
Newcastle University v Ryton
York v Blyth

Sat 11th March (Week 26)
Blyth v Newcastle University
Ryton v Beverley
Pontefract v Roundhegians
Pocklington v Selby
Old Hymerians v Ripon

Sat 8th April (Week 30)
Ripon v Pocklington
Selby v Pontefract
Roundhegians v Ryton
Beverley v Blyth
Newcastle University v York

Sat 22nd April (Week 32)
York v Beverley
Blyth v Roundhegians
Ryton v Selby
Pontefract v Ripon
Pocklington v Old Hymerians

YORKSHIRE DIVISION ONE

Sat 10th September (Week 2)
Bramley v Moortown
Goole v Barnsley
Driffield v North Ribblesdale
Cleckheaton v West Park Bramhope
Castleford v Huddersfield YMCA

Sat 24th September (Week 4)
Moortown v Castleford
Huddersfield YMCA v Cleckheaton
West Park Bramhope v Driffield
North Ribblesdale v Goole
Barnsley v Hemsworth

Sat 8th October (Week 6)
Cleckheaton v Moortown
Castleford v Bramley
Hemsworth v North Ribblesdale
Goole v West Prk Bramhope
Driffield v Huddersfield YMCA

Sat 22nd October (Week 8)
Bramley v Cleckheaton
Moortown v Driffield
Huddersfield YMCA v Goole
West Park Bramhope v Hemsworth
North Ribblesdale v Barnsley

Sat 12th November (Week 10)
Goole v Moortown
Driffield v Bramley
Cleckheaton v Castleford
Barnsley v West Park Bramhope
Hemsworth v Huddersfield YMCA

Sat 19th November (Week 11)
Castleford v Driffield
Bramley v Goole
Moortown v Hemsworth
Huddersfield YMCA v Barnsley
West Park Bramhope v North Ribblesdale

Sat 26th November (Week 12)
Barnsley v Moortown
Hemsworth v Bramley
Goole v Castleford
Driffield v Cleckheaton
North Ribblesdale v Huddersfield YMCA

Sat 14th January (Week 18)
Cleckheaton v Goole
Castleford v Hemsworth
Bramley v Barnsley
Moortown v North Ribblesdale
Huddersfield YMCA v West Park Bramhope

Sat 11th March (Week 26)
West Park Bramhope v Moortown
North Ribblesdale v Bramley
Barnsley v Castleford
Hemsworth v Cleckheaton
Goole v Driffield

Sat 8th April (Week 30)
Driffield v Hemsworth
Cleckheaton v Barnsley
Castleford v North Ribblesdale
Bramley v West Park Bramhope
Moortown v Huddersfield YMCA

Sat 22nd April (Week 32)
Huddersfield YMCA v Bramley
West Park Bramhope v Castleford
North Ribblesdale v Cleckheaton
Barnsley v Driffield
Hemsworth v Goole

YORKSHIRE DIVISION TWO

Sat 10th September (Week 2)
York RI v Doncaster
Malton & Norton v Scarborough
Bridlington v Marist
Ionians v Wath
Ilkley v Wheatley Hills

Sat 24th September (Week 4)
Doncaster v Ilkley
Wheatley Hills v Ionians
Wath v Bridlington
Marist v Malton & Norton
Scarborough v Sheffield Tigers

Sat 8th October (Week 6)
Ionians v Doncaster
Ilkley v York RI
Sheffield Tigers v Marist
Malton & Norton v Wath
Bridlington v Wheatley Hills

Sat 22nd October (Week 8)
York RI v Ionians
Doncaster v Bridlington
Wheatley Hills v Malton & Norton
Wath v Sheffield Tigers
Marist v Scarborough

Sat 12th November (Week 10)
Malton & Norton v Doncaster
Bridlington v York RI
Ionians v Ilkley
Scarborough v Wath
Sheffield Tigers v Wheatley Hills

Saturday 19th November (Week 11)
Ilkley v Bridlington
York RI v Malton & Norton
Doncaster v Sheffield Tigers
Wheatley Hills v Scarborough
Wath v Marist

Sat 26th November (Week 12)
Scarborough v Doncaster
Ilkley v Sheffield Tigers
Malton & Norton v Ionians
Marist v Wheatley Hills

Sat 14th January (Week 18)
Ionians v Malton & Norton
Ilkley v Sheffield Tigers
York RI v Scarborough
Doncaster v Marist
Wheatley Hills v Wath

Sat 11th March (Week 26)
Wath v Doncaster
Marist v York RI
Scarborough v Ilkley
Sheffield Tigers v Ionians
Malton & Norton v Bridlington

Sat 8th April (Week 30)
Bridlington v Sheffield Tigers
Ionians v Scarborough
Ilkley v Marist
York RI v Wath
Doncaster v Wheatley Hills

Sat 22nd April (Week 32)
Wheatley Hills v York RI
Wath v Ilkley
Marist v Ionians
Scarborough v Bridlington
Sheffield Tigers v Malton & Norton

YORKSHIRE DIVISION THREE

Sat 10th September (Week 2)
Old Modernians v Baildon
Leeds CSSA v Wibsey
Knottingley v Rodillians
Heath v Airebronians
Leodiensians v Yarnbury

Sat 24th September (Week 4)
Baildon v Leodiensians
Yarnbury v Heath
Airebronians v Knottingley
Rodillians v Leeds CSSA
Wibsey v Old Otliensians

Sat 8th October (Week 6)
Heath v Baildon
Leodiensians v Old Modernians
Old Otliensians v Rodillians
Leeds CSSA v Airebronians
Knottingley v Yarnbury

Sat 22nd October (Week 8)
Old Modernians v Heath
Baildon v Knottingley
Yarnbury v Leeds CSSA
Airebronians v Old Otliensians
Rodillians v Wibsey

Sat 12th November (Week 10)
Leeds CSSA v Baildon
Knottingley v Old Modernians
Heath v Leodiensians
Wibsey v Airebronians
Old Otliensians v Yarnbury

Sat 19th November (Week 11)
Leodiensians v Knottingley
Old Modernians v Leeds CSSA
Baildon v Old Otliensians
Yarnbury v Wibsey
Airebronians v Rodillians

Sat 26th November (Week 12)
Wibsey v Baildon
Old Otliensians v Old Modernians
Leeds CSSA v Leodiensians
Knottingley v Heath
Rodillians v Yarnbury

Sat 14th January (Week 18)
Heath v Leeds CSSA
Leodiensians v Old Otliensians
Old Modernians v Wibsey
Baildon v Rodillians
Yarnbury v Airebronians

Sat 11th March (Week 26)
Airebronians v Baildon
Rodillians v Old Modernians
Wibsey v Leodiensians
Old Otliensians v Heath
Leeds CSSA v Knottingley

Sat 8th April (Week 30)
Knottingley v Old Otliensians
Heath v Wibsey
Leodiensians v Rodillians
Old Modernians b Airebronians
Baildon v Yarnbury

Sat 22nd April (Week 32)
Yarnbury v Old Modernians
Airebronians v Leodiensians
Rodillians v Heath
Wibsey v Knottingley
Old Otliensians v Leeds CSSA

YORKSHIRE DIVISION FOUR

Sat 10th September (Week 2)
Old Rishworthians v Halifax Vandals
Leeds YMCA v West Leeds
Hullensians v Wetherby
Hessle v Northallerton
Dinnington v Yorkshire CW

Sat 24th September (Week 4)
Halifax Vandals v Dinington
Yorkshire CW v Hessle
Northallerton v Hullensians
Wetherby v Leeds YMCA
West Leeds v Bradford Salem

Sat 8th October (Week 6)
Hessle v Halifax Vandals
Dinnington v Old Rishworthians
Bradford Salem v Wetherby
Leeds YMCA v Northallerton
Hullensians v Yorkshire CW

Sat 22nd October (Week 8)
Old Rishworthians v Hessle
Halifax Vandals v Hullensians
Yorkshire CW v Leeds YMCA
Northallerton v Bradford Salem
Wetherby v West Leeds

Sat 12th November (Week 10)
Leeds YMCA v Halifax Vandals
Hullensians v Old Rishworthians
Hessle v Dinnington
West Leeds v Northallerton
Bradford v Yorkshire CW

Sat 19th November (Week 11)
Dinnington v Hullensians
Old Rishworthians v Leeds YMCA
Halifax Vandals v Bradford Salem
Yorkshire CW v West Leeds
Northallerton v Wetherby

Sat 26th November (Week 12)
West Leeds v Halifax Vandals
Bradford Salem v Old Rishworthians
Leeds YMCA v Dinnington
Hullensians v Hessle
Wetherby v Yorkshire CW

Sat 14th January (Week 18)
Hessle v Leeds YMCA
Dinnington v Bradford Salem
Old Rishworthians v West Leeds
Halifax Vandals v Wetherby
Yorkshire CW v Northallerton

Sat 11th March (Week 26)
Northallerton v Halifax Vandals
Wetherby v Old Rishworthians
West Leeds v Dinnington
Bradford Salem v Hessle
Leeds YMCA v Hullensians

Sat 8th April (Week 30)
Jullensians v Bradford Salem
Hessle v West Leeds
Dinnington v Wetherby
Old Rishworhtians v Northallerton
Halifax Vandals v Yorkshire CW

Sat 22nd April (Week 32)
Yorkshire CW v Old Rishworthians
Northallerton v Dinnington
Wetherby v Hessle
West Leeds v Hullensians
Bradford Salem v Leeds YMCA

YORKSHIRE DIVISION FIVE

Sat 10th September (Week 2)
Skipton v BP Chemicals
Ossett v Burley
Leeds Corinthians v Rowntrees
Sheffield Oaks v Yorkshire Main
Hornsea v Bridon

Sat 24th September (Week 4)
BP Chemicals v Hornsea
Bridon v Sheffield Oaks
Yorkshire Main v Leeds Corinthians
Rowntrees v Ossett
Burley v Phoenix Park

Sat 8th October (Week 6)
Sheffield Oaks v BP Chemicals
Hornsea v Skipton
Phoenix Park v Rowntrees
Ossett v Yorkshire Main
Leeds Corinthians v Bridon

Sat 22nd October (Week 8)
Skipton v Sheffield Oaks
CP Chemicals v Leeds Corinthians
Bridon v Ossett
Yorkshire Main v Phoenix Park
Rowntrees v Burley

Sat 12th November (Week 10)
Ossett v BP Chemicals
Leeds Corinthians v Skipton
Sheffield Oaks v Hornsea
Burley v Yorkshire Main
Phoenix Park v Bridon

Sat 19th November (Week 11)
Hornsea v Leeds Corinthians
Skipton v Ossett
BP Chemicals v Phoenix Park
Bridon v Burley
Yorkshire Mian v Rowntrees

Sat 26th November (Week 12)
Burley v BP Chemicals
Phoenix Park v Skipton
Ossett v Hornsea
Leeds Corinthians v Sheffield Oaks
Rowntrees v Bridon

Sat 14th January (Week 18)
Sheffield Oaks v Ossett
Hornsea v Phoenix Park
Skipton v Burley
BP Chemicals v Rowntrees
Bridon v Yorkshire Main

Sat 11th March (Week 26)
Yorkshire Main v BP Chemicals
Rowntrees v Skipton
Burley v Hornsea
Phoenix v Sheffield Oaks
Ossett v Leeds Corinthians

Sat 8th April (Week 30)
Leeds Corinthians v Phoenix Park
Sheffield Oaks v Burley
Hornsea v Rowntrees
Skipton v Yorkshire Main
BP Chemicals v Bridon

Sat 22nd April (Week 32)
Bridon v Skipton
Yorkshire Main v Hornsea
Rowntrees v Sheffield Oaks
Burley v Leeds Corinthians
Phoenix Park v Ossett

YORKSHIRE DIVISION SIX

Sat 10th September (Week 2)
Armthorpe Rovers v Adwick le Street
Markham v Knaresborough
Maltby v Sheffield Steels
De la Salle Sheffield v Stocksbridge
Withernsea v Granville College
Sheffield Medicals v Mosborough

Sat 24th September (Week 4)
Mosborough v Armthorpe Rovers
Adwick le Street v Withernsea
Granville College v De la Salle Sheffield
Stocksbridge v Maltby OB
Sheffield Steels v Markham
Knaresborough v Sheffield Medicals

Sat 8th October (Week 6)
De la Salle Sheffield v Adwick le Street
Withernsea v Armthorpe Rovers
Sheffield Medicals v Sheffield Steels
Markham v Stocksbridge
Maltby OB v Granville College
Knaresborough v Mosborough

Sat 22nd October (Week 8)
Mosborough v Withernsea
Armthorpe Rovers v De la Salle Sheffield
Adwick le Street v Maltby OB
Granville College v Markham
Stocksbridge v Sheffield Medicals
Sheffield Sttels v Knaresborough

Sat 12th November (Week 10)
Markham v Adwick le Street
Maltby OB v Armthorpe Rovers
De la Salle Sheffield v Withernsea
Knaresborough v Stocksbridge
Sheffield Medicals v Granville College
Sheffield Steels v Mosborough

Sat 19th November (Week 11)
Mosborough v De la Salle Sheffield
Withernsea v Maltby OB
Armthorpe Rovers v Markham
Adwick le Street v Sheffield Medicals
Granville College v Knaresborough
Stocksbridge v Sheffield Steels

Sat 26th November (Week 12)
Knaresborough v Adwick le Street
Sheffield Medicals v Armthorpe Rovers
Markham v Withensea
Maltby OB v De la Salle Sheffield
Sheffield Steels v Granville College
Stocksbridge v Mosborough

Sat 14th January (Week 18)
Mosborough v Maltby OB
De la Salle Sheffield v Markham
Withernsea v Sheffield Medicals
Armthorpe Robers v Knaresborough
Adwick le Street v Sheffield Steels
Granville College v Stocksbridge

Sat 11th March (Week 26)
Stocksbridge v Adwick le Street
Sheffield Steels v Armthorpe Rovers
Knaresborough v Withernsea
Sheffield Medicals v De la Salle Sheffield
Markham v Maltby OB
Granville College v Mosborough

Sat 8th April (Week 30)
Mosborough v Markham
Maltby OB v Sheffield Medicals
De la Salle Sheffield v Knaresborough
Withernsea v Sheffield Steels
Armthorpe Rovers v Stocksbridge
Adwick le Street v Granville College

Sat 22nd April (Week 32)
Granville College v Armthorpe Rovers
Stocksbridge v Withernsea
Sheffield Steels v De la Salle Sheffield
Knaresborough v Maltby OB
Sheffield Medicals v Markham
Adwick le Street v Mosborough

DURHAM/NORTHUMBERLAND DIVISION ONE

Sat 10th September (Week 2)
Ashington v Acklam
Rockcliff v Ponteland
Horden v Redcar
Darlington v Seghill
Hartlepool v Winlaton Vulcans

Sat 24th September (Week 4)
Acklam v Hartlepool
Winlaton Vulcans v Darlington
Seghill v Horden
Redcar v Rockcliff
Ponteland v Mowden Park

Sat 8th October (Week 6)
Darlington v Acklam
Hartlepool v Ashington JW
Mowden Park v Redcar
Rockcliff v Seghill
Horden v Winlaton Vulcans

Sat 22nd Oct (Week 8)
Ashington JW v Darlington
Acklam v Horden
Winlaton Vulcans v Rockcliff
Seghill v Mowden Park
Redcar v Ponteland

Sat 12th November (Week 10)
Rockcliff v Acklam
Horden v Ashington JW
Darlington v Hartlepool
Ponteland v Seghill
Mowden Prk v Winlaton Vulcans

Sat 19th November (Week 11)
Hartlepool v Horden
Ashington JW v Rockcliff
Acklam v Mowden Park
Winlaton Vulcans v Ponteland
Seghill v Redcar

Sat 26th November (Week 12)
Ponteland v Acklam
Mowden Park v Ashington JW
Rockcliff v Hartlepool
Horden v Darlington
Redar v Winlaton Vulcans

Sat 14th January (Week 18)
Darlington v Rockcliff
Hartlepool v Mowden Park
Ashington JW v Ponteland
Acklam v Redcar
Winlaton Vulcans v Seghill

Sat 11th March (Week 26)
Seghill v Acklam
Redcar v Ashington JW
Ponteland v Hartlepool
Mowden Park v Darlington
Rockcliff v Horden

Sat 8th April (Week 30)
Horden v Mowden Park
Darlington v Ponteland
Hartlepool v Redcar
Ashington JW v Seghill
Acklam v Winlaton Vulcans

Sat 22nd April (Week 32)
Winlaton Vulcans v Ashington JW
Seghill v Hartlepool
Redcar v Darlington
Ponteland v Horden
Mowden Park v Rockcliff

DURHAM/NORTHUMBERLAND DIVISION TWO

Sat 10th September (Week 2)
Consett v Bishop Auckland
Medicals v North Durham
Whitby v Wallsend
Hartlepool BBOB v Seaham
Billingham v Sunderland

Sat 24th September (Week 4)
Bishop Auckland v Billingham
Sunderland v Hartlepool BBOB
Seaham v Whitby
Wallsend v Medicals
North Durham v Percy Park

Sat 8th October (Week 6)
Hartlepool BBOB v Bishop Auckland
Billingham v Consett
Percy Park v Wallsend
Medicals v Seaham
Whitby v Sunderland

Sat 22nd October (Week 8)
Consett v Hartlepool BBOB
Bishop Auckland v Whitby
Sunderland v Medicals
Seaham v Percy Park
Wallsend v North Durham

Sat 12th November (Week 10)
Medicals v Bishop Auckland
Whitby v Consett
Hartlepool BBOB v Billingham
North Durham v Seaham
Percy Park v Sunderland

Sat 19th November (Week 11)
Billingham v Whitby
Consett v Medicals
Bishop Auckland v Percy Park
Sunderland v North Durham
Seaham v Wallsend

Sat 26th November (Week 12)
North Durham v Bishop Auckland
Percy Park v Consett
Medicals v Billingham
Whitby v Hartlepool BBOB
Wallsend v Sunderland

Sat 14th January (Week 18)
Hartlepool BBOB v Medicals
Billingham v Percy Park
Consett v North Durham
Bishop Auckland v Wallsend
Sunderland v Seaham

Sat 11th March (Week 26)
Seaham v Bishop Auckland
Wallsend v Consett
North Durham v Billingham
Percy Park v Hartlepool BBOB
Medicals v Whitby

Sat 8th April (Week 30)
Whitby v Percy Park
Hartlepool BBOB v North Durham
Billingham v Wallsend
Consett v Seaham
Bishop Auckland v Sunderland

Sat 22nd April (Week 32)
Sunderland v Consett
Seaham v Billingham
Wallsend v Hartlepool BBOB
North Durham v Whitby
Percy Park v Medicals

DURHAM/NORTHUMBERLAND DIVISION THREE

Sat 10th September (Week 2)
Chester le Street v Wensleydale
North Shields v Darlington RA
Hartlepool TDSOB v Washington
Prudhoe Hospital v Wearside
Guisborough v Houghton

Sat 24th September (Week 4)
Wensleydale v Guisborough
Houghton v Prudhoe Hospital
Wearside v Hartlepool TDSOB
Washington v North Shields
Darlington RA v Seaton Carew

Sat 8th October (Week 6)
Prudhoe Hospital v Wensleydale
Guisborough v Chester le Street
Seaton Carew v Washington
North Shields v Wearside
Hartlepool TDSOB v Houghton

Sat 22nd Oct (Week 8)
Chester le Street v Prudhoe Hospital
Wensleydale v Hartlepool TDSOB
Houghton v North Shields
Wearide v Seaton Carew
Washington v Darlington R A

Sat 12th November (Week 10)
North Shields v Wensleydale
Hartlepool TDSOB v Chester le Street
Prudhoe Hospital v Guisborough
Darlington RA v Wearside
Seaton Carew v Houghton

Sat 19th November (Week 11)
Guisborough v Hartlepool TDSOB
Chester le Street v North Shields
Wensleydale v Seaton Carew
Houghton v Darlington RA
Wearside v Washington

Sat 26th November (Week 12)
Darlington RA v Wensleydale

Seaton Carew v Chester le Street
North Shields v Guisborough
Hartlepool TDSOB v Prudhoe Hospital
Washington v Houghton

Sat 14th January (Week 18)
Prudhoe Hospital v North Shields
Guisborough v Seaton Carew
Chester le Street v Darlington RA
Wensleydale v Washington
Houghton v Wearside

Sat 11th March (Week 26)
Wearside v Wensleydale
Washington v Chester le Street
Darlington RA v Guisborough
Seaton carew v Prudhoe Hospital
North Shields v Hartlepool TDSOB

Sat 8th April (Week 30)
Hartlepool TDSOB v Seaton Carew
Prudhoe Hospital v Darlington RA
Guisborough v Washington
Chester le Street v Wearside
Wensleydale v Houghton

Sat 22nd April (Week 32)
Houghton v Chester le Street
Wearside v Guisborough
Washington v Prudhoe Hospital
Darlington RA v Hartlepool TDSOB
Seaton Carew v North Shields

DURHAM/NORTHUMBERLAND DIVISION FOUR

Sat 10th September (Week 2)
Barnard Castle v Richmonshire
Benton v Hartlepool Athletic
Newton Aycliffe v Sedgefield
Jarrovians v Shildon Town

Sat 24th September (Week 4)
Jarrovians v Richmonshire
Civil Service v Barnard Castle
South Tyneside Coll v Sedgefield
Benton v Shildon Town

Sat 22nd October (Week 8)
Barnard Castle v Jarrovians
Richmondshire v Newton Aycliffe
Shildon Town v South Tyneside Coll
Sedgefield v Hartlepool Athletic

Sat 12th November (Week 10)
Benton v Richmonshire
Newton Aycliffe v Barnard Castle
Jarrovians v Civil Service
Hartlepool Athletic v Shildon Town

Sat 19th November (Week 11)
Civil Service v Newton Aycliffe
Barnard Castle v Benton
Richmondshire v South Tyneside Coll
Shildon Town v Sedgefield

Sat 26th November (Week 12)
Hartlepool Athletic v Richmondshire
South Tyneside Coll v Barnard Castle
Benton v Civil Service
Newton Aycliffe v Jarrovians

Sat 14th Jan (Week 18)
Jarrovians v Benton
Civil Service v South Tyneside Coll
Barnard Castle v Hartlepool Athletic
Richmondshire v Sedgefield

Sat 11th March (Week 26)
Shildon Town v Richmondshire
Sedgefield v Barnard Castle
Hartlepool Athletic v Civil Service
South Tyneside Coll v Jarrovians
Benton v Newton Aycliffe

Sat 8th April (Week 30)
Newton Aycliffe v South Tyneside Coll
Jarrovians v Hartlepool Athletic
Civil Service v Sedgefield
Barnard Castle v Shildon Town

Sat 22nd April (Week 32)
Shildon Town v Civil Service
Sedgefield v Jarrovians
Hartlepool Athletic v Newton Aycliffe
South Tyneside Coll v Benton

MIDLANDS DIVISION ONE

Sat 10th September (Week 2)
Barker Butts v Walsall
Hereford v Newark
Stockwood Prk v Mansfield
Derby v Paviors
Wolverhampton v Solihull

Sat 24th September (Week 4)
Walsall v Wolverhampton
Solihull v Derby
Paviors v Stockwood Park
Mansfield v Hereford
Newark v Westleigh

Sat 8th October (Week 6)
Derby v Walsall
Wolverhampton v Barker Butts
Westleigh v Mansfield
Hereford v Paviors
Stockwood Park v Solihull

Sat 22nd October (Week 8)
Barker Butts v Deby
Walsall v Stockwood Park
Solihull v Hereford
Paviors v Westleigh
Mansfield v Newark

Sat 12th November (Week 10)
Hereford v Walsall
Stockwood Park v Barker Butts
Derby v Wolverhampton
Newark v Paviors
Westleigh v Solihull

Sat 19th November (Week 11)
Wolverhampton v Stockwood Park
Barker Butts v Hereford
Walsall v Westleigh
Solihull v Newark
Paviors v Mansfield

Sat 26th November (Week 12)
Newark v Walsall
Westleigh v Barker Butts
Hereford v Wolverhampton
Stockwood Park v Derby
Mansfield v Solihull

Sat 14th January (Week 18)
Derby v Hereford
Wolverhampton v Westleigh
Barker Butts v Newark
Walsall v Mansfield
Solihull v Paviors

Sat 11th March (Wek 26)
Paviors v Walsall
Mansfield v Barker Butts
Newark v Wolverhampton
Westleigh v Derby
Hereford v Stockwood Park

Sat 8th April (Week 30)
Stockwood Prk v Westleigh
Derby v Newark
Wolverhampton v Mansfield
Barker Butts v Paviors
Walsall v Solihull

Sat 22nd April (Week 32)
Solihull v Barker Butts
Paviors v Wolverhampton
Mansfield v Derby
Newark v Stockwood Park
Westleigh v Hereford

MIDLANDS DIVISION TWO WEST

Sat 10th September (Week 2)
Bedworth v Bromsgrove
Dudley v Stafford
Sutton Coldfield v Newbold
Tamworth v Old Yardleians
Worcester v Dixonians

Sat 24th September (Week 4)
Bromsgrove v Worcester
Dixonians v Tamworth
Newbold v Dudley
Old Yardleians v Burton
Stafford v Bedworth

Sat 8th October (Week 6)
Bedworth v Newbold
Burton v Dixonians
Dudley v Sutton Coldfield
Tamworth v Bromsgrove
Worcester v Stafford

Sat 22nd October (Week 8)
Bromsgrove v Burton
Dixonians v Old Yardleians
Newbold v Worcester
Stafford v Tamworth
Sutton Coldfield v Bedworth

Sat 12th November (Week 10)
Bedworth v Dudley
Burton v Stafford
Old Yardleians v Bromsgrove
Tamworth v Newbold
Worcester v Sutton Coldfield

Sat 19th November (Week 11)
Bromsgrove v Dixonians
Dudley v Worcester
Newbold v Burton
Stafford v Old Yarleians
Sutton Coldfield v Tamworth

Sat 26th November (Week 12)
Burton v Sutton Coldfield
Dixonians v Stafford
Old Yardleians v Newbold
Tamworth v Dudley
Worcester v Bedworth

Sat 14th January (Week 18)
Bedworth v Tamworth
Dudley v Burton
Newbold v Dixonians
Stafford v Bromsgrove
Sutton Coldfield v Old Yardleians

Sat 11th March (Week 26)
Bromsgrove v Newbold
Burton v Bedworth
Dixonians v Sutton Coldfield
Old Yarleians v Dudley
Tamworth v Worcester

Sat 8th April (Week 30)
Bedworth v Old Yardleians
Dudley v Dixonians
Newbold v Stafford
Sutton Coldfield v Bromsgrove
Worcester v Burton

Sat 22nd April (Week 32)
Bromsgrove v Dudley
Burton v Tamworth
Dixonians v Bedworth
Old Yardleians v Worcester
Stafford v Sutton Coldfield

MIDLANDS DIVISION TWO EAST

Sat 10th September (Week 2)
Kettering v Vipers
Leighton Buzzard v Peterborough
Lincoln v Matlock
Moderns v Stewart & Lloyds
Stoneygate v Hinckley

Sat 24th September (Week 4)
Hinckley v Moderns
Matlock v Kettering
Peterborough v Syston
Stewart & Lloyds v Lincoln
Vipers v Leighton Buzzard

Sat 8th October (Week 6)
Kettering v Stewart & Lloyds
Leighton Buzzard v Matlock
Lincoln v Hinckley
Moderns v Stoneygate
Syston v Vipers

Sat 22nd October (Week 8)
Hinckley v Kettering
Matlock v Syston
Stewart & Lloyds v Leighton Buzzard
Stoneygate v Lincoln
Vipers v Peterborough

Sat 12th November (Week 10)
Kettering v Stoneygate
Leighton Buzzard v Hinckley
Lincoln v Moderns
Peterborough v Matlock
Syston v Stewart & Lloyds

Sat 19th November (Week 11)
Hinckley v Syston
Matlock v Vipers
Moderns v Kettering
Stewart & Lloyds v Peterborough
Stoneygate v Leighton Buzzard

Sat 26th November (Wek 12)
Kettering v Lincoln
Leighton Buzzard v Moderns
Peterborough v Hinckley
Syston v Stoneygate
Vipers v Stewart & Lloyds

Sat 14th January (Week 18)
Hinckley v Vipers
Lincoln v Leighton Buzzard
Moderns v Syston
Stewart & Lloyds v Matlock
Stoneygate v Peterborough

Sat 11th March (Week 26)
Leighton Buzzard v Kettering
Matlcok v Hinckley
Peterborough v Moderns
Syston v Lincoln
Vipers v Stoneygate

Sat 8th April (Week 30)
Hinckley v Stewart & Lloyds
Kettering v Syston
Lincoln v Peterborough
Moderns v Vipers
Stoneygate v Matlock

Sat 22nd April (Week 32)
Matlock v Moderns
Peterborough v Kettering
Stewart & Lloyds v Stoneygate
Syston v Leighton Buzzard
Vipers v Lincoln

STAFFORDSHIRE ONE

Sat 10th September (Week 2)
Linley v GEC St Leonards
Cannock v Uttoxeter
Handsworth v Rugeley

Sat 8th October (Week 6)
GEC St Leonards v Uttoxeter
Linley v Burntwood
Cannock v Handsworth

Sat 22nd October (Week 8)
Rugeley v GEC St Leonards
Uttoxeter v Linley
Handsworth v Burntwood

Sat 12th November (Week 10)
GEC St Leonards v Handsworth
Burntwood v Cannock
Uttoxeter v Rugeley

Sat 26th November (Week 12)
Cannock v Linley
Rugeley v Burntwood
Uttoxeter v Handsworth

Sat 11th March (Week 26)
Rugeley v Cannock
Handsworth v Linley
Burntwood v GEC St Leonards

Sat 9th April (Week 30)
Linley v Rugeley
Burntwood v Uttoxeter
GEC St Leonards v Cannock

STAFFORDSHIRE TWO

Sat 10th September (Week 2)
Cheadle v Old Oaks
Wheaton Aston v St Matthews
Wulfrun v Rubery Owen
Wednesbury v Michelin
Eccleshall v St Georges

Sat 24th September (Week 4)
Michelin v Cheadle
Old Oaks v Eccleshall
St Matthews v Wulfrun
Wednesbury v Wheaton Aston
St Georges v Rubery Owen

Sat 8th October (Week 6)
Eccleshall v Michelin
Old Oaks v Wednesbury
Rubery Owen v Cheadle
Wheaton Aston v Wulfrun
St Matthews v St Georges

Sat 22nd October (Week 8)
Cheadle v St Matthews
Eccleshall v Rubery Owen
Michelin v Old Oaks
Wulfrun v Wednesbury
Wheaton Aston v St Georges

Sat 12th November (Week 10)
Cheadle v Wheaton Aston
Eccleshall v Wednesbury
Michelin v St Matthews
Old Oaks v Rubery Owen
St Georges v Wulfrun

Sat 26th Nov (Week 12)
Rubery Owen v Michelin
St Matthews v Old Oaks
Wheaton Aston v Eccleshall
Wulfrun v Cheadle
St Georges v Wednesbury

Sat 14th January (Week 18)
Eccleshall v Wulfrun
Michelin v Wheaton Aston
Rubery Owen v St Matthews
Wednesbury v Cheadle
Old Oaks v St Georges

Sat 11th March (Week 26)
St Matthews v Eccleshall
Wednesbury v Rubery Owen
Wheaton Aston v Old Oaks
Wulfrun v Michelin
Cheadle v St Georges

Sat 8th April (Week 30)
Cheadle v Eccleshall
Old Oaks v Wulfrun
Rubery Owen v Wheaton Aston
St Matthews v Wednesbury
Michelin v St Georges

NORTH MIDLANDS ONE

Sat 10th September (Week 2)
Newport v Evesham
Old Halesonians v Bridgnorth
Kings Norton v Camp Hill
Kidderminster v Luctonian
Malvern v Whitchurch

Sat 24th September (Week 4)
Evesham v Old Halesonians
Whitchurch v Shrewsbury
Luctonian v Malvern
Camp Hill v Kidderminster
Bridgnoth v Kings Norton

Sat 8th October (Week 6)
Kings Norton v Evesham
Old Halesonians v Newport
Shrewsbury v Luctonian
Malvern v Camp Hill
Kidderminster v Bridgnorth

Sat 22nd October (Week 8)
Newport v Kings Norton
Evesham v Kidderminster
Bridgnorth v Malvern
Camp Hill v Shrewsbury
Luctonian v Whitchurch

Sat 12th November (Week 10)
Malvern v Evesham
Kidderminster v Newport
Kings Norton v Old Halesonians
Whitchurch v Camp Hill
Shrewsbury v Bridgnorth

Sat 19th November (Week 11)
Old Halesonians v Kidderminster
Newport v Malvern
Evesham v Shrewsbury
Bridgnorth v Whitchurch
Camp Hill v Luctonian

Sat 26th November (Week 12)
Whitchurch v Evesham
Shrewsbury v Newport
Malvern v Old Halesonians
Kidderminster v Kings Norton
Luctonian v Bridgnorth

Sat 14th January (Week 18)
Kings Norton v Malvern
Old Halesonians v Shrewsbury
Newport v Whitchurch
Evesham v Luctonian
Bridgnorth v Camp Hill

Sat 11th March (Week 26)
Camp Hill v Evesham
Luctonian v Newport
Whitchurch v Old Halesonians
Shrewsbury v Kings Norton
Malvern v Kidderminster

Sat 8th April (Week 30)
Kidderminster v Shrewsbury
Kings Norton v Whitchurch
Old Halesonians v Luctonian
Newport v Camp Hill
Evesham v Bridgnorth

Sat 22nd April (Week 32)
Bridgnorth v Newport
Camp Hill v Old Halesonians
Luctonian v Kings Norton
Whitchurch v Kidderminster
Shrewsbury v Malvern

NORTH MIDLANDS TWO

Sat 10th September (Week 2)
Edwardian v Telford
Pershore v Selly Oak
Bournville v Woodrush
Aston OE v Five Ways
Ludlow v Erdington

Sat 24th September (Week 4)
Telford v Pershore
Erdington v Droitwich
Five Ways v Ludlow
Woodruch v Aston OE
Selly Oak v Bournville

Sat 8th October (Week 6)
Bournville v Telford
Pershore v Edwardian
Droitwich v Five Ways
Ludlow v Woodrush
Aston OE v Selly Oak

Sat 22nd Oct (Week 8)
Edwardian v Bournville
Telford v Aston OE
Selly Oak v Ludlow
Woodrush v Droitwich
Five Ways v Erdington

Sat 12th November (Week 10)
Ludlow v Telford
Aston OE v Edwardian
Bournville v Pershore
Erdington v Woodrush
Droitwich v Selly Oak

Sat 19th November (Week 11)
Pershore v Aston OE
Edwardian v Ludlow
Telford v Droitwich
Selly Oak v Erdington
Woodrush v Five Ways

Sat 26th November (Week 12)
Erdington v Telford
Droitwich v Edwardian
Ludlow v Pershore
Aston OE v Bournville
Five Ways v Selly Oak

Sat 14th January (Week 18)
Bournville v Ludlow
Pershore v Droitwich
Edwardian v Erdington
Telford v Five Ways
Selly Oak v Woodrush

Sat 11th March (Week 26)
Woodrush v Telford
Five Ways v Edwardian
Erdington v Pershore
Droitwich v Bournville
Ludlow v Aston OE

Sat 8th April (Week 30)
Aston OE v Droitwich
Bournville v Erdington
Pershore v Five Ways
Edwardian v Woodrush
Telford v Selly Oak

Sat 22nd April (Week 32)
Selly Oak v Edwardian
Woodruch v Pershore
Five Ways v Bournville
Erdington v Ashton OE
Droitwich v Ludlow

NORTH MIDLANDS THREE

Sat 10th September (Week 2)
Old Griffinians v Old Centrals
Ledbury v Birmingham City Off
Old Salteians v West Midlands Police
Warley v Birmingham Welsh
Redditch v Veseyans

Sat 24th September (Week 4)
Old Centrals v Ledbury
Veseyans v Kynoch
Birmingham Welsh v Redditch
West Midlands Police v Warley
Birmingham City Off v Old Saltleians

Sat 8th October (Week 6)
Old Saltleians v Old Centrals
Ledbury v Old Griffinians
Kynoch v Birmingham Welsh
Redditch v West Midlands Police
Warley v Birmingham City Off

Sat 22nd October (Week 8)
Old Griffinians v Old Saltleians
Old Centrals v Warley
Birmingham City Off v Redditch
West Midlands Police v Kynoch
Birmingham Welsh v Veseyans

Sat 12th November (Week 10)
Redditch v Old Centrals
Warley v Old Griffinians
Old Saltleians v Ledbury
Veseyans v West Midlands Police
Kynoch v Birmingham City Off

Sat 19th November (Week 11)
Ledbury v Warley
Old Griffinians v Redditch
Old Centrals v Kynoch
Birmingham City Off v Veseyans
West Midlands Police v Birmingham Welsh

Sat 26th November (Week 12)
Veseyans v Old Centrals
Kynoch v Old Griffinians
Redditch v Ledbury
Warley v Old Saltleians
Birmingham Welsh v Birmingham City Off

Sat 14th January (Week 18)
Old Saltleians v Redditch
Ledbury v Kynoch
Old Griffinians v Veseyans
Old Centrals v Birmingham Welsh
Birmingham City Off v West Midlands Police

Sat 11th March (Week 26)
West Midlands Police v Old Centrals
Birmingham Welsh v Old Griffinians
Veseyans v Ledbury
Kynoch v Old Saltleians
Redditch v Warley

Sat 8th April (Week 30)
Warley v Kynoch
Old Saltleians v Veseyans
Ledbury v Birmingham Welsh
Old Griffinians v West Midlands Police
Old Centrals v Birmingham City Off

Sat 22nd April (Week 32)
Birmingham City Off v Old Griffinians
West Midlands Police v Ledbury
Birmingham Welsh v Old Saltleians
Veseyans v Warley
Kynoch v Redditch

NORTH MIDLANDS FOUR

Sat 10th September (Week 2)
Upton on Severnv Birchfield
Ross on Wye v Tenbury
Bewdley v Market Drayton
Bromyard v Old Moselians
Birmingham CS v Oswestry
Witton v Yardley & District

Sat 24th September (Week 4)
Birchfield v Witton
Yardley & District v Birmingham CS
Oswestry v Bromyard
Old Moselians v Bewdley
Market Drayton v Ross on Wye
Tenbury v Thimblemill

Sat 8th October (Week 6)
Birmingham CS v Birchfield
Witton v Upton on Severn
Thimblemill v Market Drayton
Ross on Wye v Old Moselians
Bewdley v Oswestry
Bromyard v Yardley & District

Sat 22nd October (Week 8)
Upton on Severn v Birmingham CS
Birchfield v Bromyard
Yardley & District v Bewdley
Oswestry v Ross on Wye
Old Moselians v Thimblemill
Market Drayton v Tenbury

Sat 12th November (Week 10)
Bewdley v Birchfield
Bromyard v Upton on Severn
Birmingham CS v Witton
Tenbury v Old Moselians
Thimblemill v Oswestry
Ross on Wye v Yardley & District

Sat 19th November (Week 11)
Witton v Bromyard
Upton on Severn v Bewdley
Birchfield v Ross on Wye
Yardley & District v Thimblemill
Oswestry v Tenbury
Old Moselians v Market Drayton

Sat 26th November (Week 12)
Thimblemill v Birchfield
Ross on Wye v Upton on Severn
Bewdley v Witton
Bromyard v Birmingham CS
Market Drayton v Oswestry
Tenbury v Yardley & District

Sat 14th January (Week 18)
Birmingham CS v Bewdley
Witton v Ross on Wye
Upton on Severn v Thimblemill
Birchfield v Tenbury
Yardley & District v Market Drayton

Sat 11th February (Week 22)
Market Drayton v Birchfield
Tenbury v Upton on Severn
Thimblemill v Witton
Ross on Wye v Birmingham CS
Bewdley v Bromyard
Old Modelians v Yardley & District

Sat 25th February (Week 24)
Bromyard v Ross on Wye
Birmingham CS v Thimblemill
Witton v Tenbury
Upton on Severn v Market Drayton
Birchfield v Old Moselians
Yardley & District v Oswestry

Sat 11th March (Week 26)
Oswestry v Birchfield
Old Moselians v Upton on Severn
Market Drayton v Witton
Tenbury v Birmingham CS
Thimblemill v Bromyard
Ross on Wye v Bewdley

Sat 8th April (Week 30)
Bewdley v Thimblemill
Bromyard v Tenbury
Birmingham CS v Market Drayton
Witton v Old Moselians
Upton on Severn v Oswestry
Birchfield v Yardley & District

Sat 22nd April (Week 32)
Yardley & District v Upton on Severn
Oswestry v Witton
Old Moselians v Birmingham CS
Market Drayton v Bromyard
Tenbury v Bewdley
Thimblemill v Ross on Wye

NOTTINGHAMSHIRE, LINCOLNSHIRE, DERBYSHIRE ONE

Sat 10th September (Week 2)
Scunthorpe v Kesteven
Southwell v East Retford
Stamford v Mellish
West Bridgford v Glossop
Worksop v Chesterfield

Sat 24th September (Week 4)
Amber Valley v Worksop
Chesterfield v West Bridgford
East Retford v Scunthorpe
Glossop v Southwell
Kesteven v Stamford

Sat 8th October (Week 6)
Mellish v Kesteven
Scunthorpe v Glossop
Southwell v Chesterfield
Stamford v East Retford
West Bridgford v Amber Valley

Sat 22nd October (Week 8)
Amber Valley v Southwell
Chesterfield v Scunthorpe
East Retford v Mellish
Glossop v Stamford
Worksop v West Bridgford

Sat 12th November (Week 10)
Kesteven v East Retford
Mellish v Glossop
Scunthorpe v Amber Valley
Southwell v Worksop
Stamford v Chesterfield

Sat 19th November (Week 11)
Amber Valley v Stamford
Chesterfield v Mellish
Glossop v Kesteven
West Bridgford v Southwell
Worksop v Scunthorpe

Sat 26th November (Week 12)
East Redford v Glossop
Kesteven v Chesterfield
Mellish v Amber Valley
Scunthorpe v West Bridgford
Stamford v Worksop

Sat 14th January (Week 18)
Amber Valley v Kesteven
Chesterfield v East Retford
Southwell v Scunthorpe
West Bridgford v Stamford
Worksop v Mellish

Sat 11th March (Week 26)
East Retford v Amber Valley
Glossop v Chesterfield
Kesteven v Worksop
Mellish v West Bridgford
Stamford v Southwell

Sat 8th April (Week 30)
Amber Valley v Glossop
Scunthorpe v Stamford
Southwell v Mellish
West Bridgford v Kesteven
Worksop v East Retford

Sat 22nd April (Week 32)
Chesterfield v Amber Valley
East Retford v West Bridgford
Glossop v Worksop
Kesteven v Southwell
Mellish v Scunthorpe

NOTTINGHAMSHIRE, LINCOLNSHIRE, DERBYSHIRE TWO

Sat 10th September (Week 2)
Long Eaton v Grimsby
Market Rasen v Keyworth
Nottinghamians v Ilkeston
Sleaford v All Spartans
Spalding v Nottingham Casuals

Sat 24th September (Week 4)
All Spartans v Long Eaton
Boston v Spalding
Grimsby v Nottinghamians
Ilkeston v Market Rasen
Nottingham Casuals v Sleaford

Sat 8th October (Week 6)
Keyworth v Ilkeston
Long Eaton v Nottingham Casuals
Market Rasen v Grimsby
Nottinghamians v All Spartans
Sleaford v Boston

Sat 22nd October (Week 8)
All Spartans v Market Rasen
Boston v Long Eaton
Grimsby v Keyworth
Nottingham Casuals v Nottinghamians
Sleaford v Boston

Sat 22nd Oct (Week 8)
AZll Spartans v Market Rasen
Boston v Long Eaton
Grimsby v Keyworth
Nottingham Casuals v Nottinghamians
Spalding v Sleaford

Sat 12th November (Week 10)
Ilkeston v Grimsby
Keyworth v All Spartans
Long Eaton v Spalding
Market Rasen v Nottingham Casuals
Nottinghamians v Boston

Sat 19th November (Week 11)
All Spartans v Ilkeston
Boston v Market Rasen
Nottingham Casuals v Keyworth
Sleaford v Long Eaton
Spalding v Nottinghamians

Sat 26th November (Week 12)
Grimsby v All Spartans
Ilkeston v Nottingham Casuals
Keyworth v Boston
Market Rasen v Spalding
Nottinghamians v Sleaford

Sat 14th January (Week 18)
Boston v Ilkeston
Long Eaton v Nottinghamians
Nottingham Casuals v Grimsby
Sleaford v Market Rasen
Spalding v Keyworth

Sat 11th March (Week 26)
All Spartans v Nottingham Casuals
Grimsby v Boston
Ilkeston v Spalding
Keyworth v Sleaford
Market Rasen v Long Eaton

Sat 8th April (Week 30)
Boston v All Spartans
Long Eaton v Keyworth
Nottinghamians v Market Rasen
Sleaford v Ilkeston
Spalding v Grimsby

Sat 22nd April (Week 32)
All Spartans v Spalding
Grimsby v Sleaford
Ilkeston v Long Eaton
Keyworth v Nottinghamians
Nottingham Casuals v Boston

NOTTINGHAMSHIRE, LINCOLNSHIRE, DERBYSHIRE THREE

Sat 10th September (Week 2)
Ashbourne v Boots
North Kesteven v Barton Upon Humber
Nottinghamshire v Gainsborough
Rolls Royce v Belper
Skegness v Ashfield Swans

Sat 24th September (Week 4)
Ashfield Swans v Rolls Royce
Barton Upon Humber v Ashbourne
Belper v North Kesteven
Boots vs Nottinghamshire Police
Dronfield v Skegness

Sat 8th October (Week 6)
Ashbourne v Belper
Gainsborough v Boots
North Kesteven v Ashfield Swans
Nottinghamshire Police v Barton Upon Humber
Rolls Royce v Dronfield

Sat 22nd October (Week 8)
Ashfield Swans v Ashbourne
Barton Upon Humber v Gainsborough
Belper v Nottinghamshire Police
Dronfield v North Kesteven
Skegness v Rolls Royce

Sat 12th November (Week 10)
Ashbourne v Dronfield
Boots v Barton Upon Humber
Gainsborough v Belper
North Kesteven v Skegness
Nottinghamshire Police v Ashfield Swans

Sat 19th Nov (Week 11)
Ashfield Swans v Gainsborough
Belper v Boots
Dronfield v Nottinghamshire Police
Rolls Royce v North Kesteven
Skegness v Ashbourne

Sat 26th November (Week 12)
Ashbourne v Rolls Royce
Barton Upun Humber v Belper
Boots v Ashfield Swans
Gainsborough v Dronfield
Nottinghamshire Police v Skegness

Sat 14th January (Week 18)
Ashfield Swans v Barton Upon Humber
Dronfield v Boots
North Kesteven v Ashbourne
Rolls Royce v Nottinghamshire Police
Skegness v Gainsborough

Sat 11th March (Week 26)
Barton Upon Humber v Dronfield
Belper v Ashfield Swans
Boots v Skegness
Gainsborough v Rolls Royce
Nottinghamshire Police v North Kesteven

Sat 8th April (Week 30)
Ashbourne v Nottinghamshire Police
Dronfield v Belper
North Kesteven v Gainsborough
Rolls Royce v Boots
Skegness v Barton Upon Humber

Sat 22nd April (Week 32)
Ashfield Swans v Dronfield
Barton Upon Humber v Rolls Royce
Belper v Skegness
Boots v North Kesteven
Gainsborough v Ashbourne

NOTTINGHAMSHIRE, LINCOLNSHIRE, DERBYSHIRE FOUR EAST

Sat 10th September (Week 2)
Bourne v Cleethorpes
Rainworth v Ollerton & Bevercoates
Yarborough Bees v Meden Vale

Sat 24th September (Week 4)
Bingham v Bourne
Cleethorpes v Harworth Colliery
Horncastle v Yarborough Bees
Meden Vale v Rainworth

Sat 8th October (Week 6)
Harworth Colliery v Bingham
Ollerton & Bevercoates v Meden Vale
Rainworth v Horncastle

Sat 22nd October (Week 8)
Bourne v Harworth Colliery
Cleethorpes v Yarborough Bees
Horncastle v Ollerton & Bevercoates

Sat 12th November (Week 10)
Bourne v Harworth Colliery
Rainworth v Cleethorpes
Yarborough Bees v Bingham

Sat 19th November (Week 11)
Meden Vale v Cleethorpes
Ollerton & Bevercoates v Bingham
Rainworth v Bourne
Yarborough Bees v Harworth Colliery

Sat 26th November (Week 12)
Meden Vale v Cleethorpes
Ollerton & Bevercoates v Bingham
Rainworth v Bourne
Yarborough Bees v Harworth Colliery

Sat 14th January (Week 18)
Bingham v Meden Vale
Bourne v Ollerton & Bevercoates
Cleethorpes v Horncastle
Harworth Colliery v Rainworth

Sat 11th March (Week 26)
Horncastle v Bingham
Meden Vale v Bourne
Ollerton & Bevercoates v Harworth Colliery

Sat 8th April (Week 30)
Bourne v Horncastle
Harworth Colliery v Meden Vale
Yarborough Bees v Rainworth

Sat 22nd April (Week 32)
Cleethorpes v Bingham
Horncastle v Harworth Colliery
Ollerton & Bevercoates v Yarborough Bees

NOTTINGHAMSHIRE, LINCOLNSHIRE, DERBYSHIRE FOUR WEST

Sat 10th September (Week 2)
Bolsover v Hope Valley
Tupton v Melbourne

Sat 24th September (Week 4)
East Leake v Bolsover
Leesbrook v Tupton

Sat 8th October (Week 6)
Bolsover v Buxton
Melbourne v Leesbrook
Tupton v Hope Valley

Sat 22nd October (Week 8)
Bakewell Mannerians v Bolsover
East Leake v Tupton
Hope Valley v Melbourne

Sat 12th November (Week 10)
Leesbrook v Hope Valley
Melbourne v East Leake
Tupton v Buxton

Sat 19th November (Week 11)
Bakewell Mannerians v Tupton
Buxton v Melbourne
East Leake v Leesbrook

Sat 26th November (Week 12)
Hope Valley v East Leake
Leesbrook v Buxton
Melbourne v Bakewell Mannerians

Sat 14th January (Week 18)
Bakewell Mannerians v Leesbrook
Buxton v Hope Valley

Sat 11th March (Week 26)
East Leake v Buxton
Hope Valley v Bakewell Mannerians
Tupton v Bolsover

Sat 8th April (Week 30)
Bakewell Mannerians v East Leake
Bolsover v Melbourne

Sat 22nd April (Week 32)
Buxton v Bakewell Mannerians
Leesbrook v Bolsover

COURAGE
CLUBS CHAMPIONSHIP

STAFFORDSHIRE/ WARWICKSHIRE LEAGUE

Sat 10th September (Week 2)
Leek v Willenhall
N'ton Old Edwardians v Old Leamingtonians
Leamington v Trentham
Stratford v Newcaslt (Staffs)
Keresley v Stock OB's

Sat 24th September (Week 4)
Willenhall v Keresley
Stoke OB's v Stratford
Newcastle (Staffs) v Leamington
Trentham v N'ton Old Edwardians
Old Leamingtonians v Old Longtonians

Sat 8th October (Week 6)
Stratford v Willenhall
Keresley v Leek
Old Longtonians v Trentham
N'ton Old Edwardians v Newcastle (Staffs)
Leamington v Stoke OB's

Sat 22nd October (Week 8)
Leek v Stratford
Willenhall v Leamington
Stoke OB's v N'ton Old Edwardians
Newcastle (Staffs) v Old Longtonians
Trentham v Old Leamingtonians

Sat 12th November (Week 10)
N'ton Old Edwardians v Willenhall
Leamington v Leek
Stratford v Keresley
Old Leamingtonians v Newcastle (Staffs)
Old Longtonians v Stoke OB's

Sat 19th November (Week 11)
Keresley v Leamington
Leek v N'ton Old Edwardians
Willenhall v Old Longtonians
Stoke OB's v Old Leamingtonians
Newcastle (Staffs) v Tretham

Sat 26th November (Week 12)
Old Leamingtonians v Willenhall
Old Longtonians v Leek
N'ton Old Edwardians v Keresley
Leamington v Stratford
Trentham v Stoke OB's

Sat 14th January (Week 18)
Stratford v N'ton Old Edwardians
Keresley v Old Longtonians
Leek v Old Leamingtonians
Willenhall v Trentham
Stoke OB's v Newcastle (Staffs)

Sat 11th Marck (Week 26)
Newcastle (Staffs) v Willenhall
Trentham v Leek
Old Leamingtonians v Keresley
Old Longtonians v Stratford
N'ton Old Edwardians v Leamington

Sat 8th April (Week 30)
Leamington v Old Longtonians
Stratford v Old Leamingtonians
Keresley v Trentham
Leek v Newcastle (Staffs)
Willenhall v Stoke OB's

Sat 22nd April (Week 32)
Stoke OB's v Leek
Newcastle (Staffs) v Keresley
Trentham v Stratford
Old Leamingtonians v Leamington
Old Longtonians v N'ton Old Edwardians

WARWICKSHIRE ONE

Sat 10th September (Week 2)
Old Wheatlians v Old Coventrians
Rugby St Andrews v Dunlop
Manor Park v GEC Coventry
Broadstreet v Coventry Welsh
Kenilworth v Trinity Guild

Sat 24th September (Week 4)
Old Coventrians v Kenilworth
Trinity Guild v Broadstreet
Coventry Welsh v Manor Park
GEC Coventry v Rugby St Andrews
Dunlop v Southam

Sat 8th October (Week 6)
Broadstreet v Old Coventrians
Kenilworth v Old Wheatlians
Southam v GEC Coventry
Rugby St Andrews v Coventry Welsh
Manor Park v Trinity Guild

Sat 22nd October (Week 8)
Old Wheatlians v Broadstreet
Old Coventrians v Manor Park
Trinity Guild v Rugby St Andrews
Coventry Welsh v Southam
GEC Coventry v Dunlop

Sat 12th November (Week 10)
Rugby St Andrews v Old Coventrians
Manor Park v Old Wheatlians
Broadstreet v Kenilworth
Dunlop v Coventry Welsh
Southam v Trinity Guild

Sat 19th November (Week 11)
Kenilworth v Manor Park
Old Wheatlians v Rugby St Andrews
Old Coventrians v Southam
Trinity Guild v Dunlop
Coventry Welsh v GEC Coventry

Sat 26th November (Week 12)
Dunlop v Old Coventrians
Southam v Old Wheatlians
Rugby St Andrews v Kenilworth
Manor Park v Broadstreet
GEC Coventry v Trinity Guild

Sat 14th January (Week 18)
Broadstreet v Rugby St Andrews
Kenilworth v Southam
Old Wheatlians v Dunlop
Old Coventrians v GEC Coventry
Trinity Guild v Coventry Welsh

Sat 11th March (Week 26)
Coventry Welsh v Old Coventrians
GEC Coventry v Old Wheatlians
Dunlop v Kenilworth
Southam v Broadstreet
Rugby St Andrews v Manor Park

Sat 8th April (Week 30)
Manor Park v Southam
Broadstreet v Dunlop
Kenilworth v GEC Coventry
Old Wheatlians v Coventy Welsh
Old Coventrians v Trinity Guild

Sat 22nd April (Week 32)
Trinity Guild v Old Wheatlians
Coventry Welsh v Kenilworth
GEC Coventry v Broadstreet
Dunlop v Manor Park
Southam v Rugby St Andrews

WARWICKSHIRE TWO

Sat 10th September (Week 2)
Coventrians v Atherstone
Spartans v Pinley
Silhillians v Old Warwickians
Standard v Earlsdon
Old Laurentians v Harbury

Sat 24th September (Week 4)
Atherstone v Old Laurentians
Harbury v Standard
Earlsdon v Silhillians
Old Warwickians v Spartans
Pinley v Coventry Saracens

Sat 8th October (Week 6)
Standard v Atherstone
Old Laruentians v Coventrians
Coventry Saracens v Old Warwickians
Spartans v Earlsdon
Silhillians v Harbury

Sat 22nd October (Week 8)
Harbury v Spartans
Earlsdon v Coventry Saracens
Old Warwickians v Pinley
Coventrians v Standard
Atherstone v Silhillians

Sat 12th November (Week 10)
Spartans v Atherstone
Silhillians v Coventrians
Standard v Old Laurentians
Pinley v Earlsdon
Coventry Saracens v Harbury

Sat 19th November (Week 11)
Old Laruentians v Silhillians
Coventrians v Spartans
Atherstone v Coventry Saracens
Harbury v Pinley
Earlsdon v Old Warwickians

Sat 26th November (Week 12)
Pinley v Atherstone
Coventry Saracens v Coventrians
Spartans v Old Laurentians
Silhillians v Standard
Old Warwickians v Harbury

Sat 14th January (Week 18)
Standard v Spartans
Old Laurentians v Coventry Saracens
Coventrians v Pinley
Atherstone v Old Warwickians
Harbury v Earlsdon

Sat 11th March (Week 26)
Earlsdon v Atherstone
Old Warwickians v Coventrians
Pinley v Old Laurentians
Coventry Saracens v Standard
Spartans v Silhillians

Sat 8th April (Week 30)
Silhillians v Coventry Saracens
Standard v Pinley
Old Laurentians v Old Warwickians
Coventrians v Earlsdon
Atherstone v Harbury

Sat 22nd April (Week 32)
Harbury v Coventrians
Earlsdon v Old Laurentians
Old Warwickians v Standard
Pinley v Silhillians
Coventry Saracens v Spartans

WARWICKSHIRE THREE

Sat 10th September (Week 2)
Claverdon v Berkswell & Balsall Cmn
Shipston on Stour v Coventry Post Office
Alcester v Caludon Castle
Rugby Welsh v Warwick
Coventry Tech v Lanchester Poly

Sat 24th September (Week 4)
Berkswell & Balsall Cmn v Coventry Tech Coll
Lanchester Poly v Rugby Welsh
Warwick v Alcester
Caludon Castle v Shipston on Stour
Coventry Post Office v Shottery

Sat 8th October (Week 6)
Rugby Welsh v Berkswell & Balsall Cmn
Coventry Tech Coll v Claverdon
Shottery v Caludon Castle
Shipston on Stour v Warwick
Alcester v Lanchester Poly

Sat 22nd October (Week 8)
Claverdon v Rugby Welsh
Berkswell & Balsall Cmn v Alcester
Lanchester Poly v Shipston on Stour
Warwick v Shottery
Caludon Castle v Coventry Post Office

Sat 12th November (Week 10)
Shipston on Stour v Berkswell & Balsall Cmn
Alcester v Claverdon
Rugby Welsh v Coventry Tech Coll
Coventry Post Office v Warwick
Shottery v Lanchester Poly

Sat 19th November (Week 11)
Coventry Tech Coll v Alcester
Claverdon v Shipston on Stour
Berkswell & Balsall Cmn v Shottery
Lanchester Poly v Coventry Post Office
Warwick v Caludon Castle

Sat 26th November (Week 12)
Coventry Post Office v Berkswell & Balsall Cmn
Shottery v Claverdon
Shipston on Stour v Coventry Tech Coll
Alcester v Rugby Welsh
Caludon Castle v Lanchester Poly

Sat 14th January (Week 18)
Rugby Welsh v Shipston on Stour
Coventry Tech Coll v Shottery
Claverdon v Coventry Post Office
Berkswell & Balsall Cmn v Caludon Castle
Lanchester Poly v Warwick

Sat 11th March (Week 26)
Warwick v Berkswell & Balsall Cmn
Caludon Castle v Claverdon
Coventry Post Office v Coventry Tech Coll
Shottery v Rugby Welsh
Shipston on Stour v Alcester

Sat 8th April (Week 30)
Alcester v Shottery
Rugby Welsh v Coventry Post Office
Coventry Tech Coll v Caludon Castle
Claverdon v Warwick
Berkswell & Balsall Cmn v Lanchester Poly

Sat 22nd April (Week 32)
Lanchester Poly v Claverdon
Warwick v Coventry Tech Coll
Caludon Castle v Rugby Welsh
Coventry Post Office v Alcester
Shottery v Shipston on Stour

EAST MIDLANDS/ LEICESTERSHIRE LEAGUE

Sat 10th September (Week 2)
Aylestone St James v Towcestrians
Bedford Athletic v Long Buckby
Belgrave v Wellingborough
Northampton Trinity v Loughborough
Oadby-Wyggestonians v Wigston

Sat 24th September (Week 4)
Long Buckby v Oadby-Wyggestonians
Loughborough v Luton
Towcestrians v Belgrave
Wellingborough v Northampton Trinity
Wigston v Aylestone St James

Sat 8th October (Week 6)
Aylestone St James v Long Buckby
Belgrave v Wigston
Luton v Wellingborough
Northampton Trinity v Towcestrians
Oadby-Wyggestonians v Bedford Athletic

Sat 22nd October (Week 8)
Bedford Athletic v Aylestone St James
Long Buckby v Belgrave
Towcestrians v Luton
Wellingborough v Loughborough
Wigston v Northampton Trinity

Sat 12th November (Week 10)
Aylestone St James v Oadby-Wyggestonians
Belgrave v Bedford Athletic
Loughborough v Towcestrians
Luton v igston
Northampton Trinity v Long Buckby

Sat 19th November (Week 11)
Bedford Athletic v Northampton Trinity
Long Buckby v Luton
Oadby-Wyggestonians v Belgrave
Towcestrians v Wellingborough
Wigston v Loughborough

Sat 26th November (Week 12)
Belgrave v Aylestone St James
Loughborough v Long Buckby
Luton v Bedford Athletic
Northampton Trinity v Oadby-Wyggestonians
Wellingborough v Wigston

Sat 14th January (Week 18)
Aylestone St James v Northampton Trinity
Bedford Athletic v Loughborough
Long Buckby v Wellingborough
Oadby-Wyggestonians v Luton
Wigston v Towcestrians

Sat 11th March (Week 26)
Loughborough v Oadby-Wyggestonians
Luton v Aylestone St James
Northampton Trinity v Belgrave
Towcestrians v Long Buckby
Wellingborough v Bedford Athletic

Sat 8th April (Week 30)
Aylestone St James v Loughborough
Bedford Athletic v Towcestrians
Belgrave v Luton
Long Buckby v Wigston
Oadby-Wyggestonians v Wellingborough

Sat 22nd April (Week 32)
Loughborough v Belgrave
Luton v Northampton Trinity
Towcestrians v Oadby-Wyggestonians
Wellingborough v Aylestone St James
Wigston v Bedford Athletic

EAST MIDLANDS ONE

Sat 10th September (Week 2)
North'ton Men's Own v Brackley
Biggleswade v Daventry
Northampton BBOB v Rushden & Higham
North'ton Old Scouts v Old Northamptonians
Huntingdon v Ampthill

Sat 24th September (Week 4)
Brackley v Huntingdon
Ampthill v North'ton Old Scouts
Old Northamptonians v Northampton BBOB
Rushden & Higham v Biggleswade
Daventry v St Neots

Sat 8th October (Week 6)
North'ton Old Scouts v Brackley
Huntingdon v North'ton Men's Own
St Neots v Rushden & Higham
Biggleswade v Old Northamptonians
Northampton BBOB v Ampthill

Satu 22nd October (Week 8)
Ampthill v Biggleswade
Old Northamptonians v St Neots
Rushden & Higham v Daventry
North'ton Men's Own v North'ton Old Scouts
Brackley v Northampton BBOB

Sat 12th November (Week 10)
Biggleswade v Brackley
Northampton BBOB v North'ton Men's Own
North'ton Old Scouts v Huntingdon
Daventry v Old Northamptonians
St Neots v Ampthill

Sat 19th November (Week 11)
Huntingdon v Northampton BBOB
North'ton Men's Own v Biggleswade
Brackley v St Neots
Ampthill v Daventry
Old Northamptonians v Rushden & Higham

Sat 26th November (Week 12)
Daventry v Brackley
St Neots v North'ton Men's Own
Biggleswade v Huntingdon
Northampton BBOB v North'ton Old Scouts
Rushden & Higham v Ampthill

Sat 14th January (Week 18)
North'ton Old Scouts v Biggleswade
Huntingdon v St Neots
North'ton Men's Own v Daventry
Brackley v Rushden & Higham
Ampthill v Old Northamptonians

Sat 11th March (Week 26)
Rushden & Higham v North'ton Men's Own
Old Northamptonians v Brackley
Daventry v Huntingdon
St Neots v North'ton Old Scouts
Biggleswade v Northampton BBOB

Sat 8th April (Week 30)
Northampton BBOB v St Neots
North'ton Old Scouts v Daventry
Huntingdon v Rushden & Higham
North'ton Men's Own v Old Northamptonians
Brackly v Ampthill

Sat 22nd April (Week 32)
Ampthill v North'ton Men's Own
Old Northamptonians v Huntingdon
Rushden & Higham v North'ton Old Scouts
Daventry v Northampton BBOB
St Neots v Biggleswade

EAST MIDLANDS TWO

Sat 10th September (Week 2)
Dunstablians v Bedford Queens
Wellingborough OG v Corby
Cutler Hammer v St Ives
Colworth House v Oundle
Vauxhall v Westwood

Sat 24th September (Week 4)
Bedford Queens v Vauxhall
Westwood v Colworth House
Oundle v Cutler Hammer
St Ives v Wellingborough OG
Corby v Northampton Casuals

Sat 8th October (Week 6)
Colworth House v Bedford Queens
Vauxhall v Dunstablians
Northampton Casuals v St Ives
Wellingborough OG v Oundle
Cutler Hammer v Westwood

Sat 22nd October (Week 8)
Dunstablians v Colworth House
Bedford Queens v Cutler Hammer
Westwood v Wellingborough OG
Oundle v Northampton Casuals
St Ives v Corby

Sat 12th November (Week 10)
Wellingborough OG v Bedford Queens
Cutler Hammer v Dunstablians
Colworth House v Vauxhall
Corby v Oundle
Northampton Casuals v Westwood

Sat 19th November (Week 11)
Vauxhall v Cutler Hammer
Dunstablians v Wellingborough OG
Bedford Queens v Northampton Casuals
Westwood v Corby
Oundle v St Ives

Sat 26th November (Week 12)
Corby v Bedford Queens
Northampton v Dunstablians
Wellingborough OG v Vauxhall
Cutler Hammer v Colworth House
St Ives v Westwood

Sat 14th January (Week 18)
Colworth House v Wellingborough OG
Vauxhall v Northampton Casuals
Dunstablians v Corby
Bedford Queens v St Ives
Westwood v Oundle

Sat 11th March (Week 26)
Oundle v Bedford Queens
St Ives v Dunstablians
Corby v Vauxhall
Northampton Casuals v Colworth House
Wellingborough OG v Cutler Hammer

Sat 8th April (Week 30)
Cutler Hammer v Northampton Casuals
Colworth House v Corby
Vauxhall v St Ives
Dunstablians v Oundle
Bedford Queens v Westwood

Sat 22nd April (Week 32)
Westwood v Dunstablians
Oundle v Vauxhall
St Ives v Colworth House
Corby v Cutler Hammer
Northampton Casuals v Wellingborough OG

EAST MIDLANDS THREE

Sat 10th September (Week 2)
Bedford Swifts v North'ton Heathens
Potton v Ramsey
Bretton v Bugbrooke

Sat 24th September (Week 4)
Deepings v Rae Bedford
Bugbrooke v Potton
Ramsey v Bedford Swifts
North'ton Heathens v Old Wellingburians

Sat 8th October (Week 6)
Bretton v Deepings
Old Wellingburians v Ramsey
Bedford Swifts v Bugbrooke

Sat 22nd October (Week 8)
Deepings v Potton
Bugbrooke v Old Wellingburians
Ramsey v North'ton Heathens

Sat 12th November (Week 10)
Bedford Swifts v Deepings
Bretton v Rae Bedford
North'ton Heathens v Bugbrooke

Sat 19th November (Week 11)
Rae Bedford v Potton
Deepings v Old Wellingburians
Bugbrooke v Ramsey

Sat 26th November (Week 12)
North'ton Heathens v Deepings
Bedford Swifts v Rae Bedford
Potton v Bretton

Sat 14th January (Week 18)
Bretton v Bedford Swifts
Rae Bedford v Old Wellingburians
Deepings v Ramsey

Sat 11th March (Week 26)
Bugbrooke v Deepings
North'ton Heathens v Rae Bedford
Old Wellingburians v Bretton
Bedford Swifts v Potton

Sat 8th April (Week 30)
Potton v Old Wellingburians
Bretton v North'ton Heathens
Rae Bedford v Ramsey

Sat 22nd April (Week 32)
Bugbrooke v Rae Bedford
Ramsey v Bretton
North'ton Heathens v Potton
Old Wellingburians v Bedford Swifts

LEICESTERSHIRE ONE

Sat 10th September (Week 2)
Aylestonians v New Parks
Coalville v Lutterworth
Kibworth v Old Bosworthians
Market Bosworth v Melton
South Leicester v West Leicester

Sat 24th September (Week 4)
Aylestonians v South Leicester
West Leicester v Coalville
Lutterworth v Kibworth
Old Bosworthians v Market Bosworth
New Parks v Melton

Sat 8th October (Week 6)
Coalville v Aylestonians
Kibworth v West Leicester
Market Bosworth v Lutterworth
Melton v Old Bosworthians
South Leicester v New Parks

Sat 22nd October (Week 8)
Aylestonians v Kibworth
South Leicester v Coalville
Lutterworth v Melton
New Parks v Old Bosworthians
West Leicester v Market Bosworth

Sat 12th November (Week 10)
Market Bosworth v Aylestonians
Coalville v New Parks
Kibworth v South Leicester
Old Bosworthians v Lutterworth
Melton v West Leicester

Sat 19th November (Week 11)
Aylestonians v Melton
Coalville v Kibworth
New Parks v Lutterworth
South Leicester v Market Bosworth
West Leicester v Old Bosworthians

Sat 26th November (Week 12)
Old Bosworthians v Aylestonians
Market Bosworth v Coalville
Kibworth v New Parks
Lutterworth v West Leicester
Melton v South Leicester

Sat 14th January (Week 18)
Aylestonians v Lutterworth
Coalville v Melton
Kibworth v Market Bosworth
New Parks v West Leicester
South Leicester v Old Bosworthians

Sat 11th March (Week 26)
West Leicester v Aylestonians
Old Bosworthians v Coalville
Melton v Kibworth
Lutterworth v South Leicester
Market Bosworth v New Parks

LEICESTERSHIRE TWO

Sat 24th September (Week 4)
Old Ashbeians v Anstey
Braunstone v Birstall
Shepshed v Burbage
Oakham v Old Newtonians

Sat 8th October (Week 6)
Burbage v Anstey
Birstall v Old Ashbeians
Old Newtonians v Braunstone
Shepshed v Oakham

Sat 22nd October (Week 8)
Anstey v Birstall
Braunstone v Shepshed
Oakham v Burbage
Old Ashbeians v Old Newtonians

Sat 12th November (Week 10)
Old Newtonians v Anstey
Birstall v Burbage
Oakham v Braunstone
Shepshed v Old Ashbeians

Sat 19th November (Week 11)
Anstey v Shepshed
Birstall v Old Newtonians
Burbage v Braunstone
Old Ashbeians v Oakham

Sat 26th November (Week 12)
Oakham v Anstey
Shepshed v Birstall
Braunstone v Old Ashbeians
Old Newtonians v Burbage

Sat 14th January (Week 18)
Anstey v Braunstone
Birstall v Oakham
Burbage v Old Ashbeians
Old Newtonians v Shepshed

SOUTH WEST DIVISION ONE

Sat 10th September (Week 2)
Bridgwater v Berry Hill
Clifton v Weston
High Wycombe v Torquay
Maidenhead v Taunton
Oxford v St Ives

Sat 24th September (Week 4)
Berry Hill v Clifton
St Ives v Reading
Taunton v Oxford
Torquay v Maidenhead
Weston v High Wycombe

Sat 8th October (Week 6)
Clifton v Bridgwater
High Wycombe v Berry Hill
Maidenhead v Weston
Oxford v Torquay
Reading v Taunton

Sat 22nd October (Week 8)
Berry Hill v Maidenhead
Bridgwater v High Wycombe
Taunton v St Ives
Torquay v Reading
Weston v Oxford

Sat 12th November (Week 10)
High Wycombe v Clifton
Maidenhead v Bridgwater
Oxford v Berry Hill
Reading v Weston
St Ives v Torquay

Sat 19th November (Week 11)
Berry Hill v Reading
Bridgwater v Oxford
Clifton v Maidenhead
Torquay v Taunton
Weston v St Ives

Sat 26th November (Week 12)
Maidenhead v High Wycombe
Oxford v Clifton
Reading v Bridgwater
St Ives v Berry Hill
Taunton v Weston

Sat 14th January (Week 18)
Berry Hill v Taunton
Bridgwater v St Ives
Clifton v Reading
High Wycombe v Oxford
Weston v Torquay

Sat 11th March (Week 26)
Oxford v Maidenhead
Reading v High Wycombe
St Ives v Clifton
Taunton v Bridgwater
Torquay v Berry Hill

Sat 8th April (Week 30)
Berry Hill v Weston
Bridgwater v Torquay
Clifton v Taunton
High Wycombe v St Ives
Maidenhead v Reading

Sat 22nd April (Week 32)
Reading v Oxford
St Ives v Maidenhead
Taunton v High Wycombe
Torquay v Clifton
Weston v Bridgwater

SOUTH WEST DIVISION TWO

Sat 10th September (Week 2)
Barnstaple v Abbey
Bournemouth v Redingensians
Brixham v Newbury
Cinderford v Launceston
Dev & C Const v Henley

Sat 24th Sept (Week 4)
Abbey v Bournemouth
Henley v Matson
Launceston v Dev & C Const
Newbury v Cinderford
Redingensians v Brixham

Sat 8th October (Week 6)
Bournemouth v Barnstaple
Brixham v Abbey
Cinderford v Redingensians
Dev & C Const v Newbury
Matson v Launceston

Sat 22nd October (Week 8)
Abbey v Cinderford
Barnstaple v Brixham
Launceston v Henley
Newbury v Matson
Redingensians v Dev & C Const

Sat 12th November (Week 10)
Brixham v Bournemouth
Cinderford v Barnstaple
Dev & C Const v Abbey
Henley v Newbury
Matson v Redingensians

Sat 19th Nove (Week 11)
Abbey v Matson
Barnstaple v Dev & C Const
Bournemouth v Cinderford
Newbury v Launceston
Redingensians v Henley

Sat 26th November (Week 12)
Cinderford v Brixham
Dev & C Const v Bournemouth
Henley v Abbey
Launceston v Redingensians
Matson v Barnstaple

Sat 24th September (Week 4)
Abbey v Bournemouth
Henley v Matson
Launceston v Dev & C Const
Newbury v Cinderford
Redingensians v Brixham

Sat 8th October (Week 6)
Bournemouth v Barnstaple
Brixham v Abbey
Cinderford v Redingensians
Dev & C Const v Newbury
Matson v Launceston

Sat 22nd Oct (Week 8)
Abbey v Cinderford
Barnstaple v Brixham
Launceston v Henley
Newbury v Matson
Redingensians v Dev & C Const

Sat 12th November (Week 10)
Brixham v Bournemouth
Cinderford v Barnstaple
Dev & C Const v Abbey
Henley v Newbury
Matson v Redingensians

Sat 19th November (Week 11)
Abbey v Matson
Barnstaple v Dev & C Const
Bournemouth v Cinderford
Newbury v Launceston
Redingensians v Henley

Sat 26th November (Week 12)
Cinderford v Brixham
Dev & C Const v Bournemouth
Henley v Abbey
Launceston v Redingensians
Matson v Barnstaple

Sat 14th January (Week 18)
Abbey v Launceston
Barnstaple v Henley
Bournemouth v Matson
Brixham v Dev & C Const
Redingensians v Newbury

Sat 11th March (Week 26)
Dev & C Const v Cinderford
Henley v Bournemouth
Launcester v Barnstaple
Matson v Brixham
Newbury v Abbey

Sat 8th April (Week 30)
Abbey v Redingensians
Barnstaple v Newbury
Bournemouth v Launceston
Brixham v Henley
Cinderford v Matson

Sat 22nd April (Week 32)
Henley v Cinderford
Launceston v Brixham
Matson v Dev & C Const
Newbury v Bournemouth
Redingensians v Barnstaple

WESTERN COUNTIES

Sat 10th September (Week 2)
Cirencester v Avonmouth OB
Clevedon v Truro
Crediton v Devonport Services
Gordon League v Tiverton
Newquay Hornets v Redcliffians

Sat 24th September (Week 4)
Devonport Services v Newquay Hornets
Avonmouth OB v Clevedon
Redcliffians v Okehampton
Tiverton Crediton
Truro v Gordon League

Sat 8th October (Week 6)
Clevedon v Cirencester
Crediton v Truro
Gordon League v Avonmouth OB
Newquay Hornets v Tiverton
Okehampton v Devonport Services

Sat 22nd October (Week 8)
Devonport Services v Redcliffians
Avonmouth OB v Crediton
Cirencester v Gordon League
Tiverton v Okehampton
Truro v Newquay Hornets

Sat 12th November (Week 10)
Crediton v Cirencester
Gordon League v Clevedon
Newquay Hornets v Avonmouth OB
Okehampton v Truro
Redcliffians v Tiverton

Sat 19th November (Week 11)
Avonmouth OB v Okehampton
Cirencester v Newquay Hornets
Clevedon v Crediton
Tiverton v Devenport Services
Truro v Redcliffians

Sat 26th November (Week 12)
Devonport Services v Truro
Crediton v Gordon League
Newquay Hornets v Clevedon
Okehampton v Cirencester
Redcliffians v Avonmouth OB

Sat 14th January (Week 18)
Avonmouth OB v Devonport Services
Cirencester v Redcliffians
Clevedon v Okehampton
Gordon League v Newquay Hornets
Truro v Tiverton

Sat 11th March (Week 26)
Devonport Services v Cirencester
Newquay Hornets v Crediton
Okehampton v Gordon League
Redcliffians v Clevedon
Tiverton v Avonmouth OB

Sat 8th April (Week 30)
Cirencester v Tiverton
Clevedon v Devonport Services
Crediton v Okehampton
Avonmouth OB v Truro
Gordon League v Redcliffians

Sat 22nd April (Week 32)
Devonport Services v Gordon League
Okehampton v Newquay Hornets
Redcliffians v Crediton
Tiverton v Clevedon
Truro v Cirencester

SOUTHERN COUNTIES

Sat 10th September (Week 2)
Banbury v Aylesbury
Bletchley v Windsor
Marlow v Swindon
Oxford Marathon v Swanage & Wareham
Slough v Wimborne

Sat 24th September (Week 4)
Aylesbury v Bletchley
Swanage & Wareham v Oxford OB
Swindon v Oxford Marathon
Wimborne v Marlow
Windsor v Slough

Sat 8th October (Week 6)
Bletchley v Banbury
Marlow v Windsor
Oxford Marathon v Wimborne
Oxford OB v Swindon
Slough v Aylesbury

Sat 22nd October (Week 8)
Aylesbury v Marlow
Banbury v Slough
Swindon v Swanage & Wareham
Wimborne v Oxford OB
Windsor v Oxford Marathon

Sat 12th November (Week 10)
Marlow v Banbury
Oxford Marathon v Aylesbury
Oxford OB v Windsor
Slough v Bletchley
Swanage v Wareham v Wimborne

Sat 19th November (Week 11)
Aylesbury v Oxford OB
Banbury v Oxford Marathon
Bletchley v Marlow
Wimborne v Swindon
Windsor v Swanage & Wareham

Sat 26th November (Week 12)
Marlow v Slough
Oxford Marathon v Bletchley
Oxford OB v Banbury
Swanage & Wareham v Aylesbury
Swindon v Windsor

Sat 14th January (Week 18)
Aylesbury v Swindon
Banbury v Swanage & Wareham
Bletchley v Oxford OB
Slouth v Oxford Marathon
Windsor v Wimborne

Sat 11th March (Week 26)
Oxford Marathon v Marlow
Oxford OB v Slough
Swanage & Wareham v Bletchley
Swindon v Banbury
Wimborne v Aylesbury

Sat 8th April (Week 30)
Aylesbury v Windsor
Banbury v Wimborne
Bletchley v Swindon
Marlow v Oxford OB
Slough v Swanage & Wareham

Sat 22nd April (Week 32)
Oxford OB v Oxford Marathon
Swanage & Wareham v Marlow
Swindon v Slough
Wimborne v Bletchley
Windsor v Banbury

GLOUCESTERSHIRE & SOMERSET LEAGUE

Sat 10th September (Week 2)
Cleve v Avon & S Cons
Combe Down v Whitehall
Coney Hill v O Culverhaysians
Gordano v Spartans
Keynsham v Minehead

Sat 24th September (Week 4)
Avon & S Cons v Combe Down
Minehead v Midsomer Norton
O Culverhaysians v Gordano
Spartans v Keynsham
Whitehill v Coney Hill

Sat 8th October (Week 6)
Combe Down v Cleve
Coney Hill v Avon & S Cons
Gordano v Whitehill
Keynsham v O Culverhaysians
Midsomer Norton v Spartans

Sat 22nd Oct (Week 8)
Avon & S Cons v Gordano

Cleve v Coney Hill
O Culverhaysians v Midsomer Norton
Spartans v Minehead
Whitehall v Keynsham

Sat 12th November (Week 10)
Coney Hill v Combe Down
Gordano v Cleve
Keynsham v Avon & S Cons
Midsomer Norton v Whitehall
Minehead v O Culverhaysians

Sat 19th November (Week 11)
Avon & S Cons v Midsomer Norton
Cleve v Keynsham
Combe Down v Gordano
O Culverhaysians v Spartans
Whitehall v Minehead

Sat 26th November (Week 12)
Gordano v Coney Hill
Keynsham v Combe Down
Midsomer Norton v Cleve
Minehead v Avon & S Cons
Spartans v Whitehall

Sat 14th January (Week 18)
Abon & S Cons v Spartans
Cleve v Minehead
Combe Down v Midsomer Norton
Coney Hill v Keynsham
Whitehall v O Culverhaysians

Sat 11th March (Week 26)
Keynsham v Gordano
Midsomer Norton v Coney Hill
Minehead v Combe Down
O Culverhaysians v Avon & S Cons
Spartans v Cleve

Sat 8th April (Week 30)
Avon & S Cons v Whitehall
Cleve v O Culverhaysians
Combe Down v Spartans
Coney Hill v Minehead
Gordano v Midsomer Norton

Sat 22nd April (Week 32)
Midsomer Norton v Keynsham
Minehead v Gordano
O Culverhaysians v Combe Down
Spartans v Coney Hill
Whitehill v Cleve

CORNWALL & DEVON LEAGUE

Sat 10th September (Week 2)
Exeter Saracens v Bideford
Exmouth v Teignmouth
Falmouth v Sidmouth
Hayle v Penzance & Newlyn
Illogen Park v Penryn

Sat 24th September (Week 4)
Bideford v Exmouth
Penzance & Newlyn v Illogen Park
Sidmouth v Hayle
Teignmouth v Falmouth

Sat 8th October (Week 6)
Exmouth v Exeter Saracens
Falmouth v Bideford
Hayle v Teignmouth
Illogen Park v Sidmouth
Paignton v Penzance & Newlyn

Sat 22nd October (Week 8)
Bideford v Hayle
Exeter Saracens v Falmouth
Penzance & Newlyn v Penryn
Sidmouth v Paignton
Teignmouth v Illogen Park

Sat 12th November (Week 10)
Falmouth v Exmouth
Hayle v Exeter Saracens
Illogen Prk v Bideford
Paignton v Teignmouth
Penryn v Sidmouth

Sat 19th November (Week 11)
Bideford v Paignton
Exeter Saracens v Illogen Park
Exmouth v Hayle
Sidmouth v Penzance & Newlyn
Teignmouth v Penryn

Sat 26th November (Week 12)
Hayle v Falmouth
Illogen Park v Exmouth
Paignton v Exeter Saracens
Penryn v Bideford
Penzance & Newlyn v Teignmouth

Sat 10th January (Week 14)
Penryn v Paignton

Sat 14th January (Week 18)
Bideford v Penzance & Newlyn
Exeter Saracens v Penryn
Exmouth v Paignton
Falmouth v Illogen Park
Teignmouth v Sidmouth

Sat 11th March (Week 26)
Illogen Park v Hayle
Paignton v Falmouth
Penryn v Exmouth
Penzance & Newlyn v Exeter Saracens
Sidmouth v Bideford

Sat 8th April (Week 30)
Bideford v Teignmouth
Exeter Saracens v Sidmouth
Exmouth v Penzance & Newlyn
Falmouth v Penryn
Hayle v Paignton

Sat 22nd April (Week 32)
Paignton v Illogen Park
Penryn v Hayle
Penzance & Newlyn v Falmouth
Sidmouth v Exmouth
Teignmouth v Exeter Saracens

GLOUCESTERSHIRE ONE

Sat 10th September (Week 2)
Dings Crusaders v Tredworth
Drybrook v St Mary's OB
Longlevens v O Patesians
N Bristol v Bream
Saintbridge v Widden OB

Sat 24th September (Week 4)
Bream v Saintbridge
O Patesians v O Colstonians
St Mary's OB v Longlevens
Tredworth v Drybrook
Widden OB v Dings Crusaders

Sat 8th October (Week 6)
Dings Crusaders v Bream
Drybrook v Widden OB
Longlevens v Tredworth
O Colstonians v St Mary's OB
Saintbridge v N Bristol

Sat 22nd October (Week 8)
Bream v Drybrook
N Bristol v Dings Crusaders
St Mary's OB v O Patesians
Tredworth v O Colstonians
Widden OB v Longlevens

Sat 12th November (Week 10)
Dings Crusaders v Saintbridge
Drybrook v N Bristol
Longlevens v Bream
O Colstonians v Widden OB
O Patesians v Tredworth

Sat 19th November (Week 11)
Bream v O Colstonians
N Bristol v Longlevens
Saintbridge v Drybrook
Tredworth v St Mary's OB
Widden OB v O Patesians

Sat 26th November (Week 12)
Drybrook v Dings Crusaders
Longlevens v Saintbridge
O Colstonians v N Bristol
O Patesians v Bream
St Mary's OB v Widden OB

Sat 14th January (Week 18)
Bream v St Mary's OB
Dings Crusaders v Longlevens
N Bristol v O Patesians
Saintbridge v O Colstonians
Widden OB v Tredworth

Sat 11th March (Week 26)
Longlevens v Drybrook
O Colstonians v Dings Crusaders
O Patesians v Saintbridge
St Mary's OB v N Bristol
Tredworth v Bream

Sat 8th April (Wek 30)
Bream v Widden OB
Dings Crusaders v O Patesians
Drybrook v O Colstonians
N Bristol v Tredworth
Saintbridge v St Mary's OB

Sat 22nd April (Week 32)
O Colstonians v Longlevens
O Patesians v Drybrook
St Mary's OB v Dings Crusaders
Tredworth v Saintbridge
Widden OB v N Bristol

GLOUCESTERSHIRE TWO

Sat 10th September (Week 2)
Barton Hill v Ashley Down
Brockworth v O Bristolians
Bristol Saracens v O Cryptians
Cheltenham v Gloucester OB
Chelt Saracens v Cheltenham NO

Sat 24th September (Week 4)
Ashley Down v Brockworth
Cheltenham NO v Cotham Park
Gloucester OB v Chelt Saracens
O Cryptians v Cheltenham CS
O Bristolians v Bristol Saracens

Sat 8th Oct (Week 6)
Brockworth v Barton Hill
Bristol Saracens v Ashley Down
Cheltenham CS v O Bristolians
Chelt Saracens v O Cryptians
Cotham Park v Gloucester OB

Sat 22nd October (Week 8)
Ashley Down v Cheltenham CS
Barton Hill v Bristol Saracens
Gloucester OB v Cheltenham NO
O Cryptians v Cotham Park
O Bristolians v Chelt Saracens

Sat 12th November (Week 10)
Bristol Saracens v Brockworth
Cheltenham v Barton Hill
Chelt Saracens v Ashley Down
Cotham Park v O Bristolians
Cheltenham NO v O Cryptians

Sat 19th November (Week 11)
Ashley Down v Cotham Park
Barton Hill v Chelt Saracens
Brockworth v Cheltenham CS
O Cryptians v Gloucester OB
O Bristolians v Cheltenham NO

Sat 26th November (Week 12)
Cheltenham CS v Bristol Saracens
Chelt Saracens v Brockworth
Cotham Park v Barton Hill
Cheltenham NO v Ashley Down
Gloucester OB v O Bristolians

Sat 14th January (Week 18)
Ashley Down v Gloucester OB
Barton Hill v Cheltenham NO
Brockworth v Cotham Park
Bristol Saracens v Chelt Saracens
O Bristolians v O Cryptians

Sat 11th March (Week 26)
Chelt Saracens v Cheltenham CS
Cotham Park v Bristol Saracens
Cheltenham v Brockworth
Gloucester OB v Barton Hill
O Cryptians v Ashley Down

Sat 8th April (Week 30)
Ashley Down v O Bristolians
Barton Hill v O Cryptians
Brockworth v Gloucester OB
Bristol Saracens v Cheltenham NO
Cheltenham CS v Cotham Park

Sat 22nd April (Week 32)
Cotham Park v Chelt Saracens
Cheltenham NO v Cheltenham CS
Gloucester OB v Bristol Saracens
O Cryptians v Brockworth
O Bristolians v Barton Hill

GLOUCESTERSHIRE THREE

Sat 10th September (Week 2)
Chipping Sodbury v Cainscross
Chosen Hill v Thornbury
Frampton Cotterell v Tewkesbury
Dursley v Painswick
O Elizabeths v Smiths

Sat 24th September (Week 4)
Cainscross v Chosen Hill
Smiths v Kingswood
Painswick v O Elizabeths
Tewkesbury v Dursley
Thornbury v Frampton Cotterell

Sat 8th October (Week 6)
Chosen Hill v Chipping Sodbury
Frampton Cotterell v Cainscross
Dursley v Thornbury
O Elizabeths v Tewkesbury
Kingswood v Painswick

Sat 22nd October (Week 8)
Cainscross v Dursley
Chipping Sodbury v Frampton Cotterell
Painswick v Smiths
Tewkesbury v Kingswood
Thornbury v O Elizabeths

Sat 12th November (Week 10)
Frampton Cotterell v Chosen Hill
Dursley v Chipping Sodbury
O Elizabeths v Caincross
Kingswood v Thornbury
Smiths v Tewkesbury

Sat 19th November (Week 11)
Cainscross v Kingswood
Chipping Sodbury v O Elizabeths
Chosen Hill v Dursley
Tewkesbury v Painswick
Thornbury v Smiths

Sat 26th November (Week 12)
Dursley v Frampton Cotterell
O Elizabeths v Chosen Hill
Kingswood v Chipping Sodbury
Smiths v Cainscross
Painswick v Thornbury

Sat 14th January (Week 18)
Cainscross v Painswick
Chipping Sodbury v Smiths
Chosen Hill v Kingswood
Frampton Cotterell v O Elizabeths
Thornbury v Tewkesbury

Sat 11th March (Week 26)
O Elizabeths v Dursley
Kingswood v Frampton Cotterell
Smiths v Chosen Hill
Painswick v Chipping Sodbury
Tewkesbury v Cainscross

Sat 8th April (Week 30)
Cainscross v Thornbury
Chipping Sodbury v Tewkesbury
Chosen Hill v Painswick
Frampton Cotterell v Smiths
Dursley v Kingswood

Sat 22nd April (Week 32)
Kingswood v O Elizabeths
Smiths v Dursley
Painswick v Frampton Cotterell
Tewkesbury v Chosen Hill
Thornbury v Chipping Sodbury

GLOUCESTERSHIRE FOUR

Sat 10th September (Week 2)
Aretians v All Blues
BAC v Dowty
Bishopston v Newent
Bristol Tels v O Cothamians
Broad Plain v Minchinhampton
Gloucester CS v Hucclecote OB

Sat 24th September (Week 4)
All Blues v BAC
Aretians v Gloucester CS
Dowty v Bristol Tels
Minchinhampton v Hucclecote OB
Newent v Broad Plain
O Cothamians v Bishopston

Sat 8th October (Week 6)
BAC v Aretians
Bishopston v Dowty
Bristol Tels v All Blues
Broad Plain v O Cothamians
Gloucester CS v Minchinhampton
Hucclecote v Newent

Sat 22nd October (Week 8)
All Blues v Bishopston
Aretians v Bristol Tels
BAC v Gloucester CS
Dowty v Broad Plain
Newent v Minchinhampton
O Cothamians v Hucclecote OB

Sat 12th November (Week 10)
Bishopston v Aretians
Bristol Tels v BAC
Broad Plain v All Blues
Gloucester CS v Newent
Hucclecote v Dowty
Minchinhampton v O Cothamians

Sat 19th November (Week 11)
All Blues v Hucclecote OB
BAC v Bishopston
Bristol Tels v Gloucester CS
Dowty v Minchinhampton
O Cothamians v Newent

Sat 26th November (Week 12)
Bishopston v Bristol Tels
Broad Plain v BAC
Gloucester CS v O Cothamians
Hucclecote OB v Aretians
Minchinhampton v All Blues
Newent v Dowty

Sat 14th January (Week 18)
All Blues v Newent
Aretians v Minchinhampton
BAC v Hucclecote OB
Bishopston v Gloucester CS
Bristol Tels v Broad Plain
Dowty v O Cothamians

Sat 11th March (Week 26)
Broad Plain v Bishopston
Gloucester CS v Dowty
Hucclecote OB v Bristol Tels
Minchinhampton v BAC
Newent v Aretians
O Cothamians v All Blues

Sat 8th April (Week 30)
All Blues v Dowty
Aretians v O Cothamians
BAC v Newent
Bishopston v Hucclecote OB
Bristol Tels v Minchinhampton
Broad Plain v Gloucester CS

Sat 22nd April (Week 32)
Dowty v Aretians
Gloucester CS v All Blues
Hucclecote OB v Broad Plain
Minchinhampton v Bishopston
Newent v Bristol Tels
O Cothamians v BAC

DEVON LEAGUE ONE

Sat 10th September (Week 2)
D'port HSOB v Totnes
Honiton v Cullompton
Ivybridge v South Molton
Kingsbridge v Newton Abbot
O Technicians v Plymouth CS

Sat 24h September (Week 4)
Cullompton v D'port HSOB
Newton Abbot v O Technicians
Plymouth CS v Plymouth ARG
South Molton v Kingsbridge
Totnes v Ivybridge

Sat 8th October (Week 6)
D'port HSOB v Honiton
Ivybridge v Cullompton
Kingsbridge v Totnes
O Technicians v South Molton
Plymouth ARG v Newton Abbot

Sat 22nd October (Week 8)
Cullompton v Kingsbridge
Honiton v Ivybridge
Newton Abbot v Plymouth CS
South Molton v Plymouth ARG
Totnes v O Technicians

Sat 12th November (Week 10)
Ivybridge v D'port HSOB
Kingsbridge v Honiton
O Technicians v Cullompton
Plymouth ARG v Totnes
Plymouth CS v South Molton

Sat 19th November (Week 11)
Cullompton v Plymouth ARG
D'port HSOB v Kingsbridge

Honiton v O Technicians
South Molton v Newton Abbot
Totnes v Plymouth CS

Sat 26th November (Week 12)
Kingsbridge v Ivybridge
Newton Abbot v Totnes
O Technicians v D'port HSOB
Plymouth ARG v Honiton
Plymouth CS v Cullompton

Sat 14th January (Week 18)
Cullompton v Newton Abbot
D'port v Plymouth ARG
Honiton v Plymouth CS
Ivybridge v O Technicians
Totnes v South Molton

Sat 11th March (Week 26)
Newton Abbot v Honiton
O Technicians v Kingsbridge
Plymouth ARG v Ivybridge
Plymouth CS v D'port HSOB
South Molton v Cullompton

Sat 11th March (Week 26)
Newton Abbot v Honiton
O Technicians v Kingsbridge
Plymouth ARG v Ivybridge
Plymouth CS v D'port HSOB
South Molton v Cullompton

Sat 8th April (Week 30)
Cullompton v Totnes
D'port HSOB v Newton Abbot
Honiton v South Molton
Ivybridge v Plymouth CS
Kingsbridge v Plymouth ARG

Sat 22nd April (Week 32)
Newton Abbot v Ivybridge
Plymouth ARG v O Technicians
Plymouth CS v Kingsbridge
South Molton v D'port HSOB
Totnes v Honiton

DEVON LEAGUE TWO "A"

Sat 10th September (Week 2)
Jesters v Prince Rock
O Plym & Mann v Victoria
O.P. Oaks v Tamar Saracens
Plymouth YMCA v St Columba

Sat 24th September (Week 4)
Prince Rock v O Plym & Mann
St Columba v Plympton
Tamar Saracens v Plymouth YMCA
Victoria v O.P. Oaks

Sat 8th October (Week 6)
O Plym & Mann v Jesters
O.P. Oaks v Prince Rock
Plymouth YMCA v Victoria
Plympton v Tamar Saracens

Sat 22nd October (Week 8)
Jesters v O.P. Oaks
Prince Rock v Plymouth YMCA
Tamar Saracens v St Columba
Victoria v Plympton

Sat 12th November (Week 10)
O.P. Oaks v O Plym & Mann
Plymouth YMCA v Jesters
Plympton v Prince Rock
St Columba v Victoria

Sat 19th November (Week 11)
Jesters v Plympton
O Plym & Mann v Plymouth YMCA
Prince Rock v St Columba
Victoria v Tamar Saracens

Sat 26th November (Week 12)
Plymouth YMCA v O.P. Oaks
Plympton v O Plym & Mann
St Columba v Jesters
Tamar Saracens v Prince Rock

Sat 14th January (Week 18)
Jesters v Tamar Saracens
O Plym & Mann v St Columba
O.P. Oaks v Plympton
Prince Rock v Victoria

Sat 11th March (Week 26)
Plympton v Plymouth YMCA
St Columba v O.P. Oaks
Tamar Saracens v O Plym & Mann
Victoria v Jesters

DEVON LEAGUE TWO "B"

Sat 10th September (Week 2)
Dartmouth v Topsham
North Tawton v Tavistock
Withycombe v Salcombe

Sat 24th September (Week 4)
Ilfracombe v Withycombe
Tavistock v Salcombe
Topsham v North Tawton

Sat 18th October (Week 6)
Dartmouth v Ilfracombe
Salcombe v Topsham
Tavistock v Withycombe

Sat 22nd October (Week 8)
Ilfracombe v North Tawton
Topsham v Tavistock
Withycombe v Dartmouth

Sat 12th November (Week 10)
North Tawton v Dartmouth
Salcombe v Ilfracombe
Withycombe v Topsham

Sat 19th November (Week 11)
Dartmouth v Salcombe
Ilfracombe v Tavistock
North Tawton v Withycombe

Sat 26th November (Week 12)
Salcombe v North Tawton
Tavistock v Dartmouth
Topsham v Ilfracombe

BUCKS & OXON LEAGUE ONE

Sat 10th September (Week 2)
Grove v Chinnor
Littlemore v Chiltern
Pennanians v Buckingham
Witney v Bicester

Sat 24th Septembe (Week 4)
Bicester v Drifters
Buckingham v Witney
Chiltern v Pennanians
Chinnor v Littlemore
Milton Keynes v Grove

Sat 8th October (Week 6)
Beaconsfield v Bicester
Drifters v Buckingham
Littlemore v Milton Keynes
Pennanians v Chinnor
Witney v Chiltern

Sat 22nd October (Week 8)
Buckingham v Beaconsfield
Chiltern v Drifters
Chinnor v Witney
Grove v Littlemore
Milton Keynes v Pennanians

Sat 12th November (Week 10)
Beaconsfield v Chiltern
Bicester v Buckingham
Drifters v Chinnor
Pennanians v Grove
Witney v Milton Keynes

Sat 19th November (Week 11)
Chinnor v Beaconsfield
Chiltern v Bicester
Grove v Witney
Littlemore v Pennanians
Milton Keynes v Drifters

Sat 26th November (Week 12)
Beaconsfield v Milton Keynes
Bicester v Chinnor
Buckingham v Chiltern
Drifters v Grove
Witney v Littlemore

Sat 14th January (Week 18)
Chinnor v Buckingham
Grove v Beaconsfield
Littlemore v Drifters
Milton Keynes v Bicester
Pennanians v Witney

Sat 25th February (Week 24)
Drifters v Beaconsfield

Sat 11th March (Week 26)
Beaconsfield v Littlemore
Bicester v Grove
Buckingham v Milton Keynes
Chiltern v Chinnor
Drifters v Pennanians

Sat 8th April (Week 30)
Grove v Buckingham
Littlemore v Bicester
Milton Keynes v Chiltern
Pennanians v Beaonsfield
Witney v Drifters

Sat 22nd April (Week 32)
Beaconsfield v Witney
Bicester v Pennanians
Buckingham v Littlemore
Chiltern v Grove
Chinnor v Milton Keynes

BUCKS & OXON LEAGUE TWO

Sat 10th September (Week 2)
Chesham v Abingdon
Cholsey v Wheatley
Didcot v Phoenix
Gosford AB v Olney

Sat 24th September (Week 4)
Abingdon v Chipping Norton
Olney v Harwell
Ploenix v Gosford AB
Wheatley v Didcot

Sat 8th October (Week 6)
Chipping Norton v Chesham
Cholsey v Abingdon
Gosford AB v Wheatley
Harwell v Phoenix

Sat 22nd October (Week 8)
Abingdon v Didcot
Chesham v Cholsey
Phoenix v Olney
Wheatley v Harwell

Sat 12th November (Week 10)
Cholsey v Chipping Norton
Didcot v Chesham
Gosford AB v Abingdon
Olney v Wheatley

Sat 19th November (Week 11)
Abingdon v Harwell
Chesham v Gosford AB
Chipping Norton v Didcot
Wheatley v Phoenix

Sat 26th November (Week 12)
Didcot v Cholsey
Gosford AB v Chipping Norton
Harwell v Chesham
Olney v Abingdon

Sat 14th January (Week 18)
Abingdon v Phoenix
Chesham v Olney
Chipping Norton v Harwell
Cholsey v Gosford AB

Sat 11th March (Week 26)
Gosford AB v Didcot
Harwell v Cholsey
Olney v Chipping Norton
Phoenix v Chesham
Wheatley v Abingdon

Sat 8th April (Week 30)
Chesham v Wheatley
Chipping Norton v Phoenix
Cholsey v Olney
Didcot v Harwell

Sat 22nd April (Week 32)
Harwell v Gosford AB
Olney v Didcot
Phoenix v Cholsey
Wheatley v Chipping Norton

BERKS, DORSET & WILTS LEAGUE ONE

Sat 10th September (Week 2)
Bracknell v Weymouth
Chippenham v Sherborne
Devizes v Aldermaston
Dorchester v Wootton Bassett
Marlborough v Corsham

Sat 24th September (Week 4)
Aldermaston v Dorchester
Corsham v Chippenham
Sherborne v REME Arborfield
Weymouth v Marlborough
Wootton Bassett v Bracknell

Sat 8th October (Week 6)
Bracknell v Aldermaston
Dorchester v Devizes
Chippenham v Weymouth
Marlborough v Wootton Bassett
REME Arborfield v Corsham

Sat 22nd October (Week 8)
Aldermaston v Marlborough
Chippenham v Aldermaston
Marlborough v Devizes
REME Arborfield v Wootton Bassett
Sherborne v Weymouth

Sat 19th November (Week 11)
Alermaston v REME Arborfield
Devizes v Chippenham
Dorchester v Marlborough
Weymouth v Corsham
Wootton Bassett v Sherborne

Sat 26th November (Week 12)
Chippenham v Dorchester
Corsham v Wootton Bassett
Marlborough v Bracknell
REME Arborfield v Devizes
Sherborne v Aldermaston

Sat 14th January (Week 18)
Aldermaston v Corsham
Bracknell v Chippenham
Devizes v Sherborne
Dorchester v REME Arborfield
Wootton Bassett v Weymouth

Sat 11th March (Week 26)
Chippenham v Marlborough
Corsham v Devizes
REME Arborfield v Bracknell
Sherborne v Dorchester
Weymouth v Aldermaston

Sat 8th April (Week 30)
Aldermaston v Wootton Bassett
Bracknell v Sherborne
Devizesv Weymouth
Dorchester v Corsham
Marlborough v REME Arborfield

Sat 22nd April (Week 32)
Corsham v Bracknell
REME Arborfield v Chippenham
Sherborne v Marlborough
Weymouth v Dorchester
Wootton Bassett v Devizes

BERKS, DORSET & WILTS LEAGUE TWO

Sat 10th September (Week 2)
Hungerford v Bradford on Avon
Lytchett Minster v Supermarine
Minety v Puddletown
North Dorset v Poole
Trowbridge v Swindon Colleges

Sat 24th September (Week 4)
Bradford on Avon v Trowbridge
Poole v Oakmedians
Puddleton v North Dorset
Supermarine v Minety
Swindon Colleges v Lychett Minster

Sat 8th October (Week 6)
Lychett Minster v Bradford on Avon
Minety v Swindon Colleges
North Dorset v Supermarine
Oakmedians v Puddletown
Trowbridge v Hungerford

Sat 22nd October (Week 8)
Bradford on Avon v Minety
Hungerford v Lytchett Minster
Puddletown v Poole
Supermarine v Oakmedians
Swindon Colleges v North Dorset

Sat 12th November (Week 10)
Lytchett Minster v Trowbridge
Minety v Hungerford
North Dorset v Bradford on Avon
Oakmedians v Swindon Colleges
Poole v Supermarine

Sat 19th November (Week 11)
Bradford on Avon v Oakmedians
Hungerford v North Dorset
Supemarine v Puddletown
Swindon Colleges v Poole
Trowbridge v Minety

Sat 26th November (Week 12)
Minety v Lytchett Minster
North Dorset v Trowbridge
Oakmedians v Hungerford
Poole v Bradford on Avon
Puddletown v Swindon Colleges

Sat 14th January (Week 18)
Bradford on Avon v Puddletown
Hungerford v Poole
Lytchett Minster v North Dorset
Swindon Colleges v Supermarine
Trowbridge v Oakmedians

Sat 11th March (Week 26)
North Dorset v Minety
Oakmedians v Lytchett Minster
Poole v Trowbridge
Puddletown v Hungerford
Supermarie v Bradford on Avon

Sat 8th April (Week 30)
Bradford on Avon v Swindon Colleges
Hungerford v Supermarine
Lytchett Minster v Poole
Minety v Oakmedians
Trowbridge v Puddleton

Sat 22nd April (Week 32)
Oakmedians v North Dorset
Poole v Minety
Puddletown v Lytchett Minster
Supermarine v Trowbridge
Swindon Colleges v Hungerford

BERKS, DORSET & WILTS LEAGUE THREE EAST

Sat 24th September (Week 4)
Amesbury v Calne
Larkhill Gunners v Tadley
Melksham v Thatcham

Sat 8th October (Week 6)
Calne v Berks S Hall
Colerne v Amesbury
Thatcham v Larkhill Gunners

Sat 22nd October (Week 8)
Amesbury v Larkhill Gunners
Berks S Hall v Colerne
Tadley v Melksham

Sat 12th November (Week 10)
Colerne v Calne
Larkhill Gunners v Berks S Hall
Melksham v Amesbury
Thatcham v Tadley

Sat 19th November (Week 11)
Amesbury v Tadley
Berks S Hall v Melksham
Calne v Larkhill Gunners
Colerne v Thatcham

Sat 26th November (Week 12)
Larkhill Gunners v Colerne
Melksham v Calne
Tadley v Berks S Hall
Thatcham v Amesbury

Sat 24th January (Week 18)
Berks S Hall v Thatcham
Calne v Tadley
Colerne v Melksham

Sat 11th March (Week 26)
Berks S Hall v Amesbury
Melksham v Larkhill Gunners
Tadley v Colerne
Thatcham v Calne

BERKS, DORSET & WILTS LEAGUE THREE WEST

Sat 24th September (Week 4)
Blandford v Dorset West
Portcastrians v Westbury

Sat 8th October (Week 6)
Dorset West v Bridport
Plessey v Blandford

Sat 22nd October (Week 8)
Blandford v Portcastrians
Bridport v Plessey
Westbury v Warminster

Sat 12th November (Week 10)
Plessey v Dorset West
Portcastrians v Bridport
Warminster v Blandford

Sat 19th November (Week 11)
Blandford v Westbury
Bridport v Warminster
Dorset West v Portcastirans

Sat 26th November (Week 12)
Portcastrians v Plessey
Warminster v Dorset West
Westbury v Bridport

Sat 14th January (Week 18)
Dorset West v Westbury
Plessey v Warminster

Sat 11th March (Week 26)
Bridport v Blandford
Warminster v Portcastrians
Westbury v Plessey

SOMERSET LEAGUE ONE

Sat 10th September (Week 2)
Bristol Harlequins v Burnham
Frome v Yatton
Hornets v St Brendans
N Petherton v Walcott OB
Oldfield OB v Old Sulians

Sat 24th Septemer (Week 4)
Burnham v Frome
Old Sulians v St Bernadettes
St Brendans v N Petherton
Walcott OB v Oldfield OB
Yatton v Hornets

Sat 8th October (Week 6)
Frome v Bristol Harlequins
Hornets v Burnham
N Petherton v Yatton
Oldfield OB v St Brendans
St Bernadettes v Walcott OB

Sat 22nd October (Week 8)
Bristol Harlequins v Hornets
Burnham v N Petherton
St Brendans v St Bernadettes
Walcott OB v Old Sulians
Yatton v Oldfield OB

Sat 12th November (Week 12)
Hornets v Frome
N Petherton v Bristol Harlequins
Old Sulians v St Brendans
Oldfield v Burnham
St Bernadettes v Yatton

Sat 19th November (Week 11)
Bristol Harlequins v Oldfield OB
Burnha v St Bernadettes
Frome v N Petherton
St Brendans v Walcott OB
Yatton v Old Sulians

Sat 26th November (Week 12)
N Petherton v Hornets
Old Sulians v Burnham
Oldfield OB v Frome
St Bernadettes v Bristol Harlequins
Walcott OB v Yatton

Sat 14th January (Week 18)
Bristol Harlequins v Old Sulians
Burnham v Walcott OB
Frome v St Bernadettes
Hornets v Oldfield OB
Yatton v St Brendans

Sat 11th March (Week 26)
Old Sulians v Frome
Oldfield OB v N Petherton
St Bernadettes v Hornets
St Brendans v Burnham
Walcott OB v Bristol Harlequins

Sat 8th April (Week 30)
Bristol Harlequins v St Brendans
Burnham v Yatton
Frome v Walcott OB
Hornets v Old Sulians
N Petherton v St Bernadettes

Sat 22nd April (Week 32)
Old Sulians v N Petherton
St Bernadettes v Oldfield OB
St Brendans v Frome
Walcott OB v Hornets
Yatton v Bristol Harlequins

COURAGE
CLUBS CHAMPIONSHIP

SOMERSET LEAGUE TWO

Sat 10th September (Week 2)
Avonvale v Wells
Bath OE v Avon
Blagdon v Winscombe
Crewkerne v Stoth & Pitt
Wellington v Westland
Yeovil v Imperial

Sat 24th September (Week 4)
Avon v Blagdon
Bath OE v Yeovil
Stoth & Pitt v Wellington
Wells v Crewkerne
Wewtland v Imperial
Winscombe v Avonvale

Sat 8th October (Week 6)
Avonvale v Avon
Blagdon v Bath OE
Crewkerne v Winscombe
Imperial v Stoth & Pitt
Wellington v Wells
Yeovil v Westland

Sat 22nd October (Week 8)
Avon v Crewkerne
Bath OE v Avonvale
Blagdon v Yeovil
Stoth & Pitt v Westland
Wells v Imperial
Winscombe v Wellington

Sat 12th November (Week 10)
Avonvale v Blagdon
Crewkerne v Bath OE
Imperial v Winscombe
Wellington Avon
Westland v Wells
Yeovil v Stoth & Pitt

Sat 19th November (Week 11)
Avon v Imperial
Avonvale v Yeovil
Bath OE v Wellington
Balgdon v Crewkerne
Wells v Stoth & Pitt
Winscombe v Westland

Sat 26th November (Week 12)
Crewkerne v Avonvale
Imperial v Bath OE
Stoth & Pitt v Winscombe
Wellington v Blagdon
Westland v Avon
Yeovil v Wells

Sat 14th January (Week 18)
Avon v Stoth & Pitt
Avonvale v Wellington
Bath OE v Westland
Blagdon v Imperial
Crewkerne v Yeovil
Winscombe v Wells

Sat 11th March (Week 26)
Imperials v Avonvale
Stoth & Pitt v Bath OE
Wellington v Crewkerne
Wells v Avon
Westland v Blagdon
Yeovil v Winscombe

Sat 8th April (Week 30)
Avon v Winscombe
Avonvale v Westland
Bath OE v Wells
Blagdon v Stoth & Pitt
Crewkerne v Imperial
Wellington v Yeovil

Sat 22nd April (Week 32)
Imperial v Wellington
Stoth & Pitt v Avonvale
Wells v Blagdon
Westland v Crewkerne
Winscombe v Bath OE
Yeovil v Avon

SOMERSET LEAGUE THREE

Sat 10th September (Week 2)
Bath CS v Backwell
Castle Cary v Cheddar
Chew Valley v O Ashtonians
Morganians v Chard
TOR v Wincanton
Wiveliscombe v Aller

Sat 24th September (Week 4)
Backwell v Castle Cary
Bath CS v Wiveliscombe
Chard v TOR
Cheddar v Chew Valley
O Ashtonians v Morganians
Wincanton v Aller

Sat 8th October (Week 6)
Aller v Chard
Castle Cary v Bath CS
Chew Valley v Backwell
Morganians v Cheddar
TOR v O Ashtonians
Wiveliscombe Wincanton

Sat 22nd October (Week 8)
Backwell v Morganians
Bath CS v Chew Valley
Castle Cary v Wiveliscombe
Chard v Wincanton
Cheddar v TOR
O Ashtonians v Aller

Sat 12th November (Week 10)
Alle v Cheddar
Chew Valley v Castle Cary
Morganians v Bath CS
TOR v Backwell
Wincanton v O Ashtonians
Wiveliscombe v Chard

Sat 19th November (Week 11)
Backwell v Aller
Bath CS v TOR
Castle Cary v Morganians
Cheddar v Wincanton
Chew Valley v Wiveliscombe
O Ashtonians v Chard

Sat 26th November (Week 12)
Aller v Bath CS
Chard v Cheddar
Morganians v Chew Valley
TOR v Castle Cary
Wincanton v Backwell
Wiveliscombe v O Ashtonians

Sat 14th January (Week 18)
Backwell v Chard
Bath CS v Wincanton
Castle Cary v Aller
Chew Valley v TOR
Cheddar v O Ashtonians
Morganians v Wiveliscombe

Sat 11th March (Week 26)
Aller v Chew Valley
Chard v Bath CS
O Ashtonians v Backwell
TOR v Morganians
Wincanton v Castle Cary
Wiveliscombe v Cheddar

Sat 8th April (Week 30)
Backwell v Cheddar
Bath CS v O Ashtonians
Chew Valley v Wincanton
Morganians v Aller
TOR v Wiveliscombe

Thurs 13th April (Week 30)
Chard v Castle Cary

Sat 22nd April (Week 32)
Aller v TOR
Chard v Chew Valley
Cheddar v Bath CS
O Ashtonians v Castle Cary
Wincanton v Morganians
Wiveliscombe v Backwell

CORNWALL LEAGUE ONE

Sat 10th September (Week 2)
Bude v Bodmin
Helston v Wadebridge
Lankelly v Veor
Liskeard-Looe v Saltash
Redruth Albany v St Austell

Sat 24th September (Week 4)
Bodmin v Helston
St Austell v St Agnes
Saltash v Redruth Albany
Veor v Liskeard-Looe
Wadebridge v Lankelly

Sat 8th October (Week 6)
Helston v Bude
Lankelly v Bodmin
Liskeard-Looe v Wadebridge
Redruth Albany v Veor
St Agnes v Saltash

Sat 22nd October (Week 8)
Bodmin v Liskeard-Looe
Bude v Lankelly
Saltash v St Austell
Veor v St Agnes
Wadebridge v Redruth Albany

Sat 12th November (Week 10)
Lankelly v Helston
Liskeard-Looe v Bude
Redruth Albany v Bodmin
St Agnes v Wadebridge
St Austell v Veor

Sat 10th November (Week 11)
Bodmin v St Agnes
Bude v Redruth Albany
Helston v Liskeard-Looe
Veor v Saltash
Wadebridge v St Austell

Sat 26th November (Week 12)
Liskeard-Looe v Lankelly
Redruth Albany v Helston
St Agnes v Bude
St Austell v Bodmin
Saltash v Wadebridge

Sat 14th January (Week 18)
Bodmin v Saltash
Bude v St Austell
Helston v St Agnes
Lankelly v Redruth Albany
Wadebridge v Veor

Sat 11th March (Week 26)
Redruth Albany v Liskeard-Looe
St Agnes v Lankelly
St Austell v Helston
Saltash v Bude
Veor v Bodmin

Sat 8th April (Week 30)
Bodmin v Wadebridge
Bude v Veor
Helston v Saltash
Lankelly v St Austell
Liskeard-Looe v St Agnes

Sat 22nd April (Week 32)
St Agnes v Redruth Albany
St Austell v Liskeard-Looe
Saltash v Lankelly
Veor v Helston
Wadebridge v Bude

CORNWALL LEAGUE TWO

Sat 10th September (Week 2)
Perranporth v Redruth GSOB
RNAS Culdrose v Roseland
St Just v Stithians

Sat 24th September (Week 4)
Redruth GSOB v St Just
RNAS Culdrose v Perranporth
Roseland v Stithians

Sat 8th October (Week 6)
Perranporth v St Just
Roseland v Redruth GSOB
Stithians v RNAS Culdrose

Sat 22nd October (Week 8)
RNAS Culdrose v Redruth GSOB
St Just v Roseland
Stithians v Perranporth

Sat 12th November (Week 10)
Perranporth v Roseland
Redruth GSOB v Stithians
RNAS Culdrose v St Just

Sat 19th November (Week 11)
Redruth GSOB v Perranporth
Roseland v RNAS Culdrose
Stithians v St Just

Sat 26th November (Week 12)
Perranporth v RNAS Culdrose
St Just v Redruth GSOB
Stithians v Roseland

Sat 14th January (Week 18)
Redruth GSOB v Roseland
RNAS Culdrose v Stithians
St Just v Perranporth

Sat 11th March (Week 26)
Perranporth v Stithians
Redruth GSOB v RNAS Culdrose
Roseland v St Just

Sat 8th April (Week 30)
Roseland v Perranporth
St Just v RNAS Culdrose
Stithians v Redruth GSOB

LONDON LEAGUE ONE

Sat 24th September (Week 4)
North Walsham v Ipswich
Streatham/Croydon v Dartfordians
Sutton & Epsom v Guildford & Godalming
Ruislip v Lewes
Old Gaytonians v U.S. Portsmouth

Sat 8th October (Week 6)
Ipswich v Old Gaytonians
U.S. Portsmouth v Ruislip
Lewes v Sutton & Epsom
Guildford & Godalming v Streatham/Croydon
Dartfordians v Basingstoke

Sat 22nd October (Week 8)
Ruislip v Ipswich
Old Gaytonians v North Walsham
Basingstoke v Guildford & Godalming
Streatham-Croydon v Lewes
Sutton & Epsom v U.S. Portsmouth

Sat 12th November (Week 10)
North Walsham v Ruislip
Ipswich v Sutton & Epsom
U.S. Portsmouth v Streatham/Croydon
Lewes v Basingstoke
Guildford & Godalming v Dartfordians

Sat 19th November (Week 11)
Streatham/Croydon v Ipswich
Sutton & Epsom v North Walsham
Ruislip v Old Gaytonians
Dartfordians v Lewes
Basingstoke v U.S. Portsmouth

Sat 26th November (Week 12)
Old Gaytonians v Sutton & Epsom
North Walsham v Streatham/Croydon
Ipswich v Basingstoke
U.S. Portsmouth v Dartfordians
Lewes v Guildford & Godalming

Sat 14th January (Week 18)
Dartfordians v Ipswich
Basingstoke v North Walsham
Streathamm/Croydon v Old Gaytonians
Sutton & Epsom v Ruislip
Guildford & Godalming v U.S. Portsmouth

Sat 28th January (Week 20)
Ruislip v Streatham/Croydon
Old Gaytonians v Basingstoke
North Walsham v Dartfordians
Ipswich v Guildford & Godalming
U.S. Portsmouth v Lewes

Sat 11th February (Week 22)
Lewes v Ipswich
Guidford & Godalming v North Walsham
Dartfordians v Old Gaytonians
Basingstoke v Ruislip
Streatham/Croydon v Sutton & Epsom

Sat 25th February (Week 24)
Sutton & Epsom v Basingstoke
Ruislip v Dartfordians
Old Gaytonians v Guildford & Godalming
North Walsham v Lewes
Ipswich v U.S. Portsmouth

Sat 11th March (Week 26)
U.S. Portsmouth v North Walsham
Lewes v Old Gaytonians
Guildford & Godalming v Ruislip
Dartfordians v Sutton & Epsom
Basingstoke v Streatham/Croydon

LONDON LEAGUE TWO NORTH

Sat 24th September (Week 4)
Norwich v Upper Clapton
Hertford v Old Merchant Taylors
Cheshunt v Grasshoppers
Woodford v Barking
Thurrock v Bishop's Stortford

Sat 8th October (Week 6)
Upper Clapton v Thurrock
Bishop's Stortford v Woodford
Barking v Cheshunt
Grasshoppers v Hertford
Old Merchant Taylors v Old Albanians

Sat 22nd October (Week 8)
Woodford v Upper Clapton
Thurrock v Norwith
Old Albanians v Grasshopper
Hertford v Barking
Cheshunt v Bishop's Stortford

Sat 12th November (Week 10)
Norwich v Woodford
Upper Clapton v Cheshunt
Bishop's Stortford v Hertford
Barking v Old Albanians
Grasshoppers v Old Merchant Taylors

Sat 19th November (Week 11)
Hertford v Upper Clapton
Cheshunt v Norwich
Woodford v Thurrock
Old Merchant Taylors v Barking
Old Albanians v Bishop's Stortford

Sat 26th November (Week 12)
Thurrock v Cheshunt
Norwich v Hertford
Upper Clapton v Old Albanians
Bishop's Stortford v Old Merchant Taylors
Barking v Grasshoppers

Sat 14th January (Week 18)
Old Merchant Taylors v Upper Clapton
Old Albanians v Norwich
Hertford v Thurrock
Cheshunt v Woodford
Grasshoppers v Bishop's Stortford

Sat 28th January (Week 20)
Woodford v Hertford
Thurrock v Old Albanians
Norwich v Old Merchant Taylors
Upper Clapton v Grasshoppers
Bishop's Stortford v Barking

Sat 11th February (Week 22)
Barking v Upper Clapton
Grasshoppers v Norwich
Old Merchant Taylors v Thurrock
Old Albanians v Woodford
Hertford v Cheshunt

Sat 25th February (Week 24)
Cheshunt v Old Albanians
Woodford v Old Merchant Taylors
Thurrock v Grasshoppers
Norwich v Barking
Upper Clapton v Bishop's Stortford

Sat 11th March (Week 26)
Bishop's Storford v Norwich
Barking v Thurrock
Grasshoppers v Woodford
Old Merchant Taylors v Cheshunt
Old Albanians v Hertford

LONDON LEAGUE TWO SOUTH

Sat 24th September (Week 4)
Tunbridge Wells v Gravesend
Old Mid Whitgiftians v K.C.S. O.B.
Old Alleynian v Camberley
Old Reigatian v Purley
Odl Brockleians v Esher

Sat 8th October (Week 6)
Gravesend v Old Brockleians
Esher v Old Reigatian
Purley v Old Alleynian
Camberley v Old Mid Whitgiftians
K.C.S. O.B. v Worthing

Sat 22nd October (Week 8)
Old Reigatian v Gravesend
Old Brockleians v Tunbridge Wells
Worthing v Camberley
Old Mid Whitfigtians v Purley
Old Alleynian v Esher

Sat 12th November (Week 10)
Tunbridge Wells v Old Reigatian
Gravesend v Old Alleynian
Esher v Old Mid Whitgiftians
Purley v Worthing
Camberley v K.C.S. O.B.

Sat 19th November (Week 11)
Old Mid Whitgiftians v Gravesend
Old Alleynian v Tunbridge Wells
Old Reigatian v Old Brockleians
K.C.S. O.B. v Purley
Worthing v Esher

Sat 26th November (Week 12)
Old Brockleians v Old Alleynian
Tunbridge Wells v Old Mid Whitgiftians
Gravesend v Worthing
Esher v K.C.S. O.B.
Purley v Camberley

Sat 14th January (Week 18)
K.C.S. O.B. v Gravesend
Worthing v Tunbridge Wells
Old Mid Whitgiftians v Old Brockleians
Old Alleynian v Old Reigatian
Camberley v Esher

Sat 28th January (Week 20)
Old Reigatian v Old Mid Whitgiftians
Old Brockleians v Worthing
Tunbridge Wells v K.C.S. O.B.
Gravesend v Camberley
Esher v Purley

Sat 11th February (Week 22)
Purley v Gravesend
Camberley v Tunbridge Wells
K.C.S. O.B. v Old Brockleians
Worthing v Old Reigatian
Old Mid Whitgiftians v Old Alleynian

Sat 25th February (Week 24)
Old Alleynian v Worthing
Old Reigatian v K.C.S. O.B.
Old Brockleians v Camberley
Tunbridge Wells v Purley
Gravesend v Esher

Sat 11th March (Week 26)
Esher v Tunbridge Wells
Purley v Old Brockleians
Camberley v Old Reigatian
K.C.S. O.B. v Old Alleynian
Worthing v Old Mid Whitgiftians

LONDON LEAGUE THREE NORTH EAST

Sat 24th September (Week 4)
Eton Manor v Met Police, Chigwell
Brentwood v Old Cantabrigian
Saffron Walden v Ipswich Y.M.C.A.
Chingford v Cambridge
Old Westcliffians v West Norfolk

Sat 8th October (Week 6)
Met Police, Chigwell v Old Westcliffians
West Norfolk v Chingford
Cambridge v Saffron Walden
Ipswich Y.M.C.A. v Brentwood
Old Cantabrigian v Colchester

Sat 22nd October (Week 8)
Chingford v Met Police, Chigwell
Old Westcliffians v Eton Manor
Colchester v Ipswich Y.M.C.A.
Brentwood v Cambridge
Saffron Walden v West Norfolk

Sat 12th November (Week 10)
Eton Manor v Chingford
Met Police, Chigwell v Saffron Walden
West Norfolk v Brentwood
Cambridge v Colchester
Ipswich Y.M.C.A. v Old Cantabrigian

Sat 19th November (Week 11)
Brentwood v Met Police, Chigwell
Saffron Walden v Eton Manor
Chingford v Old Westcliffians
Old Cantabrigian v Cambridge
Colchester v West Norfolk

Sat 26th November (Week 12)
Old Westcliffians v Saffron Walden
Eton Manor v Brentwood
Met Police, Chigwell v Colchester
West Norfolk v Old Cantabrigian
Cambridge v Ipswich Y.M.C.A.

Sat 14th January (Week 18)
Old Cantabrigian v Met Police, Chigwell
Colchester v Eton Manor
Brentwood v Old Westcliffians
Saffron Walden v Chingford
Ipswich Y.M.C.A. v West Norfolk

Sat 28th January (Week 20)
Chingford v Brentwood
Old Westcliffians v Colchester
Eton Manor v Old Cantabrigian
Met Police, Chigwell v Ipswich Y.M.C.A.
West Norfolk v Cambridge

Sat 11th February (Week 22)
Cambridge v Met Police, Chigwell
Ipswich Y.M.C.A v Eton Manor
Old Cantabrigian v Old Westcliffians
Colchester v Chingford
Brentwood v Saffron Walden

Sat 25th February (Week 24)
Saffron Walden v Colchester
Chingford v Old Cantabrigian
Old Westcliffians v Ipswich Y.M.C.A.
Eton Manor v Cambridge
Met Police, Chigwell v West Norfolk

Sat 11th March (Week 26)
West Norfolk v Eton Manor
Cambridge v Old Westcliffians
Ipswich Y.M.C.A. v Chingford
Old Cantabrigian v Saffron Walden
Colchester v Brentwood

LONDON LEAGUE THREE NORTH WEST

Sat 24th September (Week 4)
Bacavians v Letchworth
Mill Hill v Kingsburian
Fullerians v Hendon
Tabard v Hemel Hempstead
St Mary's Hospital v Finchley

Sat 8th October (Week 6)
Letchworth v St Mary's Hospital
Finchley v Tabard
Hemel Hempstead v Fullerians
Hendon v Mill Hill
Kingsburian v Harrow

Sat 22nd October (Week 8)
Tabard v Letchworth
St Mary's Hospital v Bacavians
Harrow v Hendon
Mill Hill v Hemel Hempstead
Fullerians v Finchley

Sat 12th November (Week 10)
Bacavians v Tabard
Letchworth v Fullerians
Finchley v Mill Hill
Hemel Hempstead v Harrow
Hendon v Kingsburian

Sat 19th November (Week 11)
Mill Hill v Letchworth
Fullerians v Bacavians
Tabard v St Mary's Hospital
Kingsburian v Hemel Hempstead
Harrow v Finchley

Sat 26th November (Week 12)
St Mary's Hospital v Fullerians
Bacavians v Mill Hill
Letchworth v Harrow
Finchley v Kingsburian
Hemel Hempstead v Hendon

Sat 14th January (Week 18)
Kingsburian v Letchworth
Harrow v Bacavians
Mill Hill v St Mary's Hospital
Fullerians v Tabard
Hendon v Finchley

Sat 28th January (Week 20)
Tabard v Mill Hill
St Mary's Hospital v Harrow
Bacavians v Kingsburian
Letchworth v Hendon
Finchley v Hemel Hempstead

Sat 11th February (Week 22)
Hemel Hempstead v Letchworth
Hendon v Bacavians
Kingsburian v St Mary's Hospital
Harrow v Tabard
Mill Hill v Fullerians

Sat 25th February (Week 24)
Fullerians v Harrow
Tabard v Kingsburian
St Mary's Hospital v Hendon
Bacavians v Hemel Hempstead
Letchworth v Finchley

Sat 11th March (Week 26)
Finchley v Bacavians
Hemel Hempstead v St Mary's Hospital
Hendon v Tabard
Kingsburian v Fullerians
Harrow v Mill Hill

LONDON LEAGUE THREE SOUTH EAST

Sat 24th September (Week 4)
Bognor v Charlton Park
Old Dunstonian v Old Juddian
Westcombe Park v East Grinstead
Beckenham v Crawley
Old Colfeians v Horsham

Sat 8th October (Week 6)
Charlton Park v Old Colfeians
Horsham v Beckenham
Crawley v Westcombe Park
East Grinstead v Old Dunstonian
Old Jiddian v Old Beccehamians

Sat 22nd October (Week 8)
Beckenham v Charlton Park
Old Colfeians v Bognor
Old Beccehamians v East Grinstead
Old Dunstonian v Crawley
Westcombe Park v Horsham

Sat 12th November (Week 10)
Bognor v Beckenham
Charlton Park v Westcombe Park
Horsham v Old Dunstonian
Crawley v Old Beccehamians
East Grinstead v Old Juddian

Sat 19th November (Week 11)
Old Dunstonian v Charlton Park
Westcombe Park v Bognor
Beckenham v Old Colfeians
Old Juddian v Crawley
Old Beccehamians v Horsham

Sat 26th November (Week 12)
Old Colfeians v Westcombe Park
Bognor v Old Dunstonia
Charlton Park v Old Beccehamians
Horsham v Old Juddian
Crawley v East Grinstead

Sat 14th January (Week 18)
Old Juddian v Charlton Park
Old Beccehamians v Bognor
Old Dunstonian v Old Colfeians
Westcombe Park v Beckenham
East Grinstead v Horsham

Sat 28th January (Week 20)
Beckenham v Old Dunstonian
Old Colfeians v Old Beccehamians
Bognor v Old Juddian
Charlton Park v East Grinstead
Horsham v Crawley

Sat 11th February (Week 22)
Crawley v Charlton Park
East Grinstead v Bognor
Old Juddian v Old Colfeians
Old Beccehamians v Beckenham
Old Dunstonian v Westcombe Park

Sat 25th February (Week 24)
Westcombe Park v Old Beccehamians
Beckenham v Old Juddian
Old Colfeians v East Grinstead
Bognor v Crawley
Charlton Park v Horsham

Sat 11th March (Week 26)
Horsham v Bognor
Crawley v Old Colfeians
East Grinstead v Beckenham
Old Juddian v Westcombe Park
Old Beccehemians v Old Dunstonian

LONDON LEAGUE THREE SOUTH WEST

Sat 24th September (Week 4)
Old Emanuel v Guy's Hospital
Old Guildfordians v Jersey
Old Walcountians v Winchester
Portsmouth v Eastleigh
Old Whitgiftians v Gosport

Sat 8th October (Week 6)
Guy's Hospital v Old Whitgiftians
Gosport v Portsmouth
Eastleigh v Old Walcountians
Winchester v Old Guildfordians
Jersey v Alton

Sat 22nd October (Week 8)
Portsmouth v Guy's Hospital
Old Whitgiftians v Old Emanuel
Alton v Winchester
Old Guildfordians v Eastleigh
Old Walcountians v Gosport

Sat 12th November (Week 10)
Old Emanuel v Portsmouth
Guy's Hospital v Old Walcountians
Gosport v Old Guildfordians
Eastleigh v Alton
Winchester v Jersey

Sat 19th November (Week 11)
Old Guildfordians v Guy's Hospital
Old Walcountians v Old Emanuel
Portsmouth v Old Whitgiftians
Jersey v Eastleigh
Alton v Gosport

Sat 26th November (Week 12)
Old Whitgiftians v Old Walcountians
Old Emanuel v Old Guildfordians
Guy's Hospital v Alton
Gosport v Jersey
Eastleigh v Winchester

Sat 14th January (Week 18)
Jersey v Guy's Hospital
Alton v Old Emanuel
Old Guildfordians v Old Whitgiftians
Old Walcountians v Portsmouth
Winchester v Gosport

Sat 28th January (Week 20)
Portsmouth v Old Guildfordians
Old Whitgiftians v Alton
Old Emanuel v Jersey
Guy's Hospital v Winchester
Gosport v Eastleigh

Sat 11th February (Week 22)
Eastleigh v Guy's Hospital
Winchester v Old Emanuel
Jersey v Old Whitgiftians
Alton v Portsmouth
Old Guildfordians v Old Walcountians

Sat 25th February (Week 24)
Old Walcountians v Alton
Portsmouth v Jersey
Old Whitgiftians v Winchester
Old Emanuel v Eastleigh
Guy's Hospital v Gosport

Sat 11th March (Week 26)
Gosport v Old Emanuel
Eastleigh v Old Whitgiftians
Winchester v Portsmouth
Jersey v Old Walcountians
Alton v Old Guildfordians

SURREY LEAGUE ONE

Sat 24th September (Week 4)
Old Surbitonians v Old Blues
Old Tiffinians v Warlingham
Effingham v Dorking
Old Rutlishians v Old Wimbledonians
Merton v Cranleigh

Sat 8th October (Week 6)
Old Blues v Merton
Cranleigh v Old Rutlishians
Old Wimbledonians v Effingham
Dorking v Old Tiffinians
Warlingham v Old Cranleighans

Sat 22nd October (Week 8)
Old Rutlishians v Old Blues
Merton v Old Surbitonians
Old Cranleighans v Dorking
Old Tiffinians v Old Wimbledonians
Effingham v Cranleigh

Sat 12th November (Week 10)
Old Surbitonians v Old Rutlishians
Old Blues v Effingham
Cranleigh v Old Tiffinians
Old Wimbledonians v Old Cranleighans
Dorking v Warlingham

Sat 19th November (Week 11)
Old Tiffinians v Old Blues
Effingham v Old Surbitonians
Old Rutlishians v Merton
Warlingham v Old Wimbledonians
Old Cranleighans v Cranleigh

Sat 26th November (Week 12)
Merton v Effingham
Old Surbitonians v Old Tiffinians
Old Blues v Old Cranleighans
Cranleigh v Warlingham
Old Wimbledonians v Dorking

Sat 14th January (Week 18)
Warlingham v Old Blues
Old Cranleighans v Old Surbitonians
Old Tiffinians v Mertonq
Effingham v Old Rutlishians
Dorking v Cranleigh

Sat 28th January (Week 20)
Old Rutlishians v Old Tiffinians
Merton v Old Cranleighans
Old Surbitonians v Warlingham
Old Blues v Dorking
Cranleigh v Old Wimbledonians

Sat 11th February (Week 22)
Old Wimbledonians v Old Blues
Dorking v Old Surbitonians
Warlingham v Merton
Old Cranleighans v Old Rutlishians
Old Tiffinians v Effingham

Sat 25th February (Week 24)
Effingham v Old Cranleighans
Old Rutlishians v Warlingham
Merton v Dorking
Old Surbitonians v Old Wimbledonians
Old Blues v Cranleigh

Sat 11th March (Week 26)
Cranleigh v Old Surbitonians
Old Wimbledonians v Merton
Dorking v Old Rutlishians
Warlingham v Effingham
Old Cranleighans v Old Tiffinians

SURREY LEAGUE TWO "A"

Sat 24th September (Week 4)
Chobham v Wimbledon
Kingston v Farnham
Raynes Park v Harrodians
St Thomas' Hospital v Old Haileyburians
Old Freemans v Old Reedonians
University Vandals v Charing X/West Hosp

Sat 8th October (Week 6)
Wimbledon v Old Freemans
Old Reedonians v St Thomas' Hospital
Old Haileyburians v Raynes Park
Harrodians v Kingston
Farnham v Charing X/West Hosp
Chobham v Universtiy Vandals

Sat 22nd October (Week 8)
St Thomas' Hospital v Wimbledon
Old Freemans v Chobham
Charing X/West Hosp v Harrodians
Kingston v Old Haileyburians
Raynes Park v Old Reedonians
University Vandals v Farnham

Sat 12th November (Week 10)
Chobham v St Thomas' Hospital
Wimbledon v Raynes Park
Old Reedonians v Kingston
Old Haileyburians v Charing X/West Hosp
Harrodians v Farnham
Old Freemans v University Vandals

Sat 19th November (Week 11)
Kingston v Wimbledon
Raynes Park v Chobham
St Thomas' Hospital v Old Freemans
Farnham v Old Haileyburians
Charing X/West Hosp v Old Reedonians
University Vandals v Harrodians

Sat 26th November (Week 12)
Old Freemans v Raynes Park
Chobham v Kingston
Wimbledon v Charing X/West Hosp
Old Reedonians v Farnham
Old Haileyburians v Harrodians
St Thomas' Hospital v University Vandals

Sat 14th January (Week 18)
Farnham v Wimbledon
Charing X/West Hosp v Chobham
Kingston v Old Freemans
Raynes Park v St Thomas' Hospital
Harrodians v Old Reedonians
University Vandals v Old Haileyburians

Sat 28th January (Week 20)
St Thomas' Hospital v Kingston
Old Freemans v Charing X/West Hosp
Chobham v Farnham
Wimbledon v Harrodians
Old Reedonians v Old Haileyburians
Raynes Prk v University Vandals

Sat 11th February (Week 22)
Old Haileyburians v Wimbledon
Harrodians v Chobham
Farnham v Old Freemans
Charing X/West Hosp v St Thomas' Hospital
Kingston v Raynes Park
University Vandals v Old Reedonians

Sat 25th February (Week 24)
Raynes Park v Charing X/West Hosp
St Thomas' Hospital v Farnham
Old Freemans v Harrodians
Chobham v Old Haileyburians
Wimbledon v Old Reedonians
Kingston v University Vandals

Sat 11th March (Week 26)
Old Reedonians v Chobham
Old Haileyburians v Old Freemans
Harrodians v St Thomas' Hospital
Farnham v Raynes Park
Charing X/West Hosp v Kingston
University Vandals v Wimbledon

SURREY LEAGUE TWO "B"

Sat 24th September (Week 4)
Shirley Wanderers v Old Wandsworthians
Old Suttonians v John Fisher O.B.
Old Epsomians v Old Pelhamians
Law Society v King's College Hosp
Mitcham v Old Johnians
Bec Old Boys v Chipstead

Sat 8th October (Week 6)
Old Wandsworthians v Mitcham
Old Johnians v Law Society
King's College Hosp v Old Epsomians
Old Pehlamians v Old Suttonians
John Fisher O.B. v Chipstead
Shirley Wanderers v Bec Old Boys

Sat 22nd October (Week 8)
Law Society v Old Wandsworthians
Mitcham v Shirley Wanderers
Chipstead v Old Pelhamians
Old Suttonians v King's College Hosp
Old Epsomians v Old Johnians
Bec Old Boys v John Fisher O.B.

Sat 12th November (Week 10)
Shirley Wanderers v Law Society
Old Wandsworthians v Old Epsomians
Old Johnians v Old Suttonians
King's College Hosp v Chipstead
Old Pelhamians v John Fisher O.B.
Mitcham v Bec Old Boys

Sat 19th November (Week 11)
Old Suttonians v Old Wandsworthians
Old Epsomians v Shirley Wanderers
Law Society v Mitcham
John Fisher O.B. v King's College Hosp
Chipstead v Old Johnians
Bec Old Boys v Old Pelhamians

Sat 26th November (Week 12)
Mitcham v Old Epsomians
Shirley Wanderers v Old Suttonians
Old Wandsworthians v Chipstead
Old Johnians v John Fisher O.B.
King's College Hosp v Old Pelhamians
Law Society v Bec Old Boys

Sat 14th January (Week 18)
John Fisher O.B. v Old Wandsworthians
Chipstead v Shirley Wanderers
Old Suttonians v Mitcham
Old Epsomians v Law Society
Old Pelhamians v Old Johnians
Bec Old Boys v King's College Hosp

Sat 28th January (Week 20)
Law Society v Old Suttonians
Mitcham v Chipstead
Shirley Wanderers v John Fisher O.B.
Old Wansworthians v Old Pelhamians
Old Johnians v King's College Hosp
Old Epsomians v Bec Old Boys

Sat 11th February (Week 22)
King's College Hosp v Old Wandsworthians
Old Pelhamians v Shirley Wanderers
John Fisher O.B. v Mitcham
Chipstead v Law Society
Old Suttonians v Old Epsomians
Bec Old Boys v Old Johnians

Sat 25th February (Week 24)
Old Epsomians v Chipsted
Law Society v John Fisher O.B.
Mitcham v Old Pelhamians
Shirley Wanderers v King's College Hosp
Old Wandsworthians v Old Johnians
Old Suttonians v Bec Old Boys

Sat 11th March (Week 26)
Old Johnians v Shirley Wanderers
King's College Hosp v Mitcham
Old Pelhamians v Law Society
John Fisher O.B. v Old Epsomians
Chipstead v Old Suttonians
Bec Old Boys v Old Wandsworthians

SURREY LEAGUE THREE

Sat 24th September (Week 4)
Battersea Ironsides v B.B.C.
London Fire Brigade v Haslemere
Reigate & Redhill v Old Croydonians
Shene Old Gramm's v Old Caterhamians
Surrey Police v Old Bevonians

Sat 8th October (Week 6)
B.B.C. v Old Bevonians
Battersea Ironsides v Surrey Police
Old Caterhamians v Reigate & Redhill
Old Croydonians v London Fire Brigade
Shene Old Gramm's v Haslemere

Sat 22nd October (Week 8)
Old Caterhamians v B.B.C.
Old Bevonians v Battersea Ironsides
Old Croydonians v Shene Old Gramm's
Haslemere v Reigate & Redhill
Surrey Police v London Fire Brigade

Sat 12th November (Week 10)
Battersea Ironsides v Old Caterhamians
B.B.C. v Old Croydonians
Haslemere v Surrey Police
Old Bevonians v Shene Old Gramm's
Reigate & Redhill v London Fire Brigade

Sat 19th November (Week 11)
Haslemere v B.B.C.
Old Croydonians v Battersea Ironsides
Old Caterhamians v Old Benonians
Reigate & Redhill v Surrey Police
London Fire Brigade v Shene Old Gramm's

Sat 26th November (Week 12)
Old Bevonians v Old Croydonians
Battersea Ironsides v Haslemere
B.B.C. v London Fire Brigade
Old Caterhamians v Surrey Police
Shene Old Gramm's v Reigate & Redhill

Sat 28th January (Week 20)
Reigate & Redhill v B.B.C.
London Fire Brigade v Battersea Ironsides
Haslemere v Old Bevonians
Old Croydonians v Old Caterhamians
Surrey Police v Shene Old Gramm's

Sat 11th February (Week 22)
Old Caterhamians v Haslemere
Old Bevonians v London Fire Brigade
Battersea Ironsides v Reigate & Redhill
B.B.C. v Shene Old Gramm's
Surrey Police v Old Croydonians

Sat 25th February (Week 24)
Surrey Police v B.B.C.
Shene Old Gramm's v Battersea Ironsides
Reigate & Redhill v Old Bevonians
London Fire Brigade v Old Caterhamians
Haslemere v Old Croydonians

SURREY LEAGUE FOUR

Sat 24th September (Week 4)
British Aerospace v Economicals
Surrey University v Oxted
Lightwater v Racal Decca

Sat 8th October (Week 6)
Lightwater v British Aerospace
Economicals v Royal Holloway
Racal Decca v Oxted

Sat 22nd October (Week 8)
British Aerospace v Oxted
Royal Holloway v Lightwater
Racal Decca v Surrey University

Sat 5th November (Week 9)
Racal Decca v British Aerospace
Oxted v Economicals
Surrey University v Royal Holloway

Sat 12th November (Week 10)
British Aerospace v Royal Holloway
Economicals v Racal Decca
Lightwater v Oxted

Sat 19th November (Week 11)
Racal Decca v Lightwater
Royal Holloway v Economicals
Surrey University v British Aerospace

Sat 26th November (Week 12)
Economicals v Surrey University
Lightwater v Royal Holloway
Oxted v Racal Decca

Sat 7th January (Week 17)
British Aerospace v Racal Decca
Surrey University v Economicals
Oxted v Lightwater

Sat 14th January (Week 18)
Economicals v British Aerospace
Surrey University v Lightwater
Royal Holloway v Oxted

Sat 28th January (Week 20)
British Aerospace v Lightwater
Oxted v Surrey University
Racal Decca v Royal Holloway

Sat 11th February (Week 22)
Surrey University v Racal Decca
Lightwater v Economicals
Royal Holloway v British Aerospace

Sat 25th February (Week 24)
Royal Holloway v Surrey University
Oxted v British Aerospace
Racal Decca v Economicals

Sat 11th March (Week 26)
Economicals v Lightwater
British Aerospace v Surrey University
Oxted v Royal Holloway

Sat 18th March (Week 27)
Royal Holloway v Racal Decca
Lightwater v Surrey University
Economicals v Oxted

HAMPSHIRE LEAGUE ONE

Sat 24th September (Week 4)
Fareham Heathens v Esso
Guernsey v Rushmoor
Millbrook v Sandown & Shanklin
Isle of Wight v Southampton
Fordingbridge v Tottonians

Sat 8th October (Week 6)
Esso v Fordingbridge
Tottonians v Isle of Wight
Southampton v Millbrook
Sandown & Shanklin v Guernsey
Rushmoor v Trojans

Sat 22nd October (Week 8)
Isle of Wight v Esso
Fordingbridge v Fareham Heathens
Trojans v Sandown & Shanklin
Guernsey v Southampton
Millbrook v Tottonians

Sat 12th November (Week 10)
Fareham Heathens v Isle of Wight
Esso v Millbrook
Tottonians v Guernsey
Southampton v Trojans
Sandown & Shanklin v Rushmoor

Sat 19th November (Week 11)
Guernsey v Esso
Millbrook v Fareham Heathens
Isle of Wight v Fordingbridge
Rushmoor v Southampton
Trojans v Tottonians

Sat 26th November (Week 12)
Fordingbridge v Millbrook
Fareham Heathens v Guernsey
Esso v Trojans
Tottonians v Rushmoor
Southampton v Sandown & Shanklin

Sat 14th January (Week 18)
Rushmoor v Esso
Trojans v Fareham Heathens
Guernsey v Fordingbridge
Millbrook v Isle of Wight
Sandown & Shanklin v Tottonians

Sat 28th January (Week 20)
Isle of Wight v Guernsey
Fordingbridge v Trojans
Fareham Heathens v Rushmoor
Esso v Sandown & Shanklin
Tottonians v Southampton

Sat 11th February (Week 22)
Southampto v Esso
Sandown & Shanklin v Fareham Heathens
Rushmoor v Fordingbridge
Trojans v Isle of Wight
Guernsey v Millbrook

Sat 25th February (Week 24)
Millbrook v Trojans
Isle of Wight v Rushmoor
Fordingbridge v Sandown & Shanklin
Fareham Heathens v Southampton
Esso v Tottonians

Sat 11th March (Week 26)
Tottonians v Fareham Heathens
Southampton v Fordingbridge
Sandown & Shanklin v Isle of Wight
Rushmoor v Millbrook
Trojans v Guernsey

HAMPSHIRE LEAGUE TWO

Sat 24th September (Week 4)
Ellingham v Andover
Overton v Jersey United Banks
Nomads v Romsey
I.B.M. v Ventnor
New Milton v Waterlooville
Petersfield v Pegasus

Sat 8th October (Week 6)
Andover v New Milton
Waterlooville v I.B.M.
Ventnor v Nomads
Romsey v Overton
Jersey United Banks v Pegasus
Ellingham v Petersfield

Sat 22nd October (Week 8)
I.B.M. v Andover
New Milton v Ellingham
Pegasus v Romsey
Overton v Ventnor
Nomads v Waterlooville
Petersfield v Jersey United Banks

Sat 12th November (Week 10)
Ellingham v I.B.M.
Andover v Nomads
Waterlooville v Overton
Ventnor v Pegasus
Romsey v Jersey United Banks
New Milton v Petersfield

Sat 19th November (Week 11)
Overton v Andover
Nomads v Ellingham
I.B.M. v New Milton
Jersey United Banks v Ventnor
Pegasus v Waterlooville
Petersfield v Romsey

Sat 26th November (Week 12)
New Milton v Nomads
Ellingham v Overton
Andover v Pegasus
Waterlooville v Jersey United Banks
Ventnor v Romsey
I.B.M. v Petersfield

Sat 14th January (Week 18)
Jersey United Banks v Andover
Pegasus v Ellingham
Overton v New Milton
Nomads v I.B.M.
Romsey v Waterlooville
Petersfield v Ventnor

Sat 28th January (Week 20)
I.B.M. v Overton
New Milton v Pegasus
Ellingham v Jersey United Banks
Andover v Romsey
Waterlooville v Ventnor
Nomads v Petersfield

Sat 11th February (Week 22)
Ventnor v Andover
Romsey v Ellingham
Jersey United Banks v New Milton
Pegasus v I.B.M.
Overton v Nomads
Petersfield v Waterlooville

Sat 25th February (Week 24)
Nomads v Pegasus
I.B.M. v Jersey United Banks
New Milton v Romsey
Ellingham v Ventnor
Andover v Watelooville
Overton v Petersfield

Sat 11th March (Week 26)
Waterlooville v Ellingham
Ventnor v New Milton
Romsey v I.B.M.
Jersey United Banks v Nomads
Pegasus v Overton
Petersfield v Andover

EASTERN COUNTIES LEAGUE ONE

Sat 24th September (Week 4)
Bury St Edmunds v Lowestoft & Yar
Harlow v Canvey Island
Shelford v Ely
Crusaders v Romford & G.P.
Rochford v Basildon

Sat 8th October (Week 6)
Lowestoft & Yar v Rochford
Basildon v Crusaders
Romford & G.P. v Shelford
Ely v Harlow
Canvey Island v Redbridge

Sat 22nd October (Week 8)
Crusaders v Lowestoft & Yar
Rochford v Bury St Edmunds
Redbridge v Ely
Harlow v Romford & G.P.
Shelford v Basildon

Sat 12th November (Week 10)
Bury St Edmunds v Crusaders
Lowestoft & Yar v Shelford
Basildon v Harlow
Romford & G.P. v Redbridge
Ely v Canvey Island

Sat 19th November (Week 11)
Harlow v Lowestoft & Yar
Shelford v Bury St Edmunds
Crusaders v Rochford
Canvey Island v Romford & G.P.
Redbridge v Basildon

Sat 26th November (Week 12)
Rochford v Shelford
Bury St Edmunds v Harlow
Lowestoft & Yar v Redbridge
Basildon v Canvey Island
Romford & G.P. v Ely

Sat 14th January (Week 18)
Canvey Island v Lowestoft & Yar
Redbridge v Bury St Edmunds
Harlow v Rochford
Shelford v Crusaders
Ely v Basildon

Sat 28th January (Week 20)
Crusaders v Harlow
Rochford v Redbridge
Bury St Edmunds v Canvey Island
Lowestoft & Yar v Ely
Basildon v Romford & G.P.

Sat 11th February (Week 22)
Romford & G.P. v Lowestoft & Yar
Ely v Bury St Edmunds
Canvey Island v Rochford
Redbridge v Crusaders
Harlow v Shelford

Sat 25th February (Week 24)
Shelford v Redbridge
Crusaders v Canvey Island
Rochford v Ely
Bury St Edmunds v Romford & G.P.
Lowestoft & Yar v Basildon

Sat 11th March (Week 26)
Basildon v Bury St Edmunds
Romford & G.P. v Rochford
Ely v Crusaders
Canvey Island v Shelford
Redbridge v Harlow

EASTERN COUNTIES LEAGUE TWO

Sat 24th September (Week 4)
Thetford v Diss
P.L.A. v Old Edwardians
Upminster v East London
South Woodham Ferrs v Wanstead
Woodbridge v Braintree

Sat 8th October (Week 6)
Diss v Woodbridge
Braintree v South Woodham Ferrs
Wanstead v Upminster
East London v P.L.A.
Old Edwardians v Chelmsford

Sat 22nd October (Week 8)
South Woodham Ferrs v Diss
Woodbridge v Thetford
Chelmsford v East London
P.L.A. v Wanstead
Upminster v Braintree

Sat 12th November (Week 11)
P.L.A. v Diss
Upminster v Thetford
South Woodham Ferrs v Woodbridge
Old Edwardians v Wanstead
Chelmsford v Braintree

Sat 26th November (Week 12)
Woodbridge v Upminster
Thetford v P.L.A.
Diss v Chelmsford
Braintree v Old Edwardians
Wanstead v East London

Sat 14th January (Week 18)
Old Edwardians v Diss
Chelmsford v Thetford
P.L.A. v Woodbridge
Upminster v South Woodham Ferrs
East London v Braintree

Sat 28th January (Week 20)
South Woodham Ferrs v P.L.A.
Woodbridge v Chelmsford
Thetford v Old Edwardians
Diss v East London
Braintree v Wanstead

Sat 11th February (Week 22)
Wanstead v Diss
East London v Thetford
Old Edwardians v Woodbridge
Chelmsford v South Woodham Ferrs
P.L.A. v Upminster

Sat 25th February (Week 24)
Upminster v Chelmsford
South Woodham Ferrs v Old Edwardians
Woodbridge v East London
Thetford v Wanstead
Diss v Braintree

Sat 11th March (Week 26)
Braintree v Thetford
Wanstead v Woodbridge
East London v South Woodham Ferrs
Old Edwardians v Upminster
Chelmsford v P.L.A.

EASTERN COUNTIES LEAGUE THREE

Sat 24th September (Week 4)
Campion v Maldon
Harwich & Dovercourt v Wisbech
Lakenham/Hewett v Wymondham
Ilford Wanderers v Holt
Old Bealonians v Beccles

Sat 8th October (Week 6)
Maldon v Old Bealonians
Beccles v Ilord Wanderers
Holt v Lakenham/Hewett
Wymondham v Harwich & Dovercourt
Wisbech v Newmarket

Sat 22nd October (Week 8)
Ilford Wanderers v Maldon
Old Bealonians v Campion
Newmarket v Wymondham
Harwich & Dovercourt v Holt
Lakenham/Hewett v Beccles

Sat 12th November (Week 10)
Campion v Ilford Wanderers
Maldon v Lakenham/Hewett
Beccles v Harwich & Dovercourt
Holt v Newmarket
Wymondham v Wisbech

Sat 19th November (Week 11)
Harwich & Dovercourt v Maldon
Lakenham/Hewett v Campion
Ilford Wanderers v Old Bealonians
Wisbech v Holt
Newmarket v Beccles

Sat 26th November (Week 12)
Old Bealonians v Lakenham/Hewett
Campion v Harwich & Dovercourt
Maldon v Newmarket
Beccles v Wisbech
Holt v Wymondham

Sat 14th January (Week 18)
Wisbech v Maldon
Newmarket v Campion
Harwich & Dovercourt v Old Bealonians
Lakenham/Hewett v Ilford Wanderers
Wymondham v Beccles

Sat 28th January (Week 20)
Ilford Wanderers v Harwich & Dovercourt
Old Bealonians v Newmarket
Campion v Wisbech
Maldon v Wymondham
Beccles v Holt

Sat 11th February (Week 22)
Holt v Maldon
Wymondham v Campion
Wisbech v Old Bealonians
Newmarket v Ilford Wanderers
Harwich & Dovercourt v Lakenham/Hewett

Sa 25th February (Week 24)
Lakenham/Hewett v Newmarket
Ilford Wanderers v Wisbech
Old Bealonians v Wymondham
Campion v Holt
Maldon v Beccles

Sat 11th March (Week 26)
Beccles v Campion
Holt v Old Bealonians
Wymondham v Ilford Wanderers
Wisbech v Lakenham/Hewett
Newmarket v Harwich & Dovercourt

EASTERN COUNTIES LEAGUE FOUR

Sat 24th September (Week 4)
Fakenham v Gothic
Southwold v Bancrofts
Felixstowe v Mayfield Old Boys
Stowmarket v Chigwell
Clacton v Old Brentwoods

Sat 8th October (Week 6)
Gothic v Clacton
Old Brentwoods v Stowmarket
Chigwell v Felixstowe
Mayfield Old Boys v Southwold
Bancrofts v Old Palmerians

Sat 22nd October (Week 8)
Stowmarket v Gothic
Clacton v Fakenham
Old Palmerians v Mayfield Old Boys
Southwold v Chigwell
Felixstowe v Old Brentwoods

Sat 12th November (Week 10)
Fakenham v Stowmarket
Gothic v Felixstowe
Old Brentwoods v Southwold
Chigwell v Old Palmerians
Mayfield Old Boys v Bancrofts

Sat 19th November (Week 11)
Southwold v Gothic
Felixstowe v Fakenham
Stowmarket v Clacton
Bancrofts v Chigwell
Old Palmerians v Old Brentwoods

Sat 26th November (Week 12)
Clacton v Felixstowe
Fakenham v Southwold
Gothic v Old Palmerians
Old Brentwoods v Bancrofts
Chigwell v Mayfield Old Boys

Sat 14th January (Week 18)
Bancrofts v Gothic
Old Palmerians v Fakenham
Southwold v Clacton
Felixstowe v Stowmarket
Mayfield Old Boys v Old Brentwoods

Sat 28th January (Week 20)
Stowmarket v Southwold
Clacton v Old Palmerians
Fakenham v Bancrofts
Gothic v Mayfield Old Boys
Old Brentwoods v Chigwell

Sat 11th February (Week 22)
Chigwell v Gothic
Mayfield Old Boys v Fakenham
Bancrofts v Clacton
Old Palmerians v Stowmarket
Southwold v Felixstowe

Sat 25th February (Week 24)
Felixstowe v Old Palmerians
Stowmarket v Bancrofts
Clacton v Mayfield Old Boys
Fakenham v Chigwell
Gothic v Old Brentwoods

Sat 11th March (Week 26)
Old Brentwoods v Fakenham
Chigwell v Clacton
Mayfield Old Boys v Stowmarket
Bancrofts v Felixstowe
Old Palmerians v Southwold

EASTERN COUNTIES LEAGUE FIVE

Sat 24th September (Week 4)
Dereham v Norwich Union
Haverhill v Rayleigh Wyverns
Sawston v Loughton
March v London Hospital

Sat 8th October (Week 6)
Norwich Union v Swaffham
London Hospital v Sawston
Loughton v Haverhill
Rayleigh Wyverns v Thurston

Sat 22nd October (Week 8)
March v Norwich Union
Swaffham v Dereham
Thurston v Loughton
Haverhill v London Hospital

Sat 12th November (Week 10)
Dereham v March
Norwich Union v Sawston
London Hospital v Thurston
Loughton v Rayleigh Wyverns

Sat 19th November (Week 11)
Haverhill v Norwich Union
Sawston v Dereham
March v Swaffham
Rayleigh Wyverns v London Hospital

Sat 26th November (Week 12)
Swaffham v Sawston
Dereham v Haverhill
Norwich Union v Thurston
London Hospital v Loughton

Sat 14th January (Week 18)
Rayleigh Wyverns v Norwich Union
Thurston v Dereham
Haverhill v Swaffham
Sawston v March

Sat 28th January (Week 20)
March v Haverhill
Swaffham v Thurston
Dereham v Rayleigh Wyverns
Norwich Union v Loughton

Sat 11th February (Week 22)
London Hospital v Norwich Union
Loughton v Dereham
Rayleigh Wyverns v Swaffham
Thurson v March
Haverhill v Sawston

Sat 25th February (Wek 24)
Sawston v Thurston
March v Rayleigh Wyverns
Swaffham v Loughton
Dereham v London Hospital

Sat 11th March (Week 26)
London Hospital v Swaffham
Loughton v March
Rayleigh Wyverns v Sawston
Thurston v Haverhill

EASTERN COUNTIES LEAGUE SIX

Sat 24th September (Week 4)
Witham v Orwell
Hadliegh v Ongar

Sat 8th October (Week 6)
Orwell v Brightlingsea
Ongar v Old Cooperians

Sat 22nd October (Week 8)
Billericay v Orwell
Brightlingsea v Witham

Sat 12th November (Week 10)
Witham v Billericay
Orwell v Thames Sports

Sat 19th November (Week 11)
Hadleigh v Orwell
Thames Sports v Witham
Billericay v Brightlingsea

Sat 26th November (Week 12)
Brightlingsea v Thames Sports
Witham v Hadleigh
Orwell v Old Cooperians

Sat 14th January (Week 18)
Ongar v Orwell
Old Cooperians v Witham
Hadleigh v Brightlingsea
Thames Sport v Billericay

Sat 28th January (Week 20)
Billericay v Hadleigh
Brightlingsea v Old Cooperians
Witham v Ongar

Sat 11th February (Week 22)
Ongar v Brightlingsea
Old Cooperians v Billericay
Hadleigh v Thames Sport

Sat 25th February (Week 24)
Thames Sport v Old Cooperians
Billericay v Ongar

Sat 11th March (Week 26)
Ongar v Thames Sport
Old Cooperians v Hadleigh

MIDDLESEX LEAGUE ONE

Sat 24th September (Week 4)
Hampstead v Twickenham
Old Abbotstonians v Old Paulines
Old Haberdashers v Staines
London New Zealand v Sudbury Court
Lensbury v Uxbridge

Sat 8th October (Week 6)
Twickenham v Lensbury
Uxbridge v London New Zealand
Sudbury Court v Old Haberdashers
Staines v Old Abbotstonians
Old Paulines v Centaurs

Sat 22nd October (Week 8)
London New Zealand v Twickenham
Lensbury v Hampstead
Centaurs v Staines
Old Abbotstonians v Sudbury Court
Old Haberdashers v Uxbridge

Sat 12th November (Week 10)
Hampstead v London New Zealand
Twickenham v Old Haberdashers
Uxbridge v Old Abbotstonians
Sudbury Court v Centaurs
Staines v Old Paulines

Sat 19th November (Week 11)
Old Abbotstonians v Twickenham
Old Haberdashers v Hampstead
London New Zealand v Lensbury
Old Paulines v Sudbury Court
Centaurs v Uxbridge

Sat 26th November (Week 12)
Lensbury v Old Haberdashers
Hampstead v Old Abbotstonians
Twickenham v Centaurs
Uxbridge v Old Paulines
Sudbury Court v Staines

Sat 14th January (Week 18)
Old Paulines v Twickenham
Centaurs v Hampstead
Old Abbotstonians v Lensbury
Old Haberdashers v London New Zealand
Staines v Uxbridge

Sat 28th January (Week 20)
London New Zealand v Old Abbostonians
Lensbury v Centaurs
Hampstead v Old Paulines
Twickenham v Staines
Uxbridge v Sudbury Court

Sat 11th February (Week 22)
Sudbury Court v Twickenham
Staines v Hampstead
Old Paulines v Lensbury
Centaurs v London New Zealand
Old Abbotstonians v Old Haberdashers

Sat 25th February (Week 24)
Old Haberdashers v Centaurs
London New Zealand v Old Paulines
Lensbury v Staines
Hampstead v Sudbury Court
Twickenham v Uxbridge

Sat 25th February (Week 24)
Old Haberdashers v Centaurs
London New Zealand v Old Paulines
Lensbury v Staines
Hampstead v Sudbury Court
Twickenham v Uxbridge

Sat 11th March (Week 26)
Uxbridge v Hampstead
Sudbury Court v Lensbury
Staines v London New Zealand
Old Paulines v Old Haberdashers
Centaurs v Old Abbotstonians

MIDDLESEX LEAGUE TWO

Sat 24th September (Week 4)
Barclays Bank v St Bart's Hospital
Old Meadonians v Old Hamptonians
H'ersmith & Fulham v Old Millhillians
Civil Service v Orleans F.P.
Haringey v Richmond Thamesians

Sat 8th October (Week 6)
St Bart's Hospital v Haringey
Richmond Thamesians v Civil Service
Orleans F.P. v H'ersmith & Fulham
Old Millhillians v Old Meadonians
Old Hamptonians v Hackney

Sat 22nd October (Week 8)
Civil Service v St Bart's Hospital
Haringey v Barclays Bank
Hackney v Old Millhillians
Old Meadonians v Orleans F.P.
H'ersmith & Fulham v Richmond Thamesians

Sat 12th November (Week 10)
Barclays Bank v Civil Service
St Bart's Hospital v H'ersmith & Fulham
Richmond Thamesians v Old Meadonians
Orleans F.P. v Hackney
Old Millhillians v Old Hamptonians

Sat 19th November (Week 11)
Old Meadonians v St Bart's Hospital
H'ersmith & Fulham v Barclays Bank
Civil Service v Haringey
Old Hamptonians v Orleans F.P.
Hackney v Richmond Thamesians

Sat 26th November (Week 12)
Haringey v H'ersmith & Fulham
Barclays Bank v Old Meadonians
St Bart's Hospital v Hackney
Richmond Thamesians v Old Hamptonians
Orleans F.P. v Old Millhillians

Sat 14th January (Week 18)
Old Hamptonians v St Bart's Hospital
Hackney v Barclays Bank
Old Meadonians v Haringey
H'ersmith & Fulham v Civil Service
Old Millhillians v Richmond Thamesians

Sat 28th January (Week 20)
Civil Service v Old Meadonians
Haringey v Hackney
Barclays Bank v Old Hamptonians
St Bart's Hospital v Old Millhillians
Richmond Thamesians v Orleans F.P.

Sat 11th February (Week 22)
Orleans F.P. v St Bart's Hospital
Old Millhillians v Barclays Bank
Old Hamptonians v Haringey
Hackney v Civil Service
Old Meadonians v H'ersmith & Fulham

Sat 25th February (Week 24)
H'ersmith & Fulham v Hackney
Civil Service v Old Hamptonians
Haringey v Old Millhillians
Barclays Bank v Orleans F.P.
St Bart's Hospital v Richmond Thamesians

Sat 11th March (Week 26)
Richmond Thamesians v Barclays Bank
Orleans F.P. v Haringey
Old Millhillians v Civil Service
Old Hamptonians v H'ersmith & Fulham
Hackney v Old Meadonians

MIDDLESEX LEAGUE THREE

Sat 24th September (Week 4)
London Cornish v Belsize park
Wembley v Antlers
Old Grammarians v Osterley
Old Isleworthians v Pinner & Grammarians
Northolt v Quintin

Sat 8th October (Week 6)
Belsize Park v Northolt
Quintin v Old Isleworthians
Pinner & Grammarians v Old Grammarians
Osterley v Wembley
Antlers v Old Tottonians

Sat 22nd October (Week 8)
Old Isleworthians v Belsize Park
Northolt v London Cornish
Old Tottonians v Osterley
Wembley v Pinner & Grammarians
Old Grammarians v Quintin

Sat 12th November (Week 10)
London Cornish v Old Isleworthians
Belsize Park v Old Grammarians
Quintin v Wembley
Pinner & Grammarians v Old Tottonians
Osterley v Antlers

Sat 19th November (Week 11)
Wembley v Belsize Park
Old Grammarians v London Cornish
Old Isleworthians v Northolt
Antlers v Pinner & Grammarians
Old Tottonians v Quintin

Sat 26th November (Week 12)
Northolt v Old Grammarians
London Cornish v Wembley
Belsize Park v Old Tottonians
Quintin v Antlers
Pinner & Grammarians v Osterley

Sat 14th January (Week 18)
Antlers v Belsize Park
Old Tottonians v London Cornish
Wembley v Northolt
Old Grammarians v Old Iselworthians
Osterley v Quintin

Sat 28th January (Week 20)
Old Isleworthians v Wembley
Northolt v Old Tottonians
London Cornish v Antlers
Belsize Park v Osterley
Quintin v Pinner & Grammarians

Sat 11th February (Week 22)
Pinner & Grammarians v Belsize Park
Osterley v London Cornish
Antlers v Northolt
Old Tottonians v Old Isleworthians
Wembley v Old Grammarians

Sat 25th February (Week 24)
Old Grammarians v Old Tottonians
Old Isleworthians v Antlers
Northolt v Osterley
London Cornish v Pinner & Grammarians
Belsize Park v Quintin

Sat 11th March (Week 26)
Quintin v London Cornish
Pinner & Grammarians v Northolt
Osterley v Old Isleworthians
Antlers v Old Grammarians
Old Tottonians v Wembley

MIDDLESEX LEAGUE FOUR

Sat 24th September (Week 4)
Roxeth Manor O.B. v Bank of England
Hayes v Meadhurst
Enfield Ignatians v Old Actonians
Feltham v S.T. & C.

Sat 8th October (Week 6)
Bank of England v U.C.S. O.B.
S.T. & C. v Enfield Ignatians
Old Actonians v Hayes
Meadhurst v London French

Sat 22nd October (Week 8)
Feltham v Bank of England
U.C.S. O.B. v Roxeth Manor O.B.
London French v Old Actonians
Hayes v S.T. & C.

Sat 12th November (Week 10)
Roxeth Manor O.B. v Feltham
Bank of England v Enfield Ignatians
S.T. & C. v London French
Old Actonians v Meadhurst

Sat 19th November (Week 11)
Hayes v Bank of England
Enfield Ignatians v Roxeth Manor O.B.
Feltham v U.C.S. O.B.
Meadhurst v S.T. & C.

Sat 26th November (Week 12)
U.C.S. O.B. v Enfield Ignatians
Roxeth Manor O.B. v Hayes
Bank of England v London French
S.T. & C. v Old Actonians

Sat 14th January (Week 18)
Meadhurst v Bank of England
London French v Roxeth Manor O.B.
Hayes v U.C.S. O.B.
Enfield Ignatians v Feltham

Sat 28th January (Week 20)
Feltham v Hayes
U.C.S. O.B. v London French
Roxeth Manor O.B. v Meadhurst
Bank of England v Old Actonians

Sat 11th February (Week 22)
S.T. & C. v Bank of England
Old Actonians v Roxeth Manor O.B.
Meadhurst v U.C.S. O.B.
London French v Feltham
Hayes v Enfield Ignatians

Sat 25th February (Week 24)
Enfield Ignatians v London French
Feltham v Meadhurst
U.C.S. O.B. v Old Actonians
Roxeth Manor O.B. v S.T. & C.

Sat 11th March (Week 26)
S.T. & C. v U.C.S. O.B.
Old Actonians v Feltham
Meadhurst v Enfield Ignations
London French v Hayes

MIDDLESEX LEAGUE FIVE

Sat 24th September (Week 4)
Middlesex Hospital v G.W.R.
Brunel University v H.A.C.
British Airways v Royal Free Hospital
Kodak v St Nicholas O.B.

Sat 8th October (Week 6)
G.W.R. v St Mary's College
St Nicholas O.B. v British Airways
Royal Free Hospital v Brunel University
H.A.C. v Southall Tech Coll

Sat 22nd October (Week 8)
Kodak v G.W.R.
St Mary's College v Middlesex Hospital
Southall Tech Coll v Royal Free Hospital
Brunel University v St Nicholas O.B.

Sat 12th November (Week 10)
Middlesex Hospital v Kodak
G.W.R. v British Airways
St Nicholas O.B. v Southall Tech Coll
Royal Free Hospital v H.A.C.

Sat 19th November (Week 11)
Brunel University v G.W.R.
British Airways v Middlesex Hospital
Kodak v St Mary's College
H.A.C. v St Nicholas O.B.

Sat 26th November (Week 12)
St Mary's College v British Airways
Middlesex Hospital v Brunel University
G.W.R. v Southall Tech Coll
St Nicholas O.B. v Royal Free Hospital

Sat 14th January (Week 18)
H.A.C. v G.W.R.
Southall Tech Coll v Middlesex Hospital
Brunel University v St Mary's College
British Airways v Kodak

Sat 28th January (Week 20)
Kodak v Brunel University
St Mary's College v Southall Tech Coll
Middlesex Hospital v H.A.C.
G.W.R. v Royal Free Hospital

Sat 11th February (Week 22)
St Nicholas O.B. v G.W.R.
Royal Free Hospital v Middlesex Hospital
H.A.C. v St Mary's College
Southall Tech Coll v Kodak
Brunel University v British Airways

Sat 25th February (Week 24)
British Airways v Southall Tech Coll
Kodak v H.A.C.
St Mary's College v Royal Free Hospital
Middlesex Hospital v St Nicholas O.B.

Sat 11th March (Week 26)
St Nicholas O.B. v St Mary's College
Royal Free Hospital v Kodak
H.A.C. v British Airways
Southall Tech coll v Brunel University

KENT LEAGUE ONE

Sat 24th September (Week 4)
Betteshanger v Park House
Old Elthamians v Tonbridge
Canterbury v Gillingham Anch
Bromley v Medway
Snowdown Colliery v Thanet Wanderers

Sat 8th October (Week 6)
Park House v Snowdown Colliery
Thanet Wanderers v Bromley
Medway v Canterbury
Gillingham Anch v Old Elthamians
Tonbridge v Erith

Sat 22nd October (Week 8)
Bromley v Park House
Snowdown Colliery v Betteshanger
Erith v Gillingham Anch
Old Elthamians v Medway
Canterbury v Thanet Wanderers

Sat 12th November (Week 10)
Betteshanger v Bromley
Park Hosue v Canterbury
Thanet Wanderers v Old Elthamians
Medway v Erith
Gillingham Anch v Tonbridge

Sat 19th November (Week 11)
Old Elthamians v Park House
Canterbury v Betteshanger
Bromley v Snowdown Colliery
Tonbridge v Medway
Erith v Thanet Wanderers

Sat 26th November (Week 12)
Snowdown Colliery v Canterbury
Betteshanger v Old Elthamians
Park House v Erith
Thanet Wanderers v Tonbridge
Medway v Gillingham Anch

Satt 14th January (Week 18)
Tonbridge v Park House
Erith v Betteshanger
Old Elthamians v Snowdown Colliery
Canterbury v Bromley
Gillingham Anch v Thanet Wanderers

Sat 28th January (Week 20)
Bromley v Old Elthamians
Snowdown Colliery v Erith
Betteshanger v Tonbrige
Park House v Gillingham Anch
Thanet Wanderers v Medway

Sat 11th February (Week 22)
Medway v Park House
Gillingham Anch v Betteshanger
Tonbridge v Snowdown Colliery
Erith v Bromley
Old Elthamians v Canterbury

Sat 25th February (Week 24)
Canterbury v Erith
Bromely v Tonbridge
Snowdown Colliery v Gillingham Anch
Betteshanger v Medway
Park House v Thanet Wanderers

Sat 11th March (Week 26)
Thanet Wanderers v Betteshanger
Medway v Snowdown Colliery
Gillingham Anch v Bromley
Tonbridge v Canterbury
Erith v Old Elthamians

KENT LEAGUE TWO

Sat 24th September (Week 4)
Nat West Bank v Lloyds Bank
Old Shootershillians v New Ash Green
Midland Bank v Dover
Sevenoaks v Linton
Greenwich v Folkestone

Sat 8th October (Week 6)
Lloyds Bank v Greenwich
Folkestone v Sevenoaks
Linton v Midland Bank
Dover v Old Shootershillians
New Ash Green v Ashford

Sat 22nd October (Week 8)
Sevenoaks v Lloyds Bank
Greenwich v Nat West Bank
Ashford v Dover
Old Shootershillians v Linton
Midland Bank v Folkestone

Sat 12th November (Week 10)
Nat West Bank v Sevenoaks
Lloyds Bank v Midland Bank
Folkestone v Old Shootershillians
Linton v Ashford
Dover v New Ash Green

Sat 19th November (Week 11)
Old Shootershillians v Lloyds Bank
Midland Bank v Nat West Bank
Sevenoaks v Greenwich
New Ash Green v Linton
Ashford v Folkestone

Sat 26th November (Week 12)
Greenwich v Midland Bank
Nat West Bank v Old Shootershillians
Lloyds Bank v Ashford
Folkestone v New Ash Green
Linton v Dover

Sat 14th January (Week 18)
New Ash Green v Lloyds Bank
Ashford v Nat West Bank
Old Shootershillians v Greenwich
Midland Bank v Sevenoaks
Dover v Folkestone

Sat 28th January (Week 20)
Sevenoaks v Old Shootershillians
Greenwich v Ashford
Nat West Bank v New Ash Green
Lloyds Bank v Dover
Folkestone v Linton

Sat 11th February (Week 22)
Linton v Lloyds Bank
Dover v Nat West Bank
New Ash Green v Greenwich
Ashford v Sevenoaks
Old Shootershillians v Midland Bank

Sat 25th February (Week 24)
Midland Bank v Ashford
Sevenoaks v New Ash Green
Greenwich v Dover
Nat West Bank v Linton
Lloyds Bank v Folkestone

Sat 11th March (Week 26)
Folkestone v Nat West Bank
Linton v Greenwich
Dover v Sevenoaks
New Ash Green v Midland Bank
Ashford v Old Shootershillians

KENT LEAGUE THREE

Sat 24th September (Week 4)
Vigo v Met Police Hyes
Deal v Cranbrook
Sheppey v Thames Polytechnic
Old Gravesendians v Old Williamsonians
Orpington v Old Olavians

Sat 8th October (Week 6)
Met Police Hayes v Orpington
Old Olavians v Old Gravesendians
Old Williamsonians v Sheppey
Thames Polytechnic v Deal
Cranbrook v Sittingbourne

Sat 22nd October (Week 8)
Old Gravesendians v Met Police Hayes
Orpington v Vigo
Sittingbourne v Thames Polytechnic
Deal v Old Williamsonians
Sheppey v Old Olavians

Sat 12th November (Week 10)
Vigo v Old Gravesendians
Met Police Hayes v Sheppey
Old Olavians v Deal
Old Williamsonians v Sittingbourne
Thames Polytechnic v Cranbrook

Sat 19th November (Week 11)
Deal v Met Police Hayes
Sheppey v Vigo
Old Grasendians v Orpington
Cranbrook v Old Williamsonians
Sittingbourne v Old Olavians

Sat 26th November (Week 12)
Orpington v Sheppey
Vigo v Deal
Met Police Hayes v Sittingbourne
Old Olavians v Cranbrook
Old Williamsonians v Thames Polytechnic

Sat 14th January (Week 18)
Cranbrook v Met Police Hayes
Sittingbourne v Vigo
Deal v Orpington
Sheppey v Old Gravesendians
Thames Polytechnic v Old Olavians

Sat 28th January (Week 20)
Old Gravesendians v Deal
Orpington v Sittingbourne
Vigo v Cranbrook
Met Police Hayes v Thames Polytechnic
Old Olavians v Old Williamsonians

Sat 11th February (Week 22)
Old Williamsonians v Met Police Hayes
Thames Polytechnic v Vigo
Cranbrook v Orpington
Sittingbourne v Old Gravesendians
Deal v Sheppey

Sat 25th February (Week 24)
Sheppey v Sittingbourne
Old Gravesendians v Cranbrook
Orpington v Thames Polytechic
Vigo v Old Williamsonians
Met Police Hayes v Old Olavians

Sat 11th March (Week 26)
Old Olavians v Vigo
Old Williamsonians v Orpington
Thames Polytechnic v Old Gravesendians
Cranbrook v Sheppey
Sittingbourne v Deal

KENT LEAGUE FOUR

Sat 24th September (Week 4)
Citizens v STC Foots Cray
East Peckham v Lordswood
Edenbridge v Darenth Valley

Sat 8th October (Week 6)
STC Foots Cray v Bexley
Darenth Valley v East Peckham
Lordswood v Whistable

Sat 22nd October (Week 8)
University of Kent v STC Foots Cray
Bexley v Citizens
Whitstable v Darenth Valley

Sat 12th November (Week 10)
Citizens v University of Kent
STC Foots Cray v Edenbridge
Darenth Valley v Lordswood

Sat 19th November (Week 11)
East Peckham v STC Foots Cray
Edenbridge v Citizens
University of Ketn v Bexley

Sat 26th November (Week 12)
Bexley v Edenbridge
Citizens v East Peckham
STC Foots Cray v Whitstable

Sat 14th January (Week 18)
Lordswood v STC Foots Cray
Whitstable v Citizens
East Peckham v Bexley
Edenbridge v University of Kent

Sat 28th January (Week 20)
University of Kent v East Peckham
Bexley v Whitstable
Citizens v Lordswood
STC Foots Cray v Darenth Valley

Sat 11th February (Week 22)
Darenth Valley v Citizens
Lordswood v Bexley
Whitstable v University of Kent
East Peckham v Edenbridge

Sat 25th February (Week 24)
Edenbridge v Whitstable
University of Kent v Lordswood
Bexley v Darenth Valley

Sat 11th March (Week 26)
Darenth Valley v University of Kent
Lordswood v Edenbridge
Whitstable v East Peckham

HERTFORDSHIRE LEAGUE ONE

Sat 8th October (Week 6)
Royston v Barnet
Old Elizabethans v Old Ashmoleans
Welwyn v Old Verulamians
Harpenden v Stevenage

Sat 22nd October (Week 8)
Old Elizabethians v Barnet
Old Ashmoleans v Old Verulamians
Stevenage v Welwyn
Harpenden v Royston

Sat 12th November (Week 10)
Royston v Old Elizabethians
Barnet v Old Ashmoleans
Old Verulamians v Stevenage
Harpenden v Welwyn

Sat 26th November (Week 12)
Old Elizabethans v Old Verulamians
Old Ashmoleans v Welwyn
Stevenage v Royston
Barnet v Harpenden

Sat 28th January (Week 20)
Royston v Old Ashmoleans
Welwyn v Old Elizabethans
Stevenage v Barnet
Old Verulamians v Harpenden

Sat 11th February (Week 22)
Old Verulamians v Barnet
Old Ashmoleans v Stevenage
Welwyn v Royston
Harpenden v Old Elizabethans

Sat 25th February (Week 24)
Royston v Old Verulamians
Barnet v Welwyn
Old Elizabethans v Stevenage
Old Ashmoleans v Harpenden

HERTFORDSHIRE LEAGUE TWO

Sat 8th October (Week 6)
Tring v Watford
St Albans v De Havilland
Datchworth v Hitchin

Sat 22nd Oct (Week 8)
Watford v Datchworth
Hitchin v St Albans
De Havilland v Hatfield Polytechnic

Sat 12th November (Week 10)
St Albans v Watford
Datchworth v Tring
Hatfield Polytechnic v Hitchin

Sat 26th November (Week 12)
Tring v St Albans
Watford v Hatfield Polytechnic
Hitchin v De Havilland

Sat 28th January (Wek 20)
St Albans v Datchworth
Hatfield Polytechnic v Tring
De Havilland v Watford

Sat 11th February (Week 22)
Datchworth v Hatfield Polytechnic
Watford v Hitchin
Tring v De Havilland

Sat 25th February (Week 24)
Hatfield Polytechnic v St Albans
De Havilland v Datchworth
Hitchin v Tring

SUSSEX LEAGUE ONE

Sat 24th September (Week 4)
Brighton v Uckfield
Eastbourne v Sussex Police
Crowborough v Hove
Chichester v Hellingly
Burgess Hill v Seaford

Sat 8th October (Week 6)
Uckfield v Burgess Hill
Seaford v Chichester
Hellingly v Crowborough
Hove v Eastbourne
Sussex Police v Haywards Heath

Sat 22nd October (Week 8)
Chichester v Uckfield
Burgess Hill v Brighton
Haywards Heath v Hove
Eastbourne v Hellingly
Crowborough v Seaford

Sat 12th November (Week 10)
Brighton v Chichester
Uckfield v Crowborough
Seaford v Eastbourne
Hellingly v Haywards Heath
Hove v Sussex Police

Sat 19th November (Week 11)
Eastbourne v Uckfield
Crowborough v Brighton
Chichester v Burgess Hill
Sussex Police v Hellingly
Haywards Heath v Seaford

Sat 26th November (Week 12)
Burgess Hill v Crowborough
Brighton v Eastbourne
Uckfield v Haywards Heath
Seaford v Sussex Police
Hellingly v Hove

Sat 14th January (Week 18)
Sussex Police v Uckfield
Haywards Heath v Brighton
Eastbourne v Burgess Hill
Crowborough v Chichester
Hove v Seaford

Sat 28th January (Week 20)
Chichester v Eastbourne
Burgess Hill v Haywards Heath
Brighton v Sussex Police
Uckfield v Hove
Seaford v Hellingly

Sat 11th February (Week 22)
Hellingly v Uckfield
Hove v Brighton
Sussex Police v Burgess Hill
Haywards Heath v Chichester
Eastbourne v Crowborough

Sat 25th February (Week 24)
Crowborough v Haywards Heath
Chichester v Sussex Police
Burgess Hill v Hove
Brighton v Hellingly
Uckfield v Seaford

Sat 11th March (Week 26)
Seaford v Brighton
Hellingly v Burgess Hill
Hove v Chichester
Sussex Police v Crowborough
Haywards Heath v Eastbourne

SUSSEX LEAGUE TWO

Sat 8th October (Week 6)
Plumpton v St Francis
Pulborough v British Caledonian
Midhurst v Heathfield
Brighton Polytechnic v Hastings & Bexhill

Sat 22nd October (Week 8)
St Francis v Brighton Polytechnic
Hastings & Bexhill v Midhurst
Heathfield v Pulborough
British Caledonian v Sussex University

Sat 12th November (Week 10)
Midhurst v St Francis
Brighton Polytechnic v Plumpton
Sussex University v Heathfield
Pulborough v Hastings & Bexhill

Sat 19th November (Week 11)
Plumpton v Midhurst
St Francis v Pulborough
Hastings & Bexhill v Sussex University
Heathfield v British Caledonian

Sat 26th November (Week 12)
Sussex University v St Francis
Pulborough v Plumpton
Midhurst v Brighton Polytechnic
British Caledonian v Hastings & Bexhill

Sat 28th January (Week 20)
Brighton Polytechnic v Pulborough
Plumpton v Sussex University
St Francis v British Caledonian
Hastings & Bexhill v Heathfield

Sat 11th February (Week 22)
Heathfield v St Francis
British Caledonian v Plumpton
Sussex University v Brighton Polytechnic
Pulborough v Midhurst

Sat 25th February (Week 24)
Midhurst v Sussex University
Brighton Polytechnic v British Caledonian
Plumpton v Heathfield
St Francis v Hastings & Bexhill

Sat 11th March (Week 26)
Hastings & Bexhill v Plumpton
Heathfield v Brighton Polytechnic
British Caledonian v Midhurst
Sussex University v Pulborough

SUSSEX LEAGUE THREE

Sat 8th October (Week 6)
Old Brightonians v W Sussex I.H.E.
Arun v Ditchling
Newick v R.M.P. Chichester
Robin Hood v Sunallon

Sat 22nd October (Week 8)
W Sussex I.H.E. v Robin Hood
Sunallon v Newick
R.M.P. Chichester v Arun
Ditchling v Azurians

Sat 12th November (Week 10)
Newick v W Sussex I.H.E.
Robin Hood v Old Brightonians
Azurians v R.M.P. Chichester
Arun v Sunallon

Sat 19th November (Week 11)
Old Brightonians v Newick
W Sussex I.H.E. v Arun
Sunallon v Azurians
R.M.P. Chichester v Ditchling

Sat 26th November (Week 12)
Azurians v W Sussex I.H.E.
Arun v Old Brightonians
Newick v Robin Hood
Ditchling v Sunallon

Sat 28th January (Week 20)
Robin Hood v Arun
Old Brightonians v Azurians
W Sussex I.H.E. v Ditchling
Sunallon v R.M.P. Chichester

Sat 11th February (Week 22)
R.M.P. Chichester v W Sussex I.H.E.
Ditchling v Old Brightonians
Azurians v Robin Hood
Arun v Newick

Sat 25th February (Week 24)
Newick v Azurians
Robin Hood v Ditchling
Old Brightonians v R.M.P. Chichester
W Sussex I.H.E. v Sunallon

Sat 11th March (Week 26)
Sunallon v Old Brightonians
R.M.P. Chichester v Robin Hood
Ditchling v Newick
Azurians v Arun

COURAGE CLUBS CHAMPIONSHIP

MATCHES WATCHED – 1988–89

DATE	FIXTURE	VENUE	TEAM (HOME)

TEAM	RESULTS		